ENCYCLOPEDIA OF Juvenile Justice

This book is dedicated to Rebecca Oprysk, ShiAnn Griffin, Lindsey Williams, and Matthew Williams, the great children in our lives.

Marilyn D. McShane ▪ Frank P. Williams III
University of Houston   Prairie View A&M University

EDITORS

ENCYCLOPEDIA OF
Juvenile
Justice

A Sage Reference Publication

SAGE Publications
International Educational and Professional Publisher
Thousand Oaks ▪ London ▪ New Delhi

For information:

Sage Publications, Inc.
2455 Teller Road
Thousand Oaks, California 91320
E-mail: order@sagepub.com

Sage Publications Ltd.
6 Bonhill Street
London EC2A 4PU
United Kingdom

Sage Publications India Pvt. Ltd.
B-42 Panchsheel Enclave
Post Box 4109
New Delhi 110 017 India

Printed in the United States of America

Library of Congress Cataloging-in-Publication Data

Encyclopedia of juvenile justice / Marilyn D. McShane, Frank P. Williams III, editors.
    p. cm.
Includes bibliographical references and index.
ISBN 0-7619-2358-6
    1. Juvenile justice, Administration of—United States—Encyclopedias.
2. Juvenile delinquency—United States—Encyclopedias. 3. Juvenile delinquents-Rehabilitation—United States—Encyclopedias. 4. Juvenile corrections—United States—Encyclopedias. I. McShane, Marilyn D., 1956–
II. Williams III. Franklin P.
HV9104 .E58 2002
364.36′03—dc21

                                  2002015866

This book is printed on acid-free paper.

03   04   05   06   07   10 9 8 7 6 5 4 3 2 1

Editorial Assistant:	Sara Tauber
Development Editor:	Vince Burns
Copy Editor:	Barbara McGowran
Production Editor:	Denise Santoyo
Typesetter:	C&M Digitals (P) Ltd.
Cover Designer:	Ravi Balasuriya

Contents

List of Entries

Reader's Guide

Delinquency Theories and Theorists

Biological Theories
Constitutional Theories
Cycle of Violence
Sociological Theories
Psychological Theories
Ruth Shonle Cavan
Richard Cloward
Albert Cohen
Lamar T. Empey
Sheldon and Eleanor Glueck
Stanley G. Hall
Travis Hirschi
Joan McCord
Solomon Kobrin
Henry McKay
Walter Miller
Walter Reckless
Lloyd Ohlin
Thorsten Sellin
Clifford Shaw
Edwin Sutherland
James Short
Fredrick Thrasher
Marvin Wolfgang

Historical References:
People and Projects

Boys Town
Cambridge-Somerville Study
Community Treatment Project

Chicago Area Project
Child Saving
Augusta Bronner
Deinstitutionalization Movement
Stanley G. Hall
Jerome Miller
William Healy
National Youth Survey
Philadelphia Birth Cohort
Provo Experiment
Reformatories, Reform schools
Silverlake Experiment

Delinquent Behavior

alcohol abuse
arson
computer/internet crime
Drugs
Gangs
Guns
Graffiti and Tagging
Matricide/Patricide
Prostitution
Race and Delinquency
Female Delinquency
Teen Pregnancy
Runaways
Sex offenders
school violence
status offenders
self-report studies
serious/violent offenders

Treatment and Interventions for Delinquency

Aftercare
Alternative Schools
Assessment
Boot Camps
Boys and girls Clubs
community action boards
curfews
Culturally Specific Programming
Group Homes
DARE
Detention Facilities
family therapy
group therapy
victim offender mediation
Prevention strategies
police responses to delinquency
probation
out of home placement
Scared Straight
Teen courts
Wilderness Programs

Juvenile Law and Legislative Initiatives

California Street Terrorism Enforcement &
   Prevention
California Youth Authority

Death Penalty
Diversion
Education of Handicapped Children Act
Foster Care
Guardian Ad Litem
Juvenile Courts
Juvenile Law
Juvenile Justice and Delinquency Prevention Act
parens patriae
Parental liability laws
National Council of Juvenile & Family Court Judges
National Council on Crime & Delinquency
Office of Juvenile Justice and Delinquency
   Prevention
Waivers to Adult Court

Juvenile Issues and Public Policy

At-risk Youth
Child Abuse
Child Sexual Abuse
Missing children
Learning Disabilities
Mental Health Issues
Public Opinion on Juvenile Justice Issues
Victimization of juveniles
School Violence
School Responses to Juvenile Violence

Illustrations

Contributors

Allen, Leana C.
Indiana University, Bloomington, IN

Andrus, Tracy
Prairie View A&M University, Prairie View, TX

Armstrong, Gaylene Styve
Arizona State University-West, Phoenix, AZ

Azubuike, Eric E.
Prairie View A&M University, Prairie View, TX

Bailey, Charles
Prairie View A&M University, Prairie View, TX

Bailey, Frankie Y.
State University of New York, Albany, NY

Bailey, Laura J.
Prairie View A&M University, Prairie View, TX

Batton, Candice L.
University of Nebraska, Omaha, Lincoln, NE

Belbot, Barbara A.
University of Houston–Downtown, Houston, TX

Benekos, Peter
Mercyhurst College, Erie, PA

Binder, Arnold
University of California, Irvine, CA

Bing, Robert L., III
University of Texas, Arlington, TX

Bishop, Natalie
Urban Pathway's Cluster House, New York, NY

Bloom, Barbara
Sonoma State University, Rohnert Park, CA

Bohm, Robert M.
University of Central Florida, Orlando, FL

Brooks, Willie M., Jr.
Prairie View A&M University,
Prairie View, TX

Buffkin, Jana
Drury University, Springfield, MO

Caeti, Tory J.
University of North Texas, Denton, TX

Caldwell, Dawn M.
Charleston Southern University, Charleston, SC

Carona, Anthony
Prairie View A&M University, Prairie View, TX

Carter, Andrea M.
University of Arkansas, Little Rock, AR

Casey, Verna
Eastern Kentucky University, Richmond, KY

Cassiday-Shaw, Aimee
Bakersfield, CA

Catlin, Dennis W.
Northern Arizona University, Tucson, AZ

Chima, Felix O.
Prairie View A&M University, Prairie View, TX

Cintrón, Myrna
Prairie View A&M University, Prairie View, TX

Davis, Laura
San Bernardino County Probation, San
Bernardino, CA

DeLisi, Matthew J.
Iowa State University, Ames, IA

Dodge, Mary
University of Colorado, Denver, CO

Dolny, H. Michael
California State University, Stanislaas, CA

Dunnuck, Sandra
Montgomey County Probation, Conroe, TX

Eggleston, Carolyn
California State University, San Bernardino, CA

Eggleston, Elaine P.
University of Maryland, College Park, MD

Engram, Peggy A.
University of Houston–Downtown, Houston, TX

Farr, Kathryn Ann
Portland State University, Portland, OR

Farrar, Jon R.
University of Texas, Tyler, TX

Ferrell, Jeff
Southern Methodist University, Dallas, TX

Ford, Frederick
Prairie View A&M University, Prairie View, TX

Ford, Marilyn Chandler
Volusia County Dept of Corrections,
Daytona Beach, FL

French, Laurence A.
Western New Mexico University, Silver City, NM

Freng, Adrienne
University of Wyoming, Laramie, WY

Fritsch, Eric J.
University of North Texas, Denton, TX

Gaines, Larry K.
California State University, San Bernardino, CA

Gardner, Betina
Eastern Kentucky University, Richmond, KY

Gehring, Thom
California State University, San Bernardino, CA

Geis, Gilbert
University of California, Irvine, CA

Gibbons, Don C.
Portland State University, Portland, OR

Gibson, Camille
Prairie View A&M University, Prairie View, TX

Golden, James
University of Arkansas, Little Rock, AR

Gordon, Jill A.
Virginia Commonwealth University,
Richmond, VA

Grabowski, Michael J.
Prairie View A&M University, Prairie View, TX

Grimes, Ruth-Ellen M.
California State Polytechnic University,
Pomona, CA

Hagan, Frank E.
Mercyhurst College, Erie, PA

Heck, William P.
Northeastern State University, Tahlequah, OK

Heide, Kathleen M.
University of South Florida, Tampa, FL

Henningsen, Rodney J.
Sam Houston State University, Huntsville, TX

Hickey, Thomas J.
University of Tampa, Tampa, FL

Hirsch, Claudia Rios
Prairie View A&M University, Prairie View, TX

Hirsch, Philip
Prairie View A&M University, Prairie View, TX

Jenkins, Jeffrey A.
Roger Williams University, Bristol, RI

Jerin, Robert A.
Endicott College, Beverly, MA

Johnson, Wesley
Sam Houston State University, Huntsville, TX

Josi, Don A.
Armstrong Atlantic State University,
Savannah, GA

Knox, George W.
National Gang Crime Research Center,
Peotone, IL

Krause, Wesley
San Bernardino County Probation,
San Bernardino, CA

Laub, John H.
University of Maryland, College Park, MD

Lawrence, Richard
St. Cloud State University, St. Cloud, MN

Lovett, Marilyn D.
Prairie View A&M University, Prairie View, TX

Lowe, R. Steve
Pacific Youth Ministries, San Bernardino, CA

Luttrell, Vickie
Drury University, Springfield, MO

MacKenzie, Doris Layton
University of Maryland, College Park, MD

Maddan, Sean A.
University of Arkansas, Little Rock, AR

Mays, G. Larry
New Mexico State University, Las Cruces, NM

McConnell, Elizabeth H.
Charleston Southern University, Charleston, SC

McGowen, Bridgett L.
Prairie View A&M University, Prairie View, TX

McShane, Marilyn D.
University of Houston–Downtown, Houston, TX

McWhorter, Richard
Prairie View A&M University, Prairie View, TX

Mebane, Dalila
Prairie View A&M University, Prairie View, TX

Merlo, Alida V.
Indiana University of Pennsylvania, Indiana, PA

Moriarty, Laura J.
Virginia Commonwealth University,
Richmond, VA

Moyer, Imogene L.
Indiana University of Pennsylvania, Indiana, PA

Mupier, Robert M.
Prairie View A&M University, Prairie View, TX

Myers, David L.
Indiana University of Pennsylvania, Indiana, PA

Palmer, Ted
California Youth Authority, Ret., Sacramento, CA

Patenaud, Allan
University of Arkansas, Little Rock, AR

Pelz, Beth
University of Houston–Downtown, Houston, TX

Penn, Everette B.
Prairie View A&M University, Prairie View, TX

Peterson, Dana
The University at Albany, NY

Pisciotta, Alexander W.
Kutztown University, Kutztown, PA

Richter, Michelle
Sam Houston State University, Huntsville, TX

Roberts, Lisa M.
Albion, PA

Rosenbaum, Dennis P.
University of Illinois, Chicago, IL

Rubenser, Lorie
Sul Ross State University, Alpine, TX

Rush, Jeffrey P.
University of Tennessee, Chattanooga, TN

Russo-Myers, Bernadette V.
Sam Houston State University, Huntsville, TX

Samuels, Lorraine
Prairie View A&M University, Prairie View, TX

Scarpitti, Frank R.
University of Delaware, Newark, DE

Schauer, Edward J.
Prairie View A&M University, Prairie View, TX

Scheidegger, Amie R.
Charleston Southern University, Charleston, SC

Schram, Pamela
California State University, San Bernardino, CA

Sechrest, Dale K.
California State University, San Bernardino, CA

Shelden, Randall G.
University of Nevada, Las Vegas, NV

Shichor, David
California State University, San Bernardino, CA

Sims, Barbara
Pennsylvania State University, Harrisburg,
Middletown, PA

Skonovd, Norman
California Youth Authority, Sacramento, CA

Snell, Cletus
Prairie View A&M University, Prairie View, TX

Snow, Terry A.
Prairie View A&M University, Prairie View, TX

Steinmann, Rick M.
Lindenwood University, St. Charles, MO

Taylor, Morris
Southern Illinois University, Edwardsville, IL

Taylor, Terrance J.
Georgia State University, Atlanta, GA

Thistlethwaite, Amy B.
Northern Kentucky University,
Highland Heights, KY

Tibbetts, Stephen G.
California State University,
San Bernardino, CA

Tischler, Chloe
Radford University, Radford, VA

Turk, Austin T.
University of California, Riverside, CA

Van Houten, Amy
University of Arkansas, Little Rock, AR

Vandiver, Donna M.
Illinois State University, Normal, IL

Veneziano, Carol
Southeastern Missouri State University, Cape
Girardeau, MO

Veneziano, Louis
Southeastern Missouri State University,
Cape Girardeau, MO

Walker, Jeffrey T.
University of Arkansas, Little Rock, AR

Websdale, Neil
Northern Arizona University, Flagstaff, AZ

Williams, Frank P., III
Prairie View A&M University, Prairie View, TX

Willingham, Tonya Y.
Prairie View A&M University, Prairie View, TX

Worrall, John
California State University, San Bernardino, CA

Acknowledgments

The patience and kindness of many people go into the production of any scholarly endeavor. We would like to thank our good friend Leo Balk for suggesting this project to us. We also want to extend a huge thank you to all the contributors, whose conscientious efforts made this volume possible and many of whom volunteered again, even after the *Encyclopedia of American Prisons*. We would also like to thank the wonderful faculty and staff at Prairie View A&M University and at the University of Houston–Downtown for assisting us in this effort.

Foreword

We hope we have risen to the challenge of the *Encyclopedia of Juvenile Justice* in producing a mix of historical works, current perspectives, people, and ideas related to the field of juvenile justice. We are confident, at least, that the entries will invite comments and generate a lively debate. One thing is certain: Our selection is as wide ranging as it is far reaching. Here is an incredible collection for the reader, who will find that every entry provides a fascinating insight into the field of juvenile justice.

The encyclopedia features the work of many talented authors who have made their mark by producing detailed coverage of many controversial issues. More important, however, are the references, as you dip in and out of the alphabetical listing of topics from intervention and prevention programs, to legal perspectives, mental health concerns, and theories that focus on delinquency.

Each section of the volume has successfully accomplished the task of bringing a large body of knowledge together and making it understandable not only to those who work in the field but also to those who are newly interested in the problems of juvenile justice and delinquency prevention. The contributors all deserve considerable credit for their accomplishment. Most of all, recognition must be given to the editors, Marilyn McShane and Frank Williams III, who conceptualized and molded this volume into its present form. I recommend it to you and salute the authors and editors for a job well done.

Dr. H. Elaine Rodney, Dean
School of Juvenile Justice
and Psychology
Prairie View A&M University

Preface

In recent years, much attention has been focused on the juvenile offender, perceived changes in the types and seriousness of crimes being committed by the juvenile, and a controversial variety of possible treatment interventions, such as boot camps, corporal punishments, and culturally specific programs. Stories of school shootings, violent gangs, and murders being perpetrated by 7-year-olds have dominated the newspapers and sent practitioners and policymakers scrambling to develop ways to prevent crime, predict and intercept high-risk offenders, and implement treatment strategies that will both rehabilitate the offender and protect society. Unfortunately, these sensational events tend to color the public's view of juvenile crime and distort perceptions of its nature. Myths abound about the causes of and cures for delinquency. Neither research, common sense, nor logical strategy can keep up with the laws, policies, and other political "Hail Marys" flung desperately into the end zone of the juvenile justice system.

This work was compiled with the belief that everyone should be familiar with the history and current operations of the juvenile justice system. Many of the entries in this encyclopedia begin with a historical discussion to help frame the issues. Any understanding of contemporary problems must begin with an appreciation for where we have been. The more we know about juvenile justice issues, the better we can plan for and implement realistic, workable solutions for the future.

The entries included here are by no means exhaustive. We circulated lists of topics and received feedback from many respected colleagues in narrowing the subjects to this manageable volume. We apologize, in advance, if we were not able to include a personal favorite topic.

As a reference work, this encyclopedia seeks to provide an accurate and readable resource for students of juvenile justice, criminology, and criminal justice. May this be the starting point for your research efforts and serve to interest and inform you about many challenging and critical issues for our society today. To assist in this process, each entry includes a bibliography listing the most important references related to the topic as well as other related topics that might enlighten the reader further. Another function of this volume is to highlight the cumulative knowledge and insights of the experts featured here. We are constantly impressed with their ability to summarize issues and speak to the heart of matters vitally important to the quality of life we profess to value.

There are many popular claims made today about juveniles and the best way to approach the problems of delinquency. We invite the reader to evaluate these ideas and form your own opinion about what is needed to best serve children today.

Marilyn D. McShane
Frank P. Williams III
(Editors)

About the Editors

Marilyn D. McShane
Professor of Criminal Justice,
University of Houston–Downtown
Director, Community Justice Institute
Ph.D. (1985) Sam Houston State University

Specialization: Institutional and community corrections, child abuse, criminal justice system management, and criminological theory

Dr. McShane is currently working in research and faculty development at the University of Houston–Downtown. For her previous work at California State University, San Bernardino's School of Social and Behavioral Sciences, she received the 1994 Faculty Professional Development Award. She was also Chair of the Department of Criminal Justice at Northern Arizona University. Dr. McShane has served on a number of national criminal justice professional organization boards and often consults for the National Institute of Justice. Professor McShane has a consistent record of publication and grantsmanship (more than 50 books and articles, and many grants). Her editorial work includes a series for LFB Scholarly Publishing, featuring the most recent and notable dissertations in the field, and the award-winning *Encyclopedia of American Prisons* (1996), both of which she coedited. Her most recent book is the third edition of *Criminological Theory* (1999), coauthored with Frank P. Williams III.

Franklin P. Williams III
Professor of Juvenile Justice,
Prairie View A&M University
Coordinator, Juvenile Justice Doctoral Program
Professor Emeritus, California State
University, San Bernardino
Ph.D. (1976) Florida State University

Specialization: Criminological theory, corrections, fear of crime, drug abuse, methodology, and statistics

Dr. Williams has taught at departments in five universities and has published a substantial number of articles, research monographs and government reports, and books. He has served as Department Chair (California State University at San Bernardino) and Assistant Director for Research (Sam Houston State University) and has directed numerous research projects and two centers. He has served on the boards of national scholarly organizations, chaired a major division of a national organization, and chaired or served on numerous national and regional committees. He has been an editor or associate editor for several journals and publisher's book and monograph series. He is currently serving as coeditor of two book series and is beginning work on the fourth edition of a popular theory textbook. His most recent book is *Imagining Criminology* (1999).

ADOPTION ASSISTANCE AND CHILD WELFARE ACT

The Adoption Assistance and Child Welfare Act (AACWA) of 1980 (Public Law 96-272) was enacted by Congress to create an individual entitlement for foster care and adoption assistance and to establish a national program of child welfare services for children who are victims of maltreatment. The official federal government involvement in foster care began in 1961, when Louisiana denied aid to 22,000 poor African American children who were otherwise eligible for Aid to Families With Dependent Children (AFDC) because their homes were considered unsuitable and their mothers were ineligible for public assistance (Everett, 1995). Congress enacted Title IV of the Social Security Act of 1935 to ensure that these children would receive adequate care outside their homes.

In the 1960s and 1970s, before the enactment of P.L. 96-272, state child welfare systems had focused primarily on removing children from unsafe environments, or "child saving," rather than on prevention services, family reunification, or "family saving" (Petr, 1998). A 1959 study found that there were about 260,000 children in foster care and estimated that no more than 25 percent of those children had a chance of returning to their own homes. The study also concluded that roughly 168,000 children were in danger of staying in foster care throughout their childhood years (Popple and Leighninger, 1996). Thus thousands of children were growing up in foster care with few permanent ties to family. The child welfare system kept too many children in long-term foster care in a kind of limbo status instead of supporting permanent relationships in biological or adoptive families. This practice left thousands of children without the permanent bonds and supports generally thought to be essential to healthy development (Everett, 1995; Popple and Leighninger, 1998). Consequently, societal priorities in child welfare shifted from out-of-home care to serving children in their homes. With the passage of the AACWA, the preservation of families became a major goal of the child welfare systems.

INTENTS OF THE ADOPTION ASSISTANCE AND CHILD WELFARE ACT

The AACWA, commonly referred to as P.L. 96-272, is considered the most momentous piece of federal legislation to affect child welfare practices. It was designed to promote the permanency of children who come to the attention of child welfare authorities (Petr, 1998) and was enacted to combat the documented, extraordinarily high numbers of children remaining in foster care or some form of institutional care for long periods. The AACWA provides federal funding incentives to states as a way of achieving permanency-planning objectives. Placing a new emphasis on family preservation and reunification, the act requires states to develop plans for preventive and reunification services and adoption subsidies.

To continue to receive federal funding, states must develop their plans in cooperation with the courts (Johnson and Schwartz, 1997) and rewrite their laws governing child welfare to meet the requirements of P.L. 96-272. For states to be eligible for federal reimbursement, they must submit plans with a commitment to make "reasonable efforts" to provide services that return children to their natural families or to make permanent arrangements for children through placement with relatives through adoption.

REASONABLE EFFORTS MANDATE OF THE AACWA

A strong mandate present in the AACWA is that of "reasonable efforts" (Johnson and Schwartz, 1997), which means that family dysfunction affecting children is best treated by intervention with the family unit without removing the children, if possible. Thus an explicit goal of this legislation is the preservation of families. If placement is necessary, the state must make reasonable efforts to clear the child's legal status for permanent placement outside the natural home. Although the law does not specify what constitutes reasonable efforts, this determination must, and should, be made on an individual, case-by-case basis (Petr, 1998).

The AACWA of 1980 is contained in both Title IV-B and Title IV-E of the Social Security Act (Liederman, 1995). Title IV-B of the act states that services must be designed to (1) intervene early with problems that might result in abuse, neglect, exploitation, or delinquency; (2) prevent family breakup and the separation of children from their families; (3) secure appropriate out-of-home care for children necessarily separated from their families; (4) reunify children with their families whenever possible after separation; and (5) place children with adoptive families when reunification with their families of origin is not possible.

General guidelines and range of services for making reasonable efforts (Petr, 1998) include (1) crisis intervention with intensive home-based family services and counseling; (2) cash payments for emergency needs, including transportation, food and clothing, housing, emergency shelter, respite care, and child day care; (3) treatment for substance abuse and for physical, sexual, and emotional abusers and their victims; and (4) household management and homemaker services, parenting-skills training, and life-skills training. Ultimately, attainment of these goals will increase the safety and stability of the child and obviate the unnecessary removal of children from the family into state custody.

Title IV-E of the AACWA provides support for children who have been separated from families who are unable or unwilling to care for them and who have been placed in out-of-home care (that is, in family foster care, kinship care, group homes, or residential facilities or with adoptive families). This section of the act requires states to ensure that children who are taken into the custody of the state and placed in foster care have a permanent home within a reasonable period. It also contains a means-tested entitlement program under which states are partially reimbursed for the cost of caring for children up to age 18 who have been removed from their parents' custody if the children receive (or are eligible to receive) benefits under AFDC or Supplemental Security Income. The law sets forth certain standards that states must meet to receive federal funds, including a subsidy program to meet the special needs of children who are adopted.

OVERVIEW OF THE AACWA OUTCOME

Despite reforms mandated by the AACWA, permanency planning for children in foster care and other substitute care situations continues to be a problem for the child welfare system. Based on outcome evaluation of the AACWA, an estimated 502,000 children were in foster care in 1977. By 1980, this number had dropped to 302,000, declining to a low of 275,000 in 1983. Also, the number of foster homes declined from 137,000 to 100,000 nationwide between 1984 and 1989 (Everett, 1995; Popple and Leighninger, 1998). It appeared, for a while, that the problem of foster care was under control when the permanency approach was implemented in the late 1970s and 1980s.

Nevertheless, the number of children in foster care began to increase substantially in the mid-1980s. By 1991, the number had risen to 429,000, with 442,000 at the end of fiscal year 1992. An estimated 500,000 to 600,000 children were living in foster care placements nationwide in 1998. Explanations for the mixed outcome of AACWA, particularly for the increase in the foster care system, include budget cuts, cultural factors, substance abuse, HIV/AIDS, the court system, and health care issues. Popple and Leighninger (1996) noted that the funds promised by P.L. 96-272 never materialized because of the widespread service cuts during the Reagan administration.

Children who are members of racial and ethnic minority groups are disproportionately represented in the child welfare system, particularly in out-of-home care and the juvenile justice system, and remain in these systems for longer periods than do white children (Liederman, 1995). Increasing minority populations challenge the cultural competence of the child welfare system. The acceptance and integration of culture and ethnicity as central factors in the planning and provision of services to children and their families in a pluralistic social environment need to be emphasized. Substance abuse is another major factor that contributed to the low AACWA success. The drug abuse epidemic of the mid-1980s profoundly affected the safety and protection of children and young people. Alcoholism and drug abuse, particularly among women, increase the number of child maltreatment cases and are a primary reason that children enter out-of-home care.

HIV/AIDS infections have increasingly affected children, young people, and their families. The child welfare system is challenged to identify both extended and adoptive families to care for children and youths who are orphaned by AIDS. The role of the juvenile court has expanded in recent years, thus resulting in a caseload crisis. Courts are required to hear an escalating number of severe and complex child maltreatment cases, often involving drug and alcohol abuse.

The accessibility of health care and related social services for at-risk populations is critical to the child welfare system. Issues related to health care, especially mental health care, substance abuse prevention and treatment, and child development services have serious implications for the existing managed-care system and the child welfare delivery system. Thus reform is definitely needed.

Felix O. Chima

See also Children's Aid Society; Child-Saving Movement; Foster Care; Group Homes; Guardians *Ad Litem*

Bibliography

Everett, J. E. 1995. Child foster care. Pp. 375–389 in R. L. Edwards (ed.), *Encyclopedia of Social Work*, 19th ed. Washington, DC: NASW Press.

Johnson, L. C., and C. L. Schwartz. 1997. *Social Welfare: A Response to Human Need*, 4th ed. Needham Heights, MA: Allyn & Bacon.

Liederman, D. S. 1995. Child welfare overview. Pp. 424–433 in R. L. Edwards (ed.), *Encyclopedia of Social Work*, 19th ed. Washington, DC: NASW Press.

Petr, C. G. 1998. *Social Work With Children and Their Families: Pragmatic Foundations*. New York: Oxford University Press.

Popple, P. R., and L. Leighninger. 1996. *Social Work, Social Welfare and American Society*, 3rd ed. Needham Heights, MA: Allyn & Bacon.

Popple, P. R., and L. Leighninger. 1998. *The Policy-Based Profession: An Introduction to Social Welfare Policy for Social Workers*. Needham Heights, MA: Allyn & Bacon.

 AFTERCARE

Juvenile aftercare is simply the monitoring of youth within the community after a period of confinement. Rather than a sentence imposed by a judge, aftercare is the final component of a youth's institutionalization (the original sentence). Its most basic function is to supervise the youth in the community. Coming after an institutional sentence with a rigorous schedule, aftercare is designed to help the youth make the transition to the "real world."

With its roots dating back to the 1700s, juvenile aftercare is not a new concept. It is often viewed as having similarities with juvenile probation and adult parole. During the last decade, to reflect the more punitive stance currently taken in the criminal justice system, juvenile aftercare has become more intensive. This entry offers a historical perspective, links juvenile aftercare to juvenile probation and adult parole, and addresses the issue of intensive aftercare.

HISTORICAL PERSPECTIVE

During the 18th century, youth were placed in an apprenticeship at about age 8 to learn a skill, responsibility, and discipline. The practice began to decline in popularity in the latter half of the 18th century, leading to a breakdown in the supervision of youth. The result was that disorderly youth had time to be involved in antisocial extracurricular activities—crime.

Due to the increasing number of unsupervised and unruly youth, there was a rise in the number and type of individuals being detained. Hence the early 1800s witnessed a move to separate detained children from detained adults. The first facility exclusively for children opened in 1825. The New York House of Refuge detained vagrant, neglected, and criminal youth in the hope of providing them with a more positive environment. Children were required to attend school and were taught a trade during their incarceration, which lasted between one and three years. An assessment committee determined the length of the youth's detainment. The committee had to establish the youth's readiness for release into the community, based on his or her behavior within the House of Refuge.

After a period of detainment, the youth was released to a family to work in a private home as an indentured servant. This has been seen as the beginning stages of the current juvenile aftercare movement. The goal of the indentured phase was to provide supervision to the youth while in the community and teach the child a job skill. In addition, this step provided the youth with a nurturing environment to try to reduce the factors that may have led her or him to engage in illegitimate behaviors. Starting in the late 1860s, the indentured committee, which originally granted release, required an official agent to check on the youth's progress.

The indentured component of the House of Refuge ended in the late 19th century because it was no longer viewed as profitable. However, many argue that it did not truly disappear; rather, the job titles changed (Pisciotta, 1993). *Indentured* changed to *aftercare*, or parole, and visiting agents became parole agents. The only difference is that the indentured process released youth to "masters," whereas the aftercare/parole method releases youth to their families or guardians.

JUVENILE AFTERCARE COMPARED WITH JUVENILE PROBATION AND ADULT PAROLE

Juvenile Aftercare and Juvenile Probation

The difference between aftercare and probation is the legal foundation of the sanctions. In both instances, the youth was brought to the court and there was sufficient evidence to convict the youth of an offense. The difference lies in the judicial sentence received by the youth. A judge sentences a youth to probation, which means the youth will remain in the community under a series of rules and regulations. However, the judge cannot sentence a youth to aftercare; instead, the youth is sentenced to a period of incarceration, and aftercare is a final component of the sentence.

As such, the similarity between aftercare and probation is the need to provide community supervision, counseling, and any additional services to the youth. The basic goal of both is to enforce the conditions of release into the community. These conditions of release can entail abiding by curfew, attending school or sustaining employment, maintaining contact with an officer of the court, counseling, attending services (e.g., substance abuse services, sex offender programs, family services), and avoiding criminal activity. It is the responsibility of the aftercare/probation officer to monitor the conditions of release, because violating any or all the conditions of release can result in a period of incarceration. Thus when you examine the rules and regulations, the officer has two conflicting functions: enforcer and counselor.

As an enforcer, the officer must verify all terms of community release. If the youth is not complying with any of the conditions of aftercare/probation, the officer must use his or her discretion, with options ranging from warning the youth to contacting the judge for a revocation hearing. As a counselor, the officer must help the youth not to commit the same behaviors by discussing the importance of responsibility and maintaining prosocial behaviors. On one hand, the officer must be compassionate and caring (the role of the counselor), and on the other hand, she or he must apply and monitor the conditions of aftercare/probation.

Juvenile Aftercare and Adult Parole

The functions of aftercare and parole are the same—monitoring and assisting offenders who have been released from a period of confinement. The difference between the two is philosophical. The juvenile court system was created as an establishment that assists youth by looking out for their well-being. Because of his or her age, a youth could be treated or taught how to behave according to societal rules. In contrast, the mission of the adult court is to identify guilt and dispense punishment proportionate to the offense to protect the public and control crime. Therefore, the competing foundations of the criminal justice systems (juvenile and adult) are the reason for the terminology differences, although the basic functions of aftercare and parole are the same.

INTENSIVE AFTERCARE PROGRAM MOVEMENT

In general, the use of juvenile aftercare has been unsuccessful (Altschuler and Armstrong, 1990; Palmer, 1990). That is, the traditional monitoring of the youth within the community, while providing limited services and carrying large caseloads, is not a very effective means to successfully transition youth within the community. Several factors may influence the lack of success: (1) a lack of communication between institutional staff and aftercare staff during the transitional period, (2) the inability to identify appropriate service providers for youth, (3) large caseload sizes for aftercare workers, and (4) selection of inappropriate youth for aftercare. This has led to the availability of funds to try to improve the success of aftercare.

More specifically, the Office of Juvenile Justice and Delinquency Prevention has funded the implementation of the Intensive Aftercare Program (IAP), which is designed to (1) improve the transition from confinement to the community and (2) enhance the aftercare portion of a youth's sentence (Altschuler and Armstrong, 1994). This funding has been granted because of research showing the inability of youth to maintain the lessons learned from confinement when they reenter society. Namely, youth released to the community do not seem to maintain the prosocial behaviors they may have learned while institutionalized. In addition, research has found that outcomes of the release process are more favorable when a highly structured program is in place. Thus the IAP movement seeks to ease the transition from institutional confinement by a reintegrative confinement approach and intensive aftercare.

The goal of reintegrative confinement is to begin integrating the youth back into the community while he or she is still institutionalized. This transition process is accomplished by preparing the youth for the challenges ahead (e.g., how to deal with peers and temptations), identifying services and programs available within the community (e.g., substance abuse counseling), and making certain all parties uphold the conditions of release (e.g., services are provided, the youth reports as told). In sum, this phase involves detailing all the decision-making processes of release, including a youth's living arrangements.

An additional judgment to be made is who is appropriate for intensive aftercare. Research has found that when a youth who has a low likelihood of committing another crime is placed on intensive aftercare, which has tight controls, the youth is likely to behave inappropriately. In other words, the impact of aftercare can be detrimental to "low-risk" youth.

Two broadly defined groups can be selected for intensive aftercare. The first group comprises the chronic offenders—those who have long histories of nonviolent behavior. The second group is youth who have specific problems that can benefit from specialized treatment (e.g., substance users, sex offenders). Research has shown that these two "high-risk" groups

can benefit from a highly structured program, so it is of utmost importance for an aftercare program to specify whom the program will admit.

Furthermore, a successful aftercare program should be concerned with protecting the community, stressing responsibility for one's actions to the offender, providing the youth with suitable services (family intervention, health-related issues, living arrangements, job placement, and so on), identifying and solidifying community resources for the youth, and monitoring and evaluating the offender's progress. To accomplish these goals, aftercare emphasizes both surveillance and treatment. As previously discussed, surveillance and treatment have been seen as counterproductive; however, one objective of the IAP model is to combine the two functions so that treatment becomes a requirement of release. Simply attending the treatment service is a surveillance function, and the information gathered at that meeting is a treatment function.

The Office of Juvenile Justice and Delinquency Prevention provided funding to implement an IAP model in four states: Colorado, Nevada, New Jersey, and Virginia. The IAP model implemented is based on criminological theories (strain, social learning, and social control), selects appropriate high-risk offenders, and combines surveillance and treatment into a highly structured program. As of 1999, each pilot site has been improving the implementation of the multifaceted IAP model; thus a formal evaluation of the program's impact has not yet been completed. It has been suggested that the IAP model proposed by Altschuler and Armstrong (1990) contains many favorable notions that have been supported by the literature (MacKenzie, 1999), but if a community juvenile justice system cannot implement the program effectively, problems can arise. In other words, although the written model contains necessary components, success can only be achieved if all the mechanisms are implemented consistently and accordingly.

CONCLUSION

Juvenile aftercare is not a new idea. Its foundations date to the 18th century, when youth were released to "masters" for additional training. Today youth are released to their families or guardians and monitored by the court. This process is viewed by many as an important step to assist youth, because institutional confinement does not sufficiently prepare youth for release into the community, and once in the community, youth fail to maintain the skills learned within institutions without additional support. Thus aftercare today is concerned with creating a smooth transition from institution to community, identifying community support systems and resources for youth, assisting in the development of positive peer interaction, and monitoring youth's progress.

During the past decade, there has been a move to increase the success of aftercare by targeting youth most in need. Specifically, the IAP model is designed to provide increased contact and service delivery to youth who are assessed as high risk. The IAP model, on face value, looks promising because it selects appropriate youth, limits caseload size, provides highly structured programs, and is grounded in theory. The goal of the model is that future criminal behavior will be reduced through the combination of treating youth, assisting their transition by finding suitable resources, and slowly granting them greater freedom.

Jill A. Gordon

See also Probation, Juvenile

Bibliography

Altschuler, D. M., and T. L. Armstrong. 1990. Intensive aftercare of the high-risk juvenile parolee: Issues and approaches in reintegration and community supervision. Pp. 45–84 in T. Armstrong (ed.), *Intensive Interventions With High-Risk Youths: Promising Approaches in Juvenile Probation and Parole.* Monsey, NY: Criminal Justice Press.

Altschuler, D. M., and T. L. Armstrong. 1994. *Intensive Aftercare for High-Risk Juveniles: An Assessment.* Washington, DC: Office of Juvenile Justice and Delinquency Prevention.

MacKenzie, D. L. 1999. Commentary: The effectiveness of aftercare programs: Examining the evidence. Pp. 15–20 in D. Altschuler and T. Armstrong (eds.), *Reintegration, Supervised Release, and Intensive Aftercare.* Washington, DC: Office of Juvenile Justice and Delinquency Prevention.

Palmer, T. B. 1990. Intervention with juvenile offenders: Recent and long-term changes. Pp. 85–120 in T. Armstrong (ed.), *Intensive Interventions With High-Risk Youths: Promising Approaches in Juvenile Probation and Parole.* Monsey, NY: Criminal Justice Press.

Pisciotta, A. W. 1993. Child saving or child brokerage? The theory and practice of indenture and parole at the New York House of Refuge, 1825–1935. Pp. 533–555 in A. Hess and P. Clement (eds.), *History of Juvenile Delinquency.* Aalen, Germany: Scientia Verlag.

ALCOHOL ABUSE

Alcohol abuse refers to an excessive use of alcoholic beverages, including liquor. An examination of adolescent drinking patterns and problems requires consideration of (1) the quantity and frequency of consumption, (2) alcohol-related negative life consequences, and (3) alcohol-dependence symptoms (Bailey and Rachal, 1993).

PREVALENCE OF ADOLESCENT ALCOHOL ABUSE

In terms of prevalence, the 1994 national student survey data showed that 25 percent of 8th graders and 50 percent of 12th graders reported consuming alcohol within the previous month (Johnston, O'Malley, and Bachman, 1995). A substantial proportion of those drinkers consumed heavily: 15 percent of 8th graders and 28 percent of 12th graders reported having five or more drinks in a row in the previous two weeks, and just under 3 percent of 12th graders reported daily use of alcohol. The prevalence of adolescent drinking varied along demographic lines. Boys reported more heavy drinking than did girls, and among high school seniors, white adolescents reported more heavy drinking than did Hispanic or African American adolescents. For example, 1994 national data for 12th graders found that 32 percent of non-Hispanic Caucasians, 24 percent of Hispanics, and 14 percent of African Americans reported consuming five or more drinks in a row in the previous two weeks (Johnston et al., 1995). However, the researchers cautioned that ethnic differences could be due to differences in school dropout rates instead of drinking. One needs to remember that inconsistent definitions, as well as inter- and intracultural diversity, make comparisons among ethnic groups especially difficult. In general, however, compared with other ethnic groups, Native American adolescents typically report the highest consumption rates, and Asian American youth report the lowest.

The lack of empirical work on the prevalence of clinical alcohol abuse or dependence among adolescents of high school age or younger is rather shocking. The contrast between the remarkable increase in alcohol-related problems after the high school years and the allegedly low rates before and during high school is likely a product of poor diagnoses in those early years.

To diagnose the drinking patterns and problems that occur during early and middle adolescence, it is essential to use age-relevant criteria instead of applying diagnostic criteria designed for adults. Actually, criteria used tend to vary with the instrument: Different instruments use one or a combination of criteria.

For example, in a study by Rodney and Mupier (1997) on African American male adolescent children of alcoholics (COAs), the instrument used to assess the level of alcohol abuse was the Children's Structured Assessment of the Genetics of Alcoholism (C-SAGA). The C-SAGA uses the standardized diagnostic criteria for alcohol abuse as established in *Diagnostic and Statistical Manual of Mental Disorders* (*DSM-III-R*) of the American Psychiatric Association. A similar study by Fergusson and Horwood (2000) assessed alcohol-related problems at ages 15 and 16 using the Rutgers Alcohol Problem Index and measured alcohol abuse or dependence using the same *DSM-III-R* criteria. In both studies, the categorization as an alcohol abuser is rigorous.

For instance, in the C-SAGA, to be classified as an alcohol abuser, the adolescent must use alcohol six times or more during her or his lifetime and exhibit three or more of the symptoms categorized in nine groups. The first group includes the following symptoms: drinking caused others to tell the adolescent respondent that she or he drinks too much, drinking caused respondent to get into physical fights, drinking made respondent feel depressed for more than 24 hours, drinking caused problems with respondent's concentration for more than 24 hours, or respondent drank three or more times knowing a physical condition would be made worse. The second group identified the following symptoms: drinking caused respondent three or more times to miss school, work, or to do chores; respondent's grades went down because of alcohol use; or respondent three times or more accidentally got hurt when drinking. The third group identified the following: respondent quit school, activity, job, or doing things with friends. Increased tolerance by at least 50 percent made up the fourth group, and those who three times or more wanted to drink less made up the fifth group. Those who three times or more drank more than intended, and three times or more drank alcohol to relieve or avoid withdrawal symptoms made up the sixth and seventh groups, respectively. The eighth group consisted of experiencing withdrawal (shakes and at least one other symptom), and the last group consisted of

spending a lot of time getting alcohol, drinking, or trying to feel better after using alcohol.

The use of alternative measures can increase or diminish the discrepancy between prevalence rates for younger and older adolescents. For example, common adult symptoms of alcohol abuse and dependence are rare in adolescents. In addition, many adolescents with no previous alcohol-dependence diagnosis need a higher level of alcohol to attain a desired effect (i.e., their tolerance level increases). In fact, an obvious increase in consumption may be a typical feature of adolescent drinking rather than a result of dependence. Efforts should be geared toward refining methods for diagnosing clinical alcohol abuse and dependence in adolescents.

In Rodney and Mupier (1997), alcohol abuse or dependence was diagnosed when an adolescent reached a certain score by assigning 1 point when he or she fell into one group and zero otherwise. The total score obtained ranged from zero to 9, with zero indicating the absence of alcohol abuse and 1 to 9 indicating increasing degrees of alcohol abuse. Comparisons between COAs and non-COAs on the degree of alcohol abuse showed that COAs had a significantly higher mean (4.13) than did non-COAs (2.84). It should be noted that 23 percent of the adolescents were COAs, and 27 percent of the COAs were alcohol abusers compared with 17 percent of non-COAs.

The same study showed that 91.5 percent of the adolescents (COAs and non-COAs) who abused alcohol were also involved in conduct disorder compared with 66 percent of those who did not abuse alcohol. When conduct disorder was broken down into specific subtypes, it showed that alcohol abusers had a greater chance than the nonabusers (COAs and non-COAs) of engaging in all but one subtype of conduct disorder (forcing sexual activities). Also, the COA abusers had a greater chance than the COA nonabusers of engaging in all but four categories of conduct disorder. Finally, the COA abusers had a greater chance than did the non-COA abusers of engaging in those delinquent acts. What emerged from these findings was a very strong relationship between alcohol abuse and conduct disorder, especially for COAs.

ALCOHOL AND DELINQUENCY

The Rodney and Mupier (1997) study lends support to others who maintain that the use and abuse of alcohol by young people is a factor that contributes to criminal behaviors (Greenfield and Weisner, 1995). It is believed that heavy alcohol consumption generates disinhibiting effects that may increase tendencies to risk-taking, antisocial, and violent behaviors. Therefore, young and vulnerable people have an increased risk of and susceptibility to criminal behaviors. Various research studies have shown that (1) among those who criminally offend, rates of alcohol abuse are high; or (2) among those who abuse alcohol, rates of criminal offending are high. Other findings from laboratory-based research have shown in controlled settings that antisocial behaviors, and particularly aggression, tend to increase with increasing alcohol consumption. While the relationship between alcohol consumption patterns and antisocial behaviors can be observed, the pattern of causality in these relationships is still controversial (Wagner, 1996). However, in a study where both observed and unobserved sources of confounding were controlled, Fergusson and Horwood (2000) were able to suggest the presence of a possible causal association between alcohol abuse and juvenile offending. Other researchers found alcohol abuse to be one of the predictors of recidivism among juvenile offenders (Myrner, Santman, Cappelletty, and Perlmutter, 1998).

OTHER NEGATIVE EFFECTS OF ALCOHOL ABUSE

The consequences of alcohol abuse extend beyond delinquency and criminality. A few studies have shown the medical consequences of alcohol abuse in adolescents, such as liver damage and poor language function. Adolescents who abuse alcohol also demonstrate higher rates of multiple drug use. Adolescent alcohol consumption is correlated with the three leading causes of death in this age-group: unintentional injuries, homicide, and suicide. More than half of all fatal motor vehicle crashes among 15- to 24-year-olds involve alcohol, and approximately half of all homicides in this age-group are associated with alcohol use. National data also suggest that alcohol use is associated with suicidal thoughts and suicide attempts. Another public health issue is the association between adolescent alcohol consumption and risky sexual behavior. Adolescent alcohol use is associated with earlier initiation of sexual activity, more frequent sexual activity, and less frequent condom use, all of which raise the risk for HIV infection and other sexually transmitted diseases. Again, the association between

adolescent drinking and these serious negative health risks does not imply a causal relationship.

Some researchers believe that adolescent alcohol use is associated with personality characteristics such as impulsiveness and sensation seeking. It is these underlying personality characteristics, rather than simply alcohol use, that increase the risk for automobile crashes, risky sexual behavior, violence, and suicide.

Alcohol use is said to affect adolescent psychosocial development, such as the development of emerging adolescent competencies, including social and coping skills. Paradoxically, drinking in adolescence is also associated with enhanced social functioning, less loneliness, and more positive emotional states (i.e., positive affect) in early adulthood.

ALCOHOL AS A GATEWAY DRUG

Researchers consider alcohol a gateway to other drugs. Alcohol is used at earlier ages than are other drugs, and alcohol use increases the risk for later use of illegal drugs. Studies indicate that alcohol and marijuana use often begin early. In the 1997 *Monitoring the Future* study, a nationwide survey, more than 54 percent of respondents reported that they had consumed alcohol and 23 percent reported that they had used marijuana by the eighth grade (Johnston, O'Malley, and Bachman, 1998). Early onset of alcohol use (i.e., before age 15) is associated with greater risk for other substance use and the development of later alcohol-related problems. However, it is not well established that alcohol use "causes" such substance use. Meanwhile, age at alcohol initiation is strongly linked to later alcohol misuse and is a key mediator of other predictive factors for subsequent alcohol misuse. Similarly, age at onset of alcohol use can be a predictor of progression to other drugs, which suggests that delaying onset of use could be an important target for prevention efforts.

RISK FACTORS

Although it is important to learn about the consequences of alcohol abuse, it is perhaps more important for prevention purposes to examine the risk factors associated with adolescent drinking. Those risk factors can be organized into categories that include sociocultural, family, peer, and intrapersonal factors as well as factors related to adolescent beliefs about alcohol.

Sociocultural factors include, among others, the adolescent's degree of access to alcohol. It appears that greater alcohol availability is associated with higher rates of drinking. In contrast, greater regulation of alcohol availability is associated with older ages of initiation, decreased consumption, and fewer alcohol-related problems.

Empirical studies based on social control theory, social learning theory, and problem-behavior theory have consistently supported the idea that families in which parents use alcohol to excess show high levels of antisocial behavior (including antisocial personality disorder). What parents do in this case is to provide a model of alcohol-abusing behavior. Families with low levels of social support, little monitoring of children's behavior, inconsistent discipline practices, high levels of conflict, and low levels of closeness—known as family socialization factors—also are more likely to have adolescent children who use alcohol.

Adolescent drinking has often been associated with peer drinking and peer acceptance, and adolescent drinking often occurs in peer social contexts. Adolescents whose friends frequently drink are more likely to increase their own drinking over time, and adolescents who frequently drink are more likely to increase their affiliations with alcohol-using peers. Thus adolescents who drink are more likely to select friends who drink, and those friends in turn are likely to influence other adolescents' drinking.

A number of personality traits lead to high levels of alcohol consumption, essentially because of low levels of self-regulation. Adolescents in this category are more likely to be aggressive and tend to have high attitudinal tolerance for deviant behavior. They have low value of and low expectations for academic success and high levels of sensation seeking and impulsivity. However, the effect of other intrapersonal factors is more controversial. For example, the relationship between adolescent alcohol use and depression is not quite clear. It is also unclear whether negative emotional states are a cause or a result of adolescent alcohol use, although depressive disorders and anxiety disorders have been associated with clinical alcoholism in adolescence. Also, the combination of low self-regulation and high levels of negative emotional states (i.e., negative affect) may be associated particularly with adolescent alcohol use.

Alcohol expectancies, or the beliefs adolescents have about alcohol before they even consume it, seem to be associated with their drinking behavior. Because many influences such as the media, peers, and family can shape adolescents' beliefs about alcohol, which in turn affect adolescents' drinking behavior, it is essential for prevention purposes to pay close attention to alcohol expectancies.

Robert M. Mupier

See also Drugs; Learning Disabilities; Mental Health; National Youth Survey; Pregnancy, Teenage

Bibliography

Bailey, S. L., and J. V. Rachal. 1993. Dimensions of adolescent problem drinking. *Journal of Studies on Alcohol* 54:555–565.

Fergusson, D. M., and L. J. Horwood. 2000. Alcohol abuse and crime: A fixed-effects regression analysis. *Addiction* 95:1525.

Greenfield, T. K., and C. Weisner. 1995. Drinking problems and self-reported criminal behavior, arrests and convictions: 1990 US alcohol and 1989 county surveys. *Addiction* 90:361–373.

Johnston, L. D., P. M. O'Malley, and J. G. Bachman. 1995. Prevalence of drug use among eighth, tenth, and twelfth grade students. Pp. 39–76 in *National Survey Results on Drug Use From the Monitoring the Future Study, 1975–1994. Vol. 1, Secondary School Students.* Rockville, MD: National Institute on Drug Abuse.

Johnston, L. D., P. M. O'Malley, and J. G. Bachman. 1998. *National Survey Results on Drug Use From the Monitoring the Future Study, 1975–1997. Vol. 1, Secondary School Students.* Rockville, MD: National Institute on Drug Abuse.

Myrner, J., J. Santman, G. Cappelletty, and B. Perlmutter. 1998. Variables related to recidivism among juvenile offenders. *International Journal of Offender Therapy and Comparative Criminology* 42:65–80

Rodney, H. E., and R. Mupier. 1997. Alcohol abuse and conduct disorder among African-American male adolescent COAs and nonCOAs. *Journal of Child and Adolescent Substance Abuse* 7(2):37–51.

Wagner, E. F. 1996. Substance use and violent behavior in adolescence. *Aggression and Violent Behavior* 1:375–387.

 ALTERNATIVE SCHOOLS

Alternative schools are individualized schools of instruction and curriculum that operate differently from regular public schools. School districts nationwide are using many methods, approaches, and alternatives to

the traditional style of teaching to serve an ever changing population. To combat major problems like rising school dropout and truancy rates and disruptive students, school districts have been forced to offer alternatives to the regular learning environment. Alternative schools give students a number of changes to the learning environment, instruction, and curriculum that are designed to meet their individual needs. School districts around the nation are using this form of education as a means to reach a youth population that has been classified as "at risk." Instruction and curriculum are often designed to use different methodology and learning styles that are based on education research. Personality and behavior factors are also taken into account when designing an alternative school setting.

These schools take on a number of different names, depending on the locale; however, they all provide the same type of educational service. They provide the core curriculum mandated by most states—math, science, English, and history—which are taught for the number of required hours each day. In addition, alternative schools provide several social programs, including behavior/anger counseling.

Public school funding plays a major role in the development and operation of alternative schools. By law, children are entitled to a free and appropriate education. The local, state, and federal governments share the cost of alternative education. Each level of government develops its own guidelines for the use of such funds in all school programs. Local taxpayers usually fund additional costs for the operation of alternative schools in most school districts. The availability of funds often determines if an alternative school will be operated at the school site or at a different location.

HISTORY

The education of children in alternative settings is not new. The early colonists from England understood the need for the education of their children. Although education of children has long been the responsibility of the parents, as early as the mid-1600s, the colonists began formal education outside the home environment. Early progressive thinkers such as Thomas Jefferson and John Dewey helped develop the concept of public education (Applied Research Center, 2001). By 1790, the Pennsylvania Constitution called for free public education for poor children; New York and Boston followed with similar laws (Applied Research Center,

2001). The movement in northern states ventured south but excluded slaves from receiving a free public education. The nation's wealthy continued to educate their children at home. This practice of approved home-schooling programs and charter schools is still used today as a type of alternative education.

In 1845, the Massachusetts Reform School at Westboro (the Lyman School), a new type of alternative school, was developed (Platt, 1991). The reform school movement in education was initiated to combat the growing number of delinquent youth in the industrialized cities in the North (Platt, 1991). An increase in Irish immigrants before the Civil War, as well as an increasing number of African Americans afterward, produced a public image of unmanageable youth who were not attending public schools. The formation of reform schools as a type of alternative school for "wayward" youth developed throughout the late 19th and early 20th centuries.

During this same period, a group of political and social reformers called "the child savers" helped develop education for the underclass (Platt, 1991). As a result of their efforts and the nation's perception of a need for stronger supervision of children, a juvenile justice system developed in the United States. On July 1, 1899, Illinois passed legislation to establish the first juvenile court in this nation to handle the acts of school-age delinquent children (Platt, 1991). Many other states quickly adopted similar statutes using *parens patriae* as a means of gaining social control and educating children. These acts of legislation allowed the state to remove children from their homes and place them in reform and trade schools.

The U.S. Supreme Court ruled in *Plessy v. Ferguson* (1896) that the state of Louisiana had the right to "separate but equal" railroad cars to accomodate African Americans and European Americans. This landmark decision served as the basis for separate and unequal facilities for African Americans. The passage of laws in southern states regarding racial segregation in public schools had a major effect on public education, producing an alternative system of education for a part of the country's population that had been denied legal education for generations. The Supreme Court in *Brown v. Board of Education of Topeka* (1954) ruled that segregated schools are "inherently unequal" and must be abolished, ending this practice by school districts.

From 1900 to 1954, progressive educators examined the old methods of education. These progressive thinkers ruled education in the 1930s. However, the majority of school districts remained unchanged. The Life Adjustment Movement by a group of educators in the late 1940s and 1950s had little effect on changing public education (Miller, 2001). The period in history that shaped alternative schooling in the 20th century was the political unrest of the youth in the 1960s and early 1970s. A new generation of writers and progressive thinkers wrote books that created a new vision for public education. Authors like A. S. Neill, John Holt, Herbert Kohl, and Jonathon Kozol challenged tradition and inspired thousands to make changes to a system that was failing the majority of American youth (Miller, 2001).

Alternative education was at the forefront of the country's consciousness throughout the 1970s and 1980s, when home schooling and charter schools began to appear in greater numbers (Miller, 2001). Educators are now attempting to create a more human and caring environment as the nation is asking them to help solve some of the ills of today's youth, particularly crime and delinquency. Today's alternative schools house a great number of juvenile delinquents. They are being asked, like the child savers of the late 1800s, to find solutions to juvenile crime and at the same time educate a youth population that is changing ethnically and socially.

CHARACTERISTICS OF ALTERNATIVE SCHOOLS

Alternative schools do not follow any prescribed pattern or method of operation. They often vary in characteristics from school district to school district and from state to state. However, some basic characteristics hold true in almost all alternative schools. These schools offer a clearer and more defined mission statement that assists the student in understanding the school's expectations. The mission statement is often written in the form of a personal contract that the student signs, thus giving him or her ownership of the learning process. In some school districts, alternative schools not only use a contract with a mission statement and goals but also totally incorporate the students in the governance of the school.

The characteristics of the alternative classroom are different from those of the regular public school environments. With lower enrollments, alternative schools can offer many progressive services, including smaller student-to-teacher ratios, greater school counselor commitments, student mentors, and tutor programs. In contrast, some alternative schools often have a self-paced curriculum that uses less teacher support and more personal guidance. This allows students to take complete control of the pace of their instruction.

Further, research has shown several characteristics to be common elements in most alternative programs and schools. Improved grades, school attendance, and graduation rates; decreased disruptions and suspensions; and a better sense of self are used to measure the success of the school or program (Mohr and Abbott, 2001). These common characteristics include but are not limited to the following: high academic standards and expectations, high standards for interpersonal/social interactions, student-centered education and intervention plans, low teacher/student ratio, site-based management/flexibility, parent and community involvement, "program" versus "school," and location (Mohr and Abbot, 2001). Research continues to indicate that school districts that are progressive in creating alternative schools based on these characteristics will meet the need of an ever changing population.

The characteristics of alternative schools have proven to be effective; however, research into the long-term effect of alternative schools as a whole has not been very supportive. Very few studies have dealt with the overall effects of alternative schools (Gottfredson, 1987). Because the schools vary in nature, student composition, structure, and purpose, researchers outside the field of education have yet to determine the alternative school's true effectiveness (Gottfredson, 1987). In theory, they offer an excellent second means for receiving a free and appropriate education.

ALTERNATIVE SCHOOL POPULATION

Traditionally, the alternative school population has been unsuccessful in the public high school setting. This population often displays the following common traits or patterns while attending public school: suspension, delinquency, truancy, and disruptive behavior. Alternative schools have been used at times as a means to separate children with these traits from the general population in an effort to provide them with a different learning environment. The students are often retained a grade and fail to meet state proficiency standards. Compared with the average student, these students frequently find themselves socially, politically, and economically disadvantaged.

Socially, many feel alienated from the public school setting, which usually results in poor school attendance, performance, and behavior. They are often found in negative peer groups without involvements in extracurricular activities. Politically, students who attend alternative schools are classified as "at risk" by the independent, county, and rural school districts. The definitions of *at risk* vary from state to state, but in general, an at-risk student is any student who, due to a wide range of individual, personal, financial, family, social, behavior, or academic factors, may experience school failure without proper intervention (Ward and Kirk, 2000). The "at risk" label often follows students throughout their school careers. Economically, state funds are often tied to the number of students that a district labels as "at risk." Such students are also often referred to as the "economically disadvantaged."

Any single circumstance or combination of factors does not necessarily put a student at risk of school failure; however, research in the field of education indicates that the chances are greater for these individuals (Mohr and Abbott, 2001). The chances increase when the factor of delinquency is added. States are now providing alternative school systems for troubled youth. The circumstances surrounding crime have produced an alternative school population different from the population needing an alternative learning style to succeed in public schools. Students who commit status offenses now commonly find themselves in alternative settings. Furthermore, after the "get tough on crime" legislation in the 1980s and 1990s, students who commit felonies are mandated to alternative locations. Such legislation makes it common practice to place students returning from juvenile placement facilities in alternative schools as a transitional phase before reintegrating them into public schools.

In recent times, a large number of youth in the juvenile justice system have been assigned by the school districts and the states to alternative schools due to criminal offenses. Alternative schools are now beginning to be used more frequently as places for troubled youth. Public outcry is demanding that these delinquents be placed in alternative schools for the protection of the general student population. Alternative schools are becoming dumping grounds for all troubled students regardless of the crime or the offense. Further, state facilities are housing thousands of youth throughout this country and must provide educational services for them. The number of special education and mentally ill students in both private and public facilities continues to grow.

Alternative schools located in juvenile correctional institutions are operated by the state. The educational programs are usually conducted during "normal" school hours. In most states, the educators in these facilities are certified teachers with certifications in several different subjects. Students in need of specialized services, which fall under the guidelines of the Individuals With Disabilities Education Act, receive the educational and behavioral modifications needed to succeed. Historically, the philosophy of these alternative schools was trade based. Most students received instruction for four hours in language arts, history, science, and math. Vocational teachers conducted the remainder of the school hours in a physical trade classroom or workshop.

More recently, the age of the youngest students attending alternative schools has decreased to 10. This could be caused by the recent enactment of laws by certain states that allow children as young as age 10 to be arrested for criminal offenses. School districts nationwide are developing programs and schools to teach a younger population in the alternative setting. This trend will most likely continue into the next century.

Frederick Ford

See also At-Risk Youth

Bibliography

Applied Research Center. 2001. *Expose Racism and Advance School Excellence. Resources for Journalists: Historical Timeline of Public Education in the U.S.* Available at http://arc.org/erase/j_timeline.html.

Gottfredson, G. D. 1987. American education, American delinquency. *Today's Delinquent* 6:5–70.

Miller, R. 2001. *Public Education, Alternative Schools, and Democracy.* Originally published by The Foundation for Educational Renewal, Brandon, VT. Available at http://www.haven.net/edge/council/miller.htm.

Mohr, N., and G. M. Abbott. 2001. *Alternative Education for Students at Risk. National Association of State Boards of Education, Policy Update.* Arlington, VA: Educational Research Service.

Platt, A. M. 1991. *The Child Savers: The Invention of Delinquency*, 2nd ed. Chicago: University of Chicago Press.

Ward, M., and P. Kirk. 2000. *Alternative Learning Programs and Schools: Definitions Approved by NCSBE.* North Carolina State Board of Education, Department of Public Instruction. Available at http://www.dpi.state.nc.us/alternative/definitions.html.

ARSON

The largest single cause of property damage due to fire in the United States is arson and suspected arson. The National Fire Protection Association (2000) reports that the costs of direct property damage to structures and vehicles is nearly $1.2 billion. The most common targets are residential properties, which account for 60 percent of arson or suspected arson targets, and uninhabited or abandoned properties and mobile properties such as boats or trailers, which equally account for the remaining 40 percent. The final cost reaches close to $2 billion after the addition of outdoor fires or fires with unidentified causes.

The cost of arson is extreme, yet despite popular myths, arson is not the fastest growing crime, and rates remain fairly stable. However, another issue concerning arson is the high amount of juvenile involvement and arrest. In 1999, the Federal Bureau of Investigation reported a total of 76,045 arson offenses. Persons under age 18 were involved in 48 percent of these arson incidents cleared by law enforcement. Of the eight index crimes studied by the Federal Bureau of Investigation, arson was the most frequently occurring criminal activity for which juveniles were convicted. This high percentage of juvenile involvement began in the late 1970s and since 1980 the amount has not fallen below 35 percent (National Fire Protection Association, 2000).

CAUSES OF JUVENILE ARSON

Juvenile arson and fire setting are extremely complex acts with numerous motivational factors operating at the same time. Therefore, no single theory can adequately explain why juveniles set fires. Early theories speculated that young children have a naturally inborn arson impulse. However, current explanations explore the influence of curiosity and underlying psychological and social problems. The psychosocial factors become problematic when normal interest in fire is disrupted by various individual characteristics, social circumstances, and environmental conditions.

Curiosity and Accidents

A common cause of juvenile fire setting is a combination of curiosity and lack of proper supervision and instruction on the dangers of fire. Curiosity toward fire can first be observed in children as young as 3 to 5 years of age. Usually by age 6, a child will have developed either fire-risk or fire-safe behaviors. A natural curiosity about fire along with a child's tendency to explore the environment may result in an instance of fire play. Fire play, a common phenomenon that often precedes arson, typically involves playing with matches and is most common in children under 7 years old.

Psychological Problems

Juvenile arsonists have more psychiatric symptoms and mental disorders than do other juvenile offenders. In addition, juvenile arsonists suffer from a mental illness as much as adult arsonists (Räsänen, Hakko, and Väisänen, 1995). The most common psychiatric diagnoses include conduct disorder and attention deficit disorder with hyperactivity. Conduct disorder involves the emerging antisocial personality traits, which are commonly seen in adult criminals. The more severely disturbed offenders often come from abusive families, and their pathology is evident in their disorganized and abnormal thinking patterns. *Pyromania* is a common term associated with fire setting, yet it is extremely rare and a term usually reserved for adult offenders who experience conversion and dissociative symptoms. Juveniles with these problems are generally categorized as pathological fire setters whose behavior results from mental disturbances.

In addition, psychological problems can include motivating factors that range from expression of anger to seeking revenge for real or imagined injustices. Juveniles with these difficulties are often viewed as troubled and crying for help due to their serious emotional problems. Social learning theory explains fire setting as an aggressive act that results from a fear of directly expressing anger. Through modeling, the juvenile has learned to use aggressive acts to express emotions that are generally hostile, anxious, and full of self-anger. This theory views the fire setter as using fire to displace anger because of difficulty handling aggression. The anger the fire setter feels is often directed toward parents and may result from extended abuse, an absent father figure, or a rejecting mother.

Social Problems

Setting fires may also be an expression of power or control due to underlying failures at a social level. Juvenile fire setters often feel intense anger at insults and teasing from both peers and adults. When a situation is experienced as hostile and unrewarding, setting a fire allows some mastery and control over an otherwise unbearable situation. Some juvenile arsonists and fire setters are also viewed as delinquents. Setting a fire is often an act of vandalism, a source of excitement, or a way to cover up another crime, such as burglary. The cause is typically malicious mischief and may result from peer pressure and influence or be an act of striking out against authority. Poor social judgment plays a role since there is often a failure to consider the potential for damage or injury.

Dynamic behavioral theory further explores the influence of the juvenile arsonist's environment. Fire setting is seen as influenced by modeling, imitation, and inconsistent negative reinforcement. A fire setter's environment is considered replete with aggressive acts and stress. There is a lack of reinforcing prosocial behavior and a failure to punish antisocial behavior. For exmple, poor family dynamics create an atmosphere in which setting fires allows the juvenile to gain attention from an otherwise unavailable parent who may be low in both affection and supervision. The type of attention is irrelevant, thus punishment has no effect.

PROFILE OF THE JUVENILE FIRE SETTER

A profile of a juvenile fire setter contains physical, cognitive, emotional, and social characteristics. Although these characteristics do not represent all juvenile fire setters, the majority of the characteristics offer a composite profile. Gender is a powerful variable as opposed to race. As with most crimes, more males than females set fires. Motives are similar, except females tend to be more self-destructive and set fires to their own property. Male fire setters come from a variety of socioeconomic backgrounds and have a higher than average incidence of physical illness, bed wetting, and psychiatric diagnoses.

Another feature to the profile includes a history of playing with matches, lighters, or fire. The juvenile may also display an excitement about fire in general and actively seek out flammable or combustible materials. From a cognitive perspective, juvenile fire setters have normal ranges of intelligence but display below average academic performances. There is also a history of school behavioral problems, such as truancy.

Poor peer relationships are common, and rage is felt from insults, teasing, or disrespect from both adults and peers. The inability to express aggression appropriately often causes juvenile fire setters to have revenge fantasies and a history of cruelty to animals and peers. Emotionally, these juveniles tend to experience inappropriate, intense anger while lacking the normal range and depth of other feelings such as guilt or remorse. For example, juvenile fire setters rarely admit to or put out fires they set despite the damage. Impaired social judgment is seen by fire setters' poor impulse control and inability to understand cause and effect relationships. These juveniles choose to react to instead of reflect on situations.

Juvenile fire setters' social characteristics are marked by a high incidence of family instability and stress. Single-family homes and parental pathology or disorganization is common. These juveniles view their parents as depressed, low in affection, lacking in supervision, and unavailable. This negative view of parental figures causes juvenile fire setters to feel bitter, rejected, hurt, or neglected. The juveniles are less able to handle stress and to establish and maintain interpersonal relationships.

SOLUTIONS TO JUVENILE ARSON

Although the juvenile justice system handles arson in a way similar to that used in adult arson cases, incarceration and sentencing are rare because judges usually choose alternatives to punishments and believe that every effort should be made to avoid the court's involvement. As a result, numerous programs have been established with the goal of terminating recurrent nonproductive fire starts. Most of the programs are housed within the U.S. Fire Administration, but other entities are closely involved, including mental health agencies, law enforcement, and schools. Overall, programs work toward utilizing primary prevention, early identification, and early intervention.

Preventive and Educational Approaches

Prevention involves teaching communities how to prevent fire setting through the presentation of information. Most approaches focus on reaching children at the critical age of their initial fire interest and awareness. The goals are to teach appropriate behaviors and basic fire safety rules, primarily through programs involving the fire department and local schools. The National Fire Protection Agency's Learn Not to Burn fire safety curriculum is a widely used program aimed at elementary school children. The curriculum establishes competency in 25 behaviors dealing with fire protection and prevention and has been shown to be successful in helping both at-risk and normal youths.

Prevention and education can also be effective with the high-risk group of middle school youths. The St. Paul Fire Education Program uses a curriculum that teaches fire and crime prevention through topics such as arson, vandalism, and the juvenile justice system. Local law enforcement agencies are encouraged to participate, and the final goal is that the middle school youths will apply their knowledge by teaching elementary school children. However, prevention and education programs are not limited to school curriculums. Multiple methods, such as public service announcements, brochures, newsletters and seminars, are useful in communicating with youth, parents, and the general public. In addition, local firefighters may act as role models, because findings indicate that juveniles from homes with absent or inattentive fathers are more likely to set fires. The Firehawk Children's Program provides a comprehensive set of services to juveniles and their families by training firefighters to act as mentors.

Psychological Treatment and Intervention

Juveniles often obtain psychological services due to referrals or as an alternative to incarceration as ordered by judges. This approach targets recurrent and psychologically disturbed fire setters and can take place in an inpatient or outpatient setting. Outpatient settings are used more often because of the concern that fires may be set during treatment at inpatient settings such as hospitals. However, placement is not an option when juvenile fire setters have severe mental disturbances that can be a source of danger to themselves or others. In addition, the problem may stem from the environment, thus removal from the home is vital to treatment. Inpatient treatment often requires follow-up to monitor reentry into the family and the community.

Treatment involves individual, family, and group therapy along with continued education. Individual therapy often uses a cognitive-behavioral approach, which works to eliminate the fire-setting behavior by teaching socially appropriate ways of expressing emotions when the urge to start a fire is recognized.

Another option is the behavioral approach, which uses the threat of punishment in combination with positive reinforcement. This approach rewards positive behavior, such as selecting toys instead of fire-starting materials, thereby encouraging insight into the fire-setting behavior. Group therapy often explores self-esteem and relationship issues, and family therapy may use psychotherapy as a way to adjust problematic environmental conditions.

Diversion Programs

Diversion programs use strategies aimed at helping juveniles avoid detention and incarceration. First-offender programs are common and involve juveniles with no prior history of arrest. An example is the Juvenile Firesetter Program in Texas, which assesses the needs of both the youth and the family through group meetings focusing on topics like anger management, parental control, and bad decision making. Once the program is successfully completed, no additional contact is required.

Day camps are another popular alternative and use a combination of physical exercise, work detail, victim awareness, and education. For example, participants may help fight forest fires, make trips to local fire stations, or visit burn units in hospitals. Another approach is suggested by Operation Extinguish in Maryland, which requires restitution for damage through community service.

Natalie Bishop

See also Theories of Delinquency—Psychological

Bibliography

Gaynor, J., and C. Hatcher. 1987. *The Psychology of Child Firesetting: Detection and Intervention.* New York: Brunner/Mazel.

National Fire Protection Association. 2000. *United States Arson Trends and Patterns.* Quincy, MA: National Fire Protection Association.

Räsänen, P., H. Hakko, and E. Väisänen. 1995. A portrait of the juvenile arsonist. *Forensic Science International* 73:41–47.

Sakheim, G. A., and E. Osborn. 1994. *Firesetting Children: Risk Assessment and Treatment.* Washington, DC: Child Welfare League of America.

Wooden, W. S., and M. Berkey. 1984. *Children and Arson: America's Middle Class Nightmare.* New York: Plenum.

ASSESSMENT

I. Needs

Once a juvenile offender is identified, *assessment* refers to the process of determining factors related to the original delinquent behavior, potential treatments and amenability to that treatment, and the degree of risk or danger to the community posed by the offender. There are two basic types of assessment: needs and risk. Needs assessment focuses on locating the offender's problems and pinpointing interventions to reduce subsequent delinquency. The task in needs assessment is to find ways to assist and rehabilitate the juvenile, most commonly involving outside services delivered by various treatment agencies. The primary purposes of risk assessment are estimating the likelihood of recidivism and of controlling the delinquent. Most risk assessment approaches are either actuarial (existing characteristics related to future behavior) based on a psychological interview model with various screening tests, or experience-based subjective choices made by probation officers and administrators.

THE PROCESS OF NEEDS ASSESSMENT

After a juvenile is detained by police and referred to the probation department, the needs assessment process begins. The juvenile court (or family court, depending on the state) will normally request an assessment of the juvenile, and a variety of tests will be run. Face-to-face contact, coupled with a battery of psychological tests, is the basis for assessing a juvenile delinquent's needs and subsequently making a referral to appropriate services. The probation officer or other person doing the assessment will also contact and gather information from the delinquent's family and school. These contacts may help uncover additional needs or determine services aimed at resolving the delinquent's needs.

The following factors are frequently identified as juvenile needs:

1. The prevalence of abuse and neglect, particularly an abusive and traumatized home life.

2. Alcohol and other drug use.

3. Mental health problems.

4. Stress-related illnesses.

5. Teenage pregnancy (for females).

6. HIV risk behavior.

7. Educational deficits.

8. Poor family and social functioning, including a seriously troubled home life and weak family structure.

9. Lack of positive identification with adults.

10. Poverty.

11. Low self-esteem.

12. Alienation from school or family.

These factors also match those found in theories of delinquency and are supported by years of research. To the extent that some can be resolved, the probability of delinquency decreases. Thus the juvenile court and the persons doing the assessment seek to locate solutions once the assessment is made and problems identified.

SERVICE BROKERAGE

The concept of service brokering implies that, based on needs assessment, the treatment plans developed are tailored to the individual. Caseworkers or treatment teams prioritize certain types of treatment, such as drug addiction, educational problems, emotional needs, family environment, and the like, and choose available placements from their networks. While needs vary immensely among individuals, the services offered are often contracted among a limited number of vendors or providers, or are programs open to the public. Therefore, services available to delinquents are often part of an established, consistent system of interagency cooperation.

THE STATE OF JUVENILE NEEDS ASSESSMENTS

Even though we have described needs assessments as routine and part of the juvenile court and probation process, the fact is that most states do not have formal, systemwide needs assessment procedures. All states do, however, have some form of needs assessment, although they appear at various points in the juvenile justice process. A 1992 survey (Towberman, 1992) found that the most frequently measured needs were substance abuse, emotional and/or psychological dysfunction, violent behavior, sexual abuse and deviancy, family dysfunction, peer association problems, educational and vocational deficits, and physical problems.

In addition to variations in the process and instruments, the quality and point of initiation of needs assessment also vary among states. In some states, court psychologists conduct thorough clinical assessments of juvenile offenders at intake. Probation officers serve the function in other states, while in still other states, juveniles do not receive needs assessment until after commitment to the correctional system. Regardless, there is no uniform instrument or approach to needs assessment, and in many cases, the assessment instrument (if it even exists) is not based on any sound research.

Beginning in the late 1990s, juvenile justice agencies around the country began to explore the advantages of implementing community assessment centers (CACs) and/or juvenile assessment centers (JACs). In July 1995, the Office of Juvenile Justice and Delinquency Prevention (OJJDP) reviewed CACs already in operation, outlining their potential benefits and limitations. By definition, juvenile assessment centers are essentially screening and classification programs that assess the nature and extent of risks to and from detained juveniles. An assessment is often completed in a short time and within one facility, thus reducing transportation and security concerns. Officials also hope that more concentrated and in-depth assessment will ensure that placement decisions are sound and youth do not have to return to the courts to be reassigned, interrupting their progress in the system. Identifying, assessing, referring, and ensuring that referred services for such juveniles are delivered and received is vitally important, given the current levels of violent crime and drug use among youth in the United States.

Previous problems associated with not having JACs include concerns that juveniles were not obtaining needed services, creation of gaps in services, and a lack of communication among service providers, causing children to fall into the cracks. Therefore, JACs are necessary to unmask the depth of juveniles' ancillary social risk factors (besides law violation) and provide specific, valid, and reliable assessments of the often serious multiple personal and family problems exhibited by youth entering the juvenile justice system. Without this information, the prospects for directing youth to the most appropriate remediation and rehabilitation resources are diminished.

Following a careful assessment via a variety of tests, the youth is then routed to the recommended campus or placed in a specific treatment program such as those for sex offenders or the chemically dependent. Most of the CACs and JACs support the concept of a single point of entry, whether youth are received from the courts, county mental health facilities, or alternative schools.

CONCLUSION

Needs assessment is one of the critical ingredients of the juvenile justice system. In fact, much more time is spent on juvenile needs assessment than is spent on adults in the criminal justice system. Thus one argument against transferring juveniles into the adult system is the lack of appropriate assessment. At the adult level, risk and needs assessments have recently been merged to prioritize the needs (criminogenic needs) that are also potent risk factors, such as antisocial associates, antisocial attitudes, and substance abuse. This approach might also serve juvenile populations well.

Regardless of the importance of needs assessment, the fact is that even the juvenile justice system does not provide validated and adequate assessment procedures and instruments across the states. Much of what passes for needs assessment is merely a routine set of questions with an anticipation of standard answers. Therefore, the services brokered to juveniles based on their "needs" are frequently standard ones provided to almost all delinquents. It is clear that more research and well-developed instruments are necessary in most jurisdictions.

Frank P. Williams III and Terry A. Snow

Bibliography

Oldenettel, D., and M. Wordes. 2000. The community assessment center concept. *Juvenile Justice Bulletin*. Washington, DC: Office of Juvenile Justice and Delinquency Prevention.

Rivers, J. E., and R. Anwyl. 2000. Juvenile assessment centers: Strengths, weaknesses, and potential. *Prison Journal* 80:96–113.

Towberman, D. B. 1992. National survey of juvenile needs assessment. *Crime and Delinquency* 38:230–238.

ASSESSMENT

II. Risk

The term *at-risk juveniles* could be used to identify juveniles who are at risk for dropping out of school, getting pregnant, getting involved in drugs, becoming delinquent, or engaging in school violence. All those factors can be directly or indirectly involved in sending the juvenile into the juvenile justice system or the adult system. Risk assessment in the criminal justice system is a process of determining the risk that an offender would recidivate, which is not the same concept as dangerousness.

Recidivism can refer to reoffending, being reincarcerated, or attending an additional court referral after the initial offense. For instance, recidivism in parole can refer to an offender committing a new violation of law or to an offender being reincarcerated due to violating the technical requirements of parole, such as failing a drug test, violating curfew, or not maintaining employment.

DEFINING AND MEASURING RISK

Typically, risk factors are either static, dynamic, or environmental. Static risk factors, the most common of the three types, are fixed and unchangeable. These factors usually involve an offender's criminal record such as the age that an offender was first arrested (the younger the age, the higher the recidivism rate), the total number of arrests, the number of felony convictions, and the number of times an offender has failed on probation or parole. These factors are used most often in an initial risk assessment. The more factors an offender has working against her or him, the higher is the risk that she or he will violate the law again. Because criminal history variables are so important to assessment, this presents a challenge to those in the juvenile justice system—juveniles have less history to evaluate.

Dynamic risk factors, such as antisocial attitudes and behaviors, can be changed, thus a successful strategy focuses on assessing dynamic risks and meeting the needs underlying them. Juveniles may need counseling, substance abuse treatment, life-skills development, or job placement assistance. Research has found that intervention strategies focusing on cognitive or behavioral approaches work better than person-centered

therapies. Additionally, programs that provide intensive services (lasting at least three to nine months), work on developing prosocial networks (such as a juvenile wilderness retreat), and are centered on the learning style of the offender can serve to reduce the risk of recidivism.

An additional risk factor is the offender's environmental circumstances. Family bonds, including drug abuse by family members, criminal history of family members, and residential instability, are often key factors determining risk. Additionally, factors related to education and employment, such as low IQ, poor educational attainment, and frequent unemployment, have been found to be critical ingredients in recidivism.

RISK INSTRUMENTS

Risk assessment can be done informally, usually by probation officers or parole agents. Although sometimes necessary in emergencies, informal risk assessment is less valid and reliable than is formal assessment.

The most common form of formal risk assessment is a risk prediction scale, a checklist that adds an offender's scores on certain variables. This score is compared with those of previous offenders who have violated in the past to determine an overall risk of recidivism. Formal risk assessment instruments usually classify youths' risk of reoffending as high, medium, or low. Two well-known examples of risk assessment instruments are the Canadian Level of Supervision Inventory (LSI), an intensive, interview-based approach; and the Wisconsin model, an actuarial approach. Clinical assessment also may be made with standardized measures, such as the Minnesota Multiphasic Personality Inventory (MMPI).

Instruments developed specifically for juveniles include the Ministry Risk/Need Assessment Form (MRNAF) used in Ontario, Canada, and the Arizona Juvenile Risk Assessment Form. The Arizona form uses nine variables: age, prior referrals, prior parole violations, runaway behavior, offense type, school, peer associations, alcohol or drug abuse, and family dynamics. Some forms are shorter, using as few as four to six variables. Almost all forms include information about an offender's criminal history and demographics. Other factors, such as environmental factors, clinical assessments, and the offender's attitudes and behaviors, are also common.

In general, criminal history variables, including the number of prior referrals, age at first arrest (or referral), and previous parole violations are fairly strong predictors of recidivism. Those who have been in the system before, are younger at first arrest or referral, and have violated parole previously are more likely to violate parole in the future. Demographic variables have produced mixed results in research studies. While younger age has generally been associated with recidivism, some research studies on gender and race have suggested that both males and minorities have greater levels of recidivism; other studies have not found these to be significant variables. Family dynamics and educational variables seem to have some predictive power, but they generally are not as strong as the criminal history variables. Unstable employment and poor peer associations are also frequently mentioned as positive contributors to recidivism.

ADVANTAGES OF THE PROCESS

Risk assessment is important for two reasons. First, it is an attempt to find the appropriate level of supervision for an offender—whether a person should be placed at a high, medium, or low level of supervision. If staff can correctly identify high-risk offenders, closer supervision or appropriate services may prevent future crimes.

Second, risk assessment helps to devote scarce financial resources efficiently and where they will do the most good. Many states are dealing with budget constraints and workload issues. As the number of offenders in the system increases, resources have to be devoted to offenders who are most in need of them. Since probation or parole officers cannot devote equal time and resources to each offender, risk assessment provides a means to decide which juveniles need to be contacted most frequently. Additionally, research has indicated that treatment dollars might be best expended on higher-risk groups than on lower-risk groups.

Risk assessment often overlooks the concept of stakes, which is the harm or damage caused by potential reoffending. While risk deals with the *probability* of a future offense occurring, stakes deals with the likely *consequences* of that future offense. For instance, drug offenders are likely to reoffend but with little damage or harm to society. In contrast, murderers are much less likely to reoffend, but the consequences to society are much greater if they do.

Another aspect of stakes is seen in the perceived threat of reoffending. The public is more afraid of violent crime, although violent offenders are less likely to recidivate than are property offenders. Sensationalized cases create greater public scrutiny, outcry, and fear. One type of offender who would be categorized as both high risk and high stakes is a gang member. Gang members have high recidivism rates for violent offenses, and they generally carry with them antisocial attitudes, negative peer influences, and substance abuse histories. Juvenile gangs also arouse high levels of concern in the general public. Sometimes the concept of stakes is included in risk assessment via a "clinical override," in which certain types of offenders, such as sex offenders, are automatically upgraded in risk, even if they score as a low risk for reoffending.

VALIDITY

Validity is a methodological concept referring to whether a measurement instrument is measuring what it is supposed to measure. For instance, stepping on an accurate scale provides a valid measure of your weight but not necessarily a valid measure of your level of fitness or future risk for disease. Risk assessment measures are often criticized for a lack of predictive validity. While some models have been successful in predicting recidivism or nonrecidivism somewhere between 60 percent and 80 percent of the time, this still leaves a high error level and room for improvement. In one study from California in the late 1960s, risk assessment measures vastly overpredicted the number of violent offenses juvenile offenders would commit. Additionally, most models are able to account for only a tiny fraction of the variance in outcome. While current instruments can predict recidivism to some degree, they do not provide an understanding of why a juvenile may reoffend or offer an appropriate intervention or supervision strategy. Research into risk assessment has often failed to incorporate theoretical perspectives from criminology, which compounds the instrument's inability to explain recidivism.

An additional concern with validity is referred to as discriminant validity. Can an instrument distinguish between two related concepts, such as racism and fear of crime? Clinical assessments are especially challenged in discriminant validity because a juvenile who is truly emotionally disturbed may not be distinguishable from one who is alienated or a nonconformist. Additionally, risk assessment instruments would need to be able to discriminate between high, medium, and low offenders by predicting different levels of recidivism for each.

Since recidivism is a variable with only two outcomes—the offender reoffends or doesn't—there are two possible errors. If an offender does reoffend despite an expectation that recidivism will *not* occur, the error is a false negative. A risk instrument that minimizes false negatives is desirable in an effort to reduce the risk of future criminality. Avoiding false negatives also reduces negative publicity, potential legal liability, and loss of legitimacy for the system.

The second error, a false positive, occurs if the offender does not reoffend, although the risk assessment instrument predicted that he or she would. False positives are expensive to the juvenile justice system—a particular concern in this era of limited resources and correctional overcrowding. In addition, false positives are tragic for offenders and their families.

Risk assessment instruments are subject to validation to see if they can accurately measure recidivism. That is, an instrument may only be accurate with the group used to create it. Thus a test with another group is necessary to determine how accurately the instrument can predict success and failure. However, once an instrument is validated, there is still a need to revalidate on occasion. Factors may lose salience, offender populations may change, and newer, more improved instruments may be constructed. There has been a wide discrepancy in validation procedures; some instruments were implemented without validation and used for decades before research showed their lack of validity. Periodic revalidation, perhaps every two years, has been recommended.

An additional validity issue is external validity or generalizability. An instrument that works in one jurisdiction does not necessarily predict recidivism well for juveniles in other jurisdictions. Some measurement instruments are validated on populations where everyone is similar and may not be generalizable to more diverse populations. It is still unclear whether separate instruments should be used for boys and girls or for different ethnicities (such as Native American offenders who have distinctly different cultural characteristics) and whether special populations, such as sex offenders and gang members, should be assessed with unique instruments.

RELIABILITY

Reliability refers to the ability of a measurement instrument to produce similar results with repeated use. A scale that measures a person's weight at 180 pounds on three successive attempts can be considered reliable, provided the subject is the same each time (i.e., not wearing different clothing or having eaten in between). Risk assessment measures have been shown to have greater reliability than less formal measures, such as a probation officer's personal assessment that a juvenile is a bad risk, which are more likely to be prone to random error. Reliability can often be enhanced through interrater reliability—that is, having two different professionals use the instrument and then comparing the results. Criminal history variables also tend to have greater reliability than clinical assessments, which may be subjective in nature.

REASSESSMENT

Although initial risk assessment has been written about extensively, less attention has been paid to reassessment. Reassessment is particularly important for juvenile justice, since juveniles are simultaneously more prone to either positive or negative changes in their lives. Many jurisdictions have no formal procedures for reassessment. It is often done for administrative reasons—for example, every six months—as opposed to being dictated by changes in the offender. Static risk factors, such as age at first arrest or previous violations of probation or parole, may not be as important in a reassessment as these factors do not vary from one assessment to another.

CONCLUSION

Risk assessment is a necessary yet challenging aspect of the juvenile justice system. Future research will attempt to validate and revise current measures in addition to specifying the populations for which these instruments are best suited. Debate will likely continue on their use with special populations, such as sex offenders, who may not be adequately assessed with current instruments. Research will continue to search for the most appropriate static, dynamic, and environmental risk factors, and future instruments assessing related concepts, such as stakes, may come under increasing examination.

H. Michael Dolny

See also At-Risk Youth; Prevention Strategies; Probation, Juvenile; Serious and Violent Juvenile Offenders; Sex Offenders

Bibliography

Ashford, J. B., and C. W. LeCroy. 1990. Juvenile recidivism: A comparison of three prediction instruments. *Adolescence* 25:441–450.

Clear, T. 1988. Statistical prediction in corrections. *Research in Corrections* 1:1–40.

Funk, S. J. 1999. Risk assessment for juveniles on probation: A focus on gender. *Criminal Justice and Behavior* 26:44–68.

McShane, M. D., and F. P. Williams III. 1998. *Predicting Parole Success.* Sacramento, CA: California Department of Corrections, Parole and Community Services Division.

 # AT-RISK YOUTH

The concept of risk factors is at the core of a large body of research on juvenile delinquency. A risk factor is any variable that is related to a juvenile becoming or not becoming a delinquent. The answer to what puts a child at risk is elusive because some research on the subject is contradictory. Often the identification of risk has focused on the trivial and simplistic: rock and roll, rap, and punk music; pornography; the Internet; television violence; violent video games; media coverage of crime; the glorification of crime and violence in movies; and so on. The simple fact is that juveniles have always been crime-prone. The reasons why a juvenile commits delinquent acts should be considered *multivariate* in nature. In other words, there is no single variable, such as television or music, that causes a juvenile to commit crime. However, certain variables (risk factors) are correlated with a juvenile becoming delinquent. Hence it is important to understand the difference between a causal factor and a risk factor.

A causal factor is a variable that *causes* a juvenile to be delinquent. A risk factor is a variable that, by its presence or absence, is correlated with the youth's becoming delinquent. A juvenile who possesses several risk factors will not necessarily become a delinquent. Similarly, the absence of all risk factors does not guarantee that a juvenile will not commit delinquent acts. In addition, the concept of protective factors (variables that correlate with not committing delinquent acts) have also been researched quite extensively. In essence, risk factors put a juvenile in greater danger of becoming delinquent while protective factors insulate a juvenile from becoming delinquent. Risk factors do not cause delinquency; protective factors do not prevent delinquency. Nonetheless, research indicates that the presence or absence of a risk or protective factor is related to delinquency. There is a cumulative effect of risk factors that tends to lead to certain risky behaviors and lifestyles, which in turn typically lead to negative outcomes and lost opportunities for the juvenile.

Efforts to design effective delinquency intervention and treatment programs have led to many research endeavors aimed at identifying the most problematic risk factors and the most important protective factors. As a result, numerous classification schemes of risk factors exist and lead to confusion regarding exactly which risk and protective factors are the most important. In addition, many identified risk factors are often beyond the youth's control (race, gender, socioeconomic status, school district) and thus do not lead to easy interventions. They may also include behaviors that children display when they are very young: hyperactivity, lying, acting out. Because these factors are relatively common in many children, intervention can be too sweeping and can identify children who really are not at risk. Another issue in the research on risk and protective factors is that the majority of youth commit some type of delinquent act, and drawing the line between "delinquent" and "nondelinquent" youth is not always clear or consistent.

WHAT IS AN AT-RISK YOUTH?

An at-risk youth can be defined in several ways. The Girls and Boys Town youth facility in Nebraska is a prominent program dedicated to the rescue of troubled youth. They define as at risk any youth who is in danger of placement outside of the home; has had negative contact with law enforcement, schools, churches, or other agencies; or who has been impacted directly by substance abuse, sexual promiscuity, or physical abuse. A more simplistic definition is that an at-risk youth possesses risk factors correlated with delinquency. The primary difficulty in defining an at-risk youth is also the primary difficulty in this area of research.

Risk factor research, like any research, must be undertaken and interpreted with some caution. So far the research has provided no clear-cut answers and has not specified certain factors that cause or prevent delinquency. The interaction between risk factors and a juvenile's mind and perceptions is practically impossible to determine. For every at-risk juvenile who becomes a delinquent there is one who does not. One thing is certain: There is no single factor that either causes or prevents all delinquency. As Huizinga, Loeber, and Thornberry (1994) noted, the methodology of prediction and the state of theory is currently insufficient to determine who will and who will not engage in delinquency.

A number of researchers have examined risk and protective factors. Most of the research in this area contains some similar general themes and similar categorical frameworks. However, the identification of specific risk and protective factors will differ depending on which source is consulted. Nonetheless, there are several common areas of risk-focused research.

RESEARCHING RISK AND PROTECTIVE FACTORS

One of the principle research projects examining risk and protective factors is actually a combination of three coordinated studies: the Denver Youth Survey, the Pittsburgh Youth Study, and the Rochester Youth Development Study. Taken together, these three projects form the Causes and Correlates of Delinquency Program. Initiated in 1986, the research is designed to improve the understanding of serious delinquency, violence, and drug use by examining how youth develop within the context of family, school, peers, and community. Each study uses a number of data sources, including interviews with the youths, their guardians, and teachers as well as information collected from official agencies. The Causes and Correlates of Delinquency Program is the largest shared-measurement approach ever achieved in delinquency research. The three research teams work together to ensure that certain core measures are identical across the sites, including self-reported delinquency and drug use; community and neighborhood characteristics; youth, family, and peer variables; and arrest and judicial processing histories. A variety of other research findings on risk and protective factors have been published in academic journals, books, and evaluations of delinquency programs.

RISK AND PROTECTIVE FACTORS

Risk and protective factors are interrelated, affecting one another as a youth develops. Six primary types of

risk factors exist in the current literature: biology and genetics, family, personality, social environment, ecological environment, and educational environment. These categories include the primary worlds that juveniles interact with—family, social, ecological, and school—and can aid in determining the behaviors and lifestyles juveniles will develop. Although the six categories interact and influence each other, the degree to which each influences the other is the subject of debate. The interaction of risk and protective factors is different for each juvenile. There is no pattern or number of risk factors that determines who will and who will not become delinquent. Again, risk and protective factors should be viewed as *predictive* and not *causal*.

Biology and Genetics

This group of risk and protective factors comprises variables that are, for the most part, out of the control of the juvenile. Like the age-old debate of heredity versus environment, the basic question researchers ask regarding these factors is, Is delinquency an inherited trait based on biology and genetics, or is delinquency the result of socialization and environment? Although a great deal of controversy arises in the academic and political arenas regarding the role of biology and genetics in delinquency, several research studies have found correlations. Most problematic is the fact that the distinction between biology and socialization is not always clear. For example, low IQ has been found to be related to delinquency. Yet how we develop IQ, socially or genetically, is still not determined.

One volatile debate in this area involves the connection between race and crime. Some research has found that there are no differences between African American and Caucasian boys at 6 years of age, but differences gradually develop, with the prevalence of serious delinquency peaking at age 16 (Browning and Loeber, 1999). As the incidence of delinquency increases, so does the average frequency of serious offending, rising more rapidly for African American than for Caucasian boys. Regarding the onset of offending among the boys involved in serious delinquency, 51 percent of African American boys and 28 percent of Caucasian boys appear to commit serious delinquent acts by age 15 (Browning and Loeber, 1999). Another common finding is that African Americans are more likely to be involved in violent offending than are whites. It is probably best to consider the role of race in the social rather than the biological context. If a person's race or ethnicity values behavior that may put them in greater contact with the system, they are more likely to be delinquent than someone whose race or ethnicity does not hold that value. Certain ethnicities have cultures that greatly value family life, which can lead to juveniles being insulated. Further, in American society, some races and ethnicities are undoubtedly more isolated in deprived urban areas, which affects delinquency rates and further obfuscates the impact of the biology/genetics risk factor.

Gender is a genetic risk factor that is a clear predictor of delinquency. Boys are more involved in more serious forms of delinquency than are girls. However, in recent years, there has been a marked increase in female involvement in delinquent acts. Between 1988 and 1994, the violent crime index arrest rate almost doubled for females and increased 60 percent for males. Meanwhile, the violent crime index arrest rate for male juveniles remains substantially higher than that for female juveniles. In addition, the property crime index arrests for female juveniles increased 42 percent between 1981 and 1997 while arrests of juvenile males increased only 15 percent. Again, males commit property crimes far more often than do females. In general, the most powerful predictors of individual violent criminality are age and gender. Boys in late adolescence and young men are much more likely to be serious high-rate offenders than are girls or older men. Study after study confirms that males are more violent, more prone to bullying and violent behavior at school, and are arrested for more violent offenses than are females.

Family

A large body of research has assessed many family characteristics and found that several family variables are risk factors. Strong risk factors include absence of parental supervision, parental rejection, child maltreatment, and lack of parental involvement; medium- and lesser-strength predictors include parental marriage status and relations, parental criminality, parental discipline, parental health, and parental absence. One particularly interesting research finding is that a small number of families produce a disproportionate number of delinquent children (Loeber and Stouthamer-Loeber, 1986). The presence of a delinquent sibling also increases the likelihood that other children in the family will become delinquent. When breaking down certain family factors, research shows that the presence of a father reduces the chances of a son

becoming delinquent, first-born children are less likely to be delinquent, and the larger the family, the more likely it is that a child in the family will be delinquent.

A large study of previous research on families found that a "broken home" has an impact on delinquency, but the effects appear to be minimal. The study also found that the correlation between a broken home and delinquency was greater in minor forms of delinquency. Some research suggests that youths who are not closely bonded with their parents are more likely to be delinquent. Finally, family structure is moderately related to delinquent behavior (Johnson, 1989). The Rochester Youth Study examined the quality of parent-child relationships to determine the impact on delinquency of factors in the family "process," such as attachment, involvement, and supervision. The study found that children who are more attached to and involved with their parents were less involved in delinquency. In addition, the relationship between family process factors and delinquency is circular; poor parenting increased the probability of delinquent behavior and delinquent behavior further weakened the relationship between parent and child. Finally, the impact of family variables appeared to fade as adolescents became older and more independent from their parents (Browning, Thornberry, and Porter, 1999).

Personality

Most research is still in its infancy in the area of personality characteristics and their relationship to youths' being at risk. The biggest problem with research conducted in this area is the way in which concepts are defined and measured. Nonetheless, there is some consistency about which personality characteristics are common to delinquents and which protective factors are common to nondelinquents. Research shows that characteristics such as hyperactivity, restlessness, risk-taking attitudes, and aggressiveness are predictors of future delinquency and drug use (Hawkins et al., 2000).

Social Environment

The effects of peers, social class, and activities and interests on juvenile delinquency have been well researched. Associating with delinquent peers is strongly and consistently related to delinquency, in part because delinquent peers provide positive reinforcement to delinquent behavior. The opposite is also true: Having peers who disapprove of delinquency is a protective factor (Hawkins et al., 2000). In addition to its findings about the presence of delinquent peers, the Rochester Youth Study also explored the relationship to delinquency of holding delinquent beliefs and engaging in delinquent behavior. Holding delinquent beliefs means that youths assess how acceptable, or wrong, it is to engage in delinquent acts. Delinquent beliefs increased involvement in delinquency. In turn, engaging in delinquent behavior had strong reciprocal effects, increasing associations with delinquent peers and the formation of delinquent beliefs (Browning et al., 1999).

One study found that "structural" position, such as social class and community of residence, had important effects on delinquency. Children from underclass backgrounds (those where there is persistent high-level poverty) were more involved in delinquency, especially serious delinquency. In this environment, economic hardship and stressful life events led to a lack of parent-child attachment and involvement and parental control over adolescents. In turn, these elements of poor parenting were significantly associated with increased delinquency (Hawkins et al., 2000). However, one school of criminological thought (labeling) disputes the findings that social class is involved in delinquency, other than the fact that lower-class youths are subjected to greater criminal justice system scrutiny.

Ecological Environment

Certain characteristics of communities predict delinquency. In fact, the number of juveniles engaging in delinquency in a particular area is strongly correlated to community crime rates and vice versa. It is a relative truism that small areas within large cities typically have disproportionately high levels of violence and crime; therefore, juveniles living in those areas tend to be more involved in crime and violence. Areas in which poverty rates are high, access to drugs and firearms is easy, neighborhood adults are involved in crime, and social relations are disorganized have all been found to be risk factors in delinquency.

Educational Environment

The school a juvenile attends can affect his or her level of delinquency—the overall level of delinquency at the school, the truancy rates, and the number of students dropping out from the school are all related

to a juvenile's delinquency. Juveniles who fail academically, have low bonding to their schools, have made frequent school transitions, or have dropped out are more likely to use drugs and persist in delinquent conduct. Juveniles who are not committed to school have higher rates of street crime, and those who commit street crimes have less commitment to school. School performance, whether measured by reading achievement or teacher-rated reading performance, and retention in grade (being held back) also relate to delinquency as either risk or protective factors.

Weak school commitment and poor school performance are associated with increased involvement in delinquency and drug use. Further, school success is associated with resilience. Youths who avoid delinquency and drug use, even though they are high-risk juveniles, are generally more attached to school and teachers and have better performance scores than high-risk juveniles who are involved in delinquency and drug use. Conversely, involvement in delinquency reduces commitment to school, and involvement in drug use increases the chances of dropping out of school. Thus it is difficult to tell which leads to which. However, juveniles who drop out of school are generally more likely to be arrested even when they get older, get a job, or get married. Higher education, then, seems to be a protective factor against delinquency.

BEHAVIOR AND LIFESTYLE

Juveniles who possess risk factors tend to engage in behaviors that are different from those of juveniles who possess protective factors. The research conducted by the Causes and Correlates of Delinquency Program, examining behavior as a whole, found that the boys generally developed disruptive and delinquent behavior in an orderly, progressive fashion, with less serious problem behaviors preceding more serious problem behaviors. The research identified three developmental pathways in which progressively more serious problem behaviors are displayed (Browning and Loeber, 1999):

1. *Authority conflict:* Youth on this pathway exhibit stubbornness before age 12 and then move on to defiance and avoidance of authority.

2. *Covert:* This pathway includes minor covert acts, such as lying, followed by property damage and moderately serious delinquency and then by serious delinquency.

3. *Overt:* This pathway includes minor aggression followed by fighting and violence.

The progression to more serious delinquency leads to a certain lifestyle that the juvenile adopts. The word *lifestyle* denotes an organized pattern of interrelated behaviors. Once a juvenile has adopted a particular lifestyle—student, achiever, gang member, delinquent—that lifestyle is reinforcing and leads to further risky or nonrisky behavior. Interestingly, many of the risk and protective factors involved in a lifestyle also relate to the odds of becoming the *victim* of a crime. Juveniles who adopt a risky lifestyle also put themselves at greater risk of being victims of assault, robbery, rape, and murder.

Several behaviors noted among juveniles who are at risk both confirm their delinquent lifestyle and further reinforce the fact that they are at risk of even becoming more serious offenders. Perhaps the most prominent behavior in this category is drug use. For some juveniles, the drug use precedes delinquency, and for others, the converse is true. Nonetheless, drug use and delinquency are correlated. A common finding is that juvenile arrestees test positive for drug use. A major study of frequent drug-abusing juveniles conducted by the National Institute on Drug Abuse (NIDA) found that the 611 juveniles studied reportedly committed 429,136 criminal acts during the 12-month period before being interviewed—an average of 702 offenses per subject. The majority (60 percent) of the crimes committed were drug transactions of some type. Over the same period, these 611 youths also committed 18,477 serious felonies, including 6,269 robberies and 721 assaults. Eighty-eight percent reported carrying a weapon most of or all the time (Inciardi, 1990). The relationship between drug use and delinquency has changed recently. The percentage of serious delinquents using hard drugs (other than marijuana) has dropped from 48 percent to 17 percent. At the same time, the percentage of hard drug users who are serious offenders has risen from 27 percent to 48 percent (Browning and Huizinga, 1999).

Risky lifestyle and behaviors also lead to increasingly formal contact with the juvenile justice and criminal justice systems. More than half (53 percent) of the youths in Denver Youth Survey who were 11 through 15 years of age in 1987 were arrested over the next five years. For many youths, arrest and processing through the juvenile justice system did not have the desired effect of deterring future delinquent involvement. When the delinquent behavior in the year following arrest for first-time arrestees was compared with that of a matched control group, the majority—about 75 percent for status offense arrests and 92 percent for serious offense arrests—of first-time arrestees displayed similar or higher levels of delinquency (Browning and Huizinga, 1999).

Antisocial, aggressive behavior found in young children is also a risk factor for future delinquency and drug use. Many youths who join gangs, regardless of the reasons, are substantially more at risk for becoming arrested or becoming a victim of crime. Research has found that those youth who remain in gangs for a long time have extraordinarily high rates of delinquency. The Rochester Youth Study found a strong relationship between gang membership and delinquent behavior, particularly serious and violent delinquency. In addition the study found that although they represented only one third of the Rochester sample, gang members accounted for 86 percent of serious delinquent acts, 69 percent of violent delinquent acts, and 70 percent of drug sales. Gang members had higher rates of violent offenses at the time they were active gang members than they did either before they belonged to the gang or after they left the gang. Finally, gang membership had a strong impact on the incidence of violent behavior, even when other risk factors, such as poverty, prior involvement in violence, and association with delinquent peers, were held constant (Browning et al., 1999).

A series of studies on juvenile violence found that accessibility of guns is a relatively strong indicator of juvenile violence in the area of access. Firearms were involved in 80 percent or more of the violent incidents involving juveniles in each of the geographic areas examined. Further, 40 percent of the youths who were surveyed reported gun possession at some point (Office of Juvenile Justice and Delinquency Prevention, 1999). Behaviors related to sexual practices, health, and safety are also risk factors that can predict delinquency and drug use. Delinquents, as a group, tend to be sexually promiscuous and to take poor care of themselves in the areas of diet and health care. They also tend to engage in a variety of unsafe conduct.

CUMULATIVE EFFECTS OF RISK FACTORS

No single risk or protective factor can predict delinquency as effectively as the cumulative effect of risk or nonrisk behavior, background, and attitude. For instance, Browning and Loeber (1999) reported that the probability of serious delinquency increased as the number of risk factors increased. When the number of risk factors exceeded the number of protective factors, the juvenile's chance of having a delinquency-free adolescence was very small. The chances of a juvenile's having a successful adolescence did not become high until the number of protective factors far exceeded the number of risk factors. The best predictors of success in the Browning and Loeber study were having conventional friends, a stable family and good parental monitoring, positive expectations for the future, and nondelinquent peers.

OUTCOMES AND OPPORTUNITIES

Engaging in risky behaviors or lifestyles typically leads to certain outcomes and opportunities or the lack of them. Conversely, avoiding risky behaviors and adopting a certain lifestyle typically lead to other outcomes and opportunities. For juveniles already involved in risky behavior, a range of serious negative outcomes is likely. Once a youth adopts a certain lifestyle, that lifestyle tends either to open or restrict access to opportunities. The more successful and protective factors youths have, the more opportunities for advancement they are likely to enjoy. It is also true that the adoption of a delinquent lifestyle, even at an early age, blocks or restricts access to opportunities.

Tory J. Caeti and Eric J. Fritsch

See also Assessment—Risk; Drugs; Gangs, Juvenile; Guns and Juveniles; Theories of Delinquency

Bibliography

Browning, K., and D. Huizinga. 1999. *Highlights of Findings From the Denver Youth Survey Series.* Washington, DC: Office of Juvenile Justice and Delinquency Prevention.

Browning, K., and R. Loeber. 1999. *Highlights of Findings From the Pittsburgh Youth Study Series.* Washington, DC: Office of Juvenile Justice and Delinquency Prevention.

Browning, K., T. Thornberry, and P. Porter. 1999. *Highlights of Findings From the Rochester Youth Development Study Series.* Washington, DC: Office of Juvenile Justice and Delinquency Prevention.

Hawkins, J., T. Herrenkohl, D. Farrington, D. Brewer, R. Catalano, T. Harachi, et al. 2000. *Predictors of Youth Violence.* Washington, DC: Office of Juvenile Justice and Delinquency Prevention.

Huizinga, D., R. Loeber, and T. Thornberry. 1994. *Urban Delinquency and Substance Abuse: Initial Findings.* Washington, DC: Office of Juvenile Justice and Delinquency Prevention.

Inciardi, J. A. 1990. The crack-violence connection within a population of hard-core adolescent offenders. Pp. 92–111 in M. De La Rosa, E. Y. Lambert, and B. Gropper (eds.), *Drugs and Violence: Causes, Correlates, and Consequences. NIDA Research Monograph* 103. Washington, DC: National Institute on Drug Abuse.

Johnson, R. 1989. Family structure and delinquency: General patterns and gender differences. *Criminology* 24:65–84.

Loeber, R., and M. Stouthamer-Loeber. 1986. Family factors as correlates of juvenile conduct problems and juvenile delinquency. Pp. 29–149 in M. Tonry and N. Morris (eds.), *Crime and Justice: An Annual Review of Research*, Vol. 7. Chicago: University of Chicago Press.

Office of Juvenile Justice and Delinquency Prevention. 1999. *Report to Congress on Juvenile Violence Research.* Washington, DC: Office of Juvenile Justice and Delinquency Prevention.

BODY-TYPE THEORIES

Nineteenth-century biologists and anatomists attempted to link the study of the body, growth patterns, and heredity to behavior. In the early 1800s, phrenologists studied the outer contours of the skull and attempted to assess problems of the mind by the various bumps and indentations. Because no one had the means to directly study the brain of a live person at that time, the skull, as the container, gave one as close an approximation as possible. This type of "form follows function" thinking was evident in early body-type theories. It was believed that the personality was influenced by the body (and vice versa) and that one could make generalizations about a person's temperament by studying her or his physique.

Constitutional or body-type theories developed out of the positivist school of criminological thought. These theorists felt that criminal traits were manifest in the physical traits of the individual. Further, criminal individuals could be distinguished from noncriminals by their differing physical features. While these theorists all seemed to agree that environment and social influences certainly played a role in the child's development, they were interested in how heredity, intelligence, and a biopsychological personality might also be influential. Several studies in the early 1900s found that delinquents were more likely to be taller and weigh more than nondelinquents. This led to controversy over whether physical superiority was linked to aggression or dominance. As Bloch and Flynn (1956:141) explained,

The crucial factor in determining the delinquent pattern of causation may be either the motivation towards leadership or the desire to be dominated; in both cases, the factors of size, stature and weight may be associated closely or remotely with the entire complex of motivation.

In 1925, German psychiatrist Ernst Kretschmer identified three criminal body types after studying more than 4,000 individuals. The first type was the leptosome (asthenic types)—a tall, thin person with prominent skeletal features. This person, Kretschmer argued, was prone to commit crimes such as petit larceny and fraud and may have schizophrenic tendencies. The second type was the pyknic—stocky and rounded, with fleshy smooth arms and legs. This person was more likely involved in fraud, deception, and crimes of violence and was noted to have tendencies toward manic-depressive states. Third, the athletic type had well-developed muscles and commonly committed crimes of violence. Kretschmer later added a fourth body-type classification, the mixed or unclassifiable type (dysplastic). Individuals in this category usually committed offenses against morality and decency.

Kretschmer's work was continued by W. A. Willemse. He looked to the onset of puberty as a potential force in delinquency, thus he compared youth on the amount of body hair, muscularity, and fat accumulation, as well as intelligence and temperament. He made detailed measurements of such features as the skull, chest, shoulders, and legs.

In the late 1940s, William Sheldon attempted to link criminal behavior in male juveniles to their body types.

With considerable methodological improvements over the work of Kretschmer, Sheldon constructed a mental and physical typology of youths and produced three physical categories and three classifications of temperament. The physical categories were the endomorph, the mesomorph, and the ectomorph. The endomorph tended to be soft and fat, the mesomorph was more muscular and had an athletic build, and the ectomorph was skinny and fragile. The temperament types Sheldon identified were the viserotonic, who was relaxed and easy-going, free from tension; the somotonic, who was generally talkative, assertive, and aggressive; and the cerebrotonic, who was introverted and generally complained of illness, allergies, and insomnia.

Sheldon studied more than 200 male juveniles living in a rehabilitation facility in Boston. The subjects were rated on their physical characteristics and personal dispositions. These body-type and temperament ratings determined the type of treatment the subjects received. From his analysis, Sheldon concluded that body type, coupled with temperament, could act as a predictor in an individual's propensity to commit crime. He concluded that the majority of the delinquents in his study were of the mesomorphic body type.

Though Sheldon's work was widely criticized by sociologists, his research went on for years. In 1995, the Smithsonian Institution removed from its collection a set of nude photos, particularly those Sheldon took of freshmen at prestigious Ivy League schools where he studied the relationship between body shape and intelligence. The photos included those of U.S. Senator Hillary Rodham Clinton and ABC-TV's Diane Sawyer as Wellesley College students and former President George Bush and New York Governor George Pataki as Yale University students.

In the 1950s, Sheldon and Eleanor Glueck conducted a comparative study of approximately 1,000 juveniles, half of whom were officially delinquent and the other half nondelinquent. The Gluecks supported Sheldon's conclusion that delinquent body types tended to be mesomorphic; further, they suggested that these youth were well suited for tasks that were concrete in meaning and tied to direct physical relationships. Their work was criticized because the researchers simply looked at pictures of youths and then classified them into body types based on visual assessment, not actual measurements. Also, some critics have noted that the Gluecks did not take into consideration the rapid body changes in males in puberty.

Body-type theories have, to date, been disputed and their influence minimized. However, their impact can still be seen in modern brain dysfunction theories and the effects of nutrition and toxins on criminal behavior. Researchers continue to explore brain neurology, genetics, intelligence, and various mental traits for their relationship to criminal behavior. Body-type theorists were among the first to approach the study of criminal behavior from an interdisciplinary perspective. Today researchers from the disciplines of criminal justice, criminology, sociology, psychology, biology, and law collaborate to find explanations for criminal behavior and strategies for its treatment and prevention.

Elizabeth H. McConnell and Dawn M. Caldwell

See also Theories of Delinquency—Biological

Bibliography

Bloch, H. A., and F. T. Flynn. 1956. *Delinquency: The Juvenile Offender in America Today*. New York: Random House.

Glueck, S., and E. Glueck. 1950. *Unraveling Juvenile Delinquency*. New York: Commonwealth Fund.

Kretschmer, E. 1925. *Physique and Character*. Trans. W. J. H. Sprott. London: Kegan, Paul, Trench, Truber.

Sheldon, W. 1949. *Varieties of Delinquent Youth*. New York: Harper & Brothers.

Willemse, W. A. 1932. *Constitution-Types in Delinquency*. New York: Harcourt, Brace.

 # BOOT CAMPS

Boot camp programs are a juvenile correctional sanction modeled after military basic training. Developed as an alternative to traditional incarceration options, such as detention centers and prisons, boot camps are typically viewed by the criminal justice system as a punishment that is less severe than prison but more severe than probation. Boot camps, which were the same as shock incarceration programs in earlier decades, exist throughout the United States and in some foreign countries for males and females and for both youth and adult offenders.

HISTORICAL OVERVIEW OF BOOT CAMP DEVELOPMENT

Boot camp programs garnered a large amount of media and political attention with the advent of the "get tough on crime" politics of the 1980s. This attention has continued into the 21st century, resulting in a proliferation of boot camp programs throughout the United States. Although it may seem that the programs are a recent trend, the roots of boot camp programs can be traced to the 1800s. This section describes the rationale for developing boot camp programs and follows their progression.

During the latter part of the 19th century, the public became concerned about the use of inmate labor for manufacturing retail goods. The results of this concern were antilabor laws, which made the inmate labor system illegal. Before the formation of antilabor laws, most of an inmate's day was spent in some form of trade or labor that resulted in marketable products. The profits from these products were used to support the daily operation of prisons. Because inmate labor was relatively inexpensive, prison officials were able to market products produced by the inmates at a significantly lower cost to the consumer, thereby undercutting the prices of other manufacturers' goods. Unions and manufacturers considered the competition from the inmate labor system unfair and rallied for legislation that restricted the use of inmate labor and inmate-produced goods. In 1905, President Theodore Roosevelt signed an executive order that prohibited the use of inmate labor on federal projects. Congress took further action against the inmate labor system in 1929 by passing the Hawes-Cooper Act, which permitted individual states to ban the importation of inmate products from other states.

One of the indirect effects of the public concern and the subsequent legislation was that prison administrators were forced to find other activities to occupy inmates' time. The New York Reformatory was among the first prisons to suggest military-style training. In 1888, due to unions' and manufacturers' concerns, the administrators of the correctional facility in Elmira decided to eliminate inmate labor on commercial products. As an alternative, military organizational components were incorporated into almost every facet of the correctional facility in Elmira, including inmate schooling, supervision of inmates, physical training, and even parole practices. The militarization of the New York Reformatory was expected to have a number of benefits in addition to occupying inmates' time. The military-style training was viewed as a tool to assist inmates in reforming their behavior and in learning various marketable, honest skills during their time in the reformatory. Additionally, the military-style discipline was thought to provide a means for obtaining obedience, attention, and organization within the prison environment.

The militarization of correctional programs eventually stopped in most U.S. prisons due to a major shift in correctional thinking in the early part of the 20th century. Because of this shift, an increased emphasis was placed on assisting offenders to remedy the errors of their ways through therapeutic programming rather than physical training. Thus much of the inmates' time was spent in treatment activities, and there was no need for old-fashioned military-style activities.

Therapeutic programming and rehabilitation of offenders remained the focus of most correctional programs until the 1970s, when a second major shift in correctional thought occurred. This second shift led prison administrators to focus on the emerging get-tough perspective on crime and criminals, downplaying the need for treatment and emphasizing punishment and deterrence, thus resulting in a revitalization of military-style correctional programs in 1983. In this new era, Georgia and Oklahoma were the first states to develop boot camp programs modeled after a military-style boot camp. The programs were supported by some of the same rationales and philosophies that were evident nearly 100 years earlier.

One of the primary factors in revitalization and subsequent proliferation of boot camp programs throughout the United States was that the harsh, physical nature of discipline and activity in these types of programs was in tune with the emerging political climate. Consequently, journalists widely publicized boot camps as an exemplar of get-tough programming. Video footage and photographs of drill sergeants yelling in the faces of boot camp participants presented an evocative image absorbed by the general population and sought after by policymakers.

Early boot camp programs, such as those developed in Oklahoma and Georgia, emphasized a military atmosphere with drill and ceremony, stern structure, physical training, and hard labor. Following the early program examples, boot camps proliferated across the country increasing both in size and number. By 1999, 31 states, 10 local jurisdictions, and the Federal Bureau of Prisons had developed boot camp programs to serve adult populations. At this time, there were over 8,000 beds dedicated to adult offenders. With the average offender in a boot camp prison spending 107 days, more than 27,000 offenders could complete the program in a one-year period.

Boot camps for juveniles also developed in an explosive trend. A survey by MacKenzie, Brame, McDowell, and Souryal (1995) of state and local correctional officials found 37 boot camp programs, the majority of which opened after 1993. Many of these early juvenile boot camps were developed in response to the passage of the 1994 Crime Act, which permitted the Department of Justice to specifically allocate funding for juvenile boot camps. The number of juvenile boot camps, with programming similar to that of adult boot camps, continues to rise.

Although the militaristic components developed over a century ago remain central to today's boot camps, rehabilitative, educational, and drug treatment services are beginning to occupy an increasingly large share of the participants' time. Individual boot camp programs vary in their focus and in the amount of emphasis placed on the military aspects of programming as opposed to therapeutic programming. Because of the numerous types of programs, it is difficult to define a typical program in current use. Generally, researchers consider a program a boot camp if it requires military-style inmate and staff uniforms, the use of military titles (e.g., captain or sergeant) when addressing staff, military drill and ceremony, or other major aspects of military protocol.

THEORETICAL PERSPECTIVES AND CONTROVERSIES

Most shock incarceration programs operate under a constructive punishment philosophy. This philosophy assumes that if a person experiences or is placed within an environment of radical change, the environment will create a reasonable amount of stress. Under this stress, the person becomes particularly susceptible to external influences. In the case of boot camps, offenders forced to engage in a very regimented lifestyle requiring extensive physical exertion and mental discipline will become stressed and thus amenable to behavioral change. Thus when treatment programs are introduced, offenders have an increased likelihood of long-term positive change.

Despite their goals of positive change in offenders, boot camps do not have universal support. Boot camps are controversial for a variety of reasons, most often related to a negative reaction to the military atmosphere (Morash and Rucker, 1990). Critics of boot camps suggest that the confrontational nature of boot camp programs is antithetical to treatment. In fact, they argue some aspects of the boot camps are diametrically opposed to a constructive, interpersonally supportive treatment environment necessary for positive change to occur. Some critics argue that boot camps hold inconsistent philosophies and procedures, set the stage for abusive punishments, and perpetuate a "we versus they" attitude suggesting newer inmates are deserving of degrading treatment. Critics anticipate that inmates may fear staff and that the boot camps will have less individualized programming than traditional correctional facilities. Thus in the long term, offenders will be less prepared for their return to the community.

An alternative viewpoint has been described as a "Machiavellian" point of view (MacKenzie and Souryal, 1995). This perspective suggests that correctional experts expect little direct benefit from the military atmosphere of the boot camp programs but are willing to support this type of programming to achieve two primary goals: early release for nonviolent offenders and additional funding for treatment programs. In their opinion, public and political support for boot camps allows for funding that would otherwise be unavailable to these offenders.

Additional unique issues have arisen in developing boot camps for juveniles. Contrary to the punitive aspects of boot camps often publicized by the media, the primary mission of the juvenile justice system has been treatment and rehabilitation, not retribution and punishment. To align themselves with the mission of the juvenile justice system, juvenile boot camps must be designed to address the needs of juvenile offenders through increased treatment and programming. More recently developed models of juvenile boot camps strive to achieve this congruency, devoting a significant amount of time to academic education and rehabilitative counseling and less time to physical training and drill. In contrast to the time adult boot camp inmates spend during the day in work activities, juvenile boot camp participants spend most of their day in academic classes.

A TYPICAL DAY IN A BOOT CAMP

The underlying focus of boot camp programs is apparent in the name used for earlier versions of this type of program—shock incarceration. The program is intended to "shock" offenders into changing their behavior. This philosophy is put into practice upon an inmate's arrival at the facility: Males are required to have their heads shaved (females may be permitted short haircuts instead), and all inmates are informed of the strict program rules. At all times, inmates are required to address staff as "Sir" or "Ma'am," to request permission to speak, and to refer to themselves in the third person as "this inmate" or "this cadet." Punishments for minor rule violations are summary and certain, frequently involving physical exercise such as push-ups or running. Major rule violations may result in dismissal from the program and full-term institutionalization. The incoming group of inmates is called a platoon. Platoons are kept together in all aspects of the program including housing, meals, physical training, and other activities. Additionally, the platoon is expected to complete the program at the same time.

In a typical boot camp, the 10- to 16-hour day begins with a predawn reveille. Inmates dress quickly and march to an exercise area where they participate in an hour or two of physical training followed by drill and ceremony. They then march to breakfast where they are ordered to stand at parade rest while waiting in line and to exercise military movements when the line moves. Inmates are required to stand in front of the table until commanded to sit and are not permitted to converse during the 10-minute eating period. After breakfast, juveniles usually spend the first few hours in school classrooms followed by an afternoon of hard physical labor, which frequently involves community service, such as cleaning state parks or highways. When the 6- to 8-hour workday is over, inmates return to the compound where they participate in additional exercise and drill. A quick dinner is followed by evening programs, which may consist of counseling, life-skills training, or drug education and treatment. The extent of therapeutic programming varies among facilities.

Boot camp inmates gradually earn more privileges and responsibilities as their performance and time in the program warrant. In some programs, a different-colored hat or uniform may be the outward display of prestige. Depending on the facility, between 8 percent and 50 percent of the entrants fail to complete the program. For those who go through boot camp successfully, an elaborate graduation ceremony occurs, with visitors and family invited to attend. Frequently, awards are given for achievements made during the program. In addition, the inmates perform the drill and ceremony they have practiced throughout their time in the boot camp.

CHARACTERISTICS OF BOOT CAMP PROGRAMS

Types of Programs

A program typically holds an offender for three to four months in lieu of their regular sentence, or it may be a front-end or back-end program. In front-end programs, inmates are incarcerated for a short time before starting a longer traditional prison sentence. Back-end programs act as an early release mechanism whereby offenders can volunteer to spend the remainder of their sentences in boot camp programs rather than prisons in return for serving a shorter period. Additionally, boot camps may be used in conjunction with probation.

Programs vary in size and length. Some boot camp programs house as few as 30 offenders at once while others, such as the program in New York State, house as many as 1,600. The average program houses between 100 and 250 offenders at one time. Boot camps typically hold offenders between 90 and 120 days. Even if an offender received a lengthier sentence, they can, in some instances, fulfill that sentence by serving time in a boot camp program.

Usually a boot camp takes in a new group of inmates, or a platoon, every 30 days and houses three or four platoons at one time. The senior platoons that are near completion of the program are expected to serve as positive role models for incoming platoons. With multiple platoons in a program, graduation ceremonies occur frequently. As noted earlier, the graduation ceremonies are an elaborate display in which military drill and ceremony exercises, among other activities, are performed for family and friends. The graduation ceremonies may also be viewed as an incentive for platoon members who are progressing through the program.

Military-Style Uniforms

In addition to the military style of the daily routine, another characteristic common to boot camp programs is military dress. Military-style fatigues are provided to inmates, who must maintain a neat appearance, including polished boots. Correctional staff are also dressed in uniforms indicative of rank and are required to pay close attention to professional military-style appearance. As part of some programs, inmates are gradually able to earn more privileges and responsibilities as their performance and time in the program warrant. The attainment of these privileges is often displayed as a different-colored hat or a badge as an outward display of prestige.

Selection Process

One of the most important differences among boot camp programs is the selection of inmates. Generally, there are two approaches to selection procedures. Using the first selection method, sentencing judges place offenders in the boot camp program and retain their decision-making authority over the offenders until they exit the program. Failure to complete the sentence would result in resentencing of the offender, possibly to prison.

In the second type of decision-making model, officials in the Department of Corrections or Youth Authority decide who will enter boot camp. Offenders are sentenced to a term in prison by the judge. The department evaluates them for eligibility and suitability for a boot camp program. The offenders who are admitted can reduce their term in prison by successfully completing the boot camp. If they are dismissed from boot camp, they are automatically sent to prison to complete their sentence.

Eligibility Requirements

Most boot camp programs for adult offenders restrict participation to offenders between the ages of 17 and 30 (MacKenzie and Souryal, 1995). Some programs permit offenders up to age 40, while other programs have no upper age limit. Regardless of age, offenders are often required to meet minimum physical requirements that exclude offenders who have physical disabilities, severe asthma, or other conditions precluding physical exertion. Participation is also frequently restricted to nonviolent, first-time felony offenders. Although 10 states report that violent and nonviolent offenders are eligible for their boot camp programs, most of their participants are, in fact, nonviolent offenders (General Accounting Office, 1993).

Eligibility requirements can undermine the success of a boot camp program. Restrictive eligibility requirements may mean that many of the boot camp beds are unoccupied, a serious problem in this era of prison crowding. For example, when Louisiana opened its first boot camp program, officials were forced to widen their original narrow eligibility criteria to identify a sufficient number of offenders to fill available beds (MacKenzie and Piquero, 1994).

Another issue related to eligibility requirements in juvenile boot camps is with the definition of the type of juvenile who should be placed in the program. The target groups for juvenile boot camps are most often nonviolent offenders with limited criminal histories. In the last 15 years, there has been a concerted effort to use incarceration less frequently for juveniles who are not a danger to themselves or others. The dilemma for boot camps is whether to admit juveniles convicted of more serious crimes or to widen the net of control to include juveniles convicted of nonviolent crimes.

Staffing

An interesting component of boot camp programs is the militaristic nature of the correctional staff. Frequently, staff employed by boot camp programs have a military background and experience, including former Marine Corps officers or officers who have served in special U.S. Army units. The primary reason for attracting staff with military experience is that the program atmosphere is a different and more difficult work environment, thus requiring major adaptation by correctional officers without military experience.

The philosophy of boot camp staff is to lead by example and to act as role models who display physical and mental fortitude as a means to gain the respect of the inmates or wards. The staff often perform the same exercises in the daily physical regime that inmates or wards are expected to perform. Additionally, correctional staff follow military codes of discipline including standing at attention, saluting superior officers, and addressing superiors as "Sir," "Ma'am," or other appropriate titles. The staff are also frequently required to use military jargon, such as referring to floors as decks and windows as portholes.

Special Populations

The diversity of boot camps not only exists within their operation but also in the populations that they serve. Although initially designed for adult male offenders, boot camps have more recently included programs for female and juvenile offenders. By 1993, 13 states and the Federal Bureau of Prisons had developed boot camp programs for adult female offenders. These programs comprise only 6 percent of the total number of incarcerated boot camp offenders. In 10 state-level boot camps, males and females are combined in one program, where they live in separate quarters but are brought together for other activities. Other jurisdictions have completely separate programs for male and female offenders (MacKenzie, 1990).

In 1992, a focus-group meeting comprising correctional experts, feminist scholars, and criminologists was held at the University of Maryland to discuss special concerns regarding females in boot camps. Members of the focus group expressed concern about the effect of male correctional officers yelling at female offenders who may have been in abusive relationships before entering the boot camp. A confrontational environment could have a negative psychological impact on these female participants. Furthermore, questions were raised about the way in which these programs address female-specific needs, such as parenting classes and vocational training.

In response to these concerns, MacKenzie and Donaldson (1996) studied six boot camps that housed female participants. Through interviews, researchers ascertained that females in boot camps experienced difficulties keeping up with the physical demands of the program. Furthermore, female participants reported extensive emotional stress because most boot camp staff and inmates were male. Thus some researchers and practitioners have argued that gender-integrated boot camps are not appropriate. MacKenzie and Donaldson concluded their study by suggesting that the boot camps they studied were designed specifically with the male offender in mind and only accepted female offenders as an afterthought. They suggested that programs be designed for female offenders and include training in parenting skills and responsibilities as well as education about domestic violence.

OUTCOMES

Participants' Perceptions of Boot Camps

Researchers who have surveyed participants' perceptions of their programs have found support for a punitive emphasis. Wood and Grasmick (1999) surveyed male and female inmates who were serving time for nonviolent offenses. They found inmates viewed boot camps as significantly more punitive than traditional imprisonment and various forms of alternative sanctions. Thus participants and potential participants reaffirm the belief held by the public and correctional officials that boot camps are "tough" and punitive. This fact, however, does not mean that boot camps are more effective.

Recidivism

Researchers who examined the effectiveness of early boot camp programs such as those in Georgia, Florida, New York, and Louisiana compared the recidivism rates of offenders who completed boot camp with the rates of offenders who were released from prison and placed on parole. No differences were found between the groups in either rearrests or reincarcerations. Some of the difficulties with these early studies were that the groups may not have been similar and were not randomly assigned to the treatment condition. Thus prisoners who have served longer sentences may have actually received more treatment than did boot camp inmates.

A second generation of boot camp research compared probationers, boot camp graduates, boot camp dropouts, and parolees in eight states on recidivism measures (MacKenzie, Brame, McDowell, and Souryal, 1995). Results demonstrated that offenders who completed boot camp programs did not necessarily perform better or worse than comparison groups. Specifically, their results indicated boot camp dropouts had a higher recidivism rate than did boot camp graduates and were more likely to recidivate than were offenders on parole. Further, boot camp graduates were more likely to commit new crimes than were offenders who received a sentence to probation. MacKenzie et al. concluded that program effectiveness had to be judged on a state-by-state basis because effects were not consistent across all programs. The second generation of research suffered from one of the same drawbacks as the first: Offenders were not randomly assigned to boot camp programs. Nonetheless, this generation of research did include offenders in the comparison groups who were more similar to the boot camp offenders.

Some tentative results of studies that have implemented a randomized design with juvenile boot camps have recently become available. Peters (1996a, 1996b, 1996c), with follow-up studies completed by Clawson,

Coolbaugh, and Zamberlan (1998) examined three juvenile boot camp programs that were willing to permit researchers to randomly assign juvenile offenders to either boot camp or an alternative. The preliminary results from these sites indicated no significant recidivism differences between boot camp youth and the control groups. The collection of data at these sites is continuing.

One of the recommendations from second-generation research was to examine specific program characteristics of boot camps. MacKenzie et al. (1995) further analyzed their data and discovered some commonalities among programs where the boot camp releasees had lower recidivism rates than comparison groups on some, but not all, measures of recidivism. These programs devoted more than three hours per day to therapeutic activities, engaged in some form of follow-up with the offenders in the community, and required offenders to volunteer for the program. From this study, researchers concluded that the military atmosphere, structure and discipline of boot camp does not significantly reduce recidivism rate; instead, it is the incorporation of therapeutic programming that leads to successful reductions in recidivism.

Following up on the examination of specific components of boot camp environments that might enhance rehabilitation efforts, Styve, MacKenzie, and Gover (2000) compared the environments of 24 juvenile boot camps with 24 traditional correctional facilities. They found that compared with juveniles in traditional correctional facilities, boot camp residents consistently perceived the environment as significantly more controlled, active, and structured, with less danger from other residents. Boot camp juveniles also perceived the environment as providing more therapeutic and transitional programming. Overall, from the perspective of the juveniles, boot camps appear to provide a more positive environment conducive to effective rehabilitation, considering almost all the conditions measured.

CONCLUSION

Boot camp programs are an alternative to traditional prison incarceration that has become increasingly popular since its rebirth in 1983. The militarization of correctional programs provides a structured environment that requires a strict physical regime to be followed by both inmates and correctional staff. Early programs that traditionally focused on the military style of training and punishment, called "shock incarceration" programs, more recently have been subsumed by boot camps, which retain the military components but also incorporate therapeutic elements into the programming. On the whole, shock incarceration programs have not been very successful in reducing recidivism levels of offenders who have graduated. It is expected, however, that with the more recent incorporation of treatment elements into boot camp programs, these programs may become more effective in reducing recidivism and thus lead to positive long-term change in offenders.

Gaylene Styve Armstrong and Doris Layton
MacKenzie

See also Reformatories and Reform Schools; Scared Straight; Wilderness Programs

Bibliography

Clawson, H., K. Coolbaugh, and C. Zamberlan. 1998. *Further Evaluation of Cleveland's Juvenile Boot Camp: A Summary Report.* Paper presented at the Annual Meeting of the American Society of Criminology, Washington, DC.

General Accounting Office. 1993. *Prison Boot Camps: Short Term Prison Costs Reduced, but Long Term Impact Uncertain.* Washington, DC: Government Printing Office.

MacKenzie, D. L. 1990. The parole performance of offenders released from shock incarceration (boot camp prison): A survival analysis. *Journal of Quantitative Criminology* 7:213–236.

MacKenzie, D. L., R. Brame, D. McDowell, and C. Souryal. 1995. Boot camp prisons and recidivism in eight states. *Criminology* 33:327–357.

MacKenzie, D. L., and H. Donaldson. 1996. Boot camp prisons for women offenders. *Criminal Justice Review* 21:21–43.

MacKenzie, D. L., and A. Piquero. 1994. The impact of shock incarceration programs on prison crowding. *Crime and Delinquency* 40:222–249.

MacKenzie, D. L., and C. Souryal. 1995. A "Machiavellian" perspective on the development of boot camp prisons: A debate. *University of Chicago Roundtable.* Chicago: University of Chicago Press.

Morash, M., and L. Rucker. 1990. A critical look at the ideal of boot camp as a correctional reform. *Crime and Delinquency* 36:204–222.

Peters, M. 1996a. *Evaluation of the Impact of Boot Camp for Juvenile Offenders: Cleveland Interim Report.* Washington, DC: Office of Juvenile Justice and Delinquency Prevention.

Peters, M. 1996b. *Evaluation of the Impact of Boot Camp for Juvenile Offenders: Denver Interim Report.* Washington, DC: Office of Juvenile Justice and Delinquency Prevention.

Peters, M. 1996c. *Evaluation of the Impact of Boot Camp for Juvenile Offenders: Mobile Interim Report.* Washington, DC: Office of Juvenile Justice and Delinquency Prevention.

Styve, G. J., D. L. MacKenzie, and A. R. Gover. 2000. Perceived conditions of confinement: A national evaluation of juvenile boot camps and traditional facilities. *Law and Human Behavior* 24:297–308.

Wood, P. B., and H. G. Grasmick. 1999. Toward the development of punishment equivalencies: Male and female inmates rate the severity of alternative sanctions compared to prison. *Justice Quarterly* 16:19–50.

BOYS AND GIRLS CLUBS OF AMERICA

The Boys and Girls Clubs of America date back to 1860 when several women in Hartford, Connecticut, concluded that it was not a good idea to have boys roaming the streets. They felt that boys engaged in productive activities would not become involved in unacceptable social behavior. From these practical and insightful observations arose, in time, a national cause.

By 1906, the Boys and Girls Clubs of America had established facilities and operational programs in all 50 states, Puerto Rico, and the U.S. Virgin Islands. The clubs were intentionally anchored in areas where the most disadvantaged youths resided. Although the Boys and Girls Clubs of America was not incorporated until 1906 by the then existing 53 clubs, it has officially served youth since 1865. In 1931, the Boys Club Federation, as it was originally known, became the Boys Clubs of America. By 1956, Boys Clubs of America celebrated the 59th anniversary of its incorporation and received a U.S. Congressional Charter evincing their success. Finally, in 1990 in recognition that girls are also part of the cause, the national organization amended its name to the Boys and Girls Clubs of America.

In 1987, the clubs recognized that youth in public housing represented a critical group at high risk for some of society's most intractable problems, such as poor health, crime and violence, alcohol and drug use, delinquency, pregnancy, and academic failure in school. Accordingly, a major effort was made to establish Boys and Girls Clubs in public housing communities throughout the nation. A three-year independent study by Columbia University found that Boys and Girls Clubs in public housing had a significant impact on juvenile crime (reduced 13 percent), drug activity (reduced 22 percent), and the presence of crack cocaine (reduced 25 percent). Additional research found that the clubs improved the overall quality of life for children and families residing in public housing (Schinke, Cole, and Orlandi, 1991; Schinke, Orlandi, and Cole, 1992).

Another study, *Evaluation of Boys and Girls Clubs in Public Housing* (National Institute of Justice, 1995), found that new "full-service" clubs designed to offer an array of intensive services proved to be more effective. In particular, it was found that club successes or failures were predicated on their community networking abilities and the coordination of activities for youths in concurrence with established community-based service providers such as Weed and Seed efforts. The most promising programs invested heavily in time and energy and in building trust and acceptance among local children, parents, and teachers. Furthermore, community institutions providing vital financial resources, volunteers, and other support, regardless of the age of boys and girls, were also found to be very important. Thus according to the Office of Juvenile Justice and Delinquency Prevention (1997), youths as well as younger children participating in Boys and Girls Clubs have experienced reductions in juvenile alcohol and drug use, and improved school performance. Furthermore, participation seems to insulate these youths from further involvement in crime and violent behavior.

The success of Boys and Girls Clubs became apparent early in its existence. For example, Brown's (1956) study of the Red Shield Boys Club demonstrated a 52 percent decrease in juvenile delinquency since the club's creation in 1944 through June 1955. In comparison, delinquency rates tripled in one comparable neighborhood and increased 33 percent in another.

Today the Boys and Girls Clubs of America is a comprehensive national network of 2,014 associated Boys and Girls Clubs serving more than 3 million school-age boys and girls, with more clubs poised to open. The clubs strive to serve children from all backgrounds, helping them develop qualities of good citizenship and leadership and assisting them in becoming productive, successful people. Consequently, the missionary focus of the Boys and Girls Clubs of America seeks to establish formal positive partnerships and associations among young people and concerned adults, the clubs and their supporters, and the national organization and local clubs. This type of comprehensive networking has provided technical support and organizational assistance to numerous communities by establishing new clubs at the rate of 125 per year since 1988. In spite of this growth, however, the clubs' focus remains on youths from disadvantaged backgrounds, as noted by the organization's mission statement:

> The mission of the Boys and Girls Clubs of America is to promote leadership, character, health, and career development of youth while emphasizing their social, cultural, and educational growth. With special concern for children from disadvantaged circumstances, professional staff and volunteers provide daily programs to help young people develop the self-esteem that is essential for them to become responsible leaders.

At the dawn of the 21st century, the long successful tradition of the Boys and Girls Clubs of America continues to make significant positive contributions to juvenile justice. In recognition of the clubs' success and of the continued need to address the concerns of youths, the U.S. Congress has proposed the Kids Act 2000. If approved, the act will direct the attorney general to make grants to the Boys and Girls Clubs of America to fund effective after-school technology programs intended to provide the following:

1. Constructive technology-focused activities that are part of a comprehensive program to give youth access to technology and technology training during after-school hours, weekends, and school vacations.

2. Supervised activities in safe environments for youth.

3. Full-time staffing with teachers, tutors, and other qualified personnel.

In addition, the act would do the following:

1. Direct the Boys and Girls Clubs of America to make subawards to local Boys and Girls Clubs, authorizing expenditures associated with providing technology programs, including hiring teachers and other personnel and procuring goods and services, such as computer equipment.

2. Set forth provisions regarding grant eligibility, application requirements, and criteria for making grant awards; authorizes appropriations; and allows funds to carry out this act to be derived from the Violent Crime Reduction Trust Fund.

Clearly, the Boys and Girls Clubs of America will remain an integral part of the American landscape and an indispensable aid to the juvenile justice system.

Morris Taylor

See also Chicago Area Project; Children's Aid Society; Foster Care; Mentoring Programs

Bibliography

Brown, R. C. 1956. *A Boy's Club and Delinquency: A Study of the Statistical Incidence of Juvenile Delinquency in Three Areas in Louisville, Kentucky.* New York: New York University.

Bureau of Justice Assistance. 1995. *Boys and Girls Club Fact Sheet.* Washington, DC: National Institute of Justice, Bureau of Justice Assistance.

National Institute of Justice. 1995. *Evaluation of Boys and Girls Clubs in Public Housing.* Washington, DC: National Institute of Justice.

Office of Juvenile Justice and Delinquency Prevention. 1997. *Broken Windows/Mended Kids.* Available at http://www.ojjdp.ncjrs.org/about/press/oped.html.

Schinke, S. P., K. C. Cole, and M. A. Orlandi. 1991. *The Effects of Boys and Girls Clubs on Alcohol and Other Drugs and Related Problems in Public Housing: Final Research Report.* Rockville, MD: Office of Substance Abuse Prevention.

Schinke, S. P., M. A. Orlandi, and K. C. Cole. 1992. Boys and Girls Clubs in public housing developments: Prevention services for youth at risk. *Journal of Community Psychology* 20(OSAP Special Issue): 118–128.

BRONNER, AUGUSTA FOX (1881–1966)

Trained as a psychologist, Augusta Fox Bronner is remembered for her research on juvenile delinquency and her development of treatment programs for troubled children. Born in Louisville, Kentucky, to a Jewish family, her parents encouraged her to pursue a professional career.

Bronner assisted noted educational psychologist Edward L. Thorndyke through the course of her graduate career at Columbia University Teachers College. Her dissertation, *A Comparative Study of the Intelligence of Delinquent Girls*, published in 1914, was an original application of mental testing to the questions of juvenile crime. Through this research, Bronner showed that there was no correlation between retardation and delinquency, which challenged the conventional wisdom that assumed inherited biological causes for delinquency and crime. Bronner's study had great influence on theory development, research, and programming for youth in the first half of the 20th century.

In 1913, Augusta Bronner attended a summer course at Harvard University taught by the distinguished Chicago neurologist William Healy, who had developed the individual case approach for counseling and youth treatment programs. As a result of that summer experience, Bronner was hired by Healy as a psychologist at the Chicago Juvenile Psychopathic Institute, which he headed. Together they continued to develop the clinical method of studying and treating juvenile delinquency. They taught that heredity was a minor factor as a cause of social deviance but that mental repressions, social conflicts, and family relations were serious causes of youth crime and deviance.

In 1914, when grant funding ran out for the institute in Chicago, Cook County overtook the funding. The county desired only diagnoses from the institute. Bronner and Healy found themselves increasingly frustrated with their work in Chicago as diagnosing became the chief task of the institute, leaving little time to carry out, and no money to fund, research and treatment. So Bronner sought funding from philanthropists in Boston. In 1917, the Judge Baker Foundation was established, with Healy as its director and Bronner as assistant director. The Judge Baker Guidance Center, as the foundation was later named, became the pilot model for guidance centers and clinics across the globe.

By the 1930s, Bronner and Healy shifted the focus of their work from doing diagnoses for courts to diagnosing and treating clients. They developed the team guidance concept, in which psychologists, social workers, medical personnel, and others worked together to determine treatment programs for each individual youth in their care. They also attempted to keep the size of the clinic small to ensure individualized and personal treatment. Although Bronner's work in the guidance center during this time was to schedule conferences and supervise psychological work, she continued to do research on the causes and treatment of juvenile deviance.

After his wife's death, Healy married Bronner. Although Bronner produced a considerable portion of the research results and did her fair share of the partnership's work, she purposely remained in the shadow of Healy. Bronner published few of her own research results after becoming Healy's partner, and she emphasized her determination by destroying most of her papers and unpublished manuscripts when they retired in 1946. "Though her work is forever linked to Healy, Bronner made important contributions in the fields of mental testing, delinquency, and mental health" (Winkler, 1999:601).

Little has been written concerning the professional life of this "woman behind the scenes," and few documents mention the impact of the work of Augusta Fox Bronner. The best two resources concerning Bronner's professional life and impact are Winkler's (1999) biography in Garraty and Carnes, *American National Biography;* and Healy and Bronner's autobiography in *Orthopsychiatry, 1923–1948: Retrospect and Prospect* (1948).

Edward J. Schauer

See also Chicago Area Project; William Healy

Bibliography

Healy, W., and A. Bronner. 1916. Youthful offenders. *American Journal of Sociology* 22:50.
Healy, W., and A. Bronner. 1926. *Delinquency and Criminals: Their Making and Unmaking*. New York: Holt.

Healy, W., and A. Bronner. 1936. *New Light on Delinquency and Its Treatment*. New Haven, CT: Yale University Press.

Healy, W., and A. Bronner. 1948. The child guidance clinic: Birth and growth of an idea. Pp. 14–49 in L. Lowrey and V. Sloane (eds.), *Orthopsychiatry 1923–1948: Retrospect and Prospect*. Menasha, WI: George Banta.

Healy, W., A. F. Bronner, and A. M. Bowers. 1930. *The Structure and Meaning of Psychoanalysis*. New York: Knopf.

Winkler, K. (1999). Bronner, Augusta Fox. Pp. 600–601 in J. Garraty and M. Carnes (eds.), *American National Biography*, Vol. 3. New York: Oxford.

CALIFORNIA STREET TERRORISM ENFORCEMENT AND PREVENTION ACT

In the mid-1980s, the California legislature declared that California was in a "state of crisis which had been caused by violent street gangs whose members threaten, terrorize, and commit a multitude of crimes." Gang-related homicides in Los Angeles increased by 24 percent from 1985 to 1986, and in the first half of 1987, there were 200 gang killings in Los Angeles. These concerns prompted a legislative response geared at putting a halt to the gang problem in California.

In 1987, legislation that would become the Street Terrorism Enforcement and Prevention (STEP) Act was introduced in the California legislature. The proposed legislation provided for the use of criminal prosecution, civil action, and asset forfeiture to combat the gang problem. This three-pronged approach was chosen because it was believed that existing laws served only to punish gang crime, not solve the problems that led to it.

The legislation, as it was initially proposed, met with considerable opposition. The Senate Public Safety Committee did not approve the bill until its sponsor, Senator Alan Robbins, agreed to drop the asset forfeiture provisions that would require forfeiture of gang members' property. With the asset forfeiture provisions dropped, the STEP Act was signed into law by Governor George Deukmejian on September 24, 1998.

PROVISIONS

The Street Terrorism Enforcement and Prevention Act is composed of six paragraphs. The first paragraph defines the new crime:

> Any person who actively participates in any criminal street gang with the knowledge that its members engage in or have engaged in a pattern of criminal gang activity, and who willfully promotes, furthers, or assists, in any felonious criminal conduct by members of that gang, shall be punished by imprisonment in a county jail for a period not to exceed one year, or by imprisonment in the state prison for 16 months, or two or three years.

The second through fourth paragraphs of the STEP Act lay out the sentencing scheme. The fifth paragraph defines a "pattern of criminal gang activity" as the "commission of, attempted commission of, or solicitation of, or conviction of two or more of the enumerated offenses, provided at least one of these offenses occurred after the effective date of STEP, and the last of these offenses occurred within three years of a prior offense, and that the offenses were committed on separate occasions, or by two or more persons." (The fifth paragraph further lists the 23 crimes that qualify for prosecution under STEP.)

The sixth paragraph of STEP goes on to define a "criminal street gang" as "any ongoing organization, association, or group of three or more persons having as one of its primary activities the commission of one or more of the criminal acts enumerated in [the fifth paragraph]."

Simply put, the STEP Act establishes a new crime of participation in a criminal street gang. This crime is punishable by up to one year in county jail or one to three years in state prison. A conviction under STEP requires proof of five elements: (1) the existence of a criminal street gang; (2) the defendant's membership in that gang; (3) the defendant's *knowledge* that the gang members are engaged in a pattern of gang activity; (4) the defendant's willful promotion, furtherance, or assistance in felonious criminal conduct by the gang; and (5) the pattern of gang activity itself. A pattern of gang activity occurs when two or more of the criminal acts specified in the Act are committed.

The STEP Act also contains nuisance and weapons forfeiture provisions. For example, buildings used by gang members for the commission of STEP offenses may be declared public or private nuisances. Furthermore, gang weapons used in the commission of a STEP offense may be seized and not returned if they are declared a nuisance.

CRITICISMS OF STEP

So far STEP has survived attack, and other states have modeled their own antigang statutes after it, but the arguments offered by critics are still worthy of consideration. The two primary criticisms of the STEP Act have been constitutional ones based on vagueness, overbreadth, or both. A statute can be held "void for vagueness" if it does not give adequate notice of the conduct it seeks to prohibit. A statute can be declared "overbroad" by violating constitutionally protected rights.

STEP has also been criticized on due process grounds. Critics argue that STEP punishes individuals because of their associations with others. Still other critics have argued that STEP intrudes on freedom of association rights.

The Street Terrorism Enforcement and Prevention Act has also been attacked on practical grounds. In particular, critics claim that it is difficult to show gang membership and a pattern of gang activity. Courts often rely on police officers' expert testimony to do this, but critics claim that police officers cannot be considered experts in gang activity simply because of their proximity to criminal street gangs.

RESPONSES TO STEP'S CRITICS

STEP's supporters believe that criminal gangs do not have a constitutional right to associate for criminal

purposes. They refer, in part, to the Supreme Court's statement in *Madsen v. Women's Health Center Inc.* (512 U.S. 753, 776, 1994): "Freedom of association protected by the First Amendment does not extend to joining with others for the purpose of depriving third parties of their lawful rights."

Next, STEP's supporters argue that the legislation is not unconstitutionally vague. A statute will be held void for vagueness when "men of common intelligence must necessarily guess at its meaning and differ as to its application" (*Connally v. General Const. Co.*, 269 U.S. 385, 391, 1926). Supporters argue that the words and phrases in STEP, such as "actively participates," "member," "criminal street gang," "pattern of criminal gang activity," and others, are not at all vague.

Finally, STEP's supporters argue that the statute is not overbroad, stating that because it requires "active participation" in a criminal street gang with "knowledge" that the members have committed crimes, the law is very specific about who it is intended to target. A law can only be declared overbroad if it "sweeps within its ambit other activities that in ordinary circumstances constitute an exercise of freedom of speech or of the press" (*Thornhill v. Alabama*, 310 U.S. 88, 97, 1940).

John Worrall

See also Gangs, Juvenile

CALIFORNIA YOUTH AUTHORITY

The California Youth Authority (CYA), the largest youth correctional system in the United States, houses approximately 6,000 juveniles and young adults in 11 institutions and 4 forestry camps. An additional 4,000 are under parole supervision. Operating under a treatment-and-training concept, the CYA provides an extensive array of programs that includes academic education, vocational training and work experience, sex offender treatment, substance abuse treatment, specialized counseling, and intensive mental health treatment. Through its Office of Prevention and Victims Services, the Youth Authority assists local justice agencies in delinquency prevention and intervention and provides services to victims of youth crime.

THE ORIGIN OF THE CYA

The establishment of the CYA in 1941 through legislative action is often cited as a turning point in American juvenile correctional history. The California Youth Authority Act was the first implementation of the American Law Institute's model Youth Correction Authority Act. Radically breaking with traditional thinking and practice in juvenile corrections, it proposed a model of juvenile justice based on rehabilitation instead of retributive punishment and called for state-level coordination of services. The passage of the California Youth Correction Authority Act of 1941 represents the first time an elected legislative body declared that the purpose of juvenile corrections was rehabilitation rather than punishment.

During the period leading up to the passage of the Youth Correction Authority Act in 1941, California's juvenile justice system could be described as disjointed, underfunded, and prone to brutality. The system's most serious problems appear to have been the result of no overall standards. There were no guidelines for length of stay, educational services, or the quality of correctional treatment and training. Three crowded, aging institutions and a total of nine parole agents (with caseloads sometimes as high as 200) served the entire state. They operated under the direction of the Department of Institutions, an agency that was almost totally oriented toward running mental hospitals and homes for the disabled.

Before 1941, young offenders were committed directly by the courts to one of the three state schools. If space was not available, the youth were placed in overcrowded jail facilities along with adults. Even preadolescent children were sometimes placed in jails where they mingled with adult criminals of all types. In such settings, children were exposed to continual criminal influences as well as to physical and sexual abuse. Publicized reports of children being abused in jails and in the three juvenile institutions were common. Over time, this grew into a highly emotional public issue. In 1939, public attention became riveted on the Whittier State School when the *Los Angeles Times* featured stories concerning a 13-year-old boy who died under questionable circumstances after being placed in solitary confinement. When a second boy at the Whittier State School died under almost identical circumstances a year later, public demand for change became difficult to ignore.

California, of course, was not the only state with such problems. Public commissions and other influential groups in state after state found that many juveniles coming into contact with the justice system encountered injustice and brutality. Juvenile justice committee members in New York City charged with assessing its system of juvenile justice were shocked at their findings. They became convinced, however, that the only reason brutal conditions were tolerated was that the public was generally unaware of them. To address this lack of knowledge, the committee sponsored a report that detailed the sorry state of juvenile justice in New York. This report, *Youth in the Toils*, eventually drew the attention of the American Law Institute. In 1938, the institute decided to address the problem and began looking for ways to make the administration of juvenile justice more effective and humane. The solution they hit upon was a model system that individual states could adopt. This task of developing a model system was given to a select committee of judges and attorneys along with specialists in the fields of criminology, psychology, sociology, and social casework.

In June 1940, the American Law Institute released the final version of a model system called the Youth Correction Authority Act, which called for establishing a model agency called the California Youth Authority. Almost immediately, the institute began a campaign to see the act adopted in what was considered several key states. John Ellingston, representing the American Law Institute, presented copies of the act to leading California judges, probation officers, social workers, educators, and legislators. Public meetings were held beginning in November 1940, drawing considerable interest. The Youth Correction Authority Act passed the California senate and assembly with minimal opposition and was signed into law by Governor Culbert Olson on July 9, 1941.

The Youth Correction Authority Act of 1941 declared that the purpose of the CYA was "to protect society by substituting training and treatment for retributive punishment of young persons found guilty of public offenses." The act specified that a three-member board would govern the CYA and direct the placement and treatment of juvenile offenders committed to its custody by the courts. The board was authorized to employ educators, physicians, psychiatrists, psychologists, sociologists, and social workers to provide individualized assessments and develop appropriate treatment plans. As originally designed, the CYA board was authorized to use any public institution or agency that would accept the ward. The 1941 act did not give the CYA administrative control over any of the institutions, although it was empowered to inspect them periodically. Administrative control would come about in amendments enacted in 1943 at the behest of California Governor Earl Warren, who sought to end problems such as those at the Whittier School.

Although the California act remained fairly close to the model, the state legislature added amendments that have had a strong imprint on the mission of the California Youth Authority. Probation powers were left with the courts (thereby creating a two-tiered system). The CYA was given responsibility for developing and coordinating delinquency prevention programs and for providing consultative services to other agencies charged with delinquency prevention and treatment. Following the model developed at the Whittier School by Fred C. Nelles in 1918, the CYA developed a treatment model that focused on the clinical diagnosis of individual delinquents and the development of individual treatment plans.

INNOVATION AT THE CYA

Within 20 years of its inception, the California Youth Authority had developed a national and international reputation for innovative juvenile correctional treatment and training and for experimental research. In addition to being the first to establish reception centers and clinics to diagnose and develop individual treatment programs, the CYA pioneered juvenile forestry camps, community treatment, and an inmate grievance program involving independent arbitration. These programs came to be examined and copied by correctional agencies throughout the United States and, in fact, throughout the world.

Beginning in the 1950s and continuing through the mid-1970s, the Youth Authority introduced and evaluated many new diagnostic and treatment approaches. These included guided-group interaction, therapeutic communities, group therapy, behavior modification, differential treatment, and transactional analysis. Although some of the CYA's experimental research projects produced promising results, they were modest and fell far short of the hoped-for breakthroughs. The positive achievements seemed to get lost in the disillusionment that a panacea was not to be found. CYA research staff such as Carl Jesness and Ted Palmer, nevertheless, continued to publish widely. Palmer, in fact, was practically the only criminologist to publicly reject Robert Martinson's well-known 1974 statement that "nothing works" in corrections.

The CYA also experimented with treating juvenile delinquents in the community rather than in its institutions. The widely acclaimed Community Treatment Project, directed by Marguerite Warren, tested the effectiveness of providing intensive, individualized psychological treatment in the community rather than in institutions. Although the results of this research project are controversial at best, it did appear to indicate that serious juvenile delinquents could be treated in the community at less expense and with no increase in recidivism compared with institutional programs.

Like most correctional agencies in the United States, the California Youth Authority's programs and services suffered considerably under budget cutbacks and the disillusionment of the "nothing works" environment of the 1980s and 1990s. At the same time, the cultural milieu within CYA facilities gradually took on a heavier security orientation, eclipsing in most instances the CYA's traditional training and treatment orientation. Nevertheless, its forestry camp programs continued to operate, and a number of innovative programs with a rehabilitative emphasis were introduced during this time. Among the most notable of these were the Free Venture Program, which brought private-sector industries inside CYA institutions to provide employment experience, and the LEAD program, an intensive boot camp program based on the California National Guard's officer training program. Although still operating with a training and treatment philosophy, the CYA has been the subject of litigation in recent years regarding allegations of not providing legally mandated educational and mental health services as well as for failing to adequately protect those under its supervision.

Norman Skonovd

See also Community Treatment Project; Group Therapy; Training Schools

Bibliography

Palmer, T. 1974. The Youth Authority's Community Treatment Project. *Federal Probation* 38:3–14.

Palmer, T. 2002. *Individualized Intervention With Young Multiple Offenders*. New York: Routledge.

CAMBRIDGE-SOMERVILLE YOUTH STUDY

The Cambridge-Somerville Youth Study, conducted in 1938 by Edwin Powers and Helen Witmer, was a comprehensive—if somewhat erratic—attempt to determine if helpful interventions would deter delinquency and produce other important changes in the behavior and personalities of a cohort of boys, many of whom seemed headed for difficulty. The boys largely were identified by teachers in private and parochial schools, and the group included some well-behaved youths to avoid stigmatizing the study population. The project was funded by a $500,000 grant from a foundation established in the memory of his wife by Dr. Richard Clarke Cabot, a professor of social ethics and clinical medicine at Harvard University.

The experimental design closely matched 325 boys in a treatment group with 325 boys in a control group. Large amounts of data were collected about the participants to help in the matching and to serve as correlates of outcomes in the research probe. Placement in the treatment or control group was determined by a coin toss. Each treatment boy was assigned to one of ten counselors. The counselors attempted by whatever means to guide the boys toward adjusted and law-abiding behavior.

The treatment menu included friendship, example, and kindness as well as attention to any problem that appeared to be nudging a boy toward trouble. When the program terminated, more than half the boys in the treatment group had been tutored in academic subjects, over a third received medical or psychiatric help, almost half had been sent to summer camps, and some of the boys had worked in the project's shop. Subsequent research, however, would discover that youth who had participated in summer programs with other at-risk youth had the poorest long-term outcome, presumably because of a contagion effect (Dishion, McCord, and Poulin, 1999).

The interventions also included family guidance and psychological counseling as well as the provision of an array of recreational opportunities as participants or performers. Religion also was pressed: the boys and their families were encouraged to become involved in church activities, and ministers and pastors were alerted to their possible special need for help (Powers and Witmer, 1951).

The study was begun in 1938 in two densely populated neighboring Massachusetts cities that were marked by stretches of deteriorated neighborhoods and lines of factories. The intention was to continue the work for 10 years, but World War II decimated the staff and saw some of the boys enter the armed services, forcing the research to be concluded when most of the boys had received 5 years of attention and no one boy had been involved for more than 8 years. Sixty-five boys had been dropped from the study in 1941 because they were deemed less needful of help, and by December 1945, only 75 boys remained in the study population.

The results were disappointing. An evaluation conducted in 1949 showed that, despite the efforts of the counselors, the behavior of the boys in the treatment group did not differ significantly from that of the control boys who had received no study-team attention. In fact, the treatment cadre showed a slightly higher rate of delinquency, though their offenses were somewhat less serious. Explanations for the outcome included speculation that the boys had been too old to benefit from the help (their median age when treatment began was 10.5 years), and that the counselors had not used standard social-work techniques. Later writers would claim, however, that "it is scarcely clear how family preservation [in the Cambridge-Somerville study] may have differed from traditional family casework, which has a tepid history" (Fraser, Nelson, and Rivard, 1997:148). In addition, the basic treatment thesis may have been flawed: "A child rejected by parents," Joan McCord (1992:203) would observe, "may not be best served by someone else who tries to take the role of the parent. Such a strategy might result in an exaggerated sense of loss; it might produce expectations for or dependence on assistance."

It was also noted that the counselors had spent relatively little time over the years with most of the boys; the caseload was too heavy for them to offer many services. As so often is true with treatment modalities in the field of delinquency, what actually happened was not truly what was called for by the action blueprint. The goal was to foster "intense" interaction, but the counselors on average saw the boys infrequently.

Hope was held out, despite the disappointing initial results, that the treatment might produce subsequent gains by having provided the boys with internal resources so they would cease delinquent behavior at an earlier age than would the boys in the control group and would, perhaps, engage in less crime and delinquency.

These assumptions were tested by William and Joan McCord, with the assistance of Irving Kenneth Zola, in 1955, 10 years after the Cambridge-Somerville project had terminated. An attenuated sample of 263 matched boys was analyzed, representing those who had been retained throughout the entire Cambridge-Somerville study and who were still available (along with their records). The follow-up had the advantage of being able to relate information that had been gathered before the boys' difficulties with the law, thereby avoiding the usual evaluative bias inherent in looking at the offender's earlier life after he had gotten into trouble. As one reviewer noted, the study "worked backward" (Freeman, 1960:130), so retrospective bias was eliminated. On the other hand, as another reviewer (Sanders, 1960) astutely pointed out, the McCords took into account only things that had happened to the boys years earlier; they did not have information about what might have been much more important events or circumstances that had arisen during the years since the end of the study.

In addition, Gresham Sykes (1959), in a third review, noted that the authors' contention that slum environments were not an important factor in delinquency causation was undercut by a condition that they recognized but did not stress adequately. Since all the boys were from deprived socioeconomic backgrounds, it could not be expected that this item would show up in the findings as a significant variable.

The results of the follow-up, as in the initial work, were discouraging. The McCords' conclusion is forcefully stated: "As a result of these various analyses, we were forced to conclude that the treatment program, considered in its totality, had been ineffectual as a preventive of crime" (McCord and McCord, 1959a:93).

Among other things, length of treatment did not correlate with outcome, though there were stray rays of hope that some things had worked somewhat for some people. The study showed, for instance, that female counselors had greater success with adolescent boys than did male counselors. Neither this result nor earlier blueprints (Geis and Woodson, 1956), however, have had much success in establishing what kind of gender mix works best in counseling.

A particularly encouraging finding was that the intensity of treatment showed some positive results. Boys seen every week for a minimum of six months showed a significantly smaller incidence of criminality than did those seen every other week. Unfortunately, there were only a dozen boys each in the treatment

and the matched control sample who met this criterion (McCord and McCord, 1959a:95).

The data indicated that, of all items examined, the mother's personality appeared to be the most important correlate of delinquent and criminal behavior. The research also demonstrated, at least for the boys in the sample at the time the study was conducted, the inadequacy of several popular theories of delinquency. The authors noted the following:

1. We did not find a direct relationship between criminality and disciplinary methods except when a child is rejected by his parents or has deviant parental role models.

2. We did not find that punitive, harsh discipline (in whatever form administered) prevents criminality. Under certain conditions, consistently punitive discipline may deter criminality, but erratically punitive discipline promotes it.

3. We did not find that some of the passive males turn frequently to criminality to assert their "masculinity."

4. We did not find that broken homes constitute the type of atmosphere most conducive to criminality. (McCord and McCord, 1959a:172)

The Cambridge-Somerville cases were broken down to determine the relationship between particular types of offenses and the characteristics of the offenders. The largest and most amorphous offense category embraced crimes against property, such as breaking and entering, larceny, malicious destruction, forgery, and use of an automobile without permission.

Eighty-six of the boys had been convicted at least once for a property crime. The IQ scores of the offenders were among the most unanticipated results of the McCord analysis. Thirty-nine percent of the research subjects with IQ scores between 61 and 110 committed property crimes compared with only 25 percent of those with either higher or lower intelligence test results. Negatively, the researchers found no significant relationship between property crimes and neighborhood of residence and concluded that "property crimes are not simply the result of economic poverty" (McCord and McCord, 1959b: 127–130, 151). The analysis also discovered that 65 percent of the boys raised by mothers who neglected them committed property offenses compared with only 31 percent of the sons who had received other forms of mothering. Forty-three percent of the Cambridge-Somerville experimental group who had experienced lax discipline or had been subjected to erratic punishment committed property crimes compared with only 24 percent of those disciplined in any other manner. Fifty-one percent of the fathers who had criminal records had sons who committed property offenses, compared with 35 percent of the alcoholic or sexually unfaithful fathers and 25 percent of the "nondeviant" men.

Nonplussed but undaunted, Joan McCord revisited and updated the Cambridge-Somerville project material in 1975 with a grant from the National Institute of Mental Health. She learned that two thirds of the participants believed that the program had been helpful to them, but there was a distressing discrepancy between this subjective testimony and objective outcome measures.

Cases were classified as having unsatisfactory outcomes if the youth had died young, been convicted of an index crime, or had been diagnosed as an alcoholic, schizophrenic, or manic-depressive. Results showed that 42 cases, from both the treatment and control groups, had such outcomes. For the remaining 109 cases in which the outcomes for treatment and control subjects were the same, neither boy had gone bad. But among 63 pairs, only the treatment subject had an unsatisfactory outcome. McCord notes that the likelihood of such a result occurring by chance—39 cases favoring treatment and 63 favoring no treatment—is 2 in 100.

Treatment also appeared to be no more successful for the younger boys than the older ones. Distressingly, longer, more intensive treatment was related to greater harm. In a select group of 38 boys who had in 1945 been identified by their counselors as having been particularly helped by the program, 22 appeared neither better nor worse than their control group matches. Only 4 turned out better than the matches, while 12 turned out worse. Thus McCord (1990:7; see also McCord, 1981) concluded that "even among those whom the staff believed it had helped most, the objective evidence failed to show that the program had been beneficial."

Taking the treatment and control groups together, McCord determined that 76 percent of the boys from homes rated as the worst had been convicted of at least one nontraffic crime compared with 38 percent of those from homes rated above the median. There also was strong evidence that the nature of the family environment of the boys exerted an important influence on whether they later got into trouble with the law (McCord, 1982).

The McCords offered a bittersweet summary of the Cambridge-Somerville Youth Study. The experiment itself, they note, most assuredly turned out to be a failure in regard to achieving its goals. "Yet even in its failure," they observed, "the program must be regarded as a magnificent experiment, for its provision of a control group and its careful attention to research have produced a fund of information invaluable to future studies of the causation and prevention of crime" (McCord and McCord, 1959a:96). Reminiscing recently, Joan McCord (personal communication, September 19, 2000) told about her introduction to the project: "Almost half a century ago, I first encountered the record room in Emerson Hall, at Harvard, which stored case studies from the Cambridge-Somerville Youth Study. The impact was enormous. Details in the case records provided pictures of family life that rarely can be found anywhere. In the 1930s, Dr. Cabot had created a program that remains adventurous in the following century!"

Gilbert Geis and Mary Dodge

See also Chicago Area Project; Community Treatment Project; Joan McCord; Provo Experiment; Silverlake Experiment

Bibliography

Dishion, T. J., J. McCord, and F. Poulin. 1999. When interventions harm: Peer groups and problem behavior. *American Psychologist* 54:755–764.

Fraser, M. W., K. E. Nelson, and J. C. Rivard. 1997. Effectiveness of family preservation efforts. *Social Work Research* 21:138–153.

Freeman, H. E. 1960. Book review. *American Sociological Review* 25:129–130.

Geis, G., and F. W. Woodson. 1956. Matching probation officer with delinquent. *NPPA Journal* 2:58–62.

McCord, J. 1981. Consideration of some effects of a counseling program. Pp. 394–405 in S. Martin, L. Sechrest, and R. Redner (eds.), *New Directions in the Rehabilitation of Criminal Offenders.* Washington, DC: National Academy Press.

McCord, J. 1982. A longitudinal view of the relationship between parental absence and crime. Pp. 113–128 in J. Gunn and D. Farrington (eds.), *Abnormal Offenders, Delinquency, and the Criminal Justice System.* New York: Wiley.

McCord, J. 1990. Crime in moral and social contexts. *Criminology* 28:1–26.

McCord, J. 1992. The Cambridge-Somerville Study: A pioneering longitudinal experimental study of delinquency prevention. Pp. 196–206 in J. McCord and R. Tremblay (eds.), *Preventing Antisocial Behavior: Interventions From Birth Through Adolescence.* New York: Guilford Press.

McCord, J., and W. McCord. 1959a. A follow-up report on the Cambridge-Somerville Study. *Annals of the American Academy of Political and Social Science* 326(November):89–96.

McCord, W., and J. McCord. 1959b. *Origins of Crime: A New Evaluation of the Cambridge-Somerville Youth Study.* New York: Columbia University Press.

Powers, E., and H. Witmer. 1951. *An Experiment in the Prevention of Delinquency.* New York: Columbia University Press.

Sanders, W. B. 1960. Book review. *Social Forces* 38:283–284.

Sykes, G. M. 1959. Book Review. *American Journal of Sociology* 65:323.

CAVAN, RUTH SHONLE (1896–1993)

Ruth Shonle Cavan, who received her Ph.D. in sociology from the University of Chicago in 1928, was one of the most productive scholars of that era. She also was one of the few women from the Chicago School to receive national and to some extent international recognition for her scholarship in the family, juvenile delinquency, and criminology. Over nearly 70 years, she published 18 books, including research studies and textbooks, more than 80 articles in major sociology and criminology journals, book chapters, and dozens of book reviews. Cavan credited her love for writing for her successful career.

Ruth, the third child of Annie and Charles Shonle, was born in Tuscola, Illinois, on August 28, 1896. Charles Shonle, who owned his own tailor shop, was regarded as a skilled craftsman, and the family was highly respected in the community. Cavan indicated in informal conversations, interviews, and unpublished papers that she had an uncomplicated childhood that was free from family pressures to do certain things. Her early family and school experiences seem to have laid the foundation for an inquiring mind and full development of her intellectual capacity.

Early in her childhood, she began to read whatever books were available to her at home. In 1989 she stated, "I can't remember when I didn't love to read and write." Among the events that Cavan felt may have contributed to her outstanding career as a scholarly writer was her 12th birthday, when her father took her to the public library for a library card. Thereafter, Cavan explained, she read all the time. Also, her high school principal encouraged her to enter the Carnegie Foundation for Peace essay competition, and she won $50 for third prize.

Cavan's parents encouraged interests in school but could not afford to support her college education. Ruth's sense of adventure, independence, and determination manifested themselves after high school graduation, when she moved from her hometown, population 3,000, to Decatur, which had 35,000 people and Milikin University. She rented a room and worked in an office for two years, attending business school in the evening and saving for college. When Cavan had saved $200, she enrolled at Milikin University, majoring in English. She credits those two years at Milikin as developing her writing skills. A lack of funds forced Cavan to return home to Tuscola, where she worked and saved money until she could continue her studies at the University of Chicago. In 1921, Cavan graduated from the University of Chicago with a Ph.B. in English. She then went to work as a secretary to the director of the Abraham Lincoln Center, a community center.

Eventually, Cavan enrolled as a graduate student in the sociology department at the University of Chicago, where she studied with Robert Park, Ernest Burgess, and Elsworth Faris. She took classes from all three professors, and all three served on her thesis and dissertation committees. It was Burgess who provided her with the background for her work in the family, criminology, and juvenile delinquency. Cavan earned her M.A. (1923) and her Ph.D. (1926) from the University of Chicago. Her dissertation on suicide was selected for the prestigious University of Chicago Press Sociological Series.

In 1927, Ruth married Jordan True Cavan, a doctoral student in education, whom she met when they were both living at Hull House (the settlement house in Chicago founded by Jane Addams). Jordan was a professor at Rockford College. After their marriage, Jordan returned to Rockford to teach, and Ruth continued as a research associate at the University of

Chicago and taught intermittently at Rockford College. Jordan came to Chicago on weekends to see Ruth until their family was enlarged by a daughter, Anna-Lee. From 1947 to 1962, Ruth taught full time at Rockford College as a professor of sociology. After retiring from Rockford College, she joined the faculty at Northern Illinois University in 1964 and continued teaching until her second retirement in 1977 at the age of 80. Throughout her teaching career, Cavan continued to conduct research and to make many scholarly contributions to criminology and juvenile delinquency.

Among her most outstanding scholarly works in juvenile delinquency was *The Adolescent and the Family* (1934), a study completed during President Hoover's administration for the White House Conference on Child Health and Protection, which Cavan attended. Combining her interest and training in the family and delinquency, Cavan spent nine months administering questionnaires to predelinquents in Montefiore School, delinquents in the State Training School for Girls and St. Charles School for Boys, and a control group of public school children. Analysis of the data revealed that broken homes are more prevalent among delinquent children than in public school groups. Cavan was the first to distinguish between homes broken by death and homes broken by desertion or divorce. She also concluded that delinquent children were less likely to confide in their parents and thus were on less friendly and intimate terms with their parents than were nondelinquent public school children.

In 1938, while Cavan was a research associate for the Institute for Juvenile Delinquency in Chicago, Cavan and a colleague, Katherine Howland Ranck, conducted a study of the impact of the Great Depression on the family. In this study, Cavan examined 58 families referred to the institute because of the children's truancy, stealing, lying, incorrigibility, failure in school work, sexual delinquency, and so on. The authors emphasized the process whereby the reaction of the family to the depression led to disorganization of the family and contributed to juvenile delinquency. In 1959, Cavan published an article titled "Negro Family Disorganization and Juvenile Delinquency" in the *Journal of Negro Education*, in which she examined the impact of class and family transition. She found that lower-class youth faced with resistance from both white groups and middle-class African American groups might become irresponsible, seeking recognition and self-assurance through delinquency.

Ruth Cavan is most well known by current mainstream criminologists for her successful textbooks, all of which had multiple editions: *The Family* (1942, 1953, 1963, 1969a), *Criminology* (1948, 1955, 1962), and *Juvenile Delinquency* (1962, 1969b, 1975, 1981). The third and fourth editions of the juvenile delinquency text were coauthored with Theodore Ferdinand. In addition to the influence Cavan had on students during years of teaching, her textbooks reached thousands of students, many of whom majored in criminology and became academics or practitioners in criminology. Although Cavan resisted feminism, identifying herself as "a liberated woman," her chapter on women offenders in *Criminology* and delinquent girls in *Juvenile Delinquency* influenced many students to pursue research on women and crime, thus making an impact on feminist criminology today.

Cavan also made a major contribution to the theory of juvenile delinquency. In 1960, she was elected president of the Midwest Sociological Society and was the first woman to serve in this capacity. Her inaugural address was titled "Concepts of Tolerance and Contraculture as Applied to Delinquency" and was published in the *Sociological Quarterly* (1961). In this work, Cavan challenged the sharp division most criminologists made between delinquent and nondelinquent behavior that ranked juveniles at two extremes as "good boys" and "bad boys." She used the normal curve as a tool "to assign misbehavior to a place in the total social structure." Thus she presented a continuum of behavior from extreme underconformity (Area A), through decreasing degrees of disapproved behavior to central Area C, which represents an area of flexibility and tolerance, and then through increasing decrees of good behavior to Area G, extreme overconformity. Cavan noted that overconformity usually does not constitute delinquency in the same degree as underconformity (Areas A through C) but asserted that a complete picture of the social structure and delinquency should include overconformity (Areas E through G). Cavan further argued that the behavior and achievements that are rewarded by society are much more likely to be in Areas D and E than in F and G. Finally, Cavan stated that criminologists, by concentrating only on the underconformists as delinquents, were ignoring half the social structure and thus half the behavior. She argued for viewing delinquency as a continuum of behavior instead of as a dichotomy.

Ruth Shonle Cavan was active in many sociological and criminological professional associations at the state, regional, and national levels and received many honors and awards for her scholarship and service. Among the awards she received was her designation as a fellow by both the American Sociological Association (1959) and the American Society of Criminology (1965). She was honored as professor emerita upon her retirement from both Rockford College and Northern Illinois University. After her death on August 25, 1993, the American Society of Criminology established the annual Ruth Shonle Cavan Young Scholars Award in her honor.

Imogene L. Moyer

See also Chicago Area Project

Bibliography

Cavan, R. S. 1934. *The Adolescent in the Family.* White House Conference on Child Health and Protection. Sect. III: Education and training. Committee on the Family and Parent Education. New York: Appleton-Century.

Cavan, R. S. 1942. *The Family.* New York: Crowell.

Cavan, R. S. 1959. Negro family disorganization and juvenile delinquency. *Journal of Negro Education,* 28:240–239.

Cavan, R. S. 1962. *Criminology,* 3rd ed. New York: Crowell. Previous editions published in 1948 and 1955.

Cavan, R. S. 1969a. *The American Family,* 4th ed. New York, Crowell. Previous editions published under this title in 1953 and 1963 and under *The Family* in 1942.

Cavan, R. S. 1969b. *Juvenile Delinquency: Development, Treatment, Control,* 2nd ed. Philadelphia: Lippincott. Previous edition published in 1962.

Cavan, R. S., and T. N. Ferdinand. 1981. *Juvenile Delinquency,* 4th ed. New York: Harper and Row. Previous edition under this title published in 1975 and under *Juvenile Delinquency: Development, Treatment, Control* in 1962 and 1969.

Cavan, R. S., and K. H. Ranck. 1938. *The Family and the Depression, a Study of One Hundred Chicago Families.* Chicago: University of Chicago Press.

CHICAGO AREA PROJECT

The Chicago Area Project (CAP) originated in research conducted by two prominent sociologists, Clifford Shaw and Henry McKay, who began their research relationship as graduate students at the University of Chicago. Designated as the leading sociology department in the early 1900s and called simply the Chicago School, the sociology department at the University of Chicago had two objectives: to develop sociology as a science and to use information gathered in research to inform and enact social reform.

Shaw and McKay expanded on the research of Robert E. Park and Ernest W. Burgess, two well-known professors at the Chicago School. Park and Burgess studied ecology as it related to urban development and proposed that urban areas consisted of concentric zones that radiated from the central city to the suburbs. Using this model, Shaw and McKay developed an ecological theory of delinquency that examined the role of the community in producing delinquency. Until this point, delinquency theory had concentrated on biological explanations, stating that criminal and delinquent behavior was either hereditary or a result of a biological deficiency. However, Shaw and McKay believed that the sources of delinquent behavior were the urban environment and the community in which the individual lived, not her or his inherent characteristics. Shaw and McKay's ecological theory of delinquency contained ideas similar to the central tenets of the Chicago School regarding delinquency. First, a deviant individual is a human being who has more similarities to than differences from nondeviants. Second, social context is important when examining delinquency. Finally, the community plays an instrumental role both in causing and preventing delinquency.

To test this new ecological theory of delinquency, Shaw and McKay conducted research that examined the delinquency rates in Chicago. They found that delinquency was concentrated in a particular area of the city classified by Park and Burgess as the "zone of transition"— an area changing from residential living to a business district. Shaw and McKay noted that the zone contained economically, politically, and socially disadvantaged inhabitants, often immigrants and minorities. Additionally, the area was marked by social disorganization, a condition resulting from rapid social change in which deterioration appears in the basic institutions of social control such as family, neighborhoods, and schools. Shaw and McKay also reported that social disorganization caused high rates of disease, infant mortality, delinquency, and truancy.

Further examination of the pattern of delinquency showed that delinquency decreased as the distance from the central city increased. Shaw and McKay also found that delinquency remained a problem in transition areas, regardless of who lived there. Delinquency thrived as newly arriving immigrants inhabited these areas. However, when immigrants became assimilated and moved to other sections of the city and new immigrants moved in, delinquency remained high. Therefore, Shaw and McKay concluded that delinquency resulted from social factors and to prevent delinquency, treatment should be directed toward changing the environment of the neighborhood, rather than toward changing the individual.

CREATION OF THE CHICAGO AREA PROJECT

Based on results of their earlier work, Shaw and McKay proposed that delinquency within socially disorganized areas could be decreased by addressing social and economic issues. Their solution to the delinquency problem took the form of the Chicago Area Project. The CAP involved returning power to the communities. Both Shaw and McKay grew up in rural areas and wanted to recreate the power of local, informal control found in small towns within the urban environment. This project began in 1932, largely under the direction of Clifford Shaw, who was working for the Institute for Juvenile Delinquency at the time. Originally, selection for the project included three high-delinquency areas in Chicago inhabited mainly by white immigrant groups. Later the program expanded to include other predominantly minority areas.

Shaw believed that without commitment from the community to the goals of the program, the project would fail. Thus initially, Shaw met with both formal and informal community leaders to gain commitment for the project. Once support was gained, workers from the institute worked alongside community members to develop community committees. These committees were responsible for addressing local issues such as the quality of schools, health care, law enforcement, and sanitary services. While staff were available to provide support, the eventual independence of these committees was the goal, and once committees were functioning, workers from the institute were removed.

In addition to community committees, the CAP consisted of two other key components: recreational programs and gang programs. Recreational programs included summer camps and improved recreational facilities. Through these, Shaw hoped that adults would more actively monitor youth and thus increase the sense of community. The second component developed programs aimed at decreasing the number of gangs and gang members. These programs used street workers who cultivated relationships with gang members and jointly developed alternative activities and projects.

EVALUATION OF THE PROJECT

While an empirical evaluation of the CAP would have been extremely useful, no effort was made to assess the project. Shaw reported that delinquency rates decreased in areas with the project, but no systematic evaluation was completed to ensure that the decrease was due to the program and not to other factors. Therefore, it is very difficult to determine the effectiveness of the CAP. However, several replications of the CAP using evaluation components have been completed, allowing some insight into the possible effects, or the lack thereof, of the CAP.

The Midcity Project is one such replication that began in 1954 in Boston, Massachusetts. This project used gang workers to target seven gangs in the community. Similar to the Chicago Area Project, the Midcity Project was concentrated among communities characterized as low income, inner city, and socially disorganized. However, responsibility for implementing the Midcity Project did not rest solely with the community, whereas community involvement was an integral aspect of the CAP. The Midcity Project sought to decrease delinquency by strengthening community groups and improving family needs. However, an evaluation comparing gang members receiving treatment to a control group of gang members not receiving services indicated that the Midcity Project did not prevent delinquency among gang members.

CONTRIBUTIONS AND CRITICISMS

The Chicago Area Project made several important contributions toward furthering delinquency prevention by expanding delinquency prevention and treatment beyond the individual to involve the community. Without examining delinquency within the larger context of the neighborhood, the true cause of delinquency is difficult to ascertain. Furthermore, this project indicated that communities could in fact be used effectively to develop and implement their programs.

Because of these contributions, the CAP has served as a model for other delinquency programs.

While the CAP contributed to delinquency prevention, several criticisms remain. First and foremost, a systematic evaluation was not completed, thus little is known about the actual effect of the program. Replications have shown that area projects targeting social disorganization using street workers actually do not decrease delinquency. Without empirical evaluation, it is difficult to judge the effectiveness of the CAP. A second criticism is that the emphasis on the neighborhood environment ignored the role of the larger community, the city. Without city involvement, little can be accomplished at the neighborhood level. Additionally, critics noted that Shaw and McKay were not concerned with the social forces within the larger community that contributed to the social disorganization seen at the neighborhood level. Furthermore, Shaw and McKay ignored the role that industry played in the development of delinquency. While high-delinquency areas surrounded business districts, Shaw and McKay never examined the role that these businesses played in the continuation of the conditions that led to delinquency.

CONCLUSION

The CAP was the beginning of a movement to examine and prevent delinquency within the community context. To accomplish the goal of preventing delinquency by improving the conditions within the neighborhoods and focusing on the community and not individuals, several CAP components were developed. These included the formation of recreational programs, community committees, and street-worker programs with gangs. However, it is difficult to draw conclusions regarding the project since no evaluation was completed and replications of this project have shown no measurable decrease in juvenile delinquency.

Adrienne Freng

See also Ruth Shonle Cavan; Solomon Kobrin; Henry D. McKay; Clifford Shaw; Theories of Delinquency— Sociological

Bibliography

Keys, C. 1987. Synergy, prevention, and the Chicago School of Sociology. *Prevention in Human Services* 5:11–34.

Kobrin, S. 1959. The Chicago Area Project—A 25-year assessment. *Annals of the American Academy of Political and Social Science* 322:19–29.

Lundman, R. J. 1993. *Prevention and Control of Juvenile Delinquency.* New York: Oxford University Press.

Pacyga, D. 1989. The Russell Square Community Committee: An ethnic response to urban problems. *Journal of Urban History* 15:159–184.

Schlossman, S., and M. Sedlak. 1983. The Chicago Area Project revisited. *Crime and Delinquency* 29:398–462.

Shaw, C. R., and H. D. McKay. 1969. *Juvenile Delinquency and Urban Areas.* Chicago: University of Chicago Press.

Snodgrass, J. 1976. Clifford R. Shaw and Henry D. McKay: Chicago criminologists. *The British Journal of Criminology* 16:1–19.

 # CHILD ABUSE

Child abuse takes many forms, including physical, emotional, and sexual abuse and neglect. These forms are not mutually exclusive and are often difficult to define with precision.

Physical child abuse is the excessive and unjustified use of physical force against a child. The abuse might include punching, kicking, beating, biting, burning, and shaking. Injuries from physical abuse might include welts, burns, bites, and broken bones. Physical abuse therefore differs from spanking, a common parenting practice in the United States widely perceived as appropriate and justifiable. Not all societies recognize this distinction between spanking and child abuse. A number of Scandinavian societies have passed laws against physical punishment in homes, recognizing that such punishment is inconsistent with healthy child development. The logic in these countries seems to be, "If we do not use corporal punishment with adults, why employ it against children?"

The emotional abuse of a child usually builds over time, eroding the child's sense of competence and self-esteem. Such abuse can result in serious behavioral, cognitive, emotional, or mental health problems. Abusive behaviors include name calling, ridiculing, degradation, worsening a child's fears, destroying a child's possessions, torturing or destroying a child's pet, making excessive demands, and criticizing the child to excess. More recently, experts have recognized the devastating effects of children witnessing domestic violence, typically the battering of their mothers. Estimates suggest that between 3.3 million and 10 million children in the United States witness such violence every year. These child witnesses report an array of problems, including posttraumatic stress and a plethora of social, cognitive, emotional, and behavioral difficulties.

Child sexual abuse includes fondling a child's genitals (usually to sexually gratify the abuser), intercourse, incest, rape, oral sex, sodomy, exhibitionism, and the commercial exploitation of children by prostituting them or offering their bodies to pornographers (see the Child Sexual Abuse entry). It is nearly always committed by men.

Neglect results from the failure of parents or guardians to provide for their children's healthy development and physical security. Examples include refusing to seek or delaying medical care, abandoning the child, expelling the child from the home, and refusing to take back a child who has run away from home. Parents or guardians also neglect the child when they fail to make provision for the child's education. This might include allowing the child to persistently skip school. Parents can also neglect to give their children emotional affection. Clearly, parents can neglect their children without intending to. In general, low-income parents face a much more difficult time raising children than their wealthy counterparts and may not be able to provide various "necessities" because of their poverty. Indeed, authorities normally level accusations of neglect at parents who are poor. Authorities usually label mothers the "neglectful parent." This labeling reinforces the stereotypical idea that the care of children is mostly the concern of females rather than males. This works against the interests of poor women, especially minority women, who usually work for wages at the same time they play the central role in childrearing.

ORIGINS OF CRUELTY TO CHILDREN

The idea of "cruelty to children" was "discovered" in the 1870s in much of Europe and the United States and has gradually evolved into the modern-day notion of child abuse. The abuse and neglect of a small girl, Mary Ellen, from New York City in 1874 led to the formation of the first organization aimed at protecting children from cruelty—the New York Society for the Prevention of Cruelty to Children (NYSPCC). Within 40 years, nearly 500 similar anticruelty societies had formed in the United States. Mary Ellen told a court that she had been beaten daily with a rawhide whip

and less frequently with a long cane. The severity of Mary Ellen's beating contributed to the assessment that she had been cruelly treated.

The NYSPCC and later anticruelty societies did not oppose corporal punishment within families. Indeed, to oppose parental rights to "discipline" children would have angered parents and infringed on their family privacy, thereby undermining the anticruelty crusade. Historians cite an increasing sense of humanitarianism in the aftermath of the Civil War and a contemporary need to regulate the families of immigrants (especially Irish, Germans, Italians, and Poles) as factors underlying the intervention work of these anticruelty societies.

Protecting children against abuse extended the tentacles of various organizations into the lives of families to investigate much more than cases of physical abuse. Rather, anticruelty societies saw their mandate as challenging not only physical abuse but also neglect, mistreatment, and exploitation. These interventions went hand in hand with the decisions of post–Civil War courts that parental authority be measured, humane, and reasonable.

It was largely white, upper-class women who ran charitable organizations such as the NYSPCC. These child savers were usually native-born Protestants, and in cities such as New York and Boston, their targets were usually Catholic immigrants. The tone of their investigations was highly moralistic, reflecting their condescension toward the families of the urban poor. The upper-class women behind the early child cruelty movement mostly opposed the consumption of alcohol, which they determined was at the root of much physical violence and neglect of children. As the movement became more professional during the Progressive Era (between 1890 and 1920), the moralistic tone lessened. During this period, an expanding army of social workers superseded the charitable anticruelty crusaders.

DISCOVERY OF CHILD ABUSE

Until the 1960s, people considered parents who were cruel to their children to be moral degenerates. A number of advances in the field of medicine created the conditions that led to a shift in perceptions of child abuse. Instead of amoral, perpetrators were seen as psychologically flawed and in need of help. This new approach, while retaining its interest in abusers, was more concerned with defining abuse itself. During the 1950s, radiologists began to use X rays to detect hidden injuries, such as abnormal bone healing, skull hematomas, and fractures in infants. Radiologists, psychiatrists, and pediatricians began to take an active interest in child abuse. Being far removed from the doctor-patient relationship, radiologists were in a better position to report child abuse than were family practitioners and pediatricians. They also belonged to a less prestigious branch of medicine that was in need of a boost. The contribution of two radiologists to an article in the prestigious *Journal of the American Medical Association* identifying the battered-child syndrome increased the visibility of radiology.

The word *syndrome* conveyed the impression that perpetrators of child abuse were diseased or sick and implied that a constellation of poor parenting behaviors lay at the root of child abuse, rather than merely the occasional act of corporal punishment. Indeed, like the anticruelty crusaders of the 19th century, those who argued that child abuse is a syndrome did not challenge the rights of parents to spank their children. Neither did they argue that children had an innate "right" to protection. Rather, they recommended that inadequate parents receive treatment for their transgressions against children and that children be removed from the home until treatment was successful. The word *syndrome* also encouraged more compassion because the inadequate parent needed help rather than chastisement. The discovery of battered-child syndrome also led to the passage of the first laws on reporting child abuse. Between 1963 and 1967, every state passed such laws, which mandated that involved professionals report child abuse to police.

EXTENT OF CHILD ABUSE

It has always been difficult to arrive at an accurate assessment of the extent of child abuse. Indeed, it is probably safe to say that the bulk of child abuse remains hidden. Parents, guardians, or close relatives, rather than strangers such as child molesters, commit the overwhelming majority of child abuse. Young children, the most vulnerable to abuse and neglect, are less likely to be exposed to agencies capable of identifying child abuse—for example, schools, day care facilities, and kindergartens—and are less likely to be able to speak for themselves. Even if children can speak or otherwise communicate, they may not understand that the way they are being treated constitutes

abuse and may not know to whom or how they should report their maltreatment. Some children fear that reporting maltreatment will make them more vulnerable because their parents will get in trouble. Older children may perceive what is happening to them as inappropriate or wrong but may also feel that their parents have a right to hit them or punish them severely. Indeed, children may feel responsible for their victimization, sensing that their own perceived transgressions caused their parents or guardians to abuse them. Abused children may also fear reprisal from their parents if they speak out against the way their parents treat them.

Notwithstanding these difficulties, recent studies of child abuse tap different sources of data, employ different definitions of abuse, and adopt different methodologies. Not surprisingly, these studies report differing amounts of abuse. For example, the National Incidence Study (NIS) surveys schools, hospitals, and other institutions to learn about the extent of physical, emotional, and sexual abuse. The NIS reported 3.4 cases of abuse per 1,000 children in 1980 and 5.7 per 1,000 in 1986. In 1993, the NIS surveyed 5,600 professionals involved with children and reported 42 children per 1,000 harmed or endangered by maltreatment. If researchers broaden the definition of abuse, these numbers increase. For example, the American Humane Association surveyed child protection agencies only and found a rate of 22 cases per 1,000 for major physical injuries and 154 per 1,000 for minor physical injuries. In 1997, child protection agencies determined that 54 percent of victims suffered neglect; 24 percent, physical abuse; 13 percent, sexual abuse; 6 percent, emotional maltreatment; and 2 percent, medical neglect.

It is difficult for researchers to ask children to report their own victimization. Leaving aside the issue of whether children can adequately communicate their maltreatment to researchers, most research protocols require parental permission before children can complete surveys or otherwise answer sensitive questions. Parents who maltreat their children are much less likely to give permission for their children to participate in such research.

One way to gain insights into child abuse is to ask adults about their own childhood experiences of maltreatment. Although adults may forget their childhood maltreatment or somehow recreate it inaccurately, these retroactive studies provide another window into the family and another part of the puzzle. In one such study, the Gallup Corporation noted that 12 percent of adults reported being punched, kicked, or choked during childhood by their parents or guardians.

Parents are understandably reluctant to report the abuse they inflict on their children. However, some researchers have tried to soften the way they obtain information by asking questions that reveal how parents treat their children. The National Family Violence Survey (NFVS) used a fairly strict definition of abuse that included kicking, biting, hitting with a fist, beating up, threatening with a knife or gun, or injuring with a knife or gun. The findings suggested that from 1.4 million to 1.9 million children were abused in 1975. When the researchers expanded the definition of abuse to include hitting with an object (stick or belt), the number of child victims increased to nearly 7 million. Even these comprehensive studies underestimate the extent and severity of the phenomenon because they do not include single-parent families and families in which all children are less than 3 years old.

CORRELATES OF CHILD ABUSE

Given the range of findings from the different studies, it is impossible to map the precise social correlates of child abuse. A 1994 Gallup poll found that 17 percent of respondents with annual incomes of less than $20,000 reported being punched, choked, or beaten by an adult or guardian compared with only 6 percent of respondents with incomes of $50,000 or higher. Studies of child homicide reveal a strong correlation between deaths and poverty. However, the connection between poverty and child deaths remains unclear because millions of Americans live in poverty, but only a very small number kill their children. If poverty were the principal factor, we would expect to find far more child deaths from abuse and neglect.

African American children are disproportionately more likely to die from abuse and neglect. One study of 83 child deaths in Florida found that 41 percent were black; a roughly threefold overrepresentation compared with black children's presence in the population. However, given that black children are much more likely than other children to experience acute poverty, researchers do not know if they are observing an effect of race, poverty, or some combination of the two.

In the Florida research, just over three fifths of children killed were less than 3 years old, with nearly one third less than a year old. The reasons for this vulnerability include very young children's physical fragility, particularly their relatively large head size and their inability to control head movements, and their less frequent contact with agencies such as day care centers and schools that may identify abuse and neglect problems before they escalate.

Several studies have revealed that women commit more child abuse and neglect than do men. The 1975 NFVS showed fathers abused 10.1 per 100 children compared with mothers' 17.7 per 100. The 1985 survey revealed comparable rates, 10.2 per 100 for fathers and 11.2 for mothers. This disparity reflects the fact that mothers spend more time with children than fathers do and that society expects women to bear unequally the burdens of caring for, nurturing, and disciplining children. The U.S. National Clearinghouse on Child Abuse and Neglect Information, using data from state child protection agencies, confirmed approximately a million cases of child abuse in 1996. Women constituted the perpetrators in roughly two thirds of these cases. However, compared with women, men commit more severe forms of physical child abuse, the vast majority of child sexual abuse, and the majority of child killings. In the Florida study of 83 child abuse/neglect deaths, 24 of the perpetrators were biological fathers (27.6 percent), 23 were either mother's boyfriends or stepfathers (26.4 percent), and 24 were biological mothers (27.6 percent). Men committed 14 of the 15 killings attributed to head injuries and 6 of the 9 deaths due to abdominal trauma.

The 1985 NFVS revealed that only 7 percent to 10 percent of parents who reported "no instances of marital violence" frequently abused their children. Fathers who frequently abused their wives were more likely to frequently abuse their children. Mothers beaten by their husbands reported committing more than twice the rate of child abuse compared with mothers not beaten. All these observations suggest important links between the phenomena of child abuse and woman battering. Indeed, estimates suggest that in 30 percent to 50 percent of child abuse cases, adult domestic violence also occurs in the home. Research reveals a similar link in the smaller number of child homicides. Researchers in Florida scrutinized two-parent families in which children died from abuse or neglect; in just over half the cases, men had violently abused women before the child died.

The physical, social, and political vulnerability of children lies at the heart of child abuse. Put simply, children constitute a relatively powerless group in society and as such are susceptible to violence, abuse, and neglect. Like the poor in general, children from low-income families experience a disproportionate amount of violent and abusive treatment. Some researchers explain the disproportionate victimization of poor children as a product of the high levels of stress experienced by their parents. However, this explanation fails to explain why some low-income parents abuse their children and most others do not. Another possibility is that parents who experienced abuse themselves are much more likely than parents who did not to use abusive parenting themselves (see the Cycle of Violence entry). It is also likely that the widespread social acceptance of spanking creates an environment conducive to child abuse in some families.

PREVENTION OF CHILD ABUSE

Given the relationship between child abuse and poverty, social policies designed to alleviate poverty or help parents better negotiate it might reduce victimization. Prevention programs, including parenting classes, offer some potential. Because young children are at greatest risk of abuse, parenting classes for first-time parents or parents of newborns might prove particularly valuable. Currently, home visitation provides one of the most innovative and holistic forms of child abuse prevention. Services offered by home visitation include nursing to monitor the health of the mother and the infant and in-home parent education. One of the goals of home visitation is to break down the social isolation faced by new parents, particularly young mothers, and hook them up with existing community networks.

The United States does not have a national system for providing child care. Such a system of well-trained professionals would provide much-needed support for working parents and an important break or safety valve for single parents who bear the sole burden of child rearing.

Child protection agencies and other social support systems remain understaffed and underfunded. Improving the delivery of such services might reduce victimization. The rise of child-death review teams in the late 1970s provided new insights into how and why children die. Information gleaned from such reviews provides useful insights for service providers and sharpens the communication between agencies. Such communication has recently helped experts to recognize the links between woman battering and child abuse.

As a result, advocates for battered women and child protection workers have begun an encouraging, if somewhat tense, dialogue about how to work to protect both victimized parties. In the long term, reducing child abuse will depend on blending an array of agency services, reducing poverty and its impact, and creating a cultural climate that improves the status of children.

Neil Websdale

See also Child-Saving Movement; Child Sexual Abuse; Cycle of Violence; Pregnancy, Teenage; Runaways; Sex Offenders; Theories of Delinquency— Psychological

Bibliography

Dorne, C. K. 2001. *Child Maltreatment: A Primer in History, Public Policy, and Research,* 2nd ed. New York: Harrow & Heston.
Pfohl, S. 1977. The "discovery" of child abuse. *Social Problems* 24:310–323.
Tower, C. 2001. *Understanding Child Abuse and Neglect,* 5th ed. Boston: Allyn & Bacon.

 CHILDREN'S AID SOCIETY

Founded in 1853 in New York City by Charles Loring Brace, the Children's Aid Society (CAS) has become one of the largest and most complete child welfare agencies in the United States. While the stated focus of the CAS is children, the definition used to define them is exceedingly broad, written with the vision of a child's growth on a continuum from birth to young adulthood. The myriad services offered therefore range from pregnancy prevention programs to adoption services and technical assistance for community schools to juvenile justice aftercare.

The mission of the CAS is illustrated by the society's action equation: Service + Advocacy = Change. For nearly one and a half centuries, the CAS has attempted to provide for the needs of New York City's neediest children. Its goal "is to ensure the physical and emotional well-being of children and families, and to provide every child with the support and opportunities needed to become a happy, healthy and successful adult" (CAS, 2000).

When Charles Loring Brace first came to New York City in 1848, he began working in the dangerous Five Points neighborhood just north of City Hall. After attending Yale University (in which he enrolled at age 16) to become a minister and then traveling for a year in Europe, Brace planned to become a scholar of philosophy and religion. Instead, he felt compelled to work directly with the poor of New York City. He began his work in the Five Points neighborhood with youthful enthusiasm and a zeal for making positive change in the lives of its residents. Finding his efforts in reforming adults to be futile, he quickly turned his energies toward helping children.

In 1848, some 10,000 children, reviled by the populace as "street rats," roamed the streets of New York City. Making their living by picking rags, twine twisting, pickpocketing, or prostitution, many children lived on their own or in gangs. Brace admired them, cared about them, and quickly became their champion. In 1853, at a time when children were an overlooked minority, Brace and a small group of social reformers began to espouse a revolutionary idea—an organization devoted to saving children and meeting their needs. The idea became reality with the founding of the Children's Aid Society.

In its pioneering work in the field of child welfare during the next four decades and under Brace's leadership, the CAS became involved in the lives of approximately 300,000 children. The CAS became the bellwether for change in the nation's valuation of and service to children.

In the first 50 years of its existence, the CAS showed an outstanding record of achievement. Among its successes are industrial schools for poor children, the first free school lunch program in the United States, the first parents and teachers' association, fresh air-type vacations at country homes for city mothers and children, the first physicians' and nurses' visits to tenements (which became the model for visiting nurses services), the first day nursery for infants and children of working mothers, foster care, kindergarten, day schools for handicapped children, and free classes for mentally retarded children.

In its second 50 years, 1903 to 1953, the CAS continued to develop its earlier children's projects and programs while actively seeking new avenues of service. By 1913, free dental clinics were provided in every CAS school. In 1928, services to minority students were expanded with new city centers, and in 1933, the first Homemaker Services in the city began with Eleanor Roosevelt as chair. When the city and other agencies failed to agree on a plan to meet

children's needs, the CAS absorbed the Service Bureau for Negro Children in 1943.

Since the centennial of its founding in 1953, the CAS has continued to lead in vision and accomplishment in the fields of child welfare and juvenile justice. In 1956, the Wagon Road Camp was opened with summer programs for disabled children and respite weekends for their families. Head Start classes were begun in CAS centers in 1965, and psychiatric clinics were opened in five CAS centers in 1973. In 1981, the CAS launched a program to divert troubled youth from family court, and four years later, the New York legislature wrote the program into law.

In 1983, the CAS began to serve homeless children in city welfare hotels with educational support and health care, and in 1988, a mobile unit began bringing health and dental care to as many as 10,000 children per year. In 1996, the CAS began a new aftercare program for teens released from juvenile boot camps. These and many other services have been developed by the CAS, and others have been introduced through collaboration with other organizations and agencies.

The CAS offers many meaningful volunteer opportunities. More than 1,500 volunteers presently give of their time and energies in a variety of programs. Tutoring and mentoring programs offer chances for volunteers to develop person-to-person relationships with children. Periodic events offer opportunities for people wishing to help for a few hours or for a day on intermittent intervals. The CAS even has a variety of programs that allow volunteers to help from their places of employment.

Every year, the CAS serves more than 120,000 children and their families throughout the area surrounding New York City. Beyond the city, pregnancy prevention programs and community schools have been started in almost 100 communities throughout the United States. The CAS has an annual operating budget of more than $50 million and serves 36 sites. To its credit, the CAS has a record of spending 91 cents out of every expense dollar directly on services to children.

Edward J. Schauer

See also Boot Camps; Mentoring Programs

Bibliography

Children's Aid Society (CAS). No date. *Highlights and History*. New York: The Children's Aid Society.

Children's Aid Society (CAS). No date. *Thirty Years of "Firsts."* New York: The Children's Aid Society.

Children's Aid Society (CAS). 1999. The spirit of the child: Our mission and relevance in the 21st century. In *The Children's Aid Society* 1999 *Annual Report.* New York: The Children's Aid Society.

Children's Aid Society (CAS). 2000. Service + advocacy = change. In *The Children's Aid Society 2000 Annual Report.* New York: The Children's Aid Society.

CHILD-SAVING MOVEMENT

The term *child saving* has normally been used to describe the work of a group of mostly upper-class women and men who were part of a much larger social movement during a period of U.S. history known as the Progressive Era (roughly between 1890 and 1920), a social movement that resulted in numerous reforms throughout the country. The reform known as the child-saving movement resulted in the creation of the first juvenile court, which opened in Chicago in 1899 and was followed closely by a court opening in Denver in the same year. In fact, however, child saving started much earlier in the 19th century when a group of New York reformers, calling themselves the Society for the Reformation of Juvenile Delinquents, helped pass legislation that established the New York House of Refuge in 1825.

Reformers at both ends of the century were convinced that the adult justice system was a total failure at addressing the newly discovered problem of juvenile delinquency. American society throughout the 19th century could not begin to handle the fundamental contradictions of the new republic, with great wealth on the one hand and utter misery on the other. As thousands began the migration to the "land of opportunity" in the early 1800s, the cities of the northeast were filling up with homeless children. Thousands of children wandered the streets, sleeping in alleys, accosting pedestrians for a few dollars or some food, and generally making a nuisance of themselves. Something had to be done.

Many other cities around the country followed with their own houses of refuge. The statutes contained vague descriptions of behaviors and lifestyles that were synonymous with the characteristics of the urban poor. Being homeless, begging, vagrancy, and coming from an "unfit" home (as defined from a middle-class viewpoint) are examples. Most of the youth rounded up and sent to the refuges were not hardened criminals but those in danger of becoming criminals. Today we call them status offenders—youth charged with truancy, running away from home, incorrigibility, being beyond control, and the like.

There was an assumption that houses of refuge were the ideal places for the reformation of youthful deviants or potential deviants. There was also a naive belief in the "humanitarianism" of those put in charge of the refuges. The lofty aims are illustrated by a statement from the Society for the Reformation of Juvenile Delinquents, an organization in New York responsible for establishing the first house of refuge: "The young should, if possible, be subdued with kindness. His heart should first be addressed, and the language of confidence, although undeserved, be used toward him." The child should be taught that "his keepers were his best friends and that the object of his confinement was his reform and ultimate good."

The results were disastrous, to say the least. The actions by these reformers usually did not serve the "best interests of the child." Children confined in the houses of refuge were subjected to strict discipline and control. Corporal punishments (including hanging children from their thumbs, the use of the "ducking stool" for girls, and severe beatings), solitary confinement, handcuffs, the "ball and chain," uniform dress, the "silent system," and other practices were commonly used in houses of refuge.

The justification for such bold interventions came from a doctrine known as *parens patriae*, a carryover from early English society where the king, in his presumed role as the "father" of his country, had the legal authority to take care of his people, especially those who were unable, for various reasons (including age), to take care of themselves. For children, the king or his authorized agents could assume the role of guardian and administer the children's property. By the 19th century, this legal doctrine had evolved into the practice of the state's assuming wardship over a minor child and, in effect, playing the role of parent if the child had no parents or if the existing parents were declared unfit—determined almost solely by those in authority.

This doctrine was upheld in a famous 1838 case known as *Ex Parte Crouse*. This case involved a 16-year-old girl named Mary Crouse who, without her father's knowledge, had been committed to the Philadelphia House of Refuge by her mother on the grounds that she was incorrigible. Her father argued

To the Inhabitants of the City of New-York.

FELLOW CITIZENS,

At a very large and respectable meeting held at the City Hotel on the 19th of December last, a society was formed for the " Reformation of Juvenile Delinquents."

Acting under the authority of that meeting as the Managers of the recently formed society, we beg leave to solicit your attention universally, to the important and interesting concerns of this association.

The leading object to which it is expected our attention will be directed, is the establishment of an Institution under the title of a " House of Refuge," in which the numerous and increasing class of Juvenile Delinquents in this city may find an asylum from the miseries to which they have been exposed, and be subjected to a treatment at once adapted to the punishment of their crimes, the correction of their habits, the reformation of their morals, and their preparation for honest and useful service when again restored to society.

In such an Institution, young offenders must be classed according to their degrees of criminality and depravity, all contaminating intercourse strictly prohibited, their dress cheap and simple, their food plain, and their time divided into hours of labour, of necessary instruction, and of needful repose.

On the amount of benefit which such a House of Refuge, if properly established and conducted, may confer upon hundreds and thousands of the destitute and neglected youth of this city, or the appalling evils which annually result from the want of such an asylum,—or the deplorable consequences which flow from the indiscriminate mixture of young novices in crime, with veterans in wickedness, which our city prisons produce, we deem it unnecessary here to expatiate. We would refer to the report on this subject, which has been extensively circulated as an ample demonstration of the magnitude of those evils, and of the special benefits which may rationally be hoped for from a " House of Refuge."

From this report our citizens may get the alarming information, that in the compass of a single year (1822,) no less than 450 persons, all under 25 years of age, were arraigned before the Police of this city for crimes of various die, for vagrancies and misdemeanours.

The blessings attendant upon the most favoured condition of human life, are liable to an alloy of evil. The advantages which large cities afford in the facilities of business, of domestic conveniences, of social intercourse, of intellectual activity and improvement, are unavoidably accompanied with an exhibition of abject poverty, and of the manifold evils which flow from the corruptions of our common nature, aggravated by the force of example, and by companionship in misery. To such vortices of criminality, hundreds, and perhaps thousands of innocent and helpless children in this city, are hourly exposed. And when impelled by such temptations to the commission of actual crime, ought they, in their very incipiency of guilt, to be abandoned to the terrors of a sentence which consigns them to almost irremediable and hopeless depravity? Is there no preserving power in society, which shall reach forth an arm of deliverance to these victims of poverty and corrupt example? Shall no effort be made worthy of the occasion to rescue them from the gulf into which they are hastening, to cheer them with the hopes of a restoration to virtuous society, and with the prospects of enduring happiness in the life to come?

It is under the strong conviction, fellow-citizens, that every member of our favoured community, who is duly sensible of the blessings of an exemption from such sources of evil, and of the magnitude of its injuries, will unite with heart and hand in this paternal duty, that we are induced to accept the trust reposed in us.

We are aware of the responsibility which we thus assume. We anticipate the difficulties of an untried path, unaided by example in this country. We are sensible of the time and attention it will require at our hands, and of the discretion that will be requisite in every stage of its operation. But all we want as an encouragement to perseverance, is, the promptitude and efficiency of your co-operation. Even at a time when so much feeling has been excited and liberally manifested, on behalf of the grievances and sufferings of a far distant nation, we hesitate not to prefer our claims upon the charities of the bountiful, and the sympathies of the benevolent, in favour of the wretched of our own immediate borders.

We are fully persuaded of the practicability of the scheme we have undertaken, and of its truly beneficent tendencies. Hence we propose that measures be taken to call upon every citizen for a contribution proportioned to his ability ; and, upon the result of such benefactions must it depend, whether a " House of Refuge" be established, which, in its erection and progress, shall be an honour to this metropolis. Each of the Managers will be at all times ready to receive donations for the Society, either from persons in the city or those at a distance ; and it is intended that the names of donors and subscribers be published alphabetically in the Reports of the Society.

C. D. COLDEN, No. 1, William-street.	STEPHEN ALLEN, 93, Beekman-street.
JOHN GRISCOM, Elm, corner of Grand-street.	HENRY I. WYCKOFF, 6, Broadway.
JOHN DUER, Grand, corner of Mercer-street.	SAMUEL COWDREY, 338, Pearl-street.
J. M. WAINWRIGHT, 1, Rector-street.	JOHN TARGEE, 27, Frankfort-street.
ISAAC COLLINS, 424, Broome-street.	ARTHUR BURTIS, Bellevue.
THOMAS EDDY, 220, William-street.	JOSEPH GRINNELL, 36, Market-street.
ANSEL W. IVES, 3, Park-place.	HUGH MAXWELL, 22, Howard-street.
JOHN T. IRVING, Chamber-street.	HENRY MEAD, Broome, near Goerck-street.
JOHN E. HYDE, 17, John-street.	PETER A. JAY, 398, Broadway.
CORNELIUS DUBOIS, 9, Bridge-street.	GILBERT COUTANT, Bowery, near Vauxhall garden.
JAMES W GERARD, 26, Broadway.	CORNELIUS R. DUFFIE, 24, Franklin-street.
JOSEPH CURTIS, 444, Cherry-street.	JAMES LOVETT, 41, Dey-street.
JOHN STEARNS, 169, William-street.	JOHN R. WILLIS, 22, Cherry-street.
RALPH OLMSTED, 86, Liberty-street.	WILLIAM M. CARTER, 186, Church-street.
ROBERT F. MOTT, 234, William-street.	FREDERICK SHELDON, 32, Warren-street.

Photo 1. New York City broadside from circa 1823 calling citizens' notice to the organization of a society for the "reformation of juvenile delinquents."

SOURCE: Library of Congress, Rare Book and Special Collections Division. Used with permission.

that the incarceration was illegal because she had not been given a jury trial. The Pennsylvania Supreme Court ruled against the father, stating, "May not the natural parents, when unequal to the task of education, or unworthy of it, be superseded by the *parens patriae* or common guardian of the community?" Further, the court observed, "The infant has been snatched from a course which must have ended in confirmed depravity." No evidence was brought forth to support such an assertion—because there was no evidence. The Supreme Court relied solely on the testimony of the managers of the refuge.

By the end of the 19th century, many realized that the reforms of the early part of the century were ineffective, because children were still being abused by the existing system. Also, many children were still being confined in adult institutions. The child savers of Chicago began to work toward the establishment of new methods of responding to young offenders.

The result of their efforts was the establishment of the juvenile court. The new legislation of the period (first in Chicago and Denver in 1899, then elsewhere) created new categories of offenses and extended the state's power over the lives of children and youth. The new laws defining delinquency and predelinquent behavior were broad in scope and vague: They covered the usual violations of laws also applicable to adults as well as violations of local ordinances. In addition, the laws included such catchalls as "vicious or immoral behavior," "incorrigibility," truancy, "profane or indecent behavior," "growing up in idleness," "living with any vicious or disreputable person," and many more.

The child savers conceived of the new juvenile court as a special "children's court" where the best interest of the child would be the ultimate goal. The judge of the juvenile court was to be like a benevolent, yet stern, father. The proceedings were to be informal, without the traditional judicial trappings. There was neither a need for lawyers nor constitutional safeguards because the cases were not "criminal" in nature and the court would always act in the best interests of the child. The court was to be operated like a clinic, and the child was to be diagnosed to determine the extent of his or her condition and to prescribe the correct treatment plan, preferably as early in life as possible.

Even the terminology of the juvenile court was, and to some extent still is, different. Children in many parts of the United States are referred to the court rather than being arrested; instead of being held in jail pending court action, they are detained in a detention center; rather than being indicted, children are petitioned to court; in place of a determination of guilt, there is an adjudication; and those found guilty (i.e., adjudicated) are often committed to a training school or reform school rather than being sentenced to a prison.

The juvenile court system extended the role of the probation officer, a role originally introduced in the mid-19th century in Boston. This new role was one of the primary innovations in the 20th century juvenile justice system, and the role became one of the most crucial in the entire system. One historian noted that "nothing in a child's home, school, occupation, or peer-group relations was, at least in theory, beyond" the purview of the probation officer. The probation officer "was expected to instruct children and parents in reciprocal obligations, preach moral and religious verities, teach techniques of child care and household management."

The new penology (as it was called at the time), perhaps best represented by state and county reformatories, industrial and training schools, and the like, emphasized menial labor that helped produce profits for both the state and private industry. For instance, the Illinois State Reform School (opened in 1871 in Pontiac) signed contracts with a Chicago shoe company, a company that manufactured brushes, and a company that manufactured cane-seat chairs—and this was called the "educational" program at this institution! The "training" in such institutions was supposed to, in the words of the famous penal reformer Frederick Wines, "correspond to the mode of life of working people," and should "be characterized by the greatest simplicity in diet, dress and surroundings, and above all by labor." Many of these institutions emphasized agricultural training, despite the fact that America was quickly moving toward industrialization. The reformatory regime aimed to teach middle-class values but lower-class skills. Bookishness was expressed as something undesirable, while menial labor was described as an "educational" experience.

The treatment of girls within the juvenile court reinforced the traditional double standard. Girls were far more likely than boys to be brought into the court on vague charges of "immorality," mostly having to do with their sexuality. Many girls, but hardly any boys, were brought into the court for having sexual intercourse and even in some cases for merely holding hands and necking. One researcher was later to discover widespread use of vaginal exams for girls brought into the juvenile court, noting also that girls charged with various status offenses (especially incorrigibility and running away) were far more likely than boys charged with similar offenses to be detained and subsequently incarcerated (Chesney-Lind and Shelden, 1998).

The juvenile court system rapidly spread throughout the country following the lead of Chicago and Denver. Juvenile institutions, such as industrial and training schools and reform schools, continued to develop and expand. Yet problems soon emerged and continued to plague the juvenile justice system, not the least of which was a built-in contradiction between the goals of treatment and punishment. Put somewhat differently, the court combined an iron fist with a velvet glove.

The decade of the 1960s brought about some noteworthy challenges to the juvenile court. At least two developments stand out during the period. One development was the intrusion into the business of juvenile justice by the U.S. Supreme Court. Such famous court cases as *In re Gault* (1967), *Kent v. U.S.* (1966), and *In re Winship* (1970), among others, promised significant reforms. The case of *In re Gault* involved a 15-year-old Arizona boy named Gerald Gault who was adjudicated as a delinquent in juvenile court and committed to the Arizona Industrial School for the "period of his majority" (i.e., until he was 21 years old) because he and some friends made an obscene phone call to a neighbor. The U.S. Supreme Court ruled that Gault had been denied certain fundamental rights, such as the right to counsel. Writing for the majority, Justice Abe Fortas stated, "Under our Constitution, the condition of being a boy does not justify a kangaroo court." Sadly, most of the promises were never realized, especially regarding institutionalizing youth. One problem persisted and continues to exist as we enter the 21st century: racial minorities, especially African Americans, continue to receive the most severe dispositions within the juvenile justice system and are overrepresented at every stage of the process, from arrest to incarceration.

The "crime" committed by Gerald Gault illustrates a continuing problem within the juvenile court—namely, that far too many minor offenses—and in some cases no offenses at all—end up being processed. This has often been described as "net widening," in the sense that more behaviors—typically either ignored or handled outside the court—are being formally processed. A more recent example can be seen in the fact that cases of fights and other minor disturbances on school grounds are increasingly being referred to the juvenile court, no doubt stemming from recent zero-tolerance policies.

The second development of the 1960s that had a major impact on the juvenile court came on the heels of the efforts of Jerome Miller who, as Commissioner of Youth Corrections in Massachusetts, managed to close most of the reform schools opened in the 19th century. Despite the success of the closure of most of their institutions and the development of workable alternatives throughout the country, the recent "get tough" policies do not signal hopeful signs. Critics have charged that most jurisdictions continue to rely on the use of institutions, with conditions reminiscent of reform schools 100 years ago. Far too many youthful offenders continue to be warehoused in large correctional facilities, with few receiving treatment.

Randall G. Shelden

See also Courts, Juvenile—History; Female
    Delinquency—History; Law, Juvenile; *Parens Patriae*
    Doctrine; Reformatories and Reform Schools; Status
    Offenders

Bibliography

Chesney-Lind, M., and R. G. Shelden. 1998. *Girls, Delinquency and Juvenile Justice*, 2nd ed. Belmont, CA: West/Wadsworth.

Mennel, R. 1973. *Thorns and Thistles: Juvenile Delinquents in the US, 1820–1940*. Hanover, NH: University Press of New England.

Odem, M. 1995. *Delinquent Daughters: Protecting and Policing Adolescent Female Sexuality in the United States, 1885–1920*. Chapel Hill, NC: University of North Carolina Press.

Platt, A. M. 1991. *The Child Savers: The Invention of Delinquency,* 2nd ed. Chicago: University of Chicago Press.

Schlossman, S. 1977. *Love and the American Delinquent: The Theory and Practice of "Progressive" Juvenile Justice, 1825–1920*. Chicago: University of Chicago Press.

Shelden, R. G. 2001. *Controlling the Dangerous Classes: A Critical Introduction to the History of Criminal Justice*. Boston: Allyn & Bacon.

 # CHILD SEXUAL ABUSE

Few topics capture public attention and stimulate the outrage of Americans more than do sex crimes and sexual offenders. Sex offenses have a history that begins in ancient times and continues into the present. The history of sexual abuse dates back to ancient Greece, when it was common practice for young boys to accompany warriors to battle. This practice was no longer condoned when Christianity's popularity grew. In the 18th century, China, Japan, Africa, Turkey, Arabia, and Egypt accepted adult-child sex as normal. The 19th century showed an acceptance of the sale of young girls for sex (Ames and Houston, 1990).

Recent high-profile cases, such as the deaths of JonBenet Ramsey and Megan Kanka, have received massive amounts of media attention, bringing sexual abuse to the forefront of American minds. These sensational cases have made sexual offenders a topic of interest to professionals, politicians, and parents everywhere.

CHARACTERISTICS

Current literature has brought attention to the characteristics that are both common among most sexual offenders and unique to specific offenders. Some similarities among sex offenders are a history of social ineptitude and a tendency to be age and gender specific. Areas in which sexual offenders show variation are their access techniques and recidivism risks.

Sexual offenders have a lack of attachment to significant others throughout their lives (Anechiarico, 1998). Throughout their teenage years, they have limited social interactions. When looking at offenders' pasts, researchers found that many sex offenders exhibited bizarre interests in sex, such as an interest in young children, even at an early age. These interests may have been caused by feelings of not fitting in with their peers and finding that children gave them the attention they craved.

Sex offenders show an excessive interest in children, and their associations often involve activities where children are present. They hang around schoolyards, arcades, and parks—anywhere children are present. They attend activities involving children, even though they have no children of their own (Lanning, 1992).

One of the most talked-about sex offenders is the pedophile. Pedophiles are characterized by their focus on prepubescent children (Lanning, 1992). There is some indication that pedophiles have extensive childhood victimization experiences. Pedophiles are often described as using abusive behavior as a coping mechanism and duplicating their abuse on children who are the same age they were when abused. Typically, pedophiles have specific preferences for children of a certain sex or a specific age: Those attracted to girls usually prefer 8- to 10-year-olds; those attracted to boys usually prefer children a little older than 10. The sex of the child also plays an important role in the selection of the victim. A pedophile will usually choose either males or females. Although not unheard of, it is unusual for an offender to victimize both boys and girls.

Few pedophiles are able to resist the urge to initiate sexual contact with children. They make efforts to gain access to children, they take jobs where children are easily approached, or they actively pursue youngsters by befriending parents. Single mothers are often befriended by pedophiles (Anechiarico, 1998). Pedophiles often attend events for children, coach children's sports, chaperone overnight trips, and offer babysitting services to friends, family, and neighbors with children (Lanning, 1992).

Types of Pedophiles

Pedophiles are not all alike. They are categorized by the amount of contact they have with children, victim choice, type of sexual activity, and motivation. There is a distinction made between offenders who spend a substantial amount of time in close proximity to victims and those who spend little or no time with victims outside of sexual assaults. High-contact offenders—those who spend the majority of their time, both sexual and nonsexual, with their victims—have professions that allow them repeated interaction. "The high contact pedophile is always trying to get children into situations where no other adults are present" (Lanning, 1992). They may be schoolteachers, bus drivers, babysitters, or scout leaders (Lanning, 1992).

Regressed pedophiles have led otherwise normal lives but because of outside stressors and low self-esteem, have turned to children as sexual substitutes. Typically married or in long-standing relationships, regressed pedophiles have had some life experience that has caused sexual feelings for children to develop. The most common victims of a regressed pedophile are children who are readily available. Their usual method of sex offending is to coerce children into having sex (Lanning, 1992).

Fixated pedophiles have not yet developed past the point where they, as a child, found children attractive and desirable. They are fixated at an early stage of psychosexual development. This pedophile's interest in children started during adolescence and is persistent and compulsive; there is no reasonable cause for their abuse of children. The offender has enduring relationships with the victim yet no interest in physically harming the child.

Another category is the situational pedophile, an individual who commits offenses against children to fulfill needs, without the elements of the offense being necessary for arousal and gratification. Situational pedophiles do not have a true sexual preference for children. The situational pedophile prefers vulnerable individuals and may abuse children and, later, abuse elderly or disabled individuals. Lanning (1992) wrote that situational pedophiles compose the largest number of sexual offenders, growing at a rate that is higher than any other type of sexual offender.

Certain types of pedophiles do not have a true sexual preference for children but engage in sex with children for varied reasons. The morally indiscriminate pedophile is a user of people; the abuse of children is a part of a pattern of abuse. The sexually indiscriminate pedophile has sex with children out of boredom and a need for sexual experimentation. His or her interest in children stems from the fact that the children are new and different, thus the child sexual abuse occurs alongside existing sexual activity. The sexually indiscriminate offender is the most likely of all pedophiles to have multiple victims (Lanning, 1992). The inadequate pedophile is the social misfit; this type of offender becomes sexually involved with children out of insecurity or curiosity. To this type of pedophile, children are nonthreatening and provide a means of exploring sexual fantasies. Offenders in this category often kill children (Lanning, 1992).

Hebephiles

Hebephiles are offenders who prefer postpubescent children. The hebephile is a person who would not think of having a sexual encounter with a child who has not yet reached puberty. Hebephiles interpret sexual involvement with the victim to be two-sided and define the act as "having an affair." Hebephiles generally have age-appropriate relationships. Their inappropriate behavior manifests itself in the guise of external stressors, such as marital problems or a "midlife crisis," and is impulsive (Danni and Hampe, 2000). Hebephiles are mature individuals who, once they have control over the outside stressors, are unlikely to offend again (Danni and Hampe, 2000).

INCEST OFFENDERS

Incest offenders differ from extrafamilial offenders in many ways. The extrafamilial sex offender has never been married and typically has few friends, whereas the incest offender marries and has age-appropriate friendships. The incest offender spends most of his or her time with family, primarily the preferred victim, and isolates the family as well as the victim from society. The incest offender may become paranoid and believe that the victim is too close to someone else. Once incest starts, it continues for an average period of two years. Most incest victims are between 8 and 12 years of age. Children this age are more vulnerable because they are becoming more independent and are less likely to be supervised.

ADOLESCENT SEX OFFENDERS

An adolescent sex offender is defined as any male or female between 12 and 17 years of age who commits any sexual act with a person of any age against the victim's will, without consent, or in an aggressive, exploitive, or threatening manner. Adolescent sex offenders come from all socioeconomic, ethnocultural, and religious backgrounds. They vary widely in their level of intellectual functioning, their motivation, the victims they choose, and their behaviors. Because adolescence is a time for exploration of sexual issues, adolescent sex offending has sometimes been dismissed as "boys will be boys" or "he or she is just going through a stage" (Lanning, 1992).

The victims of adolescent sex offenders are more likely to be acquaintances or siblings than are the victims of adult offenders. An adolescent offender is often trusted by the victim's family and is likely to have contact with the victim as a family member, babysitter, or other substitute caretaker (Lanning, 1992).

Categories of Adolescent Sex Offenders

As with adult offenders, researchers have developed categories of adolescent sex offenders. Researchers state that sexual abuse is not a sexually motivated behavior. Typically, it is an offense that is triggered by aggression and the need for control. There are several types of adolescent sex offenders and their acts range from kissing and fondling to those who commit serious sexual offenses.

Naive experimenters are young adolescents, typically 11 to 14 years of age, with no history of any type of offense. They engage only in nonintercourse acts—hugging, fondling, kissing, or licking their victims—and use no force or threats.

Undersocialized child exploiters show evidence of social ineptness. Unable to function properly in society, they manipulate children to gain a feeling of self-importance. Abusive behavior is chronic with these offenders and is a result of their desire to fit in.

Pseudosocialized child exploiters have excellent social skills and appear to be self-confident. Their abusive behavior often is a result of long-term abuse they have experienced themselves. They are motivated by the need to achieve sexual pleasure through exploitation and rationalize their assaults.

Sexually aggressive adolescent offenders come from abusive and disordered families. They have histories of antisocial activities and substance abuse. Angry and compelled to humiliate their victims, they are motivated by the need for power, and their assaults usually involve force.

Sexually compulsive offenders come from families that are not emotionally expressive. Very compulsive, these offenders tend to abuse their victims repetitively. Their offenses often do not involve intercourse, such as peeping, exhibitionism, or frotteurism.

Disturbed-impulsive offenders have long histories of mental illness, and their families are likely to be dysfunctional. They will also have histories of substance abuse, significant learning problems, and problems with reality. Typically, their abusive behavior is impulsive.

Group-influenced offenders normally are young, between the ages of 10 and 14. They are unlikely to have histories of delinquent behavior and only act under the pressure of peers because of their strong desire for acceptance.

FEMALE OFFENDERS

Lanning (1992) reports that men commit about 95 percent of sexual offenses, with the remaining 5 percent being committed by females. It is uncommon for female abusers to commit sexual offenses before adulthood. Cases involving women are more likely to include multiple perpetrators and multiple victims. Women are more likely to commit acts involving penetration and are more likely to abuse young children and to use physical force or threats of physical force. Female offenders have been found to be more likely to force children into sexual acts with other children and participate more in ritualistic abuse than are male offenders (Kelley, Brant, and Waterman, 1993).

RISK ASSESSMENT OF TARGETS

One of the most important aspects of child sexual abuse is how the child came to be a victim. Although no identifiable characteristics of a child can be used to predict vulnerability to sexual abuse, certain characteristics are associated with greater risk. Research shows that girls are at a greater risk than are boys; it is estimated that 1 in 4 girls and 1 in 10 boys will be the victims of sexual abuse (Finkelhor, 1993). Age also plays a role in the risk: Children between the ages of 6 and 10 have the greatest risk of becoming victims, although it is difficult to determine rates of abuse in children under 6 years old because they have not yet developed memory capabilities (Finkelhor, 1993). Research does not show that social class is an indicator

of risk; however, high rates of risk are associated with placement in foster care, poor parenting, lack of supervision, and witnessing family conflict (Finkelhor, 1993). Girls growing up in the presence of stepfathers are seven times more likely to be sexually abused than are girls growing up with their natural fathers (Finkelhor, 1993).

To gain access to children, sex offenders may frequent places where children congregate, such as parks, playgrounds, skating rinks, and libraries. Some sex offenders marry or befriend single women to gain access to their children. They may collect toys or dolls, build model planes, or perform as clowns or magicians to attract and befriend neighborhood children. Sex offenders may also become scout leaders, foster parents, coaches, or substitute teachers to gain access to children. Sex offenders try to get children into situations where no other adults are present.

Sex offenders are skilled at identifying vulnerable victims. With experience, they can watch a group of children and select potential targets, usually choosing children that are loners and come from single-parent households.

A trait that helps sex offenders in obtaining victims is that they relate well to children. They know what children are interested in and often have the most up-to-date toys and games. Sexual offenders know how to listen to children; they draw the victim toward them.

CONCLUSION

Attitudes toward sex offenses have changed dramatically since ancient times. The inception of Christianity condemned sexual abuse of children and brought the heinousness of these acts to public attention. By the 1970s, child sexual abuse became an everyday topic in American society. Research indicates that all sexual offenders are dangerous individuals and that young children in particular are at risk for becoming victims. There are many types of sexual offenders, and defining the various types aids in understanding them.

Although sex offenders have different typologies, there are some specific similarities. Sexual offenders are age and gender specific, and their victims seem to profile the abuse that the sex offenders previously received. Many offenders themselves have histories of sexual abuse, but the question that remains unanswered is why all sexually abused children do not become offenders. Sex offenders also show a lack of social skills, yet they are able to relate relatively well to children. They show excessive interest in childlike activities and attend activities where children are present even if they have no children of their own.

Sexual offenders vary in their methods; however, the intent remains the same. Sex offenders are seemingly unable to distinguish between an acceptable, consensual adult relationship and a submissive, controlling, nonconsensual relationship with a child victim. All child sexual abusers participate in a deviant sexual activity, though the type of sexual activity varies considerably.

Amy Van Houten

See also Child Abuse; Cycle of Violence; Missing Children; Prostitution, Teenage; Sex Offenders

Bibliography

Ames, A. M., and D. A. Houston. 1990. Legal, social, and biological definitions of pedophilia. *Archives of Sexual Behavior* 19:333–342.

Anechiarico, B. 1998. A closer look at sex offender character pathology and relapse prevention: An integrative approach. *International Journal of Offender Therapy and Comparative Criminology* 42:16–26.

Bolen, R. M. 2000. Extrafamilial child sexual abuse: A study of perpetrator characteristics and implications for prevention. *Violence Against Women* 6:1137–1169.

Danni, K. A., and G. D. Hampe. 2000. An analysis of predictors of child sex offender types using presentence investigation reports. *International Journal of Offender Therapy and Comparative Criminology* 44:490–504.

Finkelhor, D. 1993. Epidemiological factors in the clinical identification of child sexual abuse. *Child Abuse and Neglect* 17:67–70.

Kelley, S. J., R. Brant, and J. Waterman. 1993. Sexual abuse of children in day care centers. *Child Abuse and Neglect* 17:71–89.

Lanning, K. V. 1992. *Child Molesters: A Behavioral Analysis*. Alexandria, VA: National Center for Missing and Exploited Children.

McGrath, R. J. 1991. Sex-offender risk assessment and disposition planning: A review of empirical and clinical findings. *International Journal of Offender Therapy and Comparative Criminology* 35:328–346.

Murray, J. B. 2000. Psychological profile of pedophiles and child molesters. *The Journal of Psychology* 134:211–224.

Ward, T., S. M. Hudson, and W. L. Marshall. 1996. Attachment style in sex offenders: A preliminary study. *The Journal of Sex Research* 33:17–29.

CLOWARD, RICHARD A. (1926–2001)

Richard Cloward was a world-renowned scholar and social activist who received numerous awards for his research and his unfailing commitment to helping the poor and oppressed. Throughout his career, Cloward conducted scholarly research on and actively participated in projects geared toward improving the quality of life and alleviating social problems that plague many impoverished communities. More specifically, his work focused on issues surrounding gangs and juvenile delinquency, welfare rights, voter registration, political participation and social movements of the poor, and labor issues concerning worker-employer relations. For his professional accomplishments and contributions to social work scholarship, Cloward received numerous lifetime achievement awards from nationally recognized organizations, including the Society for the Study of Social Problems (1991), the Mandel School of Social Work at Case-Western Reserve University (1992), the American Sociological Association (1995, 2000), the Association for Community Organization and Social Administration (1995), the National Association of Social Workers (1999), and the Council on Social Work Education (2001). He also received the Dennis Carroll Award (1965) from the International Society of Criminology for his work on the book *Delinquency and Opportunity* (Cloward and Ohlin, 1960), the C. Wright Mills Award (1972) from the Society for the Study of Social Problems for *Regulating the Poor*, and the Bryant Spann Memorial Prize from the Eugene V. Debs Foundation for two articles on voter registration, "Trying to Break Down the Barriers" and "How to Get Out the Vote in 1988." Additionally, Cloward received the Jim Waltermire Award of the National Secretaries of State (1994) and the Tides Foundation Award (1996) for distinguished public service.

Although Cloward earned national and international acclaim for his contributions to the field of social work, he was best known in the fields of criminology and delinquency for his work on differential opportunity theory. This theory is rooted intellectually in Robert K. Merton's theory of anomie, Albert Cohen's research on delinquent subcultures, Clifford Shaw and Henry McKay's theory of social disorganization, and Edwin Sutherland's theory of differential association. Cloward introduced the notion of the "illegitimate opportunity structure" in his 1959 *American Sociological Review* article, "Illegitimate Means, Anomie, and Deviant Behavior," and noted that it was just as important in shaping delinquency as the legitimate opportunity structure, which was the focus of Merton's theory of anomie. In 1960, Cloward and coauthor Lloyd Ohlin discussed the illegitimate opportunity structure concept more fully in *Delinquency and Opportunity: A Theory of Delinquent Gangs*. The authors acknowledged that access to legitimate opportunities for achieving culturally valued goals was affected by social position in that few opportunities were available for juveniles in lower-class, urban communities. However, they pointed out that differential opportunities also exist in terms of access to illegitimate means for achieving cultural goals. The result was the development of distinct deviant adaptations or delinquent gang subcultures.

Cloward and Ohlin identified three delinquent subcultures. Criminal subcultures were most likely to develop in communities characterized by a high degree of integration between criminal and conventional opportunity structures. In these areas, youth gangs largely functioned to prepare youths for adult involvement in organized crime. Successful adult criminals would serve as role models for juveniles, and through these associations, youths would acquire the necessary skills and normative understandings that are favorable to law violation as well as the personal contacts that can help them, such as crooked politicians or police officers who can be bribed. In these subcultures, illegal activities would primarily be profit-oriented and involve little violence.

In communities characterized by social disorganization and a low degree of integration, neither legitimate nor illegitimate opportunities may exist. In the absence of successful (criminal or conventional) adult role models, youths fail to develop the skills necessary for achieving culturally valued goals through either legitimate or illegitimate means. As a result, they may become frustrated and alienated from adults and eventually less subject to community controls. Cloward and Ohlin (1960) theorized that under these conditions, a conflict subculture is likely to develop, where the focus is on gaining respect. Status and reputation are earned through being tough, fearless, and violent. For these gangs, illegal activities are more likely to be predatory and to involve violence, vandalism, property damage, and unpredictable behavior.

Just as access to legitimate means does not guarantee the achievement of culturally valued goals, neither does access to illegitimate means through exposure and involvement in either a criminal or conflict subculture. According to Cloward and Ohlin (1960), when youths are "double failures" because they fail to achieve success through either legitimate or illegitimate means, a retreatist subculture is likely to emerge in which the focus is often on obtaining and consuming drugs and alcohol. These youths have generally given up on both conventional and unconventional goals and means. As a result, they escape, or retreat, into a different social world where status is gained through drug use and addiction.

Cloward and Ohlin's work on differential opportunity theory formed the basis for social policy. In the 1960s, differential opportunity theory served as the foundation for Mobilization for Youth, a community-based prevention program in New York geared toward organizing lower-class communities and providing youth with access to legitimate means for achieving goals, including education, job-skills training, and job opportunities. While this particular program was never completed because of political opposition, programs with similar goals continue to be implemented today.

Cloward and Ohlin's theory also stimulated subsequent scholarly activity. For example, a significant amount of research has focused on the existence of social class differences in the distribution of gangs and the extent to which gangs are characterized by delinquent subcultures. Although research has found that gang activity tends to be concentrated in impoverished areas with disproportionate numbers of racial and ethnic minorities, little support has been found for the notion that distinct subcultures exist or that gangs specialize in types of delinquency. Despite only partial support for their research on differential opportunity theory, Cloward and Ohlin are still credited with shedding light on the manner in which lower-class youths become alienated and subcultures affect behavior.

Until his death, Cloward was a professor of social work in the school of social work at Columbia University in New York City, where he had been on the faculty since 1954. The recipient of numerous earned and honorary academic degrees, Cloward earned a bachelor's degree from the University of Rochester and a master's (social work) and a Ph.D. (sociology) from Columbia University. He has also been named Honorary Doctor of Humane Letters by both Adelphi University and Hunter College.

Candice Batton

See also Albert K. Cohen; Henry D. McKay; Lloyd E. Ohlin; Clifford R. Shaw; Edwin H. Sutherland; Theories of Delinquency—Sociological

Bibliography

Adler, F., G. Mueller, and W. Laufer. 2001. *Criminology.* Boston: McGraw-Hill.

Akers, R. 1994. *Criminological Theories: Introduction and Evaluation.* Los Angeles: Roxbury.

Cloward, R. 1959. Illegitimate means, anomie, and deviant behavior. *American Sociological Review* 24:164–177.

Cloward, R., and L. Ohlin. 1960. *Delinquency and Opportunity.* Glencoe, IL: Free Press.

Paternoster, R., and R. Bachman. 2001. *Explaining Criminals and Crime: Essays in Contemporary Criminological Theory.* Los Angeles: Roxbury.

Williams, F., III, and M. McShane. 1999. *Criminological Theory (3rd Edition).* Englewood Cliffs, NJ: Prentice Hall.

 # COHEN, ALBERT K. (1918–)

Albert K. Cohen has had a substantial influence in the field of sociology, criminology, and more specifically, juvenile justice. Cohen was born in Boston on June 15, 1918. He went to Harvard in 1935 and studied sociology under Pitirim Sorokin, Talcott Parsons, and Robert Merton. After finishing his bachelor's degree, he went on to Indiana University to begin a graduate degree, working under the direction of Edwin H. Sutherland. There he had an internship at Indiana Boys School, a school for delinquent juveniles. He received his master's degree in 1942 and returned to Harvard for his Ph.D. He wrote his dissertation on the origin of the delinquent culture and completed his degree in 1951. Cohen took his first faculty position at Indiana University, where he taught for 17 years. He moved to the University of Connecticut, from which he is now retired as professor emeritus.

Cohen has been recognized as an outstanding criminologist and sociologist in many ways. His books, *Delinquent Boys: The Culture of the Gang* (1955) and *Deviance and Control* (1966), influenced the way criminologists view juvenile gangs. His articles "An Evaluation of 'Themes' and Kindred Concepts" (1946), "The Study of Social Problems: Discussion" (1948), and "The Sociology of the Deviant Act: Anomie Theory and Beyond" (1965) were also influential in criminology and sociology.

Cohen was the president of the Society for the Study of Social Problems, vice president of the American Society of Criminology, and in 1993 received the Edwin H. Sutherland award from the American Society of Criminology. In 2000, Cohen was recognized as an American Society of Criminology Fellow.

One of Cohen's most notable works was *Delinquent Boys: The Culture of the Gang*, written in 1955. Cohen applied a combination of differential association and anomie theories to explain juvenile gang delinquency. He noted that most juvenile criminal behavior was committed by groups or gangs rather than by individuals. Furthermore, juvenile gang behavior was described as nonutilitarian, serving no useful purpose. Thus Cohen's application of theory was different from that of his predecessor, Robert K. Merton, who argued that criminal acts served cultural goals, such as acquiring monetary reward. Cohen recognized that juveniles often engaged in crime to gain status among their delinquent peers. Juvenile gangs functioned as a separate culture aside from the dominant culture. The subculture served to insulate lower-class juveniles from the mainstream culture and provided a way for them to rebel against the dominant middle-class culture and gain status of their own.

The causes of juvenile delinquency, according to Cohen (1955), included poor social skills, a lack of educational opportunities, and an inability to delay gratification. Environmental influences were key concepts in Cohen's theory of juvenile delinquency. The type of family into which one was born led to the type of interactions and opportunities one would have and, subsequently, influenced juvenile delinquency.

Another key concept of Cohen's theory of juvenile delinquency was "middle-class measuring rods." According to Cohen, those who were not middle-class would fall into one of the following categories: corner boy, college boy, or delinquent boy. The category of corner boy is the most common and includes youth who engage in petty delinquency and periodically in delinquency. The college boy accepts and strives to meet the middle-class norms. Realistically, however, college boys are doomed to fail because they do not have the capacity to achieve middle-class standards. The delinquent boy rejects middle-class norms and establishes his own set of norms, thus facilitating gangs and ganglike behavior. Cohen referred to the delinquent boy behavior as reaction formation, which includes an exaggerated response to one's inability to succeed. Youth in this category are described as engaging in "short-run hedonism," indicative of living day to day with no long-term vision in mind. The delinquent subculture, therefore, develops from an inability to attain middle-class measuring rods, and the juveniles develop behavior that is negativistic, malicious, and nonutilitarian.

Cohen's article titled "The Sociology of the Deviant Act: Anomie Theory and Beyond" (1965) was also influential in the field of criminology. In this article, Cohen discusses some of the fundamental propositions of Robert K. Merton's anomie theory, which was a major contribution to criminological thought at the time. Cohen identifies some of the strengths and weaknesses of Merton's theory and explores the processes associated with anomie theory. He notes the disjunction between the social process that is proposed and the role of the individual. He concludes by proposing that better modes of conceptualization be developed to explore the role of the individual in a social process.

Cohen's work has provided the foundation for juvenile gang theories. Later criminological theorists, such as Richard Cloward and Lloyd Ohlin, were influenced by Cohen's theory and built on some of its assumptions. In 1960, Cloward and Ohlin published *Delinquency and Opportunity,* which expanded on Cohen's basic principles, posing the theory that more than one type of subculture existed. Walter B. Miller (1958), also influenced by Cohen, developed his own theory that delinquent youth behave in accordance to the "focal concerns" that they have been exposed to in their environment.

Today gang involvement poses a problem for communities throughout the United States. Law enforcement officials are forced to handle gang and gang-related problems, confounded by those in the community who are affected by the increase of gangs. Albert K. Cohen, one of the first to develop a theory regarding gang behavior and gang formation, has remained an influence in the field of criminology as it addresses the problems associated with gangs.

Donna M. Vandiver

See also Richard A. Cloward; Walter B. Miller; Lloyd E. Ohlin; Edwin H. Sutherland; Theories of Delinquency—Sociological

Bibliography

Cavender, G. A. 1993. Doing theory: An interview with Albert K. Cohen. *American Journal of Criminal Justice* 18:153–167.

Cloward, R., and L. Ohlin. 1960. *Delinquency and Opportunity.* Glencoe, IL: Free Press.

Cohen, A. K. 1946. An evaluation of "themes" and kindred concepts. *American Journal of Sociology* 52:41–42.

Cohen, A. K. 1948. The study of social problems: Discussion. *American Sociological Review* 13:259–260.

Cohen, A. K. 1955. *Delinquent Boys: The Culture of the Gang.* Glencoe, IL: Free Press.

Cohen, A. K. 1965. The sociology of the deviant act: Anomie theory and beyond. *American Sociological Review* 30:5–14.

Cohen, A. K. 1966. *Deviance and Control.* Englewood Cliffs, NJ: Prentice Hall.

Laub, J. H. 1983. Interview with Albert K. Cohen. Pp. 182–203 in J. H. Laub (ed.), *Criminology in the Making: An Oral History.* Boston: Northeastern University Press.

COMMUNITY ACTION BOARDS AND COMMISSIONS

Our system of government holds that officials who make public policy should be accountable to the public they represent. Elected officials are held accountable through the ballot. Appointed public administrators are not subject to this process. Further, they often hold their positions through several changes of elected administrations, and they have the power to establish major public policy. One means of providing public influence to policy making by appointed administrators is through community boards and commissions. Unfortunately, in past years, public participation in many such boards and commissions reflected even greater public indifference than was demonstrated by the sparse turnout for local elections. Although the public voices considerable concern over the size and power of government bureaucracies, apathy prevails when it is time to make an effort to mitigate the problem.

In an attempt to reverse the trend toward apathy, consumer protection groups worked to increase public awareness of the need for citizen participation (Shor, 1977). The December 1975 issue of *Public Management* was expressly dedicated to the concern of community involvement. One author reflected on the spirit of the issue by noting that today's public requires more than elected officials representing the citizenry; public involvement is now crucial (Schuttler,

1975). Many felt that local government could not be trusted to ensure that the public good was represented in policy. Citizen groups became both watchdogs and possibly assets to government. Schuttler expressed the accolades of citizen involvement by stating that "community involvement can not only prevent social destruction, it can also correct the errors of ego and technical judgment inside our agencies."

But what resistance or undermining might be expected from agency administrators to the efforts of citizen groups? Might not the agency wish to control citizen participation such that it does not infringe on the programs and policies that technical judgment indicates are best for the public and the agency? Schuttler (1975) does acknowledge possible symptoms of this problem, noting that community involvement has its own special set of problems.

Do the board and commission members represent the electorate of the community? Who finds the time and inclination to participate in such committees, and are these people representative of the community at large? In an era of technological complexity, most citizens do not possess the technical knowledge necessary to evaluate programs and policy accurately. If they do not ask the right questions or understand fully the complexity of issues (including the complexity of the politics influencing policy), how can they be effective? In evaluating the role of councils and commissions in the juvenile justice system, these two points must be emphasized. Boards may be generally oriented to a policy-making role at the mission- and agenda-setting level. However, they may also intervene at the administrative and management level and even the service-delivery level.

What are the issues, who initiates the issues, and how does the commission gather and evaluate information relating to issues? The answers to these questions reveal the influence of the citizen participation on the policy and programs of the agency. At the least effective end of the influence spectrum, the participation program is perceived as an end in itself (participation for participation's sake), rather than as a means to an end (as contributing to the achievement of some goal).

HISTORY AND CURRENT EXAMPLES OF BOARDS AND COMMISSIONS

Opportunities for citizen participation in corrections in the United States have existed for more than a

century and a half. The Correctional Association of New York was established in 1844 to improve prison conditions, inmate discipline, and corrections management and to support ex-offenders. The association has had an important role in legislative debates on correctional reform and prisoners' rights. In fact, the association was integrally involved throughout the end of the 19th century and into the 20th in efforts to reform the prison system in the United States (Reich, 1994).

A citizens' committee was involved in the formation of the first juvenile court in the United States in 1899. Throughout the 20th century, the Citizens Committee on the Juvenile Court of Cook County continued to be an influence in juvenile justice policy (Bensinger, 1990).

However, the influence of many other corrections boards, commissions, and committees has been less illustrious. Juvenile justice suffers from anonymity by design. The identities of juvenile offenders are protected by law as are the proceedings of the juvenile court. Until recently, juvenile crime and court cases received minimal public attention. Citizen participation in a process that occurs behind closed doors is difficult at best.

TYPES OF BOARDS AND COMMISSIONS

Examples from California demonstrate the current variety and purposes of juvenile justice committees, boards, and commissions. California law has established a Juvenile Justice Commission in each county to represent public interests and influence public policy. Funding for the commission may be provided as a separate item in the budget of the county probation department, and when this occurs, there is generally a close working link to the funding department. The commission may also exist separately from any county department, with no provision for operational support except the modest expense budget provided by statute. In some counties, the juvenile justice commission is an arm of the superior court. There is some indication that this association substantially strengthens the role of the commission.

There is no doubt that the relationship to a county juvenile justice department affects the activities of the commission and probably the individual commissioner's perceptions of the justice system. A department that can "host" the commission is presented an opportunity to influence its activities. Probation departments, which have traditionally lacked a constituency, have welcomed the opportunity to work with the commission. Further, the juvenile institutions that must be annually inspected by the commission are operated by the probation department. The juvenile justice commissioner's resource manual (issued to all commissioners statewide) specifies the formal activities of the commission. They are delineated as follows:

1. Inquiry into the administration of juvenile justice in the county.

2. Inspection of publicly operated juvenile institutions in the county authorized under the juvenile court law.

3. The holding of hearings using the subpoena power of the juvenile court judge.

4. Recommendation for changes deemed beneficial after investigation to any administrator of the provisions of the juvenile court law.

5. Publicizing its recommendations.

6. Nomination of the probation officer.

Henry and Harms (1987) suggested two varieties of boards differentiated by the amount of authority they have. First, with the least authority is the advisory board. Second, and more powerful, is the board that has supervisory power. By its authority to subpoena, hold hearings, inspect facilities, and nominate the probation officer, the California Juvenile Justice Commissions should probably be classified into the latter category. However, a strong limitation to the commissions' authority is noted in the language of the law: They can only "recommend" change. It is left to the California Youth Authority, a state agency, to enforce the implementation of any recommendation deemed necessary for compliance with laws relating to treatment and detention of juvenile court wards.

In a study of lay council decision making in Sweden, Antoinette Hetzler (1982) found that decision making was dominated by experts. Those who possessed expertise strongly influenced other board members. In a similar fashion, these commissions are influenced by information filtered and provided to them by justice systems experts. Individuals on the boards who have the greatest effect in directing activity also are those with expertise in the juvenile justice system or a related profession (i.e., psychology or education).

It is these members who provided a focus for the commissions when program or policy was influenced.

The process of learning about the juvenile justice systems is a primary activity of both participants and executive officers. The commissions and councils present a soapbox for many individuals. Henry and Harms (1987) noted that most boards they studied operated in the mission and policy arena. Little action was directed at the administration and management activities of agencies. The Juvenile Justice Commissions rarely explore these lower-order functions of departments except as they might reflect on policy. The authors also noted how boards were steered toward a conclusion by adept agency staff.

The mere existence of public interest groups, and thus the fact that officials know that they are being watched, affects the behavior of those officials quite apart from any action that such groups may take. Knowing the lack of focus generally exhibited by the commission and the tendency of individual actors to carry their own agendas makes the commission less potentially threatening as a unit but also somewhat unpredictable. Many commissioners possess substantial individual political clout. While having difficulty carrying a program through to funding, they individually bring the attention of important political actors to an agency's activities.

A Juvenile Justice Commission is composed of individuals who represent a diversity of interests and levels of expertise. They do not mirror the demographics of the community but probably do reflect special interest groups with interests in juvenile justice activities. The predominant direction of communication is from agency to commission, with information being filtered (and probably distorted in many instances) to favor the agency. Effectiveness of the commission to act on issues initiated by itself or the agency is hampered by several factors. Among these are funding, a need for greater understanding of the juvenile justice process and the political environment in which the agencies operate, a multitude of personal agendas that prevent development of a focus on issues that could be impacted and, more generally, a lack of strong leadership within the commissions.

Another type of board was recently introduced into the California juvenile justice system: the Juvenile Justice Coordinating Council, mandated by legislation passed in 2000. The law allocated nearly $250 million to local governments for juvenile justice programs and provided the establishment of a coordinating council in each jurisdiction "to implement a comprehensive multiagency juvenile justice plan as provided in this paragraph. This plan shall be developed by the local juvenile justice coordinating council in each county" (California Assembly Bill 1913, Stats. 2000, Ch. 353). Although the council is primarily composed of juvenile justice agency administrators, the law also requires a member representing "the public at large." Clearly, this is an opportunity for public participation in major juvenile justice policy and program decisions. However, it is left to the agencies to select the public member, again introducing the opportunity for the agencies to control the direction of that public input.

An example of significant public participation and direct input into the daily decision making of line-level juvenile justice practitioners is the Youth Accountability Board. This concept originated in the state of Washington in the late 1950s and was successfully developed in several western states. It was adopted in San Bernardino County, California, in 1993. The Youth Accountability Board is a juvenile diversion program that allows minor offenses committed by juveniles to be heard by a board of community volunteers. By consent of the juvenile court and mutual agreement between the board, the minor, and his or her parents, the board develops a disposition in these cases that emphasizes community service and victim restitution. In San Bernardino County in 2000, more than 400 community volunteers participated in Youth Accountability Boards.

CONCLUSION

The opportunity and processes for public participation in juvenile justice policy making, program administration, and delivery of services was well established over the last half of the 20th century. However, through enabling legislation or other means, the power of boards and commissions is carefully controlled by the public agencies. Most likely, this control will remain unchallenged unless an intense public debate arises over the administration of juvenile justice. The obscurity of corrections in the criminal justice system and the blanket of confidentiality that still protects all but the highest-profile juvenile cases makes such public scrutiny unlikely.

Wesley Krause

See also California Youth Authority; Diversion Programs; Public Opinion on Juvenile Justice Issues

Bibliography

Bensinger, G. J. 1990. Citizens Committee on the Juvenile Court of Cook County: A case study of informing and influencing policy makers. *Perspectives* 14(2):26–30.

Henry, G. T., and S. W. Harms. 1987. Board involvement in policy making and administration. *Public Administration Review* 47:153–159.

Hetzler, A. N. 1982. The role of lay councils in democratic decision making. *International Journal of the Sociology of Law* 10:395–407.

Reich, I. K. 1994. *Citizen Crusade for Prison Reform: The History of the Correctional Association of New York.* Albany: Correctional Association of New York.

Schuttler, B. L. 1975. It works. *Public Management*, December:13–15.

Shor, E. 1977. Public interest representation and federal agencies. *Public Administration Review* 37:131–132.

Ventriss, C. 1985. Emerging perspectives on citizen participation. *Public Administration Review* 45:433–440.

Washnis, G. J. 1975. Community involvement. *Public Management*, December:2–6.

 # COMMUNITY TREATMENT PROJECT

Today community-based programs for serious delinquents are far from novel. Yet as late as 1960 they were virtually nonexistent, and no research had tried to systematically address the question, "Can some such youths be worked with in their home communities instead of being institutionalized?" From 1960 to 1961, California researchers began a study and, together with parole personnel, they developed a then unique program that gave corrections its first scientific answers to this question.

DESCRIPTION OF THE PROJECT

California's Community Treatment Project (Phases 1 and 2) was a study funded by the National Institute of Mental Health that ran from 1961 to mid-1969. It examined the feasibility and effectiveness of substituting an intensive parole program for the standard state training program. Its subjects were 802 males and 212 females, mostly aged 13 through 18 at intake, who were undergoing their first commitment to the California Youth Authority (CYA). The CYA, a large state agency, is the placement of last resort for serious and/or repeat offenders.

The study took place in Sacramento and Stockton (which together form a region the study calls the Valley) from 1961 to 1969, and in San Francisco from 1965 to 1969. Sixty-five percent of the males and 83 percent of the females who were committed to the CYA from those areas were included in the study; they were the "eligible" cases. The rest, mainly seriously assaultive cases, were excluded. Chronic or severe neuroses, occasional psychotic episodes, apparent suicidal tendencies, marked drug involvement, homosexuality, and other conditions were not grounds for exclusion. On average, the eligible cases had six official contacts with the law by the time they were sent to the CYA. In the Valley, their race or ethnicity was 57 percent Caucasian, 18 percent black, 20 percent Hispanic, and 4 percent "other"; in San Francisco, the breakdown was 25 percent, 65 percent, 4 percent, and 6 percent, respectively.

The study's intensive program was called the Community Treatment Project (CTP), although the entire study is popularly referred to by the same name. Each CTP youth was assigned directly to a small-sized caseload, 11 or 12 youths per parole agent, located in the youth's community. The youth was not sent to an institution first. Before assignment, the youth was classified ("typed") in terms of a system known as I-Level (for integration, or maturity, level), and the caseload to which each male was assigned contained mainly those "types" of youth, usually about two, with whom the parole agent seemed best suited to work ("matched"). Each CTP parole unit—that is, the intensive programs in the Valley and San Francisco—contained one female and six male caseloads. In contrast to CTP, the study's standard program usually began with the youth's approximately nine months' stay in a large, secure CYA institution. This was followed by his or her assignment to standard, nonintensive parole within the youth's community. Caseloads for the standard program averaged about 70 youths per parole agent, assignments were not based on I-Level type, and, agent/youth matches occurred only by chance. CTP and standard parole were both part of the CYA, they were located in different parts of each given city, and each often lasted two or more years.

Within CTP, a detailed diagnosis and resulting treatment/control plan was developed for each youth, and the implemented plan was later modified when necessary. In order of priority, the specifics of each plan reflected the youth's individual needs, abilities, life circumstances, and interests; his or her maturity level and type of personality; and the parole agent's preferred approaches and particular skills. Among the approaches and program elements that could be used with any CTP youth were (1) individual, group, and/or family counseling; (2) pragmatically oriented discussions, advice, and information sharing; (3) external controls: establishment of rules, limit-setting sessions, and surveillance; (4) short-term detention for given infractions and certain minor offenses; (5) group homes, individual foster homes, and other temporary or longer-term placements; (6) accredited school program, including individual and small-group tutoring, plus arts and crafts—located in the project's community center; and (7) recreational opportunities and socializing experiences within and outside the center.

Each CTP youth was exposed to about four such components during any given period—for example, a three-month interval. During his or her overall program, the youth was likely to experience various other components as well, mainly because his or her specific problems were often complex, and several areas of adjustment needed to be addressed. This multimodality, multiarea approach was called extensive intervention, and components 1 through 3 were especially common throughout parole.

Approximately two face-to-face agent-youth contacts occurred per week. This rate was described as intensive intervention. The exact rate varied considerably across youths. Not counting phone calls and very brief encounters, most Phase 1 and 2 CTP youths ended up having 150 to 250 relatively focused contacts of one kind or another with their parole agents. Many youths sometimes interacted with other CTP personnel as well, such as schoolteachers and support staff at the community center. In addition, contacts occurred between the CTP parole agent and others (e.g., employers and public school personnel), and material aid (e.g., transportation and clothing) was sometimes provided.

Most youths in the standard CYA program had varied experiences and many daily interactions with staff during their institutional stay. However, during their time on standard parole, these boys and girls were seldom exposed to a broad range of components and elements, and they usually had one face-to-face contact with their agent per month.

RESULTS OF THE INTENSIVE PROGRAM

The feasibility of the intensive portion of the program was quickly demonstrated. Despite its complexity,

CTP could be managed operationally. Moreover, it was acceptable to each local community, provided that external controls were exercised over the youths and that clear accountability existed. To scientifically compare the effectiveness of the intensive program and the standard program, all eligible cases had been randomly assigned to either CTP, also called the experimental (E) program, or to the standard program, called the control (C) program. Detailed analyses of the parole and post-CYA performance of Valley youths revealed the following:

For all Valley males combined, CTP youths had far fewer arrests (38 percent to 50 percent) and convictions than did the standard-program males. That is, the E's rates of illegal behavior, recidivism in this case, were much lower than the C's rates. This was based on official Department of Justice rap sheets, not on decision making by CYA officials and parole staff. The differences in recidivism were especially strong in connection with severe offenses (e.g., burglary, felony drug violations, and felonies against persons). This was particularly true for violent offenses (e.g., assault with a deadly weapon, robbery, forcible rape, and murder). Neither these nor other differences in recidivism resulted from factors such as age, IQ, race, socioeconomic status, type of committing offense, and, most important, level of parole risk. This was because the randomization in the program design had made the followed-up E's and C's very similar to each other.

For Valley and San Francisco males alike, CTP's lower rates of recidivism for severe and violent offenses were especially strong for individuals described as conflicted—a broad category of youths that comprised the majority of all males in the eligible samples. On the other hand, CTP was less effective than the standard program with "power-oriented" males (a much smaller category), at least those described as manipulative. The results with another moderate-sized group, passive conformists, were mixed, but mainly positive. While there were other groups, these three groups comprised almost 90 percent of all males. CTP was neither more nor less effective with respect to female arrests and convictions.

Most commitments to the California Youth Authority were found eligible for an intensive community-based program that proved operationally feasible. Reductions in the recidivism of most eligible youths (namely, males) occurred in moderately as

well as highly urbanized settings (ones with different racial compositions, as well). Youths under 16 years of age at intake were just as amenable to the intensive program (but not to the standard) as were those 16 and older. Together these findings suggested that the Community Treatment Project's methods and approaches were relevant to a broad spectrum of the serious and/or repeat offender population, and, hence, of society itself.

Using fiscal data for the early 1970s, the overall savings to society were estimated at $4,545 per CTP male. This difference between CTP and the standard CYA program mainly resulted from a combination of the higher rates of arrest and conviction on the part of controls, and these individuals' greater tendency to commit violent offenses that often led to long periods of lockup. Were one to focus on the early 1990s, the savings associated with CTP would probably have been about three times larger than that of the 1970s, mainly because daily incarceration costs had greatly increased since the early 1970s. This would be true even apart from the fact that length of incarceration had itself increased for violent offenses.

The core procedures and requirements of CTP included a careful diagnosis or highly individualized understanding of the youth and his or her situation; a relevant, detailed, and integrated treatment/control plan based on that diagnosis and understanding; and adequate implementation of the plan. Particularly critical were small-sized caseloads, intensive and/or extensive contacts, and individualization and flexibility in programming. Also very important were personal characteristics, professional orientation, specific abilities, and overall perceptiveness of the parole agent; use of explicit, detailed guidelines (intervention strategies); and long-term contacts with the youth. Other factors contributed as well, and it was clear that large differences existed in how the differing I-Level groups responded to various strategies, techniques, and type of relationship with their parole agent.

DEVELOPMENT OF TREATMENT FOR UNRESPONSIVE YOUTH

The Community Treatment Project during Phase 3 resulted from a growing recognition that, despite CTP's general success, at least 25 percent of the Phase 1 and 2 youths had been largely unresponsive and that many within this category had engaged in serious offending soon after intake. By 1967, many parole staff believed that if these unresponsive youth were treated differently, their rate of recidivism would drop. A major addition to programming (beginning the treatment/control program in a relatively short-term institutional setting operated by CTP staff and on CTP principles and then released to the intensive, community-based CTP unit) was assumed to be important.

To implement this belief, the identifying features of these especially hard to reach (EHR) youths were soon spelled out, and another random assignment study was undertaken. This study also examined the feasibility of applying the CTP to a wider range of youths. It was conducted in Sacramento, focusing on males alone ($N = 161$) because of logistic limitations. Its short-term institutional setting, a 25-person unit called Dorm 3, as well as its community-based operations extended from mid-1969 to 1973.

The main findings of this third phase of the CTP supported the suppositions of the parole staff. EHR youths who were randomly assigned to begin their treatment/control in the CTP-operated-and-oriented Dorm 3 had a rate of offending after release to the CTP's intensive community-based (ICB) unit that was more than 50 percent lower than that for EHR youths who were randomly assigned directly to the ICB program. Age, race, level of parole risk, and other factors did not affect this outcome.

The previously used eligibility criteria were successfully expanded to age 21, to committing offenses such as noninjury robbery and assault with a deadly weapon, and to adult court commitments. The concepts, treatment/control methods, and most program operations that were used during previous years in the Valley and San Francisco CTP units were shown to be applicable to these individuals as well. Most EHRs could be accurately identified as such at intake, and most did not require a long period of lockup in Dorm 3 before their intensive community programming.

CONCLUSION

As early as 1967 and continuing through the early 1970s, the Community Treatment Project's influence within juvenile corrections had become widespread in the United States and parts of Canada. Many of the individual community-based programs that had been recently established in North America had drawn directly from its concepts and operational experiences, especially in their planning stages. Even various

statewide reforms, such as the deinstitutionalization efforts in Massachusetts, Florida, and Colorado, had drawn a good deal of their original encouragement and direction from the California experiences and findings. In these respects, CTP had served, among other things, as the principal catalyst of the deinstitutionalization movement within corrections. Phase 3 showed ways in which community programming and institutionalization could significantly complement each other.

Together, the Phase 1 through 3 studies demonstrated that a wide range of multiple and otherwise serious young offenders can successfully begin their treatment/control in a CTP-type program directly within the community. Other identifiable young offenders were shown to do best after a short term in institutional settings. The CTP studies also indicated that, in each setting, intervention that is intensive, extensive, and relatively individualized can be implemented humanely and can reflect substantial offender involvement in the process of change.

Ted Palmer

See also Aftercare; California Youth Authority; Deinstitutionalization Movement; Juvenile Probation; Theories of Delinquency—Psychological

Bibliography

Harris, P. 1988. The Interpersonal Maturity Level classification system: I-Level. *Criminal Justice and Behavior* 15:58–77.

Palmer, T. 1974. The Youth Authority's Community Treatment Project. *Federal Probation* 38:3–14.

Palmer, T. 2002. *Individualized Intervention With Young Multiple Offenders*. New York: Routledge

Sullivan, C., M. Q. Grant, and J. Grant. 1957. The development of interpersonal maturity: Applications to delinquency. *Psychiatry* 20:373–395.

Warren, M. 1969. The case for differential treatment of delinquents. *Annals of the American Academy of Political and Social Science* 381:47–59.

 # COMPUTER AND INTERNET CRIME, JUVENILE

Police futurist William Tafoya predicted in 1990 that computer-related crimes would increase dramatically. He noted that high-technology crimes would

become increasingly complex, leading police to become mere report takers, lacking the technological expertise to adequately combat cybercrime.

Former Federal Bureau of Investigation (FBI) Director Louis Freeh, testifying in 2000 before the Subcommittee for the Departments of Commerce, Justice, State, the Judiciary, and Related Agencies of the Senate Committee on Appropriations stated that there were more than 100 million Internet users in the United States in 1999, and Internet use is projected to reach 177 million in the United States and 502 million worldwide by the end of 2003. During the same period, electronic commerce doubled to $100 billion from 1998 to 1999 and is expected to exceed $1 trillion by the year 2003. Once thought to be a mere nuisance, denial-of-service attacks, which deliberately flood a computer with more requests for information than it can handle, have had a dramatic impact on many people and businesses.

Meyer and Thomas (1990) examined the relationship between cybercrime and juveniles from an ethnographic standpoint. Mirroring the growth in computer technology is a "computer underground" composed of individuals who hack into computers. This behavior is often considered to be deviant behavior rather than criminal, particularly if there seems to be no monetary loss. Meyer and Thomas characterized members of the underground as, in effect, a shadow society with its own set of values, rules and regulations, and networks.

The society of "hackers" has been characterized in a number of ways, ranging from "crazy kids dedicated to making mischief" to computer saboteurs to "high-tech street gangs." Unfortunately, characterizations by the media fail to distinguish between the curious hacker who enters computer systems to see of it can be done and the criminal who enters a company's computer system to damage or destroy data or the company's ability to use the system.

EARLY FORMS OF CYBERCRIME: PHREAKING

One of the earliest forms of cybercrime involved the use of the telephone rather than the computer. Phreaking involves using either a form of technology or credit card numbers to avoid long-distance charges. Phreakers, unlike their hacker brethren, are attempting to circumvent telecommunications technology,

primarily for their own use and the use of their friends. Early phreaking methods used devices that generated keytones to trick the phone company computer into connecting the call without charging a fee to the customer. Phreaking, however, seemed to lose its appeal when telephone companies computerized their switching apparatus. After a brief resurgence with the advent of the computer bulletin board, phreaking has almost disappeared as the Internet experiences phenomenal growth.

THE INTERNET AND CYBERCRIME

In its simplest form, cybercrime is any crime committed by using a computer. As such, it can encompass a number of different criminal activities. Most states, however, do not have a broad, general law against cybercrime in place and must rely on statutes that cover fraud, unlawful intrusion, or other specific statutory provisions. There are, however, some general categories of crime that can be committed using a computer, including hacking or unlawful intrusion, pornography, theft, denial-of-service, and virus attacks. Examples of each of these crimes and examples of juveniles arrested for these crimes are discussed in the following sections.

Hacking or Unlawful Intrusion

While it is fashionable to think in terms of modern-day computer hackers and Internet crime, early hackers found their way into business computers in the early 1980s, often passing their information to others using bulletin boards, the 1980s equivalent to the Web site. In late 1984, hackers in Brevard County, Florida, were arrested for using home computers to access codes for discount long-distance telephone services, running up bills of at least $12,000 in illegal calls. Obtained codes were placed on bulletin boards so others could use them.

Nine juveniles, ranging in age from 14 to 17, were arrested in July 1987 in Mount Lebanon, Pennsylvania, and charged with illegally obtaining items ranging from clothes to skateboards through a sophisticated computer network. The juveniles hacked into a West Coast credit-card authorization center and obtained lists of credit cards and expiration dates that were subsequently used to purchase merchandise. Authorities made arrests in Dallas and San Antonio,

Texas; Omaha, Nebraska; Augusta, Georgia; New York City; Newark, New Jersey; and Toledo, Ohio. The juveniles were also charged with unauthorized use of telephone services by making long-distance telephone calls using stolen access codes.

In 1989, a 16-year-old Seattle hacker was arrested after about $100,000 in phone charges were billed to credit-card numbers he obtained by listening on ship-to-shore marine calls. The youth would obtain the numbers and subsequently post them to a computer bulletin board. Authorities linked the juvenile to calls made to computers worldwide, not just in the United States.

More recently, the case of Kevin Mitnick provides insight into the world of the cybercriminal. Mitnick was first arrested in California in 1981 for stealing computer manuals from Pacific Bell. He was subsequently arrested in 1987 for computer fraud, and in 1989, he was again arrested for computer fraud and hacking into the California Department of Motor Vehicles. His next arrest was in North Carolina in 1995 for possession of unauthorized access devices, for which he was incarcerated for 8 months. In California, he subsequently served 14 months for violation of his terms of supervised release. Finally, in 1996, he was charged with computer fraud, wire fraud, and possession of unauthorized access devices. His computer hacking spree led the FBI to name him as one of its most wanted.

He began his criminal activity at age 13, punching bus tickets to get free rides, and then moved to phone phreaking. He hacked into the North American Defense Command (NORAD) computers, providing the inspiration for the 1983 film *War Games*. While not arrested for his attack on NORAD, authorities charged him with criminal offenses after he stole $1 million in proprietary software from Digital Equipment Company.

The first juvenile hacker to serve time, according to the Justice Department, was a 16-year-old from Miami, Florida, who hacked into the Defense Department and NASA. During the intrusions, he downloaded software and data, causing NASA to shut down some of their computers for three weeks. NASA estimated the cost to repair and replace the software and data was more than $40,000.

Theft

Hackers also use their skills to steal computer programs. In 1998, authorities arrested 18-year-old Herbert Zinn and charged him with six counts of juvenile delinquency under federal law for stealing more than $1 million worth of software from AT&T and U.S. government computers. He also illegally published computer passwords on bulletin boards in Illinois and Texas, a violation of federal law prohibiting the interstate trafficking of computer passwords. Zinn had also broken into computers at the Keller Graduate School of Management in Chicago and at the *Washington Post* and into unidentified computers in Ohio, New York, and Texas.

Denial of Service

Other computer hackers deny service to regular customers of both telephones and computers. In 1998, a juvenile was arrested and charged under federal statutes for knocking out phone service to 600 residents and an airport control tower. The teenager dialed into a loop carrier system computer used to funnel signals from copper wire to fiber-optic connections. When it was disabled, communications were cut. The youth was also charged with hacking into the local pharmacy and obtaining prescription records. When arrested, the youth seemed unaware of the danger and harm.

Perhaps the biggest case to date is that of "Mafiaboy," a 16-year-old computer hacker from Montreal, Canada. Mafiaboy pleaded guilty to 56 charges relating to denial-of-service attacks on some of the busiest Web sites in the United States, including Amazon.com, CNN.com, and Yahoo.com. He also bragged about hitting the Dell.com Web site, an attack that had not been previously disclosed by Dell Computer Corporation. The FBI estimated that he caused $1.7 billion in damage by slowing or stopping Web site access for up to six hours.

One case currently under investigation clearly points out the current vulnerabilities under a denial-of-service attack. On the evening of May 4, 2001, the Steve Gibson (Gibson Research) Web site, GRC.com, was knocked offline by a packet-flooding attack. As Steve Gibson (2001) stated, "We were drowning in a flood of malicious traffic, and valid traffic was unable to compete with the torrent." Gibson embarked on his own analysis of who and why and came to the conclusion that "nothing more than the whim of a 13-year-old hacker is required to knock any user, site, or server right off the Internet" (Gibson, 2001).

Gibson ultimately determined that he was attacked by 474 different personal computers, in a total of six different attacks on his system by a 13-year-old hacker named "Wicked." Based on a dialog with the hacker, Gibson determined that the hacker was doing his denial-of-service attacks for fun, had no remorse, and did not worry about the damage he had caused because he believed he would never be caught.

Virus Attacks

Perhaps the most chilling type of denial-of-service attack is the computer virus or computer worm, which not only has the ability to flood the Internet with unwanted electronic mail but also can destroy valuable data on the computer hard drive. The two major objectives of a virus are propagation and destruction, although many viruses are of the propagate-and-annoy instead of the propagate-and-destroy variety. The virus, a small piece of code inserted into another program, often causes annoying messages, system failures, or loss of data and replicates itself through electronic mail, infected floppy disks, or Web sites.

One of the early virus cases was in 1988 when graduate student Robert T. Morris Jr. wrote and propagated a virus that infected more than 8,000 computers on the Internet. Morris, who admitted his action publicly, stated that he was only attempting to raise security awareness concerning the Internet's vulnerability to viruses.

Perhaps nothing is as frightening to the public as the threat of a virus being spread from computer to computer. Of particular interest is the type of virus that replicates through an infected user's email address book and continues to propagate to other computers, often sending email messages to everyone in the user's address book. These types of viruses are potentially more dangerous because they offer the opportunity to replicate destructive acts on a multitude of computers, often catching the users unaware unless antivirus software is running on the computer.

Fraud

Sometimes the Internet is used to defraud. Take the case of a 15-year-old Utah boy who bilked 13 Internet customers out of approximately $10,000. The juvenile, using fake identity information, established an account with an online service and subsequently used the service to post phony ads for computer parts. Customers were sent COD packages to be paid for by cashier's checks. On signing for the package and paying by check, the unsuspecting purchasers got empty boxes or blank diskettes. By the time they realized that they had been scammed, it was impossible to stop payment on the cashier's checks. The youth, who was given a computer by his mother and grandmother to keep him at home and out of trouble, also obtained a stolen credit-card number and used it to purchase computer parts. Authorities in Utah noted that Internet crime was increasing as the Internet became easier to use.

Other juveniles have used computers to counterfeit money. Five teenagers were arrested in Weston, Massachusetts, in 1997 for using school computers and color printers to print money. Six bills turned up in town, and authorities found electronic images of bills in school computers.

Pornography

One of the most common forms of Internet crime, pornography can easily involve juveniles as victims. Those who study Internet pornography estimate that most youths have at least viewed obscene pictures on the World Wide Web. Authorities have arrested adults running and participating in child pornography rings whose main source of interaction was the Internet. In addition, youth who connect to Internet chat rooms frequently are exposed to lewd comments and sometimes to obscene proposals. Some law enforcement experts believe that pedophiles operate in these chat rooms, seeking opportunities to meet with the juveniles they contact. While not a common occurrence, pedophiles have indeed enticed juveniles to meet with them.

Juveniles can also be perpetrators of pornography. In 1996, a 16-year-old male was arrested and found delinquent in a Rhode Island juvenile court for distributing child pornography using the Internet bulletin board "Unleashed Online." As part of his punishment, he was prohibited from owning and operating a bulletin board or Web site until the age of 18. He posted the pictures on his bulletin board and allowed users to view the photos for a small fee. A police officer, acting on a tip, paid the fee and was allowed to view the photos. The officer subsequently contacted state prosecutors, leading to the juvenile's arrest.

LAW ENFORCEMENT AND INDUSTRY RESPONSE

Response by the computer industry and by law enforcement has been mixed at best. Many computer companies do not want to make their intrusions public and handle investigations in-house, while others go to police and federal agencies for help. Compounding the problem is that a number of intruders have been juveniles, for which there has been limited prosecution and limited punishment for hacking.

Kevin Mitnick, for instance, only served time in California after being on probation for three previous offenses. For Mitnick, perhaps the worst punishment was that he was prohibited from using a computer for a time.

A hacker arrested in 1998 for cutting off the service to the FAA control tower at the Worcester Airport marked the first time that federal charges were brought against a juvenile for computer crime. As a result of the plea agreement, he received two years probation, during which he could not access a computer network. It was not until two years later that the first juvenile was sentenced to serve time. In this case, a 16-year-old from Miami was sentenced to six months in a detention facility for his attacks on NASA computer networks.

In answer to the question of why response is lacking, many law enforcement officials are quick to state that cybercrime is difficult to prove. In 1998, federal agencies offered 419 cases to prosecutors, who only filed on 83 of the cases. The number of cases referred to prosecutors in 1988 was up 43 percent from the previous year. Although there may be serious questions of evidence, two problems quickly emerge. One is the issue of geography, where the attack on a system in the United States may have been initiated by a citizen of a foreign country. The second is that juveniles are frequently caught, but not prosecuted, based on the prosecutorial discretion of the U.S. Attorney's Office.

The average sentence length for juveniles convicted in 1998 was five months, with more than half receiving no jail time. Since 1992, federal computer crime charges have resulted in the conviction of 196 people, with 84 imprisonments. Clearly, the risk of going to prison for cybercrime is low.

In an effort to remedy the problem of cybercrime, the FBI created the National Infrastructure Protection Center (NIPC) to serve as the government's threat assessment, warning, vulnerability, and law enforcement investigation-and-response arm to cybercrime. The FBI also created the National Infrastructure Protection and Computer Intrusion (NIPCI) program as a cybercrime investigation agency at each FBI field office. Creation of this program, however, will not significantly reduce the number of juvenile hackers without the cooperation of other agencies and the private sector.

CONCLUSION

No one really knows who the hackers are, nor why they are motivated to infiltrate computer systems. The hacker underground views itself as a misunderstood group, wrongfully portrayed by a pandering media. Hackers insist that they have an interest in technology, are motivated by ideals, and demand that information be free, rather than being kept private. Some are underachievers in school, blaming a curriculum that does not cater to their interests. Most agree that hacking is addictive, as more and more access is achieved. Others use cyberspace as a means and method for committing crimes or for simply seeing if they can shut down a Web site just for fun.

Regardless of the reasons for committing cybercrime, computer security professionals insist that penalties for juvenile hackers should be stricter. Critics, however, argue that the computer security professionals have more to worry about and should focus on closing the security loopholes, not wondering about the prospective sentence of the hacker.

Tafoya (1990) suggests that a majority of police executives either do not know enough about cybercrime or simply do not care. A decade later, that statement seems to hold true concerning juveniles and cybercrime. The complex jurisdictional nightmares, coupled with the difficulty in developing and maintaining expertise in cybercrime fighting by police, suggest that the police, either deliberately or inadvertently, have made cybercrime a low priority. The addition of programs such as NIPC, while a step in the right direction, may do little to assist local law enforcement with its cybercrime problems. After events such as the terrorist attack on the World Trade Center in New York and the possibility of cyberterrorism, federal agencies will be focused on national matters rather than local crime issues.

More than likely, local law enforcement will be responsible for developing the expertise to handle their own computer-crime-related investigations and must still fight the geographic jurisdictional problems facing crime fighting in the 21st century. These issues are exacerbated by the public's seemingly insatiable desire for instantaneous personal communications provided by the Internet. Regardless of police efforts in fighting cybercrime, society is still struggling with the issue of how to properly handle the juvenile offender who is using a computer. Until those issues are resolved, local prosecutors may well follow their federal counterparts and use tremendous discretion in dealing with the juvenile cybercriminal.

James Golden

Bibliography

Freeh, L. 2000. *Cybercrime*. Statement for the Record Before the Senate Committee on Appropriations Subcommittee for the Departments of Commerce, Justice, State, the Judiciary, and Related Agencies. Washington, DC: Government Printing Office.

Gibson, S. 2001. *The Strange Tale of the Denial of Service Attacks Against GRC.COM*. Available at http://grc.com/dos/grcdos.htm.

Meyer, G., and J. Thomas. 1990. The baudy world of the byte bandit: A postmodernist interpretation of the computer underground. Pp. 31–67 in F. Schmalleger (ed.), *Computers in Criminal Justice*. Bristol, IN: Wyndham Hall Press.

Tafoya, W. 1990. Foreword. Pp. i–iii in F. Schmalleger (ed.), *Computers in Criminal Justice*. Bristol, IN: Wyndham Hall Press.

COURTS, JUVENILE

I. History

The Chancery Courts in England were the forerunners of the juvenile court. In the 1500s, the king's chancellors dealt with orphans who had inherited property. The chancellors managed the property of these dependent children and administered their welfare until they reached age 21.

Delinquency, however, was not really under the Chancery Courts' purview. Instead, delinquent juveniles (usually over age 7) were treated the same as adults. This similar treatment meant that juveniles could be treated quite harshly and subjected to incarceration with serious adult criminals (Schwartz, 1989). When the colonists came to America, they adopted a similar approach. Children under age 7 were believed to be incapable of forming the necessary intent to commit crime, but children over age 7 could be treated as adults.

It was in the Chancery Courts that the concept of *parens patriae* was first introduced. *Parens patriae* literally means the "parent of the country." When it was originally used in England, it meant that the state (through the king) is the guardian or protector of all citizens who are unable to take care of themselves. It was specifically used for children whose parents were unable to properly care for them.

INDUSTRIALIZATION, IMMIGRATION, AND URBANIZATION IN AMERICA

In the early 1800s, America began to shift from being primarily rural and agricultural to urban and industrialized. Cities experienced a rapid growth in population in a short period. Families began to migrate to urban areas in search of jobs, and the population of the cities became more heterogeneous. Conditions in many cities were atrocious. Poverty, disease, deteriorating housing, mental illness, and crowding were all part of urban life (Bartollas and Miller, 1994). During this change from a more rural to a more urban society, some families disintegrated, leaving youth to fend for themselves on the streets. As a survival strategy, some youth became beggars, and others were involved in theft (Bernard, 1992).

Before industrialization and urbanization, there was no identifiable population of troubled youth. However, life in small towns and rural areas was very different from urban environments where the population was diverse. It was during this period of upheaval that the term *juvenile delinquent* began to be employed to describe the behavior of troubled youth. Some juvenile justice scholars suggest that the term *juvenile delinquent* was similar to *pauper* (Bernard, 1992). Paupers (poor people) were perceived by the upper class as a problem. According to this perspective, paupers were wicked and did not deserve kindness or charity. They were thought to be inherently evil, and it was assumed that their own corruption and bad behavior had caused their poverty (Bernard, 1992). Pauper children were perceived as the root of the problems that cities like New York were experiencing.

According to Bernard (1992), the term *juvenile delinquent* originally meant something like "potential pauper." However, social reformers later came to use *juvenile delinquent* to describe offensive youth behavior. In particular, lower-class youth who engaged in theft in urban areas were called juvenile delinquents (Bernard, 1992).

Photo 2. Judge Benjamin B. Lindsey (third from left) presides in the chambers of his juvenile court in Denver, Colorado, sometime between 1910 and 1915. Under parens patriae doctrine, judges dealt informally with youth. Lindsey's rehabilitation-centered and humane treatment of youth was a widely copied national model.
SOURCE: Library of Congress, Prints & Photography Division [LC-USZ62-127585]. Used with permission.

Although misbehaving youth were a focal point of the evolving juvenile justice policies, there was also concern for the youth who had not yet been involved in delinquent activities, but who might be likely to engage in such behaviors. Urban children were perceived as the victims of the twin forces of urbanization and industrialization. It was assumed that poor, urban, young males who were on the streets with other youths would routinely resort to theft in order to survive. Thus there was a need for some kind of system that would be able to intervene and prevent future offenses (Bernard, 1992:47–48).

ATTITUDES TOWARD CHILDREN

Concern for juvenile delinquents who were stealing in urban areas in 1820 was fueled by two other developments. First, there was a belief in the 1800s that children, unlike adults, were malleable, and subject to change. By contrast, adults were perceived as beyond

reform. Adults were "cemented" in their ways, whereas children were just developing and could be "reshaped" (Bernard, 1992).

Children were influenced by the people with whom they came in contact, and their behavior reflected those influences. The goal then was to intervene in the lives of children early enough to allow positive influences to shape them. Law-abiding citizens were identified as the appropriate "rescuers." Young children could be saved from the corrupt influences associated with poverty, urban life, and contact with people who might have an adverse influence on the child (Bernard, 1992).

The second development was the rise of positivism. Unlike the classical school of criminology, which assumed that youth were engaging in delinquent activities because of free will, the positive school proponents contended that their behavior was shaped by forces beyond their control. These forces included biological, psychological, economic, social, and political factors that would be identified through the use of the scientific method. Once the cause of the behavior was identified, it was believed that the youth could be "cured" (Bartollas and Miller, 1994). In short, through some kind of intervention or treatment, the youth could be reformed and become law-abiding citizens. This approach was seen to be consistent with the approach to dealing with poor children.

REFORMERS AND THE
FIRST JUVENILE INSTITUTION

In 1817, a group of citizens in New York formed an organization known as the Society for the Prevention of Pauperism and sought to determine the causes of pauperism and strategies to remedy it. In their reports, they focused on the lack of separate facilities for children. In addition to removing children from adult institutions, the organization also recommended bringing children into institutions who had not yet committed any crime but who by virtue of their poor family backgrounds might engage in crime (Bernard, 1992). The intent was to prevent potential offending before it occurred.

The society, renamed the Society for the Reformation of Juvenile Delinquents, was successful in establishing a separate institution for children. The first juvenile institution in the United States, the New York House of Refuge, opened on January 1, 1825. Rather than punishing poor children, its goal was to reform them. In a short time, houses of refuge were established in other cities, including Baltimore, Boston, and Philadelphia (Bernard, 1992).

PARENS PATRIAE AND THE
AMERICAN JUVENILE JUSTICE SYSTEM

The incorporation of *parens patriae* into the American juvenile justice system officially occurred in 1838 when the Pennsylvania Supreme Court reviewed the case of Mary Ann Crouse. Mary Ann was committed to a House of Refuge in Pennsylvania. Her father opposed her commitment and sought her release, contending that no crime had been committed and that she was being held involuntarily. In rejecting Mr. Crouse's arguments, the Court used the term *parens patriae,* which had previously been applied only to orphans who inherited property in England and were subject to the king's guardianship. In the *Ex Parte Crouse* case,

the Pennsylvania Supreme Court argued that Mary Ann's parents were unable to care for her properly (due to their poverty) and that it was legal for the state to intervene in her best interests and place her in the House of Refuge (Bernard, 1992). Later, various state legislatures in America incorporated the concept of *parens patriae* into legislation with the intent that the court (i.e., the judge) would act as a parent and in the best interests of all children in the jurisdiction.

MOBILIZATION OF THE CHILD SAVERS

In Chicago, a group of upper- and middle-class women became increasingly concerned and vocal about the plight of children in the United States. In particular, they were distressed by the number of immigrant youth living in urban areas, the number of youth living in poverty, and youth who appeared to be unsupervised for lengthy periods. Anthony Platt (1991) referred to these reformers as the child savers. It was largely through their organized support that state legislatures across the country became aware of the problem and, in an attempt to find a solution to deal with these children, drafted initiatives to create a new juvenile court (Platt, 1991).

These women reformers were not unlike those who had helped to establish the House of Refuge in New York and other cities. They, too, were determined to rescue urban American children from the corrupt influences of the streets and return the country to the rural value system that had been in existence earlier. There are two viewpoints on the rationale for the social reformers' interest in the urban poor. According to the traditionalist view, these social reformers' intentions were entirely benevolent. Convinced that being a pauper or being born into a pauper family would adversely affect the child, their only goal was to help children have a better life. The traditional perspective contends that social reformers were thoroughly committed to children, sought to address the plight of poor urban children, and wanted to make it possible for them to escape the environments where crime-producing influences were likely to occur. Although their efforts may have been misguided, their intentions were noble and their plans were laudable.

The revisionist view suggests that rather than saving children, the real agenda of the social reformers was to control poor children who were viewed as problems for society (Albanese, 1993). The movement to establish a special court for children was led by wealthy, white, conservative, Protestant women who were interested in public service and saw working in poor neighborhoods as a worthy cause consistent with their societal roles of wife and mother. Such a cause enabled them to appear before the legislature to propose a court for children. By removing these children from their homes and placing them in institutions or in alternative settings under the guise of rehabilitation, the juvenile court was a way to camouflage the real issue of controlling the urban poor, many of whom were immigrants and not entirely welcomed by the more established middle and upper classes (Bernard, 1992; Platt, 1991).

Thus the social reformers' use of the term *juvenile delinquent* is consistent with their goals. These are youth who are not yet fully committed to a life of crime. They can be redirected if subjected to the proper kind of reform. Unlike hardened adult criminals, these children are still developmentally susceptible to outside influences, and removing them from the corrupting influences associated with the urban environment was a laudable goal (Bernard, 1992). They were also primarily poor children.

THE FIRST JUVENILE COURT

A number of states began to rethink their juvenile justice practices during the 1870s. Some of these states, like Massachusetts and New York, began to provide separate proceedings for juveniles or a special advocate. During the Progressive Era (1890 to 1920), states began to draft legislation that would enable the courts to treat juveniles differently than adults. However, it was not until July 1, 1899, that the first juvenile court was established by the Illinois legislature. The specific legislation authorizing the creation of the special court for children was the *Illinois Juvenile Court Act,* or the *Act to Regulate the Treatment and Control of Dependent, Neglected, and Delinquent Children* (Bartollas and Miller, 1994). The first juvenile court was guided by the law's requirements. Children under age 16 who were alleged to have violated any state or local law or ordinance along with children who were dependent and/or neglected or who did not appear to have guardians, proper parental care, or support were subject to the jurisdiction of this new court. Children who were unruly, incorrigible, or unmanageable were also suitable subjects for juvenile court intervention.

There was no minimum age at which children could be referred to the court.

The success of the first juvenile court legislation was noteworthy. Twenty states emulated Illinois in creating special courts for children between 1899 and 1909, and by 1945, every state had created some kind of juvenile court that embodied elements of the positive school and the rehabilitation process. In some states, the upper age was 16, and in others, it was 17 or 18. Although there were variations in these courts, legislators had succeeded in establishing a separate system for children. Under the authority of *parens patriae,* juvenile courts could intervene in the lives of children without parental consent and attempt to prevent juveniles from offending. They could also treat juveniles who had already been involved in delinquent activity.

This emphasis on helping children required the juvenile court to recruit and retain staff who were educated in social work and who understood children. Juvenile court judges were expected to be educated in psychology, sociology, and law. Rather than focusing on whether the child actually engaged in the alleged conduct, they were much more concerned with identifying the factors that were related to the child's referral to the court.

There was also a special language to refer to the juvenile court proceedings. A juvenile was apprehended rather than arrested and referred to the court on the basis of filing a petition rather than an indictment or a charge. A youth was brought before the judge for a hearing rather than a trial. If the youth was adjudicated (convicted), then the judge would make a disposition (sentence) and possibly commit the juvenile to a juvenile institution. This language illustrated the differences in juvenile and adult court and emphasized its helping rather than punitive process.

The juvenile court was characterized by its informality. Unlike adversarial proceedings in the adult system, the juvenile court was civil in nature. The judge assumed the role of protector of the children brought before him or her. During the youth's detention prior to court appearances, it was assumed that the staff would interact with the youth and observe how the child related to staff. Staff members would administer intelligence and psychological tests, interview the youth, and then recommend an appropriate disposition for the youth.

The emphasis was on casework services, and the juvenile court largely acted as a caseworker to poor families (Bartollas and Miller, 1994; Bernard, 1992). The social worker or caseworker identified what could be done to help the child adjust to or deal with his or her circumstances. The juvenile court's jurisdiction encompassed dependent, neglected, delinquent, and status offenders. In some instances, the court also had authority over adults who were alleged to be committing crimes against children; for example, some juvenile courts had jurisdiction in adult cases involving "contributing to the delinquency of a minor" or "furnishing alcohol to a minor child."

It was anticipated that all youth would be referred to the juvenile court for assistance and that the court staff would determine how best to address the situation. In some instances, that meant referring the youth to another social service or child welfare agency or organization, and in other cases, it would involve using the court's authority to retain jurisdiction in the court and deal with the youth there. Bernard (1992) notes that the services that the juvenile court rendered were hardly voluntary. Acting in the best interests of the child gave the juvenile court staff coercive power to intervene in cases involving children. In short, the court could decide what to do with any youth, even deciding to incarcerate a youth, regardless of whether a delinquent act had been committed or the family agreed.

In addition to the philosophy of *parens patriae,* the juvenile court was also guided by the notion of individualized justice. Each juvenile was unique, and it was the court's obligation to determine how best to deal with each child. In its role as the guardian or protector of all children, the court had a special responsibility to ensure that children were treated as individuals.

Historically, probation was the primary disposition of the juvenile court judge. In fact, probation was frequently used when the juvenile court was first established, and it continues to be used extensively (Roberts, 1989). Through probation, the judge allowed the juvenile to remain in the community under the supervision of a representative from the court. The juvenile might be expected to attend school, remain employed, and adhere to specific rules or terms of probation. The court was responsible for monitoring the youth during this period and intervening if the circumstances warranted it.

This early period of the juvenile court was characterized by optimism. The belief that the juvenile court could serve all the children in the jurisdiction through the efforts of both volunteer and paid staff was widespread. Furthermore, the court and its advocates

assumed the judge knew what was best for the child and that the parents were not in a position to alter the situation.

EVOLUTION OF THE COURT

The era of "socialized juvenile justice" started with the official beginning of the juvenile court in 1899 and continued through 1966. Rather than due process and legal safeguards, this period was characterized by the court's emphasis on trying to determine why a child had violated the law and what steps could be taken to treat him or her. The juvenile court was not to be encumbered by the requirements of the adult legal system regarding notice, counsel, confrontation of witnesses, and proof beyond a reasonable doubt. Instead, it would be more civil in nature, and the juvenile court would have the latitude to delve into the child's past to determine what factors may have caused the behavior. Then the court staff could reform the youth.

The juvenile court had transcended the idea of simply dealing with pauper children and now viewed all children as potentially dependent or neglected (Bernard, 1992). A delinquent child was perceived as dependent because his or her parents were unable to properly supervise or guide him or her. Thus the court could intervene in the child's best interests and take whatever action it deemed necessary.

The goal of prevention also required more flexibility than was allowed by the adult system. The juvenile court had to be able to intervene in a child's life before he or she had ever actually engaged in serious misconduct. Therefore, due process protections were deemed inappropriate for the mission of the court. Supporters of the juvenile court's informal process refuted any allegations regarding denial of due process by focusing on the differences between the adult criminal court and the juvenile court.

CRITICISM OF THE JUVENILE COURT

The juvenile court was not without its critics. Although there was a brief period of euphoria after the court had been established, critics began to identify the court's shortcomings as early as 1915. In particular, these allegations focused on the harsh practices of the courts and the deplorable environments that children were placed in under the guise of treatment. After World War I, more paid staff were added to the juvenile court. Rather than focusing on the societal conditions that were related to delinquency, there was a greater emphasis on social work. The influence of Freud and his emphasis on the client's emotional feelings translated into social workers focusing on the child's mental state and the psychological problems he or she was experiencing (Bartollas and Miller, 1994).

After World War II, criticism of the juvenile court and its practices and policies began to mount. The critics focused on the fact that the juvenile court had not experienced much success in dealing with juvenile delinquents. In fact, the states' efforts at reform were characterized by inhumane treatment and lack of understanding. Criticism also focused on the informal procedures of the juvenile court and whether they violated the Constitution. The fact that the juvenile court could deprive a child of his or her liberty without a formal hearing, an attorney, and any other constitutional protections was particularly troubling.

Although the number and type of court staff varied from jurisdiction to jurisdiction, juvenile courts typically had (1) a special full- or part-time juvenile court judge; (2) an intake officer to make the initial determination of whether the juvenile would be detained and whether the case would be handled informally or formally; (3) a court psychologist to test the youth; and (4) a probation officer to perform a background investigation on the youth and his or her family, supervise the youth in the community, and identify appropriate agencies to refer the youth for treatment. All these individuals had tremendous discretion in dealing with juvenile offenders who had been referred to the court.

THE U.S. SUPREME COURT AND JUVENILE JUSTICE

The Supreme Court had been silent regarding juvenile justice. In 1955, the Court decided not to hear a juvenile justice case, *In re Holmes,* and instead reiterated that juvenile courts are not criminal courts. It was not until 1966 that the Court ruled on the issue of waiver proceedings in the case of *Kent v. U.S.* In the case of Morris Kent, the justices were asked to determine if Kent's due process protections as guaranteed by the Fourteenth Amendment had been violated when the judge transferred juvenile court jurisdiction to the district court. In *Kent,* the justices determined that certain due process protections, including the right to a hearing on the motion of waiver and the right to counsel

at a waiver proceeding, are required when the judge decides to waive jurisdiction to criminal court.

In 1967, the Court decided *In re Gault,* the most significant case of the first century of the juvenile court. In *Gault,* the justices determined that, although a juvenile delinquency proceeding was less formal than a criminal trial in the adult court, the juvenile still had certain fundamental due process protections included in the Fourteenth Amendment. The justices found that juveniles who are alleged to be involved in delinquent activity have the right to notice of the charges, right to counsel, right to confront and cross-examine witnesses, and the privilege against self-incrimination.

Having established that juveniles did have certain due process rights, the Court in 1970, addressed the issue of the standard of proof necessary to adjudicate a juvenile delinquent. In deciding *In re Winship,* the Court found that juveniles who are alleged to be delinquent, just like adults who are alleged to be criminals, must be found guilty beyond a reasonable doubt. Previously, juveniles had been adjudicated delinquent by the standard of a preponderance of the evidence, or clear and convincing evidence.

The trend toward a more formal and more adult-like juvenile justice process did not continue. In 1971, in *McKeiver v. Pennsylvania,* the Supreme Court ruled that juveniles charged with delinquent conduct do not have a constitutional right to a jury trial. In noting that the juvenile proceeding was not the equivalent of a criminal prosecution, the justices found no support for the argument that the Sixth Amendment to the Constitution provides such protections to juvenile offenders. Despite this ruling, the juvenile justice system had clearly evolved from the informal proceeding that had characterized it during the early part of the century.

THE JUVENILE COURT IN THE 1970s

Another impetus for change occurred in the 1970s regarding the deinstitutionalization of juvenile offenders. The movement originally started in the field of mental health. In particular, it was aimed at releasing and reintegrating mental patients into the community rather than holding them in state mental hospitals indefinitely. The deinstitutionalization movement began to influence the juvenile justice system. Concern over children who had been placed in secure settings like training schools or reform schools prompted Congress in 1974 to enact the Juvenile Justice and Delinquency Prevention Act (JJDPA). Specifically, this act required any state that received federal funding for delinquency prevention programs to deinstitutionalize youth involved in status offenses. Status offenders as well as dependent and/or neglected youth housed in training or reform schools were to be removed, and juveniles could not be held in facilities where they would have regular contact with adult offenders (Chesney-Lind and Shelden, 1992; Schwartz, 1989).

This legislation represented a significant shift in Congress's attitude toward the juvenile court. Until this time, the juvenile court had tremendous discretion in dealing with delinquent, dependent, and status offenders. Although Congress enacted subsequent amendments to the JJDPA, it was a significant step in changing the treatment that status offenders and dependent or neglected children received in the juvenile court.

Beginning in the late 1970s, another dramatic shift in the juvenile court occurred. The public, the legislature, and the court staff moved away from *parens patriae* and the rehabilitative ideal of the juvenile court. The legislature responded with a more punitive and adultlike stance toward juveniles; and the public endorsed this perspective. The "get tough" philosophy that has characterized the adult system has affected the juvenile court process. Issues involving transfer of jurisdiction, adult sentences, juvenile prisons, and more emphasis on accountability are all emblematic of the shift that has occurred. During this time, juveniles were again perceived as miniature adults who were not deserving of the special treatment afforded them through the juvenile court.

Juvenile justice is now viewed very differently than it was when the first juvenile court was established. The emergence of gangs, drugs, and guns in the 1970s affected the juvenile court. The public's perception of juvenile offenders has changed, and support for juvenile treatment programs has waned. It is unlikely that society will return to the earlier version of the juvenile court. However, it does appear that the juvenile court has not yet completed its evolution.

Alida V. Merlo

See also Child-Saving Movement; Juvenile Justice and Delinquency Prevention Act; *Parens Patriae* Doctrine; Reformatories and Reform Schools

Bibliography

Albanese, J. S. 1993. *Dealing With Delinquency: The Future of Juvenile Justice*, 2nd ed. Chicago: Nelson-Hall.

Bartollas, C., and S. J. Miller. 1994. *Juvenile Justice in America*. Englewood Cliffs, NJ: Prentice Hall.

Bernard, T. J. 1992. *The Cycle of Juvenile Justice*. New York: Oxford University Press.

Chesney-Lind, M., and R. G. Shelden. 1992. *Girls, Delinquency, and Juvenile Justice*. Pacific Grove, CA: Brooks/Cole.

Platt, A. 1991. *The Child Savers: The Invention of Delinquency,* 2nd ed. Chicago: University of Chicago Press.

Roberts, A. R. 1989. *Juvenile Justice: Policies, Programs, and Services*. Chicago: Dorsey Press.

Schwartz, I. M. 1989. *(In)Justice for Juveniles*. Lexington, MA: D. C. Heath.

Cases Cited

In re Gault, 387 U.S. 1, 87 S.Ct. 1428 (1967).
In re Holmes, 348 U.S. 973, 75 S.Ct. 535 (1955).
In re Winship, 397 U.S. 358 (1970).
Kent v. U.S., 383 U.S. 541 (1966).
McKeiver v. Pennsylvania, 403 U.S. 528 (1971).

COURTS, JUVENILE

II. Current Status

Juvenile courts at the beginning of the 21st century can best be described as dynamic institutions in transition. Since 1899, when the first formal juvenile court began operation in Cook County, Illinois, both the philosophy of juvenile justice and the procedures of handling young delinquents have undergone significant changes. From the view of youth as "wayward children" in need of benevolent and paternalistic intervention by the state (*parens patriae*), juvenile courts have become what some have described as scaled-down criminal courts. What was designed as a system that relied on informal hearings to determine the best interests of the child has become a mirror of the formal, legal bureaucracy that characterizes the adversarial criminal court.

Originally, the juvenile court was developed with a treatment orientation based on social work principles. This model focused on understanding (diagnosing) children, not on determining their guilt. It was based on helping and caring for youth, not on punishing them. It relied on the wisdom of the judge to individualize treatment, not on the jurisprudence of courts to impose standardized, mandatory sanctions. To demonstrate this distinction between adult courts and this new specialized court for youth, separate terminology was used to convey the philosophy of juvenile justice: *taken into custody* as opposed to *arrest*, *detention* rather than *jail*, *adjudication* and *disposition hearings* rather than *trial* and *sentencing*, and *training schools* as opposed to *prisons*.

While the "child saving" ideals and intentions of juvenile court may have been noble, by the 1960s, a growing disenchantment with abuses of the court and disappointment with failed outcomes helped precipitate a series of Supreme Court decisions that began to transform the juvenile court. In a landmark decision, the Court criticized juvenile court for being a "kangaroo court" that failed to exercise the care and patience needed to protect the juvenile (*In re Gault*, 1967). The Court noted the abuses of discretion and rejected the philosophy of *parens patriae*. It ruled that youth were denied due process and were entitled to constitutional rights that included a notice of charges, access to legal counsel, protection from self-incrimination, cross-examination of witnesses, transcript of proceedings, and appellate review.

TRANSITION

In response to the Court's decision, and in efforts to reform the juvenile court, concern about due process and protecting youth from discretionary abuses began a transformation from an informal, rehabilitative system to an adversarial, punitive one that emphasized crime control and resulted in a convergence between juvenile and criminal courts. In his critique of juvenile justice, Barry Feld (1999) examined three developments that facilitated this narrowing between adult and juvenile systems: (1) greater concern with procedural justice; (2) the shift in jurisprudence from treatment to punishment; and (3) reforms that diverted less serious youth (e.g., status offenders) into other social service agencies and transferred serious young offenders from juvenile court to criminal court jurisdiction. The exclusion of serious delinquents was based on the belief that tougher sentences would be imposed in criminal court and that public safety would be ensured. This also signaled a lack of confidence in

the ability of juvenile courts to meet these objectives. Feld concluded that these changes made the juvenile court superfluous and unnecessary and he advocated for the abolition of juvenile courts.

By the 1980s, assumptions about delinquency and attitudes toward youth were also undergoing change. The prevailing conservative "get tough on crime" ideology reflected an approach to criminality that underscored rational thinking and free will. Essentially, this model posits that individuals exercise rational choice in deciding to commit crime, should be held responsible for their behaviors, and can be deterred from wrongdoing if sanctions are severe enough. In contrast, juvenile court was established on the principles that youth are engaged in psychological and sociological transition from childhood immaturity and are not yet fully responsible for their behavior. Adolescence was recognized as a developmental stage that typified risk taking, impulsivity, irresponsibility, and shortsightedness.

However, a sharp increase in juvenile crime beginning in the mid-1980s, especially drug (crack cocaine) and gang-related violence, precipitated a moral panic against youth that led to get-tough legislation. After years of stable delinquency rates, juvenile violent crime arrests increased from a low of about 100 arrests per 100,000 youth under age 18 in 1965 to 300 in 1980 to 400 in 1990. Juvenile homicide arrest rates went from about 2 per 100,000 youth in 1965 to 12 per 100,000 in 1990 (Federal Bureau of Investigation, 1998). This wave of youth violence, which was explained as the result of youth using and dealing crack cocaine, the prevalence of youth gangs, and easy access to guns, made crime a priority issue, captured headlines, and prompted punitive legislative reforms.

ADULTIFICATION OF JUVENILE JUSTICE

In a response to demands to do something about youth violence in America, between 1985 and 1995, state legislatures enacted numerous get-tough laws that changed court proceedings by (1) opening juvenile hearings to the public; (2) allowing police to fingerprint and photograph youth; (3) releasing juvenile court records to designated authorities (e.g., media, schools); (4) prohibiting the expunging of juvenile court records; and (5) transferring more juvenile offenders into the adult criminal justice system.

While juvenile courts already had the ability to transfer certain youthful offenders to criminal court by using judicial waiver (generally violent, repeat offenders), the politicization of juvenile justice resulted in legislation that automatically excluded certain youth from the jurisdiction of the juvenile system (statutory exclusion) or shifted discretion to the prosecutor (prosecutorial discretion). These laws also included tougher and mandatory sentences for designated youth and embodied the sentiment of "adult crime, adult time."

This "legislative sentencing" focused on the nature of the offense (e.g., guns, gangs, drugs) rather than on the nature of the offender and relied on punishment, incapacitation, and deterrence to curb youth crime. The retributive ideology overshadowed the juvenile court's mission of individualized sanctions and rehabilitative interventions, and lowered the ages at which youth could be tried as adults (in some states as low as 10 years old) and sentenced to adult institutions. Previous efforts in the 1970s to separate juveniles and adults were seemingly reversed, and the demonization of youth reinforced crime control policies and the movement to treat juveniles as adults.

In spite of support for get-tough legislation, evidence did not demonstrate the effectiveness of these policies and, in fact, indicated that youth transferred to adult jurisdiction had higher rates of recidivism and were at greater risk for suicide, sexual assault, and victimization when confined with adults. However, even as juvenile crime rates were decreasing throughout the 1990s and schools were becoming increasingly safer, media reports of youth crime and exceptional school shootings helped to expand zero-tolerance policies toward youth and to raise doubts about the efficacy of juvenile courts to control youth crime. At the same time and in response to criticisms of the juvenile justice system, efforts were taken to promote new models of juvenile justice.

JUVENILE COURT PROCESSES

Generally, juvenile court decision making focuses on four hearings: detention, intake, adjudication, and disposition. After a youth is taken into custody (i.e., arrested), juvenile court intake staff determine whether or not to hold the youth in a detention facility pending court hearings. The youth may be held if he or she is viewed as a risk to the community or as a risk for failure to appear in court. Sometimes youth are held in detention centers for diagnostic evaluation. Most states require judges to review the detention decision within one to three days after confinement. In 1997, between referral and disposition, about 20 percent of all delinquency cases resulted in detention.

When a case is referred to juvenile court, a decision is made whether to handle the case informally or formally. Informal handling is based on the nature of the delinquency as well as on the youth's amenability to rehabilitation and willingness to comply with various sanctions (informal probation, community service). The case is generally held open pending successful completion of the informal disposition. If the youth fails to comply with the informal sanctions, the case can be reopened, and the youth can be formally prosecuted. In 1997, 43 percent of delinquency cases were handled informally, and 57 percent were handled formally.

In formal handling, a petition is filed with the court to proceed with an adjudication hearing. As previously noted, contrary to the original informal, private hearing held by the judge, adjudication now involves the roles of both the prosecuting and defense attorneys. If the charges are substantiated, the youth is adjudicated delinquent (i.e., found "guilty") and the court holds a disposition hearing to consider how best to respond to the youth. A social summary may be requested by the court to provide background information to help the court in determining whether to impose probation, placement, or other sanctions. The summary is prepared by the probation officer and may include recommendations for appropriate dispositions. Based on 1997 data reported by Melissa Sickmund (2000), of the formally petitioned cases, approximately 57 percent were adjudicated delinquent; of those, about one half (54 percent) received formal probation and about one third (29 percent) received placement (group home, training school, private treatment facility). Probation is generally used with low-risk offenders who are amenable to community supervision and likely to comply with the conditions imposed by the court. Placement is used with more serious, older youth who have prior court records.

Courts also handle status offenses, which are violations only if committed by juveniles (breaking curfew, running away, truancy, underage drinking). Some states have turned these cases over to child protective services and do not consider them legal violations but rather dependency cases. Of all juvenile court cases in 1997, status offenses made up about 14 percent, and most were for truancy and liquor law violations. As with delinquency cases, status cases can be handled formally or informally. In about two thirds of the cases, either a formal or informal sanction was ordered by the court. Less than 1 out of 10 cases resulted in placement, and about one third resulted in probation.

JUVENILE COURT DATA

Much of the data on juvenile offenders and juvenile courts is compiled and reported by the Office of Juvenile Justice and Delinquency Prevention (OJJDP). Recent statistics indicate that even though arrests for juvenile crimes in the late 1990s and early 2000s were decreasing, the number of cases handled by juvenile courts increased. For example, the delinquency caseload in 1997 was 1.8 million cases (a 48 percent increase from 1988). Almost half of the cases, however, involved property offenses (burglary, larceny-theft, vandalism), while violent crimes (criminal homicide, forcible rape, robbery, aggravated assault) represented 6 percent and drug law violations represented 10 percent of all delinquency cases.

As previously noted, legislative reforms that mandated adultification policies for youth were responsible for statutory exclusion of some older teens (usually 16- and 17-year-olds) from jurisdiction of the juvenile court. Of delinquency cases formally processed in juvenile courts, about 1 percent are waived to criminal court. This figure has been decreasing, partially due to an increase in the cases that are statutorily excluded from juvenile court and to the decrease in juvenile crime rates. Judicial waiver, however, is the most common transfer provision. These cases generally involve youth charged with serious crimes, those with prior records, or those who have exhausted the resources of the juvenile court. Data from 1997 indicate that of the youth under age 18 who are incarcerated, approximately 13 percent are housed in adult facilities, 8 percent in local jails, and 5 percent in adult prisons.

In addition to placement and probation, juvenile courts can impose other sanctions, such as community service, electronic monitoring, wilderness and outdoor programs, and boot camp programs. While the number of delinquency cases involving females has been increasing faster than those involving males, males still account for more than three fourths of the serious delinquent offenses handled in juvenile court.

One issue that has received greater attention in juvenile courts is the disproportionate representation of minorities, especially blacks. Black youth make up 15 percent of the juvenile population and are responsible for about one third of all the delinquency cases. White youth make up 79 percent of the juvenile population and are responsible for about two thirds of all delinquency cases. Based on their proportion of the juvenile population and controlling for the nature of the offenses, black youth are overrepresented in court caseloads, especially in cases involving secure detention. For example, in 1997, cases involving black youth were twice as likely as those involving whites to receive secure detention, and while black youth represented one third of all delinquency cases, they accounted for 44 percent of detained cases. Data indicate that this disproportional processing has been greatest for drug offenses.

BALANCED APPROACH

As juvenile courts continue handling increasing caseloads of a wide variety of youthful offenders, and as statutory exclusion policies result in increasing numbers of youth being transferred to the adult criminal justice system, new models and strategies have been promoted to provide alternatives for both courts. While prevention and early intervention programs gained support and implementation in the 1990s, challenges to the court's goal of protecting the welfare of young offenders necessitated a response that could reaffirm its mission and preserve its distinction for handling juveniles. Seeking an approach that was not at either end of the continuum represented by the "soft" *parens patriae* model and the "hard" statutory exclusion reaction, many jurisdictions adopted a moderate model, the balanced approach, to integrate crime control and rehabilitation.

The Balanced and Restorative Justice Model (BARJ) incorporates three objectives for handling delinquents: (1) holding them accountable for their behavior (punishment), (2) ensuring community safety (crime control), and (3) providing interventions to help youth develop better skills and behaviors (treatment or "competency development"). The element of restorative justice recognizes the importance of holding the youth accountable to the victim and the community with strategies such as victim mediation, community service, and restitution.

In this model, the juvenile court can exercise discretion in using various alternatives to protect the community while providing for the best interests of the youth. By involving the offender, the victim, the family, and the community, the court promotes support, compensation, assistance, and a broader mission of justice and redemption. Courts work to develop collaborative and integrated responses that require agencies and programs to form partnerships. For example, community-based probation programs place probation officers in neighborhood centers where police, treatment providers, and teachers interact with youth and their families. This provides a continuum of accountability and offers the court an important leadership role in coordinating services, protecting the community, and helping youth.

SPECIALTY COURTS

Another alternative that has not only returned discretion to the court but also incorporated a therapeutic dimension to jurisprudence is the use of specialty courts. As opposed to the decision of whether to send juveniles to either juvenile or criminal court, in this court model, depending on the nature of the offense, the offender is assessed and the court determines which type of "specialty" is indicated. For example, a nonviolent juvenile offender with drug abuse indications could be referred to drug court. Other specialties include smoking court, teen court, gun court, and felony court.

In each case, the attempt is to identify factors related to the criminal behavior and match the offender to resources and programs that maintain strict monitoring and treatment. While the array of specialty courts is limited, drug courts have been well received and have helped promote the practice of therapeutic jurisprudence. Ironically, juvenile court itself is a specialty court that was founded to recognize the special needs and status of youth.

BLENDED SENTENCES

For juveniles who are serious and violent offenders, blended sentences offer the court an alternative to housing teens with adults. To avoid the abuses and management issues that occur when confining juveniles in adult prisons, these sentencing statutes give the court the option of sending youth to juvenile facilities to serve their sentence until they reach 18 or 21 years of age. At that time, the case can be reviewed for possible release or the youth can be transferred to serve the remainder of the sentence in a prison for adult offenders. By 1997, this option of imposing both juvenile and adult correctional sentences was passed by 20 states.

FUTURE INDICATIONS

While the 1980s and 1990s were characterized by legislative policies that emphasized retribution, adultification, and punishment of youthful offenders, the emergence of BARJ helped to reaffirm the juvenile court and offer a balance between crime control and rehabilitation while responding to the victim and holding youth accountable. Contrary to the prevailing get-tough attitudes of governmental figures, evidence indicates that the public supports prevention, intervention, and treatment for youth and generally recognizes the importance of these strategies in reducing delinquency.

The decrease in crime rates at the turn of the 21st century and concern with other social issues (education, health care, social security) presents the opportunity to enact less reactive and less emotional juvenile crime policies. The 107th Congress, for example, considered legislation that underscores prevention, drug abuse education, and treatment as cornerstones of juvenile justice. Juvenile courts are already engaging in collaborative, integrated responses offering a continuum of alternatives for sanctioning youth, providing treatment interventions, and protecting the community.

Peter Benekos

See also Boot Camps; Mediation; Office of Juvenile Justice and Delinquency Prevention; Restorative Justice; Status Offenders; Training Schools; Victimization; Wilderness Programs

Bibliography

Albanese, J. 1993. *Dealing With Delinquency: The Future of Juvenile Justice,* 2nd ed. Chicago: Nelson-Hall.

Bazemore, G., and M. S. Umbreit. 1994. *Balanced and Restorative Justice: Program Summary.* Washington, DC: Office of Juvenile Justice and Delinquency Prevention.

Bernard, T. 1992. *The Cycle of Juvenile Justice.* New York: Oxford University Press.

Butts, J. A., and A. V. Harrell. 1998. *Crime Policy Report: Delinquency or Criminals: Policy Options for Young Offenders.* Washington, DC: The Urban Institute.

Federal Bureau of Investigation. 1998. *Crime in the United States, 1997.* Washington, DC: U.S. Government Printing Office.

Feld, B. 1999. *Bad Kids: Race and the Transformation of the Juvenile Court.* New York: Oxford University Press.

Merlo, A. V. 2000. Juvenile justice at the crossroads: Presidential address to the Academy of Criminal Justice Sciences. *Justice Quarterly* 17:639–661.

Sickmund, M. 2000. *Juvenile Justice Bulletin: Offenders in Juvenile Court, 1997.* October. Washington, DC: Office of Juvenile Justice and Delinquency Prevention.

Snyder, H. N., and M. Sickmund. 1999. *Juvenile Offenders and Victims: 1999 National Report.* Washington, DC: Office of Juvenile Justice and Delinquency Prevention.

COURTS, JUVENILE

 ## III. Drug Courts

The first adult drug court was developed in Miami, Florida, in 1989 in response to an overburdened justice system following on the heels of the losing "war on drugs." In an attempt to relieve the overcrowded jails, prisons, and courts, authorities, spearheaded by Judge Herbert M. Klein, developed a new model whereby the goals of the court would "go beyond" traditional expectation of prosecution and punishment. In addition, the new court would tie together the fragmented existence of court, probation, and corrections into a collaborative team. The goals of the courtroom partnership were accountability and treatment.

The concept of treatment was a novel addition that arose from recent recognition that incarceration is not the solution it was assumed to be. A complex relationship exists between drugs and crime, and this model is the most ambitious attempt to break the cycle of addiction and prevent future crime. The use of treatment, intensive supervision, and personalized case management was thought to curtail the demand for illicit drugs permanently, stopping the "revolving door" reappearance of the individual within the system. This would both reduce the number of cases in the system and prove potentially cost-effective. The average cost for incarceration is $20,000 to $60,000 per year per individual, depending on the type of custody or care required. However, reports indicate the drug court model averages around $2,000 to $7,000 per individual per year based on level of treatment, supervision, and length of time in the program.

The idea of drug court was considered too naïve by most officials in the justice system. The first drug courts were forced to fund their own programs or find alternative resources because federal and state money for the project was nonexistent. It was not until the Violent Crime Control and Law Enforcement Act of 1994 that resources were made specifically available to drug courts. At that time, $1.4 billion was allocated for the rehabilitation of first-time or nonviolent drug offenders. In the first five years since this bill was passed, the funding amount for drug courts had risen to $40 million to $50 million annually in federal funds, including any drug court, not just those for first-time or nonviolent offenders.

Despite the early lack of support, the drug court movement has gained momentum. There were 12 courts operating by 1994. After government funding became more readily available that same year, there was a remarkable expansion across the United States. As of May 1999, there were more than 600 drug courts, either operating or in the final stages of planning across the 50 states, the District of Columbia, Puerto Rico, Guam, two federal districts, and more than 15 Native American Tribal Courts (Office of Justice Programs, 1998).

CHARACTERISTICS AND PHILOSOPHIES OF DRUG COURTS

Drug courts are operated differently in different jurisdictions. The Miami or Dade County model has been developed and transformed as it was adopted by other court systems. The basic structures of the courts, criteria for admission, treatment alternatives, and approaches may differ depending on the strength of local resources. Most drug courts today focus on rehabilitation and restoration, emphasizing accountability within the community.

By the mid-1990s, research revealed that incarceration was not decreasing the use of drugs or the flow of offenders and that incarceration was neither helpful in breaking the cycle of drug abuse nor did it reduce recidivism. On the other hand, there were indications that drug abuse treatment was somewhat effective in reducing drug abuse and related crime.

Recent studies indicate that upwards of 80 percent of inmates need substance abuse treatment and that addicted drug offenders are frequently involved in crime. Reviews of criminal justice research yield the finding that "there were no studies [as of 1994] that found punishment alone reduced recidivism" (Huddleston, 1998). The new philosophy offered by the drug courts seeks to address the true cause of most crime, via treatment and offender accountability.

Program Characteristics

The drug court movement has experienced an extraordinary expansion in the number of participants over the past several years. As a result, a national organization, the National Association of Drug Court Professionals (NADCP), was developed from attempts to handle the influx of participants and standardize service. The NADCP established a benchmark of standards based on 10 basic components that are practical but flexible enough to meet the needs of local communities. These standards serve as a guide for the creation of professional drug courts and as a basis for evaluating drug courts across the nation. The 10 components may be distilled to four central tenets exemplifying the drug court philosophy:

1. *Early identification and reference:* Individuals are screened shortly after arrest to determine if they are eligible to participate in drug courts and then referred quickly to the court to begin treatment. There is no waiting list. This is different from the traditional justice courts, which rarely screen before adjudication and may subsequently recommend drug treatment while in prison.

2. *One judge continuously monitoring the case:* Defendants are brought before a single judge who oversees all phases of the case to completion. This is the same judge that will conduct frequent status hearings and apply sanctions for noncompliance and rewards for progress. In addition, the judge encourages and speaks directly to the offender concerning progress. This is different from the traditional system in that multiple visits to court are not before multiple judges; thus the drug court judge is continuously aware of the offender's status. In addition, the frequency of hearings allows the judge to stay abreast of new happenings in treatment and apply appropriate changes. There is no long wait between rearrest and incarceration. Overall, the judge becomes an expert in addiction.

3. *The drug court team:* There is a coordinated effort between judges, prosecutors, treatment providers, and the community to work in the best interests of the offender and his or her addiction. Unlike the more traditional courts, there is an absence of the adversarial approach, which isolates the prosecutor from the judge and the judge from the defendant. For example, the judge, not the lawyer, might conduct weekly conversations with the defendant.

4. *Acceptance of relapse:* The drug court recognizes that addiction is not easily overcome and as such relapses are a possible occurrence. Frequent testing for alcohol and illicit drugs provides constant monitoring of progress and alerts officials to relapse. This does not, however, mean rearrest or termination from the drug court to traditional court. Generally, defendants are allowed to remain in the program as long as they continue to meet other program conditions. In traditional probation or parole, where drug testing is a condition, a positive test would mean reincarceration. Not so for the drug court, especially in light of the fact that many offenders relapse but remain in the program, later graduating with their addiction under control.

Unique to the drug court operation is the use of health and human services in ways not accessed by the traditional courts. Incarcerated offenders are frequently not obligated to participate in treatment services, whereas participation is mandatory in the drug court approach. In addition, incarcerated offenders may be recommended for substance abuse counseling yet not receive it. The drug courts offer as conditions of participation several phases of treatment and skill development, which range in length from six months to one year. This may include diverse treatment for addiction, mental illness, and family issues. Many of these treatments can be tailored to meet the needs of specific religious, cultural, or ethnic populations. Since most relapses occur within the first six months after program completion, job training, placement, and aftercare services are seen as essential elements of success.

Entering the Program

Offenders enter the drug court system following a plea, conditional plea, contract with the court, or a similar mechanism. Thus the individual is given an option of entering the drug court program in lieu of incarceration or similar traditional sanctions if he or she meets the program criteria. Originally, criteria for drug court inclusion required individuals to be first-time, minor drug offenders with a history of nonviolence. The drug court acts in a diversionary or quasi-diversionary fashion. Several courts have expanded their roles to include more serious drug violations and more violent offenders. It is estimated that only 20 percent of current drug courts restrict entrance to first-time offenders, indicating that chronic recidivists are now being placed into the drug courts (Office of Justice Programs, 1998). Because of recent modifications, some drug courts have postadjudicatory functions, monitoring offenders who have been adjudicated for offenses in other courts. A report by American University's Drug Court Clearinghouse indicates that approximately 70 percent of all drug courts are postadjudicatory (Drug Court Program Office, 2001). It is within the postadjudicatory grouping that a variety of specialized courts have arisen, including DUI courts, family courts, teen courts, domestic violence courts, and juvenile drug courts.

Once the defendant has been assigned to a multiphase treatment program (typically, detoxification, stabilization, and aftercare) and a reporting schedule begins, there is no waiting period. Depending on the level of need, inpatient programs may be made available, although the majority are given on an outpatient basis. Also, dependent on offender need, the frequency of status hearings may be as little as once every six weeks or as much as several times a week. Due to the nature of addiction, drug testing is also done randomly throughout the program. Missing treatments, positive drug tests, or missed status hearings are met with immediate sanctions ranging from more intensive supervision to increased community service and motivational detention for a short period. Since the courts share information and the judges monitor cases closely, failure to comply with conditions is met swiftly.

RESULTS OF ADULT DRUG COURT PROGRAMS

Although caution has been recommended in interpreting drug court results, the overall indication is that drug court programs do decrease the number of re-arrests. Several studies indicate that retention rates of drug courts over the first year are approximately 60 percent, while corresponding outpatient treatment of other offenders is nearly half that (35 percent). These results may be explained by several phenomena, one of which may be the effectiveness of the judge and court team in providing support and encouragement to

remain in the program. It may also be directly linked to the fact that treatment setbacks do not result in automatic expulsion from the program and subsequent incarceration, sanctions that are likely to occur with the outpatient, nonprogram group being used for comparison. Another possible interpretation lies in the type of offenders usually sentenced to the drug courts: first-time, nonviolent offenders who are more likely to succeed. However, only 20 percent of drug courts now limit themselves to this type of offender, indicating that this interpretation may not necessarily be true.

The General Accounting Office (GAO) reported in 1997 that 71 percent of all offenders entering drug courts since their inception have either successfully completed or are actively participating within the programs. Recidivism rates for those who have fully completed the program vary across programs but range from 2 percent to 20 percent. Compared with offenders not in drug court programs, this appears to be a significant reduction. Of those who do recidivate, 95 percent of the charges were misdemeanors or technical violations rather than serious or violent crimes. These findings have been supported by research completed by the National Center on Addiction and Substance Abuse at Columbia University across 24 drug court programs. It may be asserted with caution that the goal of reducing levels of rearrests has been achieved.

However, a common theme among these evaluations is that the findings reflect only short-term goals arising from the relatively short history of drug courts. Studies completed within a longer, three-year postgraduation period in Portland, Oregon, and Las Vegas, Nevada, suggest that recidivism rates for graduates rose to 36 percent and 34 percent, respectively (Goldkamp, 2000). Studies from Maricopa County, Arizona, found no evidence that recidivism was reduced (Vito and Tewksbury, 1998). These findings are mirrored in several programs across the country and reflect a need to evaluate the success of all drug court programs across longer periods before a definitive answer can be reached.

SPECIALIZED COURTS: JUVENILE DRUG COURTS

While adult crime has decreased over the past decade, juvenile crime has increased. In particular, federal reports show that juvenile drug-related crime increased 132 percent between 1990 and 1999, making up 13 percent of all drug abuse violations. This is twice the average rate of arrests that occurred in the 1980s at the inception of the "war on drugs" and represents 198,400 arrests of juveniles in 1999. However, this is only for arrests where a drug charge represented the most serious crime. It still remains unknown how many drug charges occurred that were in conjunction with more serious charges for other offenses and thus are not included in the total. Federal reports suggest that over half of all juveniles are under the influence of alcohol or drugs at the time of their arrest. If this is true, then of the 2,268,800 juveniles arrested in 1999, more than half were under the influence of a prohibited substance, making substance abuse the most important issue of juvenile justice.

Reaction to the increase in serious juvenile crime associated with substance abuse has been punitive. Recent judicial responses to the treatment of juveniles have manifested themselves in an equally punitive swing toward the adult court system, a distinctive turn away from the traditional philosophy that the juvenile courts should act in the role of a parent. In 1995, many juvenile courts began to examine the adult drug court model as a viable alternative to decrease the number of juvenile drug cases. As a result, juvenile courts returned to a new form of rehabilitation. Juvenile substance abuse treatment is more unique and complex than adult substance abuse treatment, and the adaptation of the drug court models to juvenile courts was met with several unique challenges (Kimbrough, 1998). The altered model must address four problems:

1. Counteracting the negative influence of peers, gangs, and family members.

2. Addressing the needs of families, especially families with substance abuse problems.

3. Complying with confidentiality requirements for juvenile proceedings while obtaining the information necessary to address the juveniles' problems and progress.

4. Motivating juvenile offenders to change, especially given the sense of invulnerability and lack of maturity (Roberts, Brophy, and Cooper, 1997).

It is important to understand the distinct differences between juvenile and adult drug experiences. Adults generally have entered the dependent stages of addiction by the time they reach the drug court, while juveniles are more likely to be experimenting (primarily with marijuana, which has been linked to polydrug use and more serious delinquency) at the time of their arrest. The coerced treatment of adults relies on their having "hit bottom" and realizing that there are alternatives to both addiction and incarceration. This is difficult in the case of juveniles because they may not have developed any dependence on the substance. Experimentation with drugs coincides, or may be exacerbated by, many aspects of conduct disorders. Rarely do juveniles "hit bottom" or see the devastation that addiction may have on their lives, thus incentives offered to adults in drug courts hold little appeal for juveniles. As a result, strategies have to be developed that further increase the level of supervision and target more specific reasons for experimental drug use, both social and psychological. Juvenile drug court system strategies have the following general characteristics compared with adult drug courts:

1. Intake assessments that are earlier and more intensive.

2. Increased focus on family dynamics and the juvenile throughout the program.

3. Closer scrutiny of information pertaining to case development.

4. Increased coordination of the drug court team to include schools and community.

5. Increased use of rewards and sanctions for both juvenile and family (Roberts et al., 1997).

The components of juvenile drug courts work toward two specific goals: preventing further experimentation and targeting the social and psychological aspects of the drug use. Individualized treatment modalities can vary greatly depending on the necessary level of care and supervision. It is not uncommon to see combinations of court and probation supervision alongside various forms of treatment and drug testing. It is critical that treatment programs be flexible enough to meet the changing needs and circumstances of individualized care. The nature of drug courts, both adult and juvenile, is acceptance of "setbacks" when dealing with substance abuse. Thus individuals who meet conditions set by the court may receive rewards such as a decreased number of status hearings, drug tests, and counseling sessions.

The judge is the central figure in the drug court because she or he is a consistent figure in the offender's life and provides the necessary mix of encouragement and coercion that keeps the individual in the treatment program (Huddleston, 1998). In the event of noncompliance, the judge evaluates and applies temporary detention or smart punishment. Increased supervision or the threat of transfer to regular court may provide the incentive to remain in the program and "try harder." In addition, treatment services "need to find ways of actively engaging youth and their families" in ways that are both respectful and collaborative (Kimbrough, 1998). This form of direct involvement has been linked to increases in success and graduation from treatment, because families generally are sources of support and motivation.

JUVENILE DRUG COURT RESEARCH

If drug courts are in their infancy, it is safe to say that juvenile drug courts are newborns. In the last five years, almost 70 juvenile drug courts have been established, and many more are in the planning stages. Legislators are recognizing that the increase in juvenile drug cases is not being serviced by traditional methods and are beginning to respond to the positive outcomes documented by research on various drug court models. The Drug Abuse Education, Prevention and Treatment Act, introduced in February 2001, provided federal funds specifically designated to develop and evaluate juvenile drug courts and treatment programs for addicted juveniles. Evaluations of participants and their successes have begun to take place, and conclusions are mixed. Reports reveal that the most prevalent drugs involved in proceedings have been alcohol and marijuana, although increases in crack cocaine, methamphetamines, and toxic inhalants have been seen. An area of concern is that age at first use has generally been between 10 and 12 years.

Research in juvenile drug use has suggested that only comprehensive community and court models will effectively break the cycle of experimentation and associated crimes. Initial reports from juvenile drug courts, which incorporate this structure, appear successful. Evaluations indicate that recidivism rates are consistently lower for drug court juveniles than comparison groups. The essential element of these results is that juveniles must successfully remain in the program, thus encouragement from court staff, family, and community is of the utmost importance.

Once the program is completed, the original problems presented by the juvenile's pretreatment environment, peers, and pressures must be dealt with for success to be achieved. Drug court results, although encouraging, should be interpreted with caution. It is essential that evaluation be completed on diverse juvenile drug courts, with a variety of offenders, over a longer period before success can be claimed.

Michelle Richter and Wesley Johnson

See also Alcohol Abuse; DARE; Drugs; Gangs, Juvenile

Bibliography

Drug Court Program Office. 2001. *Fact Sheet: Drug Court Clearinghouse and Technical Assistant Project.* Washington, DC: Department of Justice, Office of Justice Programs.

Goldkamp, J. S. 2000. *What We Know About the Impact of Drug Courts: Moving Research From "Do They Work?" to "When and How They Work."* Testimony before the Senate Judiciary Subcommittee on Youth Violence.

Huddleston, C. W. 1998. Drug courts and jail-based treatment. *Corrections Today* 60(6):98–102.

Kimbrough, R. J. 1998. Treating juvenile substance abuse: The promise of juvenile drug court. *Juvenile Justice* 5(2):11–19.

National Institute of Justice. 1995. *The Drug Court Movement.* Washington, DC: Department of Justice, Office of Justice Programs.

Office of Justice Programs. 1998. *Looking at a Decade of Drug Courts.* Washington, DC: Department of Justice, Office of Justice Programs.

Perters, R. H., and M. R. Murrin. 2000. Effectiveness of treatment-based drug courts in reducing criminal recidivism. *Criminal Justice and Behavior* 27:72–97.

Roberts, M., J. Brophy, and C. Cooper. 1997. *The Juvenile Drug Court Movement.* Washington, DC: Office of Juvenile Justice and Delinquency Prevention.

Vito, G., and R. A. Tewksbury. 1998. The impact of treatment: The Jefferson County (Kentucky) drug court program. *Federal Probation* 62(2):46–53.

COURTS, JUVENILE

 ## IV. Teen Courts

Teen courts, which are sometimes termed youth courts or peer courts, are an alternative to processing in the traditional criminal justice system for selected youthful offenders. The earliest teen court programs appear to have originated in the early 1970s. One of the more prominent early programs was developed in 1983 in Odessa, Texas. The Odessa program later became the model for teen court programs nationwide (Godwin, 1998). Since that time, teen courts have proliferated throughout the United States. According to the American Probation and Parole Association (APPA), as of 1998, teen court programs had been developed in 44 states and the District of Columbia.

UNDERPINNINGS OF TEEN COURTS

The basic premise of teen court programs is that young people who have committed misdemeanor crimes or status offenses may not be well served by the traditional justice system, which can stigmatize or otherwise harm persons who often have little history of prior criminal behavior. Many teen courts handle young offenders with no prior record in the justice system. According to a recent survey conducted by the Office of Juvenile Justice and Delinquency Prevention (OJJDP), many teen courts accepted only first-time offenders, and 48 percent only rarely accepted youth with prior arrest records. In addition, 24 percent of teen court cases involved persons under age 14, and 66 percent involved youths under age 16.

A second assumption of teen court programs is that the sanctions associated with traditional juvenile courts may not be appropriate for individuals who have committed relatively minor offenses, such as underage drinking. The APPA states that teen courts stress accountability, competency development, youth empowerment, and involvement and attempt to use positive peer influence to reduce problem behavior. Consequently, most teen court programs have adopted less traditional sentencing alternatives, including community service; apology to the victim; requiring that an offender write an essay on a topic related to his or her offense, such as the effects of drug use on school performance; teen court jury duty; counseling or attendance at drug/alcohol abuse classes; monetary restitution; attendance at victim awareness classes; and attendance at driving/traffic classes.

Teen court programs may also serve an important educational role in the community by providing youthful volunteers with an opportunity to participate in important governmental processes. In some teen court programs, youths become involved directly in the trial and adjudication of improper or illegal behavior

by their peers. In most programs, however, youths participate at the sentencing stage of the proceedings, often when the offender has admitted committing a violation. Teen court volunteers then have the responsibility to determine and assign appropriate sentences.

In addition, teen court programs may help to reduce caseload congestion in the formal juvenile justice system. This may permit traditional juvenile courts to focus their resources on cases involving more serious offenses, such as crimes of violence. According to the Urban Institute's survey of youth courts and teen courts, the types of offenses accepted by most courts include those shown in Table 1.

Teen court programs have used a variety of different organizational models. In some states, teen court programs are administered by the juvenile courts or by probation departments. In others, law enforcement agencies may supervise teen courts, or nonprofit organizations, such as the YMCA, and school departments administer these programs (Godwin, 1998). The organizational model to be used in a particular place is determined by a number of factors, including state statutes, administrative law, and political forces within the community.

Different types of courtroom approaches are used in various teen court programs as well. A study by the National Youth Court Center (NYCC) has identified four central types of courtroom organization: the adult judge model; the youth judge model; the peer jury approach; and the youth tribunal approach. Approximately 47 percent of teen courts use the adult judge model, which often involves youth attorneys and a youth jury that recommends sentencing dispositions. The youth judge model has been adopted by approximately 9 percent of U.S. teen courts. Youth attorneys present the case, and a youth jury recommends sentencing dispositions. The peer jury model is used in approximately 12 percent of teen court jurisdictions. An adult judge hears the case and, although youth attorneys do not participate, a youth jury may question the defendant and recommend sentencing dispositions. The youth tribunal model is used in approximately 10 percent of teen court jurisdictions. Multiple youth judges and youth attorneys participate in the case, but no youth jury is involved.

The operating budgets of teen court programs vary greatly. Some programs are well funded, while others are barely able to operate. According to the APPA's 1994 survey, annual operating budgets averaged $32,668. Typical teen court program expenses

Table 1   Offenses Accepted by Teen Court Programs

Offense	Percentage of Programs Handling the Offense
Theft (including shoplifting)	93
Minor assault	66
Disorderly conduct	62
Alcohol possession or use	60
Vandalism	59
Marijuana possession or use	52
School disciplinary problems	33
Traffic	29
Truancy	22
Weapon possession or use	11

included office space, personnel expenses, and office supplies. Godwin (1998) reported that potential funding sources for teen court programs include the federal government, state governments, city or county governments, school districts, private grants, individual donations, service fees, and profits from special events. Possible federal funding sources that may be used to develop or support teen court programs include the National Highway Traffic Safety Administration (NHTSA), the OJJDP, the Department of Health and Human Services, and the Department of Education.

Several major problems faced by teen and youth courts include difficulties associated with funding uncertainty, keeping teen volunteers, an insufficient number of referrals, delays between the offense and the referral, and coordinating the proceedings with other justice system agencies. In addition, some respondents to the Urban Institute's survey reported additional problems with an insufficient number of adult volunteers, a lack of judicial support, problems with confidentiality issues, legal liability issues, and too many case referrals.

LEGAL ISSUES AND DUE PROCESS IN TEEN COURT PROCEEDINGS

One of the major objectives of most teen court programs is to make justice system procedures more informal and less "legalistic" for appropriate youthful offenders; however, justice system policymakers must continue to remain aware of several important legal issues surrounding teen court programs. The first issue

to be considered is whether a teen court can even exist and how much authority it can exercise under a state's law, which may identify the types of offenses and the characteristics of offenders who are eligible to participate in teen court programs. For example, a Texas statute (Texas Juvenile Justice Code, Section 54.032) provides that a juvenile court can waive formal proceedings and send a youthful offender to teen court if he or she has committed a misdemeanor offense or violated a municipal penal ordinance that is punishable by a fine only. Thus teen courts in Texas would have no authority to consider other types of cases, such as felonious assault by a youthful offender.

A second legal issue in the development of teen court programs is procedural due process: What procedures should a teen court utilize to adjudicate guilt or innocence or determine a sentence? One critical flaw in the juvenile court systems of the 1970s and 1980s was that the procedural safeguards required in adult criminal trials were de-emphasized—juvenile courts were supposed to adopt a less punitive approach for youthful offenders. It soon became clear, however, that the sentences being assigned in many of these courts were exceedingly harsh, yet many juvenile offenders had not been afforded even minimal due process protections, such as the right to counsel or to confront and cross-examine their accusers.

One factor that limits the role of due process protections in teen courts is that participation in these programs is voluntary—youthful offenders and their parents must normally agree to submit the case to a teen court. If they do not agree, the case proceeds within the formal juvenile justice system. Therefore, the full scope of due process rights provided in adult criminal proceedings may not apply to teen court hearings. It remains important, however, for teen court programs to provide for basic due process rights by developing guidelines to ensure procedural consistency. Such guidelines may be contained in teen court bylaws or developed in a more formal written constitution, which may include the right to a jury trial, the right to complete confidentiality of the proceedings, and the right to be represented by another person.

RESEARCH ON THE EFFECTIVENESS OF TEEN AND YOUTH COURT PROGRAMS

Do teen courts work? According to the OJJDP, the research on teen and youth courts is largely inconclusive at present. The most comprehensive review of teen court programs, the Evaluation of Teen Courts Project, was released in 2001. This project conducted a review of teen court evaluation studies completed in the past 20 years, and included programs from California, Florida, Kentucky, Maryland, New York, North Carolina, and Texas. The studies reviewed produced a variety of conclusions about the effect of teen courts on youthful offender recidivism. Some found low rates, ranging from 3 percent to 8 percent. Others, however, discovered rates that were much higher, sometimes ranging from 20 percent to 30 percent. (For an excellent summary of these studies, see Butts and Buck, 2000, Table 5). The project has concluded that most of the studies reviewed are flawed due to a variety of methodological problems, and therefore they provide no information about teen courts' effect on recidivism. For example, one study failed to clearly define what was meant by *recidivism* and did not account for a range of unexplored possible differences between the treatment group and the control group. In spite of the methodological difficulties, however, the project's review of various studies identifies other possible benefits of teen court programs, including youth participant satisfaction with teen courts, better perceptions of the justice system, better participant attitudes toward authority, and improved knowledge of the legal system. In any event, it is clear that additional research is needed to answer important questions about the effectiveness of these programs to assist justice system policymakers who will make key decisions about the future of teen court programs in this country.

CONCLUSION

Teen and youth court programs have expanded rapidly in recent years and appear to have the potential to make a significant contribution to the U.S. juvenile justice system. The basic premise of teen courts, that nonserious youthful offenders may be better served by a less formal alternative t⌐ ⸣ traditional justice system, is a sound one. In add̖ ⸲, teen courts' emphasis on youth involvement and peer influence to reduce problem behavior is consistent with contemporary criminological theory, particularly social control theory.

One of the major problems facing justice system policymakers regarding teen courts is the lack of sound empirical research on whether teen courts deter or rehabilitate youthful offenders. Despite significant challenges to conducting this research, attempts are

being made to provide scientifically reliable answers to this question. Moreover, the additional benefits of teen court programs, including reducing caseload congestion in the formal juvenile justice system and improving youth participant satisfaction, are compelling reasons for justice system policymakers to consider developing these important programs.

Thomas J. Hickey

See also Diversion Programs

Bibliography

Butts, J. A., and J. Buck. 2000. *Juvenile Justice Bulletin: Teen Courts—A Focus on Research*. October. Washington, DC: Office of Juvenile Justice and Delinquency Prevention.

Godwin, T. M. 1998. *Peer Justice and Youth Empowerment: An Implementation Guide for Teen Court Programs*. Washington, DC: American Probation and Parole Association.

Harrison, P., J. R. Maupin, and G. L. Mays. 2001. Teen court: An examination of processes and outcomes. *Crime and Delinquency* 47:243–264.

Hissong, R. 1991. Teen court—Is it an effective alternative to traditional sanctions? *Journal for Juvenile Justice and Detention Services* 6(2):14–23.

Minor, K. I., J. B. Wells, I. R. Soderstrom, R. Bingham, and D. Williamson. 1999. Sentence completion and recidivism among juveniles referred to teen courts. *Crime and Delinquency* 45:467–480.

Reichel, P., and C. Seyfrit. 1984. A peer jury in juvenile court. *Crime and Delinquency* 30:423–438.

Rothstein, R. 1987. Teen court: A way to combat teenage crime and chemical abuse. *Juvenile and Family Court Journal* 38:1–4.

Seyfret, C., P. Reichel, and B. Stutts. 1987. Peer juries as a juvenile justice diversion technique. *Youth and Society* 18:302–316.

CULTURALLY SPECIFIC PROGRAMMING

A number of researchers have reported positive relationships between cultural identity and other variables such as nonfighting attitudes, cumulative grade point averages, self-esteem, and social perspective taking ability. Studies related to racial and ethnic identity over the past 30 years, which in many cases have yielded beneficial results, have resulted in an array of culturally specific programming efforts.

The largest ethnic minority groups typically targeted for culturally specific programming in the United States are African Americans, Asian Americans, Hispanic Americans, and Native Americans. It must be recognized, however, that differences exist within groups. For instance, interventions for Hispanics would have a similar cultural foundation; Cubans, Puerto Ricans, and Mexicans are all categorized as Hispanics, but there are differences in cultural interpretations that exist and should be addressed. The same can be said for Asian Americans, comprising Japanese Americans, Chinese Americans, and Vietnamese Americans, among similar cultural groups.

Prevention programming for adolescents exists on three levels. Primary prevention involves intervention among adolescents exhibiting no noticeable deviant behavior. Secondary prevention is intervention among adolescents who have shown minimal amounts of aberrant functioning. Tertiary prevention is treatment intended to change rampant abnormal conduct of adolescents. Culturally specific programming tends to exist on the primary level.

One group of researchers has taken seriously the efforts to place theory into practice regarding cultural identity and its role in the lives of ethnic minority juveniles and recommends that culturally specific programming should take into consideration a variety of factors. For instance, a distinction must be made between programs that are culturally sensitive and those that are culturally specific. A culturally sensitive program may include efforts to make sure participants and service providers are members of the same racial group, but this is not always an optimal situation (Soriano, 1993). The service providers in that instance may or may not recognize the importance of racial/ethnic identity. A culturally specific program connects the significance of racial/ethnic identity to behaviors of children and adolescents.

It is also imperative to acknowledge that service providers can be culturally competent enough to draw this connection, whether or not they are members of the participant's racial group. For instance, mentors might be of the same racial group as their mentees but may not be very effective in that role if they do not express their heritage culturally or if they esteem other cultures over their own. Mentees in that situation would be better off with someone who is culturally competent. The culturally competent service provider should be able to go beyond cultural sensitivity when working with juveniles.

EXAMPLES OF CULTURAL SPECIFICITY

There are numerous examples of cultural specificity, varying from one ethnic minority group to another. For African American juveniles, emphasis of the *Nguzo Saba,* or the Seven Principles, is relevant to behavioral indicators. The principles are *Umoja* (unity), *Kujichagulia* (self-determination), *Ujima* (collective work and responsibility), *Ujamaa* (cooperative economics), *Nia* (purpose), *Kuumba* (creativity), and *Imani* (faith). A couple of studies reported that endorsement of these values predicted intolerant drug attitudes among African American children.

An example of cultural specificity for Hispanic Americans is a focus on *curanderismo,* which does not separate the mind from the body and sees the service provider as a healer on spiritual and psychological levels as well. This notion is particular to Mexican Americans, although some forms are evident in other Hispanic cultures. Prayer and ritual are usual in ensuring harmony among individuals, family, and community. In a number of cases, this practice has led to healthy psychological functioning and a decline in deviant behaviors among Hispanic juveniles.

In Native American culture, the sweat lodge ceremony may be essential and consists of prayer for purification. In essence, it serves to balance one's life. A talking circle, another culturally specific technique, is similar to group therapy except a sacred object is circulated, participants are encouraged to speak freely, sweet grass is burned, and prayer concludes the session (Gibbs and Huang, 1989). These techniques can be used with Native American children and adolescents to reconnect them to their culture.

Culturally specific programming for Asian American juveniles should consider Confucian ethics. Confucian philosophy proposes that people have roles to fill for the sake of order in the universe. Harmonious family relationships contribute to this order; therefore, interventions for children and adolescents may stress their positions within the family, whether nuclear or extended (Gibbs and Huang, 1989). It could be that positive changes in behavior may occur when juveniles, particularly Chinese Americans, are reminded of their parts.

SUBSTANCE USE PREVENTION

Substance use prevention is usually implemented as a program among children and adolescents. A small but significant quantity of culturally specific programs targeting African American juveniles involve this form of prevention. These programs operate on the past cultural research findings showing that as a youth's identity strengthens, her or his attitudes toward drugs become more negative. For example, the Africentric component of the Super Stars (Substance Abuse Prevention Education Resource/Self-Esteem Through Arts and Recreation Sessions) program focused on cultural identity and pride. It targeted 6- to 11-year-old youth who reported positive changes in their racial/ethnic identity and drug attitudes after completing the intervention (Emshoff, Avery, Raduka, and Anderson, 1996). Project Smart, also a substance use prevention program, included culturally specific programming, and the SETCLAE (Self-Esteem Through Culture Leads to Academic Excellence) curriculum, developed by Dr. Jawanza Kunjufu, and was geared toward African American sixth graders.

Some culturally specific programs have been deemed exemplary by the Ohio Department of Alcohol and Drug Addiction Services. The Youngstown Urban Minority Alcoholism and Drug Abuse Outreach Program targets prevention and treatment among both African American and Hispanic adolescents (as well as adults). This program was born out of a statewide initiative in 1980 sponsored by State Representative William Mallory of Cincinnati, Ohio, on the recommendation of Jacqueline Butler, a service provider working on the front lines of the "war on drugs." Programs similar to the Youngstown program are located in Akron, Cincinnati, Cleveland, Columbus, Dayton, and Toledo. Another program considered exemplary in 1996 was Project Impact, which focuses on truancy prevention, among other variables.

Some substance use prevention programs have targeted Native American youth. For instance, *La-quee-biel* (to prevent) was intended for Native American juveniles and emphasized, beyond cultural specificity, bicultural competence. Bicultural competence involves the ability to negotiate when to act in culturally acceptable ways. For instance, in some cases, one has to act European culturally as a means to an end. In other settings, expressing one's cultural heritage is acceptable. It was reported that six months after treatment, compared with the control group, participants in this program used alcohol, inhalants, and marijuana at lower rates (Baca and Koss-Chioino, 1997). Another described a tobacco prevention program for 10- to 14-year-old Native American youth. This program used a Seneca Nation legend to deliver their services. They were effective in a number of outcome variables related to tobacco use and general dietary habits.

ENHANCEMENT OF PROSOCIAL BEHAVIORS

A few interventions target Hispanic juveniles. Cuento Therapy is a form of play therapy for Hispanic children that decreases trait anxiety in children (Baca and Koss-Chioino, 1997). Another program had a high retention rate among the Mexican American adolescents participating, probably due to its cultural specificity. Progress was reported among the adolescents in school-related issues and family relationships; additionally, psychopathological symptoms decreased (Baca and Koss-Chionio, 1997).

A couple of culturally specific programs affected self-esteem for African American juveniles. One, using a rite of passage, was geared toward African American males ranging in age from 12 to 21 who were in foster care. They reported an increase in self-esteem, responsibility, and respect for females, among other variables. In another program, African American third and fourth graders as well as fifth through eighth graders reported a change in their problem-solving skills as a result of participating in Project Self. It also increased self-esteem and self-efficacy of the participants. The students were able to consider consequences for themselves, their families, and their communities because of knowledge about themselves and being able to recognize their contributions to humankind.

A Journey Toward Womanhood was a pregnancy prevention program designated for African American females ranging in age from 14 to 19. The average age of participants in this program was 16, and they were exposed to an Africentric curriculum focusing on cultural pride and knowledge of self. Additionally, these adolescents could take advantage of booster sessions after completion of the program in the form of monthly support groups. The control group had three times as many pregnancies as those participating in this design (Dixon and Schoonmaker, 2000).

The I Have a Future program is directed at African American youth aged 10 and older in Nashville, Tennessee. The service providers endorsed the Seven Principles (*Nguzo Saba*) and connected them to life skills. They also tackled the issues of alcohol, tobacco, and other drug abuse; violence and sexuality; and other behaviors exhibited by the juveniles. One part of the program, lasting eight weeks, was planned for girls through Charm (Choosing How to Adorn and Refine Myself) and boys through Mature (Males Adorning, Thinking, and Using Refined Energies). High school graduation rates increased and pregnancy decreased as a result of the participation of children and adolescents (Burt, Resnick, and Novick, 1998).

COMPARISONS AMONG INTERVENTIONS

There have been a couple of instances in which differences between interventions have been assessed. In one case, a culturally focused and life-skills (generic) intervention both caused participants to have negative attitudes toward drugs. A two-year follow-up revealed that those exposed to culturally specific programming were less likely to drink alcohol than were those in life-skills training. Other researchers reported social skills training geared toward African American early adolescents, one of which was Africentric and the other generically culturally specific. There was no difference noted between the two; for this sample, both interventions affected assertiveness and self-control favorably, while trait anger was reduced.

CONCLUSION

Study after study shows that culturally specific programming may be better for ethnic minority juveniles. Although culturally specific programming for Asian American children and adolescents seems to be limited, most of the available research is promising in its proposal form. Juveniles who may need the most help are being excluded, possibly due to an emphasis on generic prevention measures. It is apparent that one size does not fit all. It seems that it is the responsibility of culturally competent service providers to ensure that no child is disregarded.

The U.S. population will be 50 percent ethnic minority by 2050. It's difficult to deny the impact of culture in the lives of the juveniles. There are professional psychological organizations that encourage the use of culturally specific programming when working with ethnic minority children and adolescents. It is recommended that the Association of Black Psychologists (http://www.abpsi.org), the National Alliance for Hispanic Health (http://www.hispanic-health.org), the Society of Indian Psychologists (SIP), and/or the Asian American Psychological Association (AAPA) be contacted when considering future programming (the SIP and AAPA are accessible through the Office of Ethnic Minority Affairs of the American Psychological Association [http://www.apa.org/pi/oema/homepage.html]).

Marilyn D. Lovett

Bibliography

Baca, L., and J. Koss-Chioino. 1997. Development of a culturally responsive group counseling model for Mexican American adolescents. *Journal of Multicultural Counseling and Development* 25(2):130–141.

Burt, M., G. Resnick, and E. Novick. 1998. *Building Supportive Communities for At-Risk Adolescents: It Takes More than Services*. Washington, DC: American Psychologecal Association.

Dixon, A., and C. Schoonmaker. 2000. A journey toward womanhood: Effects of an Afrocentric approach to pregnancy prevention among African American adolescent females. *Adolescence* 35:425–430.

Emshoff, J., E. Avery, G. Raduka, and D. Anderson. 1996. Findings from SUPERSTARS: A health promotion program for families to enhance multiple protective factors. *Journal of Adolescent Research* 11:68–96.

Gibbs, J. T., and L. Huang. 1989. *Children of Color: Psychological Interventions With Minority Youth*. San Francisco: Jossey-Bass.

Martinez, K., and D. Valdez. 1992. Cultural considerations in play therapy with Hispanic children. Pp. 85–102 in L. Vargas and J. Koss-Chioino (eds.), *Working With Culture: Psychotherapeutic Interventions With Ethnic Minority Children and Adolescents*. San Francisco: Jossey-Bass.

Soriano, F. 1993. Cultural sensitivity and gang intervention. Pp. 441–461 in A. Goldstein and C. R. Huff (eds.), *The Gang Intervention Handbook*. Champaign, IL: Research Press.

 CURFEW

Curfews, or restrictions on being away from home during certain hours, have been used throughout history for many different reasons. The word itself is believed to come from the French word *couvrefeu*, meaning "cover-fire," which referred to the feudal custom of ringing a bell to signify that everyone should extinguish their home fires and go to sleep. As far back as 1068 and for almost 40 years, William the Conqueror established a strict curfew that would prohibit townspeople from gathering in the dark of night and possibly planning an uprising.

In the United States, curfews were used in the pre–Civil War period to ensure that slaves were off the streets by a certain time in the evening. Throughout the 1900s, curfews were imposed to discourage vagrancy, temper race riots, and control the movements of Japanese Americans during the Second World War. The temporary use of curfews, usually in times when the government has claimed an emergency justification related to security and safety, have been upheld by the courts. The use of curfews to restrict movement and activities of juveniles, however, has been more controversial. Such curfews have been more prone to periods of frequent use and then disuse as officials seek alternative measures to reduce juvenile delinquency.

During the early 1900s, authorities commonly used curfews. They were particularly frequent in urban areas, where it was believed that immigrant parents were not properly controlling and supervising their children. President Harrison (1890) spoke glowingly of the curfew as a way to protect youth from the sin and vice found on the streets. While the imposition of juvenile curfews waned during the civil rights era, recent concerns about juvenile crime and victimization have once again triggered a resurgence in the popularity of curfews. Today communities desperate to reduce delinquency, loitering, drug and alcohol abuse, and gang activity have passed curfew laws, many for the first time.

CURFEW LAWS TODAY

The curfew laws active today may be either revived statutes that had been laying dormant "on the books" or those newly formulated to address current social problems. For some communities, curfew laws were just one part of a larger crime prevention approach passed with other crime-fighting components, including more police officers, better equipment, gang interdiction strategies, and tougher criminal sanctions. In these jurisdictions it may be difficult, if not impossible, to tell if the curfew is working because other, concurrent efforts are in effect.

Today two types of curfews can be differentiated. First, for offenders on probation or parole, a curfew may be part of the agreement for release into the community. Thus the supervision contract may specify that the offender must be home each night by a designated hour. However, the most common use of curfews are general laws passed by some communities that require all youths to be off the streets and either

at home or school during certain specified times with limited exceptions. The exceptions can include emergencies; running necessary errands for a parent; attending religious functions, work, or a parent-approved, supervised activity; or when out with a parent or responsible adult.

Curfew enforcement periods may be during the day or night. Traditionally, night curfews start between 10:00 p.m. and midnight and end between 4:00 and 6:00 a.m., although weekends, holidays, and the summer months may offer extended free time. Most curfews target youth up to 15 to 17 years of age and, while some are citywide, others target only hot spots or high-profile areas.

Today almost 75 percent of the nation's 200 largest cities and approximately the same percentage of smaller cities have some type of curfew ordinance in effect. In 1985, about 63,000 youth had been arrested for curfew violations, and by 1995 that annual figure was more than 125,000 (Ruefle and Reynolds, 1995). Most curfews are enacted by city councils and vary from jurisdiction to jurisdiction. In addition, some states have passed legislation imposing de facto curfews by restricting anyone under a certain age from driving a motor vehicle after a certain hour.

PURPOSE

According to curfew advocates, these restrictions are aimed at reducing juvenile crime and victimization as well as providing parents and schools with an important tool for supervising and controlling young people. Many view youth as having a separate legal status without the same freedoms as adults. A second justification is that juveniles need more restrictions and limitations on their behavior to ensure their, and the general public's, health and safety. To accommodate businesses employing young people, many statutes have been specifically worded to grant working youths exemption from curfews, at least until normal closing hours. Daytime curfews are often used to ensure school attendance and allow city and school police to stop and question any youth outside school during school hours. In California, curfews have been aggressively enforced in gang areas using teams made up of various law enforcement agencies, including police, probation officers, gang units, narcotics units, sheriff's officers, and parole agents.

While the motivation for most curfew laws is crime prevention, jurisdictions vary in the way they handle violators. In some places, youth may simply be taken home and reported to their parents, while other jurisdictions may cite or arrest and sanction violators, usually through fines and community service. In a few cities, the parents may be held liable for their child's violation, particularly after multiple offenses. Regarding parental sanctions, concerns are raised about the burden of fines and court costs on already economically disadvantaged families.

CRITICISMS OF CURFEW LAWS

Critics of curfew laws argue that such ordinances are overly broad and punish many law-abiding teens because of the delinquent conduct of a relatively smaller group. While some parents do not properly supervise their children, most do. Critics believe that these laws infringe on the individual's right to assemble and, in some cases, to work. Critics also point out that youth who are arrested for curfew violations are drawn into the criminal justice system where they may be labeled and perhaps presented with more criminal opportunities than if they had simply been left alone in the first place. These laws then allow for "net widening" as more youth become subject to arrest and adjudication and possibly "official" records of delinquency. Some also argue that the laws allow for too much discretion in enforcement and that minority youth may be more often detained and more severely dealt with under these laws than nonminority youth.

ARGUMENTS IN FAVOR OF CURFEW LAWS

Those in favor of curfew laws generally argue that they meet their intended goals and purposes and provide noticeable benefits outweighing the possible harms. Public opinion surveys have indicated widespread support of such measures among both blacks and whites, and even among youth themselves. With many parents working, the curfew gives authorities the power to step in and ensure that youth are not in high-risk areas at high-risk times. However, although many jurisdictions have passed curfew laws, unless they are regularly and aggressively enforced, these areas may not obtain any benefit from having them. Some jurisdictions have noted decreases in property crimes, alcohol-related accidents, and gang-related shootings as a result of the curfews. Still, these claims are somewhat dubious given the many problems inherent in conducting research capable of determining whether curfews are effective.

RESEARCH ON THE EFFECTIVENESS OF CURFEWS

To date there have been few empirical research studies done on the effectiveness of curfews. This means that most of the conclusions made about curfews have been based on anecdotal evidence, people's personal perceptions that they either are or are not working. Often law enforcement officials, city authorities, or lawmakers simply believe that curfews are reducing juvenile crime and victimization, so no rigorous evaluation is ever done. Although officials may be able to point to lower numbers of certain crimes since the enactment of curfews, they are not able to say for sure that crime is not simply moving over to other geographic areas or into other periods or that the curfew is the reason for the decline in crime. In most cases, other plausible explanations, such as an improved economy, other crime prevention efforts, or more recreational opportunities, are equally likely.

McDowall and Loftin (2000) studied curfew laws in a dozen cities and counties and found little evidence that the laws were producing any significant benefit. While one study of Dallas curfew laws did find some support for the success of curfew/antigang enforcement in some aggressively patrolled areas, another study of Dallas and two other Texas cities did not find the same consistent results. Also, in a study of various California counties, Males and Macallair (1999) were unable to substantiate that changes in curfew enforcement were responsible for any reduction in rates of youth crime. In some studies, crime decreased during the curfew hours but increased in other periods of the day. As government data indicate, only 20 percent of violent juvenile crimes take place during the hours that curfews are usually imposed.

CONSTITUTIONALITY

Policymakers wanting to construct a legally defensible curfew law must be careful not only with the scope of proposed restrictions but exceptions to them as well. Legal challenges to the use of curfews include the argument that many are written in an overly broad and vague language and thus lack clear notice of what types of people and activities are restricted and which are exempt. For example, the courts have found ordinances that prohibit minors from "loitering, wandering, strolling, or driving aimlessly" to be unconstitutionally vague because it is hard to obtain agreement on what these terms mean and what specific conduct would be targeted.

Other challenges have stated that the laws deny some people (youth in particular) equal protection under the law and that the statutes violate both substantive and procedural due process rights. Equal protection claims argue that youth are treated in ways in which it would be unconstitutional to treat adults. Under the due process clauses of the Fifth and Fourteenth Amendments, cases have argued that curfew restrictions interfere with the right to parental autonomy. This means that parents should be able to raise their children without undue (having done nothing to warrant specific intervention) interference from the government. It has also been argued that curfew laws invade unnecessarily into the right of privacy and the right to travel.

As with the research on curfews' effectiveness, the results of legal decisions have also been conflicting. In many cases, when an ordinance has been found unconstitutional, authorities simply rewrite the contents along the lines of ordinances that have been upheld by the courts and then institute the revised versions. *City of Maquoketa v. Russell* (484 N.W.2d 179, 1992) is an example of a curfew law that the Iowa Supreme Court found to be unconstitutional, in part because it was overly vague, even though it was modeled on the outcome of a case where the same court upheld a similar curfew ordinance in *City of Panora v. Simmons* (445 N.W.2d 363, 1989). In another controversial case, parents in Dallas challenged the city's curfew law under the equal protection clause. Although the District Court agreed with the plaintiffs in *Qutb v. Strauss* (11 F.3d 488, Fifth Circuit, 1993) and struck down the law, the Fifth Circuit Court hearing the appeal found that the ordinance met current constitutional standards in conjunction with the state's compelling interest in reducing juvenile crime and victimization. During this legal controversy, Dallas officials rewrote suspect elements of the provision, and their curfew language has since been used by others crafting their own curfew laws.

Marilyn D. McShane

See also California Street Terrorism Enforcement and Prevention Act; Gangs, Juvenile—Intervention and Prevention; Parental Responsibility Laws; Police Responses to Delinquency; Prevention Strategies; Truancy

Bibliography

Chudy, P. J. 2000. Doctrinal reconstruction: Reconciling conflicting standards in adjudicating juvenile curfew challenges. *Cornell Law Review* 85:518–586.

Hemmens, C., and K. Bennett. 1999. Juvenile curfews and the courts: Judicial response to a not-so-new crime control strategy. *Crime and Delinquency* 451:99–122.

Lester, B. J. 1996. Is it too late for juvenile curfews? *Qutb* logic and the constitution. *Hofstra Law Review* 25:665–699.

Males, M. A., and D. Macallair. 1999. An analysis of curfew enforcement and juvenile crime in California. *Western Criminology Review* 1(2). Available at http://wcr.sonoma.edu/v1n2/males.html.

McDowall, D., and C. Loftin. 2000. The impact of youth curfew laws on juvenile crime rates. *Crime and Delinquency* 46:76–92.

Norton, D. 2000. Why criminalize children? Looking beyond the express policies driving juvenile curfew legislation. *NYU Journal of Legislation and Public Policy* 4:175–205.

Ruefle, W., and K. Reynolds. 1995. Curfews and delinquency in major American cities. *Crime and Delinquency* 41:347–363.

 CYCLE OF VIOLENCE

In juvenile justice literature, *cycle of violence* is a term used to describe the intergenerational transmission of violent behavior. This is not to be mistaken with the term used in domestic violence literature that refers to the relational process and behavior in an abusive relationship.

Researchers, such as Murray Straus (1991, 1994) and Kathy Spatz-Widom (1989), have studied and written about the possible correlation between childhood abuse and juvenile and adult crime. They have noted that offenders who were abused and neglected as children commit more offenses, begin criminal activity at an earlier age, and have a higher likelihood of being repeat offenders compared with offenders who were not abused or neglected as children. People who were abused or neglected as children are also more likely to commit violent crimes and to abuse their spouses and children. However, some research has also shown that these differences may be marginal at best. Other studies have found a strong correlation between childhood abuse and later family violence.

THEORETICAL MODELS

The theory that drives the cycle of violence postulates that juvenile and adult violence is a behavior that is learned in childhood. Thus the theoretical underpinnings of the cycle of violence literature include other theories such as attachment theory, social learning theory, and ecological theory.

Attachment Theory

Attachment theory is based on the assumption that human attachment and relationships are an essential aspect of behavior development. Insecure attachments, or childhood relationships that are unstable, may lead to a breakdown in internal information processing methods. In other words, children who have insecure parental relationships, which are often characterized by abuse, may fail to develop a method to interpret social cues. This failure may further lead a child to respond to ambiguous situations with aggression (Dodge, Bates, and Pettit, 1990). Furthermore, attachment theory relates the development of conscience to early maternal bonding. Poor bonds in early childhood are considered the source of the antisocial personality. Another factor related to the maternal bond's influence on the cycle of violence is domestic violence. Some researchers believe that when a mother is being battered, her ability to be sensitive to the delicate developmental needs of her child are grossly impaired, and attachment becomes difficult.

Social Learning Theory

The basic premise of social learning theory is that "what you see, you learn, and what you learn, you are." In other words, abused children may learn through experience with their parents that violence is a natural and acceptable way to respond to stress and conflict. This type of learning is achieved through modeling. Social learning theory is much more complex than this, however, and also assumes that behavior is reinforced through positive and negative consequences and rewards. Violence is either rewarded or punished, which further leads to either an increase or decrease in the behavior. Naturally, because violence is not socially acceptable, we would assume it would either be punished or not rewarded and would thus decrease. However, differential reinforcement theory, an offshoot of social learning theory, hypothesizes that the social reinforcement of rewards and punishments become secondary to internal reinforcers. Therefore, the product of violence itself may be the reinforcer.

Ecological Theories

Ecological theories all have in common the environmental influences that perpetuate violence. Situations such as poverty, a lack of resources, and lower education are considered to be factors contributing to violence. It is difficult, however, to disentangle ecological theories from social learning theories, as ecological conditions almost always reflect a social learning environment. Children who grow up in poverty may be more likely to live in neighborhoods where violence is the norm. In a situation such as this, it may be that violence is learned in the environment and not a direct cause of ecological factors. We would then consider ecological factors to be correlated with violence but not necessarily the cause of violence. However, the research on ecological correlations is inconclusive. Violence seems to occur across all groups, regardless of income, race, and education.

The basic premise of all these theories is that children who are abused grow up to be violent. The underlying assumption of most theoretical explanations for the cycle of violence is that violence is learned or a product of the environment. If violence is learned, then the implication is that it is not something natural or within our inherent nature. Therefore, violence is not genetic. If violence is indeed learned in an intergenerational cycle, the implication is that humans are basically good and only taught to behave badly. But there are competing theoretical models without the assumption that we are born good, and these may also explain the seeming correlation between childhood abuse and later violent crime.

Biology/Genetic Theories

Genetic theories support the idea that violence is not just a learned response but may be biologically related. One such idea is that the tendency toward violence is actually inherited in a gene, which could be a valid explanation for the cycle of violence phenomenon. This genetic tendency toward violence could be attributed to a biochemical imbalance that predisposes one toward violent behavior and/or low impulse control. Another related genetic factor may be mental illness. Recent research has consistently shown that many of the major mental illnesses have a genetic component. The degree to which mental illnesses are correlated with violent behavior is still unknown. Neuropsychiatry is still in its infancy but has made vast strides in recognizing brain abnormalities in violent offenders. Some hypothesize that these apparent abnormalities in violent offenders are attributed to genetics, while others hypothesize that the environment in early fetal and infant development plays a crucial role in brain formation.

CONCLUSION

Regardless of the theoretical model used, it is evident that there is at least a correlation between childhood physical abuse and later family violence. While the overwhelming majority (75 percent) of abused children do not grow up to be abusive, of those adults who are abusive, most were abused as children (Straus, 1991, 1994). There also appears to be a marginal correlation between childhood abuse and later criminality. Forty-nine percent of abused children are later arrested as juveniles or adults for nontraffic offenses, whereas only 38 percent of individuals not abused as children are arrested for nontraffic offenses (Maxfield and Spatz-Widom, 1996). This evidence indeed seems to point toward a cycle of violence and could shape the future for rehabilitation of juvenile and adult offenders. It could also assist in early prediction and prevention programs that target those who may be most at risk for abuse.

Aimee Cassiday-Shaw

See also Child Abuse; Child Sexual Abuse; Theories of Delinquency

Bibliography

Dodge, K., J. Bates, and G. Pettit. 1990. Mechanisms in the cycle of violence. *Science* 250(4988):1678–1684.

Maxfield, M., and K. Spatz-Widom. 1996. The cycle of violence: Revisited 6 years later. *Archives of Pediatric and Adolescent Medicine* 150(4):390.

Spatz-Widom, K. 1989. The cycle of violence. *Science* 244(4901):160–167.

Straus, M. 1991. Discipline and deviance: Physical punishment of children and violence and other crime in adulthood. *Social Problems* 38:101–123.

Straus, M. 1994. Beating the devil out of them: Corporal punishment in American families. Pp. 99–121 in M. Straus, *Violence and Crime*. New York: Lexington.

DARE (DRUG ABUSE RESISTANCE EDUCATION)

I. The National Program

Drug Abuse Resistance Education (DARE) is a collection of school-based drug and violence prevention programs for students ranging from kindergarten to 12th grade. Started in 1983 in Los Angeles, California, DARE is a collaborative prevention initiative between local law enforcement and public schools. Sworn law enforcement officers from state, county, and local jurisdictions receive 80 hours of formal training before administering the DARE curriculum. These uniformed instructors deliver the program in a highly structured and standardized manner in urban, suburban, and rural school settings. Students typically receive one 45-minute DARE lesson per week, and a certified teacher is expected to be present in the classroom.

DARE is, by far, the largest and most popular drug prevention program in the United States, currently being taught in approximately three fourths of all school districts nationwide. DARE has been disseminated worldwide and is being used in 54 countries. The program is viewed as highly effective by parents, school administrators, and participating police personnel.

DARE offers several curriculum components to cover the full range of 13 grade levels: early elementary (Grades K through 4), elementary "core" curriculum (Grades 5 and 6), middle school (Grades 7 and 8), and high school (Grades 9 through 12). The number of lessons varies: The K–4 component includes one to five classroom visits by a DARE officer, the core component includes 17 lessons, and the middle school and high school components offer 10 lessons each. In practice, DARE has been unevenly adopted across grade levels, thus many schools do not include all components. Most participating schools offer only the core curriculum to fifth and/or sixth graders. Schools have been reluctant to adopt DARE at other grade levels, although DARE officials are currently revising and repackaging the middle school program in hopes of capturing a larger share of that market.

Given that only the core elementary school curriculum has been widely implemented and widely studied by researchers, discussion of DARE in this entry is limited primarily to this component.

THEORETICAL FOUNDATION

DARE is grounded in the theory and research on psychosocial approaches to influencing adolescent prevention behaviors. Three main approaches have been incorporated in the curriculum: psychological inoculation, resistance skills training, and personal and social skills training. The psychological inoculation strategy, analogous to the medical use of vaccines, suggests that if you expose students to weak "dosages" of simulated temptations and pressures to use drugs, they will learn to resist them. The resistance skills approach focuses on teaching specific skills for avoiding or rejecting negative social influences to use drugs, including media influences. Personal and social skills training does not home in on resisting drugs but teaches students to develop generic, widely applicable skills for personal and interpersonal development. The DARE curriculum also seeks to enhance students' knowledge about drugs (i.e., misuse and consequences) and gives considerable attention to affective education, including techniques for building self-esteem, managing stress, making better decisions, and forming better friendships (these lesson plans are consistent with the personal and social skills approach).

RESEARCH ON DARE'S EFFECTIVENESS

During the 1990s, a heated debate occurred between DARE advocates and the research community regarding the scientific evidence about DARE's effectiveness in preventing drug use among youth. Fortunately, DARE is one of the most thoroughly researched drug prevention programs in the world, thus yielding results from dozens of evaluation studies. Some researchers have reported that DARE is effective in preventing drug use, while others have reported that DARE is ineffective. These studies vary in methodological rigor (i.e., the extent to which they meet scientific standards defining "good" research) and therefore give us more or less confidence in the reliability and validity of their conclusions. In reviewing the literature, Rosenbaum and Hanson (1998) found an inverse relationship between the quality of the research and the likelihood of positive findings: "The stronger the research design, the less impact researchers have reported on drug use measures." In other words, while a number of studies have reported that DARE is effective in preventing drug use, the strongest, and most scientifically valid studies consistently report that DARE is ineffective in preventing drug use. To be more specific, our research-based knowledge of DARE can be summarized as follows: (1) DARE has some immediate beneficial effects on students' knowledge and attitudes about drugs; (2) these effects are short-lived and usually dissipate within one or two years; and (3) DARE's effect on drug use behaviors are extremely rare and, when found, they are small in size and dissipate quickly. The two most rigorous longitudinal studies of DARE show no overall effects on drug use after 6 and 10 years, and one reported a significant increase in drug use among suburban students who participated in the program.

THE IMPETUS FOR CHANGE

As the body of negative research findings grew larger and more consistent (showing clearly that the core DARE curriculum did not have the desired effects on students' drug use), the pressure mounted to address this problem. DARE is a classic example of what can happen when science and program advocacy come into conflict. In the early years of this controversy, the debate centered on the validity of the research findings, with DARE advocates challenging the scientific merit of studies showing negative results. Thus only minor changes in the DARE curriculum were considered necessary in 1994 in light of the growing popularity of the program worldwide. Over the next several years, however, several critical events occurred: (1) Some major evaluations and review papers were published confirming DARE's ineffectiveness; (2) respected organizations and institutions, ranging from the National Academy of Sciences to the surgeon general to the National Institute of Justice, issued reports suggesting that DARE's approach to drug education is ineffective; and (3) dozens of communities across the United States began to critically reexamine the DARE program and search for more effective alternatives. The convergence of these forces led DARE America to return to the drawing board in pursuit of a new national strategy (described later in this entry). But in essence, this debate underscores the important difference between program *popularity* and program *effectiveness*. DARE is extremely popular with parents, educators, police officials, and politicians, thus policy changes have been slow and painful to all parties involved.

NEW DIRECTIONS AND RESEARCH QUESTIONS

In 1998, the U.S. Departments of Education and Justice hosted meetings between DARE officials and leading drug education researchers to resolve differences and work jointly to improve drug education programming for America's youth. The group recommended that the best available knowledge be applied to develop and test the effectiveness of new drug prevention approaches. As a product of these meetings, the Robert Wood Johnson Foundation funded the development and evaluation of a new DARE curriculum for middle schools, to be tested on

50,000 students in six cities beginning in the fall of 2001. Although other drug prevention curricula have been implemented previously with this age group and have been shown to be effective, this DARE study will determine, for the first time, whether police officers can be a positive influence on adolescent drug use. Preliminary results on the national evaluation are not yet available, although the program has been examined in Ohio middle schools with positive results for children's attitudes.

The new middle school DARE program, if well designed and implemented, may serve an important role in a school's repertoire of drug prevention strategies, but it will not address the now-salient problem of the ineffectiveness of the core elementary school program for fifth and sixth graders. Additional program modifications and evaluation research are needed at the elementary level to improve this program. Future research is also need to determine (1) whether a student's participation in sequential drug education programs will have a cumulative preventive effect; and (2) whether DARE instruction can be effective with students from different socioeconomic, ethnic, racial, educational, and community backgrounds. The idea that "one size fits all" has become less defensible as our society grows increasingly diverse. Figuring out exactly how DARE should be tailored and adapted to different environments remains an important task.

Dennis P. Rosenbaum

See also Drugs; Police Responses to Delinquency; Prevention Strategies

Bibliography

Rosenbaum, D. P., and G. S. Hanson. 1998. Assessing the effects of school-based drug education: A six-year multilevel analysis of Project D.A.R.E. *Journal of Research in Crime and Delinquency* 35:381–412.

DARE (DRUG ABUSE RESISTANCE EDUCATION)

II. The Cherokee Nation Program

As the preceding entry noted, the DARE program has recently come under attack. Critics have pointed

out that in spite of its apparent popularity among police, politicians, parents, and children, DARE has failed to produce statistical evidence of decreased drug use among its graduates. In fact, some argue that the program might actually contribute to drug experimentation by stimulating students' curiosity and identifying the substances needed to satisfy that curiosity.

The utility of DARE might best be judged by a closer qualitative examination of individual programs. Thus one can gain exposure to, and greater appreciation for, the philosophy and dedication of the officers involved as well as the vast array of social problems that are identified and addressed through the program. This entry examines a DARE program delivered in an alternative setting: schools in the counties that make up the Oklahoma Cherokee Nation.

THE CULTURAL MILIEU OF THE CHEROKEE NATION

To understand DARE's phenomenal growth and popularity in the absence of quantitative evidence, one must remember that DARE America is a multimillion-dollar corporate entity generated and propagated by "the drug war." Consequently, some see it as a national symbol of that war and of our refusal to back down. In the process, the contributions of some DARE programs to present and future community-police relations within a particular area or community remain overshadowed, unrecognized, or simply ignored. Thus to appreciate the value and contributions of the Cherokee Nation DARE program, one must first explore the cultural milieu in which it operates.

The Oklahoma Cherokee Nation comprises a 14-county area covering almost the entire eastern third of the state. Most of the schools serve a mixture of white and Native American children from several tribes, mainly Cherokee, Creek, and Choctaw. Tribal lands are vast. In the eastern counties, housing is predominantly rural and largely scattered throughout rocky, mountainous terrain, which makes transportation difficult and often impossible in harsh weather conditions. In addition to social isolation, there is extreme poverty in many areas. For some of the children, school serves as the primary, if not the only, source of food.

Predictably, in the more rural counties, poverty, isolation, and the traditional absence of law enforcement have made marijuana cultivation and drug production particularly attractive and virtually risk free.

Consequently, substance abuse, involving alcohol as well as illegal drugs, is common. Other crimes that plague these areas include burglary, larceny, arson, and vandalism. Gang behavior has also become more visible during the last several years and is discernable even in rural grade schools. Given these considerations, it is not surprising that violence, along with a variety of drugs and other dangerous substances, has become a major concern for school officials.

THE DARE PROGRAM

In 1993, the Cherokee Nation Marshal Service adopted the DARE program. One marshal, a college graduate with a degree in social work, attended the initial two-week training program for DARE officers in Phoenix, Arizona. The instruction emphasized teaching methods—including how to handle distractions or disruptive behavior—and program delivery. Instruction was also provided on how to organize and host public meetings. The training went far beyond methods to discourage substance abuse and violence among fifth graders. In fact, the DARE officers were being prepared to recognize and appropriately address a wide spectrum of underlying problems that might be identified by children or demonstrated by their behavior. They were provided with ideas and instruction on how to reach the parents and the community as well.

The Cherokee Nation marshal must complete a one-week recertification program each year. Consequently, he has seen DARE evolve toward a much broader scope that encourages its officers to adapt to the specific needs of the children and their families, as dictated by the situation and culture. In fact, he considers the DARE training to be of exceptional quality and remains quite motivated in the face of seemingly impossible odds.

Perhaps the greatest challenge facing the program today is how to serve the many schools that need and actually want DARE. At any given time, only about a dozen schools can be served across several neighboring counties. In each school, the standard classroom session is delivered, after which there is lunch with the children and time spent with them during recess. In addition, the marshal is asked to attend their ballgames, festivals, and plays after hours. Time must also be factored in to attend occasional PTA meetings and make frequent trips into the rural areas to visit families. The DARE curriculum takes 17 weeks to complete,

and the marshal presents the program to more than one grade at each school. In fact, since implementing DARE, more than 1,500 children have graduated from the first through the fourth grades and the seventh and eighth grades. In all, the Cherokee Nation DARE officer puts in at least a 60-hour workweek.

Many schools within the Cherokee Nation are still waiting for the DARE officer. It is considered especially beneficial for the Native American children to see a Cherokee Nation marshal who understands their culture and is willing to spend so much time talking with them. Because of the limitations involved in delivering the program, however, area sheriffs and police chiefs have been solicited for assistance, and the marshal offers to help them implement their own DARE programs. So far, very few have even taken the first steps to do so because of financial and personnel constraints.

CULTURAL CONCERNS

Gaining the trust of tribal citizens who have had little, if any, positive contact with law enforcement has presented a formidable challenge. Negative DARE propaganda claiming that officers try to convince children to snitch on their parents raises the stakes considerably. As a result, the DARE officer is cautious in that regard and diplomatically stops any child who begins to speak in class about potential criminal matters in the home. He instead encourages the child to speak with him privately during recess and then determines if there is a potential problem that must be addressed. In practice, the children are simply provided an opportunity to communicate with a positive role model.

Concerns have also been expressed over the belief that DARE preaches a gospel of total abstinence from all intoxicating substances, including alcohol and cigarettes. Again, this is misleading. Among the Native American people, tobacco plays an important role in medicine and religion. The officer teaches children that tobacco and alcohol use involves decisions that adults must make. Furthermore, the substances should be used with discretion. The analogy that he uses to put the point across is the effect that eating too much candy can have on the body and the teeth. The children seem to understand the concept of "too much."

The DARE officer is occasionally blamed for arrests made by officers from other departments. Where relatives of DARE students have been arrested by another agency, the students have sometimes been removed from the class at the parents' request. The assumption is that the officer gained information from students in class and passed that on to other agencies. Above all, the officer emphasizes the importance of being honest with the children and strives to help them understand from the beginning that he is a law enforcement officer as well as a DARE teacher and that they may someday see him arresting someone whom they know.

THE FUTURE OF DARE IN THE CHEROKEE NATION

As the marshal service regains its equilibrium from recent political turmoil, other law enforcement concerns have emerged and are nudging the DARE program toward a much lower priority. Oklahoma is currently experiencing a phenomenal increase in clandestine methamphetamine (meth) labs. The instability, impurity, and volatile nature of the product (the labs sometimes blow up) have brought homemade methamphetamine to the forefront in the state's drug suppression efforts. Consequently, money previously used to support DARE has been transferred to suppression of meth labs on tribal lands.

The Cherokee Nation DARE program has been largely put on hold, and the marshal is spending more time with his line-supervisor activities to help deal with the more immediate threat. Still, DARE has not been abandoned, and there are hopes that it will grow to reach all of the schools within the Cherokee Nation.

CONCLUSION

If DARE is evaluated solely in terms of the percentage of its graduates that resist the temptation to eventually experiment with drugs and other dangerous substances, it is doomed to failure. It is a simple, harsh reality that some children are being, and will continue to be, socialized within a home environment that promotes self-destructive and criminal behavior. Furthermore, as many good parents have learned, even if the home environment is sound, children can still be exposed to crime-producing conditions outside the home. In effect, we might be expecting too much of the wrong things from DARE.

The lesson from the Cherokee Nation program is that there are alternative, and desirable, products of the program. If it is looked at from a much broader,

qualitative perspective—such as the percentage who have had at least some positive contact with a law enforcement officer and acquired some useful information—the DARE program becomes much easier to appreciate and justify. Cherokee Nation children have contact with a successful, positive role model and learn that police are not bad—all in the context of their culture.

The Cherokee Nation DARE officer has been approached on and off duty by many parents and children wanting to know when he will be back. They want to know why he was not at their school's game the previous Saturday and if he might make the upcoming game. He has been invited to graduations and birthday parties, and he has been hugged by a lot of children. Some things are, indeed, difficult to measure.

William P. Heck

 DEATH PENALTY

Throughout U.S. history, the death penalty has been reserved almost entirely for the crimes committed by adult men. Fewer than 3 percent of the approximately 20,000 people executed under legal authority in the United States have been women, and fewer than 2 percent have been juveniles—that is, individuals who committed their capital crimes before their 18th birthdays. Most of the juveniles executed (about 70 percent) have been black, nearly 90 percent of their victims have been white, and approximately 65 percent of them have been executed in the South.

The first juvenile executed in America was Thomas Graunger in Plymouth colony in 1642 for the crime of bestiality. He was 16 at the time of his crime and execution. The youngest nonslave executed in the United States was Ocuish Hannah. On December 20, 1786, she was hanged at the age of 12 for a murder she had committed in New London County, Connecticut. Juveniles in America have been executed for sodomy with animals, arson, robbery, assault, rape, and murder.

Before the 1980s, the age of a capital offender received little public or legal scrutiny, probably in part because death sentences were rarely imposed on juveniles. Most death penalty states before the 1980s had statutes establishing a required minimum age at the time of the crime. Indiana's death penalty statute allowed juveniles as young as 10 years of age at the

Photo 3. Charles Starkweather was executed in 1959 for a teen crime spree that included the murder of 11 people.
SOURCE: Nebraska State Historical Society [RG0809]. Used with permission.

time of their crimes to be executed. Montana's statute provided the death penalty for juveniles as young as 12 years old. Mississippi's minimum age was 13, and other states had minimum age limits ranging from 14 to 18. Some death penalty states set no statutory minimum age limits.

SUPREME COURT DECISIONS

The U.S. Supreme Court first considered the issue of age in capital cases in *Eddings v. Oklahoma* (1982).

Monty Eddings was sentenced to death for killing a highway patrol officer. He was 16 at the time of the crime. Although on appeal Eddings challenged the constitutionality of the death penalty for juveniles, the Court vacated his death sentence on narrower grounds. The key issue for the Court was not his age, which was presented as a mitigating circumstance at trial, but the trial court's failure to consider two other mitigating factors—his unstable family life and emotional disturbances. Even though the Supreme Court sidestepped the broader constitutional question in

Eddings, it did stress that chronological age was an important mitigating factor that must be considered during the sentencing phase of a capital trial.

Between 1983 and 1986, the Supreme Court had five more opportunities to rule on the constitutionality of the death penalty for juveniles but declined in each case. Also during that period, three juveniles were executed—the first juveniles executed in more than two decades. Charles Rumbaugh was executed on September 11, 1985, in Texas; James Terry Roach in South Carolina on January 10, 1986; and Jay Pinkerton in Texas on May 15, 1986. They were all 17 years old at the time of their crimes. (At the time of their executions, Rumbaugh was 28, Roach was 25, and Pinkerton was 24.) By the end of the decade, the Court finally agreed to consider the constitutionality of the death penalty for juveniles in *Thompson v. Oklahoma* (1988).

William Thompson was one of four persons convicted and sentenced to death for the brutal murder of his former brother-in-law. Thompson was 15 years old at the time of the murder and was certified to stand trial as an adult. In *Thompson*, the Court held that the Constitution prohibits the execution of a person who is under 16 years of age at the time of his or her offense. The Court reasoned as follows:

1. Besides the special certification (as an adult) process used in the *Thompson* case, Oklahoma had no statutes, either criminal or civil, that treated anyone under 16 years of age as anything but a child.

2. Although states vary in the line they draw demarcating childhood from adulthood, there is near unanimity among the states in treating a person under 16 years of age as a minor for several important purposes.

3. Of the 18 death penalty states that have established by statute a minimum age for death eligibility, none allows the death penalty for anyone under 16 years of age.

4. Respected professional organizations and peer nations have expressed the view that the execution of persons younger than 16 years of age at the time of their offense offends civilized standards of decency.

5. The evidence of thousands of murder trials shows that jurors, as representatives of the conscience of their communities, have generally found it abhorrent to impose the death penalty on a 15-year-old.

6. The imposition of the death penalty on persons under 16 years of age has not made, nor can it be expected to make, any measurable contribution to the goals of capital punishment, especially the principal goals of retribution and general deterrence.

The Court stipulated, however, that the decision applied only when a state has not specifically legislated a minimum age for its death penalty, as was the case in Oklahoma at the time.

The next year, in the cases of *Stanford v. Kentucky* (1989) and *Wilkins v. Missouri* (1989), the Court determined that the Eighth Amendment does not prohibit the execution of persons who were 17 (in *Stanford*) or 16 (in *Wilkins*) years of age at the time of their offenses. Kevin Stanford was convicted and sentenced to death for raping, sodomizing, and murdering a female service station clerk in Jefferson County, Kentucky, on January 7, 1981. Heath Wilkins was certified to stand trial as an adult and was convicted and sentenced to die for stabbing to death a young female liquor store clerk in Avondale, Missouri, on July 27, 1985. Together, the three decisions in *Thompson*, *Stanford*, and *Wilkins* suggest that the Supreme Court will not allow the execution of persons who are under 16 years of age at the time of their offenses.

In recent years, death penalty jurisdictions have amended their death penalty statutes to conform to the Supreme Court's rulings about age. Currently, 40 U.S. jurisdictions (38 states, the U.S. government, and the U.S. military) have death penalty statutes, and 23 states and the U.S. military allow by law the execution of persons who were younger than 18 years of age at the time of their crimes. Five states have a minimum age of 17, and 18 states and the U.S. military have a minimum age of 16. No death penalty state allows by statute the execution of a person younger than 16 years of age at the time of the crime. Thus current death penalty statutes institutionalize a longstanding American tradition. Historically, fewer than 20 percent of all juveniles executed in the United States were younger than 16 years of age at the time they committed the offenses for which they were executed.

RECENT EXECUTIONS AND DEATH SENTENCES

Since the execution of the three 17-year-olds in the 1980s, 14 more young men have been executed in seven states (as of March 1, 2001). Nine of the 17 juveniles executed were white, seven were black, and one was Hispanic. More than half the 17 executions took place in Texas and more than 70 percent of them in Texas and Virginia. All but 1 of the 17 juveniles executed were 17 years of age at the time of their crimes. The other juvenile, Sean Sellars, who was executed in Oklahoma on February 4, 1999, was 16 years old at the time of his crime. The last 16-year-old (at the time of his crime) executed in the United States was Leonard Shockley in Maryland on April 10, 1959. Since 1990, the United States is one of only five countries that have executed anyone under 18 years of age at the time of the crime; the others are Iran, Pakistan, Saudi Arabia, and Yemen.

At present (March 1, 2001), 74 people who committed crimes before their 18th birthdays sit on death rows throughout the United States awaiting their executions. The typical juvenile currently on death row is a 17-year-old male who killed a white adult female after robbing or raping her. Only four females who were younger than 18 years of age at the time of their crimes have been sentenced to death since 1973 (following the landmark *Furman v. Georgia* decision and the beginning of the modern death penalty era) and none of them has been executed. A study of 14 juvenile death row inmates conducted in the mid-1980s revealed the following characteristics:

1. Fourteen of them had head injuries as children.

2. Twelve had been brutally abused physically, sexually, or both.

3. Nine had major neuropsychological disorders.

4. Seven had psychotic disorders since childhood.

5. Seven had serious psychiatric disturbances.

6. Five had been sodomized as children.

7. Only three had at least average reading ability.

8. Only two had IQ scores above 90 (between 90 and 100 is considered average).

Since 1973, jurisdictions in the United States have imposed death sentences on 196 offenders under the age of 18 at the time of their crimes, which represents less than 3 percent of all death sentences imposed during the period. Nevertheless, the chances of any juvenile currently on death row being executed are remote. Since 1973, the reversal rate for juveniles sentenced to death is about 90 percent.

PUBLIC OPINION

Whether or not juveniles should be subjected to capital punishment has received more attention of late. In a recent Gallup poll, for example, 60 percent of Americans thought that when a teenager commits a murder and is found guilty by a jury, he (the survey item did not address female teenage killers) should get the death penalty (compared with 80 percent who favored the death penalty for adults). Thirty percent opposed the death penalty for teenagers, and 10 percent had no opinion. Among those who favored the death penalty for adults, 72 percent favored the death penalty for teenage killers. When asked whether juveniles convicted of their first crime should be given the same punishment as adults convicted of their first crime, 50 percent of Americans believed juveniles should be treated the same as adults, 40 percent believed they should be treated less harshly, 9 percent responded that it depends, and 1 percent had no opinion.

When asked whether juveniles convicted of their second or third crimes should be given the same punishment as adults convicted of their second or third crimes, 83 percent of Americans believed juveniles should be treated the same as adults, only 12 percent believed they should be treated less harshly, 4 percent thought it depends, and 1 percent had no opinion. As for how juveniles who commit the same crimes as adults should be treated, 52 percent of Americans believed they should receive the same punishment, 31 percent believed that juveniles should be rehabilitated, 13 percent responded that it depends on the circumstances, 3 percent chose another sanction, and 1 percent had no opinion.

One problem with alternatives to capital punishment is that Americans have little confidence in the rehabilitative programs available to juveniles. Only 25 percent of Americans believe that rehabilitation programs for juveniles are even moderately successful. However, nearly half (48 percent) of the respondents also believed that the rehabilitation programs for juveniles had not been given the necessary money and support to be successful.

RATIONALES FOR AND AGAINST APPLYING THE DEATH PENALTY

Among the reasons for not subjecting juveniles to capital punishment are the following:

1. Our society, as represented by legislatures, prosecutors, judges, and juries, has rejected the juvenile death penalty.

2. Other nations have rejected the juvenile death penalty. (The United States and Somalia are the only two countries in the United Nations not to ratify Article 37(a) of the U.N. Convention on the Rights of the Child, which bans capital punishment for anyone under 18 years of age.)

3. The threat of the death penalty does not deter potential juvenile murderers, because juveniles often do not consider the possible consequences before committing their murderous acts and because, even if they did consider these consequences, they would realize that very few juveniles actually receive the death penalty.

4. Juveniles are especially likely to be rehabilitated or reformed while in prison, thus rendering the juvenile death penalty especially inappropriate.

5. The juvenile death penalty does not serve a legitimate retributive purpose because juveniles are generally less mature and responsible than adults and should therefore be viewed as less culpable than adults who commit the same crimes.

6. Juveniles are already treated legally different from adults in other areas of life, such as driving, voting, gambling, marriage, and jury service.

On the other hand, the following are some of the reasons for subjecting juveniles to capital punishment:

1. The evidence of a societal consensus against the juvenile death penalty is nonexistent, or at least too weak to justify a constitutional ban.

2. The views of other nations are irrelevant to the proper interpretation of our Constitution, at least absent a consensus within our own society.

3. The threat of the death penalty can deter potential juvenile murderers, or at least the judgments of legislatures and prosecutors to that effect deserve deference.

4. The most heinous juvenile murderers, who are the only ones likely to receive the death penalty, are not good candidates for rehabilitation or reform.

5. There are some juvenile murderers who are sufficiently mature and responsible to deserve the death penalty for their crimes, thus the juvenile death penalty serves a legitimate retributive purpose.

6. As for other areas of the law that distinguish between adults and juveniles, while juveniles may not vote conscientiously or drive safely, they do know that killing other human beings is wrong.

THE DISCRIMINATION ARGUMENT

What for some people makes the current practice of excluding most death-eligible juveniles from the death penalty discriminatory is that the designation of "juvenile" is arbitrary and only a proxy for more relevant characteristics. In the first place, it was not until the 16th and 17th centuries that youth began to be viewed other than as miniature adults or property. Before that time, juveniles as young as 5 or 6 were expected to assume the responsibilities of adults and, when they violated the law, were subjected to the same criminal sanctions as adults. Moreover, it is hard to locate a significant difference on any relevant social characteristic between 17- and 18-year-olds, other than what has been created by law. It may not be very meaningful to consider a 17-year-old a juvenile and an 18-year-old an adult.

In considering whether a person deserves the death penalty from a retributive standpoint, it has been argued that age is largely irrelevant. It is used because it serves as an imperfect proxy for more relevant social characteristics. Whether a murderer, regardless of age, deserves the death penalty depends not on age, in this view, but on maturity, judgment, responsibility, and the capability to assess the possible consequences of his or her actions. Some juveniles possess those characteristics in greater quantity than some adults do, or in sufficient quantities to be eligible for the death penalty; in other cases, they do not. According to the argument, because age is an imperfect proxy for the more relevant characteristics, the use of age as a basis for determining who is or is not death-eligible is discriminatory.

Regardless of one's position on the subject of the death penalty for juveniles, it remains a controversial issue.

Robert M. Bohm

See also Waiver to Adult Court

Bibliography

Bohm, R. M. 1999. *Deathquest: An Introduction to the Theory and Practice of Capital Punishment in the United States.* Cincinnati, OH: Anderson.

Bright, S. B. 1997. *Capital Punishment on the 25th Anniversary of Furman v. Georgia.* Atlanta, GA: Southern Center for Human Rights.

Cothern, L. 2000. *Juveniles and the Death Penalty.* Washington, DC: Department of Justice, Coordinating Council on Juvenile Justice and Delinquency Prevention.

Hoffmann, J. L. 1993. On the perils of line-drawing: Juveniles and the death penalty. Pp. 117–132 in V. L. Streib (ed.), *A Capital Punishment Anthology.* Cincinnati, OH: Anderson.

Moore, D. W. 1994. Majority advocate death penalty for teenage killers. *The Gallup Poll Monthly,* September:2–5.

Schneider, V., and J. O. Smykla. 1991. A summary analysis of executions in the United States, 1608–1987: The Espy file. Pp. 1–19 in R. M. Bohm (ed.), *The Death Penalty in America: Current Research.* Cincinnati, OH: Anderson.

Streib, V. L. 1988. Imposing the death penalty on children. Pp. 245–267 in K. C. Haas and J. A. Inciardi (eds.), *Challenging Capital Punishment: Legal and Social Science Approaches.* Newbury Park, CA: Sage.

Streib, V. L. 1998. Executing women, children, and the retarded: Second class citizens in capital punishment. Pp. 201–221 in J. R. Acker, R. M. Bohm, and C. Lanier (eds.), *America's Experiment With Capital Punishment: Reflections on the Past, Present and Future of the Ultimate Penal Sanction.* Durham, NC: Carolina Academic Press.

Streib, V. L. 2002. *The Juvenile Death Penalty Today: Death Sentences and Executions for Juvenile Crimes, January 1, 1973–December 31, 2001.* Available at http://www.law.onu.edu/faculty/streib/juvdeath.htm.

DEINSTITUTIONALIZATION MOVEMENT

"Less is more" is the overall message of the deinstitutionalization movement. The supporters of the movement argue that less intrusiveness, less official juvenile justice involvement, and less reliance on secure institutions will bring about more just, more effective, more economical, and more humane treatment of juvenile offenders. The deinstitutionalization movement in the juvenile justice system emerged from the noninterventionist philosophical movement in American corrections, which gained prominence in the mid-1970s and argued for minimal involvement of the official juvenile justice system in the lives and treatments of juvenile status offenders and delinquents.

Disillusionment with prevailing juvenile justice practices and institutions had become commonplace throughout American society. Many people had concluded that these traditional practices were failures that created more problems than they solved. They had come to believe that juvenile correctional institutions in particular were training schools for more criminal behavior. They contended that youth placed in such institutions were harmfully exposed to hardened criminal attitudes and behavior. Others argued that publicly defining a youth as delinquent set in motion a whole new chain of dynamics and events. The effects of harmful stigmatizing can be irreversible. The damage may affect the youth's current reputation as well as future opportunities. Many looked to the labeling and conflict theories that were popular at the time for inspiration in bringing about what they believed to be the much-needed reforms in the juvenile justice system.

FORMS OF DEINSTITUTIONALIZATION

Three distinguishable but related versions of the deinstitutionalization movement developed and are in existence today. Although differing in focus and specific purpose, all represent active forms of the noninterventionist philosophy of corrections.

Decarceration

Decarceration refers to court policies that call for the least restrictive alternative in supplying services to status offenders. These are youth who have not committed a criminal act. Their "offenses" would not be criminal if conducted by an adult. Specifically, a "least restrictive alternative" is one that involves placement in a community-based correctional program rather than in a secure facility such as a jail or training school. Whenever possible or appropriate, the less severe placement should be the goal. Additionally, the federal government should prohibit states from placing status offenders in custodial facilities that are separate but similar to those used for delinquent offenders. The facilities for status offenders should be different in their appearance, purpose, and conditions from those used for more serious delinquent offenders.

Diversion

Diversion programs are especially designed to provide services to dependent and neglected youths. They are set up to supply crisis intervention services to youths. Ultimately, the goal is to return youth to their homes. In the diversion model, the juvenile court retains jurisdiction over these youth, but law enforcement agencies, schools, parents, and so on take care of these children and provide the needed services.

Divestiture of Jurisdiction

Last, deinstitutionalization has come to refer to the "divestiture of jurisdiction." This process generally involves the removal of status offenders from the jurisdiction of the juvenile court. Agencies that are not part of the justice system are given the responsibility of providing services to the youths, including treatment or foster care. Juvenile courts do not place youths on probation or in institutions when they commit status offenses.

EARLY DEVELOPMENTS

The deinstitutionalization process has come about as the result of actions, law, and policy changes that occurred in a variety of governmental settings. An early experiment in deinstitutionalization took place in the state of Massachusetts. It was there that in 1972,

Jerome Miller, who was the commissioner of the Department of Youth Services, closed the state juvenile institutions. Miller was convinced that years of failed experiences in the state's juvenile institutions required this drastic action.

It was an action that also required the successful transformation from depending on institutions to using a statewide network of community-based programs and services. Miller decentralized the state juvenile justice agency in Massachusetts and set up seven regional offices. At the same time, he set up another program to acquire needed supplies and services from private agencies.

The commissioner had apparently assumed that closing the institutions would foster the creation of many services in the private sector. But this did not happen. Instead, few programs and services were available to the youth, and many juveniles were released from institutions without supervision or services. Not too surprisingly, many public officials and juvenile justice professionals throughout the country were stunned by Miller's actions. As frustrated and aggravated as many of them were with their respective juvenile justice systems, for the most part they were unwilling or unable to follow his actions.

THE COURTS AND DEINSTITUTIONALIZATION

Courts in some of the states were also among the first to address the issues surrounding the secure detention of status offenders. As early as 1977 the West Virginia Supreme Court of Appeals had ruled that the secure detention of juveniles violated their state constitution's provisions guaranteeing due process and equal protection and protection from cruel and unusual punishment.

Likewise, the Tennessee Supreme Court in 1988 found that the secure detention of status offenders violated the due process and equal protection provisions of their constitution. The court determined that since by definition status offenders are not "guilty" of any crime, secure detention of status offenders amounted to punishment without an adjudication of guilt. Furthermore, secure detention was ruled to be in violation of equal protection because it infringed on the fundamental right to personal liberty.

As a result of the court rulings, the legislatures of West Virginia and Tennessee adopted laws designed to deinstitutionalize status offenders in their states.

FEDERAL EFFORTS

Responding to the public's concerns about juvenile delinquency, Congress passed the Juvenile Justice and Delinquency Prevention Act (JJDPA) in 1974. This act had several important and far-reaching components that affected the deinstitutionalization movement. The provision dealing with the deinstitutionalization of status offenders (DSO) was one of the act's first mandates. The original act in 1974 required states to "provide within two years . . . that juveniles who are charged with or who have committed offenses that would not be criminal if committed by an adult shall not be placed in juvenile detention or correctional facilities, but must be placed in shelter facilities." The JJDPA also mandated that juveniles be separated by sight and sound from adult offenders in detention and correctional facilities.

Another provision of the act encouraged state and local jurisdictions to find ways of separating juvenile delinquents from status offenders and removing status offenders from the juvenile courts. It contended that other human service agencies should be brought into the processing of juvenile status offenders.

CHANGES AND MODIFICATIONS IN THE JJDPA

Over the years, several modifications in the JJDPA have been made. The substantial compliance standard was developed in 1976 as a means to clarify the DSO mandate by requiring states to reduce the number of status offenders and nonoffenders in secure confinement by 75 percent over two years.

In 1977, Congress made two important modifications: First, Congress required that juveniles be separated by both sight and sound from adult offenders in detention and correctional facilities. Second, Congress required states to comply with the DSO mandate within five years. Dependent and neglected children were included in this requirement. At the same time, Congress provided more leeway in some of the JJDPA rules. It gave states more flexibility in the range of placement options of status offenders and nonoffenders such as dependent and neglected children.

Other major changes were made in the processing of juveniles in 1980. Three of these were most important: First, Congress prohibited states from detaining juveniles in jails and lockups. Second, Congress proposed that states should examine their secure confinement policies relating to minority juveniles. If a state should find that minority youth were confined in secure facilities at disproportionately higher rates than other youth, then the state should examine the reasons and justifications for the disproportionately higher rates of their minority youth confinement. Third, Congress created an "exception" to DSO by declaring that juveniles who violated a valid court order (VCO) could for a period of time be placed in secure confinement. Many juvenile court judges had come to believe that the DSO mandate made it difficult for the courts to deal with some juveniles, most especially runaways. The VCO exception permitted the courts to institutionalize status offenders and nonoffenders if they were found to violate the court order. Although the VCO procedure provided juveniles with several procedural rights such as court hearings, confrontations, and the right to be notified of the charges against them, this change became very controversial. Critics of the VCO exception complained that it undermined the goals and practices of deinstitutionalization.

FINANCIAL INCENTIVE

Most states and territories participating in the JJDPA comply with the DSO mandate. One likely reason for this compliance is the financial incentive the federal government gives to the states. As provided by this financial incentive, states that comply with the mandates of the JJDPA, monitor their progress toward fulfilling those mandates, and provide written annual progress reports can qualify for formula grant funds. On the other hand, states that do not fulfill these requirements or make acceptable progress toward fulfilling these mandates risk becoming ineligible for the grants.

Two significant changes that dealt with the financial incentive were added to the JJDPA in 1992. First, Congress threatened to take away as much as 25 percent of its formula grant money from any participating state that did not comply with the mandates of the JJDPA. Second, a fourth mandate was added, requiring states receiving JJDPA formula money to find ways and bring about concrete plans to reduce the overrepresentation of minorities in their juvenile justice systems. The new mandate, known as the disproportionate minority confinement (DMC) mandate, would apply if a participating state had a disproportionate number of minority youths in their detention and correctional facilities compared with the proportion of minority youth in the general population.

Overall, the DSO mandate is credited with bringing major changes in the juvenile justice system in several states. Like the JJDPA in general, it represented a significant departure from previous federal juvenile justice legislation. To a much greater extent, it emphasized prevention and diversion from the juvenile justice system. The Omnibus Crime Control and Safe Streets Act of 1968 had established the Law Enforcement Assistance Administration (LEAA) to provide grants to strengthen crime control. By contrast, the JJDPA provided grants to states to promote programs that would divert most juveniles from the juvenile justice system into community-based programs. In the years since it was first put into effect, the Juvenile Justice and Delinquency Prevention Act has revolutionized the way troubled youth in this country have been handled, emphasizing treatment, prevention, diversion, and community-based programs and services.

CRITICISMS

Although most states today are in compliance with the DSO mandate, many have raised concerns about both theoretical assumptions and operational problems of deinstitutionalization.

Definitional Problems

Critics note that considerable confusion still exists regarding what exactly is included in the definition of *status offender*. For some, the term *status offenders* should apply only those who have had no prior record of involvement in delinquency. Programs with this "purist" approach will include only youth who meet the requirements of this definition in their programs. Others will not exclude status offenders who have histories of delinquency in their programs.

Relabeling

Relabeling refers to defining youths as delinquent or as emotionally disturbed who in the past would have been defined and handled as status offenders. This practice often comes from police officers that resent their loss of discretion with troublesome juvenile offenders. Some juvenile court judges likewise have resisted deinstitutionalization reforms for many of the same reasons.

Net Widening

Other critics believe that the noble objectives of the DSO movement have actually proven to be counterproductive. These critics assert that the creation and availability of new programs have had the effect of encouraging police to refer more juveniles to those programs. This in turn has had the effect of "widening the net" of the juvenile justice system. *Net widening* refers to pulling youths into the juvenile justice system who would not have been involved before. Because a new program is made available, police will be more willing to send youths to the juvenile court rather than handle the case themselves. Therefore, deinstitutionalization has created a new class of juvenile offender as well as new action alternatives for police officers to follow. The number of youths processed to court is said to have increased in many cities, reducing the antilabeling efforts of the program. It has led to exposing more juveniles to the harmful effects of labeling and stigmatizing that the deinstitutionalization movement had sought to eliminate.

Recidivism Not Reduced

Critics also point to what they believe are other faulty assumptions that have brought about unintended consequences. Early supporters of deinstitutionalization argued that secure confinement of status offenders would harden them and increase the likelihood they would commit crimes that were even more serious. Today, however, critics point to indications that the opposite is true—recidivism rates have actually been found to be higher, not lower, among those who were deinstitutionalized as opposed to those kept in secure institutions. A similar assumption widely held by deinstitutionalization advocates was that status offenders once removed from secure institutions would be placed in more caring institutions. Experience has not always supported this assumption either. Instead, it appears that often the agencies and programs to which the juveniles have been referred are poorly prepared, not well designed, or unwilling to provide the kinds of services needed by troubled youth. Critics also contend that the youth most often turned away are those most in need of the services.

A related criticism leveled against the DSO movement is that it has not had any appreciable effect in reducing the problems involving gender, minority, and socioeconomic differences of delinquent youth.

These critics point out that girls are still subjected to paternalistic treatment and that minorities and those from lower socioeconomic strata are still overrepresented in the juvenile justice systems throughout the country.

Secure Confinement Not Reduced

Perhaps the most troubling criticism comes from those who point out that deinstitutionalization has failed to substantially reduce the number of status offenders in secure confinement. The problem seems to be especially true in local areas, where the often-stated reasons juveniles are kept in secure detention include the risk of the youth hurting themselves or others, not appearing in court, or leaving or being taken out of the jurisdiction.

RETRENCHMENTS

Valid Court Order Exception

Juvenile court judges have complained that the DSO requirements have limited their options in the handling of status offenders. Responding to repeated and strongly voiced complaints, Congress in 1980 addressed these concerns. It added a provision that allows judges to place status offenders in secure detention facilities if they had violated a "valid court order." States could also adjudicate a status offender as a delinquent or use the court's contempt power to "bootstrap," or upgrade, a status offender to a delinquent status if the juvenile had been found to have violated a valid court order. Although some states allow the judge to upgrade a status offender to a delinquent, most states do not use the VCO exception. Supporters of the deinstitutionalization movement strongly object to the VCO exception. In their opinion, all the protections afforded other status offenders should also apply to VCO violators. VCO violators are still status offenders.

Chronic Status Offenders

Many critics of the deinstitutionalization movement think the juvenile justice system should maintain control over chronic status offenders—that is, those who have long histories of emotional and behavior problems, such as many runaways. All too often, juvenile justice judges and other practitioners have had trouble placing these youth in programs and have concluded that chronic status offenders do not work well in community-based programs. In the opinion of these judges and practitioners, removing the option of holding these youth also removes the opportunity to help these offenders or to keep them from hurting themselves or others.

FUTURE PROSPECTS

Current policies and practices of this country's juvenile justice system have been enormously influenced by the deinstitutionalization movement. In general, major changes in juvenile crime and public policy have successfully challenged public policymakers and juvenile justice professionals. They in turn have responded by making many significant reforms in the juvenile justice system.

Nevertheless, major challenges face the deinstitutionalization movement. Everywhere, the public has railed against the perception that juvenile crime has gone out of control. Reacting to this fear, nearly all governors and state legislatures have made reducing juvenile crime and increasing juvenile crime control and correctional services primary goals. Increasingly, these public officials must face the pressure to develop and use more punitive policies, especially when dealing with violent youth. Many proponents of the deinstitutionalization movement believe the decline of the rehabilitation perspective and practices stemming from that will inevitably follow. But others point out that the implementation of more punitive policies would probably increase the number of juvenile offenders in the juvenile justice system. This would then produce a new challenge that society would have to address. In doing so, society might turn once again to using more noninstitutional means of dealing with less serious offenders. This would complete the cycle and bring about a new chapter in the deinstitutionalization movement in the American juvenile justice system.

Rodney J. Henningsen

See also Diversion Programs; Juvenile Justice and Delinquency Prevention Act of 1974; Jerome G. Miller; Status Offenders

Bibliography

Crowe, A. H. 2000. Chapter 2: Jurisdictional and program self-assessment. Pp. 25–62 in A. H. Crowe, *Jurisdictional Technical Assistance Package for Juvenile*

Corrections. Washington, DC: Office of Juvenile Justice and Delinquency Prevention.

Feld, B. C. 1998. The juvenile court. Pp. 509–541 in M. Tonry (ed.), *Handbook of Crime and Punishment.* New York: Oxford University Press.

Holden, G. A., and R. A. Kapler. 1995. Deinstitutionalizing status offenders: A record of progress. *Juvenile Justice* 2:3–10.

Miller, J. 1998. *Last One Over the Wall: The Massachusetts Experiment in Closing Reform School,* 2nd ed. Columbus: Ohio State University Press.

Office of Juvenile Justice and Delinquency Prevention. 1995. *Unlocking the Doors for Status Offenders: The State of the States.* Washington, DC: Office of Juvenile Justice and Delinquency Prevention.

Trepanier, J. 1999. Juvenile courts after 100 years: Past and present orientations. *European Journal on Criminal Policy and Research* 7:303–327.

DELINQUENCY

 I. Definitions

Juvenile delinquency is criminal and analogously deviant behavior committed by children and adolescents under the legal age of adulthood. In most of the United States (39 states and the District of Columbia) and in the federal court system, persons under the age of 18 are considered juveniles and their unlawful actions delinquencies. Connecticut, New York, and North Carolina define delinquency as criminal misconduct occurring before age 16; and Wyoming considers persons juveniles until age 19. Children under age 7 are generally excluded from delinquent status and legal responsibility because it is assumed that they are unable to form the criminal intent (known as *mens rea,* or guilty mind) necessary to perpetrate acts of delinquency.

Persons who engage in delinquency are known as *delinquents* or *juvenile delinquents.* These terms, as well as *delinquency* and *juvenile delinquency,* are interchangeable. Although not technically correct because of the different ages of the offenders, *crime* and *delinquency* are frequently used as synonyms by the general public.

Juvenile delinquency is differentially punished depending on the severity of the offense. Dire criminal behavior such as murder, homicide, manslaughter, rape, kidnapping, armed robbery, arson, and sexual molestation can denote mandatory transfer to the adult

criminal justice system. In fact, eight states set no lower age limit in waiving or transferring juvenile cases to adult criminal court. States also vary in determining whose discretion is used to waive juvenile cases to adult court. This decision can be made by a judge (judicial waiver), district attorney (prosecutorial waiver), state statute (legislative waiver), or even the delinquent (demand waiver).

DELINQUENT OFFENSES

Juvenile delinquency comprises delinquent and status offenses. Like crimes in the adult system, *delinquent offenses* are violations of codified legal statute. They encompass but are not limited to acts of violence against a person, such as murder, rape, robbery, kidnapping, aggravated and simple assault, harassment, stalking, vehicular homicide, menacing, and child abuse, and acts against property, such as burglary, larceny, auto theft, arson, and vandalism. A variety of miscellaneous offenses of varying seriousness are also included in the definition of delinquent offenses, such as drunk driving; cruelty to animals; use of controlled substances; forgery; fraud; disorderly conduct; weapons offenses; sexual offenses such as indecent exposure, prostitution, and commercialized vice; traffic violations; and vagrancy. All these offenses are subsumed under the rubric of conventional or street delinquency. Organized crime (e.g., racketeering and extortion), corporate and white-collar crime (e.g., price fixing, pollution, embezzlement, and insider trading) and political crime (e.g., genocide and terrorism) are seldom included in studies of juvenile delinquency because youth rarely have the opportunity to commit these offenses.

Status offenses are behaviors considered inappropriate or unhealthy for children and adolescents and are proscribed precisely because of the offenders' age. Such behaviors, if committed by adults, are not illegal. Examples of status offenses include being ungovernable, violating curfew, disobeying parents, drinking or possessing alcohol, engaging in sexual behavior, idleness, incorrigibility, running away from home, smoking or using tobacco, truancy, and waywardness.

Status offending is commonly considered an antecedent condition to more serious delinquent offending, and the goal of the juvenile justice system is to prevent escalation from status to delinquent offending. The juvenile justice system attaches a variety of labels to children involved in status offending, such as CHINS (children in need of supervision), PINS (persons in need of supervision), MINS (minors in need of supervision), FINS (families in need of supervision), and YINS (youth in need of supervision).

HISTORICAL DEFINITIONS OF DELINQUENCY

Historically in the United States, *juvenile delinquency* has been variously defined and interpreted. These changing definitions have compelled alternately draconian and punitive or permissive and rehabilitative reactions from the state. This oscillatory treatment continues to the present. From the colonial period (early 17th century) to 1825, juvenile delinquency was punished under English common law. This doctrine, heavily imbued with moral and religious overtones, was rigid and harsh, evidenced by the widespread use of corporal punishments such as public whippings and dunking in water, removal from the community, and capital punishment.

By 1825, a progressive social movement, organized by people know as the child savers, emerged to challenge the definition, interpretation, and handling of juvenile delinquency. Positivistic factors such as immigration, poverty, urbanity, and poor parenting replaced religiosity as the core causes of delinquency. Consequently, the child savers sought to remove children from adverse environments and make them wards of the state. Based on the doctrine of *parens patriae* (the state as the ultimate guardian of children), juvenile delinquents were placed in Bastille-like houses of refuge. Despite the reform-minded intentions of the child savers, incarceration, penitence, and corporal punishment continued.

On July 1, 1899, the modern juvenile justice system was born with the opening of the Chicago Juvenile Court, under the auspices of Judge Julian Mack. Specialized juvenile courts and a systemic juvenile justice system spread across the nation and processed youth involved in both status and delinquent offenses. Juvenile courts were philosophically different from the punishment-minded adult criminal courts. In Judge Mack's words, the function of the juvenile courts and justice system was "not so much to punish as to reform, not to degrade but to uplift, not to crush but to develop, not to make the delinquent an offender but a worthy citizen." This tension of defining and handling juvenile delinquents as childlike innocents or youthful

degenerates has never been reconciled. Over time, the juvenile justice system was criticized for its inability to effectively reduce delinquency as a social problem and, perhaps more important, for similarly processing and incarcerating generally benign status offenders with comparatively more serious delinquent offenders (although these offense categories are not necessarily mutually exclusive).

With the social upheaval of the 1960s, a variety of liberal measures were introduced to guarantee legal rights for juveniles. These included establishing a court hearing before waiving or transferring a juvenile to criminal court (*Kent v. U.S.*, 1966), general due process (*In re Gault,* 1967), the state burden of proving guilt beyond a reasonable doubt (*In re Winship*, 1970), jury trials (*McKeiver v. Pennsylvania*, 1971), and protection from double jeopardy (*Breed v. Jones,* 1975). Moreover, the Juvenile Justice and Delinquency Prevention Act of 1974 (amended in 1977, 1980, and 1984) called for the decriminalization of abused and neglected children, deinstitutionalized status offenders, and established funding for delinquency research. Over the last quarter of the 20th century, juvenile delinquency was defined in large part by contemporary social issues such as drug abuse, illegitimacy, gangs, and school shootings. The rise of these social problems resulted in the increasingly punitive treatment of juvenile offenders, particularly the reliance on incarceration.

ACADEMIC INFLUENCE

The definitions, causes, and policies used by the state to manage juvenile delinquency are highly contingent on trends in the academic disciplines that study it. Even within academic disciplines, there are differentiating theoretical debates. Archaic definitions equated delinquency with supernatural forces, sin, vice, and other bad habits. Economists have defined delinquency as the rational outcome of the purposive cost-benefit analysis of the delinquent. Biologists have pointed to various stigmata, hormones, and other innate characteristics as the natural determinants of youthful misbehavior. Psychologists have variously defined delinquency as the maladaptive product of a defective personality, over- or underdeveloped Freudian superego, low IQ, anger management and opposition-defiant disorder, and an assortment of individual-level pathologies. In the contemporary United

States, the dominant practitioners of delinquency are sociologists who point to large-scale, structural, extraindividual phenomena as the determinants of human behavior. According to this view, delinquency is a collective and social, not an individual, pathology. Numerous theoretical camps within sociology define juvenile delinquency as the outcome of various social processes. These include interaction with delinquent peers (differential association and social learning); poverty, mobility, and neighborhood dissolution (social disorganization); unequal access to societal goals (strain/anomie); weak bonds to conventional social institutions (social control); abject parental socialization (self-control); stigmatizing involvement in the juvenile justice system (labeling); and the balkanizing effects of competing social statuses (conflict, critical, differential oppression and feminist).

As the 21st century began, a paradigm shift in the definition and interpretation of juvenile delinquency occurred. Delinquency was no longer viewed as a discrete, aberrant phase of deviant behavior to contrast with adult crime. Instead, multidisciplinary efforts framed juvenile delinquency specifically and childhood/adolescence generally in a life-course context in which delinquency was examined as one stage in the longitudinal, often developmental, criminal career. These stages include the timing of the initiation of delinquent offending (onset), the proportion of youth who are delinquent (prevalence), the number of delinquent events committed annually (incidence), the rate of delinquent offenses committed annually (lambda), the decline of involvement in delinquency (desistance), and the cessation of delinquency (termination). This research paradigm has unearthed the most valid and reliable statistical data on the magnitude and stability of juvenile delinquency. Across all social strata, it is exceedingly rare to find adolescents who have not engaged in status or benign delinquent offending. The prevalence for behaviors such as drinking alcohol, truancy, unruliness, using tobacco, engaging in sexual activity, fighting, and theft are nearly 100 percent.

NATURE OF DELINQUENCY

For most youth, delinquency is ephemeral, usually emerging between ages 13 and 15 and generally ceasing between ages 16 and 17. Involvement in more serious, felonious delinquency is less common. Annually, youth account for approximately 20 percent of the violent crime and 35 percent of the property crime in the United States. Persons who begin committing delinquency during childhood and preadolescence are at great risk of engaging in the most serious forms of delinquency, at higher levels, and for prolonged periods. Fortunately, only 5 percent of males (serious, habitual criminality is nearly nonexistent among females) demonstrate life-long, pathological criminality; and such offenders have been discovered in most industrialized nations. With the exception of homicide, which is abnormally high in the United States, violent and property delinquency in the industrialized nations, such as Australia, Belgium, Canada, Czech Republic, England, Finland, Holland, Israel, Italy, New Zealand, Poland, and Sweden, is comparable to America. (The notable exception to this is Japan, a nation with extremely low levels of delinquency.)

CONCLUSION

Throughout Western history, the adult public has mistrusted youth and been very condemning of their behavior, making juvenile delinquency an indelible part of the sociohistorical fabric and a common referent in discussions of the state of nations. Infamous cases of juvenile delinquency have galvanized the lay observer and academic elite alike and influenced the ways in which they define and interpret delinquency. From the scores of children executed for violating the stubborn child law of the Massachusetts Bay Colony in the mid-17th century to the life imprisonment of Jesse Harding Pomeroy, a 14-year-old who murdered and sexually tortured several children in 1874, juvenile delinquency has held public interest.

Moreover, incidents such as the 1924 kidnapping-murder of a young schoolboy by the youthful geniuses Nathan Leopold and Richard Loeb, the rash of lethal school shootings in the 1990s, and the 2001 murder trial and imprisonment of 14-year-old Lionel Tate greatly concern society. Sensational incidents of delinquency feed perceptions of pervasive societal decline, the inadequacy of current social institutions, the lingering role of discrimination and other social biases, and the inherent flaws of certain groups of people. The instinct to protect children coupled with the pervasiveness of personal experiences among citizens who dabbled in delinquency guarantee the tenuous interpretation of childhood misconduct and continued debate over how to respond to juvenile delinquency.

Matthew J. DeLisi

See also Child-Saving Movement; Courts, Juvenile—History; Status Offenders; Theories of Delinquency

Bibliography

Bartollas, C. 2000. *Juvenile Delinquency*, 5th ed. Boston: Allyn & Bacon.

Fagan, J., and F. E. Zimring. 2000. *The Changing Borders of Juvenile Justice: Transfer of Adolescents to the Criminal Court.* Chicago: University of Chicago Press.

Feld, B. 1999. *Bad Kids: Race and the Transformation of the Juvenile Court.* New York: Oxford University Press.

Loeber, R., and D. P. Farrington (eds.). 1998. *Serious and Violent Juvenile Offenders: Risk Factors and Successful Interventions.* Thousand Oaks, CA: Sage.

Regoli, R. M., and J. D. Hewitt. 2000. *Delinquency in Society*, 4th ed. New York: McGraw-Hill.

Siegel, L., and J. Senna. 2000. *Juvenile Delinquency: Theory, Practice, and Law*, 7th ed. Belmont, CA: Wadsworth.

DELINQUENCY

 ## II. Types of Delinquency and Delinquents

Serious attention on the part of sociologists and other scholars to juvenile misconduct was relatively rare before the 1930s. Further, it was not until the post–World War II period that the study of delinquency "took off" in the form of theorizing and research efforts. Juvenile delinquency emerged as a major social problem in the eyes of citizens after World War II and, in turn, the juvenile justice system, staffed by juvenile court workers, probation officers, and workers in juvenile institutions, expanded markedly in the second half of the 20th century.

During this period, many observers—laypersons and scholars alike—pointed out that the term *juvenile delinquency* slurs over a number of seemingly important variations among offenses or offenders. For example, joyriding (car theft) by juveniles may have little in common with jackrolling (robbery), and in the same way, juvenile fire setters may be quite different from gang delinquents or other kinds of offenders.

These commonsense observations quickly led a number of investigators to a corollary argument: If delinquents and/or delinquency come in a variety of forms, the causal influences that account for these varied patterns probably also differ from one type to another. A parallel thesis emerged among juvenile correctional workers: If these causal factors differ from one offender type to another, so too do the intervention efforts required to deflect offenders from further involvement in misconduct. In other words, "different strokes for different folks" are in order for effective treatment to occur.

Although these notions seem obvious, the identification of specific types of delinquency patterns is another matter. Much energy has been expended on efforts to sort juvenile offenders into distinct types or to identify specific patterns of delinquency, with mixed results. The discussion to follow indicates some of the major directions that have been pursued, but first, some general observations are in order with respect to classificatory or typological endeavors (also see Gibbons and Farr, 2001).

SOME GENERAL CONSIDERATIONS

First, it should be noted that delinquent types or patterns of delinquency are in the eyes of the beholder; that is, citizens or criminologists rather than delinquents identify types or patterns. In all likelihood, most offenders would be nonplussed if asked questions like, "What kind of delinquent are you?" Even more to the point, the development of classificatory schemes is a conceptual and empirical enterprise. Myriad variables might be employed as the basis of a classification, but most would not provide for a theoretically meaningful typological scheme. Additionally, as later sections indicate, a number of classificatory schemes have been put forth that have not passed the test of evidence in that researchers have failed to uncover real-life counterparts of the hypothesized types.

EARLY WORK

It would be incorrect to claim that delinquency researchers have all been attuned to variations among offenders. Indeed, some early, major studies did assume that delinquents and nondelinquents make up two distinct and homogeneous groups (Glueck and Glueck, 1950). However, a number of conjectural claims by psychiatrists about alleged "types" of delinquents, such as "pathological fire setters," began to appear in psychiatric journals in the 1940s. Also, a number of speculative claims by sociologists about car theft, middle-class delinquency, female offenders, and other specific delinquent patterns or types began to appear after World War II (Gibbons, 1970).

Special note should be given to the work of psychiatrist Richard L. Jenkins (Jenkins and Hewitt, 1944; Hewitt and Jenkins, 1944). Drawing on experiences and observations in juvenile treatment programs, Jenkins argued that there are two major forms of delinquency, engaged in by two different kinds of delinquents. *Adaptive* misconduct is the work of "pseudosocial offenders"—that is, relatively normal youths who often come from lower-class, inner-city neighborhoods, while *maladaptive* delinquency refers to acts of cruelty, violence, and the like by poorly socialized, maladjusted youngsters. Jenkins, assisted by sociologist Lester Hewitt, subjected his clinical hunches to a research test in a Michigan child guidance clinic, where they identified a number of pseudosocial (adaptive) and overly aggressive (maladaptive) delinquents, along with "overinhibited" youngsters who were not delinquents but exhibited serious personality problems. Jenkins and Hewitt also reported evidence indicating that these three patterns were linked to separate backgrounds; that is, maladaptive youths came from family backgrounds different from those that characterized the pseudosocial or overinhibited youths.

A number of other investigators have conducted parallel studies and have uncovered further evidence of the existence of two broad kinds of delinquents who are often found in probation caseloads, training schools, and elsewhere in the juvenile justice system: a large group of relatively well-socialized youths who are involved in adaptive or instrumental but illegal acts and a smaller group of psychologically troubled juveniles who often engage in violence or other maladaptive behavior (Reiss, 1952).

The Interpersonal Maturity Level (I-Level) classification system, developed in the California juvenile correctional system, bears some similarity to the aforementioned efforts and also is the most well known of the relatively few attempts to use a complex typology for correctional purposes (Warren, 1976).

The I-Level system centers on a psychological development argument to the effect that there are seven successive stages in the movement from neonatal dependence to full adult maturity and competence. Not all individuals move through the seven stages; instead, some remain fixated at lower stages than do others. Most important, the I-Levels formulation contends that juveniles who exhibit interpersonal immaturity are the ones who are most likely to become involved in youthful misconduct, while more mature youngsters are less likely to become delinquent. An additional feature is the identification of nine delinquent subtypes, such as "asocial aggressives," "manipulators," and "cultural identifiers," that are located within the three main maturity stages to which delinquents are assigned.

The basic argument about identifiable stages of interpersonal development is not at issue. However, it should be noted that the diagnostic procedures through which delinquents are assigned to I-Level subtypes are relatively subjective ones. An even more important point is that the claim about higher levels of interpersonal maturity among nondelinquents is untested, for research efforts have not been made to discover whether nondelinquents truly are more mature than delinquents.

The classification endeavors considered to this point have centered on psychological variations among delinquent offenders. Quite a different conceptualization was put forth by Cloward and Ohlin (1960), dealing with working-class, gang, or subcultural delinquency. These theorists asserted that some inner-city, working-class neighborhoods are relatively stable and characterized by relatively numerous economic opportunities of a legitimate kind as well as illegitimate or criminal pathways to economic success. On the other hand, some inner-city neighborhoods are disorganized social jungles, deficient both in legitimate and illegitimate opportunities for economic success. In relatively stable neighborhoods, gang delinquency occurs within a criminalistic subculture in which offenders are typically engaged in instrumental, predatory violations, while in disorganized communities, most gang members are caught up in violence such as gang warfare. In both forms, delinquency is most common among youths who have relatively high aspirations for accepted social and economic success but who also view their chances for such success as relatively dim. Finally, in both kinds of working-class neighborhoods, some youths are "double failures"—that is, psychologically impaired individuals with poor prospects for economic success of any kind. These are the youths who are most likely to become caught up in a "retreatist subculture" of drug use.

Gibbons (1965, 1970) drew together much of the material just described and amalgamated it in a delinquent typology involving nine hypothesized types of delinquents. This scheme included both the kinds of delinquent acts engaged in and the attitudes and self-images thought to characterize the nine types, including three kinds of gang delinquents—automobile thief joyriders, "behavior problem" delinquents, and female delinquents—and four other types. This scheme subsequently appeared in a treatise on correctional treatment (Gibbons, 1965) and in a delinquency textbook (Gibbons, 1970).

THE DECLINE OF TYPOLOGICAL THINKING

Enthusiasm among criminologists for classificatory ventures was relatively short-lived, largely because research evidence began to undermine the notion that delinquents can be sorted into distinct categories. For example, most of the findings from probings of the Cloward and Ohlin (1960) argument failed to support it. In particular, investigators reported that most gang delinquents engage in a variety of offenses rather than specializing in predatory or violent kinds of misconduct. In much the same way, other research cast doubt on the descriptions of joyriders and other alleged types of delinquents.

The proliferation of self-report studies, initiated in the 1950s, also created serious doubts among criminologists about typological categorizations. Self-report studies involved questionnaires administered mainly to ostensibly nondelinquent high school students—youths who had not been arrested or dealt with in the juvenile justice system—and sometimes to a comparison group of officially identified delinquents, such as training school residents. The results indicated that many nondelinquents had actually been involved in acts of lawbreaking, although these were generally less serious and less frequent than the violations reported by the officially labeled delinquents. The studies also suggested that few offenders, whether hidden or detected, were specialists who confined their lawbreaking to only a few kinds of misbehavior.

SOME RECENT DEVELOPMENTS

During the 1990s, considerable public concern began to be voiced regarding a pandemic of serious delinquency, much of which was violent in nature, thought to be spreading across the nation. At the same time, some criminologists turned their attention to identifying the characteristics of serious and violent offenders and to documenting the numbers of such offenders. These

efforts are probed in detail in *Serious and Violent Offenders* (Loeber, Farrington, and Waschbusch, 1998), which is the product of a 22-member study group supported by the Office of Juvenile Justice and Delinquency Prevention. This large tome deals with the characteristics of serious and violent juvenile (SVJ) offenders as well as chronic ones; risk factors in the backgrounds of SVJs; and recommended strategies and programs for dealing with SVJs.

In this study, *serious offender* was defined as a person who had committed one or more of seven specific violent offenses or one or more other specific offenses such as larceny or theft, auto theft, or carjacking (Loeber, Farrington, and Waschbusch, 1998). Thus serious and violent offenders constitute a subclass of serious offenders. Loeber and Farrington also noted that while the definitions of "chronic offenders" that have been offered by others all center on the number of offenses persons have committed, the required minimum number varies from one criminologist to another. Loeber and Farrington (1998:xx) have also indicated that "the majority of SVJ offenders of any race tend to be multiple-problem youth. They often have school problems (truancy, suspension, and dropout), substance abuse problems, and they are disproportionately victims of violence."

These working definitions of *SVJ offender* and *chronic offender* are reasonable, and the assertions about risk factors in SVJ offenders' backgrounds have been drawn from a body of research evidence. At the same time, some of the members of the study group have noted some reservations regarding the conclusions about serious and violent offenders. For instance, not all youth who qualify as SVJ offenders exhibit the indicated risk factors, and some who appear to be at risk are unlikely to turn into SVJ offenders.

Turning to a different matter, many observers have in the past commented on criminologists' lack of attention to lawbreaking by either youthful or adult females. In the case of delinquency, most of the early reports on female offenders argued that (1) lawbreaking is relatively rare on the part of young women; (2) when they do come to the attention of the police or court workers, it is largely because they are in defiance of parental restraints and, in particular, are sexually active or suspected of becoming so; and (3) their misbehavior is linked to family conflict in the way of parent-child discord (Gibbons and Griswold, 1957).

While there is some evidence in support of these contentions, the research today reveals greater complexity than indicated in these early assumptions. Overall, male delinquency is more prevalent and more serious than female delinquency. However, arrest rates of girls under age 18 have increased more dramatically than those of boys, including arrests for violent crimes. Additionally, self-report studies suggest that the gender gap in lawbreaking is not nearly as great as arrest data indicate (Chesney-Lind and Shelden, 1992).

Although there are some inconsistencies in the findings, much of the research does indicate that family problems are more frequently a source of female delinquency than male delinquency. Indeed, girls are more likely than boys to be referred to juvenile court by someone other than the police, most commonly, parents. Further, parents as well as the court continue to be more concerned about the status offenses and sexual activity of girls than about those of boys. As Chesney-Lind (1989:7) puts it, "trivial offenses, particularly status offenses, are more significant in the case of girls' [than boys'] arrests."

Female delinquents are much more likely than male delinquents to have been sexually abused in their homes and over a longer period of time (Chesney-Lind and Shelden, 1992). Girls who are sexually abused frequently develop school difficulties, become truant, and run away from home. Searching for ways to survive on their own, with few skills and little education, runaway girls often turn to the streets, where they become involved in prostitution, drug sales, panhandling, and petty theft. Once on the street, they are vulnerable to further exploitation and sexual victimization (Gilfus, 1992). Chesney-Lind (1989) argues that societal responses to this very common pattern of female delinquency amount to the criminalization of girls' survival strategies.

A longitudinal study of females under the jurisdiction of the California Youth Authority (Warren and Rosenbaum, 1986) found that girls typically first come into contact with the system through their commission of a status offense. The majority of girls who enter the system in their early teens continue their involvement in crime into adulthood. Most of their lawbreaking consists of minor property crimes, sex work, and drug offenses. It is for relatively nonserious property and status offenses that the gender gap in delinquency is smallest. These gender patterns have been found to be similar across racial groups (Datesman and Aickin, 1984; Jensen and Thompson, 1990).

Girls are much less likely than are boys to engage in serious violent crimes. As Heide (1999) points out, girls only account for about 6 percent of all arrests for juvenile homicide. When girls do kill, they are more likely than boys to kill family members and to have accomplices, typically males. Although in the 1990s, several high-profile cases of neonaticide—in which a young woman, usually acting alone, killed her newborn child—resulted in criminal prosecution, this form of homicide is rare. Finally, females who commit violent and other serious crimes are more likely than their male counterparts to be labeled as mentally ill and treated through the mental health system (Frigon, 1995; Morris, 1987).

While gang delinquency has historically been considered a male behavior (with some peripheral female involvement), one extensive survey (Esbensen and Winfree, 1998) found that girls constitute 38 percent of gang members. Like boys, girls who join gangs are frequently looking for a group to meet social, emotional, and sometimes economic needs. From her research on girl gang members, Miller (2001) concluded that three characteristics—exposure to neighborhood gangs, having family members in a gang, and having family problems—were particularly descriptive of girls in gangs.

Other than the early literature on different types of "wayward" or "beyond control" girls, the research on female delinquency has focused more on pathways and patterns of female delinquency than on types of female delinquents. Most girls' delinquency comprises minor property crimes and drug and status offenses. However, girls are clearly involved in more diverse forms of lawbreaking than was historically thought.

CONCLUSION

To date, efforts to identify types of delinquents or patterns of delinquency have resulted in one of those not uncommon instances in criminology of a vessel that is either half full or half empty. The evidence suggests not only that much lawbreaking is not patterned but also that some broad patterns of delinquency and kinds of youthful lawbreakers can be identified. Some existing classification schemes are precise enough to provide benchmarks for making sense out of the myriad kinds of offenders and offenses observed in American society.

Don C. Gibbons and Kathryn Ann Farr

See also Arson; Community Treatment Project; Theories of Delinquency

Bibliography

Chesney-Lind, M. 1989. Girls' crime and woman's place: Toward a feminist model of female delinquency. *Crime and Delinquency* 35:5–29.

Chesney-Lind, M., and R. G. Shelden. 1992. *Girls, Delinquency, and Juvenile Justice.* Pacific Grove, CA: Brooks/Cole.

Cloward, R., and L. Ohlin. 1960. *Delinquency and Opportunity.* Glencoe, IL: Free Press.

Datesman, S. K., and M. Aickin. 1984. Offense specialization and escalation among status offenders. *Journal of Criminal Law and Criminology* 75:1246–1274.

Esbensen, F., and T. Winfree. 1998. Race and gender differences between gang and non-gang youths: Results from a multisite survey. *Justice Quarterly* 15:505–526.

Frigon, S. 1995. A genealogy of women's madness. Pp. 20–48 in R. E. Dobash and L. Noaks (eds.), *Gender and Crime.* Cardiff, UK: University of Wales Press.

Gibbons, D. C. 1965. *Changing the Lawbreaker.* Englewood Cliffs, NJ: Prentice Hall.

Gibbons, D. C. 1970. *Delinquent Behavior.* Englewood Cliffs, NJ: Prentice Hall.

Gibbons, D. C., and K. A. Farr. 2001. Defining patterns of crime and types of offenders. Pp. 36–64 in S. Henry and M. Lanier (eds.), *What Is Crime?* Lanham, MD: Rowan & Littlefield.

Gibbons, D. C., and M. J. Griswold. 1957. Sex differences among juvenile court referrals. *Sociology and Social Research* 42:106–110.

Gilfus, M. 1992. From victims to survivors to offenders: Women's routes of entry and immersion into street crime. *Women and Criminal Justice* 4:63–89.

Glueck, S., and E. Glueck. 1950. *Unraveling Juvenile Delinquency.* Cambridge, MA: Harvard University Press.

Heide, K. M. 1999. *Young Killers: The Challenge of Juvenile Homicide.* Thousand Oaks, CA: Sage.

Hewitt, L. E., and R. L. Jenkins. 1944. *Fundamental Patterns of Maladjustment: The Dynamics of Their Origin.* Springfield: Illinois State Printer.

Jenkins, R. L., and L. E. Hewitt. 1944. Types of personality structure encountered in child guidance clinics. *American Journal of Orthopsychiatry* 14:84–94.

Jensen, G. F., and K. Thompson. 1990. What's class got to do with it: A further examination of power control theory. *American Journal of Sociology* 95:1009–1023.

Loeber, R., and D. P. Farrington (eds.). 1998. *Serious and Violent Juvenile Offenders: Risk Factors and Successful Interventions.* Thousand Oaks, CA: Sage.

Loeber, R., D. P. Farrington, and D. A. Waschbusch. 1998. Serious and violent juvenile offenders. Pp. 13–29 in R. Loeber and D. P. Farrington (eds.), *Serious and Violent Juvenile Offenders: Risk Factors and Successful Interventions.* Thousand Oaks, CA: Sage.

Miller, J. 2001. *One of the Guys: Girls, Gangs, and Gender.* New York: Oxford University Press.

Morris, A. 1987. *Women, Crime and Criminal Justice.* Oxford, UK: Basil Blackwell.

Reiss, A. J., Jr. 1952. Social correlates of psychological types of delinquents. *American Sociological Review* 17:710–718.

Warren, M. Q. 1976. Intervention with juvenile delinquents. Pp. 176–204 in M. K. Rosenheim (ed.), *Pursuing Justice for the Child.* Chicago: University of Chicago Press.

Warren, M. Q., and J. L. Rosenbaum. 1986. Criminal careers of female offenders. *Criminal Justice and Behavior* 13:393–418.

DELINQUENCY

III. Trends and Data

The nature and extent of juvenile delinquency in the United States is elusive for several reasons. First, measuring crime in the United States—let alone juvenile crime—presents unique problems. Second, the juvenile justice system is decentralized, with each jurisdiction maintaining separate records and collecting information differently. Third, for the most part, record keeping in juvenile justice is still subject to confidentiality and sealing restrictions in many locations. Therefore, accurate records concerning juveniles who commit delinquent acts are difficult, if not impossible, to come by. Finally, and perhaps most important, there are a multitude of options available for juveniles who come into contact with the system. The number of placements, diversionary programs, and facilities is innumerable. As a result, the true picture and extent of juvenile delinquency is subject to debate and interpretation.

Despite these shortcomings, various mechanisms are in place to measure juvenile delinquency. Each method has strengths and weaknesses, and each presents different issues in both measurement and interpretation. Policymakers and researchers use juvenile crime measurements to develop laws, theories, and a variety of programs and initiatives within the juvenile justice system. Therefore, it is crucial to understand how we measure juvenile crime and what the measurements tell us about the nature and extent of juvenile delinquency.

MEASURING THE EXTENT OF JUVENILE CRIME

Questions of how much juvenile crime exists are often answered through three main methods of gathering statistics about crime: official records, victimization surveys, and self-report surveys. Each method has strengths and weaknesses, each method collects data differently, and each method typically results in different estimates of how much juvenile crime there is. Consequently, anyone wishing to interpret crime data should first determine how it was collected. The methods discussed in the following sections are used to measure the extent of juvenile crime and provide insight into trends of juvenile offending patterns. It is important to recognize that many other measures of crime exist, but they are not specific to delinquency and therefore tell us nothing about juvenile crime.

OFFICIAL RECORDS AND MEASURES

Official statistics and measures are any data collected by city, county, state, or federal government agencies. The primary agency that stores juvenile records is typically the juvenile probation agency. The juvenile court is the centerpiece of the juvenile justice system, and the juvenile probation agency is an arm of the juvenile court. Typically, each county has its own juvenile probation agency and thus its own system of record keeping. In addition, many states have a centralized juvenile probation administration or other youth bureau. However, many states only recently have begun to develop central depositories for juvenile records. As confidentiality and other restrictions on juvenile records are eased, it is likely that more centralized records will be kept on juvenile offenders.

Although probation agencies typically house the largest amount of information on juvenile offenders, these records are not typically used to estimate or count the amount of juvenile crime outside the county or state. Official records of juvenile crime are almost exclusively based on police records and counts. In this section, law enforcement, juvenile court, and juvenile correctional statistics will be discussed.

Law Enforcement Statistics

The most comprehensive official measure of crime in the United States is the *Uniform Crime Reports* (UCR) compiled annually by the Federal Bureau of Investigation (FBI). The UCR collects information about offenses committed by both adult and juvenile offenders. A summary measure of a variety of offenses based on official police reports of crime and arrests, the UCR is broken into two parts: Part I and Part II offenses. Part I offenses, also known as index crimes, are among the most serious crimes and include the following:

1. Murder and nonnegligent manslaughter

2. Forcible rape

3. Robbery

4. Aggravated assault

5. Burglary

6. Larceny-theft

7. Motor vehicle theft

8. Arson

The UCR collects a simple count of the number of index crimes reported to police in the United States. Because these data are not broken down into juvenile and adult offenders, there is no way to tell which of the reported offenses were committed by juveniles and which by adults.

Part II offenses are all offenses not included in Part I offenses, such as vandalism, weapons violations, drug abuse violations, disorderly conduct, and fraud, to name a few. In addition, three status offenses categorized as Part II offenses—running away, curfew, and truancy—only involve juveniles and give a good idea of the number of status offenses enforced by police. Data are collected on the number and characteristics (e.g., age, gender, and race or ethnicity) of individuals arrested for both Part I and II offenses. This is where differentiation can be made between juveniles and adults. The number and characteristics of juveniles arrested for Part I and II offenses can be obtained through the UCR. From the arrest data, estimates are made of the number of juvenile arrests.

In 1999, law enforcement agencies in the United States made an estimated 2.47 million arrests of juveniles in the United States. It is estimated that 1,400 juveniles were arrested for murder and 28,000 for robbery in 1999. Juveniles accounted for 17 percent of all arrests and 18 percent of all violent crime arrests in 1999. In the late 1980s, juvenile arrests for violent crimes increased substantially and peaked in 1994. In 1999, for the fifth consecutive year, the total number of juvenile arrests for violent crime index offenses—murder, forcible rape, robbery, and aggravated assault—declined. Specifically, between 1995 and 1999, juvenile arrests for violent crime index offenses fell 23 percent. Similarly, arrests for property crime index offenses—burglary, larceny-theft, motor vehicle theft, and arson—declined 24 percent between 1995 and 1999. Therefore, from 1995 to 1999, arrests for index crimes fell 24 percent and all crimes fell 9 percent. Although many categories of juvenile crime have been decreasing in recent years, arrests for fraud, embezzlement, offenses against the family and children, driving under the influence, and liquor law violations have increased substantially.

Juvenile Court Statistics

The Office of Juvenile Justice and Delinquency Prevention collects data from state and local agencies responsible for the collection and dissemination of juvenile justice data. They collect both automated case-level data and aggregate data from more than 2,000 juvenile courts around the country. The automated case-level data describe each case's demographics and processing characteristics, and the aggregate data indicate the number of delinquency cases disposed each year. It is important to note that these statistics are *estimates* and should not be taken as a comprehensive count of court activity. Nonetheless, the information provides another method to determine how much juvenile delinquency exists. Juvenile court statistics provide data on the number and type of cases handled by juvenile court. These data are also broken down by age, gender, and race or ethnicity. Juvenile courts processed nearly 1.8 million delinquency cases in 1997. In 1997, juvenile courts disposed of approximately 400,000 juvenile cases involving violent offenses such as rape, robbery, and assault. Furthermore, juvenile courts disposed of more than 840,000 cases involving property offenses such as burglary, theft, and vandalism. In addition, more than 180,000 drug law violations were processed as well as 340,000 public order offenses, including obstruction of justice and disorderly conduct. These numbers reflect a 48 percent increase in the number of cases handled by the juvenile court from 1988 to 1997.

These statistics reveal several interesting patterns, including the "funnel effect" in processing these cases.

During 1997, law enforcement agencies arrested nearly 2.8 million juveniles. In other words, 1 million juveniles were arrested who were not handled in the juvenile court. The fact that many arrested juveniles are not formally referred to juvenile court is not all that surprising. The funnel effect is present in the adult criminal justice system as well, but the effect is much more pronounced in the juvenile justice system.

The funnel effect occurs for many reasons, the least of which is the general perception that youth deserve a second chance. Most likely, the juveniles referred to the court have had prior contact with law enforcement or committed a serious offense that merited greater attention. Once a juvenile reaches the juvenile court system, a variety of exit points further narrow the total number of juveniles formally processed. A substantial portion of cases are dismissed or handled informally. In addition, a large number of juveniles are diverted once they reach the juvenile court. In other words, the juvenile court attempts to avoid stigmatizing juveniles with a delinquency adjudication.

Juvenile Correctional Statistics

Yet another official measure of delinquency in the United States is based on correctional statistics. Simply put, the number of juveniles who are committed to public and private facilities are counted and tabulated. These counts give an accurate indication of how many juveniles have been incarcerated for delinquency. In 1997, more than 105,000 juveniles were incarcerated in public and private facilities. Of those, 33.4 percent were incarcerated for violent offenses, 30.2 percent for property offenses, 8.8 percent for drug offenses, 9.2 percent for public order offenses such as weapons offenses and obstruction of justice, 11.9 percent for probation or parole violations, and 6.5 percent for status offenses such as running away and truancy. In 1997, of the more than 2.8 million juveniles arrested and 1.8 million juveniles processed into juvenile court, only a little more than 100,000 juveniles were placed into secure correctional facilities nationwide.

STRENGTHS AND WEAKNESSES OF OFFICIAL RECORDS AND MEASURES

The chief strength of official records is that they are reliable counts of juveniles who are arrested, processed, and incarcerated by the juvenile justice system. The summary counts are based on actual cases and give a clear idea of the workload of the system. In addition, official statistics are the most comprehensive measure of juvenile crime available. They present the national picture of juvenile crime and allow for comparison between jurisdictions and areas of the country. They also show trends in arrests and processing that can ultimately affect policy-making decisions. Court and correctional statistics are excellent measures of the number of cases processed and the population in juvenile correctional facilities. However, these statistics are also limited by the fact that many juvenile dispositions occur outside formal processing, and very few juvenile offenders ever see the inside of a secure correctional facility. When they do, the juveniles have normally committed many more crimes than the one(s) for which they have been locked up. Nonetheless, official statistics are used as the primary measures of crime trends and offending patterns in the United States. They allow researchers to see trends in arrests, court filings, and incarceration.

There are, however, several problems and weaknesses with official statistics, in particular the UCR. First, not all law enforcement agencies report to the UCR, and sometimes the counts reported by law enforcement agencies are not accurate. The UCR assumes that measures and counts from law enforcement agencies from around the country are accurate, which may not always be the case. The UCR also underestimates the total amount of crime in the United States. Referred to as the dark figure of crime, UCR's underestimation occurs for several reasons.

First, not all crimes are reported to police. It is estimated that less than 40 percent of all index crimes are reported to the police. In addition, certain crimes (such as prostitution and drug dealing) are considered victimless crimes because both parties "consent" to the crime. Indeed, there are very few drug dealers and prostitutes rushing to the police station to turn themselves in. Some crimes require the police to initiate and file complaints more than others. This is especially true for juvenile status offenses such as curfew and truancy. Again, without police action, there is no case to report.

Second, the UCR uses what is termed a hierarchy rule when multiple crimes occur in one incident. In other words, when a person commits multiple crimes during the same incident, only the most serious crime is reported to the UCR. This also has added importance for juvenile crime counts because juveniles frequently commit crimes in groups or commit multiple

offenses. Third, the UCR probably underestimates juvenile crime in particular because of the broad discretion and variety of dispositional options available within the juvenile justice system. Many juvenile offenders are handled informally by the police, schools, or other authorities. In addition, there are numerous diversionary placements to which a juvenile can be referred rather than being arrested. Therefore, the incident will frequently go undocumented or unreported. While the more serious crimes are more accurately reflected, the less serious Part II offenses are more a measure of police activity than of actual juvenile crime.

In a recent study of police patrol practices, the total number of UCR crimes was analyzed. Before adopting a more aggressive patrol strategy, the city's UCR statistics showed no arrests for curfew violations over a three-year period. However, after a new chief was appointed and a new philosophy began, the number of reported curfew violations jumped to more than 1,500 in one year. There was no explosion in the number of status offenses in the city and no change in the laws. The only change was in the enforcement of the offenses. The implications for measuring delinquency through official records are clear: If the police are formally enforcing these offenses, the delinquency rates are high; if they are not, the records show low delinquency rates. It's not the crimes involving juveniles that fluctuate but police attention to those crimes.

A new system of data collection is currently being implemented in the United States that solves many of the problems with the UCR. The National Incident-Based Reporting System (NIBRS) changes the way crime data are collected from simply counting the numbers to gathering information on victim and offender. Although this new system will cure many of the problems present in official statistics, the fact remains that many victims will still not be able to tell if their victimizer was a juvenile—especially for property crimes. NIBRS has the promise of substantially increasing the accuracy and validity of official police statistics with regard to all crime as well as juvenile crime in particular.

VICTIMIZATION STATISTICS AND MEASURES

Another way juvenile crime is measured is through victimization surveys. In this type of research, randomly selected people are surveyed about any criminal victimizations they might have experienced over the past six months or year. The victimization statistics gathered from this sample are then used to generate estimates about the amount of crime occurring. The largest and most well known victimization survey, the National Crime Victimization Survey (NCVS), is conducted by the Bureau of Justice Statistics and the U.S. Census Bureau. Data are obtained from a representative sample of households in the United States each year. Roughly 50,000 households are sampled and about 100,000 people interviewed. The individuals are interviewed twice a year about the frequency, characteristics, and consequences of their victimization. The respondents are asked about victimization by rape, robbery, assault, burglary, motor vehicle theft, and theft. Basically, the offenses are the same as index crimes used in the UCR except for murder and arson. Unlike the UCR, which collects and reports summary crime statistics (counts), the NCVS reports data on criminal incidents (cases). The NCVS gets a better picture of the dark figure of crime that the UCR fails to account for and consistently shows that the UCR underestimates the total amount of crime in the United States.

STRENGTHS AND WEAKNESSES OF VICTIMIZATION STATISTICS AND MEASURES

Many measures of victimization reveal that there is a dark figure of crime that goes unreported to police. The chief strength of victimization studies is that they get at unreported crimes and tend to show a more realistic picture of the total crimes committed annually. In addition, if the survey is conducted with juveniles in a school setting, it is probably an accurate measure of juvenile victimization. In the end, victimization surveys tell us much more about juvenile victimization than juvenile offending. For victimization studies to be an accurate measure of juvenile offending, the victims must know who their victimizers were. For most of the crimes reported in the NCVS, the offender is unknown. Even if the offender were known, it may not be possible for the victim to accurately assess the age of the offender.

Victimization statistics may underreport the amount of juvenile victimization as well. A chief drawback concerning the measurement of juvenile crime is that some measures of victimization in the United States are sent to households asking for the head of the household to complete the survey. It is

therefore unlikely that a juvenile would be involved in filling out the survey. We know that juveniles frequently do not report their victimizations to police, to other officials, or to their parents. Only about 40 percent of juveniles report their victimizations. Juveniles rarely tell their parents about the victimizations they experience in their communities or schools, so it is not likely that the head of a household would know about the true extent of victimization of any child living in the household. Because about 66 percent of the juvenile victims of crime were victimized by juvenile offenders, one can logically conclude that victimization studies underestimate juvenile crime as well.

SELF-REPORT STATISTICS AND MEASURES

Self-report statistics are gathered from surveys of youth who volunteer information about their criminal and drug histories. Of the three methods, self-report surveys of juveniles are the most numerous and most diverse. In fact, these are the only statistical projects that are specifically targeted at juveniles. In a self-report survey, a juvenile is asked a battery of questions concerning their past. Self-report surveys probably provide the most accurate picture of juvenile crime currently available.

Since 1975, the National Institute of Drug Abuse has conducted an annual survey of high school seniors called Monitoring the Future (MTF). The MTF survey assesses a wide variety of behaviors, attitudes, and values of juveniles. Each spring, about 50,000 juveniles in high schools are asked to fill out computer scan sheets in response to batteries of questions that include self-reported use of alcohol, tobacco, and illegal drugs as well as involvement in delinquency and other illegal acts. A subset of about 2,400 MTF respondents from the high school samples is selected each year to receive follow-up questionnaires in the mail. The MTF survey provides a rich data source for examining trends in drug use among juveniles.

Another self-report survey of juveniles comprises three coordinated projects: the Denver Youth Survey, the Pittsburgh Youth Study, and the Rochester Youth Development Study. These projects, started in 1986, are designed to improve the understanding of serious delinquency, violence, and drug use by examining how youth develop within the context of family, school, peers, and community. The studies use several data sources, including interviews with youth, their guardians, and teachers, as well as information collected from official agencies. The three research teams worked together to ensure that certain core measures were identical across the sites, including self-reported delinquency and drug use; community and neighborhood characteristics; youth, family, and peer variables; and arrest and judicial processing histories.

STRENGTHS AND WEAKNESSES OF SELF-REPORT STATISTICS AND MEASURES

Self-report surveys measure offenses not known to the police, as well as how many times an individual commits offenses. Self-report data have shown that individuals commit far more offenses than those for which they are arrested. A juvenile may commit as many as 100 offenses before police make a formal arrest. Self-reports also allow researchers to probe into a juvenile's background and potential reasons for committing delinquent acts and to examine the trends of juvenile offending and juvenile risk-taking behavior. In short, this method is undoubtedly the most comprehensive picture of juvenile crime and offending currently available.

One of the most common criticisms leveled at self-report research on delinquency is that data gained from the juveniles may not be accurate. Issues such as memory, exaggeration, confusion over definitions, and outright lying are frequently cited. However, self-reported delinquency data have been shown to be quite accurate compared with official records. Nonetheless, issues such as juveniles lying or misstating information on self-report questionnaires is still a problem. Another problem with self-report research involves whom the researchers are surveying. Several of the most comprehensive youth surveys are typically done in school settings, so certain types of youths are excluded from the surveys, such as chronic truants and serious habitual delinquents (who may be incarcerated).

Another series of problems with self-report research concerns the questionnaires themselves. Some questionnaires focus on relatively minor offenses while excluding serious offenses. In addition, there are frequently problems with offense definitions

in some questionnaires. Many juveniles (and adults for that matter) are not well versed in what is and is not a crime, as well as what is and is not specific criminal behavior. Many people confuse robbery and burglary, for example. Finally, the question responses from which respondents choose can be misleading. Typical choices on these questionnaires include "often," "sometimes," "occasionally," and "never." There obviously can be confusion and misinterpretation by juveniles responding to such questions.

COMPARISON OF THE THREE METHODS

Comparisons of official statistics, victimization surveys, and self-report data show several striking differences. Self-report data show that nearly all juveniles break the law at one time or another; however, only a small percentage of juveniles go on to become serious or habitual delinquents. Self-reports also show that gender, race, and social class are less correlated with delinquency than is found with studies using official statistics. The best measure of juvenile crime and juvenile offending patterns comes from self-reports, and probably the least useful information comes from victimization surveys. Each of the measures has certain strengths and weaknesses, and these should be taken into account whenever conclusions are made about the true nature and extent of juvenile crime in the United States (see Table 2).

Eric J. Fritsch and Tory J. Caeti

See also Self-Report Studies; Victimization

Bibliography

Caeti, T. 1999. *Houston's Targeted Beat Program: A Quasi-experimental Test of Police Patrol Strategies*. Doctoral Dissertation, Sam Houston State University.

Finkelhor, D., and R. Ormrod. 2000. *Reporting Crimes Against Juveniles*. Washington, DC: Office of Juvenile Justice and Delinquency Prevention.

Sickmund, M. 2000. *Offenders in Juvenile Court, 1997*. Washington, DC: Office of Juvenile Justice and Delinquency Prevention.

Snyder, H. N. 2000. *Juvenile Arrests, 1999*. Washington, DC: Office of Juvenile Justice and Delinquency Prevention.

Table 2   Strengths and Weaknesses of the Three Measures of Juvenile Crime

Measure	Advantages	Disadvantages
Official statistics	1. Accurate and reliable assessments of formal juvenile offender processing 2. Allow for trend analysis and comparisons over time 3. Good measures of police activity in juvenile justice 4. Allow for comparisons to be made among different jurisdictions	1. Exclude all juveniles who were processed informally 2. Underestimate juvenile crime 3. Poor measures of status offending and victimless crimes involving juveniles 4. Some agencies don't report, and most numbers are estimates 5. Most juveniles do not report crimes to the police 6. Many juvenile offenders are handled informally by police and courts 7. Specific problems exist with how UCR data are collected
Victimization surveys	1. Get at the dark figure of crime 2. When conducted with juveniles at schools, probably the best measures of juvenile victimizations and school crime	1. Primary measure of victimization sent to heads of households and not juveniles themselves 2. Most victims don't know if they were victimized by a juvenile 3. Most juveniles don't reveal victimizations to police, officials, or parents
Self-report surveys	1. Most accurate measures of juvenile crime and offending 2. Assess victimless crimes and status offenses 3. Juveniles are the ones filling out the surveys 4. Give insight into motivation, demographics, and correlates of juvenile crime 5. Only measures that can estimate the total picture of juvenile crime 6. Data can be cross-checked with other official data	1. Memory, exaggeration, and lying by juveniles filling out survey 2. Can exclude certain juveniles such as chronic offenders 3. Manner in which the questions are asked can bias survey 4. Juveniles can misinterpret survey questions

 DIVERSION PROGRAMS

Diversion seeks to replace formal justice proceedings with informal, less punitive proceedings. In broad terms, the goal of diversion is to keep a juvenile offender out of the juvenile justice system, remove a juvenile from the system at any time in the process, or simply discontinue the case against the alleged delinquent. Thus diversion can begin at the discretion of the police officer and continue through the intake, adjudication, and sentencing phases in the juvenile justice process. Diversion can help a juvenile avoid stigmatization as a criminal or delinquent as well as the inadvertent abuses of basic human rights and dignities that can occur in a detention setting. Diversion also saves taxpayers from incurring further expenses in prosecution, adjudication, and disposition of less serious cases.

Shootings by juveniles at schools and schoolyards around the United States make it difficult, but not impossible, to argue for diversion. The primary difficulties are the lack of understanding about what constitutes diversion by the general public, the fact that diversion may not be appropriate for every juvenile offender, and the current practice of using diversion to aid the juvenile justice system rather than assist juveniles.

THE JUVENILE JUSTICE SYSTEM AS A HISTORY OF DIVERSION

Diversion is what the juvenile justice system is all about. To some, juvenile justice in the United States began in New York City in 1825 as a method of protecting children from the harshness of the criminal justice process of the day. Before that, American courts followed the practices of English courts, which discerned very little difference between juvenile and adult offenders. Not only were adults and juveniles held together prior to trial, they were also incarcerated together in situations where the juveniles were both victimized and tutored in crime by older inmates. This latter situation contributed to the creation of the New York House of Refuge in 1825, where juveniles were expected to be safe from such criminogenic conditions and to learn a trade.

Unlike adult jails or prisons, houses of refuge, or industrial schools (as the houses were sometimes labeled), held both the delinquent youth and the young person in need of protection due to parental neglect and/or abuse. "The articulated purpose of this facility," according to Eggleston (1999:138–139), "was work and education, with an emphasis on work. Students toiled under a 'contract system' where outside employers brought in raw materials for manufacture. There was little time or energy left for schoolwork." Similar houses of refuge or industrial schools were established over the next 35 years in other large cities, including Boston (1826), Philadelphia (1828), New Orleans (1847), and Cincinnati (1850; Abbott, 1938; Mennel, 1973). The

state was now involved in the upbringing of increasing numbers of its children.

The introduction of state-operated facilities for destitute juveniles and young persons in conflict with the law introduced a new concept into the way in which criminal justice was administered in the United States. The state would stand *in loco parentis* or act in place of the parents in cases that involved juveniles. This practice was a mirror of the English guardianship practices under that country's Poor Laws, which evolved into the doctrine of *parens patriae* (or "nation as parent"), whereby the state is granted authority to intervene in the lives of children who have little or no parental care and who, due to their lack of development or involvement in delinquent behavior, cannot care for themselves. Unfortunately, for both destitute and delinquent destitute juveniles of the period, the conditions within most juvenile facilities continued to deteriorate to the point where they were as bad or worse than the adult prisons from which the young persons were supposedly diverted.

The development of the first juvenile court in Chicago in 1899 may be seen as both the logical extension of the use of separate court dockets for juveniles and an achievement within a broader social reform movement. Among the factors that gave rise to this reform movement are the changing economic situation of the day, concerns about the exploitive nature of the existing juvenile facilities, and the child-saving movement (Mennel, 1973; Platt, 1991). The focus of the new juvenile courts was on youth rather than their offenses, on less formal processing and rehabilitation rather than punishment. Since the juvenile court was seeking rehabilitation and personalized justice for juveniles in a manner akin to a benevolent parent, it was believed that the formal, adversarial processes and sanctions employed in the criminal justice system were inappropriate for juvenile offenders. Thus the doctrine of *parens patriae* became one of the three competing doctrines in the processing of juveniles in conflict with the law. This is illustrated in Figure 1.

Since the turn of the 20th century, every American state has established a juvenile court, and numerous states have devolved this responsibility to the county level. Instead of *convicting* a juvenile of a criminal offence, juvenile courts *adjudicate* a young person for a *delinquency* and label him or her *delinquent* rather than *criminal*. This change in language was calculated to support the notion that juvenile offenders are diverted from the adult system of criminal justice and

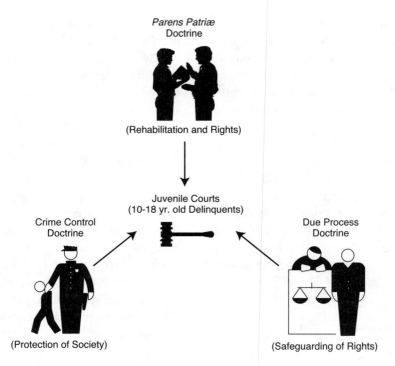

Figure 1. Competing Doctrines in Juvenile Justice.

that they remain somehow less developed and less responsible than an adult offender.

Juvenile courts represent a way to treat juvenile delinquents as wards of the state who "receive practically the same care, custody and discipline that are accorded the neglected and dependent child" (Fine, 1957:207). Care rather than custody has become the hallmark of many juvenile courts. The sanctions the courts choose to employ as juvenile court judges rely heavily on the presentence or predisposition reports completed by juvenile probation officers to create personalized justice based on the needs of the juveniles and risks they present to reoffend. The range of dispositions remain nearly the same as those available to judges in the adult criminal justice system, namely warnings, unconditional discharges, suspended sentences, conditional discharges, probation, restitution, fines, and custody. Custodial sanctions include confinement in a training school or reformatory until the juvenile reaches the age of majority or short periods within a boot camp setting followed by probation. From its beginnings, the juvenile courts have relied more on community-based rather than on custodial

sanctions. Probation supervision remains the most commonly used disposition in the United States.

Juvenile probation departments, or specialized juvenile sections within existing probation agencies, have been established to divert juvenile offenders from custodial dispositions. These specialized agencies have developed expertise in dealing with the unique needs and risks posed by juvenile offenders. The *parens patriae* doctrine continues to employ a welfare philosophy and regards the use of probation to be less restrictive than custody while still permitting for the rehabilitation of the juvenile.

One group of juveniles was diverted *en masse* from custodial sanctions when the Juvenile Justice and Delinquency Prevention Act passed in 1974. Status offenders, or youths who had not committed a criminal offence but rather offences such as truancy, underage drinking, promiscuous behavior, and curfew violations, were diverted from custodial sanctions. In the mid-1990s, two other groups were identified as worthy of diversion: first-time, young juvenile offenders (10 to 15 years of age) and juveniles charged with drug offenses. The general philosophy behind the teen and drug court movements was that relatively young first-time offenders can be dealt with more effectively and quickly by diverting them to community-based groups. This process focused on restoration and reparation by young persons, making them accountable for their actions.

IS DIVERSION APPROPRIATE FOR EVERY OFFENDER?

Simply put, the answer is no. Diversion is not appropriate for every juvenile offender, just as custody is not appropriate for many juveniles charged with violent crimes. The use of formal rather than informal processes continues to be the norm within the juvenile justice system. The formal method of handling petitioned juveniles climbed gradually from a low of 50 percent in 1990 to a high of 57 percent in 1998 (Snyder et al., 2001). For example, of all juvenile cases in 1997, the Office of Juvenile Justice and Delinquency Programs (OJJDP) estimated that 43 percent were redirected because a formal petition was not filed at intake or by diversion before adjudication within that court (OJJDP, 1999). The type of offense mattered only slightly in the decision to petition the juvenile court. Approximately 58 percent of youths accused of a personal crime were petitioned compared with 53 percent in property cases, 61 percent in public order offenses, and 63 percent of youths accused of drug law violations (OJJDP, 1999).

DETERMINING WHO WILL BE DIVERTED

One of the primary difficulties in determining eligibility for diversion is that it may occur at each decision point within the juvenile justice system. Another primary difficulty is the lack of uniform criteria across the various municipal, county, state, and federal jurisdictions. One community might offer young offenders a single chance at diversion while a neighboring community might allow multiple entries into diversion programs. One county might limit diversion to first-time offenders regardless of their offenses while a county at the other end of the state might limit diversion to persons other than those charged with violent or sexual crimes.

Eligibility criteria for diversion programs should not be exhaustive or rigidly exclusive. The decision to use diversion should consider (1) the seriousness of the current offense; (2) the offender's delinquency history, familial or other support, and willingness to participate in and complete a diversion program; and (3) the victim's acceptance of diversion by the victim. These criteria should be seen as the first steps in an informal risk assessment, and the diversion program would provide a similar needs assessment to see if the youth is appropriate for the services offered.

To date, no jurisdiction in the United States has formalized juvenile diversion to the extent that every juvenile must be considered a candidate for diversion. Although half the states had either adopted diversion or were considering changes to their juvenile justice system to increase the use of diversion by the end of 1995, the juvenile justice pendulum appears to have swung away from the welfare model espoused as part of the *parens patriae* doctrine and toward the direction of the "get tough" philosophy prevalent in the adult criminal justice system. Interestingly, the use of custody as a juvenile court sanction has changed only slightly from 10.3 percent in 1989 to a low of 9.2 percent in 1995 and rising to 10.1 percent in 1998 (Snyder et al., 2001). Juvenile probation was used as both an informal and a formal sanction, for example, in nearly 365 of every 1,000 cases processed by the juvenile justice system in 1997 compared with only 106 cases where the young person was placed into a custodial setting (OJJDP, 1999).

Today our society faces many challenges in the attempt to divert juveniles from the adult criminal justice system as well as from the more formal and punitive processes and activities within the juvenile justice system. Because of well-publicized violent events involving juveniles, many state legislatures have begun to question the applicability of the juvenile justice system, yet few legislators are advocating its abolition. The doctrine of *parens patriae* has been tested in the appellate courts and has yet to be rejected as a legal concept or declared unconstitutional in practice. Some argue that the juvenile justice system should provide a more balanced approach to dealing with young offenders, their victims, and the community as a whole through the practice of diversion whenever it is appropriate.

WHERE ARE THE DIVERSION POINTS IN THE JUVENILE JUSTICE SYSTEM?

There are several points within the juvenile justice process when juveniles and youths may be diverted away from the formal, juvenile court to less formal activities or processes. The stated goals at each of these stages have included accountability and rehabilitation of the young person (with punishment being the third and lowest concern). Currently, diversion may result from actions of well-meaning police officers, prosecutors, intake officers, and judges.

Police Diversion

As in the adult criminal justice system, individual police officers serve as the gatekeepers to the system of juvenile justice in the United States. Unlike other players in the juvenile justice system, police often have the most contact with and thereby the most knowledge about accused delinquents as well as their family situations, peers, and other factors that affect them. Informal police referrals to parents and social agencies are generally preferable to and less costly than formal judicial activities. Police officers may informally perform the role of a conflict mediator or conference facilitator when they bring together juvenile delinquents, victims, and family members to work out the repayment for a broken window or other loss.

Prosecutorial Diversion

Prosecutors can divert juveniles at two stages in the juvenile justice system. Not only do they have the ability to determine which charges are most appropriate for a given delinquency, they may also decide whether to prosecute even after an alleged delinquency is petitioned. These abilities are in keeping with the general notion of prosecutorial discretion as well as the doctrine of *parens patriae*. Prosecutors can decide not to prosecute when the interests of the juvenile and justice coincide. Indeed, these interests might be served better through alternative measures such as victim-offender mediation, counseling, and other less stigmatizing options. Prosecutors rely on information from police officers, social workers, teachers, and others in making their decisions, as well as the local political situation.

Diversion by Intake Officers

Intake officers divert more young persons than any other player in the juvenile justice system. Following local and state regulations, intake officers screen alleged delinquents and either divert them from the formal juvenile justice system or enable their processing into it by filing a petition for the juvenile court to assume jurisdiction. Lack of sufficient evidence or the potential of resolving the matter informally are the two basic reasons why a juvenile matter would not process past this stage (OJJDP, 1999). Based on the regulations, intake officers ensure that the juvenile's age, lack of prior offenses (especially violent offenses), attitude, and amenability to treatment are considered in their decision to divert or formally process the case. Intake officers divert just over 40 percent of cases that come to their attention (OJJDP, 1999).

Judicial Diversion

The juvenile court diverts the second largest number of young persons from the juvenile justice process (OJJDP, 1999). During 1997, 42 percent of cases that came before juvenile court judges were either diverted or disposed of in some manner (e.g., the juvenile wrote an essay or made a formal apology, received a warning, was given informal probation, made restitution, had to perform community service, or was referred to a social service agency) without a delinquency adjudication being made.

INTERNATIONAL EXPERIENCES WITH DIVERSION

The United States has both contributed to the development of juvenile diversion in other countries and drawn from other countries' experiences in the field of juvenile justice. The restorative justice movement has taken hold in Australia, Canada, and New Zealand as they attempt to deal effectively with juveniles from diverse backgrounds in a changing society. Each of these countries has adopted a system of graduated interventions and sanctions aimed at (1) providing accountability on the part of the youth, (2) increasing the involvement of both the victim and the community, and (3) reducing the involvement of the state and thus costs to taxpayers in proving juvenile justice services.

New Zealand developed its system of juvenile justice drawing, over time, from the Borstal system of highly disciplined training schools in England, the American juvenile court system, and the customary law and justice practices of the Maori (or Native New Zealanders). Noting that turn-of-the-century juvenile codes and a similarly antiquated system of juvenile justice were less than adequate in 1989 for dealing with increasing numbers of juvenile offenders, especially among the Maori, New Zealand began to experiment with community-based alternatives to the formal juvenile court process. Building on traditional Maori practices and modern social work concepts, the national government authorized the nationwide use of diversion and community panels known as family group conferences (FGCs) to determine the best course of action in cases involving young persons aged 14 to 17 years, inclusive (Jervis, 1996; McElrea, 1996).

The FGC process begins with a referral to and a subsequent decision by the local youth justice coordinator (a civil servant) to divert the case from the formal youth court. The youth justice coordinator brings together the accused young person, his or her family, the victim, a youth representative (if requested), a police officer (in a quasi-prosecutorial role), and a social worker (McElrea, 1996). Acting as a mediator, the youth justice coordinator facilitates an agreement among all the parties, which in turn becomes a contractual plan of action supervised by persons from the community. The agreement may involve a number of sanctions, including "apology, reparation (in money or work) for the victim, community work, curfew and/or undertaking to attend school, or not to associate with co-offenders" (McElrea, 1996:71). The case is considered closed and proceedings are withdrawn once the conditions of the agreement have been completed, or the case may be referred to the youth court, which can impose its own sanctions. This process, according to McElrea (1996:71) permits the youth court to act as "both a backstop (where FGC plans break down) and a filter (for patently unsatisfactory recommendations)" made by the FGC.

Shortly after creation of the New Zealand model for diverting juvenile offenders, several Australian states began experimenting with family conferences and other methods to deal with juvenile and other first-time offenders. As in New Zealand, several Australian states have large Aborigine (or Native Australian) populations whose approach to justice is restorative rather than punitive. The political structure in Australia is more like that of the United States than that of New Zealand, with strong state governments within a commonwealth that limit the power of the federal government to activities that are clearly delineated as federal responsibilities. There are seven states (New South Wales, Northern Territory, Queensland,

South Australia, Tasmania, Victoria, and Western Australia) and the Australian Capital Territory (which is similar to the U.S. District of Columbia), each of which has approached juvenile diversion somewhat differently (Daily and Hates, 2001).

In general, the initial Australian approach mirrored the New Zealand model in all but one aspect: the person facilitating the conference. Instead of a youth justice coordinator, a member of the local police agency, usually a sergeant or staff sergeant, creates the overall impression of "legal officialdom." This model has since been replaced with statutory-based, non-police-facilitated conferences in five of the seven state and national jurisdictions in Australia (Daily and Hates, 2001:2). Family conferences in Australia continue to operate as diversion from formal juvenile court intervention after the young person has admitted to the offense and includes all but one of the same participants as the New Zealand model, because the youth advocate is not part of the Australian model. The nature of the agreements made in these conferences are the same as those in the New Zealand model (Daily and Hates, 2001). Both the Australian and New Zealand models of family conferences have resulted in decreased numbers of youth, especially among the Aborigine and Maori, returning to the conferences and/or the juvenile court.

The effectiveness of drug courts in the United States and the United Kingdom has also been noticed in Australia. Australian legislators have taken two approaches with drug offenders: (1) diversion of minor drug offenders to the health care system and (2) tougher sentences for traffickers and importers of drugs (Makkai, 1998). At this time, drug courts remain at the pilot-project stage as Australian legislators struggle with decisions of who to divert (first-time drug offenders vs. pushers, etc.), the role of treatment, and the integration of drug courts into the adult and juvenile justice systems.

Canada has also taken juvenile diversion seriously. Like both Australia and New Zealand, Canada shared a British legal heritage and found that its turn-of-the-century Juvenile Delinquents Act (1908) did not meet the needs of young people in the changing society of the 1980s. In 1984, the Canadian Parliament repealed the earlier statute and enacted the Young Offenders Act, which formally recognized diversion. The new statute was built on the principles that young persons must be held accountable for actions, but not to the same degree that they would be as adults. Section 3(1)(d) of the new act demands that the least restrictive approaches and sanctions be applied "where it is not inconsistent with the protection of society, taking no measures or taking measures other than judicial proceedings under this Act should be considered for dealing with young persons who have committed offences." The act authorized the provinces (states) to train and appoint community volunteers to serve as members of community justice committees. The police and/or prosecutors were required to divert young persons not charged with serious or violent crimes to the committees. A committee would meet with a young offender, his or her family, the victim, and a youth officer (similar to a juvenile probation officer) to devise a behavioral contract of the same type as found in Australian and New Zealand family group conferences. Six to 12 months after the successful completion of the contract, all records of the offence and community justice committee involvement are destroyed. If the youth rejects the committee's conditions or fails to comply with them, he or she is referred to formal youth court, where material from the diversion attempt is inadmissible.

First Nations and Inuit (Native Canadian) communities have introduced the concept of "circle sentencing" into both the adult and youth justice systems. Although the practice varies somewhat between regions, Dene (a Native American tribal group) in Canada's Arctic involve the offender, the victim (if they desire to participate), the Royal Canadian Mounted Police (RCMP), defense and prosecuting attorneys, the trial judge, local elders, and any interested person from the community (Ryan, 1995). Circle sentencing can occur as either a formal youth court or as a form of diversion. For youth court, the RCMP will notify the community when court will be held and ensure that the young person is present. Unlike traditional court arrangements, all attendees sit in a large circle and can hear and see whatever is presented. The prosecutor introduces the young person to the circle and explains the charges against the youth. The youth and his or her attorney are given an opportunity to explain the youth's actions, and any person in attendance can also speak to the matter. At the end of the discussions, community input is sought regarding the best sentence, after which the judge generally concurs and sentences the offender in line with the desire of the community. When operating as an alternative to the youth court, the processes are nearly identical. The members of the court are replaced by a government-sanctioned community justice committee composed of the elders and other respected members of the community. All presentations are made within the circle, and once completed, the elders discuss the matter openly and offer a sanction that resolves the conflict and restores harmony in the community. Finally, the offender is told that on completing the sanction, she or he will be welcomed back into the community because it is the behavior that is bad rather than the person. In either scenario, the young person is brought before the formal youth court if she or he either refuses to accept or fails to complete the imposed sanction.

As with the Australian and New Zealand experiences, Canada has seen reductions in the number of aboriginal youth returning before the courts, which may be attributed to diversion and circle sentencing practices. However, many Canadian citizens and politicians are clamoring for tougher sanctions against young persons who commit violent offences, and diversion might be curtailed if pending legislation is enacted.

U.S. Experiences With Diversion

In general, American experiences with juvenile diversion have favored the judiciary and alternative sanctions at the adjudication level, partly due to the history of both the adult criminal justice system and partly to the processes employed in the system since its inception. While diversion does occur earlier, it is formalized, first at the level of the intake officer and initial intake hearing and second at the level of the juvenile court judge.

Many of the activities that the general public associates with diversion are actually prevention programs for at-risk populations or specific treatment alternatives. Prevention programs generally address one or more criminogenic factors that are correlated with delinquency, such as (1) conflict in schools, (2) conflict resolution, (3) family strengthening, (4) juvenile curfews, and (5) mentoring. Typical of this type of program is the High/Scope Perry Preschool program, which has focused for 40 years on skill development, parental support, and teacher training (Schweinhart and Weikart, 1995). These programs have general support from the public as long as increased tax resources are not required for their operation.

In the United States, preadjudication diversion programs generally occur at the level of the juvenile court intake officer or the juvenile court judge. The reasons for this are many and may have their roots within the history of corruption and abuse within the adult criminal justice system and the litigious nature of current American society in general. At the earliest possible diversion point, the police officer, departmental regulations, and prosecutorial directives often do not permit an officer to divert a case to a local service provider. Gone, too, are the days of police abuse of power, when an officer who caught a youth in a minor criminal act might have taken him or her into an alley and given the youth a beating with a warning that the commission of another crime would result in a worse beating.

In addition to police officers being restricted in their legal and extra-legal attempts to divert juveniles from formal processing, so too are prosecutors and intake officers becoming increasingly impeded in their attempts to provide diversion. Many local and state prosecutors have decided to get tough on crime regardless of the offender's age and do not want to err on the side of diversion in case a serous crime occurs later. Many intake officers similarly do not want to step outside their agency's directives and regulations to take a chance in diverting juveniles who might be marginally qualified for diversion. In addition, well-meaning prosecutors and intake officers are often constrained by the desire to avoid liability and an increasing lack of diversion resources at the local level.

The judiciary has also grown more punitive in its approaches to delinquency, however, and less likely to use diversion. Indeed, there are judges in several states who (1) do not have either the resources or the inclination to use diversion, (2) have both the resources and inclination and are using it, or (3) lack the legal ability to divert or reduce custodial sentences although wilderness programs and boot camps are operating with that incentive for participants. Despite these concerns, this does not mean the death of diversion programs in the United States.

Four programs have emerged during the last 40 years as alternatives to existing programs with which juvenile court judges have experimented. The farm or ranch alternative was used for many juveniles in conflict with the law, especially in the Midwest and West, during the 1960s. A variation of the farm or ranch concept, the wilderness program, emerged during the 1970s and was based on the success of the international Outward Bound program. In the context of the juvenile justice system, it was believed that if properly challenged and guided, troubled youth could realize that they possessed internal strengths to stand

up to crime and criminal peers. The "scared straight" movement emerged as an option for juvenile court judges during the 1970s and early 1980s. This program involved taking groups of troubled young persons into nearby state prisons wherein a group of inmates (usually doing long sentences or life) would tell them the realities of prison life and thus scare the participants into a crime-free lifestyle. During the late 1980s and 1990s, the boot camp emerged as both a sentencing alternative for judges and a method of diversion for correctional managers. Here the concept was that the structure of a quasi-military boot camp would also provide a "scared straight" message through the use of "shock incarceration."

Unlike the other juvenile justice components, juvenile corrections lacked a method to divert young people to less restrictive sanctions until the advent of the boot camp (or shock incarceration) program. This short-term, high-intensity alternative seeks to provide life-skill training, education, substance abuse intervention, and other programming in a structured environment that emphasizes both external and internal discipline. Participants are asked to volunteer for the program, which would be shorter than their original disposition, and are given the promise that they will be released from custody when they successfully complete the program. Refusal or failure to complete the program generally results in a return to the young person's original status or disposition. Mixed outcomes have been reported for this alternative.

Some critics feel that the United States has lost sight of many of the original goals of juvenile justice and is not doing what it could for delinquents compared with other countries. Today the juvenile justice system often reacts by going from no intervention at all to the maximum possible intervention, which is often akin to the adult criminal justice system's response to crime. This is based on a the lack of resources available at the community level and recent events whereby authorities have not acted on minor school threats that were later revealed to be precursors to major acts of violence.

CONCLUSION

Replacing formal justice proceedings with ones that are less formal and less punitive is the goal of diversion. Whether these diversionary practices are called alternative measures, family group conferences, or pretrial diversion does not change the intent of juvenile diversion. The philosophy and policy of diversion can be effective whether diversion is incorporated into legislation (as with the Canadian and New Zealand models) or remains as a policy decision within a criminal justice agency (as with the Australian and U.S. models). Diversion can also be incorporated as policy or legislation in the adult criminal justice system with few changes.

Diversion can, as a practice, reduce the stigmatization and labeling of the juvenile. As a practice, however, diversion appears to be less expensive and work better at the pretrial/preadjudication stages than it does once adjudication hearings and/or disposition have commenced. Diversion is one of the three legs (i.e., prevention, meaningful consequences, and rehabilitation) of effective handling of juvenile delinquency and should be regarded as such by the public and juvenile justice practitioners.

Allan Patenaud

See also Alternative Schools; At-Risk Youth; Child-Saving Movement; Courts, Juvenile—History, Drug Courts, Teen Courts; Deinstitutionalization Movement; Prevention Strategies; Scared Straight

Bibliography

Abbott, G. 1938. *The Child and the State, Vol. II: The Dependent and Delinquent Child.* Chicago: University of Chicago Press.

Daily, K., and H. Hates. 2001. *Restorative Justice and Conferencing in Australia.* Canberra: Australian Institute of Criminology.

Eggleston, C. 1999. Locking up kids: Learning from our historic legacy. *Reclaiming Children and Youth* 8(3):137–139.

Fine, B. 1957. *1,000,000 Delinquents.* New York: Signet.

Jervis, B. 1996. Developing reparation plans through victim-offender mediation by New Zealand probation officers. Pp. 417–429 in B. Galaway and J. Hudson (eds.), *Restorative Justice: International Perspectives.* Monsey, NY: Criminal Justice Press.

Makkai, T. 1998. *Drug Courts: Issues and Prospects.* Canberra: Australian Institute of Criminology.

McElrea, F. W. M. 1996. The New Zealand youth court: A model for use with adults. Pp. 69–83 in B. Galaway and J. Hudson (eds.), *Restorative Justice: International Perspectives.* Monsey, NY: Criminal Justice Press.

Mennel, R. M. 1973. *Thorns and Thistles.* Hanover: University of New Hampshire Press.

Office of Juvenile Justice and Delinquency Programs (OJJDP). 1999. Washington, DC: Office of Juvenile Justice and Delinquency Programs.

Platt, A. 1991. *The Child Savers: The Invention of Delinquency,* 2nd ed. Chicago: University of Chicago Press.

Ryan, J. 1995. *Doing Things the Right Way: Dene Traditional Justice in Lac La Martre, N.W.T.* Calgary, Canada: University of Calgary Press and Arctic Institute of North America.

Schweinhart, L. J., and D. P. Weikart. 1995. The High/Scope Perry Preschool study through age 27. Pp. 57–75 in R. Ross, D. Antonowicz, and G. Dhaliwal (eds.), *Annals of Child Development: A Research Annual,* Vol. 7. Ottawa, Ontario: Air Publications.

Snyder, H., T. Finnegan, W. Kang, R. Poole, R. A. Stahl, and Y. Wan. 2001. *Easy Access to Juvenile Court Statistics: 1989–1998.* Available at http://www.ojjdp.ncjrs.org/ojstatbb/ezajcs/.

DRUGS

I. Use Among Youth

Illegal drug use is widely considered one of the most challenging problems faced by American society today. In an annual study released in February 2001 by the National Center on Addiction and Substance Abuse (CASA) at Columbia University, teens have said that drugs are their most important concern for the sixth year in a row. In fact, most illicit drug use in the United States is by youth under the age of 18. According to the Office of National Drug Control Policy (ONDCP), there are approximately 4 million chronic drug users in the United States. Some of the problems associated with drug use affect physical and mental health, family relationships, and work performance. The drug-crime relationship has been estimated to cost society $110 billion each year (ONDCP, 1999).

Risk factors for youths becoming involved in substance abuse include the availability of drugs, community disorganization, increased mobility and instability in home life, a history of family management problems, family conflict, and parental attitudes that tolerate drug use. Poor academic performance and acting out in school are also risk factors, as are having friends who are involved with drugs and experimenting with substance abuse at an early age.

HISTORICAL PERSPECTIVES

While delinquents of the early 20th century were known to have habits involving the vices of alcohol and drug abuse, it was considered more a product of bad influences and poor parenting than anything else. Alcoholism and drug use were considered adult problems and were often cited as reasons for removing youngsters from a home. A few studies were done that tracked the incidences of youths addicted to cocaine and morphine, particularly gang members and street kids. It was also believed that excessive use of tea, coffee, and tobacco served to increase nervousness in children, making them more prone to antisocial behavior. Thus superintendents and social workers carefully catalogued the bad habits of their delinquent charges and reported on them as they did other moral deficiencies.

THEORIES OF DRUG USE

Adolescence (the period from 12 to 18 years of age) is a time of many changes in one's life: inconspicuous emotional and social changes as well as more salient biological changes. New skills, values, and attitudes develop during this period of instability. A newfound freedom from constant parental supervision also occurs, and youth look to their peers for acceptance and approval.

Explanations for drug use also reflect these changes, as do whatever current theories of human behavior are popular at the time. Research on drug and alcohol abuse, as well as intervention and treatment designs, are all patterned after particular theoretical ideas about the origin of the drug problem. Some of the major theoretical orientations include the following.

Disease or Biological Theories

These theories are based on the medical model, which views addiction as a sickness that must be cured. It is argued that an individual's genetic makeup predisposes her or him to drug and alcohol abuse or that chemical imbalances in the body or in the brain cause cravings for substances the body does not produce on its own. These are seen as lifelong conditions. The individual will always be an addict and vulnerable to cravings that, even after treatment, are simply "in remission." Family histories are studied, and medical approaches are common. Those being treated must gain physical control over their illness to become well. Proponents of this approach focus on withdrawal of the substance from the system. Clients are viewed as patients, and drugs, such as methadone, may be administered to facilitate the withdrawal process.

Psychological Theories

Psychological theories address the personal and emotional needs of the client. Weaknesses in self-esteem, ego formation, and adjustment from childhood are all analyzed as part of a personality dysfunction in which drug abuse appears mostly as a symptom. These theories are mostly behavioral in orientation. A therapist would attempt to modify the addict's interpretations of stimuli and response in the environment. It is believed that the addict receives some type of psychological reward or gratification from drug or alcohol use that must be replaced with a more appropriate substitute. Other psychological theories try to uncover subconscious anxieties related to the need for drugs or alcohol.

Sociological Theories

Sociologically oriented theories reflect the influence of an individual's peer group, family members, or even the social structure. Drug offenses are the most frequent of all delinquent behavior. While peer influence seems to be of great importance in the determination of substance abuse, juveniles are also influenced by parental substance abuse. Youth whose parents use drugs are more likely to be users than those whose parents do not use drugs. Anomie theory, social control theory, and subculture theories have all been used to explain drug use among delinquents.

Learning Theories

Some theories do not fall neatly into one of the previous disciplinary classifications. Learning theories are an example and can be considered a combination of sociological and psychological processes. They combine the influence of the individual's personality with their social environment in explaining what factors contribute to addiction. Methods of taking drugs and drinking are often respected rituals in teen circles, and status is attached to those who perform them well. Youngsters model the behavior of those around them who are respected in subcultures where drinking and taking drugs are popular.

Progression Theories

These theories concentrate on what are considered steps in the process of becoming addicted. They argue that a person can begin with casual use of less serious substances, often referred to as "gateway drugs," and progress toward more frequent use of more dangerous drugs. Some see beer or marijuana as initiating young people to the pleasure of intoxicants. The assumption is that the desire for stronger thrills and longer-lasting highs will escalate substance abuse. To date there is little support for the inevitability of escalation. While many hard drug users began with less serious substances, the process is viewed as more complex and less direct than simple escalation.

ALCOHOL USE TODAY

Alcohol has often been called the number one drug problem among youth. In 1995, according to the National Household Survey of Drug Abuse (NHSDA), 11 million drinkers were 12 to 20 years old. Of this group, 4.8 million, or more than 40 percent, engaged in binge drinking (Gfroerer, 1996). While half of the high school youth surveyed by the University of Michigan reported consuming alcohol, one third of 12th graders acknowledged binge drinking (five or more drinks in a row). Acute alcohol poisoning resulting from binge drinking takes a number of teen lives every year. Overall, alcohol kills 6.5 times more young people than all other drugs combined. In fact, it is a major factor in all three leading causes of death for young people (automobile accidents, homicides, and suicides). In a single year, 1995, over 2,000 young people (ages 15 to 20) were killed in alcohol-related auto accidents (Johnston, O'Malley, and Bachman, 2001).

According to the Monitoring the Future (MTF) study—which has measured the use of alcohol, tobacco, and other drugs by the nation's youth since 1975—illicit drug use among 12th graders declined during the 1980s but has increased since 1992 (Johnston et al., 2001). In 1998, four out of every five high school seniors said they had tried alcohol at least once, and half said they had used it in the previous month. Even among 8th graders, the use of alcohol was high: One half had tried alcohol, and almost one quarter had used it in the month before the survey (Johnston et al., 2001).

Although the number of youth arrests for drunkenness and driving under the influence are still much lower than reported in the 1980s, the number of arrests for drunken driving has risen steadily from 1993 to 1999. White males drink more than any other demographic group, and Hispanic males rank second. Black females, on the other hand, drink less than all other race/gender groups. Most teens report that alcohol is very easy to obtain, and many report that they are able to purchase it on their own (Johnston et al., 2001).

CURRENT DRUG USE

After years of continuous decline, reported marijuana and other illicit drug use by high school seniors increased after 1992. In 1998, the MTF study asked a representative sample of nearly 50,000 secondary school students in public and private schools nationwide to describe their drug use patterns through self-administered questionnaires. According to the MTF study, the proportion of high school seniors who reported they had used illicit drugs during the past month steadily increased since 1992. In 1998, 54 percent of all seniors said they had tried illicit drugs (Johnston et al., 2001).

Monitoring the Future is a survey of American adolescents, college students, and adults under the age of 40 conducted every year since 1975 by the Institute for Social Research at the University of Michigan. The adolescent surveys are given to students in the 8th, 10th, and 12th grades. In 1975, 55 percent of adolescents had used an illicit drug by the time they had graduated from high school. This level rose until 1981, when it reached 66 percent; it then declined to a low of 41 percent in 1992. Illicit drug use began to climb again during the 1990s. In 2000, the proportion of youth who had used an illicit drug before high school graduation was 54 percent. Overall, illicit drug use among 8th graders has been declining since 1996; 10th- and 12th-grade use reached a high in 1997, dropped in 1998, and has since remained steady (Johnston et al., 2001).

INDIVIDUAL LEVELS OF DRUG USE

In general, juvenile substance abusers can be classified into four categories of progressive use. The first category consists of experimental users who may occasionally try drugs out of curiosity about the effects. Social or recreational users make up the second group. Members of this group occasionally use drugs while socializing with friends and only during periods when they are not working. Juveniles in the third group spend substantial amounts of time and money on drugs. Drug use in this category is quite heavy and occurs on a regular basis; yet the youth in this category are still able to function through daily routines. Youth in the fourth and final category are considered addicted, which means that the steady use of intoxicants interferes with most aspects of their daily functioning.

TYPES OF DRUGS USED

Youth, especially recreational users, tend to prefer substances that are inexpensive, potent, and easily attainable. Beer and marijuana meet these requirements. These substances are used to achieve excitement, to enable exploration, and to escape the external world. However, drug use by addicts, rather than by recreational users, is more a way of life because users need drugs to make it through the day. Most addicts are multiple drug users.

Both the 1999 and 2000 MTF surveys of adolescents reported mixed results regarding the prevalence of specific drugs. The use of some drugs was holding steady; other drugs were increasing in use; and still others were decreasing. Overall, illicit drug use remained steady in all three grade levels for the year 2000. Specific drugs with consistent use levels include marijuana, amphetamines, hallucinogens (other than LSD), tranquilizers, barbiturates, and alcohol. According to the 2000 survey, three drugs increased in use: ecstasy (labeled a "club drug" because it is popular at night clubs and raves), steroids, and heroin. Although ecstasy use increased in all three grade levels, steroid use only increased among 10th graders. Steroids are the only drugs discussed in the MTF survey that are taken for their physical effects on the body (muscle and strength development) rather than for psychoactive effects. Almost all the increase in steroid use can be attributed to males. In fact, rates among males increased by 50 percent in one year. In 2000, prevalence rates for males were two to five times higher than those for females. Heroin use only rose among 12th graders (Johnston et al., 2001).

There are also many drugs that are declining in all grade levels, such as inhalants, LSD, crystal methamphetamine, Rohypnol, cigarettes, and smokeless tobacco. Twelfth graders also showed a decline in their use of crack cocaine and powder cocaine. The use of marijuana, crack cocaine, powder cocaine, tranquilizers, Rohypnol, inhalants, cigarettes, and smokeless tobacco has declined among 8th graders. Besides

being labeled as a "club drug," Rohypnol has also been labeled a "date rape drug" because it can cause amnesia of events occurring while an individual is under its influence and it has been used in connection with rapes. Another "date rape drug" is GHB. Questions concerning this drug were added to the MTF study in 2000, and less than 2 percent of all age groups had used GHB (Johnston et al., 2001).

Over the 25 years of the MTF survey, marijuana has remained the most widely used illicit drug. In 1998, 49 percent of high school seniors said they had tried marijuana at least once, 37 percent said they had used it in the past year, and 23 percent said they had used it in the previous month. Marijuana can be taken orally, mixed with food, or smoked in a concentrated form known as hashish. However, most consumption occurs by smoking the marijuana in cigarettes, pipes, or hollowed-out cigars. The increasing use of marijuana among high school seniors began during the 1960s and continued into the 1970s, peaking at approximately 50 percent in 1979. Marijuana use then declined until a low point in 1992, when 22 percent of high school seniors were using marijuana. Rates began to climb again, and marijuana use has remained fairly steady. The only noticeable trend is that the age at first use appears to be getting younger (Johnston et al., 2001).

Heroin, another drug that appears to be increasing in use, is an opium derivative. For years, heroin was primarily taken by injection; smoking and snorting began in the 1990s. Because of the new modes of administration, questions about routes of usage (with or without a needle) were added to the MTF survey in 1995. Equal proportions of all 8th-grade users were using each method, and one third of all 8th-grade users were using both methods. The proportion of heroin users using needles increased in each grade level. However, all the rise in usage for 12th graders in 2000 can be attributed to use without a needle (Johnston et al., 2001).

Inhalants are defined as "any gases or fumes that can be inhaled for the purpose of getting high" and include many common household products. Inhalant use in all three grades declined steadily through 1999 and remained steady in 2000. It should be pointed out that inhalant use is most common among younger adolescents, and the use of inhalants falls off as youth get older. This trend is unique to inhalants. The decline in use with age is most likely due to the fact that inhalants are seen as "kids' drugs" and that other drugs are available to older adolescents (Johnston et al., 2001).

The most widely used hallucinogen is LSD, yet its annual prevalence rate has remained below 10 percent since the inception of the study. For the first 10 years of the study, there was a slight decline in its use, with a leveling-off occurring during the last half of the 1980s. LSD use then rose from 1991 to 1996, when it peaked for all three grade levels. While use for 8th graders remained steady in 2000, use by 10th and 12th graders continued to decline (Johnston et al., 2001).

Methamphetamines are a subclass of amphetamines commonly known as speed. Speed got a bad reputation during the 1970s and consequently was not very popular for some time. "Crystal meth" or "ice" made a comeback in the 1980s, and methamphetamine use began to increase again in the 1990s (Johnston et al., 2001).

Different birth cohorts have differences in smoking rates; these differences tend to remain the same throughout the cohort's life cycle. Therefore, trends in any particular grade may not correspond to trends in other grade levels during a certain period. When measuring cigarette use, the MTF survey asked if the respondent had used cigarettes within the past 30 days. For 12th graders, this 30-day prevalence peaked in 1976 at 39 percent and dropped to 29 percent in 1981. Smoking began to greatly increase during the 1990s. Smoking peaked for 8th and 10th graders in 1996 and for the 12th graders in 1997. Cigarette use then declined, continuing to decline into 2000. Since these peak levels, prevalence rates for cigarette smoking have decreased by 30 percent for 8th graders, by 21 percent for 10th graders, and by 16 percent for 12th graders (Johnston et al., 2001).

The use of smokeless tobacco has been decreasing since the mid-1990s, when it reached peak levels. Much like steroid use, smokeless tobacco use in the United States is predominantly a male behavior. There are also some demographic differences. Use is higher in the South and in the north-central regions of the country than it is in the Northeast and West and is concentrated in nonmetropolitan areas. In addition, youth's use of smokeless tobacco is negatively correlated with the education level of their parents and is higher among Caucasians than among African Americans or Hispanics (Johnston et al., 2001).

The trends of usage for cocaine, another stimulant, have undergone some major changes over the years. Twelfth-grade usage increased in the late 1970s,

remained fairly constant during the first half of the 1980s, and then declined after 1986, dropping to 5.0 percent in 2000 (Johnston et al., 2001).

Measurement of the use of crack cocaine was added to the MTF study in 1986. Indirect indicators suggested that between 1991 and 1998, there was a steady increase in use at all three grade levels. Crack use started to decrease in 1999 in the 8th and 10th grades. Use for 12th graders peaked in 1999 at 2.7 percent. It had dropped to 2.2 percent in 2000 (Johnston et al., 2001).

ADDRESSING DRUG USE IN THE JUVENILE JUSTICE SYSTEM

Today many youth think of experimentation with drugs and recreational use of alcohol, cocaine, and marijuana as an acceptable part of the transition into adulthood. Few take seriously the potential negative consequences of HIV, accidents, teen pregnancy, violence, victimization, and mental health problems that may be related to use of illicit substances.

Although drug use among teens cuts across race, income, and gender lines, it occurs with greater frequency and intensity among youth involved in the juvenile justice system. Although the specific nature of the relationship between drug use and delinquency is a matter of research and debate, it is clear that several social, economic, political, and legal factors need to be considered to improve the environment in which young people learn and grow. Accurately identifying youth at risk for drug dependence and the creation of meaningful and individualized interventions should be a high priority in the schools and the community. The challenges of combating drug abuse will only be addressed through resources that focus both on why youth turn to drugs and why, despite all the negative messages they receive about the consequences, they remain involved with them.

Lisa M. Roberts

See also Alcohol Abuse; Courts, Juvenile—Drug Courts; DARE; Juvenile Justice and Delinquency Prevention Act of 1974; Theories of Delinquency

Bibliography

Gfroerer, J. 1996. *Preliminary Estimates From the 1995 National Household Survey on Drug Abuse.* Rockville, MD: Department of Health and Human Services,

Substance Abuse and Mental Health Services Administration.

Goode, E. 1998. *Drugs in American Society*, 5th ed. Boston: McGraw Hill.

Johnston, L. D., P. M. O'Malley, and J. G. Bachman. 2001. *Monitoring the Future—National Results on Adolescent Drug Use: Overview of Key Findings, 2000*. Bethesda, MD: National Institute on Drug Abuse.

National Center on Addiction and Substance Abuse (CASA). 2001. *National Survey of American Attitudes on Substance Abuse VI: Teens*. New York: Columbia University.

Office of National Drug Control Policy (ONDCP). 1999. *1999 National Drug Control Strategy*. Washington, DC: Government Printing Office.

DRUGS

 ## II. Treatment for Juvenile Offenders

Historically, persistent substance abuse among youth is often accompanied by school difficulties, health problems, poor peer relationships, mental health issues, and involvement with the juvenile justice system. Consequently, when young people engage in alcohol and other drug use, they, their families, and their communities usually suffer. For this reason, many treatment approaches attempt to assist clients in reestablishing ties that have been broken by the mistrust and misdeeds associated with substance abuse.

Because adolescents vary in the frequency and type of drugs they use, treatment approaches must vary as well. The variables of age, gender, urban or rural setting, social class, and availability affect the types of drugs used, the frequency of drug use, and the most appropriate treatment method.

WHAT TO TREAT—SUBSTANCE ABUSE OR CRIME?

There is little debate that youths who use drugs are more likely to engage in delinquent behavior, and the more serious the substance use, the higher the likelihood they will engage in serious forms of delinquency. Research indicates that nearly half of serious juvenile offenders were also multiple drug users. Most of these offenders reported use, beyond experimentation, of at least one illicit drug.

There are no indications that drug use is declining among "high-risk" youths, including juvenile arrestees. Moreover, there is a consistent finding that, as the seriousness of offending increases, so does the seriousness of drug use, both in terms of types of drugs used and frequency of use. Thus a greater proportion of serious and violent offenders use alcohol, marijuana, and other illicit drugs, and, on average, they use these drugs with greater frequency than do other adolescents. Reciprocally, many studies also report that a greater proportion of serious adolescent drug users, those using alcohol, marijuana, and/or other drugs, and those using these drugs with a higher frequency, are more serious delinquents. This leads us to question whether this relationship reflects that (1) drugs cause crime, (2) crime leads to drug use, or (3) the relationship is merely a product of the same underlying social and personal factors causing both.

Unfortunately, the drug-crime relationship is complex and multifaceted. It is possible for all three propositions to be true when applied to certain populations or groups of youth. For some youths, the desire for drugs may lead to various forms of delinquency, including serious delinquency, to obtain resources to buy drugs. For others, involvement in a delinquent, drug-using peer group may lead to drug use. Still other youths who do not use drugs may be involved in serious violence. In addition, there is a fourth hypothesis about the relationship of drugs and delinquency; that is, for some youth, drugs and delinquency may be reciprocally related, mutually reinforcing.

If drug involvement and delinquency are intertwined, does this also mean that a decrease in drug use is followed by a decrease in delinquent activities? There is evidence for this in interview studies of narcotic addicts. When individuals began using hard drugs less frequently, their criminal involvement also decreased. This finding is not surprising in light of the decreased need to illegally obtain funds to purchase the drugs. Results from treatment studies demonstrate similar effects on delinquency. Longitudinal studies on juveniles also showed that halting illegal drug use was associated with a decrease in delinquent activities.

Due to the strong association between substance abuse and delinquency, there is significant concern about whether the use and abuse of these substances among juvenile offenders represents a public health problem or a criminal justice problem. Because delinquent behavior is so closely associated with drug abuse, treatment and rehabilitation for underlying chemical dependency in these populations is often difficult to access and may be unavailable in some areas of the country.

THE NEED FOR EFFECTIVE DRUG TREATMENT

The connection between drug use and juvenile crime suggests that treatment services for youthful offenders should include components targeted at both behaviors. A number of research studies indicate that a small group of serious delinquents (5 percent to 8 percent) who are also serious drug users account for a disproportionate amount (well over half) of all serious crimes. Thus identifying these individuals—who clearly exemplify the serious drug–serious crime connection—and providing successful treatment interventions for them are important in reducing the overall volume of crime.

In addition, the critical transition between institution-based substance abuse treatment programs and release on parole (aftercare) remains an area of weakness for the juvenile offender and abuser. A number of studies report positive behavioral changes, higher rates of employment, and longer terms of success for juvenile offenders with a history of alcohol and/or drug abuse who receive treatment assistance as part of their community reintegration programs. Therefore, effective treatment strategies attempting to redirect or reduce future delinquency and drug use are also needed.

TREATMENT INTERVENTION FOR YOUTHFUL OFFENDERS

Most experts divide treatment programs into the following categories:

1. *Detoxification programs:* mainly short-term inpatient services in clinical settings that concentrate on working through the body's physical dependency symptoms and preparing the person for long-term counseling methods and interventions.

2. *Chemical dependency units:* also short term but concentrate on assessment and counseling in controlled hospital-like settings.

3. *Outpatient clinics:* long-term counseling provided through regularly scheduled group and individual counseling sessions. Other therapeutic programming may be used and the clients usually work and/or go to school.

4. *Residential therapeutic communities:* rigid, highly structured residential treatment plans that use self-help techniques as well as other broader educational strategies to provide alternatives to drug use.

5. *Self-help programs:* group treatment with regular meetings to provide support and control for its members. They employ storytelling and recognition of milestones in sobriety and abstinence. Example programs are Narcotics Anonymous and Alcoholics Anonymous.

When substance abuse is viewed as part of generalized deviant behavior, then removing the drug should effectively limit or stop the criminal behavior. This criminal approach teaches prosocial behavior. In contrast, 12-step programs (e.g., Narcotics Anonymous) may isolate one substance (such as cocaine) and specifically target behavior (abstinence) related to that substance. This approach does not claim to affect any behaviors other than dependency or use, emphasizing that responsibility for other destructive conduct rests with the individual.

The problem, however, does not rest solely with the fact that youthful offenders have far higher rates of alcohol and other drug use (particularly marijuana and cocaine) than other adolescents. Large proportions of juvenile offenders report experiencing negative psychological and behavioral effects related to their substance abuse. Therefore, the treatment of adolescent offenders must address substance abuse and other underlying problems in the context of concurrent psychiatric diagnoses, learning disorders, family interactions, internal conflicts, and developmental issues. In essence, the problem is both a symptom and a specific disorder.

Substance-abusing juvenile offenders with typical multiple problems may be more malleable than their adult counterparts. However, there is little evidence that the majority of substance abuse programs for youth are any more successful than are programs for adult substance-abusing offenders.

STRATEGIES WITH INCARCERATED DELINQUENTS

Typically, treatment for drug and alcohol abusers takes place in psychiatric and hospital settings for adolescents whose parents can afford it or who have third-party insurance benefits. Other youngsters, especially those substance abusers who have committed minor forms of delinquency, receive the benefits of treatment in privately administered placements, which vary tremendously in the quality of program design and implementation. However, substance abusers involved in serious forms of delinquency will likely be placed in county or state facilities whose basic organizational goal is custodial and security oriented. These youthful serious offenders generally receive some exposure to substance abuse counseling.

The approach to assessment and treatment of incarcerated youth depends significantly on the size of the facility and the duration of the stay. In short-term facilities, screening, detoxification with medical monitoring, formal assessment, and basic cognitive behavioral group education should be components of a detention-based program. A beginning 12-step group such as Narcotics Anonymous or Alcoholics Anonymous should be offered to those who want to remain drug free for longer periods of time. To date there is no clear evidence that court-ordered referral to treatment is any more effective than treatment that is not court ordered. However, it may be that for youth with few social supports and inadequate housing, court referrals allow access to treatment. Long-term facilities should include specialized services that address contributory problems such as domestic violence and parental neglect. These facilities should also provide extensive transitional services as the adolescents reenter their home communities.

Short-Term Institutionalization

In short-term facilities, like county detention centers, an educational model has generally been proposed and 12-step programs implemented. Some educational models have been expanded to include aspects of social learning theory and effective education that have been more traditionally used in therapeutic communities. One example is the Paradigm Program in the Seattle-King County Youth Detention Center. This program involves an intensive approach to education and focuses on the development of self-esteem through values clarification and the enhancement of personal skills and decision-making techniques. The program also targets general life skills relevant to the use and sale of drugs, including financial aspects, family effects, and risk of HIV infection. The offender participants receive individual and group education as

well as drug and alcohol counseling, assessment, and access to on-site mental health, physical health, and HIV diagnostic services. In addition, the Paradigm Program diagnoses chemical dependency and offers residential drug and alcohol treatment as an alternative to incarceration.

Long-Term Institutionalization

Treatment strategies in long-term facilities, like state institutions and camps, allow for intervention strategies that are more intensive than are those generally available in short-term facilities. According to Bartollas (2000), privately administered therapeutic communities (TCs) or emotional growth programs—such as Elan in Maine; Rocky Mountain in Colorado; Provo Canyon in Utah; and Cascade, Cedu, and Hilltop in California—appear to be several notches above the average substance abuse program for juvenile offenders. The TC views substance abuse as a disorder of the whole person, involving the possibility of impeded personality development and often including deficits in social, educational, and economic/survival skills. This global perspective of the problem is a multidimensional rehabilitative approach that occurs in a 24-hour setting.

The traditional TC program for adult offenders involves intense peer pressure, self-responsibility, hard physical and emotional work, and self-disclosure. Typically, adolescent offenders entering treatment have less involvement with hard narcotics, have shorter periods of drug abuse (in part, because of their younger age) although initiation of drug use is generally earlier than for adults, and have greater involvement with marijuana and alcohol than their adult counterparts. The need to accommodate developmental differences, facilitate maturation, and address differences in lifestyle, cultural, and psychosocial circumstances became increasingly evident as the number of adolescent abusers entering treatment increased. In response, many TC program participants are housed in segregated facilities within the institution.

Additionally, program facilitators have adapted the treatment structure to deal with issues unique to the youthful offender/abuser. Modifications to adolescent TC programs include reductions in program length; limited use of peer pressure focusing on positive influences, since pretreatment peer influences are generally negative; and less reliance on the use of life experiences to foster understanding about one's self and one's behaviors. Typically, adolescent residents participate in the horizontal authority structure of the TC by sharing responsibility for daily operations. However, they do not participate in the vertical authority structure of the TC; all activities are staff supervised, and the treatment staff have ultimate control over all decisions.

Evaluation results on the overall effectiveness of institution-based, therapeutic community models are limited. Typically, compared with their adult counterparts, youthful offenders are less motivated to change, do not perceive treatment as suitable for them, and are more likely to be in treatment because of external pressures.

AFTERCARE INTERVENTION STRATEGIES

Aftercare services for juvenile offenders may well be the most crucial, least understood, and most often ignored aspect of juvenile corrections. According to a report issued by the Office of Juvenile Justice and Delinquency Prevention (Altschuler and Armstrong, 1994), short-term parole failure occurs disproportionately with institutionalized juvenile offenders—all too often within the first 90 to 180 days after release. A number of studies indicate that, in addition to a persistent pattern of intense and severe criminal activity, many have a long history of alcohol and drug abuse.

Quite often, these individuals reenter the community without the support mechanisms available to nonoffending substance abusers. Many have weakened family ties, deficits in educational and employment skills, and long-standing problems with anger and stress management. Consequently, they face a greater potential of relapse by virtue of their extreme socioeconomic dislocation and exposure to drug-using peer associates, crime, poverty, and other high-risk situations. Experts seem to agree that youths are not likely to be successful in their return to the community unless they receive appropriate, specialized programming and services beginning immediately on release.

There is a considerable body of literature on the effectiveness of alcohol and drug abuse treatment programs in reducing criminal activity among youthful offenders released from an institutional setting. For these youth, the true test of recovery occurs during the initial reintegration process where many of the factors contributing to their chemical dependency remain intact. Abstinence is only the first step in recovery; the management of everyday life circumstances will test

their ability to survive on parole and successfully reintegrate into the community.

Therefore, a successful aftercare treatment program should focus on easing the juvenile offenders' transition from institution to community. To facilitate this process, basic skills must be taught, alcohol and drug abuse counseling must be reinforced, dependence on gang socialization must be reduced, employment opportunities must be enhanced, and educational/vocational challenges must be met. One example of such a program is the Lifeskills '95 aftercare treatment program designed to assist youthful offenders released from secure confinement with the California Youth Authority (CYA).

The Lifeskills '95 Program

Grounded in the dynamics of Glasser's (1965) "reality therapy" approach to offender treatment, the Lifeskills '95 paradigm was developed from Operation New Hope's Los Osos "lifestyles" substance abuse awareness program for preparoled CYA wards housed at the Paso de Robles training school. The Lifeskills '95 interactive program components assist and support the offender during their initial reintegration by using a series of lifestyle and life-skill treatment modalities in a well-integrated educational approach to healthy decision making.

The treatment is based on six principles that underlie 13 counseling modules (consolidated from the original 39 used in the nine-month Los Osos program). These principles address the behavioral antecedents believed to be most responsible for short-term parole failure. Included are efforts to achieve the following goals:

1. Stabilize the participants' length of parole by improving the basic socialization skills necessary for successful reintegration into the community.

2. Significantly reduce criminal activity in terms of amount and seriousness and alleviate the need for, or dependence on, alcohol and/or drugs.

3. Improve overall lifestyle choices (e.g., social, educational, job training, and employment).

4. Reduce participation with negative peer associates.

Counseling specific to substance abuse awareness is a major part of the life-skills approach. Topics such as the addictive personality, living with addiction, abstinence and sobriety, fear/stress and addiction, and progressive recovery are components of the program.

By design, Lifeskills '95 is an interactive 39-hour program taught over 13 consecutive weekly meetings. The sequence of the program modules is intended to enhance an individual's understanding of the lifestyle process. Each topic, however, is considered an independent unit that allows participants to begin at any point in the sequence. In other words, their participation at any given session is not dependent on previous attendance and does not affect their ability to progress and successfully complete the program.

The philosophy of Lifeskills '95, like that of similar aftercare substance abuse and life-skill models for juvenile offenders, is perhaps correct. Secure confinement in a juvenile institution does not adequately prepare youths for return to the community. Moreover, the few skills acquired, or treatment rendered, while in secure confinement are not being sufficiently built on and reinforced outside the institution. In the long run, any postrelease adjustments made will depend on the opportunities available to the juvenile offenders. A program such as Lifeskills '95 can lead parolees to opportunities, but those opportunities must be available and meaningful. Unfortunately, most aftercare programs such as this do not receive the necessary financial support or space availability for the juveniles in need of such support services.

TREATMENT SUCCESS

The popularity of drug treatment as a crime prevention strategy has led to many different approaches across the country. Some treatment programs are privately operated, while others are part of county courts or state corrections or mental health departments. While many youth are required to undergo treatment by their probation or diversion agreements, others volunteer or are placed by their families. Treatment programs also vary in the length of time spent in treatment (one month to one year) and in the intensity of services (live-in versus weekly one-hour meetings). Formats for programs range from highly structured to spontaneous and impromptu. Likewise, the costs can range from nothing to more than $1,000 per day.

The reported successes and failures of treatment programs can be confusing. Some programs simply count attendance as progress toward completion. Dropouts may not be counted as failures, although research indicates that those who do not show up for mandatory testing are more likely to be engaged in misconduct. To determine the value of research findings on drug treatment, one must carefully examine the criteria for admission, the definition of success, and the amount of tolerance the program allows for backslides or relapses. Rather than be unrealistic, some professionals argue that definitions of success should include diminished use, less dangerous substances, and occasional minor relapses. Gradual progress is seen as a more accurate reflection of the nature of addiction and as more promising for long-range success.

Don A. Josi

See also Aftercare; DARE; Family Therapy; Group Therapy; Mentoring Programs; Wilderness Programs

Bibliography

Altschuler, D. M., and T. L. Armstrong. 1994. *Intensive Aftercare for High-Risk Juveniles: An Assessment.* Washington, DC: Office of Juvenile Justice and Delinquency Prevention.

Bartollas, C. 2000. *Juvenile Delinquency*, 5th ed. Boston: Allyn & Bacon.

Glasser, W. 1965. *Reality Therapy.* New York: Harper & Row.

Johnson, B. D., E. D. Wish, J. Schmeidler, and D. Huizinga. 1991. Concentration of delinquent offending: Serious drug involvement and high delinquency rates. *Journal of Drug Issues* 21:205–291.

Josi, D. A., and D. K. Sechrest. 1993. An evaluation of substance abuse treatment outcomes for youthful parolees. *Prison Journal* 73:355–378.

Josi, D. A., and D. K. Sechrest. 1998. A pragmatic approach to parole aftercare: Evaluation of a community reintegration program for high-risk youthful offenders. *Justice Quarterly* 16:51–80.

Lyman, M., and G. Potter. 1998. *Drugs in Society*, 3rd ed. Cincinnati, OH: Anderson.

Savage, L. J., and D. D. Simpson. 1981. Drug use and crime during a four-year post-treatment follow up. *American Journal of Drug and Alcohol Abuse* 8:1–16.

Van Kammen, W. B., and R. Loeber. 1994. Are fluctuations in delinquent activities related to the onset of juvenile illegal drug use and drug dealing? *Journal of Drug Issues* 24:9–24.

E

EMPEY, LAMAR TAYLOR (1923–)

LaMar Empey was born on April 9, 1923, in Price, Utah, a trade center made famous not only by its dinosaur quarry and Native American dwellings but also by its visits from outlaws such as the Brown's Hole Gang and Butch Cassidy and his Wild Gang. In this mining and farming district in the central part of the state, Empey's father, Claudius, was a banker and his mother, Mabel Taylor Empey, raised their family. LaMar Empey served in the U.S. Army Infantry from 1943 to 1946 and remained in the reserves until 1952, reaching the rank of captain. He attended Brigham Young University (BYU), not far from his home, and married Betty Mitchell in 1949 just before graduating. He obtained his master's degree in 1951 and went on to Washington State University, where he obtained his Ph.D. in 1955. He and his wife had four children: John, Kathleen, Martha, and James.

CAREER HIGHLIGHTS

Empey's first teaching position was at BYU, where he was in the sociology department from 1955 to 1962. He left there to teach at the University of Southern California (USC) and remained there the rest of his professional career, retiring as professor emeritus.

Throughout his career, Empey focused on the study of youth. He authored many books and articles on delinquency, although he is perhaps best known for evaluation studies of the Silverlake and Provo Experiments as well as his textbook, *American Delinquency* (1978), which has been the standard

for the discipline. Now in its fourth edition, the work is currently coauthored by Mark Stafford and Carter Hay.

For Empey, the way children have been viewed and treated throughout history has varied according to whatever the current thinking was on acceptable and deviant behavior. Our responses, he argued, have evolved in formal as well as informal reactions to delinquency that have met with controversial degrees of success. For him, the historical context was important to understand the assumptions that underlie our practices and beliefs about interventions, particularly in the juvenile court. The cultural relativity of Western responses was important to Empey, and he strove to demonstrate how our theories, while varied, reflect interests and concerns basic to our society, such as our belief in due process and the desirability of community programming.

While at USC, Empey served on the research advisory committee of the California Department of Mental Hygiene and as a consultant to the U.S. Department of Labor. He worked on many grants and evaluation projects and was Director of the Youth Studies Center at USC as well as Associate Research Director of the Gerontology Center.

ENVIRONMENTAL INTERESTS

After retirement, Empey moved to Wyoming and became active in environmental issues. He and his wife founded the Clarks Fork Coalition, which led a successful effort to have the Clarks Fork River designated as wild and scenic. He was a board member of the Wyoming Outdoor Council and the Greater

Yellowstone Coalition. His commitment to grassroots activism only intensified when he lost his son-in-law, an avid outdoorsman, to a climbing accident in the Grand Tetons.

HONORS AND ELECTED SCHOLARLY POSITIONS

LaMar Empey served as Vice President (1967 to 1968, 1970 to 1971) and President (1984) of the Pacific Sociological Association and was a member of the Society for the Study of Social Problems and the American Sociological Association. He received the prestigious Edwin Sutherland Award from the American Society of Criminology in 1991.

Marilyn D. McShane

See also Provo Experiment; Silverlake Experiment

Bibliography

Empey, L. T. 1956. Social class and occupational aspiration: A comparison of absolute and relative measurement. *American Sociological Review* 21:703–709.

Empey, L. T. 1967a. *Alternatives to Incarceration.* Washington, DC: Government Printing Office.

Empey, L. T. 1967b. Delinquency theory and recent research. *Journal of Research in Crime and Delinquency* 4(1):28–42.

Empey, L. T. 1978. *American Delinquency: Its Meaning and Construction.* Homewood, IL: Dorsey Press.

Empey, L. T. (ed.). 1979. *Juvenile Justice: The Progressive Legacy and Current Reforms.* Charlottesville: University Press of Virginia.

Empey, L. T. (ed.). 1980. *The Future of Childhood and Juvenile Justice.* Charlottesville: University Press of Virginia.

Empey, L. T., and M. L. Erickson. 1966. Hidden delinquency and social status. *Social Forces* 44:546–554.

Empey, L. T., and M. L. Erickson. 1972. *Provo Experiment: Evaluating Community Control of Delinquency.* Lexington, MA: D. C. Heath.

Empey, L. T., and S. G. Lubek. 1968. Conformity and deviance in the "situation of company." *American Sociological Review* 33:760–774.

Empey, L. T., and S. G. Lubek. 1971a. *Explaining Delinquency.* Lexington, MA: D. C. Heath.

Empey, L. T., and S. G. Lubek. 1971b. *Silverlake Experiment: Testing Delinquency Theory and Community Intervention.* Chicago: Aldine.

Empey, L. T., and J. Rabow. 1961. The Provo Experiment in delinquency rehabilitation. *American Sociological Review* 26:679–695.

Erickson, M. L., and L. T. Empey. 1963. Court records, undetected delinquency, and decision making. *Journal of Criminal Law, Criminology, and Police Science* 54:456–469.

Erickson, M. L., and L. T. Empey. 1965. Class position, peers and delinquency. *Sociology and Social Research* 49:268–282.

F

 FAMILY THERAPY

Families undergo a large number of stressful events in their lives that lead to problems in the home environment. Many therapists agree that solving youth's problems depends on increasing the family's ability to communicate so there is a greater level of understanding and acceptance among all family members. Family therapy offers counseling sessions to the entire family to correct problems that make the family dysfunctional. By focusing on the entire family instead of one individual at a time, family therapy has significantly changed the nature of counseling.

There are several different models of family therapy. This entry focuses on the problem-solving model and the task-centered model. Another aspect of family therapy this entry discusses is that under very volatile circumstances, the legal system might intervene and decide that separation is best. In some such cases, the child is then returned to the home environment through a process in family therapy called reunification.

In many circumstances, family difficulties are a result of conduct problems in the children. Factors contributing to conduct problems in children include an obstinate temperament during infancy, neurological problems, a lack of cognitive or social skills, low social problem-solving skills, low academic levels in school, or genetic malformation. However, conduct problems have also been linked to the child's relationship with parents and family. There are several types of family therapy programs designed to help and teach parents how to communicate effectively with their children. This entry discusses parent management training (PMT), which includes parenting classes that teach anger management, stress reduction, and self-awareness. These training programs were originally designed in 1982 by Patterson and have since been expanded into more advanced programs.

PROBLEM-SOLVING MODEL

The problem-solving model is based on the work of Helen Perlman and J. Haley. This model involves six steps:

1. Determining the problems in the family.

2. Identifying the problem in terms of behavior.

3. Listing the problems in terms of levels of importance.

4. Realistically determining the target areas.

5. Shaping solutions to the stated problems.

6. Establishing a contract with the family.

The main purpose of this approach is to teach open communication that will enable families to resolve future conflict in a positive manner while focusing on the immediate issues at hand. Thorman (1997) suggests several guidelines for conducting a successful therapy session: (1) Members of the session should focus on the problems and possible solutions to the problems, (2) each member should be willing to work constructively to solve problems and carry out a plan of action, (3) members should be

153

willing to compromise when differences of opinions arise, and (4) sessions should be considered positive.

TASK-CENTERED MODEL

Although the task-centered model also focuses on problem solving, it is somewhat different from the problem-solving model because it actually gives the family a task to perform that can help the members solve their problems. The therapist works with the family to observe and to teach family members how to solve their problems effectively. This model is very effective in teaching problem solving to families because it teaches them how to identify and explore the problem, how to create solutions, and how to perform tasks effectively. Listening, acknowledging, and expressing oneself is very important in this model. Each person must know and understand what others are thinking and feeling to better perform the task. The assigned task should be appropriate for the abilities of the family members, and they should be able to accomplish the task in a specific amount of time. Once the task has been assigned, each family member should work toward the same results and not feel overwhelmed. Examples of techniques that facilitate completing tasks are role-playing, sculpting, exchanging positive feedback, and switching from person to person.

REUNIFICATION

Family reunification is the process that occurs when a child that has been taken out of the home environment is returned to the family. The premise behind reunification is that everyone is entitled to a family. Though it is very difficult to return a child to the family from which he or she was removed—for several reasons, inside and outside the family—reunification seeks to make the return into the home environment as successful as possible. The child and family go through six stages in the reunification process: (1) defining the family, (2) fear and distrust, (3) idealism, (4) reality, (5) a second stage of fear, and (6) return.

Recognizing the important contributors to a family environment is relatively easy for children who have lived in a steady home environment. However, when a child has moved from one foster home to another, distinguishing the people who make up a family system in the original home is much more difficult. For example, the legal system may decide that a parent has lost custody rights; therefore, when the child returns to the family structure, one parent is no longer part of the original family system. Interest also plays an important role in reunification. For example, when a child moves away from home, the family learns to deal with the absence of the child. In many cases, the child may feel as though his or her return is not wanted. Finally, a determination must be made about which family members will be reunited.

The second stage of reunification is fear and distrust. Once the family is reunited, several fears may exist, including distrust of one another. It is then very important for the therapist to remain neutral and not take any sides in the family system. This may require the therapist to work with the family members first at an individual level and then move to the group level. For reunification to be successful, the family must attend daytime therapy every week. If day visits are successful, night visits are then considered. Parents must attend every session in the therapy program, and the child must meet any behavioral requirements. Resources available to the family must be acknowledged to reduce the parents' fears of failure.

Idealism occurs when family members, in an effort to support the reunification process, try to make each other look good without considering the underlying factors that caused the separation in the first place. In this stage, the therapist tries to remind each family member that reunification is not an easy task. Many issues, conflicts, and feelings need to be resolved to keep them from reoccurring.

Reality sets in when family members begin to express their true emotions and feelings and act as themselves. The child may begin to complain, and the parents may feel rejected. This presents an opportunity for the therapist to teach the family problem-solving and conflict resolution skills. Although this may be frightening to the family, introducing new strategies that teach communication in parenting are an essential part of the reunification process. Safety becomes an important issue, and the therapist needs to make sure that a dangerous situation does not arise in the family.

With the reintroduction of conflict in the relationship, a second stage of fear and distrust happens. The child may act in an aggressive manner, and the parents may become resistant to the reunification. After all the time and energy invested in reunification, the fear of failure may also occur. Expectations of what will occur in the home environment, such as behavior and consequences, are established. The possibility of not reunifying the family at all may also be determined in this stage.

Finally, the returning phase occurs in some families. The therapist presents the family with a clear plan of action in case conflict should arise. Other support services are also discussed in preparation for the return home. Adjustment may still be difficult, however, and the therapist will continue his or her role as a consultant if necessary.

PARENT MANAGEMENT TRAINING

Poor parenting skills represent another reason for delinquent behavior. Parent management training (PMT), developed by Patterson in 1982, is one type of family therapy that seeks to improve the relationship between the child and parent by focusing on the importance of positive parenting skills. Patterson concluded that parents who consistently use negative punishment without communicating desired behavior are more likely than are other parents to raise antisocial children. Antisocial behaviors, then, are learned from the family itself. This type of therapy challenges the negative, damaging behavior with positive, prosocial behavior. Such behavior includes learning problem-solving skills and positive reinforcement techniques. There are six important areas emphasized in the PMT program according to Miller (1994):

1. Determining what is the problematic behavior.

2. Stressing the importance of positive behavior.

3. Determining the appropriate commands to use.

4. Using the appropriate discipline.

5. Communicating effectively.

6. Determining the appropriate course of action for each individual setting.

Three different parent management training programs have been used in the past. Patterson developed the first. Forehand and McMahon (1981) designed a second type of PMT program for parents of children ranging in age from 3 to 8 years. Divided into two phases, the first phase includes teaching parents how to play with their children while using positive reinforcements. The second phase includes positive methods of

dealing with discipline problems. To achieve these goals, several methods are used, including role playing between the parent and child—each separately with the therapist. Finally, homework is also assigned to give parents the opportunity to use their newly learned skills in the home.

The third type of parent management training program is called BASIC. Webster-Stratton (1984) designed this 26-hour program for parents of children between the ages of 3 and 8 years with conduct disorders. Incorporating both the Patterson (1982) and the Forehand and McMahon (1981) programs, BASIC uses videotape modeling. Parents are encouraged to view videotapes of parent-child interactions and afterward engage in group discussion with a therapist. Though children are not involved in the program training, parents use techniques that they have learned in class to complete weekly assignments with their children at home.

According to research, parent management training programs have reduced aggressive behavior in children and have been proven to alter children's behavior in general, even several years after parents complete the program. The success of the program, however, is dependent on several factors: the length of treatment, the different mechanisms of the training program, the people involved in the program, such as the therapists and counselors, and what is taught in the program. Critics of parental management training programs argue that the programs can be very expensive and, therefore, not all families in need of the program may have the opportunity to be involved.

EXPANDED PARENT MANAGEMENT TRAINING PROGRAMS

Literature has also been written on extended parent management training (EPMT) programs. Expanding on the original concepts, EPMT programs seek to help parents not only with their child but also with their marriage. They teach them how to reduce stress in their marriage so that it is easier to implement strategies learned in the parent management training program with their child. The first type of expanded parent management training program described by Patterson (1982) consists of 70 percent child-oriented therapy and 30 percent marriage therapy. Webster-Stratton (1984) called this EPMT program ADVANCE, an updated version of BASIC. It uses anger management and problem-solving techniques to further help the families in therapy. Forehand and McMahon (1981) expanded their program to teach mothers and their children how to maintain self-control. There are other types of EPMT programs that emphasize parental adjustment factors, parent support training, self-sufficiency training, and synthesis training (which teaches parents to recognize their reactions to the stressful events in their lives).

Some of the literature on EPMT programs states that they are more successful than the basic parental management training programs and that children involved in EPMT programs show considerable improvement with a longer treatment effect. However, some researchers do not agree, stating that other problems occurring outside of the family may have more to do with the conduct disorders.

Claudia Rios Hirsch and Phillip Hirsch

See also Aftercare; Culturally Specific Programming; Foster Care; Group Homes; Group Therapy; Mental Health; Mentoring Programs; Out-of-Home Placement; Parental Responsibility Laws; Restorative Justice

Bibliography

Combrinck-Graham, L., K. G. Lewis, L. Bicknell-Hentges, and R. A. Cimmarusti. 1995. *Children in Families at Risk: Maintaining the Connections.* New York: Guilford Press.

Forehand, R. L., and McMahon, R. J. 1981. *Helping the Noncompliant Child: A Clinician's Guide to Parent Training.* New York: Guilford Press.

Goldstein, A. P., and J. C. Conoley. 1997. *School Violence Intervention: A Practical Handbook.* New York: Guilford Press.

Hawkins, D. J. 1996. *Delinquency and Crime: Current Theories.* New York: Cambridge University Press.

Kopka, D. L. 1997. *School Violence: Contemporary World Issues.* Santa Barbara, CA: Deborah L. Kopka

Lawrence, R. 1998. *School Crime and Juvenile Justice.* New York: Oxford University Press.

Miller, G. E. (1994). Enhancing family-based interventions for managing childhood aggression and anger. Pp. 83–116 in M. Furlong and D. Smith (eds.), *Anger, Hostility, and Aggression: Assessment, Prevention, and Intervention Strategies for Youth.* Brandon, VT: Clinical Psychology.

Patterson, G. R. 1982. *Coercive Family Process.* Eugene, OR: Castalia.

Thorman, G. 1997. *Family Therapy: A Social Work Approach.* Springfield, IL: Charles C Thomas.

Webster-Stratton, C. 1984. A randomized trial of two parent training programs for families with conduct disordered children. *Journal of Consulting and Clinical Psychology* 52:59–69.

FEMALE DELINQUENCY

 ## I. History

The contribution of females to total delinquency is modest. Historical trends are indicative of a low level of performance in crime among girls, which may account for the lack of attention criminologists have given to this population. The kind of delinquent behavior exhibited by girls is significantly different from that of boys. Often described as childlike, manipulative, and deceitful, female delinquents tend to have a history of committing minor crimes and status offenses. In recent decades, though, the number of females arrested for aggravated and other assaults and drug offenses has increased.

THE EMERGENCE OF FEMALE CRIMINALITY

The notion of female criminality dates back as far as the 1800s, when offenders were forcibly transported from England to Australia. The women were servants or maids convicted of prostitution or the petty thefts of stealing or picking pockets. On arriving in Australia, many women returned to a life of crime, resorting to prostitution as a means of survival because no provisions had been made for the women in the new land.

Urbanization, industrialization, and class status were credited with having an effect on female offending. Criminal cases in London courts between 1687 and 1912 indicate that women were drawn to urban areas where they found work in low-paying jobs. Limited by their earnings, many began to offend, engaging in petty thievery, disorderly conduct, vagrancy, and drunkenness. Some writers who have influenced the field of female criminology, such as Cesare Lombroso, Sigmund Freud, Kingsley Davis, and Otto Pollak, argued that social and economic factors of urbanization, industrialization, and class play only a minor role in female criminality. According to Lombroso, Freud, Davis, and Pollak, a woman's criminal behavior is actually a result of her individual characteristics.

In the latter part of the 18th century, a large number of women were transported from England to the colonies for trivial offenses. Between the years of 1787 and 1852, at least 25,000 women, more than 8,000 of whom were first-time offenders, were sent to the United States (Crites, 1976). During their journey, the offenders became victims themselves as they were systematically sexually abused by the ships' crewmembers. The conditions aboard the ships were just as abusive. The holds were rat infested, and the death rate among the women was as high as one in three.

The seriousness of female offenses increased once the women reached the United States. The majority of America's early women murderers were indentured servants who were often raped by their masters. If an indentured servant gave birth to a bastard child, she would be forced to serve one to two years beyond her original term of service. Not wanting their years of punishment to be lengthened, many women went to great pains to keep their pregnancies hidden and later committed infanticide. Tired of being victims, other desperate women resorted to killing their abusive companions or husbands.

HOUSING FEMALE OFFENDERS

Females convicted of serious crimes served their sentences in central prisons in the same facilities as men, but in separate rooms. In penitentiaries, women continued to be housed with men. In many cases, one or two women would be housed in a facility with a large number of men. They received very minimal care and were considered a nuisance to prison and penitentiary administrators. Usually, females were secluded from the male population but not housed in a separate wing because there were not enough women to fill an entire wing of cells. Instead, they were frequently locked in a room above the guardhouse or mess hall and usually left on their own because it was considered extravagant to hire a matron to supervise them. Needlework and their meals were brought to them and they remained in these rooms for the duration of their sentences.

As the number of female offenders increased, by the middle of the 19th century, it became necessary to provide them with separate housing supervised by matrons. Although in separate quarters, custodial units for women provided care that was inferior to that given to male prisoners. The buildings were small, were located on the same grounds or near male

facilities, and usually had no yard for exercising. The facilities became overcrowded and fell into states of disrepair with leaking roofs and poor heating and plumbing. The head matron was able to do little about the conditions because she received orders and supplies from the nearby male prison, which focused attention on its own inmates. By the late 19th century, virtually every state was operating a custodial unit for women.

Campaigns for differential care based on gender and the new penology of rehabilitation fueled the inception of the women's reformatory movement around 1870. During the Progressive Era (1890 to 1920), the reformatory plan was able to attract support because of the period's preoccupation with prostitution. The plan offered an avenue for ridding the streets of loose women, suggesting relocation of the offenders to reformatory facilities. The women's reformatory movement was exhausted by 1935 but had achieved most of its goals, producing facilities throughout the nation. However, with the end of the movement soon came the end of the reformatory as a special type of institution. In addition, the Great Depression put a strain on government funds; states closed custodial penal units that held female felons and relocated all offenders to reformatory grounds, resulting in the former reformatories taking on the resemblance of male prisons.

Women often found institutional life difficult. It was hard on them, and they tended to crave affection. Homosexuality began to take on a particular importance in the 1960s, a theme in women's and girls' facilities that was strikingly different from men's facilities. Researchers have suggested that homosexual relationships often help lessen the pain of being imprisoned, distracting attention from the realities of the facility and forming the foundation of a pseudo-family.

THE NATURE AND CAUSES OF FEMALE DELINQUENCY

The doctrine that women should be treated the same as men is often pressed, but the rate and kind of delinquency committed by girls and women is in contrast to that of boys and men, bringing into question equal treatment in the penal system. In the first work specifically about female criminality, Cesare Lombroso, a leading positivist criminologist, focused on the individual's behavior and the traits of the offender.

His writings and theories of the late 19th and early 20th centuries suggest that women are merely "big children," insisting they are not criminal in nature (Lombroso and Ferrero, 1895:151). Lombroso suggested that women have more evil tendencies than do men and they are occasional criminals as opposed to born criminals. Although Lombroso's biological and anthropological bases of research are no longer accepted, his writings and theories greatly influenced criminology. Behaviors are influenced by definite physiological distinctions that differ between males and females. Upbringing and biology sometimes offer a link to female delinquency and criminality.

In the first modern-day book on female crime and delinquency, *The Criminality of Women*, Otto Pollak (1950) suggested that women commit as much crime as do men. Pollak contended that women poisoned untold numbers of husbands and children. However, he offered no substantial proof of this belief and has been criticized by many criminologists because of this.

The backgrounds of adult female offenders in the middle of the 20th century have suggested connections between childhood victimization and adult criminality. Coping with sexual abuse, trying to care for younger siblings, providing housework, and sometimes caring for parents who were abusive and drug dependent took a toll on many girls. Often schools were not responsive to the signs of abuse, causing the girls to lose hope for the future. Many ran away from home or turned to drugs as a solace.

African American girls tended to be at risk for victimization in a number of environments during the civil rights era. As well as victims of sexual abuse, they were often victims of class oppression. Many school administrators met them with hostility or racism and ignored possible signs of abuse in the home. Sometimes growing up in extreme poverty, African American girls would often turn to early deviant behavior, stealing to help the household. Educational neglect and parental abuse culminated in a life of delinquency for many African American girls, who often dropped out of school to live on the streets and resorted to prostitution and stealing as a means of survival.

During the women's rights movement that fueled a wave of feminist activity, a new female criminal emerged in the early 1970s. According to Federal Bureau of Investigation (FBI) statistics, there was a dramatic increase in the number of women arrested for nontraditional crimes of murder, forcible rape, and robbery. Female arrests for murder were up 105.7 percent,

forcible rape arrests by 633.3 percent, and robbery arrests by 380.5 percent (FBI, 1973:124, 1976:1919). Officials believed that these data tended to offer objective evidence that the number of women arrested was connected with the women's liberation movement.

From the past to the present, females have often turned to lives of crime because of the effects of familial, physical, and psychological injury. Literature reveals a close relationship between early victimization and later criminality. When females are abused, they have a strong inclination to internalize feelings of depression and self-blame. After reaching adulthood, flashbacks to the abuse and feelings of diminished emotional capacity often make the women vulnerable, and they may use drugs as a method of dealing with their feelings of failure.

DRUGS, CRIME, PROSTITUTION, AND GANGS

Women and girls are more likely to use drugs as a means of escape than are men, who usually indulge in illegal drug use because of peer pressure or for thrills or pleasure. Most females have histories of physical and sexual abuse; drugs provide a sort of "medication" to alleviate the pain. Those who reside in neighborhoods of extreme poverty may become further victimized in efforts to acquire drugs. The male-dominated drug culture tends to exploit women and their addiction to drugs, degrading females to engage in acts of prostitution in exchange for minimal amounts of crack or cocaine. This pattern of drug use fostered the term *crack ho*. Females involved in prostitution may consider their criminal acts more ethical than stealing or drug dealing, viewing their selling—or bartering—of sex as work or an occupation.

Another form of escape for girls is the gang. Wanting to separate themselves from problems at home or failure in school, girls may run away and become involved in gangs. Frustrated with being labeled as failures by parents, teachers, and truancy officers, they become hostile toward authority and turn to gangs as a way of being in control of their lives. Compared with their male counterparts, girls join gangs at an earlier age, commit fewer illegal acts, and are more likely to leave the gang sooner.

Females generally have lower rates of delinquency than males. Gender differences tend to be the greatest for serious violent and property crimes, with the number of male offenders far exceeding the number of female offenders in these types of crimes. While females commit fewer crimes than do males, both groups commit similar types of criminal acts, such as petty theft, robbery, burglary, and assault.

Females are the fastest-growing population in the justice system. Most women are serving sentences for nonviolent offenses, and although the number of females convicted of violent offenses is on the decline, the number of incarcerated females is continually climbing. Experts suggest that this increase is the result of mandatory prison time for drug-related crimes and sentencing laws that require those convicted to serve most of their sentences.

Bridgett L. McGowen

See also Child Sexual Abuse; Courts, Juvenile—History; Cycle of Violence; Matricide and Patricide; Missing Children; Pregnancy, Teenage; Prostitution, Teenage; Runaways; Status Offenders

Bibliography

Agnew, R. 2001. *Juvenile Delinquency: Causes and Control*. Los Angeles: Roxbury.

Binder, A., G. Geis, and D. D. Bruce Jr. 2001. *Juvenile Delinquency: Historical, Cultural and Legal Perspectives*, 3rd ed. Cincinnati, OH: Anderson.

Crites, L. 1976. *The Female Offender*. Lexington, MA: Lexington.

Federal Bureau of Investigation (FBI). 1973. *Crime in the United States—1972*. Washington, DC: Department of Justice.

Federal Bureau of Investigation (FBI). 1976. *Crime in the United States—1975*. Washington, DC: Department of Justice.

Hanson, K. 1964. *Rebels in the Streets: The Story of New York's Girl Gangs*. Englewood Cliffs, NJ: Prentice Hall.

Lombroso, C., and W. Ferrero. 1895. *The Female Offender*. London, UK: T. Fisher Unwin.

Pollak, O. 1950. *The Criminality of Women*. Philadelphia: University of Pennsylvania Press.

FEMALE DELINQUENCY

 II. Current Status

Girls and young women were invisible in the juvenile justice system until recently. To most people, the term *juvenile delinquent* refers to young men, and the juvenile justice system reflects this male focus. The system was designed to respond to the issue of male delinquency in terms of the numbers of male youthful offenders, as well as the causes, consequences, and treatment of delinquent behavior among boys and young men.

Although media attention to female juvenile crime has increased over the past decade—mostly around sensationalized issues such as "girls and gangs"—the research on issues, policy, and programs for at-risk adolescent females has, for the most part, been overlooked. Attempts to understand delinquent behavior have included few adolescent females in research studies. Much of the research on the differences between male and female adolescents centers on developmental issues. However, gender, race, and socioeconomic status also influence adolescent development. Girls and young women confront additional problems unique to their gender, such as sexual abuse and assault, teenage pregnancy, single parenthood, and disparity in educational, vocational, and employment opportunities.

Today girls are the fastest growing segment of the juvenile justice population despite an overall drop in juvenile crime. The increase in girls' arrests has outstripped that of boys for most of the last decade. Over the past several decades, there has been a marked increase in the number of girls and young women arrested, detained, and incarcerated in juvenile and adult facilities.

TRENDS IN FEMALE JUVENILE OFFENDING

Girls remain a small proportion of the juvenile justice population, but arrest, detention, and custody data show an increase in both the number and percentage of girls in the juvenile justice system. This trend runs counter to that of boys. Law enforcement agencies reported 670,800 arrests of females under the age of 18 in 1999, accounting for 27 percent of the total juvenile arrests made that year. Between 1990 and 1999, arrests of girls increased more (or decreased less) than male arrests in most offense categories (Office of Juvenile Justice and Delinquency Prevention [OJJDP] 2000b). Delinquency cases involving girls rose 83 percent between 1988 and 1997, increasing across all racial groups. Group-specific percentage increases were white, 74 percent; African American, 106 percent; and other races, 102 percent (American Bar Association and National Bar Association, 2001).

Girls accounted for 22 percent of juvenile arrests for aggravated assault and 30 percent for simple assault. They represented 36 percent of arrests for larceny-theft, much of which, particularly for girls, is shoplifting. Girls accounted for more than half (59 percent) of all juveniles arrested for running away from home. Thirty percent of curfew arrests involved girls. The increase in the number of drug abuse violation arrests between 1990 and 1999 was greater for female juveniles (190 percent) than for male juveniles (124 percent; OJJDP, 2000b).

Researchers suggest that the increase in girls' delinquency is not necessarily due to a significant rise in violent behavior but to the relabeling of girls' conflicts as violent offenses (Chesney-Lind and Okamoto, 2002). A summary of two studies on self-reported aggression reflects that while about a third of the girls reported being in a physical fight in the last year, this was true of more than half the boys in both samples. Girls are more likely to fight with a parent or sibling (34 percent compared with 9 percent for boys), whereas boys are more likely to fight with friends or strangers. Girls are less likely than their male counterparts to engage in serious, violent crime and more likely to be involved in nonviolent property and drug offenses. Status offenses, which include running away, underage drinking, truancy, and curfew violations, continue to be a key factor in female delinquency (Chesney-Lind and Shelden, 1998).

PROFILING DELINQUENT GIRLS

Females—both adults and juveniles—involved in the criminal justice system share many of the same characteristics. Most are poor, undereducated, and unskilled and are disproportionately women and girls of color. Many come from impoverished urban environments, have been raised by single mothers, or have been in foster care placement. A profile of at-risk adolescent females identifies the following common characteristics:

1. Age 13 to 18 years.

2. History of victimization, especially physical, sexual, and emotional abuse.

3. Academic failure, truancy, and dropout.

4. Repeated status offenses, especially running away.

5. Unstable family life, including family involvement in the criminal justice system, lack of connectedness, and social isolation.

6. History of unhealthy dependent relationships, especially with older males.

7. Mental health issues, including history of substance abuse.

8. Overrepresentation among communities of color.

It is important to understand the context of girls' delinquency. Current findings on female delinquency confirm that there are a number of similar correlates for delinquency between boys and girls, including low socioeconomic status, disrupted family backgrounds, and difficulties in school. However, gender-specific differences among delinquents exist and have a significant impact on their treatment and management within the juvenile justice system. For example, a growing body of research documents that delinquent girls and young women have disproportionately high rates of victimization, particularly incest, rape, and battering, preceding their offending behavior (American Correctional Association, 1990; Belknap and Holsinger, 1998). The research suggests that prior victimization, offending (e.g., running away, prostitution, and drug law violations), and subsequent incarceration are interrelated (Arnold, 1990; Chesney-Lind and Shelden, 1998; Owen and Bloom, 1998). Recent studies have identified running away from home and drug use as girls' means of coping with and surviving abuse in their homes.

The juvenile justice system's reaction to these differences has not been gender-responsive policy and programming. The current system has been designed to deal with the problems of boys and young men and, in doing so, has neglected the gender-specific programming and treatment needs of girls and young women. Girls and young women respond differently than do young males to program interventions and treatment. These differences in system response and individual reaction to treatment require separate research and planning to meet the needs of young females enmeshed in a system designed to manage and serve a predominately male population.

A 1998 California study found that while family issues (such as parental conflict, lack of family communication, and parents ill-equipped to deal with nurturing and supervising children) affect both males and females, there are multiple gender-specific dimensions that produce delinquency among girls and young women (Owen and Bloom, 1998). These specific dimensions include the following:

1. Sexual, physical, and emotional abuse are significant factors in producing risky and delinquent behavior among girls and young women. This effect is long lasting and creates problems with running away, emotional adjustments, trust and secrecy, future sexuality, and other risky behaviors.

2. Substance abuse is often a sign of other problems that lead to risky behavior. There are few focused substance abuse programs for girls and young women that provide needed services ranging from prevention to residential care.

3. Most female delinquents continue to commit relatively minor offenses. These offense patterns indicate a need for prevention and intervention programs rather than increased secure institutions. Gang involvement and fighting with peers contribute to delinquency for a small, but significant, number of girls and young women.

4. Racial, ethnic, gender, and economic discrimination may contribute to female delinquency through decreased opportunity, disparities in treatment, gender bias, and lack of program parity.

5. Girls and young women should be given special attention in prevention and education programs concerning reproductive health, pregnancy, and sexually transmitted diseases. Pregnant and parenting teens also need comprehensive health programs and services.

PROCESSING OF GIRLS' CASES IN THE JUVENILE JUSTICE SYSTEM

Girls are disproportionately charged with status offenses. Their running away propels them into the juvenile justice system and may lead to incarceration as adults. In 1999, although girls constituted 27 percent of juvenile arrests, they accounted for 59 percent of juvenile arrests for running away and 54 percent of juvenile arrests for prostitution (OJJDP, 2000b).

According to an OJJDP report (2000a), in 1997, juvenile court judges waived 400 delinquency cases involving female offenders to adult court; this was 37 percent more than in 1988. Of the cases waived in 1997, 42 percent involved a person offense as the most serious charge, 41 percent involved a property

offense, 8 percent involved a drug law violation, and 9 percent involved a public order offense. Between 1988 and 1997, the use of detention for girls increased 65 percent compared with a 30 percent increase for boys. There is evidence that girls are being detained for less serious offenses than boys. Girls are more likely to be detained for minor offenses and for technical violations of probation or parole.

A 1995 study of detention in several U.S. cities conducted by the Annie E. Casey Foundation found many more girls than boys are detained for minor offenses such as public disorder, probation violation, status offenses, and traffic offenses (29 percent girls versus 19 percent boys). Detained girls tend to have more status offenses and misdemeanors in their histories, rather than violent offenses.

African American girls make up nearly half of all those in secure detention, and Latinas constitute 13 percent. Although whites constitute 65 percent of the population of at-risk girls, they account for only 34 percent of girls in secure detention. Seven of every 10 cases involving white girls are dismissed compared with 3 of every 10 cases for African American girls.

CONCLUSION

While there is some overlap between the needs of male and female delinquents, these gender-based differences should be taken into consideration by researchers, policymakers, and practitioners. In terms of policies and programs, the juvenile justice system does not tend to identify and address the separate needs of girls and young women. Meeting the needs of delinquent girls requires specialized staffing and training, particularly in terms of relationship and communication skills, gender differences in delinquency, substance abuse education, the role of abuse, developmental stages of female adolescence, and available programs and appropriate placements.

The needs of girls and young women facing involvement in the juvenile justice system are tied to specific, identifiable risk factors. These risk factors include personal issues such as family relationships; sexual, physical, and emotional abuse; and inadequate academic and social skills. Social risk factors such as racism, sexism, and economic discrimination must also be understood in any discussion of female delinquency. Running away, truancy, early sexual behavior, substance abuse, and other predelinquent behaviors are related to these initial risk factors.

The juvenile justice system is ill-equipped to deal with the risks and needs of girls. The critical lack of early identification and assessment opportunities is exacerbated by the scarcity of appropriate and effective community-based prevention and early intervention strategies and programs. Inadequate planning and funding, the absence of a continuum of care, and the general lack of gender-appropriate programs, placement, detention, and aftercare services is further evidence of this neglect.

Girls' pathways into delinquency can be articulated through further analysis and research, as well as the development and implementation of model programs incorporating gender-specific approaches. Initiatives developed to address female delinquency should be based on the developmental, psychological, social, educational, and cultural characteristics of this population. Gender-appropriate program models should address a continuum of care and provide comprehensive services to delinquent girls and their families.

Barbara Bloom

See also Child Sexual Abuse; Cycle of Violence; Gangs, Juvenile—Organization and Activities; Juvenile Institutions; Pregnancy, Teenage; Prostitution, Teenage; Runaways

Bibliography

American Bar Association and the National Bar Association. 2001. *Justice by Gender: The Lack of Appropriate Prevention, Diversion and Treatment Alternatives for Girls in the Juvenile Justice System.* Washington, DC: American Bar Association.

American Correctional Association. 1990. *The Female Offender: What Does the Future Hold?* Washington, DC: St. Mary's Press.

Arnold, R. 1990. Women of color: Processes of victimization and criminalization of black women. *Social Justice* 17(3):153–166.

Belknap, J., and K. Holsinger. 1998. An overview of delinquent girls: How theory and practice have failed and the need for innovative changes. Pp. 31–64 in R. Zaplin (ed.), *Female Offenders: Critical Perspectives and Effective Interventions.* Gaithersburg, MD: Aspen.

Chesney-Lind, M., and S. Okamoto. 2002. Gender matters: Patterns in girls' delinquency and gender responsive programming. *Journal of Forensic Psychology Practice* 1(3):1–28.

Chesney-Lind, M., and R. G. Shelden. 1998. *Girls, Delinquency and Juvenile Justice,* 2nd ed. Belmont, CA: West/Wadsworth.

Office of Juvenile Justice and Delinquency Prevention (OJJDP). 2000a. *Female Delinquency Cases, 1997.* Washington, DC: Department of Justice.

Office of Juvenile Justice and Delinquency Prevention (OJJDP). 2000b. *Juvenile Arrests 1999.* Washington, DC: Department of Justice.

Owen, B., and B. Bloom. 1998. *Modeling Gender-Specific Services in Juvenile Justice: Final Report to the Office of Criminal Justice Planning.* Sacramento, CA: Office of Criminal Justice Planning.

 FOSTER CARE

Foster care is the temporary family substitute for children whose parents cannot or will not provide an adequate home situation. State social workers determine the adequacy of a home situation based on their education, training, and/or the policy of the state child protective services agency for which they work. The state or county may license homes to provide care to children who have been declared wards of the court. In most cases, these children have been given up by or taken away from their parents, or their homes have been designated as unfit. A juvenile having adjustment problems may be placed in temporary foster care while the entire family receives counseling.

Foster care is generally distinguished by the following:

1. It is usually arranged by a public agency.

2. The responsibility for care of the child has been removed from the child's biological parent.

3. Foster care is a full-time activity.

4. Foster care is (or at least was) designed to be a temporary arrangement, with the child either returning to his family or being adopted (Downs, Costin, and McFadden, 1996).

There are various ways to provide foster care: from individual families not related to the child, relatives of the child, a therapeutic foster home, or group homes.

CHARACTERISTICS OF CHILDREN IN FOSTER CARE

Children in foster care share certain characteristics. They have multiple moves and no stable permanent family ties. At least half of all children in foster care are there for more than two years, and many for as long as six years or more. Minority children are more likely to be placed into foster care for neglect and to stay longer than are white children. Foster care children also have higher delinquency rates and higher rates of poverty, are more likely to be young unwed mothers, and exhibit symptoms of a wide variety of other social ills. Many are illegitimate, with drug-abusing parents, a parent in prison, an absent parent, or parents who otherwise are not interested in what happens to their children. In addition, one of the most common reasons for foster care placement is the allegation of child abuse.

TYPES OF FOSTER CARE

There are essentially four types of foster care: traditional or "regular" foster care, kinship foster care, therapeutic foster care, and residential or group home care. Another form, an independent living arrangement, sometimes is used but lacks some of the normal features of regular foster care.

In traditional or regular foster care, families are recruited or offer to be a foster family. They are given basic training, paid a small monthly fee, and take children into their homes. The family must follow the dictates of the child protective service agency, but it is a "family" environment and remains so until the child is returned to her or his blood family, is moved to another foster family, or is adopted (which is rare). The expenses associated with taking care of the child are paid by the state (although to their credit, many foster families spend their own money as well) with the social worker making infrequent visits to ensure the safety of the child.

In the kinship form of foster care, the child is placed with a relative. It is thought that, while the child is not with his or her "normal" family, being with relatives provides some sense of stability and a more loving environment.

Therapeutic foster care could be considered a specialized type of foster care in which the child lives with a single family who has received specialized training in the care of "difficult" children. Children in this type of placement typically would otherwise be in a more restrictive setting (e.g., a residential group home or an institution) or might very well be in the care, custody, and control of the state department of youth services. Therapeutic foster care families receive more money per month, more training, and more support than do regular foster care families. While some would see this as discriminatory, children in therapeutic foster care require considerably more services, training, and support than would a typical foster child. These are intensely troubled children who are at great risk for further state and criminal involvement. Indeed, many children in therapeutic foster care will probably "graduate" from foster care and never be returned to their families.

Residential foster care provides care to a large number of children in a group home setting or a ranch-style environment (for instance, sheriffs' boys and girls ranches). Children live with other children of the same sex (although both sexes might live on the same grounds) and learn how to function and live in a large family. Many residential settings are privately run (or quasi-public) agencies whose support in many cases is largely made by donations. States contract with these agencies, but the payment provided by the state is substantially less than what is needed to rear growing children.

Still other children in foster care live in independent living situations, usually with one or two other children and under the supervision of a social worker. Children in independent living are usually older (16 or more years of age) and are in transition. They are in the last years of being in foster care and are preparing to enter the "real" world. Children in independent living centers are usually obtaining a GED, and they work and learn the skills necessary for survival on their own. In many cases, these are children who have been in foster care much of their lives, and independent living is the last step before becoming independent adults (i.e., being discharged from foster care).

THE NEGATIVE ASPECTS OF FOSTER CARE

While foster care may, in theory, be a positive approach to children who are not being adequately taken care of, its practice has been less than stellar. The number of children in foster care has increased dramatically since the 1960s and, for many children, foster care has been the only family setting they have ever known. The increase, contrary to assumptions, may not be because the numbers of troubled, abused, and neglected children have increased. Pelton (1989) observed that any expansion in agency responsibilities or size seemed to result in a corresponding increase in the number of children in foster care. If Pelton was correct, it would seem that the foster care industry itself is the precipitating factor.

As the money for court-ordered placements began to increase under Title IV of the 1961 Social Security Act, so too did the number of children placed in foster care. The states, it has been argued, have a financial incentive to place children out of their homes (Hagedorn, 1995:35). It has even been suggested that "if foster care dollars could be used for preventing the unnecessary placement of children, the foster care roles could be reduced from 30 to 50 percent and taxpayers could save $1 billion per year" (Besharov, 1986, in Hagedorn, 1995:35). In other words, children are removed from their homes because it is financially beneficial to the state.

At the same time, experts in the area of foster care report that a loss of funding has seriously affected the services foster care can provide. The result is that social workers have larger caseloads and make less frequent visits to the foster homes. Some systems may simply have too many foster parents for social workers to screen and monitor adequately, thereby increasing the potential for abuse.

Children in foster care (indeed throughout the child protective services system) are part of a bureaucratic quagmire in which they are sometimes forgotten, shuttled from one family (or program) to another, and abused or neglected in the very system set up to protect them. Many are, in fact, abused in foster care whether they were abused prior to entering care or not. While record keeping and statistics in child protective services are poor, the likelihood of abuse may be as high as four times that of remaining in the family. Children have also died while in foster care, an irony since it is the system designed to protect them from harm by their parent, stepparent, or other custodian.

The problems exist in most of the states, not just a few. Because foster care systems are part of the child protective services bureaucracy, they are protected by confidentiality laws. Thus details about foster care are not particularly forthcoming, and children "get lost" in the bureaucracy. Stories abound of children being moved monthly from one family to another, of being placed with known child abusers, with relatives or others who are involved with foster care just for the money, and of social workers who knew (or at least suspected) the child was not safe yet did nothing about the conditions.

MacDonald (1998:1) suggested that "the most pressing goal for welfare reform is ensuring the welfare of the children." As the family breaks down, the concerns for child welfare inevitably increase. But, some would say, the goal of foster care is to "save" or "protect" children from families who have broken down. Yet the foster care system is not oriented toward keeping families together.

For many of the children in foster care, the future holds a continued involvement with the welfare system, later finding their own children taken from them and placed in foster care. Some would say that foster care has become as much a welfare system for many foster parents (and programs) as it is a temporary care system for children.

The federal government requires that children in foster care be reunited with their families or placed for adoption within 18 months of first entering foster care. Unfortunately, this rarely happens. In most states, the goal of child protective services is family reunification (no matter how long it takes, and no matter what the role of the parent has been). As a result, many children simply languish in foster care awaiting their families to "return," and while in foster care, many children are subject to worse situations than they experienced in their families. The child's family, on the other hand, is accommodated, and may even profit from foster care.

CONCLUSION

The foster care system, as it currently exists, is in crisis. Some critics suggest it is out of control. Many states lack to ability to know what goes on in their foster care systems and "the full extent of harm children may face in foster care and how to protect children from harm in the future" (Roche, 2000:79). Child protective services agencies (of which foster care is a part) are potentially dysfunctional and seriously mismanaged, and confidentiality hurts all involved and makes oversight difficult. Many child protective service workers are significantly undertrained or indifferent to the situation (and children under their supervision), and the turnover of workers is as high as 70 percent. Very little about the foster care system inspires confidence that it will work properly.

Jeffrey P. Rush

See also Child Sexual Abuse; Family Therapy; Girls and Boys Town; Group Homes

Bibliography

Downs, S., L. Costin, and E. McFadden. 1996. *Child Welfare and Family Services*, 5th ed. White Plains, NY: Longman.

Hagedorn, J. M. 1995. *Forsaking Our Children*. Chicago: Lake View Press.

MacDonald, H. 1998. The real welfare problem is illegitimacy. *City Journal* 8:1.

MacDonald, H. 1999. Foster care's underworld. *City Journal* 9:1.

Pelton, L. H. 1989. *For Reasons of Poverty: A Critical Analysis of the Public Child Welfare System in the United States*. New York: Praeger.

Roche, T. 2000. The crisis of foster care. *Time*, November 13:74–82.

GANGS, JUVENILE

I. Introduction and Definition

Gangs are not a new phenomenon. Even though they have been studied continuously by criminologists over the past century, there is much we do not know. Further, the activities and organization of gangs seem to change over time. It is very difficult for researchers to give the term *gang* one concrete definition. *Gang* can refer to a variety of groups, some of them comprising adults and some comprising youth. The latter constitute most citizens' perception of gangs, primarily because of the media attention paid to youth gangs. For this entry, the term *youth gang* refers to any group of teenagers who participate together in deviant and delinquent activities. Police departments often have a different definition, sometimes relying on a definition provided by the state. Texas, for example, defines a criminal street gang as "three or more persons having a common identifying sign or symbol or an identifiable leadership who continuously or regularly associate in the commission of criminal activities."

Gangs have a more formal structure than do delinquent groups, but the word *gang* is used loosely to define criminal groups who commit deviant acts. Many gangs tend to come together only by territory or geography. Males have historically made up most of gang membership; however, female gangs and participation by females in mixed-sex youth gangs are becoming more common. Gangs tend to thrive in poverty-stricken neighborhoods, mostly in sections of cities where police response tends to be low.

Gangs are a way of life in some neighborhoods. They can be a problem for cities and towns, big and little, urban and rural. Historically, most youth gangs could be found in low-income neighborhoods of sizable metropolitan cities. Gang activity is still found predominantly in the inner city, but gang members are mobile and can transport their hostility wherever they want. It is a fact that gangs are a universal problem.

Topics in this entry explore in more detail some of the major issues related to youth gangs today:

1. Whether or not they are spreading and, if so, where.

2. The extent to which they are responsible for crime and violence.

3. Determining what constitutes gang membership.

4. The connection between prison and street gangs.

5. Female participation in gangs.

Phillip Hirsch and Claudia Rios Hirsch

GANGS, JUVENILE

II. History and Theories

Juvenile gangs exist in some form in all 50 states and in most communities within the United States. First documented in America's colonial period, youth gangs have been a constant in American society, have drawn from a variety of ethnic and economic backgrounds, and have consistently been viewed as destructive and threatening to the social order. Major changes in the process and structure of society have affected both the development of gangs and the fluctuating interest in their activities. Driven by periodic media pronouncements of the meteoric rise in juvenile violence, public interest and community response to gangs has vacillated over the last few decades.

Research addressing gang organization and activity has also been intermittent. The academic community that developed the sociological theories explaining why gangs exist and why gang members engage in a variety of activities seemed to have abandoned youth gang research in the late 1960s and throughout the 1970s. Researchers were heralded as "rediscovering" juvenile gangs in the 1980s. Some studies indicated that gang membership had markedly increased, while other studies suggested that gangs were "migrating" from urban centers to suburban and rural areas for a variety of reasons.

Fueled by the media's obsession with juvenile violence, the public was convinced that a new "wave" of gang activity had begun during the decade of the 1980s, and public policy addressing gang organization and activity was developed at a frantic pace. Just as the turn from the 19th to the 20th century precipitated the development of the first recognized juvenile gang in the United States, the turn from the 20th to the 21st century has provided the technology to precipitate the beginning of a movement to refocus delinquency and gang policy to more meaningful intervention and prevention strategies.

HISTORY

Reports support the existence of juvenile gangs in colonial America and gang delinquency in New England as early as the 17th and 18th centuries. Philadelphia papers reported "bands of youth hooligans" drinking, fighting, stealing, and engaging in sexual experimentation as early as 1791. However, an Irish American immigrant gang, founded in New York around 1820, is thought to be the first youth gang in the United States (Asbury, 1927/1971). This group, known as the Forty Thieves, more closely mirrored the organization and activities contemporary researchers contribute to juvenile gangs in that they were less transitory and better organized than were previous delinquent groups.

During the 19th century, citizens in several major U.S. cities expressed concerns about problems of delinquency, particularly gang-related activities. By 1855, it was estimated that New York City contained at least 30,000 young men who owed allegiance to gang leaders and the Civil War draft riots in New York City were said to have been precipitated by young Irish street gangs (Spergel, 1990b). Gang conflicts over control of turf became so violent that local police often refused to get involved until the violence subsided. Operating out of the Hell's Kitchen, Bowery, and Five Points sections of New York City, gangs such as the Pug Uglies, Bowery Boys, and Shirt Tails were involved in a variety of criminal activities, including gang wars, gambling, and robbery (Asbury, 1927/1971).

Concentrations of immigrant groups in New York and Chicago promoted the rise of ethnically organized juvenile gangs. Several Irish and Italian youth gangs operated in New York during the 19th century. The initial report of the New York Children's Aid Society (1854) described delinquent gang activity on the streets of New York. Similar to contemporary gangs, some of these gangs were highly territorial, well organized, hostile to outsiders, and occasionally had female auxiliaries (Covey, Menard, and Franzese, 1997).

20th-Century Gangs

Early-20th-century studies concluded that gangs were predatory and existed—with divergent commitment—in both middle- and lower-class neighborhoods. Recent immigrants made up most of the membership; therefore, ethnicity was a primary organizational focus. The Sugar House Gang, operating in Detroit in the 1920s, was developed to protect Jewish merchants from harassment and assault. Another major Jewish gang based in Detroit, the Purple Gang, is viewed as one of the first corporate gangs in America. Its primary activity was illegal alcohol sales.

The first extensive study of gang behavior in the United States was completed by Frederic Thrasher (1927/1963) during the 1920s. His analysis of the more than 1,000 "gangs" he was able to isolate within the neighborhoods of Chicago provided the basis on which most early gang research was conducted. He proposed that gangs begin as harmless play groups and evolve into more cohesive aggressive entities. Juveniles were originally drawn to group activity as the result of the disorganization of social institutions caused by the immense volume and rapid rate of immigration experienced in American cities during the early 1900s. This environmental conception of gang organization was supported by the work of the Chicago School and William F. Whyte within the Italian neighborhoods of Boston.

Though some Hispanic gangs formed in southern California and African American gangs in Chicago during the 1920s and 1930s, no real attention was given to them until the World War II era. During the 1940s, cities such as New York, Chicago, Detroit, and Philadelphia reported a variety of ethnic gangs roaming the streets, participating in criminal activity and waging war against each other. The public became concerned about the increase in juvenile crime, particularly juvenile gangs.

Studies indicate that African American gangs in New York (particularly in Harlem) and Chicago became more organized during the 1940s. However, although they participated in minor criminal endeavors, their primary activities were turf battles against interlopers and "hanging out." They were predominately lower-class youth from single-parent homes assuming what to them were meaningful roles in gang subcultures.

One of the most significant developments in juvenile gang history occurring during the 1940s was the emergence of Hispanic youth gangs in southern and coastal California. A few barrio gangs had already developed in these areas in response to the differences in immigrant culture, language, and the extreme poverty level. However, experts in this area agree that the "zoot suit riots" were probably the catalyst to the development of the extensive gang culture that permeates Hispanic barrios in the Pacific Southwest today.

Zoot suits (composed of baggy pants, large-shouldered jackets, and wide-brimmed hats) were so popular with young Mexican Americans that it became a symbol of their Hispanic ethnicity. The general public equated zoot suits with barrio street life, which included criminal activity. Media hype, social unrest, and racial intolerance heightened tensions and reinforced public perception of Hispanic youths as destructive and threatening to the social order. Instead of impeding the zoot suit culture, harassment by officials was the catalyst to the organization of youth gangs for mutual support and protection.

The Violent Gang

The threat of gangs and gang violence swept the public consciousness during the 1950s and early 1960s.

Movies like *West Side Story* and *Rebel Without a Cause* projected images of culturally confused juveniles engaged in increasingly violent behavior. Academics warned that lower-class allegiance to middle-class values engendered violent responses. The period reflected a significant increase in gang activity, and the media was obsessed with reporting it. Researchers were fascinated with studying gangs, and the public was terrified gang activity would invade their lives.

Internalizing these same values, California Hispanic street gang members transferred loyalties to the prisons as youth were incarcerated in adult institutions in the 1950s. Hostilities between northern agrarian and southern barrio Hispanics were intensified by the close contact of prison life.

Most of the major "supergangs" developed in the 1960s, controlling major portions of urban America and consolidating allegiances with smaller gangs in Midwestern cities. The Blackstone Rangers, Vice Lords, and Latin Kings originated in Chicago, and the Crips and the Bloods became major forces in Los Angeles.

The Watts riots of 1965 solidified African American gangs in Los Angeles in much the same way the zoot suit riots had for Hispanic gangs. Shelden, Tracy, and Brown (2001) pointed out that one of the results of the Watts riots was that both the media and the community cast young African Americans in a more negative light, causing them to view themselves as separate from the greater community. With the Chicano experience to imitate, they came together for camaraderie and protection.

Though the origin of the name has stirred considerable debate, the Crips came from Compton, California, and imitated the *cholo*, or Hispanic, tradition of wearing railroad bandannas. Blue bandannas and clothing became the "colors" for all Crip sects. Independent gangs, calling themselves Bloods and wearing red colors, soon emerged as defense against the Crips. The Compton Pirus (unaffiliated youth living on Piru Street) are believed to be the first group to use the term *blood brothers* as a gang name. Both gangs soon spread throughout the Los Angeles area and adopted many of the Hispanic gang customs. Some of these included wearing colors, using graffiti, and "jumping in" new members.

As the number of gangs, gang cohesion, and membership increased, gang activity became more violent. In his study of the violent gang, Louis Yablonsky (1962) argued that the gangs he observed were quite different from those studied by the Chicago School in the 1930s and 1940s and from those examined by the social theorists of the 1950s. Violent gangs of the 1960s were not the result of cultural violence. They were, instead, the result of sociopathic personalities formed to build "reputations" and to supply emotional gratification through power and force. Their underlying theme was hostility and aggression, and unlike the cohesive subculture organization of the social theorists, violent gangs were in a constant state of flux. The media's obsession with reporting the violent activities of large inner-city gangs fueled the public's awareness of and fascination with youth gangs. Law enforcement met the challenge of increased gang violence by developing gang control units that infiltrated gangs and arrested leaders.

At the same time, based largely on the research of Richard Cloward and Lloyd Ohlin's differential opportunity theory, delinquency prevention became a national priority in the 1960s. These researchers believed that youth who experience blockages of their efforts to achieve middle-class goals resort to illegitimate methods of attaining them in direct proportion to the level of opportunity denied them. Delinquent behavior was again explained as a search for the solution to the problem of adjustment to unattainable middle-class goals.

As the social consciousness of the nation turned to civil rights issues, some sociologists and policymakers of the period believed that gang activity could be refocused toward constructive social issues. Some supergangs became recipients of federal grants that were supposed to provide the resources to channel gang members toward productive activities. Instead of socially desirable activities, funds were used to further criminal ones.

Escalation of the Vietnam War and increased social activism among ethnic minorities drew many youth of the ages typical of gang membership. In addition, some experts speculate that increased drug use diverted many juveniles from violent, criminal gangs to retreatist, drug-using groups. Others contend that the gang-control tactics of law enforcement resulted in decreased gang activity. Whatever the reason, most gang researchers report that gang activity decreased significantly during the latter part of the 1960s.

Resurgence and Gang Migration

Walter Miller (1975) reported that by the 1970s, juvenile gangs and juvenile gang activity experienced a resurrection. Unlike their counterparts after World War II, gangs of the early 1970s embraced economic motives for their activities. Reports of gang activity in New York, Detroit, Los Angeles, Chicago, and El Paso revealed gang membership to be at an all-time high. Cities such as Cleveland, Columbus, and Milwaukee, which previously did not have serious levels of gang activity, encountered significant increases in the number of gangs, gang members, and types of activities.

Predatory crime, such as drive-by shootings, replaced the ritualistic activities of turf wars for most gangs as involvement in the drug trade became a primary focus. Many experts believe that gang activity increased because of the involvement of youth gangs in the sale and distribution of illegal drugs. In some areas, gangs replaced traditional organized crime families as the dominant suppliers of cocaine and crack. Automatic weapons, financed by drug profits, replaced the knives and handguns of traditional gangs.

Chicago gangs began operating in both Dade County, Florida, and Milwaukee, and the Crips and Bloods were reported in several Midwestern cities. Gang coordinators began talking about the "migration" of the supergangs from inner cities to America's heartland and the emergence of gangs from local dance and rap groups and neighborhood street-corner groups in midsized cities and towns.

The earliest Asian gang, Wa Ching, was formed during the 19th century by Chinese youth affiliated with adult crime groups referred to as tongs. The Joe Boys and Yu Li were formed in San Francisco during the 1960s, but it was a 1977 shootout between Chinese gangs in the Golden Dragon restaurant in San Francisco that focused national attention on Asian gangs. The end of the Vietnam War escalated immigration from South Vietnam and resulted in an influx of young, unskilled, non-English-speaking males who formed and joined gangs.

Very little research addressing gang delinquency was conducted from the mid-1960s until the early 1980s. Irving Spergel (1984, 1990b) complained that although "gang violence had reached its highest level since the turn of the twentieth century in such cities as Los Angeles and Chicago," less was known about gang behavior in the mid-1980s than in the 1960s. America seemed to rediscover youth gangs in the early 1980s. Some observers argued that when gang violence changed from being among members to being aimed at the public, the attention of law enforcement, the media, and the public was refocused.

Others suggested that a "moral panic" was purposely created by justice agencies seeking to justify federal funding of specialized units. Whatever the motivation, the media, the public, and all levels of government became fixated with gang delinquency.

During a time when criminologists were arguing that gang research was outdated and deficient, leadership in defining the issue and the solution had been seized by governmental bodies anxious for quick policy "fixes." Mayors' task forces, governors' committees, commissioners' reports, and attorneys general's summaries were the primary definition of the gang issue.

These governmental bodies also led the charge in developing policy based on information garnered from a multitude of conferences, data banks, and prevention, interdiction and suppression programs. Unfortunately, few were structured on any empirically tested theoretical base. The problem and the solution were being defined by the perceptions of parties with vested interests in the parameters of both issues. In addition, excessive media attention enhanced the radical perception of gang issues.

GANGS IN THE 1980s AND 1990s

Gang research in the 1980s and 1990s asked, "What do we really need to know about gangs to adequately understand and therefore, address 'the gang problem'?" Though there is no consensus as to stance, the following are major issues discussed in most current gang research.

Definition

An increasing number of metropolitan areas, as well as small cities and towns, have begun to maintain data on gang-related crime but do not necessarily use the same operational definition of *gang* or *gang incident* (Spergel, 1990a). Consequently, assessment of gang strength, membership, and activity differs from area to area. Definition continues to be the central issue in gang research.

Extent

Some researchers contend that we cannot begin to address the problem intelligently if we fail to adequately define the extent of gang membership, organization, and activity. Several comprehensive national studies have been conducted. However, most of what

we know comes from examining individual communities or a handful of community studies.

Nature

What are the characteristics of gangs and gang members in the 21st century? Examination of gang activity in small communities highlights the fact that gang violence is not restricted to America's urban centers. Studies have revealed that drug use is widespread and common among gangs, regardless of the city, the extent or nature of collective violence, or their organization or social processes. In addition, serious and violent behavior occurs among a majority of the gangs.

THEORIES

Theories seeking to explain the development and activities of juvenile gangs abound. Gang experts group these theories in a variety of ways. However, most gang theory can be grouped within the following six general categories: (1) social disorganization, (2) strain/anomie, (3) criminal subcultures, (4) social processing, (5) rational choice, and (6) mental disease or defect. A summary of each of the central perspectives and the major theoretical contributors for each category is included here. Covey et al. (1997:186) reminded students of gang research, "Understanding juvenile gangs requires not a single, isolated explanation, but a collection of related explanations." Why gangs form may have little to do with why individuals join gangs, and gangs may persist or disintegrate for reasons that have little to do with why they formed in the first place.

Social Disorganization

The primary focus of social disorganization theorists is the neighborhood itself. They believe that the characteristics of decaying neighborhoods so severely affect the structure of inner cities that disorganization creates crime and gang organization no matter who lives there. Often referred to as the ecological perspective, social disorganization theory views the city as a living organism decaying in neighborhoods in transition from residential to business or industrial usage.

Researchers credited with developing social disorganization theory studied the city of Chicago and became known as the Chicago School. Robert Park and Ernest Burgess argued that cities could be mapped as concentric circles or zones radiating out from the central business district. As changes occurred from one zone to the next, a pattern of social problems developed. Clifford Shaw and Henry McKay identified these high-crime and delinquency areas of change as the first three zones circling the business district. Frederic Thrasher (1927/1963:21) called these areas of constant social change "interstitial" areas, which were characterized by deteriorating neighborhoods, shifting populations, and the mobility and disorganization of the slum. In the midst of social disorganization, gangs provide the basic social needs of belonging and self-esteem for young males.

Strain and Anomie

Strain theory was developed by Robert Merton, who revised the anomie theory first developed during the 19th century by French sociologist Emile Durkheim. Historically, expectations are limited by an individual's social class. Durkheim argued that capitalism and industrialization remove traditional social filters on aspirations of the lower classes and that a constant state of dissatisfaction results from unattainable desires. Class structure and inequality create expectations of the rewards of success, such as money, power, and status, yet the lower classes do not possess the means by which to attain these goals. This discrepancy produces individual pressures or strain.

Robert Merton elaborated on this strain by developing a typology of possible individual responses to the "lack of fit" between the societal goals of success and blocked means by which to achieve them. He stated that, as *conformists*, individuals continue to accept both the cultural goals of economic success and the restrictions on their approved means of reaching those goals. *Innovation*, the adaptation most likely to produce criminal behavior, retains the goals of success but rejects the limited means in favor of unsanctioned alternative (criminal) means. *Ritualists* accept the restrictions on their means but reject the goals themselves, thereby investing themselves in the process of conformity rather than the attainment of the goals. Finally, youths who reject both the cultural goals and the means resort to either *rebellion* (replacing the goals and means with new goals and means) or *retreatism* (no interest in either the goals or means). Merton classified chronic drug users as retreatists.

Richard Cloward and Lloyd Ohlin added the concept of differential opportunity to Merton's version of strain theory. They stated that, while legitimate opportunities are blocked for lower-class youth, opportunities to substitute illegal means may not be. Therefore, those with the greatest opportunities for illegitimate means will resort to using them.

Criminal Subcultures

Albert Cohen suggested that the conflict between the lower-class boys of the ghettos and the middle-class values of mainstream society results in a "status frustration" and that the organization of the gang is used as a means of adjustment. This "reaction formation" drives the development of a separate subculture that rejects the "middle-class measuring rod" of success used by greater society. The violence of the gang is simply an expression of the rejection of these unattainable middle-class values. The delinquent subculture is a collective response to a lack of access to middle-class means necessary to attain middle-class goals.

Miller argued that delinquency is not the result of failed attempts to attain middle-class goals, as lower-class youth are "normally" in disagreement with middle-class values. He suggested that there are clearly defined focal concerns within lower-class culture and that male delinquent groups are driven by rebellion against female-dominated households. The young males adhere to the lower-class values of "trouble," "smartness," "excitement," "toughness," "fate," and "autonomy" and are automatically viewed as delinquent.

Social Processing

Social-processing theories focus on the process by which youth are socialized into American culture. Learning theory, social control theory, and labeling theory are social-processing theories. Edwin Sutherland first postulated that, as with all behavior, deviant or criminal behavior is learned. He argued that the specific attitudes, values, and skills necessary to become successful criminals are passed on through a process of differential association. Youth learn to become delinquent through excessive exposure to those with favorable attitudes toward crime rather than to persons with unfavorable attitudes concerning criminal activity. They differentially associate with those who pass on values and skills that make delinquency rewarding.

Travis Hirschi contended that involvement with delinquent peers is a result, not a cause, of juvenile gang behavior. He argued that the elements of social control—ties to school, family, legitimate peers—are weak and fail to develop commitment to societal values and behavior. Control theory assumes that antisocial, criminal activity is rewarding. Therefore, there is a natural motivation toward crime. Societal controls based on the process of bonding to society's norms of behavior prevent most people from committing crimes. Hirschi developed four elements of social bonding: (1) attachment—ties of affection and respect between children and parents; (2) commitment—the extent to which youth commit to the process of obtaining long-term goals of society (getting an education in order to obtain a good job); (3) involvement—the amount of time spent engaging in legitimate activities (working, studying, etc.); and (4) belief—the extent to which youth "buy in" to the norms of society. These processing elements work in concert with each other to develop solid bonding to mainstream goals and behavior in order to prevent juveniles from gravitating toward delinquent and gang behavior.

Labeling theory actually addresses the process of secondary deviance in that it examines the impact of the social process on youth, rather than the reasons for the initial behavior. Labeling theorists seek to explain why certain behaviors are defined as criminal, the official response to deviance, and the effect of official reaction on the labeled youths. They contend that lower-class youth are more likely than middle- or upper-class youth to be labeled as delinquents for similar behavior. Labeling is used as a tool to oppress lower-class youth. Society's reaction to marginal behavior by labeling youth "delinquent" activates a process that perpetuates future delinquency as self-fulfilling prophecy.

Rational Choice

Just as social control theories argue that natural tendencies toward criminal behavior can be overcome through internalized bonds to society, deterrence and rational choice theories argue that these natural tendencies can be overcome by threat of punishment so great as to overshadow the rewards of illegitimate behavior. Based on ideas from the 18th century's classical school of criminology, rational choice theory asserts that man is basically hedonistic, or pleasure seeking, and will participate in criminal activity for the pleasure the rewards provide him. It is a rational choice calculated on the ratio of pleasure derived from the profits to the risk of possible painful negative

sanction from society. Bentham called it a "hedonistic calculus," and Beccaria argued that "the punishment should fit the crime" as the utility of the punishment deterring crime was lessened if the pain inflicted outweighed the pleasure by too great a degree. Excessive punishment negatively affects rational choice.

Contemporary researchers have found that many juveniles today view deciding to join gangs as rational career decisions. Felix Padilla's *The Gang as an American Enterprise* (1992) examined a Latino gang in Chicago and concluded that boys joined the gang as the result of assessment of legitimate economic opportunities. The gang offered a means of achieving economic success not otherwise available to them. In addition, Spergel (1990b) found that some adolescents join gangs for personal safety rather than personal profit. Newcomers to a neighborhood or youth living in a community dominated by a different racial or ethnic background often join gangs for protection.

Modern rational choice theory recognizes that people freely choose to commit crime but that their choices are affected by a myriad of factors such as lack of information, moral values, and situational factors (Shelden et al., 2001). What may seem rational to young lower-class males, lacking family or community security, may not seem rational to mainstream America. Some researchers indicate choices made by juveniles may also be affected by mental disease or mental defect.

Mental Disease or Defect

Lewis Yablonsky's (1962) examination of the "violent gang" first suggested that juvenile gang members tended to be sociopathic youth living in disorganized slum communities. He argued that these youths lacked "social feelings" or compassion for others. He characterized them as having (1) defective social conscience with limited feelings of guilt for injury to others, (2) limited empathy for others, (3) egocentricity, and (4) manipulative behaviors for the purposes of immediate self-gratification.

More recent analysis of Los Angeles gangs by Malcolm Klein (1995) revealed that some gang members suffer from low self-concept, social disabilities, poor impulse control, and limited social and life skills. He suggested that juveniles with early onset of conduct disorder, antisocial behavior, and violent tempers are at greatest risk for gang membership. However, Klein did not believe the majority of gang members suffer from mental disease or defect.

CONCLUSION

Most gang researchers agree that no single theory or group of theories explains gang organization and activity. Elements of all categories of gang theory have proven to be useful in understanding the nature and extent of gangs, gang membership, and gang behavior. Yet a great deal of knowledge remains elusive. John Hagedorn calls for significant increases in ethnographic studies to provide the missing pieces too intimate to be reflected in historical and survey research. However, it may be that the greatest advances in understanding delinquency, specifically gang delinquency, lie within the technology of the 21st century.

Behavior is driven by functions of the brain. Reaction to strain, development of subcultures, internalizing social bonds, and making rational choices all rely on functions of the brain. Twenty-first-century technology is just beginning to explore how "misfires" within the psyche or the physical brain drive behavior. This information may help provide the last major piece of the puzzle necessary to address juvenile gang issues.

Beth Pelz

See also Richard Cloward; Curfew; Drugs; Female Delinquency; Graffiti and Tagging; Travis Hirschi; Henry D. McKay; Walter B. Miller; Lloyd E. Ohlin; Police Responses to Delinquency; Prevention Strategies; Clifford R. Shaw; Edwin H. Sutherland; Theories of Delinquency

Bibliography

Asbury, H. 1971. *Gangs of New York: An Informal History of the Underworld.* New York: Putnam. (Originally published 1927, New York: Knopf.)

Covey, H. C., S. Menard, and R. J. Franzese. 1997. *Juvenile Gangs.* Springfield, IL: Charles C Thomas.

Klein, M. W. 1995. *The American Street Gang.* New York: Oxford University Press.

Miller, W. B. 1975. *Violence by Youth Gangs and Youth Groups as a Crime Problem in Major American Cities.* Washington, DC: Office of Juvenile Justice and Delinquency Prevention.

Padilla, F. M. 1992. *The Gang as an American Enterprise: Puerto Rican Youth and the American Dream.* New Brunswick, NJ: Rutgers University.

Shelden, R. G., S. K. Tracy, and W. B. Brown. 2001. *Youth Gangs in American Society.* Belmont, CA: Wadsworth.

Spergel, I. A. 1984. Violent gangs in Chicago, IL: In search of social policy. *Social Service Review* 58:199–226.

Spergel, I. A. 1990a. Strategies and perceived agency effectiveness in dealing with the youth gang problem. Pp. 288–309 in R. C. Huff (ed.), *Gangs in America.* Newbury Park, CA: Sage.

Spergel, I. A. 1990b. Youth gangs: Continuity and change. Pp. 171–275 in M. Tonry and N. Morris (eds.), *Crime and Justice: A Review of Research*, Vol. 12. Chicago: University of Chicago.

Thrasher, F. M. 1963. *The Gang—A Study of 1,313 Gangs in Chicago.* Abridged with a new introduction by J. F. Short Jr. Chicago: University of Chicago Press. (Originally published 1927.)

Yablonsky, L. 1962. *The Violent Gang.* New York: Macmillan.

GANGS, JUVENILE

III. Organization and Activities

Of all the subcultures and deviant groups that exist in the United States, the one type of subculture that tends to dominate the public imagination is the gang. Reported here are those aspects of youth gang activities that bring members to the attention of the criminal justice system: drugs, guns, and violence. If it were not for these activities, gangs would not have the high level of public concern that they have captured over the years.

There are thousands of youth gangs with an estimated 1.5 million members in the United States alone. One out of four inmates in adult American correctional institutions are gang members. Most of the gangs that operate inside correctional institutions were imported there as result of their members being prosecuted for street gang activities. Thus most of the gangs that exist behind bars also exist by the same name and identity on the streets. Inside American correctional institutions, gangs are often referred to as security threat groups or security risk groups. Because these gangs have mostly adult members, our only concern with them here is the way in which they interact with street youth gangs.

Major gang epicenters, places from which youth gangs have formed and spread their influence, include Los Angeles, Chicago, and New York City. Los Angeles is the known gang epicenter for the Crips/Bloods gang alliance system. Chicago is the known gang epicenter for the People/Folks gang alliance system. New York City has had renegade gang factions like the Almighty Latin Kings of New York who have spread their influence throughout the East Coast, even though the original Latin Kings gang and the most powerful Latin Kings gang in the United States developed from and still persists in Chicago. In 1993, as a result of Crips meeting with Folks (most of which were Gangster Disciples) at a Chicago "gang peace treaty" summit meeting sponsored by the political arm of the Gangster Disciples, the Crips became allied with Folks. This created a national gang alliance system and forced Bloods to make allies with People gangs.

Hate groups and outlaw motorcycle clubs also meet the definition of criminal gangs but are rarely youth gangs. White racist extremist groups, in particular those predisposed toward violent bias crimes, are simply gangs whose activities are mostly known for hate, but in fact, many of these gang members have the same criminal activity profiles of other street gang members (e.g., engaging in drug sales, drug use, and criminal activity to generate income).

Some gangs have their own Web sites and spread their beliefs and values over the Internet. Most cities, large and small, in America today have some level of a gang problem. Of course, there are still cities large and small that deny the gang problem entirely as an intentional strategy, often to safeguard tourism. In 2000, all three of the youth gang epicenters previously mentioned abolished citywide gang units in their municipal police departments.

GANG ORGANIZATION

Most gangs arise out of spontaneously formed informal groups, including "party crews" or "play groups." Residential propinquity and neighborhood identification also play a role, along with race and ethnicity. The observation that most informal groups are pregang formations dates back to the 1927 classic work of Thrasher. Because not all gangs are truly organized, one way to classify gangs is to combine their formality with their organization. The following is one type of gang classification system:

1. Pregang: informal structure and group orientation.

2. Level I: formal structure with group orientation.

3. Level II: informal structure with true organization.

4. Level III: formal structure with true organization.

When an informal (pregang) group declares itself to be a collective identity, or at least operates as if

it were, often with a name for the group, it has added elements of organizational formality to the social group and can be considered the most rudimentary form of criminal or delinquent gang: a Level I gang. Many gangs are of this variety, where membership size is small, and there is typically only one unit that operates in only one geographical jurisdiction.

Anyone can watch a series of Hollywood gang movies to learn enough subcultural argot about a gang like the Crips or Bloods, visit various Web sites (some hosted by gang members) to learn about gang symbols and colors, and then basically declare him- or herself a gang member. Such individuals are called "wannabe" gang members by social control agencies and form another type of pregang. Once wannabes create their Level I gang, however, and then get arrested, they meet the real thing when placed in a correctional institution.

The Trench Coat Mafia, the group involved in the Columbine High School massacre, were, for example, a Level I gang. They existed in only one jurisdiction, did not have a large membership base, and did not have a formal written constitution and bylaws as some Level III gangs have. To see examples of gang profiles of Level III gangs, students and researchers may want to look at the Gangster Disciples and Latin Kings gang profiles available at the Web site for the National Gang Crime Research Center (NGCRC) at http://www.ngcrc.com/profile/profile.html.

GANG ACTIVITIES

Like members of other groups and organizations, gang members engage in a wide variety of social activities. Gangs have meetings, picnics, parties, raves—what gangs and gang members "do" is an endless list, including a lot of behavior that is not necessarily against the law. Gangs develop a special vocabulary of words and phrases having meaning only to gang members. Some gangs even have written constitutions and bylaws, require weekly meetings, and pay dues.

It is the illegal activities of the gang—activities related to guns, drugs, and violence—that are of interest to anyone involved in juvenile justice as well as the media and the public. Violence and drug activity are the two main factors that tend to motivate a society to respond repressively to gangs and gang members. Violence includes the many dangers involving the use and possession of firearms as well as an array of unique types of violence associated with gangs and gang members. The drug activity that a gang can engage in is such that it becomes an incipient form of organized crime; the drug dealing operations can be flagrant and sophisticated and generate a great deal of income for the gang. Unfortunately, the intense competition in the underground economy involving the distribution of illegal drugs also means another type of violence: competition with other groups and individuals involved in selling illegal drugs. If gangs and gang members did not pose a major problem in terms of violence, or a predisposition to violence, then it is doubtful that a society would be very concerned about the gang problem.

Conflict is built into the very nature of gang activity. A person who joins a Crip gang automatically takes on an opposition to any and all Blood gang members, and vice versa. The enemy is symbolic and subject to many social and psychological processes that generate ongoing conflict and violence.

One of the most unusual aspects of gang conflict is when, within one household, one sibling joins a gang like the Vice Lords (a People or Brother gang riding under the five-pointed star) and another sibling joins the Gangster Disciples (a Folks gang, riding under the six-pointed star). This happens in a variety of settings and is generally very destructive to the family as a functioning unit.

Many people think that youths join gangs for protection. Actually, only a weaker person would do that or be more susceptible to being recruited for that reason. An interesting truth about American gangs is that a gang member is actually more likely to be beaten and a victim of violence from her or his own gang than any rival gang. This is true because of the ritualistic use of corporal punishment in the gang's group context: a phenomenon called the "violation" illustrates this. The violation takes on many forms: "face work" (punches only to the face); "pumpkin head deluxe," or PHD (punches or kicks to the head); "walking the line" (taking punishment from all members present at the violation ceremony); "V30" or "V60" (30 or 60 seconds of free-for-all against the errant gang member, in the Latin Kings typically just involving punches to the chest). In extreme situations, as when a gang member betrays his or her gang, he may get a "death V" or "TOS" (terminate on sight).

ESTIMATES OF THE AMOUNT AND TYPE OF GANG ACTIVITY

Details about gang-related offenses, and even the number of gangs themselves, are not available from governmental crime statistics. The *Uniform Crime Reports* (UCR), compiled by the Federal Bureau of Investigation (FBI), have never required police departments to report whether an arrestee was a gang member or what gang was involved. There is simply no gang-related information in the UCR data. From an informational point of view, America is still in gang denial: The problem apparently is not significant enough to justify a special question or two in our major crime reporting system. Conversely, in the late 1980s, the American public was convinced that hate and bias crimes were important enough to track their patterns, and federal legislative officials passed statutes requiring the FBI to track this kind of offense pattern in the UCR.

Survey Estimates

A 1996 national random survey of 283 municipal police departments in the 48 contiguous states gives us a rough estimate of the impact of gang crime in the United States today (NGCRC, 1996). It was designed to determine the percentage of overall crime attributable to gang members. According to that study, an estimated population of 1.5 million gang members accounts for an average of 10.6 percent of all crime in the United States and about 18.5 percent of all juvenile crime in U.S. cities. These and other NGCRC law enforcement survey findings over the years are reported in Knox (2000).

Gangs and Guns. A 1995 survey provides some information on gangs and guns (NGCRC, 1995). Six gang researchers at three universities collaborated to carry out an extensive study of gangs and guns in the Midwest involving 1,206 survey respondents, which included 505 gang members. Four social contexts were used for the survey: eight county jails from the farmland to the urban central area (891 inmates), matched-pair design samples from a Chicago public high school and an inner-city program, and a sample of gang members in a private suburban probation program. A small sample of some of the findings include the following:

1. In response to a series of questions about access to and ownership of a variety of firearms and explosives, gang members were more likely to report that access was easier, and they were more likely to have been in possession, than non-gang members.

2. Gang members are more likely to report carrying concealed guns than are those who are not gang members.

3. Gang members are more likely to report having ever stolen a pistol or rifle (38.3 percent) than are nongang members (17.7 percent).

4. Gang members are more likely to report that they have ever used a sawed-off shotgun to commit a crime (22 percent) than are nongang members (3.9 percent).

5. Gang members are more likely to choose the option of retaliation as their primary solution to "wrongs" done to them (51.5 percent) than are nongang members (24.2 percent). In addition, gang members are more likely (47.7 percent) than their nongang member counterparts (33.6 percent) to believe that the best form of justice is simply "an eye for an eye."

6. Gang members are more likely (22.8 percent) to report having previously assaulted a schoolteacher than are inmates who have never joined a gang (9.5 percent).

7. Gang members are more likely to report that if they had to acquire a handgun quickly, they would go to gang associates (57.5 percent) than are nongang members (13.3 percent). Similarly, gang members are less likely (10.4 percent) to go to a "fence" than are nongang members (21.3 percent).

8. Gang members are more likely (57.1 percent) than their nongang member counterparts (32 percent) to know illegal gun merchants.

9. Gang members are more likely to shoot in all situations, whether those situations are shooting at anyone, a family member, a gang member, a police officer, or during a drug deal.

10. Gang members are more likely (73.5 percent) than other inmates (54.6 percent) to believe that gang membership helps in obtaining firearms.

Gang Activities. Another survey conducted by the National Gang Crime Research Center focused on gang activities (NGCRC, 1997; Stone, 2000). The study involved 28 researchers collecting data in 17 different states from 10,166 adults and juveniles in 85 different correctional facilities. Of this sample, 4,140 were gang members. Interesting research findings from this survey help us to understand gangs and drugs in relationship to the gang problem. Gang members were likely to do the following:

1. Report being bullies in school.

2. Report selling crack cocaine.

3. Report firing a gun at a police officer.

4. Feel that the Brady gun control bill either had no effect or made it easier to buy guns.

5. Report involvement in organized drug dealing, although that involvement was personal rather than gang oriented (as was also true for other profitable crime).

6. Report that some of their drug income was returned to the gang.

Other information gleaned from the survey indicated that gang members demonstrated greater disciplinary problems while incarcerated and that their family lives had a larger number of problems than other juveniles.

In addition, the survey provided a look at gang organization and features. Slightly over half the gang members reported that they were recruited into their gang while less than half reported that gaining protection was not a major factor in their decision to join the gang. Thus, although protection is still important as a reason for joining, recruitment appears to be the dominant mode of gaining members. Concerning organization, about two thirds reported that their gang had written rules, and over half said that there were regular weekly meetings. On the other hand, weekly dues to the gang were not common. Most gangs also appeared to have adult leaders who had been in the gang for many years. As a result, it appears that the common gang is at least semistructured (the Level II gang discussed earlier) and age structured.

When asked about nondrug activities, over half reported that they had committed a crime with their gang for financial gain. About a third reported being forced to commit a crime, and some two fifths said they knew someone who committed forcible sex with a female. While this evidence doesn't tell us much about the amount of crime committed by gang members, it does suggest that they are somewhat versatile in their offending behavior.

CONCLUSION

When we try to make sense of youth gang activity in America, it is clear that conflict is the fuel in the engine of the gang. This conflict entails much symbolic significance for gang members: They are committed to their gang identity ("us" versus "them") and by definition are at war with not only any rival gang outside their own gang alliance system (People/Folks, Crips/Bloods, Nortenos/Surenos, etc.), but often larger society as well. Gang members have a behavioral profile that includes much early exposure to various forms of violence and drug/substance abuse.

What also accentuates gang violence is the competition between gangs over the sale of illegal drugs. This kind of economic battle in the underground economy plays itself out in gang wars. Gangs today are also heavily involved in the production and distribution of illegal club drugs as well, especially methamphetamine. Thus because all drug wars declared by the various U.S. "drug czars" have been won by the drug dealers/importers/users, there is no reason to expect that "gang peace" will break out anytime soon.

There is a significant gang problem in America today. The problem is defining the extent of that problem, given our current lack of data. It would help American social policy to add gang information to the UCR. Such hard data on the gang problem would at least allow communities to know the level of the gang problem they face in terms of implementing prevention and intervention programs.

George W. Knox

See also California Street Terrorism Enforcement and Prevention Act; Delinquency—Trends and Data; Drugs—Use Among Youth; Serious and Violent Offenders

Bibliography

Knox, G. W. 2000. *An Introduction to Gangs.* Peotone, IL: New Chicago School Press.
National Gang Crime Research Center (NGCRC). 1995. *Project GANGGUNS—A Task Force Report.* Peotone, IL: National Gang Crime Research Center.
National Gang Crime Research Center (NGCRC). 1996. *The 1996 National Law Enforcement Gang Analysis Survey: A Preliminary Report.* Peotone, IL: National Gang Crime Research Center.
National Gang Crime Research Center (NGCRC). 1997. *Project GANGFACT: The Facts About Gang Life in America Today.* Peotone, IL: National Gang Crime Research Center.
Stone, S. S. 2000. *Contemporary Gang Issues: An Inside View.* Peotone, IL: New Chicago School Press.

GANGS, JUVENILE

IV. Intervention and Prevention

Youths who join gangs fall into two general types: those who freely choose to join and those who have little or no choice about joining. The first type joins a gang in search of individual pleasures by seeking material goods, status, or respect from other gang members. The second type joins a gang for survival.

The lifestyle portrayed by gang members is one with money, name-brand clothing, and large amounts of jewelry, but most important, it is a lifestyle that others emulate. In addition, gang members appear to outsiders as a closely knit group of friends. Gangs continually work to recruit new members, and members' lifestyles are important in recruitment, with members flashing their materialistic goods to others. The items in their possession come from illegal activities, sometimes from drug sales, robberies, and just plain theft. Older gang members frequently use new recruits or younger members to carry out their plans. They do this knowing that younger gang members, if caught, will receive a less severe sentence. Thus focusing on gang recruitment is one method of intervening in gang formation and continuation.

The second major reason for joining a gang, survival, is most likely for youth living in gang-infested neighborhoods. Gang members frequently use threats to get others to join, thus causing recruits to join for protection, even though that protection may be from other gang members. Some members join only because a prior relative belonged to a similar gang. Recruitment into a gang does not usually take place at one time or with one instance; acceptance takes place gradually.

Rather than concentrating on the negative, a recognition of positive reasons why youths join gangs may be valuable in locating mechanisms for gang prevention. Youth say they join gangs for reasons such as peer pressure, the need to belong to a group, and/or a need for someone to "look up to." Gangs provide their members a feeling of belonging, a family unity, and an identity. Some youths claim to acquire self-confidence and self-respect within a gang. Gang members learn that cooperation is necessary to be successful. Teamwork forces all members to work together for a common task. There is also an economic lesson to be learned in gangs. Gang members frequently learn by participating in organized theft or drug-selling activity that there are more approaches to earning money than the minimum wage jobs available to most teenagers. Intervention and prevention programs, then, must take into account these rationales for joining gangs and provide plausible alternatives.

SCHOOL-BASED INTERVENTION PROGRAMS

Gang members frequently pick up new recruits in schools. When gang members are asked why they joined the gang, they often answer that they feel as if they belong to a family. A lack of supervision from one or both parents may cause a juvenile to look for additional acceptance. Once susceptible to peer pressure and acceptance, juveniles often find gang members at school offer support and camaraderie not otherwise available.

It is difficult to separate school-based gang intervention programs from prevention programs. The following are two examples of current school-based gang intervention programs. The first, Cities in Schools (CIS), was developed as a way to lower school drop-out rates, reduce school violence, and provide more opportunities for metropolitan students. Students were offered educational assistance, as well as counseling, to develop success in academics, which is assumed to insulate students from gang participation.

Another national program is Gang Resistance Education and Training (GREAT). This is one of the newest intervention programs and works in a fashion similar to DARE. The program targets fourth and seventh graders to provide students with antidrug messages on the assumption that drugs are related to gangs. It is currently under evaluation.

GANG PREVENTION

Delinquency prevention programs have long been the most popular method of preventing crime and gang

formation. Gang prevention can be divided into four different areas: (1) community organization (neighborhood residents involved in gang prevention programs), (2) social intervention programs (counseling and treatment designed to guide behavior toward positive prevention), (3) opportunity activities (employment openings as well as anything to further the education process), and (4) suppression activities (programs that work with the criminal justice system designed to restrain gang members).

Official agencies such as police, juvenile courts, probation, community corrections, juvenile detention, and correctional institutions are examples of formal suppression activities. This system of control is primarily reactive in nature, focusing on actions to be taken after a gang member commits an offense. Official preventive mechanisms can also include examples such as police intervention with status offenders. In these cases, the idea is to intervene in children's lives before they get to the stage of delinquency and gang affiliation.

Some assume that prevention programs must begin in the home because that is where objectionable behavior begins and where the greatest gains can be made. Today families are composed of more single parents or parents who both work. This decreases the time parents have to spend with their children and increases unsupervised free time with peers. Without substantial parental care and supervision, children can come to see gangs as parental surrogates. Thus some gang prevention programs are designed to support family interaction and supervision.

Others assume that schools are the best place to prevent gangs. Gang members may declare a certain place in the school as their own and control this area by intimidating or fighting with other students. Other gang members enjoy the excitement that originates from gangs and decide school is no longer necessary. Although school is not the solution for preventing gangs, it can restrain gang members' actions while they are attending school. A common gang prevention method is to identify gang members and gang activity as soon as possible, usually by asking faculty to assist in the identification process. Most important, research findings from successful programs point out that success is more likely to occur when the community also assists. Parents share in school-based gang prevention by being involved in both before- and after-school activities and by assisting teachers in daily school operations.

CONCLUSION

While the focus of gang intervention and prevention frequently falls on schools and families, these institutions are limited in what they can do to prevent gangs. The results of various projects have shown that any one piece of the gang intervention and prevention puzzle cannot, by itself, be successful. Schools are designed to educate, not solve community problems. Similarly, families have more complex responsibilities than ever before and, in the neighborhoods where gangs commonly form, have their own unique problems. Involvement of the total community seems to be critical. Rather than assign responsibility to individual parts of the community, an integrated model with participation from the criminal/juvenile justice system, government, business, and helping agencies must be created. These components can then cooperate with the schools and families to intervene in and prevent youth gang problems.

Phillip Hirsch and Claudia Rios Hirsch

See also Curfew; DARE; Graffiti and Tagging; Prevention Strategies

Bibliography

Bender, D., B. Leone, and C. P. Cozic. 1996. *Gangs: Opposing Viewpoints.* San Diego, CA: Greenhaven.

Kinnear, K. L. 1996. *Gangs: A Reference Handbook.* Santa Barbara, CA: ABC-CLIO.

Lawrence, R. 1998. *School Crime and Juvenile Justice.* New York: Oxford University Press.

Oliver, M. T. 1995. *Gangs: Trouble in the Streets.* Springfield, IL: Enslow.

Sachs, S. L. 1997. *Street Gang Awareness.* Minneapolis, MN: Fairview Press.

 GIRLS AND BOYS TOWN

The year was 1917, and America was experiencing social crises associated with World War I, including a continued concern with the problems of wayward and delinquent youth. As an assistant pastor and director of an Omaha, Nebraska, hotel for disadvantaged workers, Father Edward Flanagan recognized the relationship between childhood problems and difficulties later in life and decided to intervene with boys before their troubles became serious. He opened Father Flanagan's Boys Home, with the goal of providing a caring, homelike atmosphere, education, and life skills to abused, abandoned, neglected, handicapped, and otherwise at-risk boys. Boys arrived, referred by the court or citizens, or on their own; none were turned away. The home had humble beginnings: Nuns volunteered their assistance, boys were driven by horse and wagon to attend local schools, and providing food and a warm, safe place was a financial struggle, dependent on community donations.

Residents soon outgrew the home, and in late 1918, they moved to the German-American Home, which had closed in the face of anti-German sentiment during WWI. There, with the generosity and volunteerism of community residents, they planted a farm, added music lessons, and began a magazine. Recognizing improvements in the lives of boys who resided at the home, judges continued to refer troubled boys. Within four years, more than 1,300 boys had received services—some staying only a few months, others much longer—and were reunited with family, were adopted, or joined the community as productive adults (Girls and Boys Town, 2001a). Not everyone, however, supported Father Flanagan's work. Some citizens objected to his nondiscriminatory policy that admitted boys of all races and religions, and others objected to having "delinquents" in the community, although only about 20 percent of the boys had delinquency records (Girls and Boys Town, 2001a).

Despite opposition, the facility persisted. After several boys experienced problems in the local schools, Father Flanagan founded an on-site grade school. Four years after the second home opened, the boys again outgrew it, and on October 22, 1921, the home moved to its current location west of Omaha. Here they cultivated another farm, constructed facilities for baseball, football, and track, and kept growing. It soon came to be called a "town," with its own post office and elected government, a means for youths to learn about citizenship and develop a sense of community. Their name changed to Boys Town after a resident vote in 1926, and in 1936, the Village of Boys Town became an official municipality of Nebraska. While in Europe to assist in the establishment of homes there, Father Flanagan died of a heart attack on May 14, 1948, but his work was carried on by Monsignor Nicholas Wegner until 1973, by Father Robert Hupp until 1985, and currently by Father Valentine Peter.

GIRLS AND BOYS TOWN TODAY

Girls were first admitted into family homes in 1979, and in the summer of 2000, Boys Town residents across the nation voted to change the name to Girls and Boys Town to recognize girls' representation. Although the Village of Boys Town retains its name, the new name applies to all national programs. In the spring of 2001, residents elected their fourth female mayor who, with a male vice mayor, serves as a liaison between village residents and program administrators.

Spreading over 900 acres, the home campus today consists of more than 95 buildings, including a middle school, a high school, both Catholic and Protestant churches, a post office, and police and fire departments. The town is run by the village board of trustees, which is responsible for maintenance of roads, buildings, utilities, and public order and safety (Boys Town, 1999). True to Father Flanagan's original intent, there are no fences at Boys Town and no locks on the doors. "I am not building a prison," said Father Flanagan. "This is a home. You do not wall in members of your family" (Girls and Boys Town, 2001a).

Today, of the more than 100 long-term residential service homes provided by Girls and Boys Town, 76 are located in the Village of Boys Town. Others are located in Brooklyn, New York; Washington, D.C.; Tallahassee and Orlando, Florida; New Orleans, Louisiana; San Antonio, Texas; Las Vegas, Nevada; and Orange County, California. These services are based on the Teaching Family Model, a "behaviorally oriented, family-style program for youth whose own families are untenable, and who are either unsuitable for foster care or have no foster care options" (Friman, 1999:2). Six to eight youths live in a "family home" with their family-teachers—trained married couples who serve as guides and mentors. Rooted in family nurture and spirituality, the model teaches youths new skills, self-empowerment, and the ability to build positive relationships (Boys Town, 1999). Key program features include a motivational token economy in which youths earn points to exchange for privileges; youth participation in rule setting and other decisions regarding daily life and treatment; a social skills curriculum; education reinforcement; and a continuous evaluation system, including youths' evaluations of their family-teachers. Youths are required to attend religious services, and if they do not already practice, must take a religion upon admission. Forty-five percent are Catholic and 49 percent Protestant, with Jewish and other religious affiliations comprising the remainder. Daily life is "normalized"; in fact, a drive through Boys Town gives one the impression of driving through a typical residential neighborhood, with families washing cars and youths playing in the yards. Youths may go off campus for work or recreation; and boys and girls interact on a daily basis and may become romantically involved if neither youth has a history of sexual aggressiveness or victimization. Girls and Boys Town police handle all law violations that occur on campus, but if youths get into trouble off campus, they must deal with local law enforcement.

Youths come to Girls and Boys Town for a variety of reasons: Some are referred by courts, parents, or other youth service agencies; others arrive voluntarily. Eighty-four percent of youths admitted to Girls and Boys Town have prior out-of-home placements, ranging from foster care to detention. Forty-five percent have substance abuse problems upon admission, 41 percent had engaged in assaultive behaviors, and 22 percent had threatened self-inflicted injury. Currently, youths served by Girls and Boys Town are 60 percent male and 41 percent minority (Boys Town, 1999). Their average age at admission is 14.4 years, and the average length of stay is 22 months (Friman, 1999).

FUNDING

Over the years, Girls and Boys Town has engaged in a variety of fund-raising activities, from a Women's Bucket Brigade in 1922, to a traveling circus during the Great Depression, to donations from citizens who learned about Father Flanagan's mission after hearing the famed Boys Town Choir or watching one of two motion pictures (*Boys Town* and *Men of Boys Town*) made about their efforts to help boys in need. Today the organization receives its funds from three major sources: public support (providing 30 percent to 40 percent of annual funds), program service revenues (25 to 35 percent), and interest and dividends from Father Flanagan's Trust Fund (30 to 40 percent).

OTHER SERVICES

In addition to the residential services program, Girls and Boys Town offers a variety of programs and services in locations across the country, many focused on aiding families. Common Sense Parenting offers help to parents, and Family-Based Services are available for families who need more intensive help in building relationships, acquiring parenting skills, and networking with community support services. There is also a 24-hour national hotline, a treatment foster care program, emergency shelter care, and a family preservation program. The Boys Town National Research Hospital specializes in hearing, speech, and language disorders and houses the Center for Abused Children With Disabilities. The National Resource and Training Center offers technological assistance to youth services professionals and organizations. In 1998, 741 youths resided at the home campus, but Girls and Boys Town as a whole provided direct treatment to more than 29,000 youths, directly assisted 380,000 through the hotline, and indirectly assisted 750,000 youths and families through other programs (Girls and Boys Town, 2001a).

OUTCOMES

The Girls and Boys Town National Research Institute for Child and Family Studies was founded in October 2000 to conduct applied research and generate collaborations with clinicians, researchers, and youth organizations (Boys and Girls Town, 2001b). In addition to this new avenue of research, many earlier studies assessed various Boys Town program effects and provided feedback for program improvement.

Pre- and posttests conducted in 1999 with Boys Town residential treatment participants indicated numerous treatment effects. Although 55 percent of youths arrived at Boys Town academically challenged, only 7 percent left with remaining academic difficulties (Boys Town, 1999). Forty percent of youths were admitted with conduct disorders, but only 7 percent still qualified for this diagnosis one year after admission, and mean scores for both internalizing and externalizing behaviors moved toward the normal range by departure (Boys Town, 1999; Friman, 1999). In addition, the percentage of youths testing positive for other conduct disorders declined from admission to one year after program participation: 10 percent to 4 percent for attention deficit hyperactivity disorder, 19 percent to near zero for substance dependence, and 15 percent to 2 percent for oppositional defiant disorder (Friman, 1999).

But how do Girls and Boys Town youths compare with youths in other treatment programs, and how long do the positive effects last?

A 10-year outcome evaluation of the residential program, the Boys Town Follow-Up Study, began in 1981. The study compared a treatment group (587 youths admitted to Boys Town) and a "treatment as usual" comparison group (84 youths who were eligible for Boys Town but received other community placements). In general, the short-term outcomes for Boys Town youth were more positive than were those of the comparison group. However, with a few exceptions, these differences tended to diminish over time (Oswalt, Daly, and Richter, 1992). The most persistent long-term effects were for religiosity and education. For example, Boys Town youths had a significantly higher grade point average, more years of school completed, and a higher graduation rate than the comparison group (Thompson et al., 1996). However, there appeared to be no long-term differences between the two groups in terms of psychological indices (self-esteem, social isolation, quality of life, or locus of control), employment, income, correctional or psychiatric placements, alcohol or drug use, or general delinquency (Oswalt et al., 1992). These researchers believe that their results suggest a need for continued treatment of at-risk youths, even after participation in long-term intensive residential programs like Girls and Boys Town (1992:159). It has been suggested that instead of following the "medical orientation" of expecting that once a problem is cured, it is cured for life, the emotional and behavioral problems should be viewed as involving learned patterns and skill deficiencies influenced by the youths' environment. From this perspective, skills and behaviors learned in the treatment environment must be continually reinforced in the posttreatment environment (Friman, 1999:13–14). Other Girls and Boys Town programs are available to assist youths and families in creating environments and building skills and relationships that can help sustain the positive effects of the residential treatment.

CONCLUSION

Girls and Boys Town has evolved over the past 84 years from a single Omaha, Nebraska, home to help wayward and troubled boys to a national organization providing a variety of services to boys, girls, and their families, but its philosophy and approach have remained the same: "Our mission: To change the way America cares for her children and families. Our values: Old-fashioned love and respect and new-fashioned science.

Our vision: To bring help, healing, and hope" (Girls and Boys Town, 2001b:6).

Dana Peterson

See also Alternative Schools; Boys and Girls Clubs of America; Children's Aid Society; Foster Care

Bibliography

Boys Town. 1999. *Outcomes '99: Mapping Success in Residential Settings*. Boys Town, NE: Father Flanagan's Boys' Home.

Friman, P. C. 1999. Family-style residential care really works: Scientific findings demonstrating multiple benefits for troubled adolescents. Pp. 2–17 in J. Austin and J. Carr (eds.), *Handbook of Applied Behavior Analysis*. Reno, NV: Context Press.

Girls and Boys Town. 2001a. *About Girls and Boys Town*. Available at http://www.girlsandboystown.org/aboutus/index.htm.

Girls and Boys Town. 2001b. *Applied Research to Help America's Children and Their Families*. Boys Town, NE: National Research Institute for Child and Family Studies.

Oswalt, G. L., D. L. Daly, and M. D. Richter. 1992. Longitudinal follow-up study of Boys Town residents: Implications for treating "at-risk" youth. Pp. 155–161 in A. Algarin and R. M. Friedman (eds.), *Proceedings for the 4th Annual Florida Mental Health Institute Research Conference. A System of Care for Children's Mental Health: Expanding the Research Base*. Tampa: University of South Florida.

Thompson, R. W., G. Smith, D. W. Osgood, T. P. Dowd, P. C. Friman, and D. L. Daly. 1996. Residential care: A study of short- and long-term educational effects. *Children and Youth Services Review* 18(3):221–242.

GLUECK, ELEANOR TOUROFF (1898–1972), AND SHELDON (1896–1980)

Sheldon and Eleanor Glueck are perhaps the most famous husband/wife research team in the field of criminology and delinquency. Sheldon Glueck immigrated to the United States from Poland as a child. He went on to earn an LL.B. and LL.M. from the National University Law School, and a master's and a Ph.D. in social ethics from Harvard. Eleanor Glueck earned a bachelor's degree in social work from the New York School of Social Work, and a master's and

a Ph.D. in education from Harvard. The couples' widely divergent educational backgrounds combined to lay the foundation for the multidisciplinary research for which they would become famous.

Sheldon's brother, Bernard Glueck, a forensic psychiatrist at Sing Sing Prison, introduced the pair. They married in 1922, and from there they embarked on a career that spanned more than 40 years and produced more than 250 publications on the causes of and potential cures for criminality.

Both Gluecks spent the majority of their careers at Harvard. Sheldon taught, first at the department of social ethics and later at the law school. He became the first Roscoe Pound Professor of Law in 1950 and a professor emeritus in 1963. Eleanor worked as a research criminologist in the department of social ethics and then as a research assistant at the law school. She never received a tenured faculty appointment.

The first major work by the Gluecks was *500 Criminal Careers* (1930). This work focused on 510 men sentenced to the Massachusetts Reformatory from 1911 to 1922. Follow-up studies of these same men produced *Later Criminal Careers* (1937) and *Criminal Careers in Retrospect* (1943). These combined works created a 15-year longitudinal study of a single group of inmates, with the goal of discovering which variables contributed to persistence (continuation) in crime and which contributed to desistence (quitting crime).

The second major study, *Five Hundred Delinquent Women* (1934), paralleled the first, but followed 500 women inmates over a period of five years. The Gluecks made an effort to distinguish factors influencing the criminality of women from those influencing men.

One Thousand Juvenile Delinquents: Their Treatment by Court and Clinic (1934) and *Juvenile Delinquents Grown Up* (1940) are the results of the third and fourth major studies conducted by the Gluecks. Both of these studies were concerned with behavior of delinquents after interaction with the criminal justice system.

It was *Unraveling Juvenile Delinquency* (1950) that brought the Gluecks the most attention as researchers of juvenile criminal behavior. In this groundbreaking study, 500 delinquent boys were matched with 500 nondelinquent boys for purposes of comparison. The groups of boys were followed over a 15-year span, resulting in the publication of *Delinquents and Nondelinquents in Perspective* (1968).

Each of the Gluecks' studies demonstrated the uniqueness of their research, marked by their reliance on a multifactor approach that departed from other models of the time. Their denial of any one theory's ability to explain crime or delinquency stood in sharp contrast to the approaches of the Chicago School and to Edwin Sutherland's differential association theory.

In spite of criticisms from theoretical purists, the Gluecks insisted on including the relevant variables from all the major schools of thought. They included biology, psychology, sociology, economics, and law as relevant sources of information to be considered in their studies. At one point, they even hired a physical anthropologist to collect material for their study.

Unfortunately, the value of their follow-up studies, with their multifactor approach, has been overshadowed by their works dealing with biological explanations for crime. In each of their major studies on delinquency, the Gluecks included biological variables, such as body type and physical abnormalities. The information gathered through these studies culminated in the publication of *Physique and Delinquency* (1956), in which it is asserted that delinquents come primarily in one body type, the mesomorph.

In the minds of many, this research placed the Gluecks in the same class as Lombroso and other biological theorists who relied on physical characteristics to predict criminality. The benefits of all the other research done by the couple fell by the wayside as they became famous for their biological work.

Despite these problems, many significant findings emerge from the work of the Gluecks. The longitudinal research conducted by the pair showed that an individual did not cease criminal activity simply by reaching a certain age. In other words, physical age and maturity level are not equivalent. In fact, the Gluecks discovered that the length of time that had elapsed since onset of criminal behavior, and even the age of onset, were more important predictors of age of cessation.

The creation of a series of prediction tables, designed to predict an assortment of outcomes related to criminal justice, was another significant result of the Gluecks' many studies. They included response to various forms of intervention and cessation of criminal activity. While admitting that further research was necessary, the Gluecks insisted that their prediction tables, or ones like them, would serve to reform the criminal justice system in the direction of greater effectiveness in rehabilitating offenders.

These tables would allow judges to compare offenders on certain characteristics that were highly correlated with offending behavior to determine which sentence was the most appropriate. The probable success ratios of each offender could be determined for each sentencing possibility. For example, an offender who, according to the tables, had no chance of succeeding if incarcerated but a high chance of success if placed on probation would be sentenced to probation.

The tables could also give the judge an estimate of the length of time before an offender ceased criminal activity. However, for the information in these tables to be useful, a wide range of sentences is necessary. For this reason, the Gluecks advocated either totally indeterminate sentencing structures or determinate structures with a wide range of sentence lengths.

The Gluecks were ahead of their time in many other ways. Their longitudinal cohort studies were a precursor to the career criminal paradigm that is currently in vogue. They were also among the first researchers to stress the role of the family and familial environment in delinquency.

Both Gluecks also published works on their own. Eleanor concentrated on schools and other social work issues. Sheldon published works on policing and on the prosecution and punishment of Nazi war criminals. This last interest came about largely because of his service as an adviser to one of the prosecutors in these trials.

Overall, the Gluecks produced a remarkable body of research that has relevance for research being conducted today. One has only to turn to any of their major studies to find a ready list of variables from a variety of disciplines that remain correlated to delinquency. This variety of variables combined with the longitudinal cohort methodology should have earned them great acclaim as innovators in the field. However, their refusal to focus on variables from only one discipline and their unique educational backgrounds caused them to remain outside the mainstream of criminological research. While they were actively researching delinquency, they were subject to harsh criticism from theoretical purists for their lack of a unified theory. Now, after they are both gone, history remembers them mostly for their biological work with body typing.

Lorie Rubenser

See also Body-Type Theories; Edwin H. Sutherland; Theories of Delinquency

Bibliography

Glueck, S., and E. Glueck. 1930. *500 Criminal Careers.* New York: Knopf.
Glueck, S., and E. Glueck. 1934. *Five Hundred Delinquent Women.* New York: Knopf.
Glueck, S., and E. Glueck. 1934. *One Thousand Juvenile Delinquents: Their Treatment by Court and Clinic.* Cambridge, MA: Harvard University Press.
Glueck, S., and E. Glueck. 1937. *Later Criminal Careers.* New York: The Commonwealth Fund.
Glueck, S., and E. Glueck. 1940. *Juvenile Delinquents Grown Up.* New York: The Commonwealth Fund.
Glueck, S., and E. Glueck. 1943. *Criminal Careers in Retrospect.* New York: The Commonwealth Fund.
Glueck, S., and E. Glueck. 1950. *Unraveling Juvenile Delinquency.* Cambridge, MA: Harvard University Press.
Glueck, S., and E. Glueck. 1956. *Physique and Delinquency.* New York: Harper.
Glueck, S., and E. Glueck. 1968. *Delinquents and Nondelinquents in Perspective.* Cambridge, MA: Harvard University Press.

 # GRAFFITI AND TAGGING

Broadly conceptualized, *graffiti* refers to the wide array of symbols, codes, and figures inscribed on the surfaces of public space. In contemporary usage, however, *graffiti* more specifically denotes illegal or officially unsanctioned public markings, and in almost every instance, graffiti has come to be associated with the individual and collective criminality of young people. In this way, contemporary conversations and public debates about graffiti reference more than the markings themselves. They invoke emerging and often contested arrangements of law, public and private property, and power; build on concerns over the status of young people in the social order; and incorporate debates as to the appropriateness of justice system responses to the graffiti "problem."

The graffiti of young people in the United States and other countries today is manifested in a remarkable range of styles and forms: exhortations to political analysis and activism; declarations of romantic love and tragic remembrance; scrawled allegiances to musical groups and sports teams; and injunctions of religious faith or spiritual skepticism. Among the many contemporary manifestations of youth graffiti in the United States, though, two forms in particular embody most directly the social and cultural tensions between power, control, and symbolic deviance, and for this reason dominate both everyday perceptions of graffiti and ongoing debates over graffiti's interconnections with youthful criminality.

HIP-HOP GRAFFITI AND TAGGING

The most widely dispersed and publicly visible form of graffiti in the United States today, hip-hop graffiti, emerged out of the minority and immigrant boroughs of New York City during the 1970s as part of a larger, homegrown hip-hop youth subculture built around rap music, break dancing, and other do-it-yourself cultural innovations. Significantly, hip-hop graffiti, like the larger hip-hop subculture, came into existence as a stylized, street-hip alternative to gang-oriented or interpersonally violent means of resolving conflict or acquiring status. Decades later, hip-hop graffiti "writers" and the "crews" to which they belong still follow the subcultural codes of status, respect, and disrespect established during the early years of hip-hop graffiti. Writing, or "tagging," their own subcultural nicknames and the names of their crews in public places, spray painting quick two-color "throw-ups," designing and spray painting larger multicolored murals, or "pieces," they operate within a highly stylized system of interpersonal honor and subcultural communication. Inscribing complimentary commentary next to a sophisticated piece executed by another writer, at other times "dissin'" or "going over"—that is, marking through or painting over—graffiti judged to be below subcultural standards, writers make this status system explicit, at least to those who can understand its codes. As such, they continue to recall and reinvent, in the public spaces of contemporary life, an elaborate form of symbolic interaction distinctive to the youthful world they occupy.

Undergirding this growing youth subculture are not only the tags, throw-ups, and pieces left behind in public places, but a key experiential dynamic involved in their production. Time and again, hip-hop graffiti writers describe their experience of writing graffiti in terms of a powerfully seductive "adrenalin rush," a rush so powerful that they regularly liken it to encounters with sex or drugs. Yet for the writers, this rush constitutes something more than the sort of indiscriminate lust for illicit kicks often ascribed to young

Photo 4. Hip-Hop Graffiti.
SOURCE: Photo by Jeff Ferrell.

people. Instead, as the writers make clear, the rush results from the opportunity to accomplish their stylized, and often long-practiced, subcultural artistry in situations necessarily fraught with immediate physical and legal danger. In this way, the experiential adrenalin rush of writing hip-hop graffiti embodies the twin dynamics that define the larger hip-hop graffiti subculture today: the organization of the subculture around artistry, image, and style, and the emergence of the subculture as a world of youthful disobedience and outlaw identities.

Since its emergence in the 1970s, hip-hop graffiti has visually saturated everyday environments in the United States because of several developments. Hip-hop graffiti writers have continued to invent new forms of tagging, including the etching of tags into glass windows, and the mass production of pretagged (and at times computer-generated) stickers that can be easily affixed in public places. They likewise have persisted in finding new outlets—some of them even semilegal—for their more elaborate design work. As part of the informal, underground economy that enlivens many urban areas, some writers now offer hip-hop-style sign painting for small, local businesses. Others are commissioned by the friends and families of street-violence victims—of those killed by gangs, drugs, or the police—to paint on-the-street RIP (rest in piece) memorials to them. Such memorials often blend hip-hop iconography and lettering with portraits of the deceased, detailed portrayals of personal effects, and various religious imagery. Further, in the context of a hip-hop graffiti subculture that public officials and others define exclusively by its criminality and delinquency, these memorials function in a way that is both ironic and revealing. They not only increase graffiti writers' opportunities for public visibility, but in many neighborhoods they serve a larger social and cultural good as well, creating informal public settings where community members can gather, grieve, and commemorate personal and interpersonal loss.

At the same time that it has increasingly come to be integrated within local communities, though, hip-hop graffiti has also continued to develop as a subculture spawning outlaw adrenalin rushes and illicit youthful identities. As with early forms of tagging—where both style and breadth of visibility measured a tagger's success—hip-hop graffiti writers continue to gain subcultural status, and to find pleasure and excitement, through various forms of spatial expansion and risk. By "tagging the heavens"—that is, by tagging the highest and most inaccessible spots on buildings or freeway signs—writers gain heightened subcultural visibility and legitimacy and clearly demonstrate their death-defying commitment to the graffiti underground itself. By dispersing their tags throughout a variety of urban neighborhoods and thus "going citywide," writers gain fame and status beyond their own particular crews, and establish a subcultural reputation that transcends particular locales.

A recent development in the hip-hop graffiti subculture has taken this expansive orientation to a certain cultural and geographic extreme. The writing of tags, throw-ups, and pieces on freight trains has emerged as perhaps the most popular contemporary form of hip-hop graffiti. This practice builds from hip-hop graffiti's longtime association with train transportation. Early in the subculture's formation, for example, tags and pieces were most often, and most spectacularly, written on urban subway cars. As the subculture developed throughout the United States, Europe, and Australia, interurban train stations and train lines likewise became focal points for graffiti writing; and given the ecology of urban areas, inner-city rail yards themselves emerged as surreptitious "playgrounds" in which writers could practice their craft. Now, with the proliferation of freight train graffiti, writers are increasingly able to use the trains to go not just citywide but nationwide, sending their images out from their initial, circumscribed points of production into nationwide, and often continent-wide, circulation. In this way, hip-hop graffiti writers continue to expand the cultural and geographic boundaries of their subculture and, interestingly, find themselves in symbolic conversation with another long-standing graffiti subculture, hobos, whose illicit messages of greeting, warning, and identification also decorate a multitude of freight trains.

GANG GRAFFITI AND GANG TAGGING

As the subculture of hip-hop graffiti writing has spread over the past two decades to large and small cities throughout the United States (and throughout Europe and beyond) and continued to emerge as a viable alternative to traditional youth gangs for many young people, the conflation of hip-hop graffiti with gang graffiti—the misperception of hip-hop graffiti *as* gang graffiti—has likewise spread. As discussed later in this entry, this misunderstanding is in many ways more a matter of careful orchestration on the part of adult authorities than it is an accident of naïve misperception. Yet whatever its origins, the conflation of hip-hop graffiti and youth gang graffiti significantly impedes the ability to understand either form of youthful graffiti, masking as it does profound subcultural differences in the dynamics of the graffiti's production and meaning. For although both hip-hop writers and youth gang members produce publicly visible graffiti, tagging illicit identities and messages on the surfaces of public space, the intent and consequences undergirding their graffiti reference sharply different subcultural orientations.

Contemporary youth gangs regularly use graffiti as a medium for negotiating individual membership status and collective gang identity, for issuing symbolic warning or threat, and for demarcating the boundaries of gang property and gang space. The particular uses and meanings of this confrontational graffiti vary widely, however, between different ethnic gangs. Latino/Latina, Chicano/Chicana, and Mexican American gang graffiti is often employed to declare and symbolize the long historical convergence between these gangs and the barrios in which they reside. Understood as a form of "barrio calligraphy," this graffiti draws on historic styles of public writing within such communities and, often, on the Mexican and Mexican American traditions of public art and public mural painting. In this cultural context, Latino/Latina, Chicano/Chicana, and Mexican American gangs mark barrio walls with their *placas*—stylized gang insignias used for defining and enforcing gang and barrio boundaries, warning off potential intruders, and communicating both the collective presence of the gang and the particular status of individuals and cliques (*klikas*) within it. Given this complex interrelationship between youth gang and barrio, such graffiti at times certainly signifies a sense of threat or discomfort within the community; yet it is as likely to be intertwined with traditional mural painting techniques and iconography and thus to function as a source of community pride and solidarity.

African American gangs, on the other hand, more often use graffiti to symbolically demarcate and reinforce internecine divisions, including most famously those between the Bloods and the Crips. In the same way, they employ graffiti as a medium for elevating gang status and for advertising the street-level power of the gang itself. This is accomplished not only by the widespread writing of a particular gang's graffiti throughout a neighborhood or community but also by the degradation of rival gangs through stylized threats (for example, Crip graffiti written "B/K" traditionally denotes "Blood Killer"); through more direct threats in the form of warnings and listings of enemy gangs and gang members; or through the systematic crossing out of rival gang graffiti. The degree of threat embedded in such graffiti can in fact be seen in hip-hop graffiti writers' response to it; when in the course of writing their own graffiti they encounter gang graffiti, they typically take care to avoid writing over it, lest their hip-hop graffiti be misunderstood as a sign of threat or disrespect to the gang involved and thus become a trigger for violent conflict.

In this sense, both Latino/Latina/Mexican American gang graffiti and African American gang graffiti incorporate a degree of symbolic threat or violence, which can, within particular situational dynamics, invite interpersonal violence or weapons-drawn intergang conflict. Often, though, this seemingly causal relationship between the symbolic violence of youth gang graffiti and broader patterns of youth gang violence remains ambiguous, and at times it is altogether reversed. In some situations, the symbolic violence of youth gang graffiti functions as a secondhand, self-congratulatory substitute for directly violent conflict, thereby displacing or diffusing more dangerous solutions to street-level disagreements. Similarly, youth gang graffiti as often includes memorials to murdered gang members or "roll calls" of those lost to gang and police violence as it does the promise of further violence; in such cases, it serves more as sorrowful warning than as violent threat. Further, by organizing the cultural space and social property of youth gangs, and setting normative and territorial boundaries for their activities, gang graffiti functions in many situations to at least regulate, if not fully obviate, intergang violence.

Interestingly, a much clearer link between symbolic violence and interpersonal/intergroup violence is found in the graffiti of groups often and erroneously omitted from discussions of youth gangs and youthful criminality: skinheads and neo-Nazis. Written on gay and lesbian gathering places, synagogues, cemeteries, and the walls of minority neighborhoods, skinhead and neo-Nazi graffiti communicates focused terror and threat and supports a broader campaign of direct and aggressive violence against those groups it targets. Incorporating Nazi iconography and symbolism, this graffiti also intentionally recalls, and in many ways resurrects, previous campaigns of terror and extermination. The exclusion of this graffiti from most discussions of youthful graffiti writing, and most debates over the graffiti "problem," suggest something of the ethnic and ideological politics surrounding graffiti and surrounding the efforts of criminal justice agencies and others to control it.

GRAFFITI, YOUTH, AND CRIMINAL JUSTICE

Though products of distinctly different dynamics, both gang graffiti and hip-hop graffiti stand as markers of particular youthful identities and subcultural affiliations. As such, both types of graffiti exist as highly visible public displays but function mostly as private conversations among those privy to their symbolic and stylistic codes. In this dual role, both gang graffiti and hip-hop graffiti at times violate the legal boundaries of public and private property; yet this violation is driven less by some sort of mindless property vandalism than by the ongoing, mindful practice of subcultural expression. Likewise, with the exception of skinhead or neo-Nazi graffiti, these youthful graffiti forms are designed and used primarily as devices for interior subcultural interaction; they are in almost every case meant to communicate and negotiate status within or between subcultural groups, rather than to communicate threat or intimidation to the public as a whole.

The widespread misperception of youthful graffiti as a form of generalized threat or violence aimed at all those who use public space, and the equally widespread and erroneous conflation of hip-hop graffiti and gang graffiti previously noted, can largely be traced to the high-profile antigraffiti campaigns that have emerged since the 1980s. Funded by a mix of corporate money and tax dollars and often coordinated among a variety of local and national criminal justice and juvenile justice agencies, such campaigns have fought youthful graffiti with increased legal penalties, police and citizen surveillance teams, helicopter patrols, undercover officers, sting operations, remote control infrared video cameras, night vision goggles, razor wire, graffiti-resistant paint, toll-free graffiti hotlines, and a host of other control technologies and techniques. They have also systematically promoted a militant antigraffiti ideology, calling for stern legal penalties, boot camps, public paddlings, canings, even physical mutilation for those young people caught writing graffiti. Further, in their zeal to generate public concern and enlist public support, these campaigns have intentionally conflated the various types of youthful graffiti, continually confused subcultural communication with external aggression, and regularly equated property violence with personal violence, at times even defining graffiti writing as a form of rape and assault.

In this way, the response of the criminal justice system and its economic and political allies has distorted and amplified the meaning of the very youthful activity that was the focus of control. As such, the campaign against youthful graffiti writing presents textbook examples of successful moral entrepreneurship and of the demonization of young people and their subcultures in such a way as to reinvent them as folk devils and foster moral panic around their activities. Moreover, as these criminological concepts would suggest, the campaign to stop graffiti writing has spawned a number of ironic consequences regarding graffiti writing itself. Failing to halt the growth of youthful graffiti writing, the campaign has accomplished the opposite; its visibility has served to recruit new writers into the graffiti underground, and its misguided militancy has, especially in the case of hip-hop graffiti, helped to reshape a youthful subculture into a youthful counterculture increasingly willing to match official attempts at control with a stylized public militancy of its own.

Jeff Ferrell

See also At-Risk Youth; Curfew; Gangs, Juvenile; Public Opinion on Juvenile Justice Issues

Bibliography

Chalfant, H., and J. Prigoff. 1987. *Spraycan Art.* New York: Thames & Hudson.

Cooper, M., and H. Chalfant. 1984. *Subway Art.* New York: Holt, Rinehart & Winston.
Cooper, M., and J. Sciorra. 1994. *R.I.P.: Memorial Wall Art.* New York: Henry Holt.
Ferrell, J. 1993/1996. *Crimes of Style: Urban Graffiti and the Politics of Criminality.* New York: Garland.
Ferrell, J. 1995. Urban graffiti: Crime, control, and resistance. *Youth and Society* 27:73–92.
Ferrell, J. 1998. Freight train graffiti: Subculture, crime, dislocation. *Justice Quarterly* 15:587–608.
Phillips, S. A. 1999. *Wallbangin': Graffiti and Gangs in L.A.* Chicago: University of Chicago Press.
Walsh, M. 1996. *Graffito.* Berkeley, CA: North Atlantic Books.

 # GROUP HOMES

Group homes (often called residential treatment centers, boarding homes, halfway houses, shelters, general child care institutions, or residential diagnostic centers) are facilities operated by a person, organization, society, or corporation, for profit or not for profit, to provide a nonsecure residential program that emphasizes family-style living in a homelike atmosphere. The group home provides 24-hour care to children not related to each other. Program goals include group living, school attendance, securing employment, returning to parents, resolving problems, and participating in the community. Though court-committed children and youth are most often found in group homes, they also house abused or neglected children and youth placed by social agencies. Group homes usually house 8 to 12 residents ranging in age from 10 to 17 with a high concentration from the 13-to-16 age group.

HISTORICAL BACKGROUND OF GROUP HOMES

Group homes date back to colonial times in the United States, when wayward and orphaned children and youth worked for town tradesmen in exchange for room, board, and training. The first group home in the United States was established in New Orleans in 1727, created by a trading company and operated by seven Ursuline nuns. Other group homes were established, mostly throughout the South. During the 1800s, increasing numbers of group homes were opened, often to house deviants and "defective" persons. Group homes during the 19th century were synonymous with almshouses, penitentiaries, juvenile reformatories, and mental asylums. During that time, group homes housed children with adults and treated children as adults and were characterized by corporal punishment, abuse, starvation, lack of outside visitors and resources, poor treatment, and isolation from the community. The State Charities Aid Association of New York, while evaluating an almshouse housing 370 people, including 60 children, remarked that there was no nurse for the sick and that children were badly clothed and fed, poorly cared for, exposed to the influences of the inmates who took care of them, showed despair, and were joyless (Bremner, 1970). Opposition to such treatment of children came from many religious, social, and civic groups. Organized opposition brought about reform, which motivated Ohio to be the first state to remove all children from almshouses. By 1900, most states had followed suit.

With reform came a new type of group home, which numbered as high as 1,600 in 1923 (Tiffin, 1982). This new type of group home no longer housed adults with children and further evolved into the contemporary group home. Three significant developments occurred during the middle and latter part of the 20th century. First, the state required all group homes to be licensed. This created a system of regulation and control through government intervention at local, state, and federal levels. Second, deinstitutionalization became the norm for design and operations. Instead of large, one-room, open-bay facilities, shared rooms and cottage-like living became the preferred style. Finally, a psychological framework for each child became the standard operating procedure in the form of an individual service plan. With this change, the underlying goal of treating the child and returning him or her to the community was established.

CONTEMPORARY GROUP HOMES

Collectively across the United States, more than 50,000 children are housed annually in group homes. Group homes operate under two basic treatment models: house parents or shift personnel. The houseparent model consists of a married couple living in the facility with their own separate bedroom and bath. Relief workers may be hired to cover the night shift and/or provide time off for the couple. Support personnel, such as social workers and psychiatric staff, may be hired. The houseparent model provides a high level of

consistency in staff and strong attachment between the residents, as well as male/female role models in the form of a stable married couple.

The shift-personnel model involves the hiring of staff to cover three 8-hour shifts. With this model, there is often a higher staff-to-resident ratio. In addition, the residents are exposed to a diversity of individuals to whom they may develop intense attachments. These workers (often called child care workers) are most often college-educated yet receive a starting pay of only $7 to $8 per hour. This low pay may explain the high staff turnover that occurs with this model. Such turnover is often damaging to the treatment of the resident.

The group home has increasingly been viewed as a significant tool for meeting the emotional, academic, and development needs of children. While these needs make the task of group homes intimidating, the financial rewards paid by states, counties, and jurisdictions to these nonprofit and for-profit businesses are substantial. Group homes charge from $60 to $250 per day per child. With the average stay at 172 days in 1993, the estimated cost is between $10,000 and $43,000 per child staying in a group home. With such costs, an increasing amount of empirical research is necessary to determine what works and why.

Everette B. Penn

See also Adoption Assistance and Child Welfare Act; Boys and Girls Clubs of America; Child-Saving Movement; Children's Aid Society; Foster Care; Girls and Boys Town; Runaways

Bibliography

Adler, J. 1981. *Fundamentals of Group Childcare: A Textbook and Instructional Guide for Child Care Workers.* Cambridge, MA: Ballinger.

American Correctional Association. 1994. *Standards for Juvenile Community Residential Facilities*, 3rd ed. Laurel, MD: American Correctional Association Press.

Bremner, R. 1970. *Children and Youth in America: A Documentation History*, Vol. 1. Cambridge, MA: Harvard Press.

Shostack, A. 1987. *Group Homes for Teenagers: A Practical Guide.* New York: Human Sciences Press.

Tiffin, S. 1982. *In Whose Best Interest: Child Welfare in the Progressive Era.* West Point, CT: Greenwood Press.

GROUP THERAPY

Group therapy, a term attributed to the late Dr. J. L. Moreno (creator of psychodrama and a contemporary of Sigmund Freud), began as a form of psychotherapy that departed from the conventional one-on-one doctor-patient relationship by allowing multiple persons to receive simultaneous care. In its most basic meaning, group therapy is a therapist facilitating a group of three or more persons who mutually benefit psychologically from interaction among themselves and the therapist.

In its inception, group therapy was a purely therapeutic modality. However, in the last 40 years, group therapy has evolved to include other facilitator–multiple-person groups for such varied purposes as providing inspirational and reeducative opportunities. In such a group, problem solving, motivation, education, sensitivity awareness, and specific training are but a few of the objectives that may be pursued by people mutually gathered for a common purpose under the leadership of a facilitator. An Alcoholics Anonymous meeting or a group of employees interacting to gain sensitivity regarding sexual harassment are examples in the evolution of the concept of *group.* However, regardless of the purpose of the group, dynamic interaction remains the essence of all group activity.

APPLICATION TO JUVENILES

Group therapy for juveniles is a natural extension of the goals and aims for which the juvenile court was created in 1899—namely, to foster care for juveniles. The concepts of treatment and rehabilitation have, over time, included the subconcepts of counseling and therapy. Line staff in juvenile facilities are often officially termed counselors, indicative of the goal of making the living environment a therapeutic milieu for positive change. Inclusive in this counseling treatment modality is the use of groups for varied purposes, a practice that became common during the 1960s.

Two different delinquency projects pioneered group therapy. The Provo Experiment (1959 to 1965) used the concept of allowing peer groups to solve problems under the structure of "guided group interaction." In the Silverlake Experiment (1964 to 1968), youths used daily group meetings to solve problems with an adult serving as a facilitator and not an authority figure. Because of these projects, most probation

departments began designing treatment approaches that depended heavily on group interaction as the focus of behavioral change.

The use of groups failed to achieve the lofty ultimate goal of reducing recidivism for the same reason many criminal justice programs fail—namely, programmatic overexpectation. Groups alone cannot accomplish short-term behavioral change and have been increasingly replaced by more confrontive methods found in boot camps, wilderness or challenge programs (such as VisionQuest), and radical behavior modification programs. However, the reduced dependence on group therapy has been premature, for research has shown that juveniles who are young, anxious, verbal, intelligent, and neurotic can benefit from group interaction.

ADVANTAGES OF GROUP THERAPY

Group therapy has three distinct advantages for juveniles: (1) enhancing basic socialization, (2) facilitating mental health, and (3) fostering training and reeducation. The following paragraphs describe these advantages in more detail.

Socialization

The adage that you cannot resocialize someone who has not been socialized is true, and groups can serve to provide remedial socialization. Groups create one more additional opportunity to learn how to behave properly. The group process intrinsically provides some form of structure in which members assume or are assigned special roles. Inherent to the group construct is the process of goals being implicitly accepted or explicitly defined. The juvenile enhances socialization as he or she learns to stay in a role, participates as a team player, and helps the group realize a common goal. The necessary external, social control results from group norms being applied with varying pressure to each group member as part of an ongoing group structure. Juveniles benefit from the social contacts made in a group setting through shared experiences that ease social tension and promote self-confidence. As group members learn to relate to each other more freely, they learn to compromise as well as give and receive.

Because juveniles bring to the group situation all the distortions and expectancies that constitute their personality structure, as they relate to others, they are able to observe distortions as they develop. Therefore, the group can become a mini-laboratory for the juvenile to begin reality-testing the differences between his and another's subjective reality. Through constant verbal and nonverbal interpersonal actions and reactions, group process fosters ongoing feedback. Groups offer an artificial environment as a testing ground for observation and experimentation with the phenomenon of group values. By developing cooperative participation, helpfulness, and friendliness, juveniles may, over time, replace destructive interpersonal feelings and behavior with more socially acceptable presentations of self.

Mental Health

Another adage—that no psychological conditions exist in isolation—is also true. By giving the group member an opportunity to relate to others in a fresh manner that transcends established dysfunctional patterns of behavior, groups may serve to provide a therapeutic environment that minimizes pathology. In this controlled social climate that values honesty and frankness, the juvenile can reveal him- or herself without having to put up the usual defensive front. This freedom expands the ability to gain self-understanding by allowing a youth to express his or her feelings in an accepting and safe milieu. The passive and fearful juvenile (who usually avoids confrontation) can incrementally increase speaking his or her mind, minimizing the perceived fear of rejection. The aggressive juvenile can learn to quietly share deeper and truer feelings, minimizing the fear of appearing weak. A youth can develop ego strength, which will enable her or him to reduce psychic conflict, thus reducing the need to feel and behave in an exaggerated (and often unacceptable) manner. Therapeutic groups that foster mental health offer the best use of clinical resources, as one or two clinical group facilitators can handle from 8 to 10 juveniles.

Training and Reeducation

The following are some examples of how group therapy encourages training and reeducation:

1. Parent-teacher or industrial groups aim at problem solving in relation to some area of concern involving all members.

2. Executive-training groups focus on resolving expressed or undefined social-emotional problems or shared anxieties.

3. Social or educational groups can supply members with solutions to personal problems.

Variations of these groups have proved helpful when they are intentionally designed to meet the specific emotional and learning needs of juveniles being emancipated and/or entering the workforce.

POTENTIAL PROBLEMS

While group therapy with juveniles may be a positive means of intervention, studies in group therapy, group process, and group dynamics reveal limitations, some minor and some potentially damaging. In conducting groups with juveniles, the following concerns must be considered:

1. *Remaining pathologies:* Pathologies may remain among and within group members and negatively affect group dynamics. Insensitive juveniles can do quick damage to members who have let their guard down in a therapeutic (and assumed safe) setting. In most juvenile groupings, a member can be identified as the negative indigenous leader (NIL) who will attempt to co-opt the group for her or his own purposes. If there is a single group facilitator (or multiple group facilitators who are untrained or naïve), manipulative and damaging behavior by the NIL may occur unnoticed.

2. *Masked impulses:* In groups focusing on reeducation, it has been observed that reeducation is often an overlay superimposed on unchanging, underlying impulses and attitudes. In situations of stress, this overlay may become fragile and newly acquired characteristics may be easily replaced.

3. *False compliance:* Juveniles can quickly determine exactly what compliant behavior is expected and simply feed it back to the group. "Cooling the group" is accomplished when a juvenile provides a seeming homogeneity of responses. Factors such as inexperienced group facilitators and limitations of time (the length of individual sessions and/or the number of sessions) hinder the group from unmasking these individuals. This may serve to give undue importance to

superficial group behavior, reinforcing the problem of juveniles seeing people as chess pieces on the chessboard of life and the perception that others exist only to be manipulated for selfish gain.

CONCLUSION

While group therapy may have obvious and potential limitations, skillful group facilitators can successfully contribute to an overall treatment process that aids juveniles in maturing out of delinquency. The action methods pioneered by J. L. Moreno (psychodrama, role playing, and role training) are especially helpful for juveniles who test low for verbal IQ, are unable to adequately grasp reality, and lack a sufficient time horizon. Group participation that is action oriented and not merely verbally oriented decreases the potential for juveniles to front, control, and manipulate. Action methods are especially helpful for diagnosing degrees of individual pathology, determining levels of potential violence, and forecasting future behavioral responses. This can be particularly helpful in assessing a juvenile's readiness to graduate from a program.

Research has demonstrated that the right juvenile in the right program with the right staff can greatly benefit from the treatment process. Group therapy, in the forms of supportive, behavioral, and confrontive groups, can be a valuable part of a successful program, particularly with selected juveniles.

R. Steve Lowe

See also Culturally Specific Programming; LaMar Taylor Empey; Mental Health; Provo Experiment; Silverlake Experiment

Bibliography

Glasser, W. 1970. *Mental Health or Mental Illness?* New York: Harper & Row.

Maletzky, B. 1990. *Treating the Sexual Offender.* Newbury Park, CA: Sage.

McShane, M., and W. Krause. 1993. *Community Corrections.* New York: Macmillan.

Moreno, J. 1946. *Psychodrama,* Vol. 1. New York: Beacon House.

Rogers, C. 1970. *Carl Rogers on Encounter Groups.* New York: Harper & Row.

GUARDIANS *AD LITEM*

A guardian *ad litem* is a special guardian of a minor child appointed by the court to protect the best interest of the child. A guardian *ad litem* may be an attorney or a lay person. In some states, the nonattorney guardian *ad litem* is called a court-appointed special advocate (or CASA). In Virginia, for example, only attorneys can be guardians *ad litem;* however, in North Carolina, lay-persons can be guardians *ad litem,* but the guardian must work with an attorney. The terminology is state specific with relatively few differences between the nonattorney guardian *ad litem* and the court-appointed special advocate.

Guardians *ad litem* represent the interests of a child when it has been alleged that child maltreatment has occurred. *Child maltreatment* refers to specific harmful acts, or a failure to act, on the part of the parents or legal guardians. The categories of offenses included in child maltreatment are emotional abuse, dependency, abandonment, neglect, and physical or sexual abuse. Some states are moving toward having guardians *ad litem* involved in divorce proceedings. To date, however, no state has formally included such cases in the duties of the guardian *ad litem.*

Representation of children in the judicial system is a relatively new concept. The Child Abuse Prevention and Treatment Act of 1974 laid the foundation for legal representation of children in the American judicial system. States vary in their approach to this representation; however, in most cases, the courts have determined that a child needs someone to speak for him or her. The key players in any maltreatment case are the parents or legal guardians of the child, the social workers, and the child. The parents or legal guardians usually have an attorney who explains how the system works and counsels the parents or legal guardians on how to behave in the courtroom. The Department of Social Services (or similar state agencies with different names) employs social workers to investigate maltreatment cases. Social workers are familiar with the legal proceedings and understand what is expected of them in court. Thus all parties in the case are represented by legal counsel. The only entity not represented is the child. The courts have determined that children need representation in such cases.

As the voice of the child, the guardian *ad litem* independently investigates the charges and makes a recommendation to the judge about both the facts of the case and what should be done with the child. It is important to remember that the guardian *ad litem* is only interested in what is best for the child. Typically, social workers are interested in keeping families together, regardless of how difficult the family situation may be. Often the parents or legal guardians are interested in avoiding legal trouble. The two perspectives often conflict, and the child is left in the middle without having anyone hear his or her wishes. The guardian *ad litem* listens to the child, presents in court what the child wants, and expresses an opinion about what is the best course of action in the given case.

The recommendations of the guardian *ad litem* are affected by the particular facts and circumstances of the case as well as the type of litigation. The role and responsibilities of the guardian *ad litem* vary from state to state. However, there are some common duties and responsibilities:

1. Act as the voice of the child.

2. Independently investigate the facts of the case.

3. Interview the parties, including the parents or legal guardians involved in the case.

4. Make recommendations to the court.

Unless the state specifically requires the guardian *ad litem* to be an attorney (as in Virginia, for example), a guardian *ad litem* can be any adult who can make independent, mature, and informed decisions on the issues of the case; can remain impartial; has an open mind; and is fair in determining what is best for the child. Special training is provided to all guardians *ad litem* in such critical areas as the court process, interviewing techniques, resources available to guardians *ad litem,* report writing, record keeping, and investigation skills. Guardians *ad litem* are taught to be respectful of cultural, ethnic, economic, and social differences. When working in a different environment—for example, on an Indian reservation—the guardians *ad litem* must understand the cultural differences and make recommendations in light of what is expected and accepted in the culture.

Guardians *ad litem* are assigned to a wide variety of family-related cases. The following case is presented to demonstrate how a guardian *ad litem* might handle a case.

A husband and wife living in Baton Rouge, Louisiana, were out shopping with their newborn child. The infant was safely secured in her car seat. The husband drove the wife to different stores, and she ran in and got what was needed while the husband stayed with the baby. This continued for a couple of hours until the shopping and errands were finished. As is common with parents of a new infant, both the husband and wife were operating on very little sleep. They both had less than 3 hours of sleep the previous night. Upon arriving home from running the errands, both the husband and wife decided they needed to rest and would take a nap. Being exhausted, they decided to wait to unload the car.

After about 30 to 45 minutes, the husband and wife awoke from their nap and could not find the infant. As they frantically looked for her, they both realized at the same time that they should check the car. The infant was still in her car seat but she was dead. The couple called the paramedics but it was too late. The infant had died of heat stroke.

A guardian *ad litem* was called to investigate this case. Even though the child had died, the court wanted an independent investigation of the facts in the case. The parents were devastated; they never intended this to happen. The guardian *ad litem* was able to determine that the parents were physically exhausted from the sleepless nights with the newborn. Both thought the other had taken the child out of the car. The guardian *ad litem* recommended no formal charges be imposed. It was obvious to her, after a full investigation, that the parents did not intentionally cause the death of their child. The death was a tragic accident.

Laura J. Moriarty

See also Parens Patriae Doctrine

 GUNS AND JUVENILES

In the early spring of 1999, Eric Harris and Dylan Klebold opened fire on their Columbine High School classmates, killing fifteen people in the process. The event has had a lasting impression on the consciousness of America (Cook and Ludwig, 2000). Snell, Mebane, Bailey, and Carona (2001) recently found that 46 percent of Texas public schools surveyed had made some change to their policies or practices due to the Columbine shootings. Moreover, these changes were directly related to increased complaints from parents and increased fear of crime among faculty and students.

It is true that school crime rates have been steadily decreasing since the mid-1990s. However, there have been 286 violent deaths in U.S. schools since the 1992-93 school year, and 77 percent of these deaths involved the use of firearms (National School Safety Center, 2001). Media attention to school shootings as well as a significant increase in the incidence of murders committed by juveniles between the mid-1980s and 1993 has focused tremendous attention on the role of guns in American society, especially as they involve youth (Cook and Ludwig, 2000).

PATTERNS OF HOMICIDES ATTRIBUTED TO YOUTH GUN VIOLENCE

There was a 65 percent increase in juvenile homicides, beginning in 1987 and peaking in 1993. Juvenile homicides have declined since that time to a level just 20 percent above that of 1987 (Snyder and Sickmund, 2000). A number of experts believe that nearly all the growth, and the subsequent decline, in juvenile homicides was directly related to firearm use by nonfamily members. Between 1980 and 1987, firearms were used in just over half (54 percent) of all homicides involving juvenile offenders. Firearm-related homicides began to increase sharply so that by 1994, 82 percent of homicides by juvenile offenders involved the use of firearms. Both the growth and decline involved substantial changes in the number of murders by acquaintances and the number of murders by older youth and African American youth (Snyder and Sickmund, 2000).

When a juvenile kills other juveniles, the victims are usually acquaintances killed by a gun. Of the juveniles killed by other juveniles between 1980 and 1997, 63 percent were age 16 or older. Family members killed only 5 percent of these older juvenile victims, 76 percent were killed by acquaintances, and 19 percent were killed by strangers. During this period, 77 percent of these older juveniles were killed with firearms.

Between 1980 and 1997, the vast majority (93 percent) of known juvenile homicide offenders were male. Slightly more than half (56 percent) were

African American, and 88 percent were juveniles aged 15 or older. Murders by the very young have been rare; between 1980 and 1997, fewer than 10 juveniles age 10 or younger were identified as participants in murders. However, firearms were involved in about half of these homicides (Snyder and Sickmund, 2000).

YOUTH HOMICIDE, ILLICIT DRUG MARKETS, AND THE DIFFUSION OF GUNS

Blumstein and Cork (1996) have theorized that the increase in juvenile homicides is due to a link between illicit drug markets, recruitment of juveniles for those markets, and the diffusion of guns among juveniles. The crack cocaine epidemic began around the mid-1980s, just before the youth homicide rate began its dramatic ascent. Unlike powdered cocaine, crack was affordable to lower-class individuals. However, because they could not afford large quantities of the drug, they had to purchase frequently. Thus many more consumers were purchasing at a higher rate, resulting in a sharp increase in the need for sellers.

The reasons juveniles were specifically recruited to sell drugs among the urban poor, according to Blumstein and Cork (1996), were that they faced less risk of punishment, were cheaper distributors, and saw drug selling as an attractive alternative to what they believed was a lack of opportunities in the legitimate economy. Drug dealers and urban youth, especially African American youth, were mutually attracted to each other.

Blumstein and Cork did not believe that the use of guns by youth in the drug industry fully accounts for the increase in juvenile homicides. They suggested that a diffusion process occurred through networks of youth connected to juvenile drug dealers (kids that go to the same school or travel in the same paths). As the availability of guns became more widespread, there was more incentive for other juveniles in even larger social networks to arm themselves. The proliferation of adolescent gangs armed with guns stimulating other gangs to obtain their own guns further facilitated this process.

PREVALENCE OF WEAPONS CARRYING BY YOUTH

Several studies have documented the relative frequency of weapon carrying by youth. In a study of 11th-grade students in Seattle, 6 percent of males reported having carried a handgun to school and 11 percent of males reported owning a handgun. Among the juvenile gun owners, 78 percent reported gang membership, involvement in drug sales, a history of school suspension, or a history of assaultive behavior. One third of these gun owners actually reported firing the handgun at someone (Callahan and Rivera, 1992).

The Rochester Youth Development Study found that 10 percent of 9th- and 10th-grade boys in Rochester public schools owned a firearm and that 7.5 percent carried it regularly (Lizotte, Tesoroero, Thornberry, and Krohn, 1994). Similarly, a 1993 national opinion poll (the Harris poll) of 6th to 12th graders found that 15 percent reported carrying a handgun in the last month.

Male juvenile offenders and inner-city youth are most likely to carry guns. In a study of male serious offenders incarcerated in six juvenile correctional centers in four states and male students attending 10 urban high schools near the correctional centers, Sheley and Wright (1993) found that 83 percent of the offenders and 22 percent of the students reported possessing a gun. Among the offenders, 55 percent reported carrying a gun most of the time within the last year or two. Of those who sold drugs, 89 percent of the offenders and 75 percent of the students usually carried a gun.

In perhaps the largest and most comprehensive study to date, Sheley and Wright (1998) examined the weapon-carrying behavior of 10th and 11th graders from 53 high schools nationwide. They found that while 29 percent of the respondents reported owning a gun, only 4 percent owned a handgun, and only 2 percent said they carried a gun all the time. Handguns (50 percent) and revolvers (30 percent) were the most common types of firearms carried.

Sheley and Brewer (1995) investigated the possibility of the spread of firearms to suburban youth populations. Public high school students from the wealthiest suburb in Louisiana were asked a variety of firearm-related questions. Among the youth, 13 percent reported owning a revolver, 9 percent reported owning an automatic or semiautomatic handgun, and 17 percent reported carrying a gun outside home. Another 23 percent of the students claimed that they had been threatened with a gun, and 40 percent reported attending a party where a gun had been fired.

REASONS FOR FIREARM ACQUISITION

In the Sheley and Wright (1998) study of 53 high schools, the most common reason given for carrying weapons was the need for protection. Holding a gun for someone was the other commonly cited response (35 percent). Less common reasons were to scare someone (18 percent), to get back at someone (18 percent), and to commit a crime (10 percent).

In the study comparing juvenile inmates and inner-city male students, also by Sheley and Wright (1993), most inmates (70 percent) and students (68 percent) said they carried guns for self-protection. More than half the inmates (52 percent) and almost one third (32 percent) of the students said they carried firearms because their enemies had guns. Fewer inmates (38 percent) and students (18 percent) admitted to carrying guns to "get someone" or to use in a crime (37 percent of inmates).

In the Sheley and Brewer (1995) study of suburban youth, 57 percent of gun owners were involved in violent crime, 44 percent were involved in drug activities, and 36 percent stated that they fired their weapons at social activities often. While they were not asked about gun carrying for self-protection, 53 percent of the students reported being threatened with a gun many times.

SOURCES OF GUNS

The 1993, the Harris national opinion poll of youth in Grades 6 to 12 found that 59 percent of the 2,508 youth surveyed said they could get a handgun if they wanted, and 35 percent maintained that it would take less than an hour to obtain a firearm. These statements demand an answer as to where and how youth are acquiring guns, because federal law prohibits the sale of shotguns and rifles and related ammunition to anyone under age 18 and other firearms and ammunition to anyone under age 21.

In the Sheley and Wright (1993) study of juvenile inmates and inner-city youth, the respondents were questioned about their likely source of guns and the actual sources of their most recently acquired handguns. When asked how they would get a gun, 45 percent of the juvenile inmates and 53 percent of the students said they would "borrow" one from family or friends, while 54 percent of the inmates and 37 percent of the students said they would get one "off the streets." More than one third of inmates (36 percent) and students (35 percent) bought guns from family members or friends. Importantly, 12 percent of inmates and 28 percent of students stated they would obtain a gun from a gun shop. Inmates actually obtained their guns primarily from friends (30 percent), drug dealers and addicts (24 percent), and the street (22 percent). Students actually acquired their guns most often from friends (38 percent) and family members (23 percent). Only 7 percent of inmates and 12 percent of students reported obtaining guns from retail outlets.

GANGS AND FIREARMS

Gang researchers generally agree that gang violence is becoming more frequent and more deadly (Klein, 1997). Gang members commonly have handguns, and many claim to have multiple firearms. Lizotte et al. (1994) found that over half of the juveniles who reported being in a gang also claimed to own guns for protection. In addition, many gang members have access to guns in their homes.

Not only are gang members carrying weapons more frequently but they are using them more often as well. According to the Los Angeles Police Department, guns were involved in 80 percent to 82 percent of all gang-related homicides in that region. Researchers have found similar percentages in other cities.

Does gun ownership by youth come before or after gang involvement? Bjerregaard and Lizotte (2001) examined this question and found that gangs were likely to recruit among juveniles who already own guns. This suggests that weapon-carrying youth join gangs because they are attracted to the role of weapons in gangs.

STRATEGIES TO REDUCE YOUTH GUN VIOLENCE

The Boston Gun Project is one gun violence program with demonstrated success. A major component of that program included efforts to interrupt the sources of illegal guns to youth. The Boston Police Department (BPD) teamed with agents from the Bureau of Alcohol, Tobacco, and Firearms (ATF) to discover sources of illegal weapons and gun-trafficking patterns. They also conducted joint inspections of licensed firearm dealers to ensure compliance with

federal, state, and local laws. Because of these inspections, 80 percent of license holders decided to surrender or not renew their licenses.

The BPD and the ATF also traced and investigated recovered guns that were used in crimes within 30 months of being sold, guns popular with youth (semi-automatic handguns), those with serial numbers removed, guns found in high-crime neighborhoods, and those guns associated with gang membership. Since the beginning of the Boston Gun Project and other youth violence prevention programs in the Boston area, the number of homicides by youth 16 and younger declined by about 80 percent in eight years. The total number of homicides in the city declined from 152 in 1990 to 43 in 1997. Based on the success of this program, the ATF has launched similar gun interdiction programs in 17 cities.

Cletus Snell

See also California Street Terrorism Enforcement and Prevention Act; Curfew; Gangs, Juvenile; School Violence; Serious and Violent Juvenile Offenders

Bibliography

Bjerregaard, B., and A. J. Lizotte. 2001. Gun ownership and gang membership. Pp. 213–227 in J. Miller, C. Maxson, and M. Klein (eds.), *The Modern Gang Reader*, 2nd ed. Los Angeles: Roxbury.

Blumstein, A., and D. Cork. 1996. Linking gun availability to youth gun violence. *Law and Contemporary Problems* 59:5–24.

Callahan, C. M., and F. P. Rivera. 1992. Urban high school youth and handguns: A school-based survey. *Journal of the American Medical Association* 267(22):3038–3042.

Cook, P. J., and J. Ludwig. 2000. *Gun Violence: The Real Costs.* New York: Oxford University Press.

Klein, M. W. 1997. *The American Street Gang: Its Nature, Prevalence, and Control.* New York: Oxford University Press.

Lizotte, A. J., J. M. Tesoroero, T. P. Thornberry, and M. D. Krohn. 1994. Patterns of adolescent firearms ownership and use. *Justice Quarterly* 11:51–74.

National School Safety Center. 2001. *Report on School Associated Violent Deaths.* Westlake Village, CA: National School Safety Center.

Sheley, J. F., and V. E. Brewer. 1995. Possession and carrying of firearms among suburban youth. *Public Health Reports* 110:18–26.

Sheley, J. F., and J. D. Wright. 1993. Motivations for gun possession and carrying among serious juvenile offenders. *Behavioral Sciences and the Law* 11:375–388.

Sheley, J. F., and J. D. Wright. 1998. *High School Youths, Weapons, and Violence: A National Survey*. Washington, DC: National Institute of Justice.

Snell, C., D. Mebane, C. Bailey, and A. Carona. 2001. *Texas School Administrator's Reaction to Recent School Violence: The Impact of Columbine*. Prairie View, TX: Texas Juvenile Crime Prevention Center.

Snyder, H. N., and M. Sickmund. 2000. *Kids and Guns*. Washington, DC: Office of Juvenile Justice and Delinquency Prevention.

H

HALL, G. STANLEY (1844–1924)

G. Stanley Hall is known as the founder of professional psychology, the father of the child study movement, and the great reformer of higher education in the United States. Hall was born February 1, 1844, in Ashfield, Massachusetts. The child of Congregational parents who made a modest living farming, Hall set an early goal of leaving the farm and making something of his life. Parental influence sent him in a theological direction, and he began his higher education in 1861 at Williston Seminary in Easthampton, Massachusetts. In 1863, he entered Williams College, where he turned his academic interests to philosophy and psychology and received his bachelor's degree in 1867.

His early academic exposures spawned an interest in character development, morality, and religion that would last throughout his life. Hall had wanted to study abroad, but lacking in funds, he continued his education for the next two years at Union Theological Seminary in New York City. He then spent the next two years in Leipzig, Germany. On his return to the United States, Hall studied with William James and Henry Bowditch at Harvard University, receiving the first American Ph.D. in psychology in 1878. At that time, he returned to Leipzig and studied for two years with Wilhelm Wundt, the father of experimental psychology.

Back in the United States, Hall briefly taught at Harvard and Williams College before accepting a position as lecturer and professor of psychology and pedagogy at Johns Hopkins University (1882 to 1888). It was here that Hall began the first American laboratory of psychology as well as founding the first psychology journal in the United States, the *American Journal of Psychology*.

In 1889, Hall became the first president of the research-oriented, graduate-level Clark University. Although experimental and applied psychologies were his greatest scholarly interests, he was interested in education at all levels. Hall viewed the study of education as a specialization within applied psychology. Hall was devoted to the development of the new American university. Based on the German model of higher education, he created a research revolution in American universities that propelled the development of graduate programs and professional schools throughout the country. It was at Clark that Hall introduced higher education as a field of study designed to further educate university administrators and education faculty in the reformation of higher education in the United States.

While revolutionizing American higher education, Hall continued his work in the development of psychology as a profession and his research in child studies. He founded and served as the first president of the American Psychological Association (1892) and completed the first systematic study of child development in the United States. Hall strongly supported the concept that children develop through stages and that each stage required a certain parenting response.

In his writings, Hall placed the primary focus of parenting on the mother, with little focus on the father. This perspective reflected American culture in the early 1900s. Only through close observation of the child would a mother be able to respond appropriately to each developmental level. The widespread influence of Hall's teachings changed American beliefs on the role of motherhood. Mothers were now to be trained in the art of child rearing and encouraged to devote themselves to the study of child guidance and development. In higher education, renewed importance was placed on female education.

The National Congress of Mothers (forerunner of the Parent Teacher Association) readily accepted and popularized the concept of the educated mother. Beginning in 1897 with a delegation of 2,000 people, the organization developed chapters in 36 states with membership of 190,000 over the next 20 years. Congress encouraged the development of courses for women in domestic science and child development and encouraged university chairs in child study to forward Hall's work.

Both public and private child welfare organizations serving dependent and delinquent children were transformed by the trend toward educated motherhood. The National Congress of Women strongly lobbied for progressive child welfare measures, such as public pensions for widows, and against the institutionalization of the orphaned and/or delinquent child. Fitting with Hall's theory, progressives recognized that the institutional environment could not meet the complexities involved in nurturing a child through developmental stages and that it would be best for families to remain together.

With an interest in genetics and evolution theory, Hall did gain some notoriety from his theory that "ontology recapitulates phylogeny." He theorized that psychic and somatic changes parallel the evolution scale of the mind and body. He suggested that people should not be prompted to think deeply until they reach the appropriate physical maturation. Although this theory had no major influence on education, it did facilitate further theoretical development. By the time he died in 1924, Hall had created significant changes in professional psychology, child development, and higher education that are with us to this day.

Anthony Carona

See also Child-Saving Movement; Mental Health

Bibliography

Goodchild, L. F. 1996. G. Stanley Hall and the study of higher education. *The Review of Higher Education* 20:69–99.

Hall, G. S. 1923. *Life and Confessions of a Psychologist.* New York: D. Appleton.

Hilgard, E. R. 1987. *Psychology in America: A Historical Survey.* San Diego, CA: Harcourt Brace Jovanovich.

Rothman, D. J. 1980. *Conscience and Convenience: The Asylum and Its Alternatives in Progressive America.* Boston: Little, Brown.

 # HEALY, WILLIAM (1869–1963)

Psychiatrist and neurologist William Healy was a pioneer in the psychological study of juvenile delinquency in early-20th-century America. The origins of psychological criminology can be traced back to his career, which set the basis of modern work on the subject.

Healy and his wife, Mary Tenney Healy, studied and wrote on forensic psychology and the diagnosis and prognosis of both juvenile and adult offenders while he taught at Harvard University.

DIAGNOSIS AND TREATMENT OF JUVENILE DELINQUENTS

Child psychiatry grew out of the newly formed juvenile courts of the late 19th and early 20th centuries, in which judges requested professional assistance in understanding the children who appeared before them in court. In 1909, Ethel Sturges Dummer, a society figure, provided substantial financing to help establish the Juvenile Psychopathic Institute in Chicago. Healy was selected as Director of the Institute and as the psychiatrist of the first child guidance clinic. The institute was linked to the juvenile court and served to evaluate and diagnose children seen by the court. Because of the belief that the use of psychiatric means could effectively treat antisocial behavior in children, such clinics proliferated and were patterned after Healy's original institute.

Healy hired one of his former students, Augusta Fox Bronner, to be a psychologist at the institute. They jointly published several pieces and, after his wife's death, Healy and Bronner married. Healy and Bronner developed the team concept of working with a patient by bringing together social workers, psychologists, and others to analyze a case.

Healy's interest in emotional aspects of personality fueled his desire to work with children who had behavior problems and delinquency issues. His book *The Individual Delinquent,* published in 1915, asserted that understanding a child's behavior was possible only by an examination of the child's unique individual history. At the institute, Healy applied the "own story" approach, a technique influenced by psychoanalysis and later relied on by Clifford Shaw in his chronicling of a boy's delinquency in *The Jackroller: A Delinquent Boy's Own Story.* Healy had examined the book's main character, Stanley, emphasizing the importance of understanding a delinquent child's attitudes and mental conflicts through the subject aspects of the life history.

By 1914, the Institute's funding was exhausted, and Cook County began to provide funding. But the county only wanted Healy's diagnoses and had no interest in the institute's research and treatment. In 1917 the newly created Department of Public Welfare assumed control of the Juvenile Psychopathic Institute, made it a part of the Division of the Criminologist, and renamed it the Institute for Juvenile Research. The institution began to serve as a research center, and it coordinated child guidance and delinquency activity to be implemented throughout the state.

OTHER SIGNIFICANT CONTRIBUTIONS

Healy was persuaded to expand on the Chicago model, and philanthropists in the Boston area provided funding to open the Judge Baker Foundation clinic in 1917, which became the international model for child guidance. Significantly aided by Bronner as director, Healy expanded on efforts to understand and help, rather than punish, delinquent children.

Healy testified in a number of cases, including a landmark case in the fight against capital punishment in the United States. He examined the defendants of the 1924 abduction-murder trial, Nathan Leopold and Richard Loeb, in which the two 19-year-old college students from one of Chicago's most affluent neighborhoods killed 14-year-old Bobby Franks. Healy's testimony revealed that Leopold had an established pathological personality before he met the other defendant, Loeb, and had he not been in association with Loeb, he would not have been tempted to kidnap and kill Franks.

Healy was significantly influenced by William James and Sigmund Freud and can be remembered for being one of the persons responsible for introducing the Binet-Simon tests into the United States. The Institute for Juvenile Research continues to operate the William Healy School as an inpatient unit, providing child guidance services to children and families, training personnel in these fields, and conducting research in the field of clinical psychiatry.

Bridgett L. McGowen

See also Augusta Fox Bronner; Chicago Area Project; Clifford R. Shaw; Theories of Delinquency— Psychological

Bibliography

Bilchik, S. 2001. *History of Juvenile Justice and Mental Health: Future Partnership for Children.* Joseph Noshpitz Memorial History Lecture. Available at http://ojjdp.ncjrs.org/about/spch991021.html.

Healy, W. 1915. *The Individual Delinquent: A Textbook of Diagnosis and Prognosis for All Concerned in Understanding Offenders.* Boston: Little, Brown.

Jones, K. W. 1999. *Taming the Troublesome Child: American Families, Child Guidance, and the Limits of Psychiatric Authority.* Cambridge, MA: Harvard University Press.

 # HIRSCHI, TRAVIS (1935–)

Travis Hirschi was born on April 15, 1935, in Rockville, Utah. He received his bachelor's degree in 1957 and his master's in 1958 from the University of Utah. In 1968, he earned his Ph.D. in sociology at the University of California at Berkeley. Hirschi began his academic career in the Sociology Department at the University of Washington, Seattle, as Assistant Professor and later became Associate Professor (1967 to 1971). From Washington, he moved to the University of California at Davis, where he was Professor of Sociology from 1971 to 1977. From 1977 to 1981, Hirschi was Professor of Criminal Justice at the State University of New York at Albany. In 1981, he moved to the Department of Sociology at the University of Arizona, Tucson, and stayed there until his retirement in 1997. Hirschi is currently Regents' Professor Emeritus at the University of Arizona.

During his illustrious career, Hirschi wrote four books: *Delinquency Research* (coauthored with Hanan Selvin, 1967), *Causes of Delinquency* (1969), *Measuring Delinquency* (coauthored with Michael Hindelang and Joseph Weis, 1981), and *A General Theory of Crime* (coauthored with Michael Gottfredson, 1990). He has also served as editor or coeditor on four volumes and has written 32 journal articles, 29 book chapters and forewords, and several book reviews and review essays covering a variety of topics in the study of crime and delinquency. The trademark of Hirschi's body of work is profound theoretical insights coupled with rigorous research methods. Over the last 25 years, Hirschi's work has dominated intellectual discussion and created the research agenda for the field of criminology.

Consider *Causes of Delinquency,* published in 1969. In this book, Hirschi developed and tested a theory of social control capitalizing on the idea of social bonding. In contrast to then popular delinquency theories that focused on motivations for delinquency, social control theories focused on the restraints and circumstances that prevent delinquency. In *Causes,* Hirschi presents the delinquent as "relatively free of the intimate attachments, the aspirations, and the moral beliefs that bind most people to a life within the law" (Hirschi, 1969, preface). The theoretical focus then is on the socialization processes that constrain antisocial and delinquent behavior that comes to all individuals naturally. The key question is, why do men obey the rules of society? For Hirschi, delinquency occurs when an individual's bond to society is weak or broken. There are four separate but interrelated elements of an individual's social bond to society: attachment (e.g., affection for and sensitivity to others); commitment (e.g., investment in conventional society); involvement (e.g., the amount of time spent on conventional activities); and belief (e.g., the extent to which people believe they should obey the rules). For example, the more strongly a juvenile is attached to his or her parents or teachers, the less likely he or she will engage in delinquent behavior. Along similar lines, a juvenile that has invested time and effort in conventional activities in school has a "stake in conformity," and he or she is less likely to jeopardize this investment by engaging in delinquent behavior.

Hirschi, perhaps more than any other delinquency theorist, also brought the family back into the picture, especially family relations. Although empirical research has consistently found that family variables, especially poor family functioning and child-rearing practices, are strongly associated with delinquent behavior, many sociological theories of delinquency ignore the family or minimize its influence relative to other factors such as poverty, social class, and neighborhood. The publication of *Causes of Delinquency* (1969) rectified this situation and marked the beginning of the era of empirical testing

of theories of delinquency to better understand the causes of delinquency and more effectively shape juvenile justice policy.

During the 1980s, Hirschi, with his longtime friend and colleague Michael Gottfredson, wrote a series of provocative papers that challenged much of the conventional wisdom in criminology, especially regarding age and crime, criminal careers, and the necessity of longitudinal research for the study of crime and delinquency. This intellectual collaboration culminated with the publication of *A General Theory of Crime* in 1990, in which Gottfredson and Hirschi attempted to "explain all crime, at all times" (117). These authors embrace a classical view of human behavior and argue that "all human conduct can be understood as the self-interested pursuit of pleasure or the avoidance of pain" (5). The cause of crime is low self-control—the tendency to pursue immediate and easy gratification with minimum regard for the long-term consequences. Thus individuals who lack self-control tend to be impulsive, insensitive, physical, risk oriented, shortsighted, and nonverbal. According to Gottfredson and Hirschi, low self-control is largely the result of ineffective child rearing—lack of care and love, poor monitoring and supervision, and inconsistent use of punishment for misbehavior.

Several ideas are central to Hirschi's self-control theory that distinguish it from earlier control theories: (1) The relationship between age and crime is invariant; (2) the distinction between crime and criminality is important; (3) individual differences to commit crime can be located in a person's level of self-control; (4) variation in self-control not only accounts for all types of crime but can also explain analogous acts that are not criminal such as smoking, drinking, and gambling; (5) the sources of variation in self-control can largely be found in child-rearing practices; (6) there is stability in crime and deviance over time; and (7) crime declines with age for one and all.

Although social control theory remains quite popular, the self-control theory advanced in *A General Theory of Crime* (1990) is arguably the major focus of research attention and critical evaluation in the field today. Like *Causes of Delinquency* (1969), *A General Theory* focuses on the family as critical to understanding the causes of crime. Self-control theory is also one source of the growing consensus that delinquency prevention and treatment should concentrate on the early years of life.

Throughout his career, Hirschi received many awards and honors, including the prestigious Edwin

H. Sutherland Award from the American Society of Criminology, given to a criminologist who has made outstanding contributions to the discipline. More recently, Hirschi was named the most-cited scholar in the field of criminology and criminal justice.

John H. Laub

See also Self-Report Studies; Theories of Delinquency— Sociological

Bibliography

Gottfredson, M. R., and T. Hirschi. 1990. *A General Theory of Crime*. Stanford, CA: Stanford University Press.

Hindelang, M. J., T. Hirschi, and J. G. Weis. 1981. *Measuring Delinquency*. Beverly Hills, CA: Sage Publications.

Hirschi, T. 1969. *Causes of Delinquency*. Berkeley, CA: University of California Press.

Hirschi, T., and H. C. Selvin. 1967. *Delinquency Research*. New York: Free Press.

I

INDIVIDUALS WITH DISABILITIES EDUCATION ACT

The Individuals With Disabilities Education Act (IDEA, P.L. 101-476) was passed in 1990 and maintained in 1997. The IDEA is a reauthorization of the Education of All Handicapped Children Act (EHA, P.L. 94-142), first passed by Congress in 1975. These pieces of legislation represent some of the most significant federal education efforts, with broad implications for public schooling in the United States. The EHA and the IDEA are unusual in educational legislation because the impetus for passage was a coalition of parents and professionals. Both acts have addressed discrimination of the disabled in public schools, offering specific provisional remedies.

The term *special education* is similar to, but not the same as, the corrections classification of "special needs" for wards and inmates. Special needs wards and inmates are those identified for special services, such as mental health, and may be found eligible for special education services. The corrections classification can also apply to wards or inmates at high risk for escape or harm from enemies in a facility. These reasons for a special needs classification would not be applicable to special education, as they are not education related. There is often overlap, however, because wards or inmates who need services for specific problems may also require special education.

The EHA was built in part on the 1973 Vocational Rehabilitation Act, considered a civil rights act for the disabled. In 1991, the Vocational Rehabilitation Act was reauthorized as the Americans With Disabilities Act. Section 504 of the Vocational Rehabilitation Act dealt with education of the disabled but was not as specific as the EHA requirements are. The EHA and the IDEA require that students with disabilities be provided educational experiences similar to students without disabilities. Schools are required to provide individualized support to meet special learning needs.

The EHA was originally designed to correct the lack of programs for educationally disabled children and youth aged 5 through 21 in public schools. It states that disabled students, *wherever they are found*, must be provided a "free, appropriate, public education" (FAPE). A disabled student's placement in a correctional facility is specifically included under the EHA. The IDEA expands and clarifies the EHA.

Before EHA was passed, students with disabilities were often removed from public education through placement in trailers, cramped classes, or separate facilities. The FAPE requirement, imposed to solve this problem, requires that disabled students be educated with regular education students to the maximum extent possible. In addition, parents of special education students do not pay more than do parents of regular education students.

EHA also required that schools actively seek potentially disabled students. This helps early identification of problems. The effort is called Child Find, designed to solve the problem of disabled students not being identified and thus not being provided appropriate services.

The federal government committed to a process of reimbursing state education agencies (state departments of education) for a portion of the extra costs for educating disabled students. Reimbursement was achieved through the provision of "flow-through" funds for local schools from the state education agency. Proposed federal funding levels have never been achieved, but there has recently been a new emphasis on increasing these levels.

Evaluation for placement into special education was a major area addressed by the EHA, and subsequently the IDEA. Before passage of special education legislation, students were often evaluated by a single professional, who might be biased or use racially and linguistically discriminatory testing instruments. Students were placed into special education after limited educational evaluation efforts and were not regularly reevaluated to determine progress. The solution to these problems was the development of multidisciplinary team evaluation. To determine student eligibility for special education services, at least four professionals must evaluate strengths and weaknesses. These professionals make up the multidisciplinary team, which must include, at a minimum, an educational evaluator/teacher, a school psychologist, a medical representative, and a social worker who completes a social history. Additional persons may be called on for evaluation when necessary, such as speech/language clinicians, or occupational or physical therapists. Together the multidisciplinary team reviews evaluation results and determines a student's placement into special education. The plan must not be limited by services that are readily available but must indicate what the student actually needs.

The EHA established 11 categories under which students could be found eligible for special education. A student must fit into one or more of the following categories to be able to access special education: specific learning disability, serious emotional disturbance, mental retardation, hearing impaired/deaf, visually impaired/blind, multiply handicapped, communication handicapped, other health impaired, orthopedically handicapped, physically handicapped, and speech impaired. The IDEA added the categories of autistic and traumatically brain injured.

Placement options for an identified special education student include such diverse alternatives as a regular classroom with some support and a residential facility placement. The student may be placed in a part-day special education program, often called a resource program, or a full-day special education program, often called a self-contained class. The critical issue is the availability of a "cascade of educational services" to meet student needs. The student is always to be placed in the least restrictive environment (LRE) possible. Emphasis is on placing the student in an LRE first and then moving on to more restrictive environments as needed. Corrections agencies have successfully negotiated this problem with the provision that educationally disabled wards or inmates be placed in the same environment as any other ward or inmate. Although the institution may be very restrictive, identified wards and inmates are treated equitably as long as they are not housed in more restrictive areas because of their disabilities.

The EHA also addressed the problem of a student being placed in special education and never reviewed for progress. The solution was found through the development of an individualized education plan, or IEP. The IEP, generated from the information collected during the multidisciplinary evaluation, contains a statement of goals and objectives for the disabled student. The initial IEP is written after the student is found eligible for special education services and must be reviewed every year. After the third year, a complete reevaluation must be done, which involves retesting by multidisciplinary team members.

One critical area addressed by the EHA and the IDEA is an increased role for parents. A lack of parental involvement was seen as a major problem before the EHA was passed. Parents might not know if their child had been evaluated for or placed in special education, and educational records were available to agencies but not to parents. The EHA and the IDEA provide for parent involvement at each stage of the special education process by allowing for a system of due process procedures in the case of disagreement about placement or program. This can conflict with confidentiality restrictions in corrections, but successful negotiations have been possible in most systems.

The EHA was initially perceived as a school-age law that overlooked the fact that disabled students need support before and after the ages first identified. To adequately serve students with disabilities during their years in school, attention had to be given to developmental periods before and after those years.

To address this concern, the IDEA developed regulations for early intervention with disabled infants and toddlers and transition for older students. Early intervention by the school can make a great difference during early developmental stages. The focus of early intervention programs is in working with families as well as directly with children with disabilities.

The problem of older students was addressed in the IDEA by the provision of transition services for students with disabilities who are age 16 or older. States must develop statements of transition needs at age 14, with services initiated at age 16. Transition services must include a set of activities specifically designed to help the student move into postschool activities. These may include training for employment, postsecondary education, or other skills or needs. The efforts must be coordinated and must address the student's individual needs and interests as well as community support options.

A transition plan is to be made part of the IEP for each disabled student. This plan is called the individualized transition plan, or ITP. The ITP is required for all disabled students, including those who are incarcerated. Corrections systems are required to go beyond the limited prerelease programs now available and develop transition plans for all identified special education wards and inmates.

Another significant area of change under the IDEA deals with the provision that students with severe disabilities be placed in integrated settings. Public school classrooms will, for the first time, be integrated to include students with severe disabilities. Although the emphasis on integration is again focused on the public schools, corrections agencies may face similar challenges.

Although the EHA and the IDEA were designed to be public school laws, they have clear applications to corrections. Many of the requirements are difficult to implement in the institution. Nevertheless, litigation in a number of states has verified that corrections must accept responsibility for special education. The most successful state corrections systems have worked closely with their state departments of education to develop special education programs that meet the spirit of the law while addressing institutional restrictions.

Several aspects of the IDEA revisions are important to correctional populations. They include the development of an additional program of support for students identified as seriously emotionally disturbed (SED). This area is of particular significance to corrections populations because of the overrepresentation of students identified as SED. Under the EHA, students who were determined to be socially maladjusted were eliminated from the category of SED. New definitions are more specific and less influenced by subjective opinions.

Corrections agencies have been slow to implement the EHA and the IDEA. Some systems, particularly adult prisons, have made no attempts. Both the EHA and the IDEA apply to corrections facilities as well as to public schools. The latest revisions have allowed adult corrections systems to provide special education only to those previously identified as special-education-eligible by the public school.

Litigation of special education in corrections has overwhelmingly supported wards' and inmates' rights to special education. Most litigation has forced states to implement special education under federal court order, the most expensive and least effective means of implementation. A much more logical approach is to take a proactive role in special education implementation.

Carolyn Eggleston and Thom Gehring

See also Alternative Schools; Learning Disabilities

J

JUVENILE DETENTION FACILITIES

Locking children away in secure detention facilities has posed problems for the juvenile system since its inception in 1899. Who should be detained and in what kind of setting are questions we are still struggling with today, and the answers depend on the prevailing political and social climate. For many years, there were no clear guidelines for detention. Children were detained for various reasons, including delinquency, neglect, abuse, or for their own safety, and in deplorable conditions, usually with adult criminals. While the rest of the juvenile system was recognizing that juveniles and adults cannot be treated the same, detained juveniles were still being treated as adults.

The removal of children from their homes and parents has always been considered a last resort. Detention can be a very traumatic event in a child's life. Studies suggest that the child's self-esteem may be damaged in the detention setting, where they are subject to strip searches, institutional clothing, and dictated routines. The child also may begin associating with negative peers and view him- or herself as a criminal, thereby promoting future criminal behavior (Kilm, 1980; Brown, 1980). For children held in adult facilities, educational, medical, and counseling services were generally nonexistent.

In light of the recognized negative effects of detention on children, the obvious answer would seem to be to detain few children. That has not been the case, however. In the 1990s, with juvenile crime receiving increased media attention, the "get tough" policies of the federal and local governments resulted in increased detention, even though the juvenile crime rate began declining in the mid-1990s.

A look at the history of juvenile detention will illustrate the difficulty this country has experienced in determining the role of the juvenile detention facility.

HISTORY

Since the first juvenile court was established in 1899, the problem of detaining children in suitable facilities has plagued the juvenile system. A 1923 report by the United States Children's Bureau and the National Probation Association addressed detention conditions and pushed for improvements. However, a study of detention centers in 1932 by the National Probation Association (NPA) found that children were still regularly detained in adult jail facilities. Detention homes were not much better than jails, and policies for detaining and releasing children were inadequate. The NPA also determined that the wrong type of children were being detained, frequently for long periods (National Council Crime and Delinquency [NCCD], 1961).

A second study by the NPA, conducted in 1945, found little change in detention conditions in the best facilities in 22 states. They found that jurisdictions varied greatly in the way they used detention, with some detaining less than 5 percent of children referred to court while others detained all children and released them with no formal court referral. Since no standards for juvenile detention centers existed at that time, the Association produced two publications: *Detention for the Juvenile Court: A Discussion of Principles and Practices* and *The Design and Construction of Detention Homes for the Juvenile Court.*

Photo 5. Boys in a Beet Field at the State Industrial School, Kearney, Nebraska, 1914.
SOURCE: Nebraska State Historical Society [RG2608]. Used with permission.

The NCCD published *Standards and Guides for the Detention of Children and Youth* in 1959 and a second edition in 1961. Standards were recommended for the education, programming, medical care, and activities for detained children as well as training and selection of staff, personnel policies, and administration of the detention centers. In spite of the increasing concern regarding the overuse of detention, studies continued to indicate most jurisdictions were not following these guidelines.

The NCCD conducted a survey of detention and correctional facilities in 1967. The study showed that nearly 320,000 children were held in secure facilities as of 1965. Most of these facilities were converted workhouses, hospitals, private homes,

and county infirmaries. Ninety-three percent of the country's juvenile court jurisdictions did not have detention centers, other than county jails. Many of the detained juveniles had not committed delinquent acts but were being held for neglect and dependency issues. There was widespread use of detention for holding children accused of noncriminal offenses, often without filing a petition, and for immediate punishment using detention as a disposition (Howell, 1998).

As a result of this survey, Congress passed the Juvenile Justice and Delinquency Prevention Act in 1974 in an effort to reduce the use of juvenile detention and provide alternatives to secure detention. The act required deinstitutionalization of status offenders, separation of juveniles from adults, and a reduction in the disproportionate confinement of minorities (Howell, 1998). Several states followed suit, passing legislation designed to restrict the allowable conditions for predetention of children. However, pervasive detention abuse continued throughout the country (Kilm, 1980).

The great latitude each jurisdiction had in making detention decisions led to vast differences in detention use. The National Advisory Committee on Standards for the Administration of Juvenile Justice issued national standards in 1976, establishing specific and objective criteria defining which juveniles were eligible for detention. These standards state that a juvenile should not be detained unless she or he meets the following criteria:

1. Is a fugitive from another jurisdiction.

2. Requests protection in writing and is in a situation that presents an immediate threat of serious physical harm.

3. Is charged with first- or second-degree murder.

4. Is charged with a serious property crime or a violent crime that, if committed by an adult, would be a felony and
   a. is already detained or on conditional release,
   b. has a record of failing to appear at court proceedings,
   c. has a recent record of violent conduct, or
   d. had a record of adjudications for serious property offenses.

5. Has no less restrictive alternative that reduces the risk of flight or harm to property or others.

Juveniles who did not meet these criteria were to be released to their parents or a nonsecure shelter (Kilm, 1980). The act also required juveniles to be removed from adult jails by 1985. Juveniles held in jail facilities had to be separated from adult inmates by sight and sound.

DEFINITION AND USE OF DETENTION CENTERS

According to the National Council on Crime and Delinquency, detention is defined as "the temporary care of children in physically restricted facilities pending court disposition or transfer to another jurisdiction or agency" (NCCD, 1961:1). The dual purpose of detention is to ensure that the child appears in court and to protect the community. Detention centers should not be confused with correctional facilities, whose purpose is the long-term confinement of juveniles committed by the court, or with residential facilities, which provide long-term treatment and rehabilitation.

In most states, local county probation departments operate juvenile detention centers. State agencies may oversee the administration of the facilities, establish standards, and monitor compliance. The American Correctional Association (ACA) has established national standards and guidelines, but these standards are voluntary for facilities choosing to be ACA-accredited.

According to a 1995 report by the Office of Juvenile Justice and Delinquency Prevention, 69,075 juveniles were held in detention centers on the day of a national count. While 96 percent of these children were charged with delinquent offenses, 2.6 percent were held for status offenses, and about 1 percent were held for other reasons, such as neglect or dependency. Half the juveniles were detained by six states: California, Ohio, Texas, New York, Florida, and Illinois. California held the most juveniles, with 28 percent of the total (Moone, 1997).

The states varied greatly in their use of detention. While nine states held only delinquent offenders, the other states included status offenders. Indiana, Iowa, Missouri, and South Dakota held the highest percentages of status offenders. Hawaii and Iowa detained the highest percentage of children held for dependency or neglect. Nineteen states did not hold status offenders (Moone, 1997).

A recent trend has been the increased use of detention centers for short, punitive incarceration sentences as well as long-term postadjudication dispositions. In some cases, these facilities are also being used for long-term lockup for children who have been charged as adults while they wait for the much slower adult criminal court process.

It could be assumed that the detention rates would decline as the juvenile crime rate declines. However, a look at the data indicates that is not the case. In the 1980s, the juvenile crime rate for all offenses declined 7 percent and for Part I offenses, 17 percent. However, the detention rate increased 24 percent and the average length of stay increased 78 percent (Annie E.

Casey Foundation, 2000). In Florida, the detention rate increased 77 percent between 1991 and 1997.

While the studies and guidelines stressed the goal of detaining only those who have been charged with serious crimes, a study of detention facilities in 1995 indicated that only 29 percent of detainees were accused of committing a violent offense. Thirty-four percent were detained for status offenses and technical violations of probation. Between 1984 and 1995, the greatest detention population increase was among drug offense cases (Poe-Yamagata, 1997). Males continue to be detained at higher rates than females. However, the female detention population is increasing. Minority youth remain overrepresented in detention centers as in other areas of juvenile justice.

Programming within detention centers varies among jurisdictions. Every center is required to provide some form of educational program. However, many jurisdictions have no standards for schooling. Other programs that may be provided include anger-management skills training, cognitive-behavior therapy, drug and alcohol groups, and most recently, female offender programs. An exercise program is usually included in the daily schedule. Some facilities keep the children locked in their rooms for long periods, while others reserve room confinements for discipline purposes. Level systems are common within the detention setting, encouraging positive behavior by providing rewards for reaching higher levels. Rewards can include later bedtimes, TV or video game privileges, increased phone contact, and longer family visits. Detention decisions can be made based on the level achieved by the juvenile.

In 1992, the Annie E. Casey Foundation launched the Juvenile Detention Alternatives Initiative, a program designed to encourage selected counties to find ways to reduce the use of detention. The counties chosen—Cook County, Illinois; Sacramento County, California; Multnomah County, Oregon; and New York City and County—were given grants to develop alternatives to detention. Some of the new procedures included restructuring the admissions process and developing screening instruments that used prescribed criteria for detention. Home detention was used, with increased supervision and electronic monitoring. Day check-in centers and evening reporting centers were established, using corporate and community resources. Last, efforts were made to reduce the time between initial contact with the juvenile and final

court disposition. All the counties experienced significant reductions in the detention population (Annie E. Casey Foundation, 2000).

CONCLUSION

In the current get-tough atmosphere, increased numbers of youths are being detained. The cost of detaining a youth is approximately $100 to $130 per day, thus the increase in detentions is costly. Detention centers have increased their capacity in the last decade to handle growing populations. A recent trend has been to use detention centers as secure postadjudication centers, usually boot camp programs, as well as temporary predetention confinement. Juveniles are given a sentence, which includes spending a designated period in the detention facility as part of the punishment. As the political climate shifts and the treatment of juveniles swings from punishment to treatment and back, use of detention centers will continue to change.

Sandra Dunnuck

See also Boot Camps; Juvenile Justice and Delinquency Prevention Act; Reformatories and Reform Schools; Training Schools

Bibliography

Annie E. Casey Foundation. 2000. *Juvenile Detention Alternatives Initiative.* Baltimore: Annie E. Casey Foundation.
Brown, M. 1980. A philosophy of juvenile detention. *Texas Journal of Corrections*, Jan/Feb:9–11.
Howell, J. C. 1998. NCCD survey on juvenile detention and correctional facilities. *Crime and Delinquency* 44:102–109.
Kilm, R. 1980. *Prohibiting Secure Juvenile Detention: Assessing the Effectiveness of National Standards Detention Criteria.* Champaign-Urbana, IL: University of Illinois Community Research Forum.
Moone, J. 1997. *States at a Glance: Juveniles in Public Facilities, 1995.* Washington, DC: Office of Juvenile Justice and Delinquency Prevention.
National Council on Crime and Delinquency (NCCD). 1961. *Standards and Guides for the Detention of Children and Youth.* New York: NCCD.
Poe-Yamagata, E. 1997. *Detention and Delinquency Cases, 1985–1994.* Washington, DC: Office of Juvenile Justice and Delinquency Prevention.

JUVENILE JUSTICE AND DELINQUENCY PREVENTION ACT OF 1974

The fundamental purpose of the Juvenile Justice and Delinquency Prevention Act of 1974 (JJDPA; P.L. 93-415) is to provide a coordinated and sound approach for reducing juvenile delinquency. The Act, having been amended numerous times since 1974, is now U.S. Code Title 42, Chapter 72. It is currently sectioned into five subchapters, each of which administers its own specific policies.

SUBCHAPTER I: CONGRESSIONAL FINDINGS AND GOALS

Subchapter I states the findings of Congress concerning juvenile delinquency and lists the purposes of the act in reaction to those findings. In its reports, Congress acknowledges the increasing arrest rate for juveniles committing serious crimes, overcrowding in juvenile courts and correctional facilities, the lack of adequate responses by existing programs, and the need for local communities to accumulate adequate resources for reducing juvenile delinquency. Congress further states that its purpose is to develop and conduct effective programs to prevent delinquency, thereby assisting states and local communities with resources to develop and implement programs. Other goals include establishing training programs for persons working with delinquent youth, developing a centralized research effort on the problems of juvenile delinquency, and creating a federal assistance program to deal with the problem of runaway youth. The remaining four subchapters of the Act are designed to fulfill those goals.

SUBCHAPTER II: PROGRAMS AND OFFICES

Subchapter II creates programs and offices to coordinate and administer proper strategies for preventing juvenile delinquency. Part A of this subchapter creates the Office of Juvenile Justice and Delinquency Prevention (OJJDP) within the Department of Justice under the general authority of the Attorney General. The administrator of this office, who is appointed by the president and approved by the Senate, is authorized to prescribe regulations to award, administer, extend, evaluate, reject, or deny all grants and contracts and applications for funds. Part B authorizes the Administrator to make grants to states and units of local government to assist them in planning and operating projects with public and private agencies for the development of more effective programs. Other general duties of the Administrator include advising the President through the Attorney General on matters relating to federally assisted juvenile delinquency programs and conducting, reviewing, and commenting on evaluations and studies on the performance of the federal programs.

To receive grants, states must submit a plan for carrying out their goals as well as an annual performance report to the Administrator that describes the progress in implementing the programs contained in the plan. The plan consists of numerous programs and challenge activities that include analysis of juvenile crime problems and delinquency prevention needs, development of an adequate research, training, and evaluation capacity within the state, an adequate system of monitoring jails, detention facilities, and correctional facilities, and the establishment of procedures for protecting the rights of recipients of services while ensuring appropriate privacy for records of those services.

The Council on Juvenile Justice and Delinquency Prevention was created under Subchapter II as an independent organization in the executive branch. The function of the council is to coordinate all federal juvenile delinquency programs and activities that detain or care for unaccompanied juveniles as well as all programs related to missing and exploited children. The Council must report to the President and Congress with recommendations for the coordination of overall policy and development objectives.

The National Institute of Juvenile Justice and Delinquency Prevention was established within the OJJDP under the direct supervision of the administrator. The purpose of the Institute is to provide a coordinating center for the collection and preparation of useful data on the prevention and treatment of juvenile delinquency as well as provide appropriate training for representatives of law enforcement officers, educators, and counselors. The Administrator is authorized through the Institute to review reports and data on the juvenile justice system, serve as an information bank by collecting data and knowledge obtained from studies and research by the public and private agencies, and conduct and coordinate research and evaluation into any aspect of juvenile delinquency including prevention and treatment.

Subchapter II also focuses on prevention and treatment programs and determines under what circumstances public and private nonprofit agencies receive grants and contracts. The purposes of such grants include establishing and maintaining community-based alternatives, establishing effective means of diverting juveniles from the juvenile justice system, developing model programs to strengthen and maintain the family unit, and establishing programs designed to prevent and reduce the incidence of hate crimes by juveniles. Any agency desiring to receive a grant or enter a contract must submit an application, which should include the program's purpose and goals. Programs are selected through a competitive process and reviewed before selection.

Part D of Subchapter II establishes an incentive for agencies and organizations to develop programs designed to produce gang-free schools and communities. The Administrator will make grants or enter contracts with public and private nonprofit agencies to carry out programs and activities designed to reduce the participation of juveniles in illegal gang activity. The goals of these programs include targeting elementary school students to steer them away from gang involvement, providing treatment to juveniles who are members of gangs, and assisting them in obtaining appropriate educational instruction.

The Administrator, in consultation with the Secretary of Health and Human Services, also has the authority to make grants for programs designed to treat juvenile offenders who have been the victims of child abuse or neglect. These programs, developed by public and nonprofit private organizations, must be designed to strengthen the relationships of juveniles with their families, facilitate the juveniles' alternative placement, prepare them to live independently, and carry out research pertaining to transitional services and treatment.

Mentoring is also established with hopes to reduce juvenile delinquency and gang participation as well as improve academic performance. These mentoring programs, administered by grants for three-year periods, are designed to link at-risk children with responsible adults, such as law enforcement officers and persons working with local businesses and community-based organizations. The goals of mentoring include promoting personal responsibility, discouraging use of illegal drugs and violence, and encouraging at-risk youth to participate in community activities. One hundred twenty days after completing the first

cycle of grants, the administrator must submit to Congress a full report on the effectiveness of the mentoring grant programs.

Ten military-style boot camps were established in Part H of Subchapter II to instill discipline and provide treatment for juveniles who are already under the laws of the state of jurisdiction and have been adjudicated as delinquent. The juvenile must agree to participate and must be assessed as having the physical and emotional capability to participate in the boot camp regimen. The boot camps, after consultation with the Secretary of Defense and the attempt of the administrator to achieve equitable geographic distribution, are to be located on existing or closed military installations on sites chosen by the agencies in one or more states.

SUBCHAPTER III: RUNAWAY AND HOMELESS YOUTH

Subchapter III of the JDDPA is devoted to runaway and homeless youth. Congress has found that homeless juveniles are at risk of developing serious health and other problems because they lack sufficient resources to obtain care and are in urgent need of temporary shelter and counseling. The Secretary of Health and Human Services has the authority to give grants to public and private entities to establish and operate local centers for runaway and homeless youth. Their primary purpose is to deal with the immediate needs of runaway and homeless youth (youth between the ages of 16 and 21 who have no safe living environment) and their families.

Projects eligible under the grant program include centers providing temporary shelter and counseling to juveniles who have left home without permission of their parents or guardians. Early intervention programs or home-based services as well as street-based services are also eligible to receive grants.

Home-based services are designed to prevent runaway and homeless youth from becoming involved in the juvenile justice system. Street-based services target runaway and homeless youth who require assistance and would not otherwise avail themselves of assistance or services without such outreach.

The Secretary of Health and Human Services also has the authority to make grants to states, localities, and private agencies to carry out research and service projects designed to increase knowledge and improve services for runaway and homeless youth. Special consideration is given to agencies proposing projects that include proper services for youth who repeatedly run away, runaway and homeless youth in rural areas, staff training in the behavioral and emotional effects of sexual abuse, and increased access to health care for runaway and homeless youth.

SUBCHAPTER IV: MISSING CHILDREN

Subchapter IV of the JJDPA focuses on missing children. The term *missing child* is defined as any individual under the age of 18 whose whereabouts are unknown to the legal custodian of the child. In their statement of findings, Congress recognizes that thousands of children are abducted or removed from parents without their consent and are placed under dangerous circumstances, including physical harm and sexual exploitation.

The Administrator of the OJJDP, either by making grants or entering into contracts with public or non-profit private agencies, is to establish a national 24-hour, toll-free telephone line by which individuals can report information regarding the location of a missing child. The Administrator is also, through grants or contracts, authorized to establish and operate a national resource center and clearinghouse. This resource center is designed to coordinate public and private programs that locate, recover, or reunite missing children with their legal custodians and provide technical assistance and training to juvenile justice agencies in the prevention, investigation, prosecution, and treatment of missing and exploited child cases. Programs receiving grants from the administrator must be designed to educate parents and children on preventing the abduction and sexual exploitation of children, provide information to assist in locating and returning missing children, and develop effective treatment programs pertaining to the psychological consequences of abduction or sexual exploitation of a child.

Federal, state, and local law enforcement agencies must report each case of a missing child under the age of 18 to the National Crime Information Center of the Department of Justice. The report is to include the name, date of birth, sex, race, height, weight, and eye and hair colors of the child as well as the date and location of the last known contact with the child. The report is entered into the National Crime and Information Center computer networks by the law enforcement agency and must be updated 60 days after its original entry with any additional information, including medical and dental records.

SUBCHAPTER V: LOCAL PROGRAM INCENTIVES

The fifth and final subchapter of the act deals with incentive grants for local delinquency prevention programs. In their findings, Congress states that it is more effective in both human and fiscal terms to prevent delinquency than to attempt to control or change it after the fact. Therefore, federal incentives are needed to assist states and local communities in mobilizing delinquency prevention policies and programs.

The Administrator is responsible for arranging to facilitate coordination and policy development among all delinquency prevention activities funded through the Department of Justice. The Administrator may also make grants, which are transmitted through the state advisory group, to units of local government. The local government must meet certain requirements to provide delinquency prevention programs and activities for youth who have had, or are likely to have, contact with the juvenile justice system. The requirements of these units of local government include developing a three-year plan outlining the unit's local front-end plans for delinquency prevention; coordinating services for at-risk youth and their families, including such programs as nutrition and housing; and agreeing to provide a 50 percent match on the amount of the grant to fund the activity.

The JJDPA has been amended and reauthorized by the OJJDP six times since 1974. The central mandate, to remove all status offenders from institutions, has essentially been accomplished and other facets of the act and its amendments now occupy the attention of the OJJDP. At this point, a majority of the states are in compliance with the various requirements of the act. A reasonable assessment would be that the act's effect on the juvenile justice system of the United States has been substantial.

Andrea M. Carter

See also Adoption Assistance and Child Welfare Act; Boot Camps; Mentoring Programs; Missing Children; Office of Juvenile Justice and Delinquency Prevention; Runaways

Bibliography

Brown, J. W. 1995. Beyond the mandates. *Juvenile Justice* 2(2):22–24.

Holden, G. A., and R. A. Kapler. 1995. Deinstitutionalizing status offenders: A record of progress. *Juvenile Justice* 2(2):3–10.

Raley, T. A. 1995. The JJDP Act: A second look. *Juvenile Justice* 2(2):11–18.

Saucier, M. E. 1995. Birth of a partnership. *Juvenile Justice* 2(2):19–21.

JUVENILES IN ADULT CORRECTIONAL FACILITIES

 ## I. Jails

American jails were originally designed in colonial times (1650) to detain or hold individuals awaiting trial and until a sentence was carried out. It was not until the turn of the 20th century that jails also became places where convicted individuals served short sentences, typically less than one year.

The earliest jails did not have individual cells. Instead, they were designed like other residences of the day, with assorted groups of prisoners housed in a series of rooms. These jails accepted both adults and juveniles. There was no separation of prisoners by age, although prisoners of different sexes were separated by the Quakers in the late 1700s when the Walnut Street Jail was established.

Children were not segregated from adults until the 19th century. In 1825, the first separate institution for juveniles, the New York House of Refuge, was established. Other houses of refuge for youth soon followed. Houses of refuge were privately operated institutions developed out of both humanitarian and social control principles. These twin themes can be traced to other efforts to control juveniles, as well as efforts to regulate adult offenders.

Following the house of refuge movement, public training schools were developed. The first one opened in 1845 in Massachusetts, and in 1876 the first public reformatory for youth—the Elmira Reformatory—was established in Elmira, New York. With the advent of the first juvenile court in 1899, specialized and totally separate detention centers and training schools for youth became commonplace. Yet this did not mean that juveniles were always confined separately from adult offenders. In many jurisdictions across the nation, juveniles were still mingled with adults in jails. It would take another 75 years for the practice of routinely jailing juveniles in adult facilities to be regulated.

Separating inmates by age is, in practice, a crude classification system for prisoners. The move to separate youth from adults is linked to developments in the fields of biology, sociology, and psychology that began in the 19th century and continued through the 1940s. Previously, youth were sometimes treated as children and at other times as adults. An individual was a child for legal purposes, such as making a contract or inheriting property, but an adult for economic reasons, such as earning money for the family. With the advent of the scientific study of individual stages of development and physiology—although research studies were few and still in their infancy—adolescence finally became recognized as a separate class.

During this same period, U.S. economic structures were changing from agrarian to industrial. Industrialization and urbanization were seen as creating separate pressures that contributed to rising dependency and poverty and, in turn, to rising youth and adult crime. A number of efforts were undertaken to mitigate the negative ramifications of industrialization upon youth. One effort was the separation of youth from adults in jails or placement in other institutions altogether (e.g., child protective services). Separating juveniles was seen as a humane alternative to the harshness of adult jails. Alternatively, it was desirable to separate juveniles from adults because mingling young and more mature offenders fostered criminal lifestyles.

These strains of thought continue in laws regulating placement and housing of juveniles in adult jails today. The major piece of legislation regulating the detention of juveniles in adult jails is the Juvenile Justice and Delinquency Prevention Act of 1974 (JJDPA). The Act was designed to prevent delinquency and encourage the rehabilitation of youth. Although it is over a quarter of a century since the Act's passage, its goals are as vibrant today as when it was enacted.

A key concern of the JJDPA was separation of juveniles, both status offenders and delinquents, from adults in pre- and postadjudication confinement. As with earlier reform efforts to separate juvenile and adult offenders, it was thought that reductions in delinquency would occur by limiting contact of nonserious juvenile offenders and more serious youthful and adult offenders. Mixing youths with adult offenders, offenders who were presumed to be more sophisticated and entrenched in the criminal lifestyle by virtue of their age, created negative opportunities for youth to learn and harden their criminal ways.

The JJDPA restricts the confinement of status offenders and delinquents in adult facilities. The placement of status offenders in adult jails is specifically prohibited under all circumstances. Jails are permitted to house youths charged as delinquents under one of three conditions. First, the juvenile is charged with, and will be processed in the adult criminal system on, felony charges. Misdemeanor and traffic offenses are excluded from this formulation and do not justify jail detention for juveniles. Failures to appear and violation of probation charges also do not qualify if the underlying or instant charge occurred in the juvenile court. Second, a youth who was previously tried as an adult and received adult sanctions will be accepted into custody by the jail under the principle that "once an adult, always an adult." If a juvenile court waived jurisdiction and a finding of guilt and sentencing in an adult court occurred, thereafter a juvenile is considered an adult for all future criminal justice processing.

The final limitation is that juveniles may be detained in the secure setting of jails on a temporary basis. This detention is justified by its limited duration, generally not beyond six hours, as well as its limited purpose. A juvenile may be (1) held after arrest and pending contact and transfer to the parents or guardian, (2) pending transfer to the closest juvenile detention facility, or (3) before and after a court appearance. In addition, a juvenile may be held up to six hours for identification purposes or, in the rare situations when bond has been authorized, to permit the posting of bond.

States were slow to comply with the JJDPA despite an initial deadline of 1978. In 1980, the act was amended, and removal of all juveniles from adult jails and police lockups by 1985 was mandated. A 1982 study of states' efforts to comply with the Act detailed slow progress in meeting its requirements. Among the barriers to achieving full compliance were ignorance of the law, a lack of commitment to follow the Act's provisions, conflict between state and federal regulations, and insufficient resources. Probably the most intractable barrier in many jurisdictions was the latter—a lack of funds to construct and staff a separate facility or jail section for juveniles. Rural states faced fiscal constraints and geographic limitations. The distance between the location of the arrest and the closest institution with separate juvenile holding capability made it impossible to meet JJDPA guidelines of release from secure custody within 6 hours of admission. As a result, amendments to the Act permit jails in rural areas to hold delinquents up to 24 hours under certain circumstances.

Compliance with the law's mandates lagged even after the first extension of the Act, and the deadline to comply was extended three years until 1988. The grace period for compliance was eventually closed by the 1988 mandate that required noncomplying states to use all their grant money for jail removal efforts or face the loss of federal juvenile justice grants to the state. This firm directive prompted many states to reinvigorate their compliance efforts. Modifications to the Act in 1996 provide states flexibility in achieving compliance, with noncomplying states sacrificing only 25 percent of the state's Formula Grant Program allocation.

Given that juveniles may be housed in adult jails if they face prosecution as an adult or have previously received an adult sentence, what other practical limits are there on jail admission and detention? Age is one delimiter. Eighteen is the typical boundary defining juvenile court and criminal court jurisdiction. Even so, nearly a dozen states specify 16 or 17 as the age of majority for criminal court processing, and in recent years, more exceptions have been carved out to permit transfer of youth for prosecution as adults.

A second restriction is that juveniles and adults must be kept completely separate for all institutional activities, such as eating, sleeping, and programming. Direct contact—referring to both "sight and sound" separation—is prohibited. The JJDPA does allow for contact that might be termed accidental or haphazard, such as when a juvenile and an adult prisoner pass each other in the hallway, but the act does not permit regular or recurring contact, such as transporting juvenile and adult prisoners in the same vehicle or permitting them to attend the same church service or educational class. Even when a juvenile is housed on a temporary basis within the rule of six hours, the sight and sound restriction applies.

From mid-1980 through the mid-1990s, juvenile crime increased nationwide. High rates of serious juvenile offending led to increased public demand to treat youth in the adult criminal justice system rather than in the juvenile justice system. For example, between 1992 and 1996, 43 of 50 state legislatures and the District of Columbia revised their laws for juveniles committing violent or serious crimes. Correspondingly, the number and proportion of juveniles housed in adult jails rose.

In 1983, 1,736 juveniles were in adult jails; in 1990, 2,301 juveniles; in 1993, 4,300 juveniles; and by 1995, 7,800 juveniles were confined in adult jails. By 1999 the number of juveniles in local correctional institutions had risen to 9,458. While the number of juveniles in adult jails declined to 7,615 in 2000, the cumulative percentage change over the past 17 years is more than 330 percent.

The June 30, 2000, total of 7,615 juveniles in custody in adult facilities represents nearly 1 percent of the total average daily inmate population in jails on that date. Eighty percent of those juveniles had been convicted or were being held for trial as adults in the criminal court. These numbers may be more readily understood by considering a "typical" county jail system. Many jails may confine none or only one juvenile on any given day, and even a megajail system—that is, a jail with a capacity in excess of 1,000 prisoners—may hold only 3 to 10 juveniles in custody on a typical day.

In comparison, the number of juveniles in jail is nearly double the number of youths confined in state prisons at midyear 2000, when 3,915 persons under 18 were serving sentences at state facilities. The overwhelming majority of those inmates were male; 3,741 were males under 18, and only 174 were females under 18. Overall, fewer than 0.5 percent of all state inmates are juveniles. There were no youths under 18 confined in federal prisons at midyear 2000.

Despite the counts from public adult jails, most juveniles are housed in institutions specifically created for them. In mid-February 1995, the date of the last census for youth in public and private juvenile detention, correctional, or shelter care facilities, 91,505 juveniles were accused or adjudicated for actions that would qualify as law violations. Combining correctional census data for jails (7,615) and for prisons (3,915) yields 11,530 persons under 18 in adult correctional settings either accused, awaiting sentencing, or serving sentences. Thus comparison of juvenile and adult correctional censuses shows roughly 90 percent of youth are held in juvenile facilities, and 10 percent are confined in adult correctional settings.

Given the rationales for separating juveniles and adults, one of the primary concerns for jail administrators is to ensure the safety and security of youths legally detained in their institutions. Jail administrators have to consider not only separating adults and youth but also protecting vulnerable juveniles. It is not enough to merely separate by age; jails must also screen and separate aggressive youth from more passive ones.

Beyond safety and security concerns are management issues tied to youthfulness. Foremost is what we know about age as it relates to behavior and perception. For example, youth are known to experience time differently and to act based on a host of physiological, social, psychological, and emotional bases that do not hold for adults. What may be acceptable punishment for adults may be unacceptable for children. For example, five minutes may seem like an eternity to a juvenile. A youth's capacity to cope with sensory deprivation is limited. These differences may explain, for example, prior studies that place the suicide risk for juveniles in jail at five times the rate of juveniles in the general population and at eight times the rate for adolescents in juvenile detention facilities.

Juvenile offenders differ from adult prisoners in other ways. It is common for both correctional officers and for older inmates to comment on the higher energy levels of young inmates, heightened levels of noise and activity, and an associated propensity for interpersonal conflicts to arise. Juvenile offenders also are often described as impulsive. These factors have implications for the amount and nature of rules violations, or disciplinary infractions, and the resulting penalties, especially when disciplinary segregation is ordered. However, while professional correctional organizations such as the American Correctional Association have established standards specific to juveniles, and many jurisdictions train staff about youthful offenders' needs, the reality is that custodial practices do little to fully address the specialized needs of the young jail detainee.

A different set of concerns arises relative to legal requirements that attach to age. Youth typically are not considered adults for purposes of consenting to medical treatment. Thus jail administrators must gain parental consent for medical services, including surgery, or, in the extreme, jail authorities end up acting *in loci parentis* when emergency and routine medical treatment is needed.

Compulsory education laws, which apply only to youth, are another concern when juveniles are housed in adult jails. Youths are required to be enrolled in school until they are 16. With increased transfer of 15-year-old (and younger) juveniles for criminal court processing, jail staff are increasingly confronting the need to offer basic educational programs. Conversely, due to the federal Individuals With Disabilities Education Act, juveniles are entitled to the benefit of specialized education programs, and such educational programming must be available to the incarcerated juvenile who seeks to attend school past normal graduation age (ranging from 21 to 22 years). The failure of some school boards and jails to provide these services has led to litigation in a number of states (e.g., Florida).

Other problems arise related to providing different programs for juveniles. Given their relatively small numbers in the average daily population, it is easy for jail administrators to overlook juveniles' special needs. The high cost of providing services to only a few inmates often becomes a justification for offering only the most rudimentary services. The perceived danger of the youth who are transferred for adult prosecution and who are detained in adult jails hampers recruitment of both paid civilians and volunteers to lead juvenile programs.

In a similar vein, juvenile inmates are, at least by law and in theory, entitled to the same privileges as adults in jails. Youth have the right to out-of-cell time and recreation privileges consistent with their custody and segregation status, mail and visitation privileges, and access to legal counsel and the courts. Unfortunately, juveniles often face restrictions on these privileges due to staffing, space, and financial constraints. Thus juveniles held in adult jails are victims of double marginality. Because federal mandates require their separation from adults and typically few youth are in custody at any one time, youth have reduced chances for regular and wide social interaction. This remains a challenge both for lawmakers who craft the regulations and authorize budgets and for jail administrators who must manage the juvenile offenders in increasing numbers.

Marilyn Chandler Ford

See also Juvenile Detention Facilities; Juvenile Justice and Delinquency Prevention Act of 1974; Probation, Juvenile; Waiver to Adult Court

Bibliography

Austin, J., K. D. Johnson, and M. Gregoriou. 2000. *Juveniles in Adult Prisons and Jails: A National Assessment.* Bureau of Justice Statistics. Washington, DC: Government Printing Office.

Beck, A. J., and J. C. Karberg. 2001. *Prison and Jail Inmates at Midyear 2000.* Bureau of Justice Statistics. Washington, DC: Government Printing Office.

Howard, S., and M. Sickmund. 1999. *Juvenile Offenders and Victims: 1999 Update on Violence.* National Center for Juvenile Justice. Washington, DC: U.S. Government Printing Office.

Strom, K. J. 2000. *Profile of State Prisoners Under Age 18, 1985–97.* Bureau of Justice Statistics. Washington, DC: Government Printing Office.

JUVENILES IN ADULT CORRECTIONAL FACILITIES

 ## II. Prisons

Until the 1800s, juveniles and adults in the court system were processed and punished similarly, and juveniles often suffered abuse during their incarceration with adults. Throughout the 19th century, the public and the justice system began to perceive juveniles as less blameworthy and more open to rehabilitation than adults. Exposing them to punishment with adult criminals was thought to cause more harm than good, and efforts were made to remove juveniles from adult facilities. The movement toward the separate processing of juveniles culminated in a separate juvenile court in 1899. Although there have always been provisions to allow for the transfer of certain juveniles to adult court, transfer was rarely used.

Between 1960 and 1975, the juvenile crime rate increased by 140 percent compared with an increase of only 13 percent for adults, and juvenile offenders were perceived as becoming more serious and violent offenders. In addition, studies produced negative evaluations of juvenile rehabilitation programs, and many people began to question the effectiveness of the juvenile justice system. The combination of fear of serious juvenile crime and the inability of the juvenile justice system to deter it led to a conservative "get tough" position emphasizing retribution and punishment for juveniles. In response to get-tough policies, the number of juveniles prosecuted, convicted, and sentenced in the adult criminal justice system increased dramatically. Many states increasingly turned from rehabilitation to punishment and deterrence as appropriate goals for the juvenile justice system.

In general, juveniles waived to adult court are more likely to be older, to have been charged with serious offenses, to have serious prior records, and to have experienced previous juvenile incarcerations. Nearly 70 percent of juveniles convicted in criminal court are incarcerated and, for those convicted of violent offenses, nearly 80 percent are incarcerated. These numbers are much higher than those in juvenile court, where only 40 percent of convictions result in some form of incarceration. Thus it appears that the process of trying juveniles in adult court leads to a greater number of youth in jails and prisons. Who are these youths, and

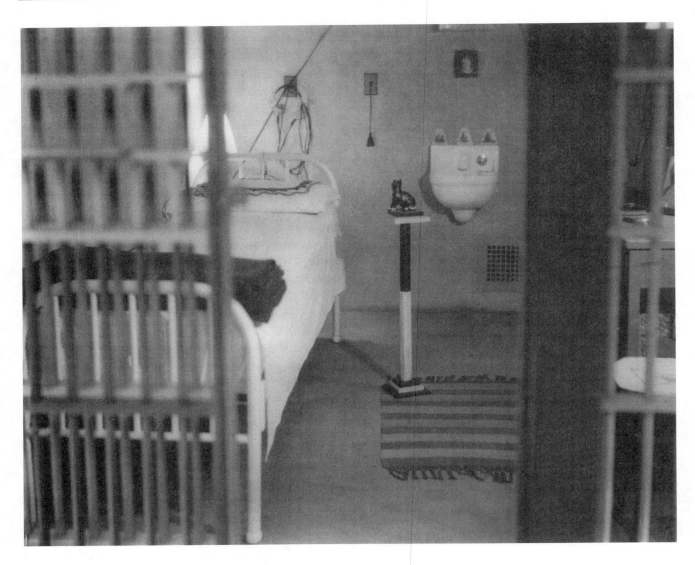

Photo 6. An Inmate Cell at Elmira, Circa 1937.
SOURCE: Correctional Photograph Archives Collection, Eastern Kentucky University Archives. Used with permission.

what are the consequences of their increased incarceration with adults?

A DESCRIPTION OF JUVENILES IN ADULT PRISONS

Since the mid-1980s, inmates under the age of 18 have consistently constituted less than 1 percent of the state prison population (Strom, 2000). However, over the last two decades, the number of juveniles held in adult jails has increased nearly 400 percent, from 1,736 in 1983 to 8,090 in 1998 (Austin, Johnson, and Gregoriou, 2000). Increases in new admissions between 1985 and 1997 were greater for juveniles (increasing by 7 percent per year) than for adults (increasing by only 5 percent per year; Strom, 2000). As expected, violent offenders accounted for most of the increase, especially those convicted of robbery and aggravated assault. In addition, the number of juvenile drug offenders admitted to state prisons increased dramatically, especially for black males.

Nearly all the juveniles held in adult prisons (97 percent) are male. By comparison, less than 80 percent of juveniles tried and sentenced in juvenile court are male. For juveniles in adult institutions, 25 percent are white and 58 percent are African American.

Almost three quarters of all juveniles in adult facilities are 17 years of age or older. Inmates in juvenile institutions are typically younger (only 18 percent are 17 or older). A majority of youths in adult facilities (61 percent) were sentenced for violent offenses compared with only 22 percent of inmates in juvenile institutions. Based on these statistics, juvenile inmates in adult institutions are more likely than their counterparts in juvenile facilities to be older minority males who were sentenced for violent offenses. Additionally, juveniles convicted in adult court are more likely to be incarcerated and to receive longer sentences than are those sentenced in juvenile court. However, the actual time served in adult prison is shorter than the possible punishment available in the juvenile system (assuming the juvenile is kept until the maximum discharge age).

CONSEQUENCES OF HOUSING JUVENILES IN ADULT PRISONS

In *Kent v. U.S.* (383 U.S. 541, 1966), the Supreme Court recognized the consequences of judicial transfer for juveniles, including lengthy incarceration and abuse in adult prisons. In 1967, the President's Commission on Law Enforcement and Administration of Justice recommended separate systems, or facilities, be established for juveniles and adults. Despite court rulings and government suggestions, juveniles are often held in the same facilities as adults. Many states have passed new regulations enabling the shared use of nonresidential areas, so juveniles and adults in the same facilities are not necessarily kept strictly separate. In most states, juveniles are housed with the general adult population. Fewer than 10 states house juveniles with youthful offenders (those up to the age of 21 or 25). Austin et al. (2000) reported that nearly 90 percent of adult institutions in the United States house juvenile offenders, but only 13 percent of them provide separate facilities or units for youthful offenders.

Management and Treatment Issues

Adult institutions expose juveniles to a vastly different environment than do juvenile institutions in terms of organization and management orientation, staffing and programming, and makeup of the inmate population. Adult prisons are generally larger than juvenile institutions, with an average daily population of 700 inmates compared with an average of only 70 in juvenile facilities. About 10 percent of juvenile institutions and nearly 20 percent of adult institutions have significant overcrowding problems.

The management orientation of juvenile and adult institutions also differs. Adult prisons emphasize punishment and retribution; their primary concern is controlling inmates. About two thirds of the personnel in adult facilities are custody or security staff. On the other hand, juvenile facilities place greater emphasis on rehabilitation and treatment. Their staff members are generally trained in counseling, with pay and promotion scales partially determined by services provided to inmates. Because of these contradictory goals, the adult prison experience for juveniles tends to be more severe than that of the juvenile system. In addition, there is evidence that the rehabilitative institutional climate seen in juvenile institutions is more likely to produce positive behavioral change than is the more custody-oriented approach seen in adult prisons.

An additional consequence of housing juvenile and adult offenders together is higher rates of misconduct. Age is one of the strongest predictors of misconduct in prison, and younger inmates have more frequent disciplinary offenses. In their analysis of misconduct among juvenile and adult inmates, McShane and Williams (1989) found that juveniles were less likely to have work assignments or earn good time and were more likely to be in more restrictive custody. Juveniles were about twice as likely to be problem inmates. While juvenile inmates may enter prison with shorter sentences, their adjustment and misconduct problems may result in the loss of good time, thus they may be in prison longer than adults with comparable sentences.

Juveniles admitted to adult institutions also receive fewer rehabilitative, medical, mental health, educational, and vocational services than do those in the juvenile system. Where education is concerned, Bishop (2000) reported that most juvenile institutions have a ratio of one teacher for every 15 inmates; between 75 and 100 percent of inmates are involved in educational programs. In adult facilities, the teacher-inmate ratio is much higher (about 1:100), and fewer than half of the inmates participate in academic programming. Juvenile institutions also appear to provide more counseling services with an average ratio of one counselor for every 25 inmates (Bishop, 2000). In adult prisons, the ratio of noncustodial staff is also one for every 25 inmates, but this includes medical and classification staff in addition to counselors.

The inmate population is also vastly different in adult institutions. Sending juveniles to adult prison exposes them to a population of inmates who are older, are physically larger and stronger, have longer criminal records, and have prior experience with incarceration. Because juveniles tend to serve longer sentences in adult prisons than they do in juvenile facilities, this exposure obviously occurs over an extended period of time. Potential consequences include a higher risk of victimization and suicide and greater exposure to the criminal influence of veteran offenders.

The suicide rate for juveniles in adult jails is lower than the rate for the adult population but nearly eight times higher than the rate for those in juvenile institutions (Austin et al., 2000). In addition to higher suicide rates, about one third of youth in adult institutions report being victims of assaults involving weapons compared with 25 percent of those in juvenile facilities (Bishop, 2000). Austin et al. reported that, in 1988, almost half the juveniles incarcerated in adult institutions suffered violent victimization. Sexual assault victimization is also five times more likely for juveniles in adult institutions compared with those held in juvenile facilities.

In addition to the increased likelihood of victimization, juveniles in adult prisons are exposed to other adult inmates with lengthy criminal records and prior incarcerations. While staff are able to provide close supervision in juvenile institutions, they are more distant in adult institutions. The higher ratio of inmates to staff and the physical construction of adult prisons increase the opportunities for private interaction between inmates. Thus juveniles have more opportunities for criminal socialization in adult prisons.

In interviews with juvenile inmates in both juvenile and adult facilities, Smith, Usinger-Lesquereux, and Evans (1992) found that the adult prison environment is perceived as significantly less positive than the juvenile system. Because of their youth and vulnerability, adolescents are more likely to be placed in protective custody, where they are isolated from others and are typically unable to participate in programs or recreation (Bishop, 2000). Bishop found that more than half the inmates in juvenile institutions were confident in their ability to become law-abiding citizens upon release. Only one third of the juveniles in adult prisons felt the same way.

RESOLVING THE PROBLEMS OF HOUSING JUVENILES IN ADULT PRISONS

Evans (1992) argued that while transferring juveniles to adult court and punishing them as adults may decrease the immediate risk to society through incapacitation, those who serve their sentences in adult prisons may pose a greater threat when they are released. Between 1985 and 1994, the number of juvenile cases transferred to adult court increased 71 percent, but research indicates that this increase did not deter crime. In fact, juvenile offenders tried and sentenced in adult court are more likely to reoffend after their release. Evans emphasized the importance of balancing rehabilitation, control, and punishment.

A task force looking at the juvenile justice system in Minnesota concluded that a more graduated transition between the juvenile and adult systems was needed. As a result, Minnesota developed the prototype for current blended sentencing strategies, or efforts to combine the juvenile ideal of rehabilitation with society's demand for accountability. The goal of blended sentencing is mainly deterrence, providing juveniles with one last chance at rehabilitation while threatening the use of adult sanctions if they fail to conform. The original Minnesota model gives violent juveniles both a juvenile sentence and a stayed adult sentence. If the offender complies with the requirements of the juvenile sentence and shows evidence of rehabilitation, the adult sentence and record may be suspended. If, however, the offender violates the juvenile sentence, the adult sentence may be invoked and the youth may be transferred to an adult correctional institution. This basic model has also been implemented in Connecticut and Montana.

Alternative sentence-blending strategies have also been developed. However, some of the models fail to adhere to the original intention. Models that provide a juvenile sentence with the threat of adult sanctions, as in the original Minnesota model, appear to be the most promising strategies. In fact, early results from Minnesota found that in its first 20 months, only 12 percent of the sentenced juveniles had violated their juvenile sentences and been transferred to adult prisons. Though there are no available studies of sentence blending, there is some early indication that strategies faithful to the original goal may reduce recidivism and violence without the immediate consequences of sending juveniles to the adult correctional system.

Leana C. Allen

See also Juvenile Justice and Delinquency Prevention Act of 1974; Waiver to Adult Court

Bibliography

Austin, J., K. D. Johnson, and M. Gregariou. 2000. *Juveniles in Adult Prisons and Jails: A National Assessment.* Washington, DC: Bureau of Justice Assistance.

Bishop, D. M. 2000. Juvenile offenders in the adult criminal justice system. *Crime and Justice* 27:81–167.

Forst, M., J. Fagan, and T. S. Vivona. 1989. Youth in prisons and training schools: Perceptions and consequences of the treatment-custody dichotomy. *Juvenile and Family Court Journal* 2:1–14.

McShane, M. D., and F. P. Williams. 1989. The prison adjustment of juvenile offenders. *Crime and Delinquency* 35:254–269.

Smith, M., J. Usinger-Lesquereux, and W. Evans. 1992. Rural juvenile first offenders describe what is working and what is not. *International Journal of Offender Therapy and Comparative Criminology* 43(3): 322–337.

Strom, K. J. 2000. *Profile of State Prisoners Under Age 18, 1985–97.* Washington, DC: Bureau of Justice Statistics.

K

KOBRIN, SOLOMON
(1910–1996)

Solomon Kobrin was a pioneer in the study of juvenile delinquency. He was born in Chicago and earned his bachelor's and master's degrees at the University of Chicago in 1937 and 1939, respectively. His Ph.D. was in sociology from the University of Southern California in 1972.

His professional and research activity was strongly influenced by the Chicago School of sociology, which had a major impact on the study of crime and juvenile delinquency in the early part of the 20th century. In the 1920s, under the leadership of Robert Park and Ernest Burgess, members and students of the Department of Sociology at the University of Chicago conducted a series of studies concerning the urban problems of the emerging American metropolis. A focus of their research was the increasing level of crime and, especially, juvenile delinquency. One of the classic works from this era was Frederic Thrasher's book *The Gang* (1927/1963). During the same period, Clifford R. Shaw and Henry D. McKay of the Chicago Institute for Juvenile Research, in cooperation with the University of Chicago, were also conducting research on juvenile delinquency in the city.

After receiving his master's degree, Kobrin started working as a research assistant at the Institute for Juvenile Research. He continued his association with the institute and in 1960 became head of the Division of Social Systems Analysis. In 1965, he received a National Institute of Mental Health Fellowship and relocated to the University of Southern California in

Los Angeles. While he was working on his Ph.D. at the Department of Sociology, he became a faculty member and a research associate in the Youth Studies Center and the Public Systems Institute of the university. In 1977, in recognition of his professional contribution to the study of juvenile delinquency, he was the recipient of the Edwin H. Sutherland Award of the American Society of Criminology, a scholarly organization that honors outstanding contributions to the discipline.

Throughout his long research career, Kobrin has focused on the study of juvenile delinquency. His first two major articles, "The Conflict of Values in Delinquency Areas" (1951) and "The Chicago Area Project: A 25-Year Assessment" (1959), became classics within the criminological literature. These articles were written in the theoretical framework of the social disorganization approach to the study of juvenile delinquency. This theory was developed by Shaw and McKay following the ecological orientation of the Chicago School and suggested that most slum neighborhoods in large urban areas are characterized by the breakdown of conventional institutions and social control. This atmosphere frees individuals, especially juveniles, to behave in ways disapproved of by the dominant social order and eventually leads to the development of cultural values favorable to delinquent behavior.

Kobrin continued to follow his research interest in juvenile delinquency among youth in slum areas. During the 1960s, he published a series of articles and book chapters on gang members, gang structure, cultural factors and delinquency, and drug use among young people in Chicago. In addition to his empirical research dealing with lower-class juvenile delinquency, Kobrin was also interested in theoretical issues concerning this topic. In a widely cited book chapter titled "The Formal Logical Properties of the Shaw-McKay Delinquency Theory" (1971), he applied principles of formal theory construction and pointed out some of the weaknesses of social disorganization theory. In a 1976 volume originally prepared for a symposium honoring Henry D. McKay, Kobrin contributed another theoretical chapter focusing on the limits and problems of labeling theory. A few years later (1982), he wrote another chapter dealing with theory development entitled "The Uses of the Life-History Document for the Development of Delinquency Theory."

After moving to the University of Southern California in 1967, Kobrin also continued his involvement in empirical research, focusing mainly on juvenile delinquency in urban areas and program evaluation of delinquency and crime-control programs. One of the most notable projects he conducted, together with Malcolm W. Klein, was a national evaluation of a federal project on the deinstitutionalization of status offenders. This large-scale study funded by the National Institute of Juvenile Justice and Delinquency Prevention led to the publication of *Community Treatment of Juvenile Offenders: The DSO Experiments* (coauthored with Klein). He also coauthored a book chapter (1980) dealing with the offense patterns of status offenders based on this project.

In the 1980s, Kobrin conducted research on the early correlates of the careers of violent offenders. His last major research project to gain national attention was a longitudinal study of Los Angeles County neighborhoods with the highest crime rates. The intent of the study was to understand how urban neighborhoods evolve into high crime areas. While this project considered various social indicators, some of the variables explored were directly related to juveniles and juvenile delinquency. To a large degree, this project was a continuation of Kobrin's community-oriented research from the early years of his career in Chicago. A book chapter on this project was coauthored with Leo Schuerman. At the time of his death, Kobrin was working on a book based on this research.

In addition to the publications cited, Kobrin presented numerous papers at professional conventions. He received grants from federal, state, and local agencies to conduct research on crime and juvenile delinquency issues and submitted research reports to these agencies. During his career, he was also a consultant to the U.S. Department of Health Education and Welfare (HEW) and chaired the HEW Task Force on Youth Development and Delinquency Prevention Administration (1973). He served on the Advisory Board for the Evaluation of Addict-Treatment Centers for the U.S. Office of Economic Opportunity (1971) and as a member of the President's Committee on Law Enforcement and the Administration of Justice (1965 to 1966). On the state level, he was a consultant to the California Council on Criminal Justice and for various agencies and research projects. Kobrin also served as President of the Illinois Academy of Criminology (1958) and later as President of the California Association for Criminal Justice Research (1975). His impact on juvenile delinquency theory and research and his reputation as a leading expert on these fields of study are well established.

David Shichor

See also Theories of Delinquency—Sociological

Bibliography

Kobrin, S. 1951. The conflict of values in delinquency areas. *American Sociological Review* 16:653–661.

Kobrin, S. 1959. The Chicago Area Project: A 25-year assessment. *Annals of the American Academy of Political and Social Science* 322:19–92.

Kobrin, S. 1971. The formal logical properties of the Shaw-McKay delinquency theory. Pp. 101–132 in H. Voss and D. Petersen (eds.), *Ecology, Crime, and Delinquency*. New York: Appleton-Century-Crofts.

Kobrin, S. 1980. The uses of the life-history document for the development of delinquency theory. In D. Shichor and D. Kelly (eds.), *Critical Issues in Juvenile Delinquency*. Lexington, MA: Lexington Books.

Snodgrass, J. 1982. *The Jack-Roller at Seventy*. Lexington, MA: D. C. Heath.

L

LAW, JUVENILE

Until the late 1800s, juveniles who committed crimes in this country received the same treatment from the criminal justice system as did adults. The criminal justice system generally did not distinguish between adults and children, although minors were accorded the defense of infancy. Under the infancy defense, children under the age of 7 were conclusively presumed incapable of criminal responsibility. Children between the ages of 7 and 14 were presumed to lack criminal capacity, and a child defendant could be punished only if the prosecution showed that the child knew and understood the consequences of his or her act.

In addition to the defense of infancy, juveniles were also accorded some degree of leniency by the legal system with respect to the punishments imposed. Nonetheless, juveniles were not exempt from the type of punishments imposed on adults for criminal behavior. They were not even excluded from the death penalty. Twenty-two executions have been documented between 1642 and 1899 for crimes committed by juveniles under the age of 16.

THE BEGINNINGS OF JUVENILE LAW

Society's treatment of juveniles was transformed beginning in the late 1800s. In 1899, the Illinois legislature established the first juvenile court of Cook County. From the juvenile court statute adopted in Illinois, the juvenile court system has spread to every state in the union, the District of Columbia, and Puerto Rico. The juvenile court system was designed to handle the punishment and rehabilitation of juveniles.

Juvenile courts were rooted in social welfare philosophy. The early reformers were appalled by adult procedures and penalties and by the fact that children could be given long prison sentences and mixed in jails with hardened criminals. Reformers saw the need for a nonpunitive *parens patriae* alternative to the criminal justice system for juvenile criminal offenders. The court proceedings were designated as civil rather than criminal. The objectives were to provide measures of guidance and rehabilitation for the child and protection for society, not to fix criminal responsibility, guilt, and punishment.

Most states prohibited the prosecution of juveniles for crimes, except when permission was granted by juvenile courts. Juvenile court jurisdiction was not limited to merely criminal behavior; instead, juvenile courts were authorized to handle status offenses, which involved noncriminal behavior deemed harmful or inappropriate. In exercising their role, juvenile courts were not concerned with procedural rules employed in traditional criminal courts. Indeed, procedural protections were deemed counterproductive in trying to rehabilitate juveniles and to fashion a remedy that was appropriate to the individual needs of a particular child. Children, unlike adults, had a right to custody, not to liberty. Juvenile courts were permitted to act as they deemed appropriate in their *parens patriae* role. Reliance was placed on social workers, probation officers, psychologists, psychiatrists, and physicians in providing information to the juvenile court in assessing and treating the needs of an individual child.

SUPREME COURT DECISIONS

The unfettered discretion of juvenile courts eventually began to erode. Courts began to question the practices of juvenile courts during the same period of time that the judicial system was vigorously enforcing the rights of defendants in criminal cases. The U.S. Supreme Court began scrutinizing the practices of the juvenile courts in the 1960s. The first significant case was *Kent v. U.S.* (1966).

Kent v. United States

The *Kent* case concerned the practices of juvenile courts in the District of Columbia. Morris Kent was placed on probation by the juvenile court when he was 14 years old. In 1961, an intruder entered a woman's apartment and raped her. The police found fingerprints belonging to Morris Kent, who was then 16 years old. Kent was taken into custody, interrogated by police, and detained for almost a week without an arraignment or a judicial determination of probable cause.

His mother retained an attorney, who contacted the social services director of the juvenile court. The attorney hired two psychiatrists and a psychologist, who determined that Kent was a "victim of severe psychopathology" and needed psychiatric care. At that point, Kent's attorney made known his opposition to the juvenile court waiving jurisdiction. The juvenile court, however, waived jurisdiction without a hearing or explanation. The juvenile court never conferred with Kent or his parents. Kent was tried in the criminal courts and convicted on six counts with a total range of punishment between 30 and 90 years in prison.

His attorney challenged the juvenile court's waiver of jurisdiction in this case, along with the failure to accord Kent basic constitutional rights that adults are entitled to receive. The Supreme Court decided to pass on the issue of Kent's constitutional rights, but the case was remanded because of the juvenile court's waiver of jurisdiction. The Supreme Court held that the waiver was invalid. Acknowledging that juvenile courts have considerable latitude when dealing with children, the Court stressed that such latitude is not complete. The governmental exercise of *parens patriae* was not an invitation to procedural arbitrariness. Citing District of Columbia statutory law and constitutional principles of due process, the Supreme Court held that Kent was entitled to a hearing before the juvenile court waived jurisdiction and that he was entitled to a statement of reasons for the juvenile court's decision.

In re Gault

The *Kent* case occurred in the District of Columbia and involved, in large part, federal statutory law. There was some question whether *Kent* would have any impact on state juvenile justice systems. The Supreme Court quickly settled these questions in deciding *In re Gault* in 1967.

Gerald Francis Gault was a 15-year-old who had been committed to the State Industrial School by a juvenile court in Arizona. He was on six months' probation when Mrs. Cook, a neighbor, made a verbal complaint that she had received a telephone call in which the caller or callers made lewd and indecent remarks. Gerald was picked up by police when both parents were at work. No notice was left that he was taken into custody. His parents sent his older brother out to look for him after they came home from work. A neighbor informed the Gault family that Gerald had been taken into custody.

On the following day, June 9, 1964, the arresting officer filed a formal petition, and a hearing was conducted. Gerald's parents did not receive a copy of the petition until more than two months later. The petition was entirely formal. It made no reference to any factual basis for the judicial action. It merely said that "said minor is under the age of eighteen years, and is in need of the protection of this Honorable Court; [and that] said minor is a delinquent minor." The hearing was conducted before a juvenile judge. Gerald's father was not there since he was working in another city. Mrs. Cook, the complainant, was not there. No one was sworn at the hearing. No transcript or recording was made. No memorandum or record was prepared.

The Supreme Court noted that the information that it had about the hearing came solely from the testimony of the juvenile judge, Mrs. Gault, and the arresting officer at a habeas corpus hearing more than two months later. There was conflicting testimony, and Gerald purportedly admitted making one of the lewd statements. Gerald was temporarily kept in a detention facility while the juvenile judge decided he would "think about it."

A second hearing was conducted on June 15. This time both parents, another juvenile and his father, and two officers were present. Mrs. Cook was not present. The arresting officer agreed that Gerald never admitted making a lewd comment, although the juvenile judge recalled at the habeas corpus hearing that Gerald made "some admission." At the conclusion of the hearing, Gerald was committed to the State Industrial School. No appeal was permitted under Arizona law, thus the parents filed a petition for a writ of habeas corpus. The Arizona Supreme Court affirmed the denial of relief concluding that the Arizona Juvenile Code "impliedly" implements due process and the commitment proceedings did not violate due process.

The U.S. Supreme Court disagreed. The Court noted that neither the due process clause of the Fourteenth Amendment nor the Bill of Rights is for adults alone. The Court also noted that the right of the state, as *parens patriae*, in dealing with juveniles was the product of the highest motives and most enlightened impulses as a means to correct the appalling procedures and penalties employed in adult criminal courts. The Court held, however, that the constitutional and theoretical bases for the juvenile system were debatable and that the results had not been entirely satisfactory.

The Court further noted that the "condition of being a boy does not justify a kangaroo court." The Supreme Court limited its decision to the procedures discussed by the Arizona Supreme Court and concluded that, contrary to the decision by the Arizona Supreme Court, a juvenile has a right to notice of charges; a right to counsel, confrontation, and cross-examination of witnesses; and to the privilege against self-incrimination.

In re Winship

The Supreme Court's next significant decision was decided three years later in *In re Winship* (1970). The Court was concerned with the standard to employ in determining whether a juvenile was a delinquent. New York law defined a juvenile delinquent as a person older than 7 years and younger than 16 years of age who does any act that, if done by an adult, would constitute a crime. New York law also provided that any determination at the conclusion of a hearing that a juvenile did an act or acts must be based on the preponderance of the evidence.

Samuel Winship was 12 years old when he was found to have entered a locker and stolen $112 from a woman's pocketbook. He was placed in a training school, and under New York law, he could be kept there until his 18th birthday. The case focused on the

issue of whether a finding of delinquency had to be based on the preponderance of the evidence or beyond a reasonable doubt. Justice Brennan, writing for the majority, noted that the due process clause of the Fourteenth Amendment requires that the "essentials of due process and fair treatment" be employed during the adjudicatory stage when a juvenile is charged with an act that would constitute a crime if committed by an adult. He also noted that the higher standard of beyond a reasonable doubt had been used in adult proceedings throughout the history of this country. The reasonable doubt standard plays a vital role in the American scheme of criminal procedure.

The Court rejected the argument that to afford juveniles the protection of proof beyond a reasonable doubt would risk destruction of beneficial aspects of the juvenile process. The Court held that when a child is charged with stealing, which could place her or him in confinement for as long as 6 years, then due process requires that the case against the child be proved beyond a reasonable doubt.

Further Extension of Rights to Children in Court Proceedings

The Supreme Court has not extended all the rights of defendants in adult proceedings to children in juvenile court proceedings. A year after the *Winship* decision, the Supreme Court held that juveniles are not entitled to jury trials in *McKeiver v. Pennsylvania* (1971). Four years later, however, the Court extended another constitutional right involving the double jeopardy clause to juvenile proceedings in *Breed v. Jones* (1975).

In this case, a California juvenile court found that Gary Jones had committed acts that, if committed by an adult, would constitute the crime of robbery. Days later, Jones was found unfit for treatment as a juvenile. The juvenile court ordered that he be prosecuted as an adult. He was found guilty of the offense of robbery in a California criminal court. The sole question before the U.S. Supreme Court concerned whether the juvenile proceedings triggered the protection of the double jeopardy clause. The Supreme Court again noted that the juvenile court system had its genesis in the desire to provide a distinctive procedure and setting to deal with the problems of youth. The Court also noted, however, that there has been a gap between the originally benign conception of the system and its realities.

The Court held that it was too late in the day to conclude that Jones was not placed in jeopardy at the juvenile proceedings, whose purpose was to determine whether Jones had committed acts that violated a criminal law and whose consequences included the possibility of a loss of liberty for many years. The Court concluded that Jones had been subjected to two trials for the same offense. The Supreme Court vacated the adult conviction and remanded the case to California with the option of either setting him free or remanding him to juvenile court for disposition.

In *Schall v. Martin* (1984), the Supreme Court was concerned with the standard employed in New York for the pretrial detention of juveniles. The Court held that pretrial detention of juveniles based on the finding that there was a "serious risk" that the juvenile "may before the return date commit an act which if committed by an adult would constitute a crime" did not violate the due process clause.

OTHER CONSTITUTIONAL RIGHTS OF JUVENILES

Apart from juvenile court proceedings, the treatment of juveniles has been the subject of other U.S. Supreme Court cases involving the application of the Constitution. *Ingraham v. Wright* (1977) concerned whether the use of corporal punishment in public schools violated the cruel and unusual punishment clause of the Eighth Amendment. Florida statutes authorized corporal punishment after a teacher had consulted with the principal or teacher in charge of the school, and the punishment was not to be "degrading or unduly severe." The Supreme Court initially noted that the use of corporal punishment in this country as a means of disciplining schoolchildren dates back to the colonial period. It has survived the changes in education over the centuries. Even though public opinion is sharply divided on the practice, the Supreme Court could not discern any trend toward its elimination. The Court went on to note that the cruel and unusual punishment clause of the Eighth Amendment was designed to protect those convicted of crimes. The Court held that it does not apply to the paddling of children as a means of discipline in public school. The Court also held that the due process clause does not require notice and hearing before the imposition of corporal punishment.

The applicability of the cruel and unusual punishment clause has also been the subject of Supreme Court cases concerning the imposition of the death penalty for juveniles. In *Thompson v. Oklahoma*

(1988), the Supreme Court was concerned with the execution of a juvenile who was 15 years old when he committed murder. The decision was a sharply divided 5-to-3 opinion. The majority of the Court stressed that the Eighth Amendment prohibits the infliction of cruel and unusual punishment. The Court noted that the authors of the amendment did not define the contours of the prohibition and delegated that task to future generations, who will be guided by the "evolving standards of decency that mark the progress of a maturing society." The Court also noted that there is near unanimity of the states in classifying a person under 16 years old as a minor and treating him or her differently from adults. The majority of the Court concluded that it offends civilized standards of decency to execute a person who was under 16 at the time of the commission of the offense.

Justice Scalia, who was joined by Chief Justice Rehnquist and Justice White, wrote a dissenting opinion. He argued that the applicability of the cruel and unusual punishment clause must be determined by examining how it was understood at the time the Eighth Amendment was adopted. He noted that Blackstone's Commentaries on the Laws of England, published in 1769, specified that the imposition of the death penalty for 14- and 15-year-old defendants was widely accepted. One scholar had documented 22 executions between 1642 and 1899 for offenses committed by persons under the age of 16. In light of the original understanding of what was "cruel and unusual punishment" at the time the Eighth Amendment was adopted, Justice Scalia concluded that the execution of a person who was only 15 at the time of the commission of the offense is not prohibited by the Eighth Amendment.

The Supreme Court revisited the issue the following year in *Stanford v. Kentucky* (1989). The Court was again sharply divided with a 5-to-4 vote. This time, however, Justice Scalia wrote the opinion for the majority. He concluded that the Eighth Amendment did not prohibit the execution of people who were 16 or 17 at the time of the commission of the offense. The difference in the two decisions was primarily the product of the way Justice O'Connor voted. In *Thompson*, she specified that a juvenile may be executed only if the state statute specifies a minimum age at which the commission of a capital crime can lead to the offender's execution. In *Stanford*, she concluded that the death penalty should not be set aside since there is no consensus forbidding the imposition of capital punishment on 16- and 17-year-old capital murderers.

CONCLUSION

The U.S. Supreme Court has been somewhat skeptical about permitting states on the basis of *parens patriae* to deprive juveniles of basic constitutional rights. Indeed, the Court has required juvenile courts to honor such rights in juvenile proceedings. The contours of such rights have been established for several years, and the Supreme Court has not issued any significant cases concerning the rights of juveniles since the 1980s. It must, nonetheless, be noted that the Supreme Court has permitted states to treat juveniles differently to some degree. States have been permitted to continue using a unique juvenile justice system for dealing with juvenile offenders, as long as the provisions in the juvenile laws do not transgress the basic constitutional rights of all people. In recent years, there have been some calls to divest the juvenile courts of delinquency jurisdiction and to have a unified criminal court system for all adults and children, although that alternative has not yet been implemented because there is some consensus that children are different and should be treated as such.

Jon R. Farrar

See also Child-Saving Movement; Courts, Juvenile; National Council of Juvenile and Family Court Judges; *Parens Patriae* Doctrine; Waiver to Adult Court

Bibliography

Gardner, M. R. 1997. *Understanding Juvenile Law.* New York: Matthew Bender.

Rosenberg, I. M. 2000. Teen violence and the juvenile courts: A plea for reflection and restraint. *Houston Law Review* 37:75–96.

Shepherd, R. E. 2000. The "child" grows up: The juvenile justice system enters its second century. *Family Law Quarterly* 33:589–605.

Streib, V. 1983. Death penalty for children: The American experience with capital punishment for crimes committed while under eighteen. *Oklahoma Law Review* 36:613–639.

Case Citations

Breed v. Jones, 421 U.S. 519, 95 S.Ct. 1779, 44 L.Ed.2d 346 (1975).

Ingraham v. Wright, 430 U.S. 651, 97 S.Ct. 1401, 51 L.Ed.2d 711 (1977).

In re Gault, 387 U.S. 1, 87 S.Ct. 1428, 18 L.Ed.2d 527 (1967).

In re Winship, 397 U.S. 358, 90 S.Ct. 1068, 25 L.Ed.2d 368 (1970).

Kent v. United States, 383 U.S. 541, 86 S.Ct. 1045, 16 L.Ed.2d 84 (1966).

McKeiver v. Pennsylvania, 403 U.S. 528 (1971).

Schall v. Martin, 467 U.S. 253, 104 S.Ct. 2403, 81 L.Ed.2d 207 (1984).

Stanford v. Kentucky, 492 U.S. 361, 109 S.Ct. 2969, 106 L.Ed.2d 306 (1989).

Thompson v. Oklahoma, 487 U.S. 815, 108 S.Ct. 2687, 101 L.Ed.2d 702 (1988).

LEARNING DISABILITIES

Compared with other explanations for delinquency, learning disabilities form a more recent area of exploration. Although the literature suggests that learning disabilities and juvenile delinquency are related, the nature of this relationship is neither strongly confirmed nor clearly described.

Since its development in 1963, the concept of *learning disabilities* has been defined differently by schools (varying by state), lawmakers, and mental health practitioners—so much so that a child may be "cured" by simply going from one state to another. This ambiguity is the major obstacle for researchers interested in examining the alleged connection between learning disabilities (LD) and juvenile delinquency (JD).

EXTENT OF LEARNING DISABILITIES

Among students at public schools (from which many delinquents come), it is estimated that 5 percent have learning disabilities. While it has long been established that school failure (especially in reading) is common among juvenile delinquents, the possible variance for which learning disabilities may be responsible is yet unknown. One problem is that many juvenile offenders are not screened for disabilities when apprehended. However, from the juveniles who are, it appears that youngsters with learning disabilities are overrepresented among those adjudicated delinquent. From these sketchy data, delinquents with learning disabilities represent about 32 percent to 36 percent of those adjudicated delinquent.

In the broadest sense, learning disabilities involve a marked and chronic discrepancy between a person's *intellect* and *achievement*. Usually, in diagnosing the condition, there will be an attempt to rule out the influence of the following:

1. Poor schooling (if others similarly situated seem to be doing well).

2. Mental retardation (if the juvenile has an IQ score greater than 70 to 85).

3. Illnesses or medication that might affect learning.

4. Impaired vision and/or hearing.

5. Comprehension problems related to having English as a second language.

6. Cultural influences.

7. Economic disadvantages.

8. The effects of absenteeism (an indication of the juvenile's motivation).

The most problematic aspect of constructing a uniform definition of *learning disabilities* to work with has been in measuring the level of achievement that an individual should possess, given a certain level of intelligence. For the most part, a standard test for measuring intelligence is the Wechsler Intelligence Scale for Children–Revised (WISC-R), for which a score above 70 (which rules out mental retardation) would be compared with a person's actual academic achievement. However, there is no standard measure for achievement. Expected achievement per grade level varies from state to state and so do the instruments that measure achievement. For example, California schools may use the California Achievement Test (CAT) while New York schools may use the Regents test.

ORIGINS OF LEARNING DISABILITIES

Also problematic in the standardization of learning disabilities is the controversy regarding their origin. There are eight main theoretical positions on the cause of learning disorders: reproductive causality, genetics, brain anatomical variations, developmental or acquired brain damage, biochemical factors, traumatic experiences, faulty teaching, and an impaired home experience.

Theories of reproductive causalities state that there are environmental factors in the pre- and postnatal periods of development that lead to learning disabilities (for example, maternal-fetal blood type incompatibility, an infant's shortage of oxygen during birth, and substance abuse during pregnancy). Genetic theories focus on dyslexia. These theories are based on family and twin studies indicating that many juveniles with reading problems also have family members with similar problems. Brain anatomical variation theories have a basic premise that learning disabilities are the result of symmetry in the temporal lobes. Normally, the left lobe is larger than the right. In LD individuals, although the left lobe is not necessarily smaller than usual, the right lobe is larger than usual, which impairs the ability to analyze stimuli related to learning and interactions.

Other theories state that developmental or acquired brain damage from nervous or infectious diseases (such as encephalitis and meningitis), accidents, poisoning from substance abuse, or continuous malnutrition leads to learning disabilities. Indeed, it is believed that in some persons, poor nutrition may even intensify not only learning disabilities but also hyperactivity and a tendency toward violence and/or substance abuse. Biochemical theories focus on the effects of metabolic substances on the brain; for example, the effects of hyperglycemia, allergies, and lead poisoning.

Other theoretical positions claim that learning disabilities are not biological at all. Instead they claim that LD is the result of either a behavioral adjustment to a traumatic experience or prolonged stress (for example, the death of a parent or continued neglect by a parent); poor teaching, which leads a child with minor learning problems to achieve at the level of a child with severe learning problems (such as mental retardation); or an impaired home environment. In the case of poor teaching, this may simply be the result of an incompatibility between the child's learning style and the teacher's techniques. This perspective suggests that increases in delinquency mirror the decline in quality public education in those locations from which most delinquents come. Where an impaired home environment is concerned, such theories state that learning disabilities may be a behavioral manifestation of home-related stress (for example, a child who is unable to meet high parental expectations despite his or her best efforts in a chaotic family environment).

VARIANCE IN THE NATURE OF LEARNING DISABILITY CASES

There are four basic types of learning disabilities—*dyscalculia* (problems with numerical calculations), *dysgraphia* (problems with writing and spelling), *dyslexia* (problems with reading, as letters appear jumbled), and a combination of the previous types. The severity of the disability varies from person to person. Often, an LD condition might be masked by the presence of a coexisting attention deficit hyperactivity disorder (ADHD) condition. This coexistence of LD and ADHD ranges from 10 percent to 92 percent in the general population. The larger percentages are attributable to the use of liberal definitions for learning disabilities.

Where LD and ADHD coexist, it becomes more difficult to say which disorder may be more responsible for delinquent behavior. Regardless, it is widely accepted that individuals with a more severe LD condition have an increased likelihood of evoking negative responses from others because of their difficulty in comprehending subtle social cues. These individuals are more susceptible to being misled as they attempt to "fit in" with peers. After experiencing social rejection from conventional peers, the LD juvenile may be easily led by the promises of false friends. These LD juveniles, lacking in the verbal finesse to defend themselves, are then more likely to be the ones caught and adjudicated delinquent.

When both hyperactivity and LD are present in a child, the family may serve as the most important moderator in determining whether or not the presence of a learning disability results in delinquency. In low-income families where resources are so limited that access to preventive intervention is rare, the likelihood of delinquency increases. Significantly, girls manifest fewer accompanying behavior problems than boys. As a result, in girls, the disorder often goes undiagnosed.

THEORIES OF LEARNING DISABILITIES AND JUVENILE DELINQUENCY

There are three main theories on a possible LD/JD relationship: school failure rationale, susceptibility theory, and the differential treatment theory.

School Failure Rationale

The school failure rationale states that learning disabilities can lead to academic failure, which in turn can lead to peer rejection. Peer rejection fosters a sense of powerlessness in LD children, who then begin to see themselves as the subjects of injustice in a school system that denies them the opportunity to defend themselves. Thus the LD child develops a negative self-image manifested by hostility toward school and teachers. Eventually, this child becomes detached from school, is suspended, and eventually drops out. LD students account for 26.7 percent of high school dropouts; another 16 percent of dropouts leave school for "unknown reasons."

Recent revisions of this theory address the negative secondary effects from initial school failure. Once that initial failure occurs, students may then find themselves on the receiving end of a "watered-down education." Of course, this leads to further academic weakness—a grave travesty because many LD children are actually very intelligent but simply take in information differently from their non-LD peers. Children who are busy excelling in school are far less likely to be engaged in delinquency.

There is evidence that LD students report more serious delinquency and are more frequently disciplined compared with non-LD students. Students with learning disabilities are also punished more frequently for misbehavior than are mentally retarded students and those with no mental disability. Not surprisingly, LD students report feeling more alienated from school than do their mentally retarded counterparts. Relatedly, LD students tend to have more unexcused absences from school. Thus LD may predispose an individual to dropping out of school and to persistent delinquency. Perhaps the weakest area of the school failure rationale is that the empirical literature indicates that LD juveniles often hold an unrealistically high perception of themselves.

Susceptibility Theory

Another theory on a possible LD/JD relationship is Charles Murray's 1976 susceptibility theory. Susceptibility theory states that the personality characteristics of LD juveniles make them more susceptible to delinquent activities. These personality characteristics include impulsivity, an inability to anticipate consequences of actions, irritability, suggestibility, and a tendency to act out. Approximately 75 percent of LD juveniles who are the most susceptible to delinquency show a lack of impulse control, a lack of reasonable judgment, and an inability to properly anticipate the consequences of actions. Nevertheless, it is unclear whether or not such traits as "impulsivity" and a "tendency to act out" are the effects of a behavioral disorder acting in conjunction with learning disabilities rather than the latter alone.

Some variations of the theory distinguish between "pseudo-" and "true" delinquency. *Pseudodelinquency* refers to a situation in which an overly trusting LD juvenile is so eager for social acceptance that the juvenile is easily misled by false friends into breaking the law (being gullible or susceptible given her or his learning deficits). *True delinquency* refers to an LD child who, after understanding the true nature of delinquent actions, persists in them.

Although some LD juveniles have little trouble understanding concrete situations, they have social cognitive deficits that affect their comprehension of other people's expressions of emotions and intentions. Having this reduced ability to interpret overtures can provoke negative reactions. Thus if the LD child feels socially isolated, the child may assume an unassertive posture among peers in an effort to gain their acceptance. However, when LD juveniles perform well in school, they are likely to feel better about themselves and are far less desperate for the social acceptance of delinquent peers.

Differential Treatment Theory

The third major theory, differential treatment, addresses arrest, adjudication, and disposition in the juvenile justice system. This theory states that LD juveniles are overrepresented in the formal justice process because of the nature of their interactions with the system. Juveniles with learning disabilities are less skilled at getting themselves out of trouble given their linguistic and pragmatic limitations. Hence their delinquent behavior, plus their expressive deficits and a poor school record all work against them and toward amassing harsher juvenile justice treatment. Not surprisingly, LD adolescent males are thus more than twice as likely to be adjudicated delinquent than are their non-LD peers. They are also more likely to fail parole and recidivate.

CONCLUSION

To better understand the possible LD/JD relationship, the definition of the disorder must be clarified to enhance the validity, replicability, and comparability of research findings. Additionally, research reports need to be more precise in reporting exactly which learning disabilities they have examined (be it dyscalculia and/or dyslexia and/or dysgraphia). Precision is also necessary in isolating the effects of depression and/or ADHD on LD. Longitudinal studies in this area are also needed because the disorder, though chronic, appears to change over time. Regardless of these problems, there are still indications of major differences between LD juveniles who persist in delinquency and those who do not. Basically, there are pseudodelinquents (LD juveniles who are momentarily misled into delinquency) and there are true delinquents (LD juveniles who after realizing the wrongfulness of their actions choose to persist in wrongdoing). The former type is more biologically determined and the latter more sociologically determined.

Currently, much of the research addresses biological or social factors in isolated contexts, instead of the way in which microbiological traits are affected by macrosociological traits. Thus the psychological connection between the biological and the sociological influences remain a major weakness in the LD/JD theories.

Additionally, the literature indicates that academic success may positively affect behavior and peer relations (especially if there is no coexisting behavior disorder). Nonetheless, it seems that the more severe the deficit, the more frustrated and resistant the juvenile may be to change through remediation efforts.

Pertaining to the treatment of LD delinquents (in particular, those with behavior disorders), some researchers advocate a combination of medication and behavioral therapy. A concern that is often overlooked, however, is the possibility that medications for behavioral disorders (such as Ritalin) may intensify disordered thinking, including symptoms of a learning disability. Hence overall, the LD/JD association, in spite of the number of theories assuming its existence, remains weak and questionable.

Camille Gibson

See also Individuals With Disabilities Education Act; Theories of Delinquency—Psychological

Bibliography

Ariel, A. 1992. *Education of Children and Adolescents with Learning Disabilities*. New York: Macmillan.

Culliver, C., and R. Stigler. 1991. The relationship between learning disability and juvenile delinquency. *International Journal of Adolescence and Youth* 3:117–128.

Fink, C. 1990. Special education students at-risk: A comparative study of delinquency. Pp. 61–81 in P. Leone (ed.), *Understanding Troubled and Troubling Youth*. Beverly Hills, CA: Sage.

Hinshaw, S. 1992. Academic underachievement, attention deficits, and aggression: Co-morbidity and implications for intervention. Special section: Co-morbidity and treatment implications. *Journal of Consulting and Clinical Psychology* 60:893–903.

Moffitt, T. 1990. Juvenile delinquency and attention deficit disorder: Boys' developmental trajectories from age 3 to age 15. *Child Development* 61:893–910.

Pearl, R., and T. Bryan. 1990. Learning disabled adolescents' vulnerability to victimization and delinquency. Pp. 139–154 in H. Swanson and B. Keogh (eds.), *Learning Disabilities: Theoretical and Research Issues*. Mahwah, NJ: Lawrence Erlbaum.

Roush, W. 1995. Arguing over why Johnny can't read. *Science* 267:1896–1898.

Simpson, S., J. Swanson, and K. Kunkel. 1992. The impact of an intensive multisensory reading program on a population of learning disabled delinquents. *Annals of Dyslexia* 42:54–66.

Waldie, K., and O. Spreen. 1993. The relationship between learning disabilities and persisting delinquency. *Journal of Learning Disabilities* 2:417–423.

LITERATURE OF DELINQUENCY

In examining the treatment of juvenile delinquency in literature, it is possible to view fictional works in the larger context of the history of childhood and the discovery of juvenile delinquency as a social problem. However, in doing so, it is important to be aware of the various social, political, economic, and religious forces of the time that shaped the literature. Since the beginning of the 19th century, various schools of literature (e.g., romanticism and naturalism) have appeared. As well as "mainstream" literature, various genres and subgenres of literary works (e.g., children's literature, African American literature, mystery fiction) have evolved. The treatment of juvenile delinquency in literature embodies not only societal changes but also the history of literary movements in the United States and abroad.

JUVENILE DELINQUENCY IN 19TH-CENTURY LITERATURE

Before the late 19th century, the treatment of delinquency in literature did not represent a significant body of work. In the 19th century, only a few works are memorable for their portrayal of juvenile characters, such as British novelist Charles Dickens's *Oliver Twist* (1837). The novel was Dickens's searing critique of the Poor Law Amendment of 1834, which made the poor dependent on workhouses for relief. Young Oliver Twist is orphaned when his mother is abused and dies at the workhouse. When he is apprenticed to an undertaker, he runs away and falls into the clutches of Fagin, a master pickpocket. With the Artful Dodger and Fagin's other child recruits, Oliver becomes immersed in a life of crime.

In the United States, another social critic, Mark Twain, wrote *The Adventures of Tom Sawyer* (1876) and *The Adventures of Huckleberry Finn* (1885). Twain's two protagonists engage in a range of pranks and minor offenses. The most serious offense from the perspective of Southern law is arguably Huck's collusion in the temporary escape of the slave Jim. However, Twain treats this offense as behavior more moral than that of many of the adults in the novel. Both *Tom Sawyer* and *Huck Finn* are described by literary scholars as classic tales of boyhood adventure. In fact, Twain's two novels, along with Thomas Bailey Aldrich's *The Story of a Bad Boy* (1869), present protagonists who are, in critic Leslie Fiedler's phrase, "good bad boys." As Aldrich recounts in this autobiographical novel, his protagonist did not hesitate to join his peers in pranks such as stealing a decaying coach and pushing it into a bonfire during Independence Day celebrations. However, he suffers no lasting consequences for his misbehavior, nor is he particularly troubled by a guilty conscience.

The conscience of the youthful offender was a matter of concern in the literature of the early 19th century, which focused on the moral education of the young characters. Literature for children was written to impart moral lessons and training in citizenship. At the same time, the literature of the period offered guidance to parents in the upbringing of their children. Rather than responding to misbehavior with anger and physical force, parents were encouraged to take a rational approach to child management, combining loving care with firmness.

In the 19th century, changes took place in the portrayal of children in literature. The rationalism of the 18th century was discarded in favor of a more romantic view of children and childhood. This change began to occur at mid-century and reflected the social trends of the country. Literature became one vehicle for protest about conditions such as urban poverty. By the late 1840s, the images of homeless and vagrant children engaged in various forms of vice that were appearing in reports of journalists and reformers were also appearing in fictional depictions of urban life.

JUVENILE DELINQUENCY AS A SOCIAL PROBLEM

With the creation of the first juvenile court in 1899, juvenile delinquency was recognized as a social problem for which a solution might be found. From the end of the 19th century to the early 20th—as more academic, sociological literature appeared about the causes of juvenile delinquency and appropriate societal responses—depictions of juvenile delinquency also appeared more often in fiction. Stephen Crane's *Maggie: A Girl of the Streets* (1893), a novel about a young woman who leaves home and is forced to become a prostitute in order to survive, was an early precursor of the literary works that would appear in the 20th century. Most would not achieve the enduring status of Crane's novel. In fact, Willa Cather's short story, "Paul's Case" (1905), about a misfit who steals money and runs away to New York, is a more compelling representation of juvenile delinquency than some longer works.

Novels during the 1920s also sometimes traced the careers of prohibition-era criminals, as in Donald Henderson Clark's *Louis Beretti* (1929), in which a boy rises from youthful lawbreaking to full-fledged gangster status. During the 1930s, James T. Farrel's *The Studs Lonigan Trilogy* (1932, 1934, 1935) presented the story of an Irish Catholic boy who became delinquent not because of poverty but because of the failure of institutions such as family and school.

WORLD WAR II AND AFTER

The treatment of delinquency in literature during the 1940s and 1950s reflected public concerns over current social issues such as inadequate parenting, gangs, drugs, and teenage sexuality. Among the first novels to deal with gang delinquency was Irving Shulman's *Amboy Dukes* (1947). Other works such as I. S. Young's *Jadie Greenway* (1947), which featured an African American protagonist, and Sara Harris's *The Wayward Ones* (1952), about an uncooperative 16-year-old who is sent to a reformatory, deal with the issues related to female juvenile delinquents, such as prostitution and teenage pregnancy. One classic novel of this era, J. D. Salinger's *Catcher in the Rye* (1951), is about a white, male, middle-class delinquent, Holden Caulfield, who is expelled from prep school and spends a few days in New York, engaging in status offenses such as drinking and consorting with a prostitute.

Several of the more popular literary works about juvenile delinquency were adapted as films. These novels included Evan Hunter's *The Blackboard Jungle* (1954), which relates the challenges of teaching and learning in a tough urban high school. Hunter's *A Matter of Conviction* (1959) was adapted to the screen under the title *The Young Savages*. Other novels made into films included Warren Miller's *Cool World* (1959), about a 14-year-old African American boy in Harlem and his world of gang delinquency, and Willard Motley's *Knock on Any Door* (1947), which features a young Italian American protagonist, Nick Romano, whose creed becomes "Live fast, die young, and have a good-looking corpse." Irving Shulman's *Children of the Dark* (1956), about the problems of juveniles in a small midwestern town, became the film *Rebel Without a Cause* and the vehicle for James Dean's rise to stardom as a symbol of alienated youth.

During the 1950s, the paperback fiction industry produced more than 300 novels about juvenile delinquency. These works had such titles as *D for Delinquent*, *Jailbait Street*, *Jailbait Jungle*, *Reefer Club*, *Teen Temptress*, *Zip-Gun Angels*, and *Girls Out of Hell*. These paperbacks were generally set in urban areas and presented worlds of poverty, violence, and hopelessness. These books were being produced during a period when congressional subcommittee hearings were being held on the causes of delinquency. Concern was being expressed by some observers about the impact of the mass media, including films, comic books, and rock and roll.

JUVENILE DELINQUENCY AFTER 1960

Since the 1960s, as the country's consciousness regarding racism, sexism, and homophobia increased and more novels by women and minorities were published, the issues of juvenile delinquency have been approached with more general sensitivity to social structural factors that contribute to delinquency. Books such as Louise Meriwether's *Daddy Was a Number Runner* (1970), a coming-of-age novel about Francie, a young black girl growing up in depression-era Harlem, and S. C. Hinton's *The Outsiders* (1967), about an orphaned 14-year-old white, lower-class gang member living with his two brothers, have presented critically acclaimed depictions of the problems of juveniles and the issue of delinquency.

Some images of juvenile delinquency have been more violent. Irish novelist Patrick McCabe's *The Butcher Boy* (1993) is a critically acclaimed novel about the son of an alcoholic father and a dysfunctional mother. Although he eventually commits murder, one stepping-stone along the way is his commitment to a reform school, where he is abused. The protagonists of Lorenzo Carcaterra's *Sleepers* (1996) suffer a similar fate when a prank leads to the serious injury of an innocent man. The four boys go from a tough but carefree existence in the infamous neighborhood of Hell's Kitchen to the nightmare of survival in an upstate New York reformatory. Carcaterra's book created controversy when it was published and later adapted as a film because of his claim that it was autobiographical. Equally controversial, though hardly autobiographical, was an earlier novel by Anthony Burgess, *A Clockwork Orange* (1962). Later adapted as a film, the book is the story of Alex, a young thug in a futuristic world. Alex is brought under the control of the justice system after a series of brutal and violent crimes committed in the company of his gang. Ironically, there is an inherent tension in Burgess's depiction of the methods used by the state to render Alex harmless.

CONCLUSION

The treatment of juvenile delinquency in two centuries of literature provides some insight into both changing perspectives on childhood and delinquency and the changing responses of society to delinquents. These works must, however, be considered in the context of the times during which they were written and the social problems that were linked to delinquency during each of those times.

Frankie Y. Bailey

Bibliography

Gordon, M. 1971. *Juvenile Delinquency in the American Novel, 1905–1965*. Bowling Green, OH: Bowling Green University Popular Press.

MacLeod, A. S. 1994. *American Childhood: Essays on Children's Literature of the Nineteenth and Twentieth Centuries*. Athens: University of Georgia Press.

M

 MATRICIDE AND PATRICIDE

A father is riddled with bullets; a mother is stabbed multiple times; a family of four—father, mother, and two of their children—is slaughtered by a son, a daughter, acting alone or with others. Crimes like these are universally viewed as abhorrent and have been for centuries. Literary themes involving such figures as Oedipus, Orestes, Alcmaeon, and King Arthur reflect that society has reacted to the killing of one's parents with horror for thousands of years.

In the early 1980s, attention in the United States began to focus on several cases of adolescents who killed one or both parents under harrowing circumstances. From that time on, the term *parricide*, while technically referring to the killing of a close relative, has become increasingly identified in the public's mind with the killing of a parent. *Patricide* and *matricide* are the precise terms used to refer to the killings of a father and a mother, respectively.

INCIDENCE AND VICTIM AND OFFENDER CHARACTERISTICS

During the last two decades in the United States, on average, four to six parents have been killed weekly by their children. Despite interest in this phenomenon, only one comprehensive study of parricides committed in the United States currently exists. Analysis of all homicides for the period 1977 to 1986, using the Federal Bureau of Investigation's *Supplemental Homicide Report,* revealed that the typical parent or stepparent slain was white and non-Hispanic and was killed in a single-victim, single-offender situation. The typical father killed was in his early 50s; the mother, in her late 50s; the stepfather, in his mid-40s; and the stepmother, in her late 40s or early 50s.

The typical offender who killed a parent or stepparent was also white and non-Hispanic. Sons were the killers in 85 percent to 87 percent of homicides involving fathers, mothers, stepfathers, and stepmothers. The percentages of males arrested for committing these types of parricides was approximately equal to their 87 percent representation among all homicide arrestees during this period. There were no significant differences in the percentages of parents and stepparents killed by juvenile and adult sons and daughters (Heide, 1993a, 1995).

In contrast to media depiction and public perception, the overwhelming majority of children who killed fathers, mothers, and stepparents in the United States between 1977 and 1986 were over age 18. Involvement of youth in parricide, however, was fairly significant given their proportionate representation in the population. Analysis of single-victim/single-offender parricides indicated that 25 percent of fathers and 15 percent of mothers were slain by biological children less than 18 years of age. The percentages of stepparents killed by youths under 18 was even higher: 34 percent of stepfathers and 30 percent of stepmothers were slain by youths under 18 (Heide, 1993a, 1995).

TYPES OF PARRICIDE OFFENDERS

Adolescent parricide offenders (APOs) are typically presented in the popular and professional literature as

239

prosocial youths in fear of their lives, often killing to protect themselves or others from death or serious physical injury or to end the chronic abuse they and other family members suffer (Heide, 1993a).

In these cases, an extensive history of abuse is often easily corroborated by interviews with relatives, neighbors, and friends. These youths increasingly come to perceive that their physical well-being is threatened or their psychological survival is at stake. They kill in response to terror or in desperation. From their perspective, there is no way out other than murder.

The severely abused child is only one of three types of parricide offenders identified to date (Heide, 1995). Youths who fit this pattern are typically diagnosed after the killing as suffering from posttraumatic stress disorder (PTSD) and/or depression. Both diagnoses, however, typically predate the killings. PTSD is a disorder that affects some individuals who have been subjected to events where their lives or those of others have been severely threatened. Individuals with this diagnosis reexperience the traumatic event, numb themselves, and avoid thoughts, feelings, and activities associated with the trauma. They have a heightened state of arousal and may react quickly to events that signify a threat to them based on their past history. Adolescent parricide offenders often experience several symptoms of depression before the killing, including sadness, feelings of hopelessness, suicidal ideation, difficulty concentrating, fatigue, and loss of interest in pleasurable activities (American Psychiatric Association, 1994).

Other types of children who kill parents include the severely mentally ill child and the dangerously antisocial child (Heide, 1995). Severely mentally ill children who murder their parents are psychotic or otherwise gravely mentally ill. Psychotic individuals do not have a solid grip on reality. Their perceptions are distorted, their communications are often hard to follow, and their behavior is frequently inappropriate. They typically have a long-established psychiatric history. They may experience bizarre delusions (false beliefs that have no basis in reality and would appear implausible to other people in the setting) and hallucinations (illusory sensory perceptions, such as seeing or hearing things that are not occurring). Individuals with psychotic disorders often do not realize that they are mentally ill. In many cases, severely mentally ill individuals require hospitalization until their mental disorders have been stabilized.

For this type of parricide offender, the killing of the parent is an underlying product of mental illness. For example, a psychotic young man might hear Satan commanding him to kill his mother as a sacrificial offering and might also believe that his lethal course of action is a necessary and moral one. A psychotic individual who has killed her or his parents may have such visible and historically documented mental illness that criminal prosecution is not completed or is halted until the individual's condition is stabilized. On the other hand, a case involving a severely mentally ill parricide offender may proceed to trial if the offender is deemed competent to stand trial because he or she knows the nature of the criminal proceeding and is able to assist counsel in preparing a defense.

Dangerously antisocial youths kill their parents for selfish, instrumental reasons. The term *dangerously antisocial youth* was used to refer to individuals who were diagnosed as having "psychopathic" or "sociopathic" personalities by professionals in the late 19th and early 20th centuries, respectively. The two terms, which are perceived as the same by the public, have been replaced in the professional literature with two more precise terms—*conduct disorder* and *antisocial personality disorder*. Which diagnosis is given depends on the age of the individual and the presence of specific criteria. Unlike individuals who are psychotic, those diagnosed as having conduct disorders or antisocial personalities are oriented in time and space and are free of delusions and hallucinations (American Psychiatric Association, 1994).

A child under age 18 may be diagnosed as having a conduct disorder when it is apparent that he or she has a pattern of disregarding the rights of others that has been ongoing for at least six months. Diagnostic criteria indicate that the youth must engage in at least three types of disruptive behavior. The severity of the conduct disorder (mild, moderate, or severe) depends on the number of conduct problems displayed by the youth and the amount of harm they cause. Of the 13 criteria specified, 9 involve physical violence against persons or property (e. g., physical cruelty to people or animals, rape, or arson) or thefts involving confrontation with a victim. The remaining behaviors are nonaggressive, including stealing without confrontation, running away from home, truancy, and often lying under conditions other than to avoid physical or sexual abuse.

The American Psychiatric Association currently recognizes three types of conduct disorders: the group type, the solitary aggressive type, and the undifferentiated type—reserved for youths who do not fit either of the other two types. If the person is at least 18 years of age, the diagnosis of antisocial personality disorder may be made if evidence of a conduct disorder existed before age 15 and the individual has continued to engage in behavior disregarding the rights of others.

TYPES OF PARRICIDE OFFENDERS AND OFFENDER AGE

Empirical studies and clinical case reports indicate that adults who kill their parents often have documented histories of psychopathology (Heide, 1995). Although abuse might have existed in the home as the adult child was growing up, it is not typically the driving force behind the parricide. Usually, adults have more choices and resources and are more mature than juveniles. If the home situation is intolerable, a healthy adult can leave. When an adult resorts to murdering a parent, she or he is likely to be severely mentally ill or psychopathic.

In contrast, when adolescents kill their mothers and fathers, severe mental illness is typically ruled out. The question frequently becomes the one litigated in the case of Lyle and Eric Menendez, who killed both their parents: Was the adolescent a severely abused child or was he or she "a psychopath"?

CHARACTERISTICS OF SEVERELY ABUSED CHILDREN WHO KILL PARENTS

Twelve characteristics are typical of a severely abused youth who has killed his or her parents (Heide, 1995):

1. *A pattern of family violence exists in the home.* Typically, more than one type of abuse is present. These children have histories of being psychologically abused by one or both parents and have often witnessed or directly experienced physical, sexual, and verbal abuse by their parents. Neglect accompanies abuse in almost all these cases. If there is a nonabusive parent, either that parent did not protect the child from known harm, or the parent was unaware of the extent of the abuse when she or he should have known and acted to end the maltreatment.

2. *The adolescent's attempts to get help have failed.* APOs typically tell others about the abuse. Those who knew about the abuse often include neighbors, teachers, friends, and classmates, as well as relatives. The youths' situations were either minimized or their pleas for help were ignored.

3. *The adolescent's attempts to escape the family situation failed.* APOs typically have considered running away, and many have done so for short periods, returning because they had no safe place to go. Many have considered suicide, and some have attempted to take their own lives.

4. *The adolescent is isolated from others and has few outlets.* Abusive parents in these cases often restrict the youths' freedom and activities. In addition, many APOs withdraw from others because of excessive obligations placed on them and due to the shame they feel regarding their parents' behavior.

5. *The family situation became increasingly intolerable.* In parricides, three phases are often discernable. In phase one, conditions experienced by the youths are abusive and difficult. In phase two, conditions deteriorate; that is, specific events can be identified that signal that home life has gone from bad to worse. In phase three, typically a triggering event occurs that propels the youth to take lethal action.

6. *The adolescent felt increasingly helpless and trapped.* Youths in these situations have become overwhelmed with life events and may reach their breaking point.

7. *The adolescent's inability to cope led to a loss of control.* In some cases, APOs, worn thin by the constant pressure, snap. They lose their hold on reality and react without giving thought to the nature of their behavior or its lethal consequences.

8. *The adolescent had little or no prior criminal record.* These youths usually are not criminally sophisticated. Many were viewed by others in their communities as "great kids" before the homicide.

9. *A gun was readily available.* Analysis of thousands of parricide cases using FBI data over a 10-year period was consistent with clinical case data. Youths who killed parents and stepparents typically used guns. APOs are significantly more likely to use firearms than are adults who kill their mothers, fathers, or stepfathers (Heide, 1993b, 1995).

10. *Parental chemical dependency is commonly found in the homes of youths who killed parents.* Alcoholism or heavy drinking is frequently found among fathers. In addition, abuse of psychotropic medication by mothers who are coping with an abusive partner is also frequently encountered.

11. *There was evidence that the youth was in a dissociative state or experienced some dissociation (alteration in consciousness) during the homicidal incident.* APOs frequently report gaps in memory occasioned by the stress they experienced during the homicidal incident. Although they accept responsibility for killing their parents, many cannot remember parts of the homicidal event.

12. *The victim's death was perceived as a relief.* APOs and surviving members of their families often express relief that the abusive parent is gone and can no longer hurt them or others.

DIAGNOSING THE DANGEROUSLY ANTISOCIAL CHILD

Accurate identification of adolescent parricide offenders is vital. If these youths are misdiagnosed, they may have the opportunity, as well as the underlying character structure, to kill again. Criminal justice personnel and mental health professionals need to address two questions in this regard. The first concerns the offender, the second focuses on the offense. A qualified mental health professional with expertise in juvenile homicide should evaluate the youth to determine if he or she meets the diagnostic criteria for conduct disorder.

In addition to making this determination, the mental health professional needs to address the second question: What propelled the homicide? If the youth meets the diagnostic criteria for conduct disorder *and* killed the parent to further his or her selfish ends, then the youth would appropriately be classified as a dangerously antisocial parricide offender.

The mere diagnosis of conduct disorder does not rule out that the youth could be a severely abused child who killed to end the abuse. Children who have been abused or neglected may adopt an antisocial way of responding to life as a means of psychic, if not physical, survival. Engaging in antisocial behavior can help youths to focus their attention away from problems at home that are too difficult to handle. Accordingly, it is important to look closely at what motivated the conduct-disordered youth to kill: Was he or she trying to end the abuse or escape from it? Or, was he or she killing to get something desired, such as more freedom or access to a parent's money or car? The answers to these questions enable the clinician to determine whether the youth is a conduct-disordered, severely abused child or a dangerously antisocial child.

IMPLICATIONS

Appropriate diagnosis of an adolescent parricide offender has important ramifications for determining effective intervention strategies. The course of treatment and the likelihood of successful reintegration into society will vary depending on the diagnosis. The prognosis for youths who are clinically depressed or suffering from posttraumatic stress disorder is typically better than for youths who are psychotic or conduct disordered (Heide, 1995).

Many clinicians are understandably pessimistic about working with "psychopathic" youth. However, not all conduct-disordered youth are alike. Some may represent more of a risk to society than others.

Ascertaining the driving force behind the homicide is critically important. It sheds light on the offender's way of coping with life events and has significant implications for intervention. A conduct-disordered, severely abused child poses less of a risk to society than a dangerously antisocial child and is probably more amenable to treatment. In short, the dangerously antisocial child is at the end of the continuum—he or she is both antisocial and dangerous. If the child is not checked, the killing of a parent may be only one of a series of deadly and destructive acts perpetrated in his or her lifetime.

Kathleen M. Heide

See also Serious and Violent Offenders

Bibliography

American Psychiatric Association. 1994. *Diagnostic and Statistical Manual of Mental Disorders*, 4th ed. Washington, DC: American Psychiatric Association.

Heide, K. M. 1993a. Parents who get killed and the children who kill them. *Journal of Interpersonal Violence* 8:531–544.

Heide, K. M. 1993b. Weapons used by juveniles and adults to kill parents. *Behavioral Sciences and the Law* 11:397–405.

Heide, K. M. 1995. *Why Kids Kill Parents: Child Abuse and Adolescent Homicide*. Columbus: Ohio State University Press.

McCORD, JOAN (1930–)

Throughout a career that so far has spanned five decades, Joan McCord has published and presented more than 100 articles. She is best known for her research on the influences of parental child-rearing practices and family socialization on delinquency, criminality, alcoholism, and psychopathy. She continues to advocate the use of the longitudinal method maintaining that it is a critical and superior methodological approach in researching and understanding the correlates of offending behavior. Indeed, McCord's early exposure to this methodology influenced her use of it over the course of her career.

Dr. McCord grew up in Tucson, where she met William (Bud) McCord. A high school friendship developed. They attended Stanford University together and subsequently were married. After graduating with a bachelor's degree in philosophy from Stanford in 1952, McCord worked as a public school teacher in Concord, Massachusetts. She credits her study of philosophy for helping her to understand the value of critical thinking and, in her own words, of enduring skepticism. Through her husband's summer employment at San Quentin penitentiary, she became interested in studying criminal behavior. A short time later, in 1956, work at a reform school led the pair to their initial interest in psychopaths and their first publication, *Psychopathy and Delinquency*. That same year, she accepted a position as a research assistant for Harvard's Laboratory of Human Development while earning her master's degree in education. In 1957, McCord embarked on a project evaluation of the Cambridge-Somerville Youth Study, an endeavor that would significantly focus and serve the majority of her lifework. McCord continued her work on juvenile and criminal behavior and earned her Ph.D. in sociology from Harvard University. While at Harvard, she served as a research assistant for Dr. Eleanor Maccoby, a pioneer in the field of human development. She credits this experience as being influential in steering the course and direction of her career.

THE CAMBRIDGE-SOMERVILLE YOUTH STUDY

The Cambridge-Somerville Youth Project began in 1938, under the direction of Richard Clarke Cabot, a professor of clinical medicine and social ethics. In the early 20th century, psychological procedures and interventions were being developed and used to assess youths appearing before the newly created juvenile courts. Services combining social work with psychology to treat youth identified as "at risk" were delivered through a growing network of child guidance clinics. As a product of the times, Judge Frederick Cabot, Richard Cabot's cousin, helped to create the Juvenile Psychopathic Institute in Chicago and hired William Healy, an established psychiatrist, as the institute's director.

Given his cousin's involvement in the field, and his own interest in the work of the Harvard research team of Eleanor and Sheldon Glueck, Dr. Cabot set out to test the notion that delinquency could be prevented by providing consistent and positive guidance for youth and their families. He selected a disadvantaged region of eastern Massachusetts as the study site, where both adjusted and maladjusted males under age 12 were matched on relevant characteristics and randomly assigned to his treatment and control groups. Interventions and services were prescribed by a multifaceted treatment staff that included social workers, psychologists, and medical personnel. Services were delivered in the form of monthly home visits, tutoring, woodworking, psychological care, counseling, participation in community youth activities, and summer camps. Extensive data were collected on the youths' school behavior, neighborhood conditions, court files, medical records, family interactions, and social environments. The study concluded in 1945.

The opportunity to conduct a follow-up study and evaluation of the Cambridge-Somerville Youth Study presented itself rather early in McCord's career. Analyses of the youth project data led to publishing the coauthored book *Origins of Crime* (1959), followed in 1960 by *Origins of Alcoholism*. Essentially, the Cambridge-Somerville Youth Study was a failure. Introducing the intervention of supportive professionals and activities into the lives of more than 200 boys seemed to make little difference in the outcome of criminality. Initial assessments conducted by McCord and her then husband/colleague, William McCord, indicated that the program not only failed to have a positive impact on adult offending behavior but actually increased the likelihood that subjects would exhibit deviant or criminal behaviors. For example, the innocuous exposure of some of the boys to summer camp seemed to accelerate deviancy potential rather than retard it. This finding was the precursor to what is now a widely recognized precept on the unintended and harmful consequences of certain intervention strategies.

The Cambridge-Somerville Youth Study, however, was not a total loss because it left behind a data set rich with multiple indicators of family and preadolescent developmental concepts. Through the diligent work of McCord, significant advances were made in delineating the components of effective parenting and the role family socialization plays in the development of criminality and alcoholism.

THE IMPORTANCE OF FAMILY INTERACTION

McCord's findings were among some of the first to help establish that the absence of positive parenting styles and family interaction promotes aggressive and delinquent behavior. Youths reared with self-confident mothers who displayed maternal affection and warmth and used consistent nonpunitive discipline were more likely to be insulated from criminal behavior. Youths raised in home environments where marital conflict and family strife were present were more likely to develop antisocial tendencies than were youths raised in either attentive single-parent homes or peaceful two-parent homes. Further, McCord's studies have documented that the socialization practices and daily interaction patterns of the family unit have a considerable effect on how biological predispositions develop into antisocial behavior.

More recently, McCord's reanalysis of the Cambridge-Somerville data led her to conclude that the lack of paternal interaction may have a differential or sleeper effect on the development of male adult criminality but is of lesser importance in predicting delinquency. The implications of McCord's research are far-reaching in framing family interactions as potentially affecting different periods of juvenile-adult criminal or noncriminal development.

Additionally, McCord's research has confirmed that children subjected to parental aggression and corporal punishments are at risk for delinquent and criminal behavior, even when administered by an otherwise competent parent. In her groundbreaking study on child abuse, which was one of the first to include a comparison group in the research design, parental rejection of a child was as criminogenic as parental neglect or abuse.

LONGITUDINAL METHODOLOGY

Her work has also been instructional on the importance and value of using the longitudinal and prospective method when determining the causes of conduct disorders. For instance, in her early analysis of the Cambridge-Somerville data, she and colleagues concluded there was a relationship between paternal alcoholism and the development of alcoholism in sons. Approximately two decades later, McCord clarified this relationship after conducting a follow-up study of her original research and subjects. She found that certain patterns of family socialization promote alcoholism as well as criminal behavior. Specifically, a male youth with an alcoholic father and a mother who respects the alcoholic father and lacks control or supervision over the son was more likely than were other youths to become an alcoholic. This and other research experiences explain why McCord is critical of using cross-sectional methodology, because it is "unable to disentangle causes from effects" (McCord, 1991:398), especially when trying to understand the precursors to, and causes of, deviant behavior. Without benefit of the longitudinal method, associations and relationships discovered in previous measures would remain unclear, unknown, misidentified, or misunderstood.

The longitudinal method also supports McCord's interest in the study of intergenerational transmission of violence by allowing cross-classification of family, social, and criminal histories. Her research in this area has shown that criminal fathers produce families rife with aggression and conflict. She continues to push for the collection of individual social histories, believing that this is the only way true advances in juvenile delinquency research can be made.

RECOGNITION

McCord's work is widely regarded and considered in the construction of prevention and intervention programs. Based on her research, McCord has demonstrated that those planning treatments for delinquents or offenders must consider strategies that go beyond simply trying to supplement or correct the past with the provision of positive influences. She has chaired (and continues to serve on) numerous panels and committees for governmental agencies overseeing policy formulation or research on children at risk for conduct disorders, delinquency, and criminal behavior. Her extensive research has earned her recognition as a nationally acclaimed and distinguished authority on juvenile delinquency. Joan McCord is currently Professor of Criminal Justice at Temple University.

Chloe Tischler

See also Cambridge-Somerville Youth Study; Chicago Area Project; Cycle of Violence; William Healy

Bibliography

McCord, J. 1991. Family relationships, juvenile delinquency, and adult criminality. *Criminology* 29:397–415.

McCord, W., and McCord, J. 1956. *Psychopathy and Delinquency.* New York: Grune & Stratton.

McCord, W., and McCord, J. 1959. *Origins of Crime.* New York: Columbia University Press.

McCord, W., and McCord, J. 1960. *Origins of Alcoholism.* Stanford, CA: Stanford University Press.

McKAY, HENRY D. (1899–1980)

Henry McKay became a graduate student in the Sociology Department at the University of Chicago when sociology, as an academic discipline, was still in its infancy. The work of McKay and his associate Clifford Shaw helped to establish the department as the leading sociology program in the United States and is considered among the most significant contributions made to the field of criminology.

Henry Donald McKay was born in 1899, the fifth of seven children in Orient, South Dakota. His parents were farmers from Scotland. Even though McKay grew up on a South Dakota farm, education was a high priority in his family. He attended college, earning a bachelor's degree from Dakota Wesleyan University in 1922 and a master's degree from the University of Chicago in 1924. McKay taught at the University of Illinois from 1925 to 1926 and returned to the University of Chicago in 1926 to pursue a Ph.D. in Sociology. Rather than finish his studies, however, McKay went to work at the Institute for Juvenile Research in 1927 and remained there until his retirement in 1972.

THE UNIVERSITY OF CHICAGO

The University of Chicago was home to the first sociology department, created in 1892. Early Chicago School sociologists were primarily interested in studying the impact of a growing industrial and urban society on the lives of individuals. Henry McKay came to the university in 1923, when sociologists interested in studying criminal behavior would begin to locate the causes of crime within an individual's social environment. The Chicago School of criminology grew out of the research being conducted by Chicago sociologists. Faculty and students were interested in studying the criminogenic quality of life in a big city. Criminologists also turned their attention to the illegal behaviors of juveniles in hopes that if the causes of delinquency could be identified and interventions begun early, delinquents would not grow up to become adult criminals.

McKay came to the University of Chicago at the encouragement of L. Guy Brown, a former graduate student in social psychology (Carey, 1972). At that time, Chicago sociologists were developing a provocative theoretical perspective known as the human ecological approach to the study of urban life. In particular, Robert Park and Ernest Burgess have been credited with pioneering this ecological approach. Park described the city as an organism that contained "natural areas" and contended that a city's development and growth could best be understood according to the social processes of invasion, dominance, and succession. Burgess's concentric zone theory describes the manner in which a city grows outward from the central business district to the suburbs. Of particular interest to Park and Burgess was the area immediately surrounding the central business district, known as the "zone of transition." They observed that this zone was characterized by high rates of residential mobility, deteriorated housing, and abandoned buildings. Park and Burgess contended that these characteristics contributed to "social disorganization" within the zone. The ecological approach and the concept of social disorganization intrigued Henry McKay, who was working under the direction of Burgess at the time.

McKay supported himself while working on his degree by writing abstracts for the *American Journal of Sociology*. He completed his master's degree in 1924 and began teaching at the University of Illinois in Champaign-Urbana. He returned to the University of Chicago in 1926 to pursue a Ph.D. in Sociology and was given a teaching assistantship (Carey, 1972). McKay also began working again with Burgess, who had turned his attention to the study of delinquency. McKay's interest in delinquency was further heightened by the work of Edwin Sutherland, who was a faculty member at the University of Chicago at the same time.

THE INSTITUTE FOR JUVENILE RESEARCH

Clifford Shaw had already started collecting data from the Cook County Juvenile Court. He began with a large map of the city and used pins to mark the home address of each juvenile who had come under the jurisdiction of the juvenile court to see if the distribution was related in any way to Burgess's concentric zones. McKay joined the project on his return to graduate school but never finished his Ph.D. Instead, McKay accepted a position in 1927 with the newly created Institute for Juvenile Research under the direction of fellow graduate student Shaw, who had left the University of Chicago a year prior.

The Institute for Juvenile Research was the successor to a clinic established by prominent psychiatrist William Healy in 1909. Organized around the Cook County Juvenile Court, clinic workers were primarily interested in helping delinquents and their families take advantage of various social services and programs. The purpose of the clinic was to help families in economically disadvantaged communities become self-sufficient. Healy recognized that the ecological research of Chicago School sociologists could contribute to this goal (Carey, 1975). Shaw was the first sociologist hired by the clinic. The Institute for Juvenile Research provided these newly trained sociologists the opportunity to incorporate their research skills into their work as community organizers. The institute served as a research center and was responsible for coordinating child guidance and delinquency prevention programs across the state.

RESEARCH AND THEORY

After McKay joined Shaw at the Institute for Juvenile Research, the two sociologists continued their research on delinquency. First, Shaw and McKay were interested in determining whether a widely held assumption about the relationship between broken homes and delinquency was valid. Research from New York City revealed that the ratio of delinquents from broken homes to those from unbroken homes was 1.5 to 1. A more careful analysis by Shaw and McKay in Chicago revealed that the ratio was actually only 1.18 to 1, a finding that has since been supported

as well. Shaw and McKay were taking advantage of newly developed quantitative research methods and statistics to refute many widely held assumptions about delinquency, including the assumption that race and ethnic origin were the causes of much delinquency in Chicago neighborhoods.

Shaw and McKay also began a thorough analysis of their prior work with Burgess involving the mapping (by hand) of the home addresses of more than 100,000 juvenile offenders in Chicago between 1900 and 1927. This research revealed that rates of officially recorded delinquency were not evenly distributed throughout the city but rather were highly concentrated in the area referred to as the zone of transition and became successively lower in each of the outward zones. What impressed Shaw and McKay the most was that regardless of which racial or ethnic group lived within the zone, delinquency was always high, leaving them to speculate that there was something about the neighborhood structure itself and *not* the characteristics of the individuals themselves that was pushing young people into a life of delinquency.

Shaw and McKay's research would become part of the *Report on the Causes of Crime* (1931) prepared for the Wickersham Commission. Established by President Hoover in 1929, the Wickersham Commission was set up in response to America's increasing concern over crime. The second part of the report was devoted to Shaw and McKay's study of the distribution of juvenile offenders in Chicago as well as other large cities around the country. The Wickersham report represented a strong endorsement of the sociological approach to the study of crime. Until that point, most of the explanations for criminal behavior were derived from the fields of psychology and biology. Shaw and McKay's research on delinquency rates were also incorporated into the *Local Community Fact Book*, a noteworthy source of information relating to all different aspects of community life in Chicago.

THE CHICAGO AREA PROJECT

Shaw was interested in more than simply discovering the causes of delinquency. He wanted to build on the research he was doing with McKay and implement a program for community change. With the assistance of McKay and others from the Chicago School and with money provided by the Rockefeller Foundation, the Chicago Area Project (CAP) was established in the early 1930s. It represented the first large-scale attempt to organize community resources in an effort to reduce delinquency. The CAP consisted of three components: structured recreational opportunities for youth, efforts to facilitate community involvement in combating delinquency, and utilizing "curbstone counselors" to mediate disputes between gang members and act as prosocial role models. Aspects of the program are still operational today, and the project serves as a model for crime and delinquency prevention programs throughout the country.

SOCIAL DISORGANIZATION THEORY

Shaw and McKay's research at the University of Chicago as well as with the Institute for Juvenile Research developed into one of the most prominent theories of delinquency. Social disorganization theory was finalized in their classic work *Juvenile Delinquency in Urban Areas* (1942). According to the theory, rates of delinquency vary geographically according to the structural characteristics of the neighborhoods in which the delinquents live. Neighborhoods characterized by high rates of poverty, population density, urban decay, residential mobility, and heterogeneous populations tend to become socially disorganized and consequently have very high rates of delinquency. Socially disorganized neighborhoods are often lacking in effective informal social control institutions. Families, churches, schools, and neighborhood organizations lose their ability to impart on the youth of the community conventional values and behaviors. Community members residing in socially disorganized neighborhoods become unable or unwilling to solve commonly experienced problems, and delinquency flourishes. The neighborhood itself ultimately becomes the cause of delinquency.

LIFE-HISTORY METHODOLOGY

McKay not only established himself as a quantitative researcher, but also he was involved in another phase of the work being carried out at the Institute for Juvenile Research that involved collecting detailed life-history studies of thousands of known delinquents. One such history traced the criminal careers of five brothers over 15 years. This research became the basis for *Brothers in Crime,* coauthored with Shaw and James McDonald in 1938 and considered an important contribution to our understanding of sibling-involvement delinquency.

RECOGNITION

Henry McKay retired from the Institute for Juvenile Research in 1972. He spent his life exploring the causes of delinquency and taking part in efforts to reduce it. His work remains an important contribution to the field of criminology. Social disorganization theory continues to be one of the most influential theories of delinquency. The recognition that structural characteristics of a community can influence behavior has kept the ecological study of crime and delinquency alive. Social disorganization theory not only advanced our understanding of delinquency but also offers communities plausible programs to combat the problem.

Amy B. Thistlethwaite

See also Chicago Area Project; Clifford R. Shaw; Theories of Delinquency

Bibliography

Carey, James T. 1972. *Personal Interview with Henry D. McKay.* Chicago: University of Chicago Library, Special Collections Department.

Carey, James T. 1975. *Sociology and Public Affairs: The Chicago School.* Beverly Hills, CA: Sage.

McKay, H. D. 1960. Differential association and crime prevention: Problems of utilization. *Social Problems* 8:25–37.

Shaw, C. R., and H. D. McKay. 1931. *Social Factors in Juvenile Delinquency. Report on the Causes of Crime to the Wickersham Commission,* Vol. 2. Washington, DC: Government Printing Office.

Shaw, C. R., and H. D. McKay. 1942. *Juvenile Delinquency in Urban Areas.* Chicago: University of Chicago Press.

Shaw, C. R., H. D. McKay, and J. F. MacDonald. 1938. *Brothers in Crime.* Chicago: University of Chicago Press.

Snodgrass, J. 1976. Clifford Shaw and Henry D. McKay: Chicago sociologists. *The British Journal of Criminology* 16:1–19.

 # MEDIATION

The terms *mediation, reconciliation,* and *restitution* are all found within the movement now called restorative justice. It appears that the adoption of the

term *restorative* is an attempt to capture all these variations in definition and approach within the framework of returning both the victim, the community, and the offender to their original conditions. Other terms are used, and several models of restorative justice exist. Basically, however, they attempt to bring together victims, offenders, and community members in a nonthreatening process that will hold offenders accountable as well as repair the harm suffered by the victims and their neighborhoods (Bazemore and Umbreit, 2001). Mediation, then, is a tool or practice available in the juvenile justice system that is consistent with the broader restorative justice model.

THE SHIFT AWAY FROM REHABILITATION

While mediation has been used with both adults and juveniles, a major application has been in the area of juvenile justice. As the philosophical foundation of the juvenile justice system began to shift in the 1980s, traditional rehabilitative goals often came into sharp conflict with a reemerging punishment ideology. This changing view of punishment challenged the juvenile and adult justice systems to provide innovative approaches. From the more liberal point of view, rehabilitation ideology emphasizing treating and protecting juveniles led to policies that, in some cases, resulted in punishments that were more severe than were those adults received for similar offenses. On the other hand, from the more conservative retributionist standpoint, juvenile court and its policies seemed to be too lenient, allowing many hard-core delinquents to "get away with crime" (see Shichor, 1983).

In spite of the hardening attitudes toward delinquents, efforts for creating alternative methods for handling juveniles, as well as adults, continued. The reasons for these efforts stem from several sources. First, juveniles are different from adults, and many of them are still amenable to change. Second, rehabilitation programs using community resources to deal with juveniles may be more effective than keeping juveniles incarcerated and isolated. Third, the cost of severe sentences puts a heavy economic burden on society. Similar to the adult system, efforts were made to differentiate between hard-core "dangerous" offenders, who are more severely punished than before, and minor offenders, for whom cheaper and more community-oriented rehabilitation programs were devised.

MEDIATION

The community's use of mediation between the offenders and their victims is based on restorative justice models that have been in place for hundreds of years, all over the world. Although disputes had traditionally been resolved informally between the feuding parties, a decisive turn away from this practice occurred in the Middle Ages, when crimes began to be defined as violations against the king. This trend continued into recent times with the increasing power of the states. A renewed interest in restorative justice during the 1960s became more formalized in 1974 with the establishment of the first Victim-Offender Reconciliation Program (VORP) in Canada.

The principal points of this philosophy are that crime should be viewed not only as lawbreaking but as a cause of injuries to victims, the community, and even the offender. The justice system should have a duty to assist in repairing those injuries. Also, the government should not have a monopoly on the response to crime.

In general, mediation programs attempt to repair the personal and social damage caused by criminal acts. Because one of the main goals of the juvenile justice system is to instill accountability, this issue became an important component of the VORP process. Most juvenile and adult systems try to achieve accountability by some kind of punishment and by laying down rules to which offenders must adhere, usually overseen by a probation agency. However, being punished, or following a set of rules, does not necessarily lead to the acceptance of full responsibility for one's behavior and/or to the repair of the harm that was caused by that behavior. Therefore, accountability involves offenders taking responsibility "for their crimes and the harm caused to victims by making amends and restoring losses. Moreover, accountability requires the victims and offenders be involved in the sanctioning process, when feasible" (Elrod and Ryder, 1999:426). Victim-offender mediation fits into this framework.

WHO SHOULD ENTER MEDIATION?

Mediation programs take on many different formats and involve a variety of participants. In most cases, the mediator who is a representative or designee of the courts works to bring together the victim and the offender in a neutral setting in a face-to-face meeting.

The purpose of the meeting is generally to discuss the genesis of the offense, its meaning and effects, and what steps can be taken to repair the harm or damage that will be acceptable to both parties. Although which offenders should be included or excluded is often controversial, most programs generally limit participation to less serious, nonviolent offenses where restitution amounts and payment formats can be arranged. Sex offenders, those in need of drug or mental health services, and chronic or serious offenders are generally ineligible. There are also parameters for victims best suited for mediation or victim-offender reconciliation. Those include victims who are not seriously or permanently injured, those who are not too angry to work through the session, or those whose physical health and mobility allow them to participate in a productive way. While some mediators are professionally employed in this function, most programs use specially trained volunteers or court personnel, such as probation officers, for this program. Some jurisdictions use a teen court model, where youthful peers serve in the mediator role.

THE MEDIATION PROCESS

The mediation process may take place before a youth's formal adjudication and in some cases, if successful, in lieu of further formal involvement in the criminal justice system. In these cases, the mediation allows for deferred adjudication, and the charges may be removed from the youth's record if all of the terms of the agreements are honored. Other models may use mediation in treatment, such as programs within prison or juvenile detention settings. Victim awareness components of many rehabilitation programs stress the importance of the offender acknowledging responsibility and maturing to see the offense through the victim's eyes and apologize. In a similar process, both Narcotics Anonymous and Alcoholics Anonymous call on participants to make amends with those who have been harmed by their actions as part of the 12-step process of recovery.

Overall, VORP requires participants to come together in mutual respect and with the interests of restorative justice at heart. Research has indicated that both victims and offenders seem to appreciate the opportunity they have to work with each other and to learn not only what motivated the offense but also how it influenced others over time. Victims often say

that the way the mediation process allows them to set aside their anger or fear and move on is more important than any restitution paid or work service performed by the offender. Victims also seem to express more satisfaction with the criminal justice system following participation in VORP.

RESEARCH ON VICTIM-OFFENDER MEDIATION

One evaluation of a victim-offender reconciliation program in Orange County, California, was completed as part of a study of six restorative justice programs in California. This evaluation included a description of the main features of a reconciliation program based on agreements achieved through mediation between victims and juvenile offenders conducted by specially trained community volunteer mediators. Analysis was completed for 170 individual juvenile offenders referred to probation and sent to VORP who were responsible for 322 offenses. The analysis compared juveniles who went through the mediation process with youth who were referred to the program but did not complete it—that is, the nonmediation group. Recidivism and cost data were provided, along with a description of the main features of this program based on agreements that were achieved through mediation between victims and juvenile offenders.

The study focused on cases referred to the program by the Orange County Probation Department during a period of 18 months between January 1, 1997, and June 30, 1998. The overview of the operation provided information about the personal characteristics of referred juveniles (age, gender, ethnicity), the number and nature of offenses for which they were referred, and the types of the victims. Pre- and post-program offense data were made available by the Orange County Probation Department, which made recidivism comparisons possible for individuals who completed mediation or conciliation and those for whom no agreement was reached. Youth for whom the mediation agreement was completed were less likely to be recidivists. Most important, it was possible to determine restitution and service agreements arrived at through mediation, the amount of restitution collected, and service hours completed.

The analysis provided information on the juveniles referred to the program by their offenses and compared 121 cases who completed the mediation process with 49 who were referred to the program but did not complete it. Findings indicated that females were referred to the program for less serious offenses than were males. The highest percentage of referrals among males were for offenses "against the person" and "nonutilitarian" charges (vandalism, malicious mischief, annoying phone calls), and for females, most charges were for "utilitarian minor" offenses (shoplifting, petty theft, stolen property). These patterns confirmed the traditional social roles based on gender. Accordingly, boys commit offenses that reinforce their masculine role of being more aggressive and daring, and girls are involved in minor offenses that may help to enhance their physical attractiveness. While these offenses are obviously against the law, the juveniles involved do not tend to violate expectations concerning their social roles.

Concerning ethnic composition, Caucasian and African American juvenile referrals were overrepresented in the program; Hispanics and Asians were underrepresented. This distribution may have indicated differential offense patterns among the various ethnic groups and/or may reflect the selection criteria implemented by the probation department. Caucasian youth had the highest percentage of mediated cases (76 percent), and Hispanics had the lowest (61 percent). Regarding the type of offenses referred to VORP by probation, more serious offenses were referred than in a previous study of referrals from four police departments (Shichor and Sechrest, 1998). It was possible that police departments had somewhat different opinions regarding the type of cases that VORP should handle than did the probation department. Police may refer only very minor cases.

Fewer than 10 percent of juveniles with prior records were referred to the program. This referral pattern may indicate that VORP can result in "net widening." There is also a concern about identifying victims. About 40 percent of the victims were individuals and the others were different kinds of organizations (mainly schools and businesses). The mediated and the nonmediated groups differed in this respect, because less than one third of the victims in the mediated group were individuals compared with more than 55 percent of victims in the nonmediated group. As was noted earlier, these figures reflect the fact that it is more difficult to establish a face-to-face relationship that facilitates mediation between an offender and an uneasy or potentially hostile victim. On the other hand, the representative of a business or organization

might be less personally involved. One of the important findings was that the agreements included close to $60,000 in restitution, of which more than $16,000 had been collected at the time of the study. Similarly, 2,742 service hours worth nearly $16,000 were completed, with 22 cases still open for more service and restitution.

Restorative justice in general and the VORP process in particular was generally considered a useful method to deal with youthful offenders who are in the beginning stages of their delinquent careers and possibly for first-time adult offenders. Meeting with their victims might increase offenders' understanding of the harm and the loss they caused their victims. Such meetings might also help offenders develop empathy toward the victims, which according to some scholars is the best, or even the only, mechanism to build protection against violence (see Pepinsky, 1998). Similarly, victims might gain more understanding of the offenders' backgrounds, motivations, and actions, while not condoning their behavior. This may temper their resentment and demands for retribution in lieu of receiving restitution and encouraging accountability in offenders.

The major findings of the study cited have been included in a recent report on six victim-offender reconciliation programs in California prepared for the California Judicial Council by its Administrative Office of the Courts (AOC; Evje and Cushman, 2000). The report to the California legislature summarized the results of six separate evaluations of VORPs serving victims and their juvenile offenders in six California counties. The purpose of the report was to assess the efficacy of six programs, each funded to complete an evaluation.

The study found that generally, compared with juveniles not participating in the program, juveniles in VORPs paid more restitution and were less likely to reoffend, and that VORP participants (both victims and offenders) were satisfied with the program. In most cases, the VORP participants performed better than legislation has called for. When the VORP groups were matched against comparison groups, they exceeded the amount of restitution collected from the comparison groups by much more than the 40 percent legislative benchmark. Five of the six programs achieved recidivism rates that were at least 10 percent less than the comparison groups' rates. Further, the VORP groups garnered satisfactory rates of participation by victims and offenders who were referred to the programs, and they received impressive participant satisfaction scores from victims, offenders, parents and guardians, mediators, probation officers, judges, and other justice system personnel. Additional indicators of success were also enumerated, including increased numbers of mediations and satisfaction from victims and system participants (Evje and Cushman, 2000).

CONCLUSION

The terms *reconciliation* and *restoration* often are used interchangeably, along with *mediation* and *restitution*. In a California VORP study, the programs are variously pursuing restoration, reconciliation, restitution, or mediation. Added to these, the term *restorative conferencing* has been introduced to describe a variety of nonadversarial community-based programs that involve both the victim and the offender working together to achieve something positive out of a negative experience (Bazemore and Umbreit, 2001). These include traditional victim-offender mediation programs, reparative boards, family group conferencing, and circle sentencing. It appears that each of these approaches represents an attempt to contribute something to the rehabilitation and restoration of the youthful offender, the victim, and the community in which they live.

Dale K. Sechrest

See also Courts, Juvenile; Restorative Justice

Bibliography

Bazemore, G., and M. Umbreit. 2001. *A Comparison of Four Restorative Conferencing Models*. Juvenile Justice Bulletin Series. Washington, DC: Office of Juvenile Justice and Delinquency Prevention.

Elrod, P., and R. S. Ryder. 1999. *Juvenile Justice: A Social, Historical, and Legal Perspective*. Gaithersburg, MD: Aspen Publications.

Evje, A., and R. C. Cushman. 2000. *A Summary of Six California Victim Offender Reconciliation Programs*. Report to the California Legislature. Sacramento, CA: The Judicial Council of California, Administrative Office of the Courts.

Pepinsky, H. 1998. Empathy works, obedience doesn't. *Criminal Justice Policy Review* 9(2):141–167.

Shichor, D. 1983. Historical and current trends in juvenile justice. *Juvenile and Family Court Journal* 34(3):61–75.

Shichor, D., and D. Sechrest. 1998. A comparison of mediated and non-mediated juvenile offender cases in California. *Juvenile and Family Court Journal* 49(2):27–40.

Umbreit, M. S. 1994. *Victim Meets Offender: The Impact of Restorative Justice and Mediation*. Monsey, NJ: Criminal Justice Press.

 MENTAL HEALTH

Juvenile justice issues and mental health disciplines often present as contravening entities within Western cultures, with the former being dichotomous and the latter falling on a continuum. Juvenile justice in the United States entered the adversarial "guilty versus nonguilty" dichotomous rubric in 1967 with the U.S. Supreme Court's decision *In re Gault*. Intended to address the abuses long associated with juvenile courts, including closed sessions and a lack of due process protections, a latent result of the *In re Gault* decision was that it opened the floodgates to the current trend of certifying younger and younger juveniles as adults and holding them to the same standard of *mens rea*, despite considerable biophysiological and neuropsychological evidence to the contrary. At the same time, the incredible growth in our knowledge of brain physiology during the past decade has provided the clinical realm with more information on child and youth behavior than has ever been compiled previously, data that clearly contradict the assumptions still held by the juvenile and criminal justice systems.

THE CLINICAL/LEGAL DILEMMA ASSOCIATED WITH *PARENS PATRIAE*

British Common Law, the basis of U.S. jurisprudence, has long made a distinction between unpremeditated, impulsive, and infantile behaviors—those behaviors most likely to occur from birth to age 7. The challenge of rehabilitating, instead of merely punishing, wayward children and youth first gained attention in the United States during the mid-1800s among those advocating progressive, proactive, preventive programs for youth. They advocated the creation of special courts for troubled youth, mostly children in need of supervision (CHINS). In 1899, Illinois became the first state to establish a juvenile code specifically addressing criminal conduct, providing the foundation for the U.S. juvenile court philosophy. By 1925, all states had adopted separate juvenile courts based on this intervention philosophy. However, because of a lack of oversight, juvenile courts deteriorated. Following the trend in the adult criminal courts during the 1950s, juvenile courts moved from a proactive clinical model to that of reactive punishment and were not really challenged until 1966 with *Kent v. U.S.*

The *Kent* case was interesting in that it represented both the clinical and criminal aspects of juvenile justice while challenging the abuses of the special conditions associated with the juvenile court's authority of *parens patriae*. In this case, Morris Kent was accused of robbery, burglary, and rape at age 16. His case was first held in juvenile court, and he admitted these offenses during the informal proceedings. His case was then transferred to adult criminal court without a hearing. His juvenile court admission was used in his trial, and he was convicted of the robbery and burglary charges but found not guilty by reason of insanity for the rape charge. He was then sentenced to 90 years in prison. The case was eventually appealed to the U.S. Supreme Court, which referred the case back to the district court, urging that the conviction be vacated and the indictment dismissed based on the grounds that the transfer from juvenile to adult criminal courts was conducted without a hearing and counsel.

The dilemma articulated by the Supreme Court in *Kent* was that the state has a responsibility to protect children and youth when it exercises its authority of *parens patriae*. Juvenile proceedings thus are considered to fall within the realm of civil justice, with its goals of guidance and rehabilitation. These proceedings are not adversarial and therefore cannot be automatically transferred to criminal courts without all the safeguards of due process afforded adult offenders being executed.

A year after *Kent,* the *Gault* decision extended due process to juvenile court. The intent of the *Gault* decision was to incorporate three due process procedural requirements into the juvenile justice system: (1) the timely notice to parents and children of the nature and terms of any juvenile adjudication; (2) sufficient notice to provide counsel adequate time to prepare for these proceedings with counsel appointed for the indigent; and (3) maintenance of a written record, or its equivalent, adequate to allow for review for appeal purposes or for collateral proceedings. Together these requirements would address the basic Fourteenth Amendment guarantees and, with the exception of a jury trial, afford juveniles the same rights to which

adults are entitled (Wadlington, Whitebread, and Davis, 1983). In 1979, the American Bar Association adopted standards for juvenile representation:

> Justice requires that all parties subject to juvenile and family court proceedings (including children, parents, and other adults) be represented. Children and their parents (or guardians) should have independent counsel at all stages of legal proceedings concerning charges of delinquency, status offenses, and cases involving child abuse, neglect, custody, and adoption, except in temporary emergencies where immediate participation of counsel cannot be arranged. (Pitts, 2001:5)

The historic right to clinical treatment for juvenile offenders was articulated by Chief Justice Burger in 1975 in *O'Connor v. Donaldson:*

> There can be little doubt that in the exercise of its police power, a state can confine individuals solely to protect society from the dangers of significant antisocial acts or communicable disease. Additionally, the states are vested with the historic *parens patriae* power, including the duty to protect "persons under legal disabilities to act for themselves." The classic example of this role is when a state undertakes to act as "the general guardian of all infants, idiots, and lunatics."

Recently, widely publicized school shootings and other juvenile violence have resulted in more states lowering the age of minority relevant to juvenile status and more children and youth being qualified and tried as adults. The case of Lionel Tate—an African American who was 12 when he killed Tiffany Eunick, was subsequently classified as an adult, convicted of first-degree murder, and sentenced to life in prison—illustrates the gross failure of the post-*Gault* juvenile justice system. The missing link in contemporary juvenile justice is new evidence documenting the way a child's or adolescent's brain functions in relation to her or his capacity to control impulsive behaviors, have sufficient insight, or exercise good judgment. The capacities to make decisions (judgment) and delay gratification (impulses) are vested in the frontal lobe. Age-specific mitigating circumstances need to be addressed when looking at juvenile offenses.

Ironically, the weight of mitigating versus aggravating circumstances was the basis for reintroducing capital punishment in the United States in 1976 (see

Gregg v. Georgia, 1976; *Jurek v. Texas,* 1976; *Proffit v. Florida,* 1976). Nine years later, the Supreme Court declassified mental retardation as a protected mental illness, thus death qualifying the mentally incompetent, including teens (*Cleburne v. Cleburne Living Center,* 1985). Today, the United States has the highest incarceration and capital punishment rates of any Western culture. Further, the United States has failed to ratify the U.N. Convention on the Rights of the Child, sharing this distinction with only one other holdout—Somalia. Currently, there are over a dozen inmates on death row who were age 17 or younger at the time of their offenses. Moreover, numerous mentally retarded individuals have been executed or await execution, which is particularly significant because a diagnosis of mental retardation requires an onset prior to age 18, with most involving prenatal and neonatal etiologies. Once again, the Supreme Court has agreed to review the constitutionality of death qualifying mentally retarded offenders, with a decision made during the 2001 docket. The two cases involve mentally retarded offenders from Texas and North Carolina. When the high court first heard a similar case in 1989, they concluded that there was no national consensus against executing the mentally retarded. Today 13 of the 38 states that have the death penalty bar the execution of the mentally retarded.

NEUROPHYSIOLOGY AND NEUROPSYCHOLOGY OF CHILD AND ADOLESCENT IMPULSIVITY

Dendrite growth—neuronal branching in the central nervous system (CNS)—occurs during the embryonic stage of gene migration and during the development of the fetus. Marked dendrite growth is associated with the prepuberty period, with excessive branches pruned at about puberty. The neurons are not fully developed during this time and lack the insulation provided by myelination. Hence, the electrical impulses that occur in the CNS (about 70 millivolts) have a propensity to "storm" or short-circuit, thus providing the "magical thinking" often associated with prepuberty children. Another neurophysiological feature of the developing child's brain is that the frontal lobe is still immature and not capable of fully controlling the subcortical impulses emitted from the greater limbic system. This accounts for the sudden change in affect within children, including impulsivity, as well as their inability to make good judgments during these excited states.

Myelination of the frontal lobe neuronet increases during adolescence from puberty until the skeletal structure, including the brain and skull, has completed its growth at about age 18. The myelin sheath, a compact wrapping of glia material around the CNS neurons, provides insulation of some neurons, allowing for more rapid conductivity of the sending and receiving electrical impulses traversing the neuronet. This is a critical factor relevant to the frontal lobe properties of executive functioning, delayed gratification (control of subcortical impulses), and insight and judgment. In essence, the child and adolescent brain and corresponding neuronet is not sufficiently developed to meet the adult definition of *mens rea*—criminal intent—on which the most severe sanctions of society are based (Pinel, 1993).

Impulsivity of childhood and adolescence is further complicated by the relationship of the greater limbic system (subcortical autonomic processes) to the endocrine system. The structures of the greater limbic system—thalamus, hypothalamus, amygdala, hippocampus, septum, and basal ganglia—play a significant role in emotions, memory, and certain aspects of movement. The thalamus plays a significant role in relaying sensory information coming in and going out of the forebrain, providing the connector between the neocortex, where interpretations are conferred to our sensations, and the limbic system—the emotional/primitive portion of the brain. The hypothalamus maintains homeostasis and provides neurocompensation whenever dysregulation occurs. The amygdala plays a major role in emotions, notably those that pertain to sex, hunger, aggression, and fear reactions, while the hippocampus plays a role in learning, memory, and alcohol withdrawal seizures. The septum, which forms the wall between the fluid-filled lateral ventricles, is associated with rage and provides neurotransmission between the hippocampus and the hypothalamus. The basal gaglia, which include the amygdala, are a set of subcortical forebrain structures that play an important role in motor systems and neurotransmission. They are part of the neuronet that assists the thalamus in processing sensory motor activity to the neocortex for interpretation and meaning.

Greater limbic structures relevant to impulsive and addictive behaviors include the substantia nigra, which provides a major neurotransmitter, dopamine. Another major associated structure is the locus coeruleus, located within the pons. It is associated with the secretion of another major neurotransmitter, norepinephrine, and has the unique capacity of firing back on its own neurons, thereby exacerbating an autonomic response to a crisis situation. These subcortical functions work in conjunction with the endocrine system, which governs the autonomic responses of the peripheral nervous system (PNS). The PNS is a division of the nervous system consisting of all the nerves not part of the CNS (the brain or the spinal cord). It includes the autonomic nervous system and its components, the sympathetic and parasympathetic response systems.

The sympathetic nervous system is responsible for mobilizing the body's energy and resources during times of stress and arousal, including impulsive reactions. This mechanism of action involves activation of the adrenal medulla, which secretes norepinephrine and epinephrine (adrenalin), two excitatory catecholamines whose actions influence the bronchi, heart, veins, and arteries to increase blood flow to muscles, the heart, and the brain for quick response to stress situations (Preston, O'Neal, and Talaga, 1994).

Involved in impulse control dysregulation is the hypothalamic-pituitary-end-organ axis. All variations involve the subcortical neuroendocrine feedback loop and the relationship of the CNS, hypothalamus, anterior pituitary, and target glands and tissues. Basic "fight or flight" sympathetic responses involve the hypothalamic-pituitary adrenal axis, while sexual aggression (paraphilias) involve the hypothalamic-pituitary-gonad axis along with the influence of the luteinizing hormone (French, 1991). These subcortical/pituitary functions pose a challenge to the neocortex for fully developed adults and are more problematic for children and youth because they do not have a sufficiently developed frontal lobe or established neuronets. When these impulses overwhelm the neocortex (the rational portion of the brain) in a pathological fashion, they are know as the "manias" accounting for the irrational behaviors associated with bipolar hypermania, brief psychotic disorders, the paraphilias, kleptomania, pyromania, trichotillomania, and intermittent explosive disorder (American Psychiatric Association, 1994).

Children and youth are more likely to experience electrical storming in the CNS as well as the impact of impulsive urges emanating from the subcortical greater limbic region. This fact, coupled with an immature frontal lobe, clearly indicates that children and youth are not operating under the same mental capacity as adults with a fully developed brain structure and therefore should not be held to the same degree of culpability relevant to their behaviors. Certainly, their clinical situation should not be relegated to an Axis II personality disorder, one which is exempt from the protections offered by Axis I clinical syndromes. Children and youth are exempt from a clinical diagnosis of a personality disorder because this capacity cannot be adequately measured during the physiological and neurological developmental periods of childhood and adolescence due to the numerous intervening variables already cited. The challenge for both the criminal justice and mental health systems is to become more aware of these factors and to provide interventions and innovative rehabilitative methods that better reflect these processes and that will benefit children, youth, and society.

Laurence A. French

See also Learning Disabilities; Theories of Delinquency—Psychological

Bibliography

American Psychiatric Association. 1994. *Diagnostic and Statistical Manual on Mental Disorders,* 4th ed. Washington, DC: American Psychiatric Association.

French, L. A. 1991. A practitioner's note on treating sexual deviance. *Psychological Reports* 68:1195–1198.

Pinel, J. 1993. *Biopsychology.* Boston: Allyn & Bacon.

Pitts, L. 2001. Beyond rhetoric: Civil rights approach to protecting children's due process rights. *North Carolina Academy of Trial Lawyers: Trial Briefs,* January:3–10.

Preston, J., J. H. O'Neal, and M. C. Talaga. 1994. *Handbook of Clinical Psychopharmacology for Therapists.* Oakland, CA: New Harbinger.

Wadlington, W., C. H. Whitebread, and S. M. Davis. 1983. Chapter III: Reshaping the juvenile justice system: Before and after *In re Gault.* Pp. 197–262 in C. H. Whitebread and S. M. Davis (eds.), *Cases and Materials on Children in the Legal System.* Mineola, NY: The Foundation Press.

Cases Cited

Cleburne v. Cleburne Living Center, 84 S.Ct. 468 (1985).

Gregg v. Georgia, 428 U.S. 153, 237–241 (1976).

In re Gault, 387 U.S. 1, 87 S.Ct. 1428, 18 L.Ed.2d 527 (1967).

Jurek v. Texas, 428 U.S. 262, 96 S.Ct. 2950 (1976).

Kent v. U.S., 383 U.S. 541, 554, 86 S.Ct. 1045, 16 L.Ed.2d 84 (1966).

O'Connor v. Donaldson, 422 U.S. 563, 95 S.Ct. 2486, 45 L.Ed.2d 396 (1975).

Proffit v. Florida, 428 U.S. 242, 252 (1976).

MENTORING PROGRAMS

A mentor is a concerned adult who helps a child understand and better deal with the world. Normally, the relationship is supportive and aims to facilitate the child's educational, social, and personal growth. Though not the usual case, a person can have more than one mentor. This adult guidance and support has been both theoretically and empirically found to enhance development from childhood to adulthood. Given the number of youth deemed at high risk, there is increased interest in promoting nonfamily adult support relationships. Research further points to such relationships as an answer to countering youth antisocial development.

Traditionally, the treatment of high-risk youth has been the job of professionals. However, more local organizations are intervening to bring paraprofessionals into service programs that interface with youth. Most of these programs seek to provide high-risk children with an alternative view of a world lacking in positive role models. Frequently, these programs target specific populations. For example, there are mentoring programs specifically for gifted children, disadvantaged youth, children at risk for dropping out of school, children with disabilities, and juvenile delinquents.

While older programs such as the Big Brothers Big Sisters are not geared to specific problems of the youth in these mentor-mentee relationships, newer programs are frequently designed by researchers and clinicians specifically to reduce maladjustments. The organizations that offer programs to help maladjusted youth are national youth-serving organizations, youth sports organizations, independent youth organizations, and broad-based private organizations.

NATIONAL YOUTH-SERVING ORGANIZATIONS

Among all organizations serving youth, this category is perhaps the largest. They include 4-H, Boy Scouts and Girl Scouts, Boys and Girls Clubs, YMCA and YWCA, Girls Incorporated, Camp Fire, Big Brothers Big Sisters, and Junior Achievement. According to the National Collaboration for Youth, more than 30 million youths are served annually by these programs. Most of the organizations promote prosocial values and life-skills building such as leadership, decision making, and problem solving. In most instances, mentors can be either paid or unpaid leaders.

The degree of autonomy afforded the local affiliates of these organizations ranges from very structured to relaxed. The scouting organizations, for example, are top-down in their structure, as is evident with the use of handbooks, uniforms, badges, and delineated management guidelines. At the other end are organizations such as YMCA and YWCA, which encourage local and more individual development dependent on the needs of the particular geographic area. There is also identifiable diversity among the youth served. For example, the children of the Boys and Girls Clubs are characteristically minorities from low-income households, while the typical scouting organization youths are not.

PUBLIC AGENCY PROGRAMS

Quinn (1999) suggests that it is not always easy to distinguish between private and public youth development sectors. While most mentoring programs are conducted by private, nonprofit organizations, a number of the organizations do receive public funds via federal, state, and local funds. Nonetheless, Quinn identifies two programs as good public programs: public library programs for young adolescents and parks and recreation services. Some of the young people who use libraries go there for more than just the books. In some neighborhoods, libraries have become a safe haven for children. Computers in the libraries are also a major attraction. In fact, library programs developed after noticing that libraries became special "hangout" locales for students. Once this phenomenon was discovered, libraries were encouraged to structure programs for this captive audience, a sizable number of which included latchkey kids.

Parks and recreation services, like libraries, provide a venue for children to have fun and learn valuable life lessons as well. As with libraries, parks and recreation services are found in most neighborhoods. They are literally ready-made areas for youth programs because they are usually fitted with community centers, parks, pools, athletic fields, playgrounds, and other facilities. The Chicago Parks Department, which established 40 new programs to service more than 4,500 children annually, is one example of the more structured programs. A similar program located in Oregon aims to provide children with constructive after-school activities. Similar programs are available across the country.

YOUTH SPORTS ORGANIZATION

Sporting activities of all kinds are popular with children. The potential to make a positive impact on children through sporting events is real, an opportunity that should not go untapped. There are numerous little leagues and similar groups throughout the country, and worldwide for that matter. Perhaps no greater opportunity may present itself for responsible, caring, and dedicated adults and older teens to influence the impressionable minds of youth. Outlets such as these are the only opportunity for a growing number of youth to have positive interactions with adults. They have the opportunity to learn to play and work alongside both adults and other children who may come from dissimilar backgrounds.

PRIVATE ORGANIZATIONS

Among the types of private organizations working to give children needed prosocial skills are religious organizations and adult service clubs. Religious organizations are estimated to serve between 33 percent and 50 percent of American youth (Quinn, 1999). These organizations have at their core an interest in youth's moral development as well as their social and emotional growth. Worship services and formal instructions are also typical community projects.

Adult service clubs include the Association of Junior Leagues, Kiwanis, and Rotary. Other organizations, such as adult fraternities and sororities, involve themselves with young people both financially and socially, by providing scholarships for children, sponsoring equipment for sporting events, and creating other outreach programs.

Lorraine Samuels

See also Boys and Girls Clubs of America

Bibliography

Grossman, J., and J. Tierney. 1998. Does mentoring work? An impact study of the Big Brothers Big Sisters Program. *Evaluation Review* 22:403–426.

Haensly, P., and J. Parsons. 1993. Creative, intellectual, and psychosocial development through mentorship: Relationships and stages. *Youth and Society* 25:202–221.

Jackson, Y. 2002. Mentoring for delinquent children: An outcome study with young adolescent children. *Journal of Youth and Adolescence* 31:115–122.

Quinn, J. 1999. Where need meets opportunity: Youth development programs for early teens. *The Future of Children* 9(2):96–111.

Rogers, A., and A. Taylor. 1997. Intergenerational mentoring: A viable strategy for meeting the needs of vulnerable youth. *Journal of Gerontology and Social Work* 28:125–140.

MILLER, JEROME G. (1931–)

Jerome G. Miller is recognized as one of the nation's leading authorities on corrections, alternative programs, and clinical work with violent juvenile and adult offenders. Dr. Miller has a Ph.D. in Psychiatric Social Work and has taught at Ohio State University. He has held positions as Commissioner of the Massachusetts Department of Youth Services, Director of the Illinois Department of Children and Family Services, and Commissioner of Children and Youth for the Commonwealth of Pennsylvania.

From 1989 to 1994, Dr. Miller was Jail and Prison Monitor for the United States Court in the Middle District of Florida. In October of 1995, Dr. Miller was appointed by the federal court to be "Receiver" of the District of Columbia's Child Welfare System. He is also Former President and Cofounder of the National Center on Institutions and Alternatives and Clinical Director of the Augustus Institute in Alexandria, Virginia. The center develops innovative criminal justice programs and services in response to institutional overcrowding and assists in creating sentencing alternatives to imprisonment.

THE MASSACHUSETTS EXPERIMENT

Jerome Miller is best known for reforming the juvenile correctional system in Massachusetts. He was appointed the first Commissioner of Youth Services for the Commonwealth of Massachusetts in 1969. In his first two years in that position, he initiated a number of reform measures in an effort to provide more humane treatment for the young persons in his department's care. From 1969 to 1972, Miller closed the state reform schools and placed the residents in community programs. The results of his actions were the release of 95 percent of the 1,200 youth from secure facilities to community-based contractors or an outright release.

Although Commissioner Miller was forced from office by the legislature, his legacy remains intact. There was no resulting juvenile crime wave. Today Massachusetts has roughly 200 secure beds, and the Department of Youth Services places more than 80 percent of juveniles in small, staff-secured programs operated by private, nonprofit agencies. Massachusetts continues to have one of the lowest rates of juvenile crime in the United States.

OTHER ACHIEVEMENTS

Dr. Miller is an advocate for developing therapeutic treatment alternatives in a noninstitutionalized setting for many juvenile and adult offenders. He strongly believes that community-based treatment programs provide a better and less expensive alternative to institutionalization with a reduction in future criminality.

His books include *Last One Over the Wall: The Massachusetts Experiment in Closing Reform Schools* (1991), which chronicles his experiences as the administrator of the Massachusetts Juvenile Correctional System. That book was the winner of the Edward Sagarin Prize from the American Society of Criminology. Another book, *Search and Destroy: African-American Males in the Criminal Justice System* (1996), systematically analyzes and critiques the overrepresentation of black males in the criminal justice system. Dr. Miller continues to work for the betterment of juvenile corrections and the juvenile justice system.

Robert A. Jerin

See also Deinstitutionalization Movement; Diversion Programs; Reformatories and Reform Schools; Training Schools

Bibliography

Coates, R. B., A. D. Miller, and L. E. Ohlin. 1978. *Diversity in a Youth Correctional System: Handling Delinquents in Massachusetts*. Cambridge, MA: Ballinger.

Miller, A. D., and L. E. Ohlin. 1985. *Delinquency and Community: Creating Opportunities and Controls.* Beverly Hills, CA: Sage.

Miller, J. 1991. *Last One Over the Wall: The Massachusetts Experiment in Closing Reform Schools.* Columbus: Ohio State University Press.

Miller, J. 1997. *Search and Destroy: African-American Males in the Criminal Justice System.* Cambridge, MA: Cambridge University Press.

Rutherford, A. 1974. *The Dissolution of the Training Schools in Massachusetts.* Columbus, OH: Academy for Contemporary Problems.

MILLER, WALTER B. (1920–)

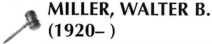

Walter B. Miller was born in 1920 in Philadelphia, Pennsylvania. He received his master's degree in anthropology in 1950 from the University of Chicago. From this field, Miller would develop his appreciation of conducting research by direct observation of people in their natural settings, called ethnography. He went on to complete his Ph.D. in Social Relations at Harvard University in 1954.

Miller worked as a researcher on various projects, including the Fox Indian Applied Anthropology Project, which looked at Native American political organization (1948–1952). Soon after, he was involved in a study of public health practices with the Harvard School of Public Health (1953–1955), where he collaborated with Dr. Benjamin D. Paul, editing a case book titled *Health, Culture and Community*. Between 1956 and 1972, Miller was active in a variety of research projects in urban studies.

CONTRIBUTIONS TO THE GANG DELINQUENCY LITERATURE

Beginning in 1955, Miller worked on the Boston Delinquency Project, serving as its director from 1958 to 1965. This privately funded demonstration project attempted to change the attitudes and activities of corner-group youth (predominantly male and Irish) through the interventions of a small group of social workers in the field. As Miller reported, the project was somewhat effective at lowering rates of law-violating behavior as well as reducing hostility towards law enforcement officials.

Drawing from these experiences, Miller made significant contributions to subcultural theories of delinquency with his work on lower-class gang members. While other theorists writing at this time viewed lower-class children as competing unsuccessfully for, and being frustrated by, middle-class standards, Miller (1958) saw lower-class lifestyles and values as separate and distinct, functional in their own surroundings. As he explained, lower-class delinquent behavior is primarily the result of pursuing values common to the cultural environment.

Building on common perceptions of the time, he theorized that broken homes were related to delinquency and gang involvement. Miller argued that many of the youth he had observed came from female-dominated households, where the mothers engaged in serial monogomy. This meant that significant male authority figures rotated in and out of the home without providing the sex-role identification and authority that the youth needed.

Young men from these working-class urban environments exhibited thought patterns and behaviors that were marked by what Miller identified as lower-class focal concerns or values, including trouble, smartness, excitement, fate, toughness, and autonomy. The youth seemed to favor a reputation for "trouble" and sought out older peers from the streets as role models who reflected their preference for maleness, status, and belonging.

Miller continued his work on youth gangs and has been responsible for, or associated with, all three phases of the federal government's Youth Gang Surveys. These surveys cover the years from 1974 to 1978, 1980 to 1993, and 1994 to 1998. Over this period, Walter Miller has arguably been the nation's foremost expert on youth gangs. In 2001, the Office of Juvenile Justice and Delinquency Prevention published his latest report on the growth of youth gangs in the United States.

ACADEMIC RECOGNITION

Dr. Miller held positions at Boston University, Brandeis University, Simmons College, the Graduate School of Education at Harvard University, and the State University of New York at Albany. In 1973, he was named a research fellow at the Center for Criminal Justice at the Harvard Law School, where he is now professor emeritus.

Marilyn D. McShane

See also Gangs, Juvenile; Theories of Delinquency

Bibliography

Miller, W. B. 1958. Lower class culture as a generating milieu of gang delinquency. *Journal of Social Issues* 14(3):5–19.

Miller, W. B. 1959. Preventive work with street-corner groups: Boston Delinquency Project. *The Annals of the American Academy of Political and Social Science* 322(March):97–106.

Miller, W. B. 1959. Implications of lower class culture for social work. *Social Service Review* 33:219–236.

Miller, W. B. 1962. The impact of a total-community delinquency control project. *Social Problems* 10:168–191.

Miller, W. B. 2001. *The Growth of Youth Gang Problems in the United States: 1970–98.* Washington, DC: Office of Juvenile Justice and Delinquency Prevention.

 # MISSING CHILDREN

Missing children, as a concept, is defined as "children whose whereabouts are unknown to their parent, guardian, or legal custodian." The term refers to children who have been abducted by either a family or nonfamily member and includes children who have been abducted within the United States and those who have been abducted from the United States to a foreign country. It includes those who may later be identified as runaway or throwaway children and those who are lured away through child exploitation. As the definition states, it may also refer to children whose whereabouts are simply unknown.

This entry is concerned primarily with nonfamily and family abductions. Experts estimate that 85 percent to 90 percent of missing-person reports to the Federal Bureau of Investigation (FBI) have to do with children. Based on this estimation, in 2000, 750,000 (or 2,100 children per day) were reported missing according to the FBI's National Crime Information Center (NCIC).

The key NCIC categories in which missing-child reports are entered are juvenile, endangered, and involuntary. Most missing-child cases are entered into the juvenile category, including some nonfamily abduction where there is no evidence of foul play. *Endangered* is defined as "missing and in the company of another person under circumstances indicating that his or her physical safety is in danger." The involuntary group includes abduction or kidnapping and is defined as "missing under circumstances indicating that the disappearance was not voluntary."

Kidnapping and murder of a child by a stranger were once thought to be the most common type of child abduction, but this is a misconception. Nonfamily abductions receive the most media attention but actually account for the smallest percentage of missing children. Teens and girls tend to be the most common victims of nonfamily abductions, but infants can also be at risk. In the majority of cases, the abductions were for relatively short periods of time and involved sexual assault. Parental abduction of children is a serious concern in the United States, where over half of all children spend time in single-parent households. The risk of international abduction is heightened in relationships where dual citizenship with the United States exists.

In 1988 the first National Incidence Study on Missing, Abducted, Runaway and Throwaway Children in America (NISMART) was conducted, with its findings published in 1990. NISMART indicated that more than 1 million children are victimized through abduction annually. This estimation, however, did not include police data on family abductions. The study established five categories of missing children for its examination: nonfamily abductions, family abduction, runaways, throwaways, and other missing children.

NISMART 2 is now under way. Researchers have expanded the number of missing children categories to eight in the current national study. The purpose is to distinguish between custodial interference and more serious family abductions. Runaway and throwaway children are combined into one category. The new version also distinguishes between general missing-child cases, in which the children are lost, and those in which the child is injured. The number of children who were sexually assaulted will be identified, and the study will account for children who were missing as a result of simple miscommunication and were not in any danger.

The National Incident-Based Reporting System (NIBRS), a comprehensive system for collecting and assembling crime information, is being tested to replace the FBI's *Uniform Crime Reports* (which largely contains arrest data). Recent data from NIBRS indicates that kidnapping of juveniles is a relatively rare crime, constituting less than 2 percent of all violent crimes against juveniles. Nonfamily abductions primarily involve strangers that isolate the juvenile in order to commit another crime, such as sexual assault or robbery. Not yet nationally recognized, NIBRS identifies a new category of acquaintance kidnapping—which has a higher percentage of female offenders than stranger abduction and the largest proportion of juvenile offenders. Even more unusual than the crime of kidnapping itself is finding a child alive after a long period of being missing. This fact was

highlighted in November 1997 when Crystal Anzaldi was found living in Puerto Rico, seven years after she had been kidnapped. Abducted from her home in San Diego, Crystal was 14 months old at the time. DNA tests confirmed that the eight-year-old girl was the daughter of Dorothy and Jeffrey Anzaldi.

KEY NATIONAL LEGISLATIVE REFORMS

The Office of Juvenile Justice and Delinquency Prevention (OJJDP) is the federal agency responsible for providing national leadership, coordination, and resources to prevent and respond to juvenile delinquency and victimization, pursuant to the Juvenile Justice and Delinquency Prevention Act (JJDPA) of 1974 (42 U.S.C. § 5601). Its Child Protection Division (CPD) administers projects, programs, and initiatives related to crimes against children and children's exposure to violence.

The Missing Children's Act of 1982 (28 U.S.C. § 534(a)) permits parents to guarantee that identifying information about their missing child is promptly entered into the NCIC computer system. The National Center for Missing and Exploited Children (NCMEC) is available to verify the information that is entered.

In 1984, Congress enacted the Missing Children's Assistance Act, Title IV of the Juvenile Justice and Delinquency Prevention Act of 1974 (42 U.S.C. §§ 5771–5780). Under this mandate, a 24-hour toll-free hotline was established to which individuals could report information regarding the location of any missing child, or other child 13 years of age or younger, whose whereabouts are unknown to her or his legal custodian. Interested individuals now have the resources for information on procedures necessary to reunite the child with her or his legal custodian.

The Missing Children's Assistance Act formed the Missing and Exploited Children's Program (MECP) under the Office of Juvenile Justice and Delinquency Prevention. MECP coordinates federal missing and exploited children activities, including exploitation prevention efforts, locating missing children and reuniting them with their families, and addressing the psychological impact of abduction on the child and the family. MECP provides funds for a variety of activities to support and coordinate a network of resources such as the National Center for Missing and Exploited Children, training and technical assistance to a network of state clearinghouses, nonprofit organizations, law enforcement personnel and attorneys, and research and demonstration programs. Under the National Child Search Assistance Act of 1990 (P.L. 101-647), federal, state, and local law enforcement are required to enter reports of missing children less than 18 years old and unidentified persons into the NCIC computer.

Congress enacted an International Parental Child Kidnaping Act (18 U.S.C. § 1204) in 1993 to protect children from international child abduction. This legislation reflects the growing concern and compounded difficulties when a child is abducted across international boarders. Since the late 1970s, more than 7,000 American children were abducted from the United States or prevented from returning to the United States by one of their parents. The Department of State reports that the Hague Convention provides a treaty obligation of involved countries to return an abducted child who is under the age of 16 if application is made within one year from the date of the wrongful removal or retention. In the past, most taking parents were fathers; now 70 percent of taking parents are mothers, and courts in some countries are reluctant to compel children's return to their fathers in the United States. Before the United States became party to the Hague Convention, only about 20 percent of abducted children were returned to the United States. Under the convention, about 72 percent of cases now result in return or access. The rate of returns from the United States to other countries is even higher, approximately 90 percent, including voluntary returns.

The most recent act relating to missing children is the Child Protection and Sexual Predator Punishment Act of 1998 (H.R. 3494). It provides for numerous sentencing enhancements and other initiatives addressing sex crimes against children. Perhaps of most importance is that it includes crimes facilitated by the use of interstate facilities and the Internet.

CHARACTERISTICS AND ESTIMATED RATES OF ABDUCTION

Nonfamily Child Abduction

Highly publicized cases of child kidnapping and victimization have generated incredible fear among parents and children. Examples highlight these abduction events as newsworthy, commanding intense media focus. This national attention makes clear the need for legislation, research, common definitions, and consistent reporting of missing children. In the face of growing evidence that few abductions are committed by strangers (the ones most highly publicized), the category of stranger abduction was renamed as nonfamily abduction, because like many crimes committed against individuals, the offender is usually someone known to the victim. The best current estimates are that approximately 3,000 nonfamily abductions occur annually, with few of these falling under the old conception of "strangers."

One such child-kidnapping case was heralded as "The Crime of the Century." In 1932, a kidnapper dared to enter the home of then America's hero, Charles A. Lindbergh, to steal his child. The 20-month-old Lindbergh baby was taken from his second-story nursery in New Jersey and a ransom note was left behind on the windowsill. The controversy surrounding the kidnapping and subsequent conviction of Richard Bruno Hauptmann for the murder continue to this day. Kidnapping was not a federal crime at the time. Fueled by the Lindbergh tragedy, Congress passed a federal kidnapping statute (18 U.S.C. § 1201) in 1932.

The abduction of 6-year-old Adam Walsh is the most widely known child kidnapping of recent history. Adam, who had been left alone by his father, disappeared from a shopping mall across from a Hollywood, Florida, police station on July 27, 1981. Two weeks later, evidence of his murder was found in a canal 120 miles away. The major suspect in the kidnapping was never tried. The story of the tragedy was dramatized in two television movies. Following the airing of the broadcasts, a roll of missing children was featured, leading to the recovery of 65 youngsters.

At the time of Adam's disappearance, there was no system in place for tracking information or leads about abducted children. Law enforcement agencies were not trained or equipped to investigate missing-child reports, and most were reluctant to get involved in missing-child cases. Adam's parents, John and Reve Walsh, turned their grief into the confrontation of bureaucratic resistance. Their tireless efforts led to the passage of the 1982 Missing Children Act and the Missing Children's Assistance Act of 1984.

The Polly Klaas Foundation of Petaluma, California, was formed in 1993 to continue the search for the missing 12-year-old Polly Klaas. Kidnapped at knifepoint from her bedroom on October 1 of that year, she and two of her friends had been tied up and gagged. Polly was abducted while her mother slept in a room nearby. Despite the assistance of thousands of volunteers from across the nation, the child was not found alive. Richard Allen Davis was convicted on

June 18, 1996, of this murder and kidnapping. The Klaas kidnapping horrified the nation and was a driving force behind the passage of a California law that prescribes a life jail term for people convicted of a third felony crime. Today the foundation assists parents and communities with the recovery of missing children, disseminates child safety materials, and provides support for child safety legislation.

America's families lived in fear of stranger child abduction, thought to be the number one worry of children and parents between 1987 and 1997. Only recently has a picture begun to emerge indicating the true extent of child abduction, which is now recognized to be vastly smaller than the original estimates. Kidnapping is not one of the crimes included in the FBI's *Uniform Crime Reports,* and individual states rarely gathered independent statistics on the event. The National Crime Victimization Survey collects data only on crimes occurring to persons 12 years of age or older.

Infant Abductions

Although nonfamily abduction of infants (birth through 6 months) is not a crime of epidemic proportion, it is still a concern for parents, health care security and risk-management administrators, and law-enforcement officials. NCMEC studied a group of 187 infants known to have been abducted by nonfamily members between 1983 and 1999, finding that approximately half of the infants were 7 days old or younger when taken. The majority of these children were recovered and returned safely to their parents, but 12 are still missing. The data do not suggest a strong gender preference in the kidnapping of these infants. A profile of the "typical abductor" emerged.

The "typical" infant abductor is female between the ages of 21 and 50, often overweight. She is likely to be compulsive and seizes the child by opportunity, yet plans the abduction. Often married or cohabiting, she is likely to have lost a baby or is incapable of having one and perceives the child as "her newborn baby." Typically, the abductor lives in the community where the kidnapping takes place, visits the local hospital nursery frequently before committing the crime, and often impersonates hospital staff.

Family Abductions

According to NISMART, family members abduct approximately 355,000 children annually, almost 90

times more frequently than nonfamily members. NIBRS differs in its determination of the frequency of family abductions. Reflecting police data, it finds family members commit a slight minority of kidna ppings. This discrepancy may suggest that most kidnappings reported to police are not actually recorded as "crimes."

The typical perpetrator is a parent of the child, yet other family members kidnap a small percentage of these victims. Family abductions can be viewed as two separate categories, according to severity. In the first are situations in which a family member takes a child in violation of a custody agreement or decree or, in violation of a custody order, fails to return a child at the end of the legal or agreed-upon visit. The second type involves an attempt to conceal the taking or whereabouts of the child or to prevent contact with the child. In such cases, the abductor may take the child out of state or may intend to keep the child indefinitely and permanently alter custodial arrangements. The vast majority of these kidnapping cases involving family occur within the context of divorce.

Almost half of family kidnappings involve an attempt to conceal the child, take him or her out of state, or permanently alter custody. A common misconception is that the child is safe because he or she is with a family member. Over half of the abductions occur in relationships with histories of domestic violence, and many of the abductors have criminal records. The majority of family abductions are quickly resolved, however. In severe cases, child victims have had their names and appearances altered and experience medical or physical neglect, unstable schooling, homelessness, and/or frequent moves.

Family perpetrators kidnap males and females in approximately equal proportions. Both males and females are equally prone to kidnap their offspring. Children under the age of 6 are most likely to be victims of family abduction. In cases where a parent has a history of violating custody or visitation agreements or has made threats to abduct his or her child in the past, there is a risk.

NONABDUCTION CATEGORIES: RUNAWAY AND THROWAWAY CHILDREN

There are approximately 1.3 million runaway and homeless youth in the United States, according to the National Runaway Switchboard. The number of throwaway children may actually be a large portion of this figure, since young people living in shelters and on the street often report that an adult caretaker either asked them to leave or did not care whether they left. According to the Department of Health and Human Services, up to 300,000 prostituted children may live on the streets in the United States. Many are only 11 or 12 years old, and some are as young as 9.

RESOURCES FOR LOCATING MISSING CHILDREN

Every state has set up programs to help parents in locating and recovering their missing children. While the scope and extent of each program varies, they include statewide photo dissemination and assistance in obtaining information from state agency records. As time elapses on a case, parents or law enforcement authorities may request age progression of the child's photograph using computer technology and graphics.

The Child Protection Division administers federal programs related to crimes against children and provides leadership and funding in the areas of enforcement, intervention, and prevention. The Jimmy Ryce Law Enforcement Training Center at NCMEC provides a national training program that promotes awareness of FBI and other federal resources that assist law enforcement agencies investigating missing children cases.

A voluntary partnership between law enforcement agencies and broadcasters called the AMBER Plan activates an urgent bulletin through the Emergency Alert System in the most serious child abduction cases. The NCMEC, the Vanished Children's Alliance, and the Polly Klaas Foundation are examples of organizations dedicated to assisting parents, law enforcement, and the community on missing children issues.

Lorraine Samuels

See also Foster Care; Prostitution, Teenage; Runaways; Victimization of Juveniles

Bibliography

Best, J. 1990. *Threatened Children: Rhetoric and Concern About Child-Victims*. Chicago: University of Chicago Press.

Finkelhor, D., and N. Asdigian. 1996. New categories of missing children: Injured, lost, delinquent, and victims of caregiver mix-ups. *Child Welfare* 75(4): 291–310.

Finkelhor, D., G. Hotaling, and A. Sedlak. 1990. *Missing, Abducted, Runaway and Thrown Away Children in America*. Collingdale, PA: DIANE.

Forst, M. L., and M. E. Blomquist. 1991. *Missing Children: Rhetoric and Reality*. New York: Lexington Books.

N

NATIONAL COUNCIL ON CRIME AND DELINQUENCY

The National Council on Crime and Delinquency (NCCD), a private organization, was established in 1907. Its earliest work involved expanding the juvenile court movement as a means of keeping children out of the criminal justice system. The Council also developed model laws and standards to strengthen the newly developing professions of probation and parole. In addition, the NCCD assisted many states in organizing their first juvenile court systems and in developing programs to rehabilitate offenders without resorting to incarceration (NCCD, 2001).

In 1954, the NCCD launched a major research and consultation program to involve citizens in criminal justice reform efforts, and during the 1960s, the NCCD received financial support from the Mary Babcock Reynolds Foundation, the Rockefeller Brothers Fund, and the National Institute of Mental Health, which allowed the NCCD to expand its research and training.

The nature of the Council's work today encompasses a multitude of functions that include, among other projects, providing program evaluations of correctional programs, providing strategic planning for juvenile detention systems, and helping correctional and child welfare agencies manage limited resources. Since 1982, the NCCD has also provided accurate planning models and forecasts for prison, jail, training school, secure detention, and parole and probation populations in over 30 states (NCCD, 2001). The well-respected professional journal *Crime and Delinquency* is published by Sage Press, in cooperation with the NCCD. Long-term editor Don C. Gibbons, a professor at Portland State University, retired as editor in 2000 and was succeeded by Ron E. Vogel of California State University at Long Beach.

The NCCD is headquartered in Oakland, California, and the Midwest office is in Madison, Wisconsin. Work is also conducted out of a Washington, D.C., office.

The NCCD recognizes and honors with special awards outstanding practitioners, public officials, and scholars in the fields of criminal and juvenile justice and child protective services. Recent recipients were Norval Morris of the University of Chicago, for outstanding contributions in criminology, and U.S. Senator Patrick Leahy, for forceful leadership in implementing effective crime prevention and control policies that are fair, humane, and economically sound. The organization also presents media awards to print and broadcast journalists, TV news and feature reporters, producers and writers, and those in film and literature who try to focus on criminal and juvenile systems in a thoughtful and balanced manner. The media awards, which have continued for eight years, place special emphasis on media efforts that help the public understand the causes of crime and what must be improved or changed to prevent and control crime.

MEMBERS OF THE ORGANIZATION

The staff at the NCCD includes more than 20 professional employees spread out through its various offices. Barry Krisberg has been the president of the NCCD for the last 14 years. Toni Aleman serves as Director of Administration, and S. Christopher Baird is Senior Vice President and has directed the Midwest office in Madison, Wisconsin, since 1984. Robert E. DeComo is Director of Research in the Oakland office and has been employed at the NCCD since 1989. The current Chairperson of the Board of Directors is Chase Riveland of Riveland Associates, and the preceding chair was Allen F. Brand, a criminal justice consultant.

NCCD President Barry Krisberg (1998) produced a summative article in a special January anniversary edition of *Crime and Delinquency* titled "The Evolution of an American Institution," which highlighted the accomplishments of the NCCD as it celebrated its 90th year in service to the nation. Krisberg related the history of the NCCD, from its beginnings in 1907, when 14 probation officers met in Minneapolis, to the 1950s, when the organization made greater use of citizens and benefited from a five-year grant from the Ford Foundation. Krisberg further discussed how in the 1970s the NCCD expanded its research, training, and technical assistance programs. He also described how in the early 1980s the organization experienced a period of hardship but bounced back through the generous financial backing of groups like the Edna McConnell Clark Foundation, Bristol Meyers, AT&T, and several private philanthropists.

In addition to providing a historical overview of the NCCD, Krisberg reemphasized that the following principles continue to guide the organization:

1. A separate court system for children is of crucial importance.

2. Community-based alternatives to incarceration are necessary.

3. The link between the pursuit of social justice and the achievement of domestic tranquility is crucial.

In his article, Krisberg also described other prominent contributors to the special anniversary issue, who not only celebrated the accomplishments of the NCCD but also discussed the need for additional reform efforts in the future. For instance, Allen Breed and Marvin Wolfgang wrote about the need to rekindle professional leadership and the continuing struggle to end capital punishment in America. Janet Reno wrote a piece titled "Taking America Back for our Children," and Albert Blumstein wrote "Rising Prison Populations and Stable Crime Rates." Other recognized scholars and practitioners who provided articles for the special issue included John Irwin, James Austin, Shay Bilchik, James C. Howell, Peter Greenwood, and Lloyd Ohlin.

ACTIVITIES OF THE ORGANIZATION

The NCCD is engaged in many activities. NCCD staff, for instance, have extensive experience implementing programs and conducting rigorous process and outcome evaluations in diverse settings. Examples of the NCCD's recent single and multisite evaluation work include the following:

1. Completion of a five-site process and outcome evaluation of drug treatment programs in local jails funded by the National Institute of Justice to provide policy-relevant recommendations for jail-based treatment programs.

2. Completion of a process and outcome evaluation of the Los Angeles County adult boot camp, known as the Regimented Inmate Diversion (RID) Program.

3. Completion of a four-jurisdiction process evaluation of the Bureau of Justice Assistance's Correctional Options Demonstration Program and continued work as the national evaluator of this multisite program.

4. Ongoing process evaluation of the Federal Office of Juvenile Justice and Delinquency Prevention's Intensive Aftercare Program (IAP) Model currently being implemented in four jurisdictions. An outcome analysis is expected to be funded in the near future, with the NCCD as the national evaluator (NCCD, 2001).

Another example of a major research undertaking by the NCCD is illustrated in a 1994 report entitled "Prisoners Who Don't Need to Be Imprisoned," completed by James Austin (1994). In this report, the NCCD was asked to undertake a study of the Florida Department of Corrections' inmate population. The study was part of an ongoing effort by the NCCD to provide Florida's policymakers, and the public at large, with information and analysis on the state's use of incarceration to help control crime. Based on this study, the NCCD advanced the proposition that a significant number of inmates who were incarcerated were low-risk inmates who could have been safely placed in alternative sanctions without increasing the risk to public safety and at considerable savings to Florida taxpayers.

Another role that the NCCD plays is to regularly issue policy (position) statements on current issues in juvenile justice and the criminal justice system in general. For example, the NCCD recently issued a call for protection of children from gun violence, calling on the federal government to initiate action to support localities that are addressing this issue. Among the suggestions were to (1) provide funding to hire 100,000 new school counselors, (2) fund programs to help create policy and programmatic solutions to reduce violence in their communities and schools, and (3) support the restructuring of ineffective zero-tolerance programs (NCCD, 2001).

A brief sample of other policy statements issued by the NCCD include the topics of females in the criminal justice system, the link between child welfare and juvenile delinquency, the struggle to stop domestic violence, and the NCCD's July 2000 board of directors' call for a death penalty moratorium.

CONTRIBUTIONS TO RESEARCH AND POLICY ON JUVENILE JUSTICE

A key question arises as to what impact NCCD research has had in the field of juvenile justice. In other words, does the work of the NCCD make a difference in the lives of individuals, particularly children and young adults?

During the 1960s, the President's Commission on Law Enforcement and the Administration of Justice asked the NCCD to survey state and local correctional agencies and institutions throughout the United States. In addition to juvenile detention and correctional facilities, the survey also encompassed juvenile probation, juvenile aftercare, and adult correctional institutions. As a result of this massive survey project, the NCCD recommended standards for juvenile detention and juvenile institutions and also proposed various statutory provisions relative to these two areas. By means of this one study, the NCCD made a very significant contribution to the improvement of juvenile justice in America (NCCD, 2001).

Today the NCCD continues its efforts in the field of juvenile detention. For instance, the NCCD has developed a strategic planning process to help jurisdictions evaluate their need for secure detention bed space and to consider alternatives to total confinement. This approach is based on the NCCD's experience in detention policy analysis and in the implementation of detention alternatives in state and local jurisdictions across the country, including New York City, Cook County (Chicago), Milwaukee County (Wisconsin), San Francisco County (California), and Multnomah County (Portland, Oregon). The effect of the research has been to develop plans that seek to manage future juvenile detention populations more safely and with substantial savings (NCCD, 2001).

Another area in which the NCCD has had an influence on juveniles is in the field of structured decision making as it pertains to the NCCD's Children's Research Center. The burden of child welfare agencies is to provide services to neglected and abused youngsters with limited public resources, in a climate of increasing demand for those services. The Children's Research Center works with state agencies to implement the various components of structured decision making to provide workers with simple, objective, and reliable tools with which to make the best possible decisions for individual cases. The center also provides managers with information for improved planning and resource allocation. The NCCD annually hosts, with other social service–related agencies, a conference for child protective services' administrators that addresses nationwide issues in the field (NCCD, 2001).

The NCCD has likewise had an impact in the field of workload studies. Both child welfare agencies and corrections agencies benefit from the concepts of workload management and budgeting, which is based on studies of the time required to handle various types of cases. In the last decade, the NCCD has conducted more than 60 workload studies, providing a wealth of comparative data to assist with workload budgeting needs. The upshot is that NCCD researchers can estimate the total number of staff needed by an agency to fulfill its mandate to the court and the community while maintaining an adequate standard of performance.

MILESTONES AND IMPORTANT ACHIEVEMENTS

The NCCD is nationally recognized as an expert in conducting risk assessment studies and implementing case classification studies. Many agencies employ risk assessment as a critical component of their decisions about how to allocate scarce resources for supervising or incarcerating offenders among growing correctional populations. Over the past 10 years, the NCCD has conducted these programs in more than 20 adult probation and parole agencies and in 10 juvenile correctional agencies. NCCD literature indicates that no other correctional research agency has more experience in this area.

Two examples of recent risk assessment studies include those done for Rhode Island and Arizona. In the former, NCCD experts were retained by the Rhode Island Division of Children, Youth and Families for a juvenile risk assessment and supervision workload study. The NCCD studied the outcome of 535 juveniles entering probation or aftercare services in Rhode Island. Study findings were used to examine the behavior of youths while on supervision and to revise the agency's current risk assessment instrument and case classification system. The second study was for the Arizona Department of Juvenile Corrections. In that study, the NCCD provided research, technical assistance, and training to the department in designing management systems, including risk assessment classification, workload reporting, and computerized management information systems. NCCD experts also conducted a risk assessment study of 1,000 youths to assist in classification for initial placement and aftercare supervision.

The NCCD has also completed research in the area of correctional population projections. Faced with increasing correctional populations and decreasing resources, decision makers are under pressure to accurately forecast resource needs and identify policies that most influence overall population growth and the distribution of key offender subpopulations throughout the system. Since 1982, the NCCD has provided accurate planning models and forecasts for prison, jail, parole, and probation populations in more than 30 states across the country.

In a related area, the NCCD has received recognition for providing relief from correctional system decrees. A vast number of state prison, jail, and juvenile correctional systems are currently legally obligated to adhere to specific requirements outlined in settlement agreements, consent decrees, or orders set forth by the federal court. The NCCD has an extensive track record in helping more than 20 state and local

governments achieve compliance with court mandates and stipulations, thus terminating the court's jurisdiction over their correctional systems.

A more recent undertaking by the NCCD has been its efforts on behalf of the criminal justice system and racial equality. In September 1998, the NCCD and Clark Atlanta University cosponsored a two-day conference designed to address the impact of racism on the criminal justice system and the nation as a whole. Because of the conference, attended by more than 500 people, the NCCD developed a model to ameliorate the conditions that foster racial discrimination in the administration of criminal justice.

Through the Institute on Race and Justice, the NCCD is establishing a process to systematically involve communities of color academically and personally as stakeholders in developing research-based solutions. The institute is a collaborative venture comprising several historically black colleges and universities, prestigious national research organizations, and professional associations of minority criminal justice practitioners.

Each year, the institute will address such topics as racial profiling, disproportionate minority confinement, crime and victimization, sentencing, women in prison, and criminal justice policy. The institute represents an effort to affect the degree to which emerging leadership in communities of color perceive the role and practice of criminal justice and law enforcement. This is being done by increasing the number of young people of color who are actively interacting with policymakers and criminal justice practitioners as partners—as opposed to victims.

After a relatively successful 94 years (in 2002), the NCCD appears well positioned to face the juvenile/adult justice system research challenges of the 21st century.

Rick M. Steinmann

Bibliography

Austin, J. 1994. Prisoners who don't need to be imprisoned. Pp. 1–15 in J. Austin, *National Council on Crime and Delinquency Internal Report*. San Francisco: NCCD.

Krisberg, B. 1998. The evolution of an American institution. *Crime and Delinquency* 44:5–8.

National Council on Crime and Delinquency. 2001. Web site at http://www.nccd.crc.org.

NATIONAL COUNCIL OF JUVENILE AND FAMILY COURT JUDGES

The National Council of Juvenile and Family Court Judges (NCJFCJ) is America's oldest national judicial membership organization. The name of the organization has changed several times through its history, from its beginning as the National Association of Juvenile Court Judges to the National Council of Juvenile Court Judges to its current name. The generic term *council* is used in this entry to designate all the entities.

Membership, which is approximately 2,000, is open to juvenile and family court judges, referees, and commissioners, as well as court services personnel, police and probation officers, attorneys, and other professionals and volunteers in the field of juvenile justice. From its headquarters in the National Center for Judicial Education on the campus of the University of Nevada at Reno, the Council conducts a program of continuing education, publication, technical assistance, and research designed to improve the effectiveness of the nation's juvenile courts.

In 2000, the Council conducted or assisted in conducting 191 educational programs for more than 25,000 judges, court administrators, social and mental health workers, police, probation officers, and others working in the juvenile and family courts through its Louis W. McHardy National College of Juvenile and Family Justice. This training and continuing education is conducted at its education site in Reno and numerous other sites throughout the country.

Through its various departments, the Council maintains ongoing projects in the areas of permanency planning, victim advocacy, family violence, and alcohol and substance abuse. The National Center for Juvenile Justice is the Council's research arm. Founded in 1973 and headquartered in Pittsburgh, Pennsylvania, the Center responds to the practical concerns and research needs of the country's juvenile justice system.

COUNCIL PUBLICATIONS

The Council has an extensive publishing effort that includes regularly scheduled publications, a textbook series, and numerous specialty publications. The regularly scheduled publications are briefly described in the following paragraphs.

Juvenile and Family Court Journal

Published quarterly, the *Journal* presents articles on topics related to the field of juvenile justice and family law. At least once a year, an issue is devoted to a single timely and relevant subject, such as child abuse, permanency planning, or domestic violence.

Juvenile and Family Law Digest

Distributed monthly, the *Digest* includes summaries of recent case law classified under one of over 250 categories relating to juvenile and family law matters. The level of jurisdiction of cases included in the *Digest* ranges from the local trial court level to Supreme Court cases.

Juvenile and Family Justice TODAY

A quarterly newsmagazine, *TODAY* updates members and subscribers on news of the council and on major events in the field of juvenile and family law.

Textbook Series

Titles include *Learning Disabilities and the Juvenile Justice System; Juvenile Probation: The Balanced Approach; Juvenile Justice: The Adjudicatory and Dispositional Process; Child Sexual Abuse: Improving the Systems Response;* and *Child Abuse and Neglect.* In addition, specialty publications are issued from time to time. These publications contain reports of special studies, grant projects, or recommendations from special conferences.

HISTORY

The NCJFCJ had its genesis as the National Association of Juvenile Court Judges, which came into being on May 22, 1937. Judge Harry Eastman, an Ohio juvenile court judge, is credited with first proposing the idea of such an association in the fall of 1935 when he addressed the annual meeting of the New York State Association of Children's Court Judges. In that address, Judge Eastman proposed, "The leadership in developing juvenile courts should be assumed by the judges of these courts. To do so effectively, some form of mutual association is imperative." Judge Eastman became the first president of the association and went on to serve four consecutive terms as president. The purposes of the organization as set forth in its charter are as follows:

1. To improve the standards, practices, and effectiveness of the juvenile and family courts of the United States.

2. To make available the collective experiences of all members to persons and agencies, private and government, in any manner affecting juvenile justice.

3. To encourage and afford opportunity for members to keep abreast of developments and principles relating to juvenile and family courts.

4. To engage in educational, training, and research activities to further the foregoing objectives.

The membership and the work of the association grew steadily during the 1940s and 1950s. The first issue of the *Juvenile Court Judges Journal* was published in September 1950 and continues to be published today as the *Juvenile and Family Court Journal*. Also in 1950, the council promoted the creation of the National Juvenile Court Foundation, Incorporated. The Foundation was chartered to stimulate and conduct research and educational and instructive activities relating to the work of the juvenile courts throughout the United States and further the betterment of the treatment and training of all children coming under the jurisdiction of juvenile courts. Over the years, the Foundation has received private contributions, grants from other foundations, and federal government grants to promote the work of the council.

In 1962, the Council established its first headquarters office with an executive director and paid staff at the American Bar Association Center in Chicago. The Council obtained a grant from the Fleischmann Foundation in 1969 that covered the costs for basic operations and provided matching funds for grants from federal agencies and private foundations. The training conducted under the Fleischmann Grant was centered at the Judicial College Building on the campus of the University of Nevada at Reno. Therefore, the entire operation of the council moved to Reno. These events culminated in the 1969 establishment of the College of Juvenile and Family Law. The Council now conducts its operations from the Midby-Byron National Center for Judicial Education.

SYSTEM IMPACT

Throughout its history, the Council has had a significant impact on the juvenile justice system. As early as 1943, the Council became active in national issues affecting children. In that year, the Council "presented a multi-point program to a United States Senate Committee investigating juvenile delinquency. The Council urged, among other things, the construction of adequate facilities for delinquent children, educational programs for juvenile police officers, and federal responsibility for the return to the home state of interstate runaways" (Whitlatch, 1987:6). The Council was an early leader in the continuing education of judges on both the national and local levels. Early on, juvenile and family court judges, through the work of the council, took the initiative for their own continuing professional development.

The Council continues to play a leadership role in the current issues affecting children and families by engaging in programs and projects to improve standards, practices, and effectiveness in juvenile and family courts. This is evident in the Council's active research efforts by the National Center for Juvenile Justice as well as the Council's programs and projects on child neglect and abuse, including permanency planning, family violence, victims' rights, and disproportionate confinement of minority youth.

The National Center for Juvenile Justice is the only nonprofit research organization in the United States whose resources are concentrated solely on the juvenile justice system and the prevention of juvenile delinquency, child abuse, and child neglect. It provides research, services, and technical assistance in the areas of program planning and evaluation, facility evaluations and planning, court and court services administrations, and juvenile code statute analysis. The Center maintains a unique resource in the National Juvenile Court Data Archive, which contains more than 10 million cases from more than 1,600 court jurisdictions nationwide. The records are electronically stored in case-level format and support applications that range from estimating future caseloads to analyzing reentry rates by type of referral offense to demographic profiling of first offenders. The Center also maintains electronic files of *Uniform Crime Reports* data, Children in Custody data, *Uniform Crime Reports Supplemental Homicide Report* data, as well as other electronically stored data sets.

Council members have led state efforts to improve the court and child protective systems response to child abuse and neglect. The Council has been instrumental in establishing 23 model courts engaged in efforts to improve juvenile and family court handling of child abuse and neglect cases nationwide. The council published *Adoption and Permanency Guidelines: Improving Court Practice in Child Abuse and Neglect Cases*, which provides best-practice recommendations to expedite complex termination of parental rights hearings and to ensure the safe, timely movement of children out of foster care into adoption and other permanent placements. Training and technical assistance are delivered to judges and other professionals in all 50 states and the District of Columbia. Training programs in calendar year 2000 numbered 128, including 54 national and 74 state and regional programs. An estimated 40,218 judges, court personnel, attorneys, agency representatives, volunteer advocates, and others received training and follow-up technical assistance.

The Council's Family Violence Project was established in 1987 to develop, test, and promote improved court responses to family violence. Since that time, the project has evolved into the Family Violence Department (FVD) and has grown significantly to become a major force in addressing the issues of family violence in the country. The Resource Center on Domestic Violence: Child Protection and Custody provides access to the best possible source of information and tangible assistance to those working in the field of domestic violence and child protection and custody.

Through its National Judicial Institute on Domestic Violence, the Council conducts training in the skills necessary to handle appropriately and effectively both civil and criminal cases involving domestic violence. The Institute, a partnership between the Council and the Family Violence Prevention Fund (FVPF), is funded by the Violence Against Women Office of the Department of Justice.

In 1994, the Council published the *Model Code on Domestic and Family Violence*. The Code was drafted by a multidisciplinary advisory committee comprising judges, battered women's advocates, attorneys, law enforcement officers, and other professionals. The five chapters of the Code include General Provisions, Criminal Penalties and Procedures, Civil Orders for Protection, Family and Children, and Prevention and Treatment.

The juvenile court's attention to victims' rights can be seen in its early and extensive use of restitution in adjudication. The restitution programs can be viewed as a precursor to the current restorative justice movement. The Victim Advocacy Department of the council is dedicated to ensuring that the juvenile courts are victim friendly. It maintains a resource center for juvenile courts interested in improving the treatment of victims.

As a recognized leader on matters of state, national, and international juvenile and family law, the council is often called upon to submit amicus briefs and testify before Congress and other legislative bodies.

Dennis W. Catlin

See also Courts, Juvenile

Bibliography

Hurst, H. 1987. A history of the National Center for Juvenile Justice. Part II. *Juvenile and Family Court Journal* 38(2):19–22.

National Council of Juvenile and Family Court Judges. 2001. Web site at http://www.ncjfcj.unr.edu/index.html.

National Council of Juvenile and Family Court Judges. No date. *End Product—Less Delinquency*. Reno, NV: National Council of Juvenile and Family Court Judges.

Ruffin, J. 2000. After 31 years, NCJFCJ bids a fond farewell, Marie. *Juvenile and Family Justice Today*, Summer:14–15.

Whitlatch, W. G. 1987. A brief history of the national council. *Juvenile and Family Court Journal* 38(2):1–13.

 NATIONAL YOUTH SURVEY

One of the weaknesses of past juvenile delinquency research was that it often focused on the youths who were already in the system, those with official records who were easy to access in juvenile halls and state reformatories. These samples were less likely to include middle- and upper-class youths who were often diverted from the system before formal statistics counted them.

A solution to the bias evident in early methods was for researchers to use self-report techniques in research and to seek permission to survey general school populations or households. Findings seemed to indicate that delinquent behavior was more "normal" and accepted among youths of all backgrounds than was originally believed. These observations led to significant changes in delinquency theory and in prevention efforts.

LONGITUDINAL RESEARCH

Still, juvenile self-report studies had limitations as well. One was that certain factors thought to be related to crime could be present in a youth's life and could affect the youth, but if those factors were not having an effect at the time of the study, they would be missed in the research. Another problem was that of causal ordering—the fundamental "chicken or the egg" dilemma. For example, researchers could not tell whether having delinquent friends influenced youths to engage in criminal activities or whether by committing delinquent acts youths were more likely to find themselves in the subsequent company of other troubled kids.

One method used to address this problem is a longitudinal study. With this method, researchers identify a large sample of youth and not only gather a significant amount of information about them but also track them over the years to see what activities and outcomes they encountered. One of the most famous longitudinal studies on delinquency was the Wolfgang and Sellin cohort study, which tracked most of a sample of youths in Philadelphia from birth to 18 years of age and some even longer.

THE DEVELOPMENT OF THE NATIONAL YOUTH SURVEY

The National Youth Survey is an 800-item questionnaire administered to a random sample of 1,725 youths nationwide who were born between 1959 and 1965. The information was gathered in confidential face-to-face interviews.

The survey was originally funded by the National Institute of Mental Health (Department of Health and Human Services). Over the years, supplemental funding was provided by the Department of Justice through the Office of Juvenile Justice and Delinquency Prevention and the National Institute of Justice.

The survey was initiated by Dr. Delbert S. Elliot and his colleagues at the University of Colorado, Boulder. Dr. Elliot is currently Director of the Program on Problem Behavior and Director of the Center for the Study and Prevention of Violence, both at the Institute of Behavioral Science, University of Colorado, Boulder.

THE COLLECTION OF DATA IN WAVES

As in other longitudinal studies, the researchers go back and contact the original participants to readminister the questions at regular intervals. Fortunately, most of the participants continued in the survey over the years, and only a relatively small number dropped out. This helps the survey's results maintain comparative value or significance. Each survey respondent and a parent or legal guardian were first interviewed in 1977 about events and behaviors occurring during 1976. Researchers revisited the homes each year until 1981 and then again in 1984, 1987, 1990, and 1993, each time asking about events and attitudes relative to the previous year. These seven repeated administrations of the survey are called waves. Most research studies use only part of this data in their designs, and they are careful to note which waves their findings are based on.

WHO ARE THE SURVEY RESPONDENTS?

Of the 2,360 youths originally targeted by this multistage cluster sampling design, 1,725 agreed to participate and signed informed consent documents. There were approximately 250 youths of each age in the group. The youths who participated in this survey were between 11 and 17 years old during the first year of the interview. By 1993, the original participants were 27 to 33 years old. According to the research design, they will continue to be followed into their late 30s and early 40s.

The sample of youths who took part in the survey, according to the authors, appeared to match the characteristics of youths of the same age in the general population, as indicated by the U. S. census. Thus one could say that the study sample was representative of youth nationwide.

CONTENT OF THE QUESTIONNAIRE

Although there were some additions to the survey questions over time, the basic format was the same year to year. The National Youth Survey asked respondents about any delinquent activity they may have participated in during the past year. It also asked participants to report on the nature of family relationships, their own attitudes toward delinquency, as well as their prosocial (conforming) activities and about their friends and associates. The survey attempted to obtain information about the frequency and nature of certain behaviors as well as changes in behaviors over time, including disruptive events in the home. It asked about parental aspirations for the youths, any arrests or other labeling events, the integration of family and peers, and whether the youths are socially isolated.

The instrument also measured attitudes toward deviance in adults and juveniles, parental disciplinary methods, a youth's level of community involvement, respondents' educational aspirations, employment, skills, exposure and commitment to delinquent peers, self-reported depression, self-reported delinquency, attitudes toward sexual assault, victimization, pregnancy, abortion, use of mental health and outpatient services, neighborhood problems, the use of violence by the respondents and/or their acquaintances, the use of controlled substances (both illicit drugs and alcohol), sexual activity, and sex roles. Finally, the survey collected a number of demographic variables and indicators of socioeconomic status.

The survey responses can be broken down into three broad categories: self-reports of delinquency; parental appraisals of their children; and the youths' internal appraisals of themselves from the standpoint of parents, friends, and teachers.

INITIAL FINDINGS FROM THE RESEARCH

As with other self-report studies on delinquency, results from the National Youth Survey indicate that only a small portion of those who admit to committing crimes are officially arrested. Further, police arrested only about one quarter of those who say they committed an act for which they could have been arrested.

Using five waves of the data, Elliot, Huizinga, and Ageton (1985) concluded that delinquent friends exerted more influence on an individual's behavior than did an individual's behavior predict the association with delinquent peers. They also found that drug use did not appear to be related to social class, even though use is reported more in urban areas.

In later studies, it became clearer that the progression of an originally nondelinquent person escalated from involvement with a slightly more delinquent peer group to engagement in some minor delinquent acts to movement into a more delinquent peer group and then committing some index offenses (categorized by police in official statistics) to becoming almost exclusively involved with a delinquent peer group. This supports theories of progressive or incremental delinquency that look to interventions to interrupt or terminate the escalating pattern of criminal behavior.

The researchers also concluded in subsequent analyses that there is a relationship between delinquent bonding and committing both less serious and more serious offenses.

It has also been reported that more than half of the participants with records of violent behavior began to engage in this behavior between the ages of 14 and 17. In addition, after age 20, the risk of initiating a pattern of violent behavior was found to be close to zero. The researchers also indicate that association with delinquent peers seems to come before the initiation and progression of serious violent offenses in 90 percent of the cases.

CONTINUED USE OF NATIONAL YOUTH SURVEY DATA

The data from the National Youth Survey have been available for criminologists to access and use in conducting research. (Publications based on this research appear in the bibliography at the end of this entry.) Many studies using the data have tested theories of delinquency, particularly social control theory and differential association. Today the data from the National Youth Survey can be found in the National Archives of Criminal Justice Database.

In addition to the many research reports and theoretical studies that have been generated by the National Youth Survey, other states and jurisdictions have undertaken their own surveys based on the National Youth Survey model. Either by using the same methods of surveying or by using parts of the actual National Youth Survey instrument, the field has been enriched by this type of research. The Oregon Youth Study, the Rochester Youth Development Study (which concentrated on youth who are at high risk for serious delinquency), and the National Gang Youth Study all have benefited from the initial work done in the National Youth Survey.

Myrna Cintrón and Marilyn D. McShane

See also Philadelphia Birth Cohort; Self-Report Studies

Bibliography

Dunford, F. W., and D. S. Elliott. 1984. Identifying career offenders using self-reported data. *Journal of Research in Crime and Delinquency* 21(1):57–86.

Elliott, D. S. 1987. Self-reported driving while under the influence of alcohol/drugs and the risk of alcohol/

drug-related accidents. *Alcohol, Drugs, and Driving: Abstracts and Reviews* 3(3-4):31–43.

Elliott, D. S., S. S. Ageton, and R. J. Canter. 1979. An integrated theoretical perspective on delinquent behavior. *Journal of Research in Crime and Delinquency* 16(1):3–27.

Elliott, D. S., and D. H. Huizinga. 1983. Social class and delinquent behavior in a national youth panel: 1976–1980. *Criminology* 21(2):149–177.

Elliott, D. S., D. H. Huizinga, and S. S. Ageton. 1985. *Explaining Delinquency and Drug Use*. Beverly Hills, CA: Sage.

Elliott, D. S., D. H. Huizinga, and S. Menard. 1989. *Multiple Problem Youth: Delinquency, Substance Use, and Mental Health Problems*. New York: Springer-Verlag.

Elliott, D. S., D. H. Huizinga, and B. J. Morse. 1986. Self-reported violent offending: A descriptive analysis of juvenile violent offenders and their offending careers. *Journal of Interpersonal Violence* 1(4):472–514.

Huizinga, D. H., and D. S. Elliott. 1987. Juvenile offenders: Prevalence, offender incidence, and arrest rates by race. *Crime and Delinquency* 33(2):206–223.

Huizinga, D. H., S. Menard, and D. S. Elliott. 1989. Delinquency and drug use: Temporal and developmental patterns. *Justice Quarterly* 6(3):419–455.

Menard, S., and D. S. Elliott. 1990. Longitudinal and cross-sectional collection and analysis in the study of crime and delinquency. *Justice Quarterly* 7(1):11–55.

Menard, S., and D. S. Elliott. 1994. Delinquent bonding, moral beliefs and illegal behavior: A three-wave panel model. *Justice Quarterly* 11(2):173–188.

OFFICE OF JUVENILE JUSTICE AND DELINQUENCY PREVENTION

The Office of Juvenile Justice and Delinquency Prevention (OJJDP) was established in 1974 when Congress passed the Juvenile Justice and Delinquency Prevention Act (JJDPA). At this time, many were concerned about young status offenders being labeled and exposed to more serious criminals when incarcerated. With many states deinstitutionalizing juveniles and looking for community alternatives, the legislation tasked the agency with providing national leadership in the process of coordinating, developing, and implementing the most effective methods for both preventing juvenile victimization and responding to delinquency. One of the Office's major functions was to study and to assist others in evaluating the most effective techniques for combating juvenile delinquency.

THE ORGANIZATION OF THE OJJDP

The organizational structure of the OJJDP in the early years had the agency positioned under the Director of the Law Enforcement Assistance Administration (LEAA). The OJJDP supported two operating divisions. One was the Office of Programs, which administered grants throughout the 50 states and technical assistance to law enforcement and juvenile justice agencies at all levels of government. This office also provided staff assistance for two boards: (1) the Coordinating Council, where federal agency heads provided oversight for developing a federal agenda on

juvenile interests and for reviewing the programs and policies of their agencies; and (2) the National Advisory Committee for Juvenile Justice and Delinquency Prevention, a 21-member committee appointed by the president to make recommendations on policies and programming initiatives for the OJJDP.

The second division was the National Institute of Juvenile Justice and Delinquency Prevention, which offered training for those already working in or preparing for work in the field of juvenile justice. To this end, the OJJDP established a clearinghouse of information on these topics, the Juvenile Justice Clearinghouse (JJC), and became a sponsor, administrator, and publisher of research in the areas of juvenile justice and delinquency prevention. During this period, the OJJDP funded many studies on diversion and restitution programs in hopes of finding more appropriate sanctions for youthful offenders.

RESTRUCTURING AND REDIRECTING PRIORITIES

Over the years, the OJJDP weathered financial difficulties, a result of often not receiving the full funding appropriated to it, and criticisms of focusing too much on one juvenile population at the expense of others. However, by analyzing funded research, one can see that the OJJDP responded to changes in priorities in justice initiatives and our interest in new problems as they were recognized by society. When the LEAA was dissolved, the OJJDP was reorganized and placed directly under the attorney general. In 1984, the Office also took on a number of responsibilities related to addressing missing children. In 1988, the OJJDP became involved in initiatives in the areas of gang intervention and prevention as well as treating teenage drug abuse. In 1992, the Victims of Child Abuse Act delegated additional responsibilities to its agenda.

Although the work of the OJJDP had been instrumental in reducing the number of young, less serious offenders in institutions, in 1987, the JJDPA was amended to allow status offenders to be detained in lockups if they violated court orders. By 1993, the OJJDP focused on developing comprehensive strategies for serious, violent, and chronic offenders. Research and funded initiatives used risk prediction models to try to identify youth most likely to persist in delinquent behavior. Providing services to juveniles in secure confinement has also been an area of concern for the OJJDP as well as studying the effectiveness of boot camps and aftercare programs for youths released from state and county facilities.

THE OJJDP TODAY

A governmental reorganization in 1998 moved the OJJDP under the Office of Justice Programs administered by the National Institute of Justice. This umbrella agency is under the Justice Department, so the OJJDP remains under the authority of the Attorney General. The OJJDP is located in Washington, D.C., while the clearinghouse is in Rockville, Maryland. In 2001, the budget for the OJJDP was almost $600 million, which included $12 million for gang issues, $16 million for mentoring programs, $23 million to address missing children, $25 million for initiatives related to underage drinking, $8 million for research and programming on victims of child abuse, and $15 million under the Safe Schools Initiative.

Through research grants, many of the country's experts in juvenile justice are able to evaluate new ideas for treating and preventing delinquency. This gives policymakers and practitioners valuable insights into the best methods for serving the needs of not only youth in custody and in the court system but also those who are most at risk for future delinquency in the community. Some examples of recent reports published by the OJJDP include *Bridging the Child Welfare and Juvenile Justice Systems; Curfews: An Answer to Juvenile Delinquency and Victimization;* and *Keeping Young People in School: Community Programs That Work.* The OJJDP publishes approximately 100 of these reports, bulletins, and fact sheets per year. They have also developed Portable Guides, which are practical references for

law enforcement and other professionals conducting investigations of child abuse and neglect. Other publications include *Juvenile Court Statistics* and *Juvenile Arrests,* as well as training guides for those who work with young offenders.

Throughout its distinguished history, the Office of Juvenile Justice and Delinquency Prevention has attempted to respond to the problems society has considered most pressing among our youth. The agency has continually searched for viable programs to address solutions for delinquency, sponsored research on and evaluations of those efforts, and made all this information available through a system of reports and press releases disseminated in a variety of formats. Further information may be found at the OJJDP Web site, http://ojjdp.ncjrs.org, which includes the most recent issues of *Juvenile Justice,* a periodic journal that provides current information on research reports and funding opportunities.

Marilyn D. McShane

See also Juvenile Justice and Delinquency Prevention Act of 1974

Bibliography

Olson-Raymer, G. 1984. National juvenile justice policy: Myth or reality? Pp. 19–57 in S. Decker (ed.), *Juvenile Justice Policy: Analyzing Trends and Outcomes.* Beverly Hills, CA: Sage.

 # OHLIN, LLOYD E. (1918–)

With the dominant criminological theories of the 1950s and early1960s concentrating on juvenile delinquency, most theorists' efforts were devoted to the explanation of gang development and the types of gangs that existed. The dominant approach at the time relied heavily on the concept of subcultures. Lloyd Ohlin was one of the criminologists most associated with gangs and gang subculture. His work influenced the entire field of criminology and delinquency.

BACKGROUND AND EARLY ACADEMIC YEARS

Lloyd E. Ohlin was born in Belmont, Massachusetts, on August 27, 1918, to Swedish immigrant parents. The second of four sons, he lived a middle-class lifestyle because of his father's successful bakery business. Ohlin's youngest brother died at age 7 due to a brain tumor, an event that would later lead to Ohlin's interest in psychology.

As he grew up, Ohlin demonstrated a passion for reading and was studious in school. After making his mark through excellence in the classroom and participation in track, Ohlin graduated from Belmont High School in 1936. The following summer, he enrolled in Brown University, his second choice of colleges to attend. His first choice, Harvard, was financially out of reach for his family, with his oldest brother already a student there. Because of this economic obstacle, Ohlin chose to attend Brown, which was near his home.

At Brown, Ohlin devoted himself to the study of sociology and psychology, while also participating in intercollegiate track. A former high school friend who was his college roommate had chosen sociology as a major, and this fostered Ohlin's interest in the study of sociology. His interest in psychology was motivated not only by the death of his younger brother but also by the literature itself. In 1940, Ohlin graduated from Brown University with honors, receiving a bachelor's degree in sociology and a minor in psychology.

While attending Brown, Ohlin developed an interest in the study of criminology through his contact with the new Chair of the Psychology Department, Walter Hunter. Ohlin eventually married Hunter's daughter, Helen, and the couple attended graduate school together in 1946 at the University of Chicago.

Ohlin believed the study of crime was intertwined with the fields of sociology and psychology. With this interest in the study of crime, Ohlin intentionally applied to the graduate program at Indiana University to study with Edwin Sutherland. Ohlin was accepted into the program, and his interactions with Sutherland significantly influenced his approach to criminology. In 1942, Ohlin received his master's in sociology from Indiana University. He then entered the military and was assigned to the counterintelligence corps in the European Theater. Ohlin credits his background in criminology as the reason for his assignment in military intelligence.

Ohlin also claims that much of his theorizing and work in criminology stems from his earlier days at Indiana University through his academic relationship with Nathaniel Kantor of the Psychology Department. This similar pattern of influence also occurred while Ohlin was working on his Ph.D. in Sociology at the University of Chicago. During this particular experience, Ohlin met another professor who would influence his career—his Ph.D. adviser, Ernest Burgess.

In the fall of 1947, Lloyd Ohlin was hired by the Illinois Parole and Pardon Board for the position of sociologist-actuary at the Stateville-Joliet Penitentiary. He accepted this offer of employment because it allowed him to be compensated while pursuing his dissertation in the area of adult corrections. Originally, Ohlin had considered the idea of pursuing a dissertation under the direction of Shaw and McKay in the Chicago Area Project, but with pressing family obligations, his only practical choice was to take the Illinois position. In 1950, he was transferred to the Chicago office, where he was promoted to the position of supervising sociologist. In addition to his duties related to parole research, Ohlin was also given the responsibility of developing inservice training programs for Illinois correctional workers.

In 1953, Ohlin accepted a position with the University of Chicago as the director of the Center for Education and Research in Corrections. A short time after accepting this position, in 1954, he received his Ph.D. in Sociology from the University of Chicago. With his new degree, Ohlin continued to serve as the director of the center while also serving in various consulting capacities. During this time, his consulting career included research projects with the American Bar Foundation and the sheriff of Cook County, Illinois, in reorganizing the corrections division.

DIFFERENTIAL OPPORTUNITY THEORY

In 1956, Ohlin accepted a position as Professor of Sociology in the doctoral program at Columbia University's School of Social Work. It was during this period that he began his greatest contribution to the field of criminology, a study of juvenile delinquency. While serving as director of Columbia's newly created research center, he shifted his focus from the study of adult corrections to that of juvenile delinquency. Ohlin became intensely involved with the study of delinquency through professional liaisons and memberships in organizations that included the National Institute of Mental Health, the Ford Foundation, the journal *Children,* the Social Science Research Council Committee on the Sociocultural Contexts of Delinquency, the Professional Council of the National Council on Crime and Delinquency, and the Youth Center Study of Syracuse University.

During the fall of 1957, Ohlin and colleague Richard A. Cloward began a three-year comparative study of two private and public juvenile institutions in New York. This joint effort, sponsored by the Ford Foundation, provided Ohlin and Cloward with the opportunity to explore inmate subcultures in juvenile institutions. Together, they formed the assumption that these two contrasting official structures would each produce different kinds of inmate subcultures. Their professional collaborations during this study led directly to their well-received book, *Delinquency and Opportunity: A Theory of Delinquent Gangs* (1960).

Cloward and Ohlin attempted to explain subcultural delinquency through a theory that became familiarly known as differential opportunity theory. They examined the relationship between communities and socially defined patterns of youth opportunity in the community. Cloward and Ohlin proposed that communities have defined sets of legitimate and illegitimate opportunities that establish the type and amount of deviance in a subculture. They contended that lower-class boys have the same material dreams of success that middle-class boys do. Because lower-class boys have decreased access to legitimate means of attaining their goals, they perceive their chances of success as limited. The severe chasm between their aspiration levels and their expectations creates pressures or strain that results in deviance and crime. To reach their goals, many youth will use available illegitimate means. From this, Cloward and Ohlin found that dominant patterns formed as youth subcultures based on the degree of integration of illegitimate opportunity structures in the community.

Their coordinated efforts in the Ford Foundation study were temporarily postponed in 1959 when both were asked by a coalition of the Lower East Side Community Settlement House in Manhattan to design and conduct a "saturation of service" project for youth. This study became the groundwork for testing their institutionally based opportunity theory in a community framework.

Results of this project spawned programs like Mobilization for Youth under the Kennedy administration. With his recent publication on delinquency and gangs and his understanding of model youth programs, Ohlin was asked by then Attorney General Robert F. Kennedy to serve as Special Assistant to the Secretary of Health, Education, and Welfare. Ohlin's role was to act as an in-house academic expert on delinquency. Ohlin served in this capacity from 1961 to 1962, while on leave of absence from Columbia University.

LATER CONTRIBUTIONS AND AWARDS

In 1962, Ohlin returned to Columbia to teach and resume his duties as the director of the research center. During his remaining three years at Columbia, he was asked to participate in other areas related to his area of professional expertise. From 1963 through 1964, the National Council on Crime and Delinquency asked for his assistance in organizing and publishing a new journal, *Research in Crime and Delinquency*. He was also appointed Vice Chairman of the International Conference on Poverty Research. In 1964, Ohlin was named as a U.S. delegate to the International Conference on Social Work in Athens, Greece. While on leave of absence from Columbia from October 1965 to June 1967, he served as Associate Director of the President's Commission on Law Enforcement and Administration of Justice. After leaving this post, he went on to Harvard, where he became Professor of Criminology.

While at Harvard, Ohlin continued to actively pursue his research and writing interests in the area of juvenile delinquency. In 1969, the importance of Ohlin's work was recognized by the American Society of Criminology when he was awarded the prestigious Edwin H. Sutherland Award. During the spring of 1982, he accepted a position as Visiting Professor in the School of Criminal Justice at the State University of New York at Albany. Ohlin retired from Harvard in the summer of 1982 as the Touroff-Glueck Professor of Criminal Justice, Emeritus. After his retirement, Ohlin and his wife moved to Maine, where he has remained active in research and writing. In 1986, he served as the president of the American Society of Criminology. He also served in the capacity of Codirector of the Program on Human Development and Criminal Behavior, a project to develop plans for large-scale and long-term longitudinal studies.

Michael J. Grabowski

See also Richard A. Cloward; Theories of Delinquency— Sociological

Bibliography

Cloward, R. A., and L. E. Ohlin. 1960. *Delinquency and Opportunity: A Theory of Delinquent Gangs*. Glencoe, IL: Free Press.

Laub, J. H. 1983. *Criminology in the Making*. Boston: Northeastern University Press.

Martin, R., R. J. Mutchnick, and W. T. Austin. 1990. *Criminological Thought: Pioneers Past and Present*. New York: Macmillan.

Miller, A. D., and L. E. Ohlin. 1985. *Delinquency and Community: Creating Opportunities and Controls*. Beverly Hills, CA: Sage.

 # OUT-OF-HOME PLACEMENT

When a juvenile in trouble has a questionable family life, the family is contributing to the juvenile's delinquency, or there are undesirable associates at the home, the youth may be temporarily removed to some facility until the home problems are resolved. Such cases are referred to as out-of-home placements.

Out-of-home placement is one of the many options available to probation officers. The Office of Juvenile Justice and Delinquency Prevention (1996) indicated that 65,300 juveniles were in out-of-home placement by court commitment in February 1995. Additionally, 67 percent of the offenders were in public facilities—those owned and operated by state or local government agencies—and 33 percent were in private facilities. The average length of stay for a youth committed to a public facility and released in 1994 was 147 days, while a youth in a private facility stayed an average of 109 days. The number of placements between 1987 and 1996 increased across all racial groups. However, between 1987 and 1996, the number of cases resulting in placement increased the least for Caucasian youth (43 percent) compared with African American youth (58 percent) and all other races (128 percent). Males made up the vast majority of offenders in placements at 86.5 percent (Gallagher, 1997).

Although the court orders an offender into placement, the probation officer is required to arrange appropriate placement in a group home, ranch, camp, or institution. The probation officer works directly with treatment facilities on the implementation of the youth's rehabilitation plan. While the juvenile is in a placement, the probation officer is responsible for monitoring the quality of services the offender receives as well as supplying supplemental casework services as needed. These placements often offer a different environment for the offender away from the atmosphere and associations that may have aided in his or her delinquency.

Laura Davis

See also Group Homes; Probation, Juvenile

Bibliography

Gallagher, C. A. 1997. *Juvenile Offenders in Residential Placement, 1997*. Washington, DC: Office of Juvenile Justice and Delinquency Prevention.

Office of Juvenile Justice and Delinquency Prevention. 1996. *Residential Placement of Adjudicated Youth, 1987–1996*. Washington, DC: Office of Juvenile Justice and Delinquency Prevention.

 ## PARENS PATRIAE DOCTRINE

Parens patriae is one of the essential tenets upon which the U.S. juvenile court system is built. This doctrine, literally translated from the Latin as "state as parent," was adopted during the child-saving movement of the late 1890s and early 1900s from the British Common Law system.

HISTORICAL FOUNDATION OF *PARENS PATRIAE*

The child-saving movement was born of the Reformation. The child savers were predominantly Anglo-Saxon, Protestant, middle- to upper-class women whose intentions were to prevent the children of the immigrant working class from developing criminality. This movement was spirited by a duality in goals: the humanitarian rehabilitation and reform of youth, and social control to protect the privileged positions of the middle and upper class (Platt, 1995:16).

The majority of the women involved in the child-saving movement held strong convictions regarding the need for women to nurture and take care of children. As the child savers possessed the financial means to provide child care for their own children by employing nannies and domestic help, they turned their attention to those they perceived to be in need of their assistance. They held the view that criminals were a distinct and separate class, spawned of the working-class culture, and a threat to mainstream society (Platt, 1995:19). Concurrently evolving during

this period was the medical, or therapeutic, approach to criminality. The control and reform of youth and the therapeutic approach to crime congealed to produce fertile ground for the rationale for juvenile court, *parens patriae*.

LEGAL PRECEDENTS IN THE EVOLUTION OF *PARENS PATRIAE*

The 1838 case of *Ex Parte Crouse* served to establish precedent for the legal standing of *parens patriae* in the American court system. Mary Ann Crouse was committed to the Philadelphia House of Refuge by her mother for incorrigibility, against her father's wishes (Elrod and Ryder, 1999:113). Mr. Crouse contended Mary Ann had not committed a criminal offense and therefore should not be punished. The Pennsylvania Supreme Court held the following:

1. The function of the house of refuge was to reform and rehabilitate children, not to punish them.

2. As Mary Ann was not being punished, the formal due process protections afforded to adults in criminal proceedings were not applicable to Mary Ann.

3. The state has a legal obligation to protect children when parents are either unable or unwilling to do so.

The protection intended by the court was to prevent the child from engaging in further delinquency and future criminality.

Photo 7. Students in front of the Industrial School for Boys, Kearney, Nebraska, 1909. Judges acting under the parens patriae doctrine institutionalized many youth in the belief that it was the best option for them.

SOURCE: Nebraska State Historical Society [RG2608]. Used with permission.

In 1870, the Illinois Supreme Court ruled in the case of *People v. Turner* that placement in the house of refuge was a punishment, not a preventative protection. Similar to the case of Mary Ann Crouse, Daniel O'Connell had been placed in the house of refuge without having committed any criminal offense, based on the perception that he was in danger of becoming a criminal (Elrod and Ryder, 1999:114). This decision threatened the precedent established in *Ex Parte Crouse*. The child savers viewed this ruling as an impediment to efforts to assist, reform, and control youth. This concern shortly thereafter led to the establishment of the first juvenile court in Cook County, Illinois, with the passage of the 1899 Juvenile Court Act.

The rationale for the establishment of juvenile court was to protect the welfare of the child through state intervention when necessary. The state, in this forum, was to act as ultimate parent whose primary focus was the rehabilitation, protection, and supervision of the child. The child was viewed as not being of full legal capacity and, as such, was in need of the court's benevolent intervention.

CURRENT TRENDS

The drug wars of the 1980s and early 1990s greatly affected the position of youth in the criminal justice system. The intentions of the child savers to protect children from a downward progression from delinquency to criminality were overshadowed by the use of children as pawns by the illegal drug industry. The former contention, fundamental to the establishment of the juvenile court system, that children are not of full legal capacity, was overshadowed by media images portraying children committing adult offenses. Children, sometimes as young as age 13 years, were used to conduct illicit drug transactions, as they were afforded the protections of the juvenile court. A possible 20-year sentence for an adult convicted of drug trafficking translated into detention in a youth facility until the age of majority for the same crime committed by a juvenile. Public outcry, fueled by media frenzy for harsher sentencing and a crime-control, punitive atmosphere swept the country in the wake of the drug wars.

At the same time, the media focused on violent crimes by juveniles, particularly homicides connected with the drug trade. A false prediction of violent juvenile "superpredators" emerging in the next decade also fueled the punitive debate. Although there was little evidence of a massive increase in juvenile violence (indeed, there was a decrease in youth violence throughout the 1990s), legislators and the public assumed the worst. In the face of this, the public demanded a more punitively oriented juvenile court or even the abolition of juvenile courts in favor of treating all juveniles as adults.

The doctrine of *parens patriae* as a means to protect youth through government intervention, the ideal of the state as the ultimate parent whose focus was to save and reform the child when the child's family could not or would not, was all but lost in the punitive climate of just deserts. The age of majority for certain crimes and sentences was lowered, and adult transfer rates increased at an alarming rate. The informal "parental" approach to dealing with juvenile issues gave way to formal due process as juveniles became increasingly subjected to prosecution as adults.

Bernadette V. Russo-Myers

See also Child-Saving Movement; Courts, Juvenile; Law, Juvenile; Waiver to Adult Court

Bibliography

Bilchik, S. 1999. *Juvenile Justice: A Century of Change.* Juvenile Justice Bulletin, National Report Series. Washington, DC: Office of Juvenile Justice and Delinquency Prevention.

Elrod, P., and R. S. Ryder. 1999. *Juvenile Justice: A Social, Historical, and Legal Perspective.* Gaithersburg, MD: Aspen.

Platt, A. 1995. The child-saving movement and the origins of the juvenile justice system. Pp. 13–27 in P. Sharp and B. Hancock (eds.), *Juvenile Delinquency: Historical, Theoretical, and Societal Reactions to Youth.* Englewood Cliffs, NJ: Prentice Hall.

PARENTAL RESPONSIBILITY LAWS

Parental responsibility laws are, in general, statutes that deal with issues regarding the responsibility of parents for the deviant activity of their children. Statutes that address parental responsibility range from status offenses, such as truancy, to violent felony offenses. The statutes vary widely and address a variety of issues, including parental liability for failing to adequately supervise children (especially during curfews), lack of parental participation in a child's postadjudication rehabilitation, parental responsibility for property damage and/or injury caused by a child's acts, and parental liability for the costs of a child's rehabilitation or treatment program (for further elaboration, see Lansing, 1999).

Although parental responsibility laws have typically addressed the issues just noted, contemporary discussions have broadened the relevant issues to include a more comprehensive, and ever expanding, view of parental responsibilities. For example, some parental responsibility laws have been so broadly worded that they can be interpreted in ways that would include such factors as the psychological effects that a student had on other students due to their actions or threats. This factor has only recently been acknowledged by individuals who have been direct, or even indirect, victims of mass murders by students at schools, such as the shootings at Columbine High School in Colorado.

In addition, the state of California in 1996 implemented the Street Terrorism Enforcement and Prevention Act (called the STEP Act), which permits the arrest of parents whose child becomes a suspect in a crime and who consciously fail to control or supervise their child. Although such far-reaching cases of holding parents responsible are still somewhat rare, the use of these laws is growing rapidly due to strong public demand in a time of relatively conservative views regarding crime and crime control.

Legal scholars have argued that these laws result in parents being unjustly punished for the acts of their children. In spite of this, empirical studies and public opinion polls have shown that the public generally believes that parents are largely responsible for the behavior of their children. Consequently, most citizens strongly support the creation and enforcement of parental responsibility laws.

OBJECTIVES OF PARENTAL RESPONSIBILITY LAWS

Parental responsibility laws have several intended goals. Most important, the statutes are meant to prevent and/or reduce delinquent behavior in children. It is commonly believed, by both experts and the public, that parental supervision and discipline are perhaps the most important factors in controlling the deviance of juveniles. Another significant reason for such laws is to hold the persons whom many consider to be responsible for crimes committed by juveniles—the parents—responsible for their children's crimes. Such feelings among the general public, whether warranted or not, are that if the parents did their job, their children would not engage in delinquency. A further rationale behind parental responsibility laws is that the actual or potential victims of juvenile crime are interested in having a more likely source of compensation for crimes committed against them by children. Such attitudes make sense because, after all, most juveniles do not have the resources to pay court-ordered restitution. However, the parents of these juveniles often have the ability to pay. Other reasons for parental responsibility laws exist, including the fact that politicians often use such concepts in their reforms so they will appeal to the public. However, the primary reasons for the statutes are those previously noted.

HISTORY OF PARENTAL RESPONSIBILITY LAWS

The idea of imposing legal responsibility on parents for the deviant behavior of their children has been present in the American juvenile justice system for at least the last 35 years. To compare the attitude in other industrialized countries, the issue of parental responsibility has long been part of their legal philosophies. For example, recent studies summarized in a report by the National Association for Care and Resettlement of Offenders have shown that the French juvenile justice system has long emphasized the responsibility and accountability of the family in the behavior of their juveniles. In fact, the French word for education connotes parenting, or bringing up. In addition, a former prison governor of England, David Wilson, recently discussed the fact that new legislation on delinquency in the British justice system (such as the British Criminal Justice Act of 1991) that includes provisions for parental responsibility laws is simply a rehashing of rules and policies rooted in old laws. He believes the new laws contain little that is innovative. This history is likely a result of European culture, which has always expected a level of accountability on the part of parents; the use of laws was simply a manifestation of this phenomenon.

Despite a history of international focus on parental accountability, America has only recently emphasized the role of parents in the offending of their children. One of the first noted presentations of a parental responsibility law was in 1967 in Pennsylvania. In that case, the state legislature passed a bill that imposed liability on parents for the willful, tortuous acts of children under age 18. The rationale behind the statute was that tax-paying parents would be induced to have greater control over their offspring. However, this statute did not differentiate between parents who attempted to control their children and those who did not.

Some research has generally shown that there is no correlation in delinquency rates between parents who have been legally required to control their children and those who have not. However, some communities may have more success than others with some statutes. Furthermore, it is possible that, if such laws are implemented, the community will become both psychologically and legally removed from controlling and assuming any responsibility for delinquent behavior of their youth.

Parental responsibility laws seen in 1967 as well as most modern versions inherently inject the financial interests of the parents into decisions made by members of the juvenile court. Despite some shortcomings, the 1967 Pennsylvania law demonstrated an early American interest in attributing the responsibility of deviant acts by youths to their parents or caregivers. This law started a trend that has caught on in most U.S. jurisdictions. Geis and Binder (1990) reported in a survey of current laws that all states, except New Hampshire, had enacted laws allowing victims to collect compensation directly from parents for the intentional criminal activities of their children. However, it should be acknowledged that these laws have evolved in such a way that there is a wide range of types. Furthermore, the different criteria included in each are likely to influence their effectiveness on reducing delinquency and improving parental accountability.

In contemporary times, the use of parental responsibility laws is much more common, largely due to public outcry for such legislation. Also, many state advisory boards, such as the Virginia Commission on Youth, have recommended the creation of more statutes that mandate more accountability on the part of parents in controlling their offspring. Federal advisory boards, such as the Office of Juvenile Justice and Delinquency Prevention and the National Council of Juvenile and Family Court Judges, have recently released reports discussing the growing use of parental responsibility laws. However, the issue of whether such laws have an effect is still very much in question.

RESEARCH ON PARENTAL RESPONSIBILITY LAWS

Empirical studies of the impact of parental responsibility laws have been completed, but only on a limited basis and usually only in one state. For example, Silas and Lieb did a study for the Washington State Institute of Public Policy (WSIPP) of the effectiveness of curfew and parental responsibility ordinances in the state of Washington. They found mixed support regarding the number of citations issued for such violations. A second study by Slavick and Aos for the WSIPP reviewed curfew and parental responsibility ordinances in three jurisdictions. Examining juvenile crime before and after the ordinances were passed, the statistical analysis showed that more active parental involvement led to a reduction in delinquency. Furthermore, a study by Roy (1994) of 177 juveniles on home detention with electronic monitoring in Indiana showed that 87 percent of participants received successful discharges. Only 13 percent of the youths were committed for new offenses during the follow-up period. Roy attributed the high degree of successful program completion to the high level of parental responsibility that was a cornerstone of the program. However, the cause of the success might have been related to other unexamined factors. Perhaps parental accountability is the answer to making many contemporary juvenile programs (e.g., those dealing with curfew, house arrest, truancy) work. The empirical research suggests that this might be true.

There are a number of recent suggestions transcending the idea that the activity of youth is a parental responsibility. For example, New York has considered laws that would make local commissioners responsible for financial aspects of various stages of juvenile justice processing, including the initiation of support hearings, the collection of court-ordered payments by juveniles, and probation fees for juveniles. However, this type of accountability has not yet been seen in the United States.

Still, there may come a day when parental responsibility laws transform into community responsibility laws, in which the larger community is held responsible for the behavior of their youth, instead of simply vesting responsibility in the parents/caregivers of the juvenile. As Hillary Rodham Clinton claimed, "it takes a village to raise a child." If one follows this line of thought, the parents are not solely responsible for the behavior of their children. Rather, the entire neighborhood and/or community is accountable. Historically, there is ample precedent for such a position.

Stephen G. Tibbetts

See also California Street Terrorism Enforcement and Prevention Act; Curfew

Bibliography

Geis, G., and A. Binder. 1990. Sins of their children: Parental responsibility for juvenile delinquency. *Notre Dame Journal of Law, Ethics, and Public Policy* 5:303–322.

Lansing, S. 1999. *Parental Responsibility and Juvenile Delinquency: A Comparative Analysis of Laws in New York and Other States.* Office of Justice Systems Analysis Public Policy Report. Albany, NY: Division of Criminal Justice Services.

Roy, S. 1994. Electronic monitoring of juvenile offenders in Lake County, Indiana: An exploratory study. *Journal of Offender Monitoring* 7:1–8.

Wilson, D. 1999. Still waiting for a "Third Way" in criminal justice: New Labor and young people in Britain. *Current Issues in Criminal Justice* 10:319–325.

PHILADELPHIA BIRTH COHORT

The Philadelphia Birth Cohort study is renowned as the first large-scale longitudinal birth cohort study focusing on crime and delinquency in the United

States. The methods and results are compiled in *Delinquency in a Birth Cohort,* by Marvin E. Wolfgang, Robert M. Figlio, and Thorsten Sellin (1972). This study represents a breakthrough in delinquency research, and its findings have guided subsequent research in the field over the past 30 years. Before the Philadelphia Birth Cohort study, researchers primarily relied on information in the FBI's *Uniform Crime Reports* (UCR) or self-report surveys to uncover trends and patterns of crime and delinquency. However, the cross-sectional nature (examining behavior at a single point in time) of these data sources limits one's ability to uncover longitudinal patterns of individual behavior. A cohort study, on the other hand, follows the same group of individuals over a long period and therefore allows for a separate analysis of the incidence (frequency) and prevalence (participation) of delinquent behavior. Thus the Philadelphia Birth Cohort study has had significant theoretical and policy implications for the field.

DESCRIPTION OF THE STUDY

The study began with an in-depth investigation of 9,945 males (29 percent nonwhite and 71 percent white; 54 percent high socioeconomic status and 46 percent low socioeconomic status) who were born in 1945 and resided in Philadelphia between the ages of 10 and 18. Public, private, and parochial school records were used to determine who was eligible for inclusion in the cohort. Once the cohort was established, the researchers collected data on the 3,475 delinquents with official nontraffic police contacts during ages 7 to 18 from the Juvenile Aid Division of the Philadelphia Police Department. This information included offense type, seriousness, and other related information about each contact as well as the type of disposition imposed. Researchers also collected information on demographic, school, and other social characteristics for the cohort. These data allowed the investigation of a number of outcomes regarding delinquent careers, such as age of onset, offense sequence, offense seriousness, and recidivism.

FINDINGS

The first finding from this cohort study was that the probability of committing an offense is directly related to age. For this sample of boys, the highest percentage (25 percent) of all offenses was committed at age 16.

The mean age of onset was 14.4 years, and the modal age was 16 years. Some differences by race with respect to onset occurred in that nonwhites were more likely to have an earlier onset than whites. Lower income nonwhites had their first contact the earliest.

Prevalence and Incidence of Delinquency

The most notable set of findings from this study concerns the prevalence and incidence of delinquency. With respect to the prevalence of offending, 35 percent of the 9,945 boys in the cohort had at least one police contact between ages 7 and 18. Thus a large percentage of juveniles offended at least once, indicating that offending during adolescence may be more typical than anomalous. Among the background characteristics employed in this study, race and socioeconomic status were the strongest predictors of delinquent involvement. For the entire cohort, 50 percent of the nonwhites and 29 percent of the whites had at least one police contact; 26 percent of the high-income boys and 45 percent of the low-income boys were delinquent.

The second key finding involves the incidence of offending. Fifty-four percent of the delinquents were recidivists who committed a mean number of 4.62 offenses each. These recidivists tended to be more serious offenders than were nonrecidivists; for instance, recidivists in the cohort were more likely to commit index offenses than were one-time offenders. Moreover, these recidivists did not appear to specialize in a crime type, and there was little evidence of escalation in offense seriousness for individual offenders. With respect to background characteristics, recidivists were more disadvantaged compared with one-time offenders and nonoffenders in the cohort. For instance, recidivists had the lowest IQ scores and were more likely to have low socioeconomic status and lower education levels.

Recidivism

Because 54 percent of delinquents recidivated, it follows that approximately half (46 percent) of those with one offense did not reoffend (1,613 of the 3,475 delinquents). Moreover, among the 1,862 boys who had a second police contact, 650 (35 percent) did not incur a third contact. This seemingly "natural" desistance raises the issue of appropriate juvenile justice intervention strategies. In addition, the disposition findings show that the juvenile justice system does little to deter juvenile offenders. In fact, the dispositions of probation or incarceration do not appear to influence whether or not a juvenile commits a subsequent offense. Thus, following the publication of *Delinquency in a Birth Cohort*, the effectiveness of the juvenile justice system was questioned. The authors of this study recommended official intervention after the third offense based on the fact that the probability of desisting levels off after the third offense. This approach was thought to be more cost-effective while having a similar effect on curbing delinquency. Drawing on these findings, a "hands off" approach, particularly for first-time offenders, became a popular idea in the 1970s.

Chronic Offenders

The most influential finding from the Philadelphia Birth Cohort study stems from the discovery that a small group of offenders are responsible for the majority of juvenile crime. *Chronic offenders* in this study were defined as boys with five or more police contacts between the ages of 7 and 18. Among the delinquents in the cohort, 18 percent (627 of the 3,475 delinquents) were classified as chronic offenders and were responsible for 52 percent of the total offenses (5,305 of the 10,214 offenses committed) and 63 percent of the UCR index offenses (i.e., homicide, robbery, larceny, motor vehicle theft, etc.). These chronic offenders made up 6 percent of the entire cohort and are frequently referred to as "the chronic 6 percent." Although the idea of chronic offending was not new at the time, this study provided documented evidence that these chronic offenders existed, constituted a small percentage of the cohort, and were responsible for a large proportion of crime.

Again, there were race and socioeconomic differentials among the recidivists and chronic offenders. Nonwhites were not only more likely to be recidivists but were 4.5 times more likely to be chronic offenders than whites. In addition, lower-income boys were more likely to be recidivists and chronic offenders than were higher-income boys. The pattern of race differentials remained prominent even after socioeconomic status was held constant, suggesting that race was a stronger indicator of delinquency among this cohort of boys.

Selective incapacitation strategies have been proposed under the assumption that if these chronic offenders can be identified and incarcerated, then the volume of crime committed by juveniles would be reduced by 50 percent. However, the critical element of a successful selective incapacitation policy is the ability to accurately identify chronic offenders in advance. The Philadelphia Birth Cohort study identified the "chronic 6 percent" retrospectively. The issue of prospectively identifying which juveniles will become chronic offenders and which ones will desist or remain low-rate offenders has been problematic. To date, the empirical evidence on this predictive ability has been less than encouraging.

FOLLOW-ON STUDIES

One lasting contribution of the Philadelphia Birth Cohort study is the subsequent research and cohort studies following the original study. There have been two extensions of Wolfgang's original Philadelphia Birth Cohort Study, which provide additional information about offending patterns. A study by Marvin E. Wolfgang, Terence P. Thornberry, and Robert M. Figlio (1986) investigated the continuity and discontinuity of offending into adulthood for 10 percent of the original 1945 birth cohort from ages 18 to 30 (975 males). Overall, the study presents a picture of continuity among these subjects in that the delinquent juveniles were likely to become adult offenders while the nondelinquent juveniles were likely to be nonoffenders. However, it is interesting to note that 22 percent of the juvenile chronic offenders had no contacts as adults, indicating the possibility for change and the presence of discontinuity in criminal careers.

The second extension of Wolfgang's Philadelphia Birth Cohort study was a replication study conducted by Paul E. Tracy and Kimberly Kempf-Leonard (1996). This replication study, known as the Philadelphia Birth Cohort II study, used a 1958 birth cohort. The investigation used data collection and methodological techniques similar to the original Philadelphia Birth Cohort study to analyze the offending patterns of 27,160 males and females through age 26. The findings from the 1958 cohort concurred with the original 1945 birth cohort with respect to the prevalence and incidence of juvenile offending. Approximately 33 percent of the birth cohort had at least one police contact, and 7.5 percent of the cohort were classified as chronic offenders (23 percent of the delinquents). These chronic offenders were responsible for 61 percent of the offenses (9,240 of the 15,248 offenses committed) and 68 percent of the UCR index offenses. The addition of females is informative; with respect to prevalence, only 14 percent of the females in the cohort had at least one police contact by age 18, showing that males were 2.5 times more likely to commit a delinquent act than were females. There was also a small number of female chronic offenders who were responsible for a large percentage of the female crime.

CONCLUSION

Marvin Wolfgang and his Philadelphia Birth Cohort study influenced the field by using longitudinal empirical data to investigate the problem of delinquency. His study gave rise to a number of subsequent birth cohort studies initiated in the United States and abroad. In the United States, there are the 1945 and 1958 birth cohort extensions of the original Philadelphia Birth Cohort study mentioned earlier and Lyle Shannon's study of three birth cohorts (1942, 1949, and 1955) in Racine, Wisconsin. On the international level, Wolfgang and his colleagues conducted a 1970 birth cohort study in Puerto Rico and a 1973 birth cohort study in China. Although the field is still in need of more longitudinal data of this kind, as more studies are conducted in the tradition of the Philadelphia Birth Cohort study, new scientific data about the nature of juvenile delinquency are being discovered.

Elaine P. Eggleston

See also Johan Thorsten Sellin; Marvin Eugene Wolfgang

Bibliography

Nevares, D., M. E. Wolfgang, P. E. Tracy, and S. Aurand. 1990. *Delinquency in Puerto Rico.* Westport, CT: Greenwood.

Tracy, P. E., and K. Kempf-Leonard. 1996. *Continuity and Discontinuity in Criminal Careers.* New York: Plenum.

Tracy, P. E., M. E. Wolfgang, and R. M. Figlio. 1990. *Delinquency in Two Birth Cohorts.* New York: Plenum.

Wolfgang, M. E. 1996. *Delinquency in China: Study of a Birth Cohort.* Washington, DC: Department of Justice.

Wolfgang, M. E., R. M. Figlio, and T. Sellin. 1972. *Delinquency in a Birth Cohort.* Chicago: The University of Chicago Press.

Wolfgang, M. E., T. P. Thornberry, and R. M. Figlio. 1986. *From Boy to Man, From Delinquency to Crime.* Chicago: University of Chicago Press.

POLICE RESPONSES TO DELINQUENCY

Juveniles represent a unique population that poses many problems for the police. This population is unique for several reasons. First, juveniles are processed through a juvenile justice system that has a number of similarities with the adult justice system but, in many instances, is quite different. Second, our society gives more deference to juveniles as opposed to adult criminals. Society has a greater expectation that we should attempt to rehabilitate juveniles or guide them away from a life of delinquency and criminality. The police are seen as the frontline defense for this purpose. Third, the police are called on to intervene in juvenile offenses such as truancy, curfew violations, and teen drinking—offenses that are not applicable to the adult population. Enforcement of these offenses is seen as a way of preventing future criminality. This uniqueness results in the police having to pay special attention when dealing with juvenile offenders or victims.

Today juvenile involvement in violent crime is of particular interest to society. This interest has been spawned by the rash of mass murders committed by juveniles that have occurred in schools across the country. The frequency of these killings over the last decade has heightened public fear and the expectation that the police do something about juvenile violence. However, it should be noted that contrary to media and political forecasts, juvenile violent crime has not surged to unprecedented levels and has remained fairly stable. Although juvenile violent crime has increased somewhat over the past decade, it has not grown to epidemic proportions as some experts predicted. Indeed, juveniles continue to account for only a small fraction of the total violent crime in the United States.

Most medium and large police departments have specialized juvenile units to deal with juveniles and delinquency. Although most of a department's contact with juveniles is by patrol officers, juvenile officers generally process youths who are placed in custody and coordinate programs designed to reduce juvenile delinquency. Departments developed juvenile units because often juvenile cases are complex and many patrol officers do not remain familiar with how juvenile cases are processed. Juvenile courts have implemented specific rules to protect the juvenile, and these rules are quite different from criminal procedures. The juvenile unit maintains all files relating to juvenile cases and works with other officers in presenting their cases in juvenile court. This unit is generally housed in the criminal investigation or detective division within the department.

THE FUNCTIONS OF POLICE JUVENILE UNITS

The juvenile unit has a number of functions other than processing juvenile cases. One function of this unit is to investigate or supervise cases of child neglect, abuse, missing or runaway children, and domestic violence involving children. The police have substantial latitude in dealing with juveniles. The judicial philosophy used in juvenile court is *in loco parentis*. This philosophy dictates that the primary mission of the police and the courts is to protect, rather than punish, juveniles. Juveniles are immature and become influenced by the wrong role models, which sometimes requires "parental intervention" by the state to assist them in becoming productive citizens. It also gives the police broad powers to intervene in status offenses. Status offenses are offenses or situations where the police would have no authority if the situation or act involved an adult. Some examples of status offenses include possessing alcoholic beverages, running away, violating curfew, and truancy. The broad powers of the police in dealing with juveniles enable authorities to intervene in the early stages of delinquency and, it is hoped, prevent future criminality.

In addition to processing juvenile cases, many juvenile units are responsible for a number of other functions. Gang eradication programs are often housed in juvenile units. Since the crack epidemic in the 1980s and early 1990s, gangs have become a primary target for the police. The police implement programs designed to reduce gang involvement and gang violence. These include education programs for youths in neighborhoods where gangs are prevalent. Such programs are designed to educate potential gang members about the risks and problems should they become associated with a gang. Departments also have a number of gang enforcement programs. These programs are designed to target gangs and gang members. Typically, the police target gang leaders and violent gang members for enforcement efforts. Another part of this function is to gather intelligence information on gang activities and membership. Today most large departments maintain files of gang activities and membership.

Many departments have their Drug Abuse Resistance Education (DARE) or drug education officers working out of the juvenile unit. A large number of departments have implemented DARE programs in an effort to combat the drug problem. Unfortunately, research tends to indicate that these programs are not successful in reducing future drug use. However, departments keep them for several reasons. First, they hope the program will have a positive effect on some juveniles. Even if only a few juvenile participants are swayed from using drugs, the program is worthwhile. Second, the program affords the police an opportunity to develop positive relations with juveniles. DARE officers can meet with and interact with large numbers of students. Finally, a drug education program tends to be one of the police department's best public relations tools. The program meets parents' expectations that the police are proactive in drug eradication in the schools.

Currently, a large number of departments have school resource officers (SROs). In an SRO program, officers are assigned to schools (primarily junior high schools and high schools) and serve to prevent crime and delinquency. These programs are designed to develop rapport between students and the police, to investigate crimes occurring on campus, and to prevent crime from occurring. SROs are particularly helpful at sporting events, at which fights and other disorders often occur. In addition, SROs are becoming more involved in drug intervention on school grounds because the courts have given school officials broader authority to conduct searches of students and their lockers.

SROs generally work out of juvenile units or work closely with juvenile officers to alleviate crime and drug problems in the schools. One of the important functions of an SRO program is for the police and schools to advise each other about criminal behavior involving students. For example, schools should be notified when a student has been involved in drug trafficking or a violent crime, even when the crime did not occur on school grounds. This would alert school officials about potential problems and allow them to investigate the student's activities on campus or to take other preventive measures. At the same time, school officials should notify the police of a violent student or one who has been caught trafficking or possessing drugs on school grounds. Historically, the police and schools have not communicated, which has led to a number of problems when students commit crimes on campus. SRO programs not only link the police with schools, they allow juvenile units to collect better information about delinquents who may be violent, possess weapons, or deal in drugs.

JUVENILE PROCEDURE AND THE POLICE

As previously noted, the procedures used by the police in handling juveniles are different from those used when dealing with adults. The primary objectives of these procedures are to protect juveniles and prevent future victimization or delinquency. The overriding concern in adult cases is "probable cause." Once the police have probable cause that an adult has committed a crime, they arrest the adult and build a case; then the court makes a final determination about guilt and punishment. The police use probable cause in dealing with juveniles, but once they decide to detain a juvenile, the justice system mandates that everything be done to protect the juvenile. Juveniles also have the same constitutional rights as adults, so it is more complicated for police officers as they go about protecting juveniles while presenting their cases.

Typically, the police do not arrest juveniles. Instead, they take them into custody or detain them. Detention is the time during which the police or a probation officer holds a juvenile until the arresting officer files a petition. During detention, a juvenile normally cannot be placed in a jail or other facility used to house adult offenders. Most juvenile detention facilities are completely detached and separate from adult jails. This is done to protect the juvenile from the undue influences of more mature criminals and to prevent the juvenile's victimization while in detention.

The police are restricted in how they can investigate a juvenile case, particularly in the areas of fingerprinting and photographs. Typically, police officers fingerprint and photograph all arrestees because some of those arrested have committed a number of offenses. The fingerprints are used to match suspects to other crime scenes, while the photographs are sometimes used to show witnesses and link suspects to other crimes. However, most states have restrictions on when the police can photograph or fingerprint juveniles who are taken into custody. Normally, juveniles cannot be photographed or fingerprinted, except in specific circumstances. For example, if the police, as a part of an investigation, suspect that a juvenile has been involved in a crime, they may take photographs and fingerprints for comparison purposes. Once the investigation is completed, the fingerprints and photographs must be separated from adult files, and

restrictions are placed on access. Some jurisdictions require that these items be destroyed at the completion of the investigation. Other jurisdictions allow the police to retain juvenile photographs and fingerprints as long as they are separated from any adult files. Access by the public is also limited. In some jurisdictions, the police can access juvenile files only in specific situations, such as during an active investigation. Regardless, files are destroyed after the juvenile becomes an adult.

Following an investigation, the investigating officer completes a petition. If an officer not assigned to the juvenile unit initiated the case, a juvenile detective usually assists the officer in completing and processing the petition. The petition essentially is an affidavit that details the particulars of the case. It is different from a warrant used in adult cases in that, in addition to explaining how probable cause in the case was developed, it also provides information about the juvenile's situation and circumstances. Once the petition is completed, it is submitted to juvenile court and a hearing date is set. The hearing itself can be an arduous process for the officer. There may be a number of meetings with the defense counsel, probation officers, judge, police officer, and others to determine the best course of action for the juvenile.

POLICE DISCRETION
IN HANDLING JUVENILES

Police officers are afforded a great deal of discretion when deciding how to handle a case or situation. The police are charged with enforcing literally hundreds of criminal statutes but, surprisingly, there are only a few instances where the statutes mandate that the police take action. Most states now require the police to make an arrest in cases of domestic violence, and some states require officers to arrest in cases of driving under the influence of intoxicants (DUI). Otherwise, the police officer is given substantial freedom when dealing with crimes and offenses.

When a police officer encounters a juvenile who has violated a law, the officer can choose among a variety of options when dealing with the case, including the following:

1. Warn the juvenile and release him or her.

2. Release the juvenile to his or her parents or guardians.

3. Take a report detailing the juvenile's problems or activities and then release him or her.

4. Release the juvenile but file a report to initiate a juvenile petition for processing.

5. Detain the juvenile and initiate informal meetings and processing with the juvenile's parents or guardians.

6. Detain the juvenile, write a petition, and refer the juvenile to juvenile court.

The police consider a number of factors when deciding how to handle a case. The primary factor is the nature of the offense. Police officers tend to use less discretion when a serious crime has been committed. Police officers generally refer any case involving violence, weapons, or drugs, or in which an injury occurred, to juvenile court. Minor cases tend to be handled more informally. The crime victim's feelings and attitude are often considered when deciding how to process a case. If a victim is adamant about detaining a juvenile suspect, the police often consider this in making a decision. Also, if a victim is innocent and the attack or victimization was unprovoked, the police are likely to refer the case to juvenile court. Similarly, police are likely to give elderly victims and female victims more consideration than they give to younger males when deciding how to process a case. Finally, the demeanor of the juvenile is a key ingredient in the decision. If the juvenile is repentant, the police are more likely to use some informal option.

We find that the police use a substantial amount of discretion when they encounter juveniles. The police take a juvenile into custody in only about 10 percent of the cases in which they come into contact with juveniles. In many of these cases, the police ultimately drop the charges or release the juvenile. This occurs in about one half of the cases where a detention by an officer occurred. If the police do not drop the charges, the case is referred to juvenile court intake. There a juvenile detention counselor or juvenile probation officer reviews the case. The juvenile detention counselor informally handles about one half of the cases referred by the police. The detention process results in fewer juveniles being processed up the system. Ultimately, less than 3 percent of the juveniles who come into contact with the police are processed in juvenile court.

There are several reasons for this. First, many police officers will initiate contact with juveniles for minor infractions. Police officers often exercise their role of juvenile delinquency prevention by stopping or talking with juveniles who appear suspicious or who appear to be unsupervised. For example, police officers often will stop and question juveniles who are on the streets late at night. Second, the police perceive that the parents or guardians can best handle many juvenile problems. Thus when an officer takes a juvenile into custody, the parent is called to the police station, where both the parent and juvenile are counseled about the problem. Finally, and perhaps most problematic, the police tend not to use the juvenile justice process because it is complicated and time-consuming. When an officer decides to detain a juvenile, the processing time is likely to be substantial. Even when juvenile detectives process the case, the detaining officer generally must be present and participate in any counseling sessions or the decision to forward the case to juvenile intake. If the case is forwarded to juvenile intake, the officer ultimately must spend a considerable amount of time in juvenile court. Thus in many cases, police officers see juvenile detentions as being too labor-intensive. Many juvenile courts have contributed to this problem by making the hearing process extremely complicated and time-consuming.

COMMUNITY POLICING AND JUVENILE CRIME

American policing has undergone a major change over the past decade. Most police departments have embraced the idea of community policing, which has affected, to some extent, how they deal with juveniles and juvenile crime. Community policing dictates that the police become more involved in problem solving and community partnerships. Problem solving is a process in which the police attempt to develop effective solutions to problems that result in increased crime and disorder. Historically, the police primarily responded to calls for service and dealt with crime and disorder, rather than attempting to investigate their causes. Problem solving requires a more in-depth response to situations and problems. Community partnerships, on the other hand, require police to work more closely with other community and government agencies to solve problems. In terms of combating juvenile delinquency, the police should work with social service agencies and neighborhood groups to develop programs for reducing juvenile crime and delinquency.

Before community policing, most police departments only had a few limited programs to prevent juvenile delinquency. Police officers generally saw their role as detaining and processing juvenile suspects. Some departments had a wider range of programs, but that was rare. The two most common programs were Officer Friendly programs and police athletic leagues (PALs). The Officer Friendly programs consisted of officers visiting schools and making presentations about how the police operated. They were primarily intended to develop better relations with students. The PAL programs, which still exist, consist of involving youth, especially those from disadvantaged families, in sports programs. The police organize and sponsor baseball, basketball, and football programs. Both programs were designed to mentor youth, provide them with positive experiences, and keep them from wandering the streets and becoming involved in delinquency.

Today police departments have substantially expanded their arsenal of programs, as previously discussed. The programs are primarily enforcement programs designed to attack specific crime problems. In addition, the police have used intensified patrol operations that include aggressive field interrogations and pretextual traffic stops and searches of juveniles' cars. The purposes of these aggressive tactics are to deter gang activity, look for evidence of the commission of a crime, and confiscate contraband such as drugs and weapons. The police tend to believe that aggressive policing, especially in high gang and crime neighborhoods, is the most effective way to deal with juvenile crime, particularly violent crimes.

Unfortunately, the police have concentrated their community policing efforts on problem solving and enforcement rather than expending increased resources on community partnerships. Although problem solving is an important ingredient in reducing juvenile crime, it is limited in that it does not assist in developing nurturing types of relations and safer conditions for juveniles, especially those who are considered high-risk cases. The police should work with neighborhood groups, churches, schools, and other social service agencies to develop neighborhood-level programs that mentor juveniles and provide them with positive role models. Programs such as PAL should be expanded to teach juveniles teamwork and help occupy their time. Moreover, there is a need for programs that enhance juveniles' life skills. The overwhelming majority of juvenile delinquents have deficient life skills, and programs such as after-school tutoring, vocational education, and pregnancy and birth control counseling could assist at-risk youth in resisting criminality.

CONCLUSION

The police are extensively involved in juvenile crime problems. Because of community policing, the police now have a plethora of programs aimed at reducing juvenile crime. Unfortunately, programs aimed at building juveniles' capacity to resist delinquency are still in short supply. The police have a difficult task that they cannot accomplish successfully on their own. The police must work with other community groups in reducing juvenile delinquency, and these groups must willingly become involved in this effort.

Larry K. Gaines

See also DARE; Gangs, Juvenile

Bibliography

Black, D. J., and A. J. Reiss Jr. 1979. Police control of juveniles. *American Sociological Review* 35:63–77.

Browning, S. L., F. Cullen, L. Cao, R. Kopache, and T. Stevenson. 1994. Race and getting hassled by the police. *Police Studies* 17:1–11.

Leiber, M. J., M. K. Nalla, and M. Farnworth. 1998. Explaining juveniles' attitudes toward the police. *Justice Quarterly* 15:151–174.

Piliavin, I., and S. Briar. 1964. Police encounters with juveniles. *American Journal of Sociology* 70:206–214.

Portune, R. 1971. *Changing Adolescent Attitudes Toward Police.* Cincinnati, OH: Anderson.

 PREGNANCY, TEENAGE

Statistics suggest that at the end of the 1990s, teenage pregnancy rates in the United States were steadily declining to a rate lower than was the case throughout most of the 20th century, and teens were becoming parents less frequently than their counterparts in the 1950s. From 1992 to 1996, teenage pregnancies among 15- to 19-year-olds decreased by 13 percent, while the teen birth rate fell by 20 percent (Henshaw and Feivelson, 2000). Despite this good news, the perception is that an epidemic is upon us. Numerous politicians, activists, and researchers are quick to point out that about one million young females get pregnant annually, and our country continues to have higher rates of teen pregnancy and childbearing than do most other developed countries, particularly Western European nations.

The costs of teen pregnancy, in terms of loss of social and economic potential, are often mentioned in accounts expressing great concern with this phenomenon. Specifically, it has been noted that teen mothers and fathers tend to fall behind in the areas of education and employment and thus are less successful in adulthood, perhaps living in poverty. This entry provides an overview of teenage pregnancy, beginning with a historical review of its construction as a social problem. It contains a review of the risk factors associated with this problem, what is known about its connection to delinquent behaviors, and the characteristics of those who become parents. The conclusion focuses on an evaluation of various strategies that have been undertaken to combat teen pregnancy and early parenthood.

THE EMERGENCE OF TEENAGE PREGNANCY AS A PROBLEM

Two factors are salient when examining teenage pregnancy from a historical perspective: the emergence of adolescence as a distinct period of human development and changing norms regarding female sexuality. Both factors occurred as our nation's economic base shifted from agrarian to industrial. In colonial America, young men and women generally married at younger ages than they do today, and although not necessarily considered ideal, premarital sex and adolescent parenthood were treated as somewhat inevitable. The Puritans, for example, socially approved of premarital sex between individuals of all ages, provided the parties involved had entered a "precontract," a practice that made engagements legally binding. However, since unwed motherhood violated social norms, the wedding date was simply moved forward if the young woman became pregnant (Hymowitz and Weissman, 1978). The precontract and similar practices suggest that adults in early America at least tacitly acknowledged and accepted the fact that young people would engage in sexual activities, which could result in pregnancy. Adolescent parenting was common and was viewed as nonproblematic in the context of marriage. Therefore, to understand current concerns about "kids having kids," one must look to the late 1800s, when views on

adolescence in general, and teenage pregnancy in particular, were altered.

Most accounts attribute the advent of adolescence, as a distinct phase of development, to industrialization—particularly the post–Civil War period. The concept of childhood had developed to some degree in the 15th and 16th centuries, but the family's reliance on all its members for economic subsistence stifled any remarkable changes in the treatment of children. Differences for children began when the growth in industry enticed workers away from the farm and the increasing mechanization of the factory (and agriculture) required fewer workers. Growing labor unions pressed for restrictions on cheap child labor in some sectors, while increasing numbers of immigrants were available to work in the nonunion plants. Conditions were ripe for the passage of child labor laws promoted by unions and humanitarian groups.

By 1914, all but one state had statutes forbidding children, generally under age 14, from working in factories. Thus for the first time in our country's history, there were large numbers of young people with nothing constructive to fill their days. This period of idleness was short-lived, however, as compulsory education was promoted as a means to encourage the moral and social development of children and adolescents and to train young people to be good workers. Whether schools ever achieved those goals did not seem as important as their function of controlling large numbers of young people freed from the confines of the factory and the farm by industrialization.

One of the reasons why adults believed young people needed to be controlled was that they might engage in sexual experimentation and possibly become young parents. Those espousing this concern adhered to Victorian morality, which had been gaining steam throughout the 1800s alongside the expansion of industry. Proponents of this line of thought argued that sexual experience threatened the moral character of children and adults alike and that females were degenerate if they had any sexual feelings at all. Although Freud soon informed us that Victorian moralists and the medical authorities backing them had erred, the strict norms governing sexual conduct at the time were powerful enough to be evidenced in laws. By 1900, for instance, the age of consent was raised from around age 10 or 12 years to age 16 in most states. Male sexuality was not considered benign by Victorian thinkers, but since women were deemed morally superior and devoid of sexual urges, the force of this movement soon focused almost exclusively on the most controllable females, young girls. To illustrate, almost all the girls appearing in the early juvenile courts were charged with immorality or waywardness, buzzwords signifying that those females could be sexually experienced and must be stopped. Too frequently, these girls were institutionalized until of marriageable age (Chesney-Lind and Shelden, 1998).

As America moved through the 20th century, society explicitly promoted a concept of successful adulthood that included the postponement of sex until marriage and the postponement of marriage until schooling was completed and marketability achieved. Normative constraints on sexual conduct, combined with industrial-age regulations on labor market participation and school attendance, had lowered the respectability of teenage pregnancy and childbirth. But the behaviors of teenagers had not changed. Statistics tracking these events, as well the Kinsey reports released in the late 1940s and early 1950s, revealed that sexual activity and pregnancy among teens had not disappeared. As in the past, the desired responses to teen pregnancy—adoption or marriage—were often achieved. However, the pregnancy itself was treated with contempt because it jeopardized the ideal purpose of adolescence, which emphasized preparing for adult roles, not participating in them.

Contempt turned to outrage in the 1970s, when the teenage population expanded, thus producing more teen mothers in absolute terms, and when teens who got pregnant did not overwhelmingly select preferred options. As Skolnick (1992) explained, from the late 1960s to the early 1970s, births legitimized by marriage declined from 65 percent to 35 percent. In addition, by the 1980s, only 10 percent of pregnant teenagers were giving their babies up for adoption, representing a complete turnaround from the 1960s when 90 percent of teen mothers chose that alternative.

RESEARCH ON TEENAGE PREGNANCY

Disillusion with war on poverty programs, coupled with increasing numbers of unmarried teenage mothers, many of whom relied heavily on government assistance, translated into a panic over teenage pregnancy and childbirth. Research examining the risk factors correlated with teenage pregnancy and childbirth rapidly expanded as a result of this anxiety.

Most of the research on those topics relied on self-reports and was conducted on individuals in clinical or institutional settings or schools. Although school surveys had been administered on a national level, many studies focused exclusively on adolescents from urban areas, where young people are believed to be at risk for multiple problem behaviors. It is difficult to make generalizations from some of these studies because the samples were unrepresentative. Moreover, causal processes are hard to detect because most of the existing research is cross-sectional, and many studies lack control variables. Despite these shortcomings, some tentative conclusions can be drawn regarding the risk factors associated with teenage pregnancy, the link between teenage pregnancy and delinquency, and the characteristics of those most likely to become teenage parents.

The most undisputed risk factors for teenage pregnancy are behavioral and include age of onset of sexual intercourse, frequency of intercourse, number of sexual partners, and the use of contraceptives. Simply put, when adolescents start having sex at a young age (12 or 13 years of age), have sex often with different people, and do not use contraceptives, pregnancy becomes more likely. The controversy, however, centers on which of the more than 100 antecedents of those practices have the greatest predictive value. No single risk factor stands above the rest across all studies, but some precursors appear more relevant than others. We will focus attention on those factors, beginning with the most widely examined influences of the family.

Miller, Benson, and Galbraith (2001) synthesized more than 100 studies on teenage pregnancy and childbearing, and although results were discrepant, it was concluded that relationships within the family may be crucial. Specifically, research consistently demonstrates that higher levels of attachment to parents may reduce the risk of pregnancy. Adolescents who are closer to their parent(s) are more likely to postpone sexual intercourse, have fewer sexual partners, and use contraceptives more consistently. Many have assumed that the relationship between connectedness and decreased pregnancy risk may be mediated by more frequent and open communication between adolescents and parents. Findings regarding this association, however, are mixed. Some studies have found that communicating the values of abstinence and/or protected intercourse may have more significance than the quantity of discussions about sex or the degree of openness on the issue.

Another commonly examined potential mediator of the relationship between family attachment and pregnancy risk is parental supervision. Most studies show that parental regulation of adolescents' conduct is inversely related to teenage pregnancy, but level and type of control qualify this relationship. When supervision is too extreme and intrusive or is lacking, the relationship between parental control and pregnancy risk likely becomes curvilinear. In summary, it appears that behavioral risks for teenage pregnancy are reduced when supportive parents, who stress abstinence and/or safer sex, effectively regulate their children's interactions without being overbearing. It should be noted that these family-based contingencies may shed light on often-noted positive correlations between teenage pregnancy and parental alcohol and drug abuse and child physical and sexual abuse. The parent-child relationship necessary to reduce risk is obviously strained by those factors.

Other familial factors have also received considerable research attention, such as sibling pregnancy, family structure, and socioeconomic class. Having older siblings in the home who have been involved in a teenage pregnancy increases risk, perhaps through imitation of risk-taking behaviors, but this relationship only holds for younger sisters whose older sisters became pregnant as teens. Adolescent males do not appear to be affected by sibling teenage pregnancy (East and Jacobson, 2001). Regarding family structure, cross-sectional studies frequently find that being from a single-parent home is associated with teenage pregnancy. This factor, however, appears to be conditioned by family socioeconomic status.

Single-parent homes typically include the mother and her children, and for a variety of reasons, these families are more likely to be poor or to live in poverty (Coley and Chase-Lansdale, 1998). Numerous studies show that adolescents from families with low socioeconomic status are more at risk of becoming involved in teenage pregnancy than are their counterparts in more economically secure families. Although there is some speculation that the differential availability of contraceptives explains this relationship, the precise influence of socioeconomic status on teenage pregnancy is unknown. The section on teen parenthood that follows revisits this issue. For now, this section reviews the literature examining how school experiences, career aspirations, and other attitudinal variables influence teenage pregnancy.

Measures of teenage attitudes toward school and future employment opportunities are not included as often in studies of teenage pregnancy as are the familial variables discussed thus far, yet when they are analyzed, the findings are consistent. Compared with other teens, those who have higher educational expectations, a more positive attitude toward school, and higher career aspirations are more likely to desire to postpone pregnancy until their goals are achieved. Consequently, these teens are less likely to engage in intercourse or have multiple partners, and they are more likely to use contraceptives. Having a more egalitarian view toward females also seems to reduce behavioral risk for teenage pregnancy through increased use of contraceptives. If mothering or fathering is perceived as less disruptive to the future or something that would be pleasing to family or friends, contraceptive use decreases (Plotnick, 1992). Some findings have suggested that teens likely to become involved in pregnancy have more deviant attitudes or possess more antisocial characteristics than do teens who do not get pregnant. This proposed relationship merits more detailed examination.

As the body of research on teenage pregnancy expanded after the 1970s, analysts began to notice that the phenomenon could often be linked to a wide range of deviant behaviors, such as alcohol or drug use, theft, and use of aggression. These findings encouraged researchers to explore whether delinquency may be an antecedent of teenage pregnancy or vice versa. Several longitudinal studies were conducted in the late 1980s and early 1990s, and the results tend to be uniform and consistent: When multiple problems are found, they are usually co-occurring or syndrome-like (e.g., Huizinga, Loeber, and Thornberry, 1993). There is some evidence that delinquency, particularly alcohol and drug use, may precede teenage pregnancy, but the more important issue is risk taking in general, including numerous forms of delinquency. Clearly, not all adolescents involved in pregnancy are delinquent, but delinquents who become involved with pregnancy exhibit more severe patterns of problem behaviors. The onset of those problematic behaviors typically precede the teenage years.

The behavioral, familial, and economic circumstances that may either increase or minimize pregnancy risk, as discussed thus far, are not equally applicable across all ages, races or ethnicities, or socioeconomic groups, nor do they hold when considering males versus females. For example, parent-child relationships are not as consistently significant when the subjects are African American. More research is needed to examine differential influences and interactive effects.

A final issue deserving attention concerns the biological correlates of teenage pregnancy. Findings in the biological arena are mixed, but age of puberty onset, age of menarche (which has slowly declined from around age 14 in the 1950s to approximately age 13 today), dopamine receptor genes, androgen hormone levels, and other biological variables have been shown to affect sexual behaviors, such as age at first intercourse. Further research is necessary to determine whether biological influences interact with environmental variables or operate independently to increase behavioral risk taking (e.g., Miller et al., 2001).

PROFILE OF TEENAGE PARENTS

Our knowledge about the temporal order and statistical significance of the various precursors related to teen pregnancy is limited, and few researchers have considered the potential explanatory power of a biosocial model. However, these shortcomings do not hamper our ability to provide a profile of the typical teenage parent. Teen fathers tend to be about two or three years older than teen mothers and are more likely to have been involved in illegalities and to have been arrested. Otherwise, there are few differences between the sexes. Teenage parents are likely to have dropped out of school and to have been raised by single parents in poverty. They will likely experience unemployment. Teenage parents are also likely to be Hispanic or African American. This is not surprising given that, compared with white youth, Hispanics and blacks report that they have sex at a younger age, have sex more often, and have more sexual partners (Warren et al., 1998). As Coley and Chase-Lansdale (1998) and others hypothesize, the relationship between teenage childbearing and these descriptive variables may be explained by socioeconomic status. Living in poverty affects family stability, school experiences, and job opportunities. Faced with few life options, the perceived costs of parenthood among minority youth may be lower, leading to behavioral risk taking. In addition, poorer teenagers may have less access to contraceptives and abortions.

EFFORTS TO REDUCE TEENAGE PREGNANCY

Given the likelihood of adverse outcomes, various strategies have been implemented to combat teen pregnancy and early parenthood. Unfortunately, few intervention strategies have focused on the broader structural forces that are related to teenage pregnancy and other problem behaviors among at-risk populations. Those programs that have tackled the issue of building social and human capital have typically been aimed at teen parents, especially mothers. Evaluations reveal little success in terms of quality educational advancement, job training, or earnings increases. In some of these programs, repeat pregnancies and births have occurred. Part of the problem lies in ineffective service delivery and lack of proper funding, but the target population itself presents special considerations. Program participants are often multiply disadvantaged and do not meet minimum standards to receive some services (Coley and Chase-Lansdale, 1998). Early intervention is the key when dealing with at-risk populations, which is likely why programs like the Perry Preschool Project receive positive evaluations. This comprehensive intervention strategy is not designed to combat teenage pregnancy alone but problem behaviors in general. It is a developmentally focused, multi-pronged strategy with individual and family services accompanied by school-based and community programs. Pregnancy rates have been reduced in areas where the program has been implemented.

Most of the programs geared toward reducing teenage pregnancy have not been as comprehensive as the early intervention efforts. A plethora of techniques have been applied to the problem, ranging from abstinence-based programs to contraceptive distribution or sex education. Many of these programs are so unique or geographically specific that they have not attracted the attention of evaluation researchers, but sex education and the provision of contraceptives have not suffered from lack of attention. Given the controversial nature of speaking candidly to adolescents about sexual behaviors and providing them with the means of achieving safer sex, these programs have received much scrutiny.

Although the long-term effects are questionable, evaluations have been somewhat positive, especially among programs that include a parent education component. More adolescents understand the risks associated with sexual behavior and are using contraceptives more reliably due to their increased availability in some communities. In addition, more parents are becoming aware that sexuality is something that has to be addressed in the home. The problem is primarily political and is tied to the Victorian ideology that still strongly exerts itself, particularly when teenage sexuality is the issue: Sex education and contraceptives do not promote abstinence. Approximately half of all teens in Grades 7 through 12 report that they have had sexual intercourse (Warren et al., 1998), and large, vocal segments of the population are as concerned with teens having sex as they are with teenage pregnancy. People in this camp want abstinence programs of the "Just Say No" variety. Despite congressional backing for such programs to the tune of $250 million in 1996, there is no credible evidence to suggest that this is a worthy expenditure (Coley and Chase-Lansdale, 1998).

The Teen Outreach program, which seeks to reduce school failure and suspension as well as teenage pregnancy, is not politically unpopular and does appear to work. This intervention strategy is school based and developmentally oriented. The program uses two primary techniques: structured volunteer service and classroom discussions. Participants receive mentoring while working on a community project of interest to them. In the classroom, the volunteer service is explored and there is a forum for discussing relationships, life choices, and career opportunities. If the school already teaches sex education, no new material is introduced. In any case, only 15 percent of the written curriculum deals with the topic. None of the target behaviors is given much direct attention. Teen Outreach was evaluated over five years at 25 sites across the country, and substantially positive results were found, particularly among female participants (Allen, Philliber, Herrling, and Kuperminc, 1997). How the program operates to reduce these behaviors is a matter of speculation rather than empirical fact. Those involved suggest that enough autonomy is offered to foster increased competence, which combines with connectedness to the others in the program and the larger community to produce more mature decision makers. This strategy is exciting for two reasons: It successfully combats multiple problematic behaviors, and it should be appealing to all communities given the lack of emphasis on adolescent sexuality. The lingering question revolves around whether this program can meet the challenges provided in high-risk communities. It is unlikely that Teen Outreach will be able to counter all the negatives facing adolescents disadvantaged by dire living conditions and a paucity of life options. However, it shows promise and may be blended with needed health and social services to lower involvement in behavioral risks leading to teenage pregnancy and childbearing.

Jana Buffkin and Vickie Luttrell

See also At-Risk Youth; Prostitution, Teenage

Bibliography

Allen, J., S. Philliber, S. Herrling, and G. Kuperminc. 1997. Preventing teen pregnancy and academic failure: Experimental evaluation of a developmentally-based approach. *Child Development* 64:729–742.

Chesney-Lind, M., and R. G. Shelden. 1998. *Girls, Delinquency and Juvenile Justice*, 2nd ed. Belmont, CA: West/Wadsworth.

Coley, R., and P. Chase-Lansdale. 1998. Adolescent pregnancy and parenthood: Recent evidence and future directions. *American Psychologist* 53:152–166.

East, P., and L. Jacobson. 2001. The younger siblings of teenage mothers: A follow-up of their pregnancy risk. *Developmental Psychology* 37:254–264.

Henshaw, S., and D. Feivelson. 2000. Teenage abortion and pregnancy statistics by state, 1996. *Family Planning Perspectives* 32:272–280.

Huizinga, D., R. Loeber, and T. Thornberry. 1993. Longitudinal study of delinquency, drug use, sexual activity, and pregnancy among children and youth in three cities. *Public Health Reports* 108:90–96.

Hymowitz, C., and M. Weissman. 1978. *A History of Women in America*. New York: Bantam Books.

Miller, B., B. Benson, and K. Galbraith. 2001. Family relationships and adolescent pregnancy risk: A research synthesis. *Developmental Review* 21:1–38.

Plotnick, R. 1992. The effects of attitudes on teenage premarital pregnancy and its resolution. *American Sociological Review* 57:800–811.

Skolnick, A. 1992. *The Intimate Environment: Exploring Marriage and the Family*, 5th ed. New York: Harper Collins.

Warren, C., J. Santelli, S. Everett, L. Kann, J. Collins, C. Cassell, et al. 1998. Sexual behavior among U.S. high school students, 1990–1995. *Family Planning Perspectives* 30:170–172.

PREVENTION STRATEGIES

Prevention strategies attempt to stop juvenile crime from occurring, while intervention strategies look at

Photo 8. 1936 Work Projects Administration poster promoting planned housing as a method to deter juvenile delinquency, showing silhouettes of a child stealing a piece of fruit and a child involved in armed robbery.

SOURCE: Library of Congress, Prints & Photographs Division, WPA Poster Collection [LC-USZ62-59985]. Used with permission.

ways to educate, reform, or treat those who have already committed offenses and have come to the attention of the criminal justice system. While some intervention strategies are more informal, such as diversion and teen courts, they still focus on the small percentage of youth who face the risk of being labeled juvenile delinquents.

Prevention efforts, on the other hand, can be aimed at all youth in broadly focused programs offered in schools or communities. Delinquency prevention programs are identified by their philosophies or target populations. Positive preventive efforts are those aimed at encouraging socially appropriate behaviors and rule-abiding interactions rather than those that seek to deter behavior with the threat of sanctions or punishments. Social control theorists look at ways of reinforcing ties to conventional norms in society, either through activities, such as Boy Scouts or 4-H, or through bonds to significant others, such as teachers, Big Brothers Big Sisters, or religious leaders.

There are three basic phases of prevention. Primary prevention addresses children at risk of becoming juvenile offenders, and secondary prevention involves intervention with young offenders in the early stages of delinquency to help them avoid further involvement in the justice system. Tertiary prevention deals with the rehabilitation or intervention efforts applied to more serious offenders, such as those who are sent to detention centers or other court placements. Programming at this phase is geared toward reintegrating the offender back into society with no further involvement in crime.

HISTORICAL EFFORTS AT PREVENTION

For centuries, sacred and secular initiatives have made attempts to guide parents in delinquency prevention. Phrases such as "spare the rod and spoil the child" indicate that corporal punishment was viewed as an acceptable if not necessary aspect of discipline and control.

The Industrial Revolution was marked by immigration, the growth of urban centers, and a wave of juvenile crime and delinquency thought to be linked to everything from social disorganization to poor breeding and absent, ill-mannered parents. While trying to address the proposed underlying causes of delinquency, sociologists from the Chicago School attempted to assist communities in preventing delinquency with holistic, grassroots initiatives in the

format of the Chicago Area Project (CAP). One of the oldest and longest running programs, CAP used local community leadership to effect bonding and self-help within the neighborhood units.

New York City was also very proactive in organizing delinquency prevention programs, particularly those that involved police officer participation. The Juvenile Aid Bureau dates back to the 1930s, as do the police athletic leagues (PALs) and precinct coordinating councils.

GOVERNMENT INITIATIVES IN DELINQUENCY PREVENTION

In 1968, Congress passed the Juvenile Delinquency Prevention and Control Act, which was revised in 1974 and renamed the Juvenile Justice and Delinquency Prevention Act. The Office of Juvenile Justice and Delinquency Prevention (OJJDP) evolved from that initiative and is geared to assisting states and local communities in researching and setting up effective prevention programs. The OJJDP acts as a clearinghouse of information on best practices and provides technical assistance to agencies as they initiate and evaluate programs.

One of the juvenile crime prevention strategies funded under the OJJDP is the JUMP program, which sponsors one-on-one mentoring initiatives for youth at risk for failing in school, or becoming involved in gangs or substance abuse. The government has prioritized this program for areas with high juvenile arrest rates, high dropout rates, and youth poverty rates. Another program is Students Taking On Prevention (STOP). The Family, Career and Community Leaders of America (FCCLA) developed this national peer-to-peer outreach program funded by the OJJDP, which challenges youth to "recognize, report and reduce" violence.

PROBLEMS IN MEASURING PREVENTION

One of the difficulties of prevention programming is how to show results or effects from the "treatment." The difficulty in evaluating prevention efforts is that when they work, there is nothing to measure, yet it is often difficult to discount the myriad of other factors in daily life that may also have been responsible for the positive outcome, such as the influence of relatives or peers or simply self-control.

The effects of intervening life events are particularly problematic for education or awareness programs, such as those for sex abuse prevention or AIDS awareness. Media and public information campaigns in our society make it almost impossible to isolate the effects of any one delivery mechanism. Children today receive input from many sources (television, parents, friends), and it could hardly be said that one particular source is the sole influence. Our youth do not live in a laboratory, so most prevention efforts do not attempt to evaluate their outcomes in terms of future behavior. Instead, most use basic pre- and posttest assessments that simply indicate whether the content of the program has been conveyed, which is measured by a positive increase in the participants' knowledge relative to that subject.

Another difficulty in determining which prevention efforts work is that many programs do not include an evaluation component, so they do not even attempt to determine if their efforts have achieved their goals. Often, staff and parents relate anecdotal evidence as to the success of a program, but only scientifically controlled, randomized experiments can supply meaningful feedback on prevention efforts. In addition, other evaluations have been based on such small treatment groups that it is not meaningful to draw any conclusions from the outcomes. Some outcome evaluations have found positive effects, but those findings are either not replicated or, if replicated, are unable to duplicate the successful outcomes.

PREVENTION PROGRAMS TODAY

Scholars have long debated the utility of the various delinquency prevention strategies. Some focus on the health model (prevention is recognized as a health problem by the Centers for Disease Control) and look at the risk and protective factors, whereas others focus on a child's assets, strengths, and capabilities. Across the country, hundreds of volunteers and paid professionals work in various delinquency programs every day and evening.

Program components often include academic enhancement, cultural competence, personal development, leisure and recreation, career development, and family-focused approaches. Strategies often include mentoring, tutoring, life-skills training, cultural awareness, drug awareness, gang awareness, career exploration, conflict resolution, anger management, health and fitness, field trips, and structured family therapy and celebrations.

Federal, state, and local governments are always eager to identify and share information on model programs—those that are considered the most successful, those that are able to demonstrate effectiveness through rigorous scientific evaluation in achieving their goals and objectives. Model programs appear to share similar characteristics in that they target the current and critical needs of the youth, they and their staff members have excellent reputations in their communities, and they have good working relationships with a broad range of community stakeholders. Some of the more successful model programs have been highlighted in the media as well as evaluated in research studies.

Recreational Programs

These programs seek to provide alternatives to the boredom and less constructive activities that may lead to delinquency. Soccer, little league, and midnight basketball all attempt to instill positive values such as teamwork, physical fitness, and competition as well as mentoring with coaches and other positive role models. In Maryland, officials claim that the late-night basketball program has been associated with a 60 percent decrease in drug-related offenses. In Phoenix, Arizona, it is reported that nights with recreational sports have lower juvenile crime rates than nights without (Bilchik, 1997).

Educational/Awareness Programs

Some educational/awareness programs are generically aimed at preventing all types of crime and delinquency and promoting sensitivity toward crime victims. Others target specific behaviors, such as joining gangs or taking drugs (see the DARE entry). Most teach healthy alternative responses to anger and conflict as a way of avoiding fights, retaliation, and self-destructive behavior.

Some educational efforts directly address not delinquency but behaviors that are thought to be related to or risk indicators for future delinquency, such as dropping out of school, teen pregnancy, and smoking.

Prevention Through Legislation

New laws are passed each year that seem to be designed to control delinquency by curfews, restrictions on drivers licenses for young teens, and antiloitering measures. Such statutes have been adopted in many communities as a way to prevent juvenile crime and victimization. Many complain that because of a small percentage of problem youth, the rest are made to suffer under the restrictions of these laws. The courts have, for the most part, upheld such legislation. In some California cities, regulations ban gang members from associating on street corners; driving, walking, or gathering together; and harassing anyone who has complained about them (gang abatement injunctions).

Prevention Through Environmental Control

Reducing the opportunities for crime is the goal of environmental strategies. This means "target hardening," or the provision of extra security and surveillance in areas that may be subject to juvenile crime, such as parks, school yards, and shopping malls. Video cameras, metal detectors, sensor alarms, and high-intensity lighting are just a few of the approaches communities may take to reduce crime in public places. In addition, ordinances that prohibit congregation, shrubbery that discourages trespassing, and the prompt elimination of graffiti are all considered environmental controls. Vandalism, which is typically a crime committed by juveniles, has been successfully reduced by strategies that increase adult scrutiny and a sense of territorial protection by residents in areas where there is unsupervised youth activity.

THE POLICE ROLE IN PREVENTION

Criminologists continue to look at the role of police in crime prevention as one of ensuring safety as well as deterring crime. Popular emphasis on community policing involves law enforcement in many delinquency prevention activities, including patrolling parks, skating rinks, malls, pool halls, and other places where youth may congregate. Police are also encouraged to look into allegations of bullying, underage drinking, and unsupervised recreation. Such activities may lead to safety risks as well as potential criminal victimization.

In the aftermath of the shootings by two students at Columbine High School in Colorado, a number of elementary and secondary schools have established partnerships with local law enforcement agencies to provide uniformed police officers on campus. It is not uncommon to see uniformed police officers in schools serving as school resource officers (SROs). SROs

teach Drug Abuse Resistance Education (DARE) and Gang Resistance Education and Training (GREAT) classes and are visible on campus to interact with youth and to build positive relationships that may extend beyond the campus and beyond graduation.

THE SCHOOL'S ROLE IN PREVENTION

When schools install cameras, surveillance equipment, and metal detectors and hire police officers, they are said to be "target hardening," or attempting to reduce crime through equipment and services that make the environment less conducive to victimization. Some research indicates, however, that more punitive methods of control may increase antisocial responses in children.

While many prevention programs such as DARE are offered in the schools, those viewed as most effective use modeling and differential reinforcement techniques to reward positive behavior and emphasize social-skills training. These proactive efforts are thought to provide "replacement behaviors" for inappropriate conduct that will be learned by the students if applied fairly and consistently.

PARENTS' ROLE IN PREVENTION

Historically, parents are most often blamed for the delinquent conduct of their children, but more recently, programs have aggressively addressed the issue of assisting parents in filling the "supervision" gaps that fall between school and adult work schedules. Public opinion polls seem to indicate that unsupervised children are a significant social problem and that more after-school programming should be provided. Parenting classes, family therapy, and the use of parental role models such as Big Brothers Big Sisters have all been part of delinquency prevention over the years.

Efforts to increase parents' communication with their children and allow for more quality parent-child activities can also be viewed as preventive measures. Surveillance efforts such as cell phones and pagers allow parents oversight while still recognizing the child's need for independence. In addition, home drug test kits allow parents to address concerns about substance abuse privately without involving formal law enforcement responses. But more formal measures are found in parental liability laws. In Rhode Island, for example, parents face a $500 fine and up to six months in jail when their children miss excessive amounts of school.

THE COMMUNITY'S ROLE IN PREVENTION

To ensure that community leaders work together to address delinquency prevention, both federal and state funding sources often require local agencies to form councils and coordinate on both financing and operating programs. Often grants require that communities match any funds they are awarded with their own resources and demonstrate that they are networking effectively in coordinated program efforts. Rather than just copy programs that appear to have been successful elsewhere, communities must decide what needs or problems to prioritize and what unique characteristics of their area must be taken into consideration during planning. In Mississippi, officials fund coordinated efforts between families, schools, and local agencies to provide after-school mentoring and other attitude- and performance-enhancing activities in a program called Save Our Students (SOS).

THE ECONOMICS OF PREVENTION

Legislators, criminal justice workers, teachers, and taxpayers all understand the value of effective prevention efforts. According to estimates, one juvenile offender can cost society more than $2 million, factoring in the direct and indirect expenses related to crime, drug abuse, and dropping out of school. It is estimated that for every dollar invested in crime prevention, $1.40 is saved.

Increases in federal and state support for after-school programming reflect the realization that not only is juvenile crime costing taxpayers money, but also working parents are a necessary part of a healthy economy. The 21st Century Community Learning Center program, funded under the Elementary and Secondary Education Act, has allowed more than 3,600 public schools to become after-school programming facilities. In 2001, more than $846 million was appropriated by Congress to maintain and expand these programs.

Still, the economics of prevention are controversial. For example, many businesses argue that although curfews may prevent some crimes, they are bad for nighttime recreation and entertainment industries geared for youth. Curfews also may take younger, less costly employees out of the labor force. On the other hand, Oregon passed a tax credit incentive that rewards businesses that hire at-risk juveniles under the First Break Program.

CONCLUSION

Prevention and intervention strategies have been based on traditional assumptions about what causes crime, and these assumptions have remained somewhat constant over time. Some argue that prevention programs waste resources by incorporating too large a population as a base, such as all sixth graders, even children who would not resort to criminal activity anyway. On the other hand, although singling out high-risk individuals for education and prevention efforts might be more efficient, it would mean possible error and bias in focusing attention on certain traits, such as low income or poor neighborhoods.

Prevention strategies, like other crime-related efforts, are subject to trends and fads that appeal to policymakers and the general public. Even in the face of conflicting scientific evidence, programs may be implemented or continued because they "sound good" or appear "tough" regardless of whether or not they have any impact on crime.

Overall, prevention programs that address youth risk issues at an early age, those that are school-based, and those that stress conflict resolution and other social-skill-building exercises appear to be most popular today. Most experts agree that a continuum of services that address a range of needs and risk factors is the optimum strategy for delinquency prevention.

Charles Bailey

See also Chicago Area Project; Curfew; Boys and Girls
    Clubs of American; Diversion Programs; DARE;
    Office of Juvenile Justice and Delinquency Prevention;
    Parental Liability Laws

Bibliography

Bilchik, S. 1997. *Juvenile Justice Reform Initiatives in the States: 1994–1996*. Program Report. Washington, DC: Office of Juvenile Justice and Delinquency Prevention.

Flannery, R. B. 1999. *Preventing Youth Violence*. New York: Continuum.

Gottfredson, D. C. 2002. Quality of school-based prevention programs: Results from a national survey. *The Journal of Research in Crime and Delinquency* 39:3–35.

PROBATION, JUVENILE

Probation is the most common disposition ordered by juvenile courts today. The reformists of the Progressive Era (1890 to 1920) were the original developers of the probation system. Shortly after the turn of the 19th century, juvenile courts and probation for juvenile offenders were adopted in several states. By 1918, a survey of 321 juvenile courts across the United States revealed that each offered some type of probation program. In addition, the juvenile courts took responsibility for appointing and supervising juvenile probation staff and programs, thereby establishing themselves as the decision makers for the policies and direction that probation would take—a trend that still holds true today.

During World War II, community activists were once again concerned over appropriate child care, including the treatment of delinquency. The Fair Labor Act of 1938 abolished child labor, and at the same time, Dr. Benjamin Spock's book on child rearing became a household requirement for many women across the country. In the 1960s, a number of cases, including *Kent v. U.S.,* took a close and critical look at the treatment of juveniles in the criminal justice system. This resulted in a reformation of the juvenile courts, giving children additional protection, including the right to counsel. Although this reform intended that children should have the same level of protection afforded to adult offenders, the juvenile institutions continued to be plagued by reports that they were lacking in rehabilitative programs while continuing in their harsh and neglectful treatment of juvenile wards. In the 1970s, anti-institutional attitudes surfaced, and the Juvenile Justice and Delinquency Prevention Act of 1974 resulted in federal funding of community correction alternatives to institutionalization of juvenile offenders. The trend toward community corrections resulted in the development of diversion programs and home supervision, which are still in place today (McShane and Krause, 1993).

According to a report published in 1999 by the Office of Juvenile Justice and Delinquency Prevention (OJJDP), the number of delinquency cases handled by the country's juvenile courts increased by 48 percent from 1988 to 1997. This increase was disproportionately represented by juveniles involved in weapon, drug, and personal offenses. In 1998, however, juvenile arrests for violent crimes declined by 19 percent

from the 1994 peak. Arrests for murder decreased 48 percent from 1994 to 1998. Despite continued growth in the juvenile population, the number of arrests for each violent crime has declined. However, the juvenile arrest rate for drug violations in 1998 was twice the average rate in the 1980s and was far greater for juveniles than it was for adults. In addition, there was a substantial increase in arrests for simple assault, curfew, and loitering violations from the 1980s until 1998. In 1997, the juvenile courts processed nearly 1.8 million delinquency cases (Sickmund, 2000). Although arrests for violent crimes have decreased, detention populations have soared. On any day, there are approximately 25,000 children held in some 500 secure detention facilities nationwide (Annie E. Casey Foundation, 2000). More than one third of these facilities are overcrowded. The increase in arrests for nonviolent crimes, coupled with overcrowding in detention facilities, has enhanced the need for programming that addresses these issues. Numerous alternatives to detention are currently offered nationwide, including diversion programs, first-time offender programs, placements and aftercare, electronic monitoring, and intensive home supervision.

In 1994, 55 percent of adults under some form of correctional supervision were on probation. In 1992, 30 percent of the felony sentences resulted in a grant of probation for adults while 56 percent of adjudicated youth were given probation according to the Department of Justice (Sickmund, 1997). The number of juvenile cases placed on probation grew 32 percent between 1985 and 1994. The caseload demographics indicate that 80 percent of juveniles placed on probation are males. The proportion of offenders involving Caucasian youth decreased from 73 percent in 1985 to 68 percent in 1994, while the African American population increased from 25 percent in 1985 to 29 percent in 1994. The proportion of youth of other races remained the same overall at 3 percent.

PROBATION OPTIONS

Juvenile offenders were more likely to receive probation for property offenses than for personal offenses. Probation departments throughout the nation receive referrals from the courts, law enforcement personnel, schools, parents, and other agencies, which must be assessed. After assessing the juvenile offender's level of risk to the community and need for services, the probation officer has several options. Probation may be used at the front end or the back end of the justice system. Some juveniles are first-time offenders who agree to comply with a brief period of informal probation. Others are high-risk offenders who are ordered by the court to terms of probation and must follow specific terms and conditions.

Diversion is an option that has been explored with varying offender populations within the juvenile justice system. Diversion is the "halting or suspension, before conviction, of formal criminal proceedings against a person, conditioned on some form of counter performance by the defendant" (Fields, 1994). Many states provide diversion for a number of offenses, including drug abuse, domestic violence, traffic violations, and passing bad checks. The goal of diversion programs is to reduce overcrowding and costs within the system while giving offenders a second chance to stay away from criminal activity. At the same time, diversion programs take advantage of counseling, education, and other treatment options.

Today, the term *diversion* is used to describe a formal and organized effort to use alternatives to the traditional processing of offenders in the juvenile justice system. The majority of arrests involving juveniles with diversion as an option usually result in diverting them before they reach the court process. Formal proceedings stop before adjudication or true finding is made. Diversion is more likely to be used with status or misdemeanor offenders than with felony cases. Traditionally, probation officers implement and monitor diversion programs.

There are a number of approaches to diversion programs for juveniles. One of the earlier diversion programs was a referral to military service to avoid further adjudication. Although referral to military service is not an option today, wilderness programs that attempt to build self-esteem, self-confidence, teamwork, and problem-solving skills have been developed as diversions. Dispute resolution is another diversion program available to youth. This program allows for community volunteers to bring the juvenile offender and crime victim together, with a volunteer playing the part of a mediator. Together the parties attempt to reach a mutually agreeable resolution, which most commonly includes informal probation, restitution, and community service. These diversion programs are usually an option for first-time offenders or those at low risk for reoffending. Diversion programs are also available for youth involved in drugs, petty theft or shoplifting, domestic violence, and vandalism, if damage is minimal.

A second option available to probation officers is to settle the case out of court with no further intervention. Offenders who are deemed eligible for this option are assigned appropriate sanctions, which range from writing a letter of apology or making restitution to the victim to entering treatment that will benefit the youth. Diversion may also be an alternative in these cases.

For a more serious offense, the probation officer may determine that referral to the juvenile justice system is necessary. The probation officer then files a petition with the juvenile court. Once filed, the court and the probation department work together to determine an appropriate alternative for the juvenile, including formal probation or intensive probation supervision, placement outside the home, detention in a juvenile facility, or a recommendation to a state-run corrections facility. Additional alternatives that have become more popular include boot camps and specialized high-risk supervision units that are available in some states.

ROLE OF THE PROBATION OFFICER

Probation officers supervising juvenile offenders use a variety of techniques to balance protection of the community with rehabilitation of the youth. The degree of risk to the community and individual needs of each juvenile are assessed through a classification system. This system is designed to help the probation officer establish a plan to effectively supervise the offender via employment referrals, educational counseling, psychological counseling, drug testing, and searches for contraband.

Offenders determined to be at the highest risk level receive intensive supervision from a field probation officer. These juveniles are given an opportunity to receive highly structured, close supervision before they are removed from their homes. Most of these offenders are juveniles who have been adjudicated for more than one offense or who have been adjudicated for a serious or violent offense. The intensive supervision programs routinely require offenders to pay victim restitution, attend school, face curfew requirements, and participate in regular drug and alcohol testing, regular home and school checks to ensure compliance, and any programs required by the probation officer.

Many of these programs nationwide require the probation officer to have contact with the juvenile offender on a regular basis, conduct home checks to ensure compliance with curfew requirements, engage in regular contact with schools and guardians regarding the offender's compliance, test for drug and alcohol use, and monitor restitution payments. The juvenile's failure to comply with the conditions of their supervision can result in a recommendation for detention in a juvenile facility or removal from the home and a referral to either an out-of-home placement or a corrections facility. Progress reports to the court are routinely required for juveniles assigned to intensive supervision. Because of the amount of supervision work required, these probation officers normally have a limited caseload.

PROGRAMS FOR JUVENILES IN THE COMMUNITY

Young offenders released from placements or juvenile detention are eventually reintegrated into their communities. Probation officers in the aftercare units are required to monitor and supervise these offenders. Research has shown that an increased level of supervision for high-risk youth released to the community is essential (OJJDP, 1994). Such supervision includes the involvement of noncorrectional agencies, such as educational and mental health professionals, frequent drug and alcohol testing, assessment of special needs and referrals to necessary programs, and high levels of surveillance and control similar to that in intensive supervision units.

Many specialized programs have been developed to address the unique issues of juvenile offenders. Because police frequently make contact with juveniles on probation, teams of probation officers and police officers have been organized. These teams work together, making contact with juveniles and adults within the neighborhoods, using a combination of community policing and supervision of probation caseloads.

High-risk gang units are another program that has developed due to the increase in gang activity in the community. Gang units can comprise probation officers alone or police officers teamed with probation officers. These officers receive specialized training to enable them to supervise high-risk offenders who have been identified as gang members or affiliates.

Another specialized program involves placement of a probation officer in a school environment. These officers work directly with a school or school district and are on campus and available for students and staff of the school. Multidisciplinary teams are composed of probation officers, child protection caseworkers, mental health professionals, and educational staff who work together to aid youthful offenders as well as their families. A team focuses on every aspect of the family dynamic to solidify the family and subsequently decrease the chance for potential delinquency of the juvenile and other family members.

Other programs in various stages of development throughout the country are first-time sex offender programs, teen courts in which community teenagers aid in the determination of low-risk or first-offender punishments, and prevention programs that focus on stopping deviant behavior before it leads to a more serious offense. Most of these programs involve both the court system and the probation department either to monitor juveniles or provide direct supervision.

CONCLUSION

Although the juvenile crime rate declined in the late 1990s, the juvenile justice system continues to consider strategies that are effective in preventing delinquency. According to the National Institute on Drug Abuse, there are a number of "prevention principles," including family-focused efforts, media campaigns, community programs, skill development programs, age-specific interventions, and programs that enhance protective factors while reducing known risk factors (Merlo and Benekos, 2000). Juvenile justice officials must educate the community to the programs that are both rehabilitative and cost-effective. Probation is an alternative that is appropriate for meeting those goals.

Laura Davis

See also Assessment—Risk; Diversion Programs; Juvenile Detention Facilities; Mediation; Wilderness Programs

Bibliography

Annie E. Casey Foundation. 2000. *Juvenile Detention Alternatives Initiative*. Available at http://www.aecf.org/publications/juvenile/rising.htm.

Fields, L. L. 1994. Pretrial diversion: A solution to California's drunk driving problem. *Federal Probation* 58(4):20–30.

Gallagher, C. A. 1997. *Juvenile Offenders in Residential Placement, 1997*. Washington, DC: Office of Juvenile Justice and Delinquency Prevention.

McShane, M. D., and W. Krause. 1993. *Community Corrections*. New York: Macmillan.

Merlo, A.V. 2000. Juvenile justice at the crossroads: Presidential address to the Academy of Criminal Justice Sciences. *Justice Quarterly* 17(4):639–661.

Merlo, A.V., and P. J. Benekos. 2000. *What's Wrong With the Criminal Justice System: Ideology, Politics, and Media.* Cincinnati, OH: Anderson.

Office of Juvenile Justice and Delinquency Prevention. 1994. *Intensive Aftercare for High-Risk Juveniles: A Community Care Model.* Washington, DC: Office of Juvenile Justice and Delinquency Prevention.

Office of Juvenile Justice and Delinquency Prevention. 1999. *Juvenile Arrests.* Washington, DC: Office of Juvenile Justice and Delinquency Prevention.

Sickmund, M. 1997. *The Juvenile Delinquency Probation Caseload, 1985–1994.* Washington, DC: Office of Juvenile Justice and Delinquency Prevention.

Sickmund, M. 2000. Offenders in juvenile court, 1997. *Juvenile Justice Bulletin.* Washington, DC: Office of Juvenile Justice and Delinquency Prevention.

 # PROSTITUTION, TEENAGE

Prostitution is a big business that continues to draw countless numbers of people. With a long history in different societies and cultures, it has survived despite changes in laws, changes in attitudes about sex, and the women's liberation movement. Historically, most definitions of *prostitution*, and even research on the topic, have focused on adult female prostitutes.

Since the 1970s, both definitions of and research on prostitution have expanded to encompass other types of people. Now the focus includes prostitution among adolescent females, adult males, boys, homosexuals, and bisexuals, as well as prostitution by phone and online services. This entry presents an overview of information on the topic of teenage prostitution, including the different types of prostitution in which teens are involved, the extent of teenage prostitution, motivations for turning to prostitution, and the risks involved for teenage prostitutes.

TEENAGE PROSTITUTION

Prostitution is usually thought of as the act of performing, offering to perform, or agreeing to perform a sexual act for hire. Also, prostitution can be defined as engaging in, agreeing to engage in, or offering to engage in sexual conduct with another person under a fee arrangement with that person or any other person. Sexual acts include intercourse, oral copulation, and sodomy. Payment usually comes in the form of cash but can include drugs, shelter, clothing, or jewelry. Teenage prostitutes often compete with each other as well as adult prostitutes in selling their bodies.

It is impossible to obtain an accurate account of how many prostitutes there are. The best indicator of the amount of prostitution comes from official arrest data. The problem with this data source is that only a fraction of prostitutes are ever arrested, which means that official arrest data offer only the relatively limited view of prostitutes' involvement in the justice system. Aside from these arrest statistics, there are few reliable sources assessing the amount of prostitution in the United States. Because most prostitutes manage to elude law enforcement, their true numbers may never be known.

Arrest data indicate that teens under age 18 account for a small fraction of those arrested for prostitution. Arrests peak at age 17 and decline with the prostitutes' age. The research indicates that the average age of entry into prostitution falls between 13 and 14 years. Also, the data indicate that teenage prostitution occurs most often in cities.

More teenage prostitutes are female than are male. Although there is little research on male prostitution in general, the research indicates that teenage male and female prostitutes have many similarities. There are two subcultures behind teenage male prostitution: the peer-delinquent subculture and the gay subculture. The gay subculture differentiates male and female prostitutes. In the gay subculture, youth may engage in prostitution as one outlet for their sexuality. Prostitution as a means of identification for the homosexual male is the primary difference between male and female teenage prostitution.

There are various classes of prostitutes, which range from apparently respectable to the well-established women on the street. Flowers (1998) identified seven different categories of prostitution: streetwalker, call girl, massage parlor prostitute, house prostitute, madam or pimp, mistress or gigolo, and barterer. A streetwalker overtly solicits men on the street and offers sexual favors for pay. A call girl works in a residence or a hotel and solicits clients there or solicits by phone. A massage parlor prostitute offers sexual services in a massage parlor, not always limited to massages or fondling. A house prostitute works in an establishment created specifically for prostitution. A madam or pimp supplies other prostitutes to customers for a percentage of the fee. A mistress or gigolo is mainly supported by one person at a time or sees only one person at a time for paid sexual favors. A barterer exchanges sexual relations for professional or other services or for material goods. Besides these types of prostitution, three others are emerging: phone sex, lap dances in "gentlemen's clubs," and cybersex on the Internet.

Prostitution is a relatively closed system (Gray, 1973). Fees for prostitution are hierarchically structured—generally low for a streetwalker and high for an attractive, well-dressed call girl. Streetwalkers rarely transfer to the call girl trade; upward mobility for prostitutes is difficult or impossible. Downward movement is more likely over the course of a prostitute's career. Further, if the market or submarkets in a city are clearly defined, a streetwalker of one area cannot necessarily work in another area.

Because teenage prostitutes come from every conceivable background (social class, race, and ethnicity), they cannot be singularly categorized. The majority of teenage prostitutes are streetwalkers. In fact, one fifth of all streetwalkers are believed to be teenage girls. Teens can also be found in every position of Flowers's typology.

ENTRY INTO TEENAGE PROSTITUTION

Females and males enter prostitution for a myriad of reasons. Explanations range from financial gain to psychological abnormalities to sexual deviance to thrill seeking to violence and coercion. Even though many prostitutes fail to realize the anticipated financial rewards, money is the primary reason individuals turn to prostitution. Most teenage prostitutes enter the business on a part-time basis, but prostitution can quickly become a full-time profession. Generally, the transition to full time occurs within eight months to a year after the prostitute's first experience.

Studies of prostitutes indicate that inadequate family relationships and broken homes may be factors leading to prostitution. Weak parental ties and attachments result in a lack of supervision, intimacy in communication and attention, and affection. Family instability can cause the teen to run away from home, which has a clear relationship with becoming involved in prostitution. Indeed, the majority of teenage prostitutes are runaways.

Evidence also indicates a strong relationship between early sexual abuse and entry into prostitution. Many of these damaged children and teens will experience prostitution, and some will become regularly active in the lifestyle. The extent and nature of this relationship is not fully understood. Even if the prostitute does not have sexual abuse in his or her history, Gray (1973) found that the majority of teenage prostitutes had extensive knowledge of sexual intercourse before age 12.

In Gray's study, all the subjects reported having known someone on a regular basis who was involved in prostitution. The subjects also deliberately sought out the experienced individuals before making any firm decision to enter prostitution themselves. They flirted with the idea and were curious to learn more about prostitution. After deciding to enter prostitution, subjects had little or no training period before their first acts of prostitution.

OCCUPATIONAL RISKS OF TEENAGE PROSTITUTION

The costs of being a prostitute fall into four categories: physical, financial, legal, and psychological. Physical costs include violence from customers and pimps. The chances of being assaulted by a customer are as likely for the teenage prostitute as being assaulted by the pimp. Physical violence also comes from the threat of sexually transmitted diseases (STDs), a risk always faced by prostitutes (Reynolds, 1986). Financial costs depend on the market segment in which a prostitute works. These costs include clothing, makeup, and coiffure expenditures and any expenses associated with providing an assignation site. Legal costs include retainers paid to lawyers, bail bond agents, or fines and fees ordered by the court. Also, legal costs entail the lost wages that could have been earned in the time the prostitute was attending to the court proceedings or jail time. The psychological costs of prostitution are argued to be the greatest cost. The prostitutes' attitude toward their customers and sex with men in general, their attitudes about society, and their attitudes about themselves become jaded.

Teens involved in prostitution face terrible risks. Murder, torture, and slavery are among the most serious, but other troublesome risks exist.

Pimps can be one of the greatest risks for prostitutes. A prostitute's history of abuse, sexual victimization, and feelings of abandonment can explain the relationship between the prostitute and the pimp. Bracey (1983) wrote that pimps control their prostitutes by supplying attention, approval, and understanding that the prostitutes did not receive at home; this is especially critical to the female juvenile prostitute.

The pimp-prostitute relationship ranges from businesslike to shockingly brutal. Pimps do not necessarily force individuals into prostitution. The pimp is not essential for an individual turning to prostitution, but a pimp is essential if the novice prostitute is to remain in the business. If violence at the beginning of the pimp-prostitute relationship is rare, it becomes more common. The mutual attraction that may mark the beginning of the relationship is often replaced by fear and hostility later (Gray, 1973). A pimp's threats of violence eventually turn into violence itself. Pimps can be possessive and generally wish to control decisions about when a prostitute may leave. Thus career changes for prostitutes are difficult, and the consequences can be severe for those who attempt to leave on their own.

CONCLUSION

Prostitution can be a lucrative occupation for teens, even if they do not keep much of the income. Individuals show similarity in their motives for engaging in prostitution with respect to their social class, parental neglect or abuse, lack of conventional ties, and their initial sexual experiences (abusive or natural). The risks associated with teenage prostitution range over a large spectrum that includes violence and exposure to STDs.

Research on prostitution has primarily addressed three issues: accounting for the existence of prostitution in society, explaining why certain individuals enter prostitution, and elaborating on the criminal justice system's reaction. The majority of research on prostitution has dealt with adult female prostitutes, although this emphasis has shifted since the 1970s. Research has consistently shown relationships between teenage prostitution and broken homes, sexual abuse, and school problems. These types of situations can cause a teen to run away and subsequently enter the world of prostitution. Research has also shown a connection between teenage prostitution and substance use or abuse.

Reynolds (1986) argued that prostitution will continue to exist even if it is prohibited by law. However, it is possible for citizens, lawmakers, and law enforcers to affect both the kind and amount of prostitution occurring in their communities. Because criminal legislation has a poor record in reducing prostitution, current public policies regarding prostitution should be changed for the good of society itself.

External mechanisms do not work to keep prostitution completely out of a town or city. Areas without prostitution occur only because other nearby areas offer such services. If laws are passed to contain certain types of prostitution, participants in the affected areas will change strategies to find alternative ways to continue prostitution. Reynolds (1986) noted that just as a chameleon changes colors, so too will the method of solicitation or point of assignation change to overcome the effect of the new laws limiting prostitution.

Sean A. Maddan

See also Female Delinquency; Runaways; Status Offenders

Bibliography

Bracey, D. H. 1983. The juvenile prostitute: Victim and offender. *Victimology* 8(3):151–159.

Flowers, R. B. 1998. *The Prostitution of Women and Girls.* Jefferson, NC: McFarland & Company.

Gray, D. 1973. Turning out: A study of teenage prostitution. *Urban Life and Culture* 1(4):401–425.

Jolin, A. 1994. On the backs of working prostitutes: Feminist theory and prostitution policy. *Crime and Delinquency* 40(1):69–80.

McMullen, R. J. 1986. Youth prostitution: A balance of power. *International Journal of Offender Therapy and Comparative Criminology* 30(3):237–244.

Reynolds, H. 1986. *The Economics of Prostitution.* Springfield, IL: Charles C Thomas.

Snell, C. L. 1995. *Young Men in the Street: Help-Seeking Behavior of Young Male Prostitutes.* Westport, CT: Praeger.

Weisberg, D. K. 1985. *Children of the Night: A Study of Adolescent Prostitution.* Lexington, MA: Lexington Books.

 PROVO EXPERIMENT

The Provo Experiment was an activist research project developed by LaMar T. Empey and Maynard L. Erickson as a way of testing the effects of community control on delinquent recidivism. The project spanned six years (1959 to 1965) in Utah County, Utah, before being disbanded in the wake of political turmoil surrounding the experiment. Serving as an intermediate intervention between probation and institutionalization, the Provo Experiment was one of the first programs of its kind.

The experiment consisted of two components: a program and a simultaneous evaluation of the program. The program consisted of a community-based, nonresidential, unstructured, group-oriented approach aimed at reducing recidivism. Treatment consisted of intensive group-oriented counseling sessions and work opportunities for youth. The treatment facility was named Pinehills.

THEORY AND PROCESS

The Provo program was theoretically guided. Delinquency was viewed as resulting from the lack of legitimate opportunities available to lower-class youth. These youth were believed to share the same desires (e.g., money, social status) as nondelinquent, upper-class youth but were less able to achieve those goals through legitimate means (e.g., employment, family support). To achieve the goals, the lower-class youth turned to a variety of illegitimate means, including involvement in delinquency. Eventually, a social system of delinquent groups was spawned from this pool of youth who had conventional goals but no legitimate opportunities.

To counter this system, the Provo program provided youth with legitimate employment opportunities in various city and county capacities (e.g., parks, streets). The employment opportunities were intended to provide delinquent youth with the resources (e.g., money, skills) necessary to achieve their goals without returning to a delinquent lifestyle.

Additional elements were also incorporated. With the exception of the employment component, however, a lack of formal structure was a centerpiece of the program. The program was guided by unstructured activities and a reliance on group-centered change within the peer group. Youth who entered the program were immediately exposed to an environment without structure other than mandated daily attendance at the program grounds and expectations of hard work on the job. Youth were given the option of attending group counseling sessions, which consisted of the youth and adult counselors sitting, possibly talking, but with no predetermined focus.

This lack of formal structure served an important function. Individual youth became anxious at the unfamiliar lack of structure, eventually turning to the peer group for support. Under the theoretical framework on which the project was developed, the peer group was deemed the primary mechanism of delinquent involvement. Youth were believed to engage in delinquent activities as part of their involvement in a social system that included values, beliefs, and rationalizations supporting such activities. Consequently, to reduce youth's involvement in delinquent activities, the social system supporting such activities needed to be replaced with an equally viable peer group that did not favor such activities. Once the youth involved in the program began looking to one another for support, the groundwork was set for creating a new prosocial peer group.

Program administrators reported that the youth responded well to this unstructured environment. While the youth were given considerable latitude in determining the course of the program, an informal structure became evident quite early. When adults involved in the program played an inactive role by refusing to answer questions posed by the youth or offer any direction for the session, the initial counseling session amounted to nothing more than the youth silently sitting around. However, when the counseling session was held the next day, the youth became uncomfortable at the silence. Following a suggestion by an adult in attendance, the youth began talking about the circumstances and consequences of their prior delinquent activities. As time progressed, the youth became more open about their experiences, eventually realizing some sort of group cohesion with other members and resulting in the positive peer group intended by the program.

The unstructured nature of the program also allowed the youth to control the situations or the situations to occur naturally, providing an opportunity to observe and evaluate youth interactions in their natural setting. Once in the program, the youth were not exposed to any types of individual-oriented diagnoses or treatments—the instruments traditionally used to gather information on institutionalized delinquents. To gain the information necessary for successful change, the youth were observed in the naturally occurring group interactions. The program evaluators felt that this setting would allow them to gain more insight about the program and its participants than would other, more artificial, settings.

EVALUATION RESULTS

An evaluation of the program was also incorporated. The program evaluation consisted of analyses of juvenile arrest records spanning four years after the respective treatments for three separate groups of youth: those assigned to the program, those assigned to probation, and those sentenced to the Utah State Industrial School. During the course of the experiment, 326 male habitual offenders were assigned to one of the three groups. The design of the experiment was intended to work in the following way. First, judges would determine whether a youth should be placed on probation or in a reformatory. Once this determination was made, the judge would choose an envelope from a corresponding stack marked "probation" or "reformatory." Inside each envelope was a slip of paper marked "control group," where the youth would be placed on probation or in the reformatory, or "treatment group," where the youth would be placed in Pinehills for treatment. In this way, the design was intended to contain a mix of logistical practicality and scientific rigor suitable to both the juvenile court judges and the program evaluators.

In practice, however, the design needed modification because the juvenile court judge rarely committed youth to the reformatory. The number of youth who would have been committed to the reformatory under the original design would have been too small to yield meaningful comparisons between the control and experimental groups. Therefore, the actual design that was implemented worked like this: All youth who were committed to the reformatory by the county judge were instead directed to the program (treatment group), and a comparison group was developed consisting of youth from throughout the state who were committed to the Utah State Industrial School. One implication of the design modification was that the comparison group consisted of more serious delinquents than the experimental group, thus reducing the confidence in any program effects which may have been found. The component of the design allowing comparisons between youth assigned to the program and youth assigned to probation was implemented as intended.

Few other requirements were specified for the experiment's participants. To be eligible, boys had to be between the ages of 15 and 17 and not identified as highly disturbed or psychotic by the presentence investigation to be eligible for the program. Most participants were from upper-lower-class or lower-middle-class backgrounds, and program participation typically lasted between five and seven months.

Many outcomes of the program were reported by the evaluators. First, few differences were found between probationers and program participants in the number of arrests up to four years after release. In other words, the Provo program was found to be neither more nor less effective than probation at reducing future delinquency. Differences were, however, found between the program participants and youth committed to the reformatory. Specifically, reformatory youth had accumulated many more arrests than program participants in each of the years following their release. The long-term effects of the program were particularly striking, as reformatory youth averaged nearly twice as many arrests as program youth three and four years after release. These findings supported the notion that community treatment programs, like the Provo program, were more effective than incarceration at reducing recidivism.

FUNDING PROBLEMS

The Provo Experiment was financed through county funds and grants provided by the Ford Foundation. In Utah, the juvenile court and corrections systems were under the control of the state, a unique situation in the 1950s. However, program administrators felt there were good reasons to avoid state funding when implementing the Provo Experiment. For one thing, the funding provided by the Ford Foundation and Utah County was sufficient to cover the costs of the initial stages of the project, and the program administrators were confident that state money would be made available once the program had proven its effectiveness and the grant money had run out. In addition, the program administrators were wary that state funding would be accompanied by additional binds, such as reduced autonomy from state governmental demands.

However, the initial decision to avoid state funding later turned out to be a fatal mistake for the project. Of primary importance was the volatile nature of county politics surrounding the project. At the outset, the project was supported by the county and its public constituents. Within two years, however, the political winds had shifted from a relatively liberal county commission to a much more conservative one. Under the new administrative shift, the Provo Experiment became a political issue. In 1961, the newly elected county commissioner (ironically, a former deputy sheriff) proclaimed that the Provo Experiment was illegal, as it should have been run at the state level. During 1962, in the midst of a countywide fiscal shortage, the commission appropriated a number of budget cuts, one of which was funding for the experiment. The issue was twice heard by the Utah Attorney General, who first stated that county funds should not be used to finance Ford Foundation research, but later stated that funding for the Provo Experiment would be justified to pay staff if they were specially deputized as probation officers. By this time, however, the county funds had been reappropriated to other agencies.

In addition, the county commission continued to proclaim that the experiment was illegal because the project staff, now acting as "deputy probation officers," as required by the attorney general, were not fully certified state probation officers. Even after experiment employees passed the State Merit System Exam, thereby certifying them as Utah state probation officers, the county commission refused to fund the project. Additional pressure from state authorities did not change the county commission's stance on the issue, and later appeals to the state for funding were not granted. While the project continued operating on funds provided by the Ford Foundation for several years, it was officially disbanded in 1965 due to lack of funds.

CONCLUSION

The Provo Experiment has had a lasting effect on juvenile justice policy and theory. Of particular importance to juvenile justice practitioners is the finding that community treatment programs can be equally, or more, successful than other methods, including probation and incarceration, at curbing juvenile recidivism. In addition, the experiment capitalized on the relationship between theory and practice, beginning with a theoretical explanation of the causes of a problem (in this case, juvenile delinquency) and resulting in a program designed to address the problem. Finally, despite the relatively small scale of the experiment and the deviations from the intended design, the experiment employed a reasonable scientific method to determine the effectiveness of the program, resulting in more rigorous information to guide juvenile justice policy.

Terrance J. Taylor

See also Community Treatment Project; Diversion Programs; LaMar Taylor Empey; Silverlake Experiment

Bibliography

Empey, L. T., and M. L. Erickson. 1972. *The Provo Experiment: Evaluating Community Control of Delinquency.* Lexington, MA: Lexington Books.

Empey, L. T., and J. Rabow. 1970. The Provo Experiment in delinquency rehabilitation. Pp. 431–448 in H. L. Voss (ed.), *Society, Delinquency and Delinquent Behavior.* Boston: Little, Brown.

Lundman, R. J. 1993. Chapter 7: Community treatment. Pp. 171–204 in R. J. Lundman, *Prevention and Control of Juvenile Delinquency.* New York: Oxford University Press.

PUBLIC OPINION ON JUVENILE JUSTICE ISSUES

Over the past quarter century, the American public has grown progressively more conservative in its ideology and more punitive toward juvenile delinquents. Without question, America is one of the most punitive industrialized nations in the world. In terms of the number of people incarcerated, it is second only to Russia. Nevertheless, the American public continues to call for ever more punitive sanctions to combat criminal activity. Some observers now contend that the purpose of criminal sanctions has changed from righting wrongs committed against society to incapacitation and retribution.

A punitive philosophy has long been present in the adult criminal justice system. Now, resulting largely from public sentiment, such a philosophy is taking hold in the juvenile justice arena. Some members of the public assert that the aggression of today's juveniles is much different than that of the past. Therefore, changes in juvenile aggression must be met by changes in the law. Regardless of competing punitive positions, there is clearly a shift in public opinion toward holding juveniles more accountable for criminal violations. The results of this movement have yielded more severe sentencing, less emphasis on helping juveniles, less concern with differences between youths and adults, and a call to eliminate juvenile courts in favor of using the adult criminal justice system.

EXTENT AND SOURCES OF PUNITIVE PUBLIC OPINION

The move toward criminalization of juveniles, spurred on by public opinion, has dramatically affected the landscape of juvenile justice. Delinquency is now seen as an escalating crime problem. Indeed, there have been predictions of a new breed of juvenile "superpredator." Not only have these predictions been false and misguided, but juvenile offenses, particularly violent offenses, decreased in the 1990s to their lowest levels in more than three decades. Regardless, the public continued to believe that the juvenile crime problem was getting increasingly worse. In addition to perceiving that people make their own decisions to engage in deviant behavior, a growing segment of the public views juveniles more as rational young adults than as impulsive adolescents with a poorly formed sense of right and wrong. Therefore, public sentiment toward juvenile offenders has matched that toward adults in a "lock 'em up" approach.

Such public attitudes and approaches to juvenile justice issues have engendered a shift from rehabilitative to punitive policies. The law is more punitive toward juveniles today than at perhaps any other time in American history. It is not uncommon to send juveniles to boot camps for small offenses or to long prison sentences for more serious offenses. In several states, a juvenile as young as 14 may be certified to stand trial as an adult for certain offenses. Such laws exist because public sentiment is so robust that concern about a juvenile's *mens rea* (guilty mind) is taken less into consideration as the seriousness of the offense rises.

The public opinion shift to more punitive sanctions stems more from the public's perceptions of juvenile delinquency than actual empirical data. School shootings in California, Colorado, Georgia, Florida, Kentucky, Michigan, Oregon, and other states have served to increase the public's fear of juveniles and fuel their cry for more punitive sanctions. Parents are under the impression that their children are more susceptible to violence among their peers than ever before (see the School Violence entry). Fueled largely by various media outlets, which tend to sensationalize and overanalyze criminal incidents involving juveniles, parents are held captive by events occurring hundreds or thousands of miles away.

Some would argue that the public's fear of juvenile crime and dissatisfaction with the juvenile justice system is based largely on the reality that the juveniles who are committing these sensational crimes are not very different from their own children. The school shooting at Columbine High School in Colorado was very disheartening and difficult for the public to digest because the shooters were not poor, their parents were not criminals, and their community was not in decay. In fact, the juvenile shooters were the products of an affluent community and upper-class families. The public has an idea of what a juvenile offender should be; when that stereotype fails to fit the reported facts, a degree of uncertainty develops. The public tends to feel safer when the perceived threat matches the stereotype.

THE EFFECT OF PUBLIC OPINION

For many years, the perceived threat of delinquency has centered on this stereotype of urban, minority, underclass youth. These youth are seen as preying on society because their value systems and codes of ethics and conduct are different from those of society in general. Decades of criminological research have demonstrated that an individual or group whose behavior contrasts with that of the dominant society risks being labeled as deviant. Such labeling becomes detrimental to the stereotyped youth because public perception is inevitably passed along to legislative bodies and law enforcement agencies.

One criminologist, Nels Christie (1993), noted that social distance occurs because the lower-class youth provide examples of "improper behavior" and unseemly living conditions. The negative depictions of these youth in movies, magazines, newspapers, television shows, and news programs are translated into "real life" views harbored by the majority of Americans. These perceptions form stereotypes that may contribute to worsening living conditions and even differential law enforcement (see the Race and Processing of Juvenile Offenders entry).

Others contend that the reflection of these urban lower-class youth is a product of a capitalistic system. Overall, these youth, like the youth of most American subcultures, strive to accomplish the American dream (e.g., money, prestige, property), but the path to their dreams is riddled with obstacles. Consequently, the most efficient way for many minority and/or lower-class youth to achieve their goals is through illegitimate means.

These perceptions are consistent with strain theories of delinquency, which typically view delinquent behavior as the outcome of frustrations in attaining desired goals. Strain theories assume that pressure to deviate from societal norms is created by a discrepancy between goals and means. The juvenile internalizes societal goals but, because legitimate means are blocked, uses illegitimate means to obtain them. A study by Vowell and May (2000) of Mississippi high school students revealed that the perception of blocked opportunities was associated with violent behavior and gang membership. The resulting illegal behaviors of these youth serve to validate public opinion and stereotypes, with subsequent increases in the punitive nature of juvenile justice legislation. In turn, the effects of these punitive policies serve to reduce life opportunities of the youth, and a cyclical process develops.

Another front in delinquency research has consistently shown that many delinquents lack proper early socialization because of a range of factors from fatherless homes to poverty in homes and schools to violence in their neighborhoods. Many in the public and more in the field of juvenile justice have come to understand that a child's formative years are very important in determining the nature and extent of law-abiding or delinquent behavior in the future. Government programs have already been proposed, and funded, in an attempt to alleviate these problems before delinquency occurs.

CONCLUSION

Whether public sentiment on juvenile justice issues centers on rehabilitative approaches or punitive ones, juveniles are now being held more accountable for their actions. The alarming arrest numbers of American youth, in the minds of some, reflect the fact that they are more prone to criminality today than ever before. In the minds of others, the arrest numbers are indications that America is out of touch with the needs and conditions of today's youth. Regardless, arguments about factors that contribute to delinquency will continue to persist. More important, the sentiment of public opinion and an increase in the number of youth arrests will affect the social fabric of America

for years to come. Based on these premises, public opinion is already having a significant effect on the application and structure of juvenile justice. As long as public sentiment toward juveniles is represented by a "get tough" philosophy, America will continue to invoke punitive measures to control juvenile behavior.

This reactionary approach to juvenile justice issues is clearly not based on empirical research. It is also clear that this perspective will lead many to label youth as present and future law violators. Such negative labels may have the effect of reducing life opportunities, thus predisposing some juveniles to future criminality as a way of achieving goals. The public, as well as justice officials, must come to the realization that stiffer penalties may not be the answer to solving juvenile crime issues and building public support. Currie (1985: 275) noted, "If we do not find new ways of including the displaced within the bonds of a supportive and enriching social life, we are likely to see harsher efforts to contain the consequences of their anger and demoralization."

Willie M. Brooks Jr.

See also Courts, Juvenile; Death Penalty; Delinquency—Trends and Data; Gangs, Juvenile; Literature of Delinquency; Race and Processing of Juvenile Offenders; School Violence; Theories of Delinquency—Sociological

Bibliography

Christie, N. 1993. *Crime Control as an Industry.* Oslo, Norway: Scandinavian University Press.

Currie, E. 1985. *Confronting Crime: An American Challenge.* New York: Random House.

Vowell, P., and D. May. 2000. Another look at classic strain theory: Poverty status, perceived blocked opportunity, and gang membership as predictors of adolescent violent behavior. *Sociological Inquiry* 70:42–60.

R

RACE AND PROCESSING OF JUVENILE OFFENDERS

The issue of race remains pervasive and controversial in American society. Hacker (1992) reminds us in his book *Two Nations: Black and White, Separate, Hostile, Unequal* that American society is divided along racial lines. The issue of race is also manifested in the research foci of many social scientists (e.g., Pope and Feyerherm, 1990a, 1990b). For more than 30 years, social scientists (Bishop and Frazier, 1988; Bridges and Steen, 1998; Piliavin and Briar, 1964) have attempted to address the issue of discrimination in our juvenile justice system. Despite legal safeguards mandated by the Supreme Court decision of *In re Gault* (1967), juveniles remain at greater risk of having their rights compromised (Feld, 1989) and minority youth continue to be overrepresented in the juvenile justice system.

RESEARCH ON RACIAL DISPARITIES IN PROCESSING

Pope and Feyerherm (1990a, 1990b) are often cited in the juvenile justice literature for their review of early studies on the role of race in the handling of juvenile cases. They found that more than 70 percent of the research identifies race as a determinant in the outcome of a case. Further, both qualitative and quantitative research yields similar findings of disproportionality—system biases can occur at any stage. The net effect of the Pope and Feyerherm report was a demand that states participating in the federal Juvenile Justice and Delinquency Prevention Act explore the issue of minority overrepresentation.

Addressing the issue of race, the Office of Juvenile Justice and Delinquency Prevention (OJJDP) has provided funding to several states to examine the role of race in the processing of juveniles. The result of each study has yielded findings of race discrimination or a race effect in the disposition of juvenile cases. Georgia and Pennsylvania were among the first of many states to receive funding from the OJJDP. In both studies, there were patterns of discrimination based on race.

Not surprisingly, in some of the funded studies, there has been much debate about research methods that were employed and the terms that were used in the technical reports. For example, in a study conducted in Missouri, researchers disagreed on appropriate phraseology—specifically, whether to use the phrase "race effect" or "apparent race discrimination." The Missouri study, like others, refers frequently to findings of a race effect, which was one way to politically and politely charge findings or patterns of racial discrimination without offending state agencies. The politics of funded research on this topic are discussed later in this entry.

Other findings from Missouri, such as the notion of "justice by geography" (Feld, 1991), reveal that black youth were more likely than any other group to be detained in urban areas. In rural areas, the researchers found that black juveniles, compared with their white counterparts, were at greater risk for removal from the home and referral to a residential program. In sum, two very different justice systems in Missouri emerged, one urban and the other rural. In rural parts of the state, juveniles were afforded the least number of procedural safeguards. More generally, future researchers are encouraged to further explore racial disparities based on geography.

While past studies reviewed by Pope and Feyerherm (1990a, 1990b) found evidence of racial disparity, more recent research (e.g., Bishop and Frazier, 1996; Leiber and Jamieson, 1995; Wu, 1997) also points toward race effects in juvenile justice settings. Many of these decisions are amplified on the front and back ends of the juvenile justice system. At the front end, minority youth are more likely to be detained and treated differentially. At the back end, black youth are more likely to be referred to restrictive residential programs.

THE POLITICS OF RACE RESEARCH

As suggested earlier, it would be a mistake not to consider political input in the research. We need to be concerned about the potential political motivations of the researchers. The author's experience in Missouri suggests that even when confronted with findings of disparate treatment (based on race), there might be pressure to use terminology that mitigates against actual findings. Astute students of this issue must understand the realities behind use of aggregate data: Findings of no discrimination at the macro level do not preclude the possibility of discriminatory findings when the data are disaggregated. On this subject, any serious attempt to explore the role of race in the processing of juvenile offenders must be multistage in design. Clearly, single-stage reports can conceal patterns of discrimination at other levels within the juvenile justice system.

There is another concern as well: questions about the researchers themselves. There are few black scholars and researchers working on discriminatory juvenile processing, thus their total contribution to research in disparate treatment of minority offenders is relatively small. The point here is not so much the differences between majority and minority researchers but an assumption that minority researchers can bring a certain sensitivity in field settings that their white counterparts might dismiss or discount as not worthy of additional exploration.

Aside from the politics, the role of race in the processing of juvenile offenders is profound. The point is made that terminology preferences, single-stage analyses, and the use of aggregate data can obscure significant findings.

CONCLUSION

The preponderance of the literature provides evidence of disparate treatment for minority youth in the juvenile justice system. One finding after another (e.g., Bishop and Frazier, 1996; Kempf, Decker, and Bing, 1990; Wu, 1997) confirms that biases exist. Black youth are likely to be detained and more likely to receive out-of-home referrals to restrictive settings than are their white counterparts. In fact, much of the research suggests that the greatest bias against poor people and visible minorities occurs at the detention stage (Wu, 1997). The data from many of these same studies reveal that black youth are more likely to admit their wrongdoing. This finding begs the question of why this is so.

In addition, black youth are more likely than similarly situated and similarly arrested white youth to have petitions filed against them. This fact cannot be easily dismissed as evidence of greater criminality among black youth. One plausible explanation might be related to the social construction of black youth with a greater proclivity toward crime. In other words, black youth may be seen as more threatening than their white counterparts (e.g., Bridges and Steen, 1998; Leiber and Jamieson, 1995). In sum, nonlegal variables, such as race and use of stereotypes, continue to shape decisions by juvenile justice officials, resulting in a greater representation of minority youth at most stages of the juvenile justice system.

Robert L. Bing III

See also At-Risk Youth; Delinquency—Trends and Data; Public Opinion on Juvenile Justice Issues

Bibliography

Bishop, D., and J. Frazier. 1988. The influence of race on juvenile justice processing. *Journal of Research in Crime and Delinquency* 25:242–263.

Bishop, D., and C. Frazier. 1996. Race effects in juvenile justice decision making: Findings of a statewide analysis. *The Journal of Criminal Law and Criminology* 86:392–414.

Bridges, G., and S. Steen. 1998. Racial disparities in official assessments of juvenile offenders. *American Sociological Review* 63:554–570.

Feld, B. 1989. The right to counsel in juvenile court. *Journal of Criminal Law and Criminology* 79:1185–1346.

Feld, B. 1991. Justice by geography: Urban, suburban and rural variations in juvenile justice administration. *Journal of Criminal Law and Criminology* 8:156–210.

Hacker, A. 1992. *Two Nations: Black and White, Separate, Hostile, Unequal*. New York: Scribners.

Kempf, K., S. Decker, and R. L. Bing III. 1990. *An Analysis of Apparent Disparities in the Handling of Black Youth Within Missouri's Juvenile Justice Systems*. Technical Report. St. Louis: University of Missouri.

Leiber, M., and K. Jamieson. 1995. Race and decision making within juvenile justice: The importance of context. *Journal of Quantitative Criminology* 11:363–386.

Piliavin, I., and S. Briar. 1964. Police encounters with juveniles. *American Journal of Sociology* 70:206–214.

Pope, C., and W. Feyerherm. 1990a. Minority status and juvenile justice processing: An assessment of the research literature—Part 1. *Criminal Justice Abstracts*, June:327–335.

Pope, C., and W. Feyerherm. 1990b. Minority status and juvenile justice processing: An assessment of the research literature—Part 2. *Criminal Justice Abstracts*, September:527–542.

Wu, B. 1997. The effect of race in juvenile processing. *Juvenile and Family Court Journal* 48:43–51.

RECKLESS, WALTER C. (1899–1988)

Walter Cade Reckless was a pioneer in the sociological study of juvenile delinquency and juvenile justice. He advocated the importance of structural variables in understanding adolescent misbehavior at a time when most legal and behavioral analysts emphasized individual factors as the causes of crime and deviance. Throughout his long and productive career as a teacher and researcher, Reckless never wavered from his belief that "problem children" are the products of faulty socialization that can be modified in the right environment. This conviction was the basis of his commitment to social reform and activism intended to prevent crime and delinquency in the young, while offering the opportunity for behavioral change to those already labeled as lawbreakers.

Walter Reckless was born in Philadelphia and educated at the University of Chicago. After completing an undergraduate history major in 1921, he was offered a graduate assistantship in the Department of Sociology and an opportunity to work with Robert Park and Ernest Burgess. These noted scholars were then conducting a series of studies of social problems in Chicago using the participant observer method. This approach appealed to Reckless, who, as an accomplished violinist, was earning extra funds playing his instrument in a roadhouse and observing various types of vice and law violation. This led to his doctoral dissertation, a study of prostitution titled *Natural History of Vice Areas in Chicago* (1925). A year before receiving his doctoral degree, he accepted the position of Assistant Professor at Vanderbilt University, where he remained until 1940. He was then lured to Ohio State University, accepting a professorship in the Department of Social Work with a joint appointment in the Department of Sociology. He moved to Sociology on a full-time basis in 1958 and remained until he retired in 1969. During his 29 years at Ohio State, he built a criminology program that attracted students from around the world, and he trained many academics and practioners who have played instrumental roles in criminological research and correctional reform. In the 1960s, he revived a moribund American Society of Criminology, serving as President for three terms and seeing it become the discipline's premier professional association.

EARLY WORK IN JUVENILE DELINQUENCY

Reckless's first publication on "problem children" was an article in the *Journal of Educational Sociology* (1928) in which he outlined techniques for a sociological study of youngsters with behavioral problems. He placed sociological variables in the context of other relevant factors and advocated a holistic approach to understanding children with problems. More interesting, however, is observing the seeds of ideas he would use much later in his major theoretical contribution to the etiology of delinquency—namely, self-image, "good" boys, and "bad" boys. A year later, he published *Six Boys in Trouble: A Sociological Case Book* (1929). In this monograph, he sought a picture of the child in his world, the total situation, to understand him and his behavior. Delinquency, he claimed, is a situational matter, "not a direct expression of inner mental life." This was a gentle but obvious criticism of psychological and psychiatric approaches to understanding delinquent and problem children. Throughout his earliest writings, he maintained repeatedly that the juvenile offender is not an abnormal child. This, of course, was at a time when individual factors of causation were espoused by most "experts."

Juvenile Delinquency (1932), the first textbook on the subject, was coauthored with his colleague Mapheus Smith. This comprehensive text depicted delinquency as the result of social and structural variables, the result of one's social experience. The authors concluded that "delinquent children are pretty much the same as other children." Demonstrating his early training in social psychology (the year before he coauthored a text on the subject) at Chicago, where he studied with the symbolic interactionists Herbert Blumer and George Herbert Mead, Reckless pointed out the detrimental effects on children of being stigmatized by labels of delinquent and criminal. He also demonstrated his commitment to activism in this text by advocating treatment and clinical intervention to prevent delinquency and rehabilitate the delinquent.

CONTAINMENT THEORY

By the mid-1950s, after several decades of researching and writing about prostitution, corrections, jail administration, probation, female crime, and various related topics, Reckless once again turned his attention to juvenile delinquency. By this time, he had begun to crystallize a control theory of delinquency, which he would ultimately call containment theory. Containment theory is an explanation of both deviancy and conforming behavior, positing a system of outer and inner factors that may work together or in isolation to account for behavior. Outer or external containment are those "structural buffers" operating in the social world that work to keep the youth from deviating toward unacceptable behavior. One's family and community are the most important of a number of external constraints on one's behavior. When external constraints are strong, they can work to handle the social pressures one may encounter to violate the law. When they are weak, however, they must be reinforced by inner containments.

Inner containments are what Reckless called self-components, the primary one of which is the individual's self-concept. A well-developed and prosocial self-concept is the product of positive interactive experiences and the internalization of nondeviant attitudes and values. The self-concept protects one against the pressures or pulls of deviance, especially when external controls are inadequate. In areas of social disorganization, for example, outer controls on a youth's behavior are weak, perhaps nonexistent, and the direction of his or her actions will depend on the actor's self-image. A good self-concept is usually strong enough to prevent delinquency, even when external controls are weak. A poor self-concept cannot contain the individual under such circumstances. This is not to say that a poor self-concept is a gross lack of ego and superego control. Instead, it is a normal lack of inner controls that have potential for positive change if and when the individual favorably internalizes the right kind of experiences later in life.

Working with his long-time collaborator and close friend Simon Dinitz, Reckless conceived and supervised studies of so-called "good" boys and "bad" boys to test the efficacy of his theory. Sixth graders living in high delinquency areas were nominated by their teachers as either "good" or "bad" boys—that is, headed for trouble with the law or not. They and their mothers were interviewed and asked numerous questions designed to assess the boys' self-concepts. Four years later, at age 16, the boys and their mothers were interviewed again. At both times, the self-concepts of the "good" boys were determined to be more positive than those of the "bad" boys. Reckless and Dinitz (1967) and their students used this and related research to help substantiate containment theory.

Based on this research, Reckless and Dinitz (1972) launched an innovative prevention program in the Columbus, Ohio, public school system designed to enhance the self-concepts of seventh-grade students. Children in the experimental classes were exposed to instruction infused with techniques thought to improve self-image and provide positive role models. Those in the control classes had standard instruction. Judged by four years of school and police records, the project could not show that potential delinquents in the experimental classes fared any better than those in the control classes. These results were a disappointment to Reckless, who thought it might be possible, with such special programs, to "vaccinate" a youth against the adversities of a bad environment. In addition, this disappointment was compounded by professional criticism of the "good" and "bad" boy studies based on claims of both theoretical and methodological shortcomings in the research. He remained optimistic, however, believing in the possibility of preventing delinquency through structural changes that have the potential for containment.

RECOGNITION

For some 50 years, Walter C. Reckless influenced the theory and research on delinquency through his creative scholarship and pioneering spirit. Before it was fashionable among criminologists, he emphasized structural factors in delinquency causation, saw value in the principles of symbolic interaction, posited an early and seminal control theory, and worked tirelessly to demonstrate the essential link between social research and its policy applications. As a teacher, lecturer, consultant, world traveler, and humanitarian, his influence was felt by scholars and practitioners around the world. The American Society of Criminology honored Reckless's many contributions to the field with its Edwin H. Sutherland Award in 1965.

Frank R. Scarpitti

See also Theories of Delinquency

Bibliography

Reckless, W. C. 1928. Suggestions for the sociological study of problem children. *Journal of Educational Sociology* 2:156–171.

Reckless, W. C. 1929. *Six Boys in Trouble: A Sociological Case Book*. Ann Arbor, MI: Edwards Brothers.

Reckless, W. C., and S. Dinitz. 1967. Pioneering with self-concept as a vulnerability factor in delinquency. *Journal of Criminal Law, Criminology and Police Science* 58: 515–523.

Reckless, W. C., and S. Dinitz. 1972. *The Prevention of Juvenile Delinquency: An Experiment*. Columbus: Ohio State University Press.

Reckless, W. C., and M. Smith. 1932. *Juvenile Delinquency*. New York: McGraw-Hill.

REFORMATORIES AND REFORM SCHOOLS

Juvenile reformatories have been one of the ideological and programmatic cornerstones of the American juvenile justice system since the first House of Refuge opened more than 175 years ago. However, an examination of the origin, development, operation, and impact of key reformatories, as well as the general contours of the movement as a whole, reveals that the purpose, structure, and character of juvenile correctional institutions have changed over time.

EARLY HISTORICAL EVENTS

During the colonial period there were no reformatories in the United States. Juvenile delinquency was a relatively minor problem. Juvenile offenders were disciplined by parents, relatives, neighbors, or local religious leaders. Serious offenses—and in some colonies, acts that violated community morals (such as blasphemy, heresy, and improper dress)—were handled by adult courts. Convicted juvenile offenders were subjected to a range of punishments, including corporal punishment and incarceration in adult jails, county penitentiaries, and prisons.

New York House of Refuge

The opening of the nation's first juvenile reformatory—the New York House of Refuge (NYHR)—on January 1, 1825, was a pivotal event in the history of the American justice system. This institution is historically significant for three reasons. First, the opening of the NYHR marked the birth of the juvenile reformatory movement. Second, this institution laid the foundation for the rise of a separate juvenile justice system in the United States. Third, many 19th-century child savers believed that the keepers of the NYHR had discovered the cure for juvenile misbehavior and delinquency. Consequently, the goals, structure, and programs of the NYHR served as the undisputed model for new juvenile reformatories.

The NYHR was founded by an organization known as the Society for the Reformation of Juvenile Delinquents (SRJD). The members of the SRJD—prominent upper-class, white, male reformers—were concerned about perceived increases in crime, delinquency, and social disorder. They were also concerned with reports that juvenile offenders sentenced to adult correctional facilities were being mistreated and abused. The SRJD successfully lobbied state legislators to appropriate funds to open a reformatory in New York City. The new institution had two key aims: remove juveniles from adult correctional institutions and introduce an innovative program of reform aimed at helping and treating troublesome children.

The NYHR was carefully designed to achieve this rehabilitative end. The commitment criteria were broad. Delinquent, dependent, neglected, and incorrigible children were eligible for admission. Female offenders could be committed and incarcerated to the age of 18; males could be committed and incarcerated to the age of 21. The regimen of reform was designed to instill moral values and prepare the inmates, who were largely from the lower class, to assume their "proper place" in society. Academic education was

Photo 9. New York State Reformatory, Elmira.
SOURCE: Correctional Photograph Archives Collection, Eastern Kentucky University Archives. Used with permission.

introduced to teach reading, writing, and arithmetic. Inmates worked in shops where, in theory, they learned the habits of order, discipline, and self-control, as well as skills that would prepare them to find jobs after release. A carefully structured classification and mark system (an early form of behavior modification) was designed to reward good behavior and measure fitness for release. Religious instruction instilled moral values and provided the word of God. After exhibiting contrition and working their way through the mark and classification system, inmates were indentured. Boys were placed in a variety of occupations—typically, farming, blacksmithing, and painting. Females were usually indentured as domestic servants.

The keepers of the NYHR were confident that their efforts to remove children from adult correctional institutions and initiate a new approach to juvenile reform were a complete success. Their annual reports declared that 70 percent, 80 percent, and even 90 percent of their charges were saved from a life of crime. The NYHR was widely hailed as one of the nation's most innovative and important correctional institutions. Child savers from across the county and around the world came to New York to study the model institution. The success of the NYHR's "congregate system" (where the youth worked together) laid the foundation for the rise of the juvenile reformatory movement. Social reformers in Massachusetts and Pennsylvania, inspired by these promising reports, opened the Boston House of Reformation (1826) and the Philadelphia House of Refuge (1828). By 1857, 13 reformatories were opened in the United States. By 1876, 51 institutions were receiving children. The juvenile reformatory movement had supplanted the adult prison system as the most innovative and hopeful part of the American penal system.

The Lancaster Industrial School for Girls

The opening of the Lancaster Industrial School for Girls in 1856 in Lancaster, Massachusetts, was a pivotal event in the history of the juvenile reformatory movement. The Lancaster Industrial School was significant for two reasons. First, it was the nation's first juvenile reformatory exclusively for girls. Second, it introduced a new approach to reform known as the cottage, or family, system. Borrowed from juvenile institutions in France and Germany, the Lancaster Industrial School rejected New York's large-scale congregate reformatory system. Under the new plan, institutions were located in the country, away from the corrupting influences of big cities. Inmates were housed in cottages containing, under ideal conditions, 10 to 15 children. House parents, who served as role models, taught the girls domestic skills and provided a "family setting."

The opening of the Lancaster Industrial School for Girls and the nation's first cottage institution for boys, the Ohio Reform School (1858), sparked a major debate among juvenile reformers: Which system, cottage or congregate, was more effective at helping and treating juveniles? Although the NYHR had served as the model for the first half of the 19th century, the congregate system quickly fell into disfavor. Juvenile reformatories opened between 1860 and 1900 generally adopted the cottage system. Some early congregate reformatories, including the Philadelphia House of Refuge, closed and reopened in the country as family institutions.

Late-19th-Century Contributions

Late-19th-century reformatory keepers introduced a number of innovations while they were debating the merits of the cottage and congregate systems. Recreational programs were expanded. Traditional academic education and labor systems were supplemented with systematic vocational education. The indenture system was replaced with parole. A number of reformatories introduced military drill. Inmates were dressed in uniforms, assigned ranks, and drilled in daily parades. Reflecting these trends, an increasing number of juvenile correctional facilities adopted new names: industrial schools, training schools, or reform schools.

Research by modern criminal justice historians has revealed, however, that the late-19th-century debate between proponents of the congregate and cottage systems was misleading. In fact, a critical analysis of historical data sources reveals there was a wide disparity between the promise and practice of both child-saving systems. Juveniles in congregate and cottage reformatories were subjected to a variety of harsh punishments. In many institutions, children were whipped and subjected to severe corporal punishment; in others, they were locked in dungeons, handcuffed, and fed only bread and water. Labor systems, particularly in congregate reformatories, did not teach children skills or the habits of industry. Child workers were abused and exploited for profit. Religious instruction was often sectarian, resulting in conflicts between the Catholic Church and the keepers of institutions, who were often Protestant. Indentured and paroled inmates were, in some instances, abused and exploited by their masters or by community supervisors. Inmate gangs, violence, escapes, sexual encounters, and smuggling disrupted the daily operation of reformatories. The keepers of congregate and cottage reformatories were primarily preoccupied with the task of maintaining order and security; rehabilitation was a secondary concern.

Nineteenth-century reformatories were particularly harsh on black and female offenders. In fact, there were four versions of "treatment" and "reform." White males were the primary concern of 19th-century reformatory keepers. They were trained to assume their "proper places" as skilled workers (farmers, blacksmiths, carpenters). White females, reflecting conditions in the broader social structure, were trained to be domestics and wives to lower-class workers. Black males were often excluded from academic programs and prepared for positions as obedient lower-class laborers. Black females were doubly stigmatized by their race and gender and received custodial care. In some states, black children were placed in separate "colored reformatories." In some southern states, they were admitted to reformatories with white children, but their sole purpose was to serve as menial laborers and support staff.

TWENTIETH-CENTURY REFORMATORIES

Juvenile reformatories lost their place as the central focus of the juvenile justice system at the beginning of the 20th century. The opening of the first juvenile court in Chicago in 1899 marked the birth of the juvenile court movement and the rise of the second key component of the American juvenile justice system.

The Progressive Era

During the Progressive Era (about 1900 to 1920), juvenile courts spread quickly across the country. Child savers were confident that these new juvenile courts—which were grounded on the goal of rehabilitation and the legal doctrine of *parens patriae*—would provide individualized treatment and reform. The proliferation of juvenile probation, which was often included in legislation founding juvenile courts, provided judges with new sentencing, treatment and supervision options. Juvenile court judges would, in theory, make certain that every child received individualized care. Reformatories became a more peripheral treatment-control strategy reserved for serious and less promising offenders.

During the Progressive Era, the keepers of congregate and cottage reformatories continued to articulate the goal of rehabilitation. But reflecting conditions in the broader social structure, in particular the pervasive nativism and eugenics movements, reformatory keepers became decidedly less optimistic about the malleability of many of their charges.

Eugenic Concerns

In reaction to these concerns, psychologists and physicians opened psychological laboratories and psychopathic clinics in juvenile reformatories. Newly developed psychological tests produced distressing results: many juveniles (sometimes more than 90 percent of the inmates tested) were classified as morons, idiots, dullards, or incorrigibles. Reformatory keepers responded by introducing two treatment-control regimens. More hopeful inmates were exposed to traditional rehabilitative programs: academic education, vocational education, recreation, the mark and classification system, and parole. Hopeless inmates were excluded from treatment and exposed to a regimen structured around custody.

Eugenic criminology reached its high point in 1921 with the opening of the Eastern Reformatory in Napanoch, New York. This institution was designed to serve as a dumping ground for New York's more hopeless "defective delinquent offenders." Reflecting nativistic and eugenic sentiments, Napanoch was designed to isolate unsalvageable, so-called defective delinquent offenders for long periods. Proponents of the institution believed it would protect the public from crime and prevent dangerous defectives from producing offspring who would, no doubt, create another generation of misfits. The Eastern Reformatory continued to isolate New York's incorrigibles until it closed in 1966.

The Midcentury Period

Juvenile justice was not a central concern of Americans over the next three decades. With isolated exceptions, the central aims, structure, programs, and problems of reformatories remained unchanged. During the 1930s, Americans were consumed with the Great Depression and the threat posed by adult crime. The publication of the FBI's 10-most-wanted list reinforced the notion that adult criminals, not juveniles, were a central threat to social order. During the 1940s, Americans focused their attention on defeating Nazi Germany and winning World War II. The threat posed by juvenile delinquents and the failings of juvenile institutions remained secondary concerns.

Americans became alarmed at perceived increases in delinquency during the 1950s. Concerns with juvenile gangs, adolescent misbehavior, and the rise of a "youth culture" attracted an increasing amount of attention. Experts on juvenile justice cited a variety of causes for the rise in misbehavior: lack of parental discipline, the attraction of gangs, bad schools, erotic music, and even comic books. Authorities called for more scientific diagnostic techniques and an increased emphasis on treatment in reformatories. However, 19th-century treatment strategies such as academic education, vocational education, and religious instruction continued to serve as the foundation of reform.

The 1960s—A Period of Change

The 1960s was a pivotal decade in the history of American society. Protests against the Vietnam War, the civil rights movement, urban riots, the drug crisis, and perceived increases in crime and delinquency presented serious challenges to the legitimacy of political, social, and economic institutions. These criticisms carried over to the criminal and juvenile justice systems. Labeling theorists raised the possibility that the justice system could actually make juvenile and adult offenders worse. The President's Crime Commission's *Task Force Report: Juvenile Delinquency and Youth Crime*, written in 1967 by some of the country's most respected experts on crime, lashed out at the juvenile justice system. The report charged that juvenile courts were run by incompetent judges who were making arbitrary, capricious, and harmful decisions. They went on to charge that juvenile reformatories—the historical foundation of the juvenile justice system for more than 130 years—were providing little treatment and reform. In fact, juvenile correctional institutions were miniature prisons and schools of crime.

The President's Commission, along with academicians and reformers across the country, proposed radical solutions to deal with the deficiencies of juvenile courts and reformatories. Drawing on labeling theory, reformers called for diversion programs, which were aimed at keeping children out of juvenile court. The President's Commission and many academicians urged legislators and correctional officials to expand the use of community-based corrections to remove offenders from juvenile reformatories. Community-based corrections would, in theory, spare offenders the harm of incarceration, reduce stigmatizing labels, save the state money, and perhaps most important, provide effective treatment in the community. The reintegrative model was most fully implemented in Massachusetts. The head of the division of youth services, Jerome Miller, actually closed the state's reformatories, moving his charges (except for roughly 100 of the most dangerous offenders) into a variety of community settings. During the 1960s, America's juvenile reformatories were experiencing unprecedented scrutiny and criticism.

THE CONTEMPORARY REFORMATORY PERIOD

The movement to shut down juvenile reformatories was, however, short-lived. The country moved in a more conservative direction in the 1970s. Sustained criticisms of the government gradually abated. Conservatives and liberals increasingly denounced diversion and deinstitutionalization programs, but for a variety of conflicting reasons. The popularity of labeling theory, one of the key theoretical foundations for attacks on reformatories and support for community based corrections, faded. Academicians, politicians, and the public increasingly supported more conservative theories of crime and delinquency, especially classical theory. Advocates of this perspective believed that adult and juvenile offenders were free, rational, and hedonistic actors who needed and deserved punishment. Juvenile reformatories and

adult prisons were, then, necessary for deterrence and social defense.

The election of Ronald Reagan to the presidency in 1980 reflected and reinforced these trends. Conservative administrators at the Office of Juvenile Justice and Delinquency Prevention called for a new "get tough" approach to delinquency. Juvenile justice policymakers at the federal and state levels called for and implemented a variety of delinquency prevention and control strategies based on classical theory. More specifically, the call for punishment and deterrence led to a war on chronic juvenile offenders, reductions in diversion and deinstitutionalization programs, more juvenile waivers to adult courts, increasing use of restitution programs, longer sentences for juvenile offenders, and finally, more juvenile reformatories. These conservative strategies have continued to guide American juvenile justice policy through modern presidential administrations.

CONCLUSION

Modern American juvenile reformatories are not, to be sure, clones of the NYHR and the Lancaster Industrial School for Girls. Federal legislation has prohibited the incarceration of status offenders (dependent, neglected, and incorrigible children) with delinquents in reformatories. Whipping and other forms of barbaric punishment have been prohibited. Child workers are no longer exploited by unscrupulous prison contractors. Blatant religious proselytizing has been eliminated. A variety of innovative treatment programs have been introduced over the past few decades: group counseling, individual counseling, group psychotherapy, individual psychotherapy, therapeutic communities, reality therapy, transactional analysis, transcendental meditation, family therapy, and relaxation therapy. A number of states have privatized the supervision of juvenile institutions. Correctional architects have developed unit management cell designs, introduced new technologically advanced surveillance equipment, and employed color therapy to brighten up the walls of reformatories in an effort to reduce violence and foster treatment.

However, a closer look at modern juvenile reformatories reveals that they are, in many ways, products of the past. Many correctional institutions are still structured as congregate or cottage institutions. Gangs, violence, smuggling, theft, drugs, predatory sex, and the threat of arson and suicide continue to plague many reformatory keepers. Modern reformatories, especially public institutions, continue to incarcerate the children of the "dangerous classes": poor, city-raised blacks, Hispanics, and "white trash." And perhaps most important, modern juvenile reformatory keepers continue to confront ageless questions concerning the causes of delinquency and appropriate ways for a civilized society to help, treat, and reform troublesome children.

Alexander W. Pisciotta

See also Courts, Juvenile—History; Juvenile Detention Facilities; Jerome G. Miller; *Parens Patriae* Doctrine; Training Schools

Bibliography

Brenzel, B. M. 1983. *Daughters of the State: A Social Portrait of the First Reform School for Girls in North America, 1856–1905*. Cambridge, MA: MIT Press.

Hawes, J. M. 1971. *Children in Urban Society: Juvenile Delinquency in Nineteenth Century America*. New York: Oxford University Press.

Mennel, R. M. 1973. *Thorns and Thistles: Juvenile Delinquents in the United States, 1825–1940*. Hanover, NH: University Press of New England.

Pickett, R. S. 1969. *House of Refuge: Origins of Juvenile Reform in New York State, 1815–1857*. Syracuse, NY: Syracuse University Press.

Pisciotta, A. W. 1994. *Benevolent Repression: Social Control and the American Reformatory-Prison Movement*. New York: New York University Press.

Rothman, D. J. 1971. *The Discovery of the Asylum: Social Order and Disorder in the New Republic*. Boston: Little, Brown.

Rothman, D. J. 1980. *Conscience and Convenience: The Asylum and Its Alternatives in Progressive America*. Boston: Little, Brown.

Schlossman, S. L. 1977. *Love and the American Delinquent: The Theory and Practice of "Progressive" Juvenile Justice, 1825–1920*. Chicago: University of Chicago Press.

 RESTORATIVE JUSTICE

Restorative justice is a different way of thinking about crime, a new view of the crime problem that has been gaining support in many parts of the world over the last two decades. There is significant controversy about the definition of restorative justice and what should and should not be included under its umbrella. There is agreement, however, that restorative justice begins with the premise that crime is more than law-breaking and that justice cannot be achieved by simply punishing the wrongdoer. Van Ness and Strong (1997) have identified three core principles of restorative justice:

1. If crime is about harm, then justice requires healing or repair. There may be a number of different ways to repair harm, and repair will have different meanings in different contexts.

2. Harm cannot be repaired without input from those most affected by crime. Victims, offenders, and community members must be provided with opportunities for input and participation in the justice process.

3. Repairing harm requires that society rethink the roles of government and community in the response to crime. Justice systems and justice professionals should offer legal authority, policy support, and resources in a facilitative approach to problem solving as opposed to serving as experts in a case-driven response.

Under the restorative justice paradigm, crime is defined by the harm done to victims. Therefore, the primary reaction to crime should not be punishing or even rehabilitating the offender but repairing and compensating for the harm caused by the crime. Harm can include material losses, physical injuries, psychological consequences, relationship problems, and social dysfunctions, for which the offender is held accountable and is primarily responsible for repairing. Focusing on repairing harm does not preclude efforts to rehabilitate offenders but actually supports those efforts because sincere rehabilitation requires that offenders acknowledge the harm they caused and work toward making amends. Repairing the harm, in turn, sets the stage for reintegrating offenders into the community.

Unlike the formal justice system, which directs most of its attention toward establishing guilt and determining punishment for offenders, restorative justice focuses on allowing victims to have significant input into plans for holding offenders accountable and for repairing the harm the victims have suffered. Victims include the individual victim, those close to him or her who were affected, and also the community. Communities are affected by crime, and members of a community are considered stakeholders in the restorative justice process. The community plays an important role in setting the terms of reparation agreements and in monitoring and supporting offenders through their completion.

According to John Braithwaite (1989), restorative justice is essentially a community solution. Crime is best controlled when members of a community are the primary controllers, actively participating in shaming offenders and then helping them to reintegrate into the community. Justice systems and justice professionals should no longer dominate the business of crime control; however, they are important in helping facilitate, provide resources, and enforce agreements designed to repair harm and hold offenders accountable. Restorative justice is sometimes described as a three-dimensional balanced approach to crime because it views victims, communities, and offenders as "customers" of the justice process. All three receive services under a balanced approach, and all three should be actively involved as participants in the system (Bazemore and Umbreit, 1997).

The restorative justice movement is relatively new to the United States, but it has deep roots in many ancient societies that relied on forms of conflict resolution that closely resemble many of the more recent restorative justice programs. Restorative practices are not just the stuff of ancient history, however. Indigenous people such as the Aborigines, the Inuit, and North and South American Indians have been using different restorative justice approaches for centuries, approaches that now serve as models for programs being piloted in the dominant European-style criminal and juvenile justice systems. The restorative justice movement is international in scope, although practices and policies differ widely both between and within countries.

To date the intensity of activity around restorative justice has centered on juvenile justice and responses to youth crime. Most of the significant restorative justice projects have been implemented as alternatives to the traditional juvenile justice process. For example, in New Zealand, family group conferencing has become the dominant option for dealing with all but the most serious and chronic youthful offenders. Many victim-offender mediation programs in the United States are focused primarily on juvenile crime. Why has youth crime become the focal point of restorative justice initiatives? All over the world, the juvenile justice system

faces a crisis of confidence. The public and juvenile justice professionals are frustrated by the inability of the current system to respond effectively to rising levels of violent youth crime. Many nations, led by the United States, have moved toward a more retributive juvenile justice model, implementing harsher penalties for juveniles with less concern for rehabilitation and more emphasis on punishment and incapacitation. Advocates for restorative justice fear that the juvenile justice system will continue to lose legitimacy and its authority will increasingly shrink, possibly resulting in its eventual abolition. They propose a radical transformation of the juvenile justice system, based on new principles and policies that go beyond both the retributive/punishment model and the traditional treatment/ "best interests of the child" model. They see the current crisis in confidence as an opportunity to preserve a separate juvenile justice system by offering a third alternative built on a more balanced restorative paradigm.

Contributing to the intensity level of restorative justice around juvenile crime are justice professionals who also realize that the current system is in crisis and are searching for ways to cope with the tug between retribution and treatment. Many of these professionals have opened the doors for experimentation to projects designed on restorative justice principles. Even among a retributive-minded public, there remains a sense that young people are somewhat less blameworthy than adults are. Because the public is still receptive to flexible approaches to addressing youth crime, restorative justice projects may be more politically feasible in the juvenile justice system. Although restorative justice goes beyond the traditional treatment model, it remains compatible with treatment while and at the same time appeals to a more retributive sentiment by stressing that offenders must accept responsibility for the harm they caused and take steps to eliminate the damage. Finally, juvenile justice, unlike what happens in the adult system, has always recognized that parents, siblings, school personnel, religious advisors, and other interested parties play an important role in juvenile court and in helping the offender reintegrate into the community. Restorative justice principles are built on the need to incorporate families and communities in the process, whether in victim-offender mediation, family group conferencing, or circle sentencing. Because of the unique cultural and structural context of the response to youth crime, proponents are optimistic about the prospects for implementing restorative justice models in juvenile justice systems.

Bazemore and Umbreit (1997) described four restorative conferencing models that encompass a range of strategies to bring the victim, offender, and other members of the community together in a nonadversarial, community-based process. The goal of the process is to hold the juvenile offender accountable and to repair the harm suffered by the victim and the community. The four models—victim-offender mediation, community reparative boards, family group conferencing, and circle sentencing—are currently implemented in programs in North America, Australia, New Zealand, and parts of Europe. Although the models are not exhaustive of the possibilities for restorative justice, they illustrate the common themes that link the models together as well as their differences in design and approach.

Victim-offender mediation, also called victim-offender reconciliation and victim-offender dialogue, has a 20-year history in the United States, Canada, and Europe. There are currently 320 such programs in the United States and Canada and more than 700 in Europe. The largest number of cases referred to mediation involve less serious property crime; however, the process is used increasingly in response to more serious and violent youth crime. In the mediation process, victims voluntarily meet offenders in a safe, structured setting and, with the assistance of a trained mediator, the victim is able to tell the offender about the crime's physical, emotional, and/or financial impact; ask the offender questions about the crime; and be involved in developing a restitution plan for the offender. For additional information about victim-offender mediation and youth crime, see the Mediation entry.

Community reparative boards are composed of small groups of citizens who have received intensive training and conduct public, face-to-face meetings with offenders who have been ordered by the court to participate. During the meeting, board members discuss with the offender the nature and seriousness of the offense. The boards develop agreements that sanction offenders, monitor compliance, and submit reports to the court. Community reparative boards involve citizens directly in the justice process and increase their ownership of the system. Board members are trained to confront offenders in a constructive manner to assist them in taking personal responsibility for their offense. Reparative boards also help reduce the cost of the formal justice system. The Vermont Department of Corrections implemented its Reparative Probation Program in 1995. The state has used reparative boards primarily with nonviolent, adult offenders, but recently it has begun using them for youthful offenders as well. There is limited data on the effectiveness of community reparative boards. Experience has demonstrated that although they are intended to provide an opportunity for victims and community members to confront an offender, in practice they may better serve community input.

Ancient sanctioning and dispute resolution traditions of the Maori people of New Zealand provide the basis for the family group conferencing model. The New Zealand legislature adopted a modern version of the tradition in 1989 to dispose of all but the most violent and serious cases of juvenile delinquency. In South Australia, another form of family group conferencing is known as Wagga Wagga, because it was developed by the Wagga Wagga Police Department. The Wagga Wagga model is used in cities in Minnesota, Montana, Pennsylvania, and Vermont and in several parts of Canada. According to Bazemore and Umbreit (2001), Wagga Wagga is the primary family group conferencing model that has taken hold in North America and has been used to deal with cases of theft, minor assault, arson, vandalism, and drug crimes. The model has been implemented in schools, probation departments, police agencies, residential programs, neighborhood groups, and mediation programs. Used most frequently as a diversion from the official juvenile justice system, Wagga Wagga can also be used after a youth has been adjudicated to address unresolved issues or to determine the specifics of restitution.

To initiate a family group conference, a trained facilitator contacts the victim and the offender to explain the process and invite them to participate. The victim and offender are asked to identify key members of their support system who will also be asked to attend. Participation is voluntary. The conference usually begins with the offender describing the incident, after which the other participants describe how the incident has affected their lives. In some conferences, the victim begins the conference. Through this process, offenders must confront their behavior and the impact it has had on the victims, those close to the victims, and their own families and friends. Victims can ask questions and express their feelings. After the discussion, the facilitator asks the victim what he or she wants the outcome of the conference to be. All participants can contribute suggestions about how the harm can be repaired, and an agreement is reached that outlines what is expected of the offender.

A study in New Zealand found that families of offenders who go through conferencing are more involved in the justice process than are families who go through the formal juvenile justice system. All the participants—victims, offenders, families, and friends—described conferencing as helpful. Preliminary research in the United States indicates that victims are very satisfied with conferencing, and there are high rates of offender compliance with the agreements reached during a conference (Bazemore and Umbreit, 1997).

The fourth restorative conferencing model is circle sentencing, based on traditional practices of aboriginal peoples in Canada and the Native Americans in the United States. Circle sentencing has been used most extensively in Saskatchewan, Manitoba, and in the Yukon. In 1996, a pilot project in circle sentencing was launched in Minnesota. It has been used with both adult and youthful offenders. Circle sentencing includes participation of the victim, offender, both of their families and friends, personnel from the justice agency, police department and relevant social service agencies, and interested community members who together develop a sentencing plan that addresses the concerns of all of the parties. After an offender petitions to participate in a circle, a healing circle is formed for the victim, a healing circle is formed for the offender, a sentencing circle is formed to reach consensus on a reparation plan, and a follow-up circle takes responsibility for monitoring the enforcement of the agreement. Of all four models, circle sentencing places the most emphasis on community empowerment in responding to crime.

The specific circle process necessarily varies from community to community because it must be customized to meet the needs and culture of each local area. It requires a strong and healthy relationship between the formal justice process and the community and participants who are trained in consensus building. The circle process takes time, experience, and flexibility to grow. How it is used will depend not only on the personalities of the victim and offender but also on the experience and dedication of the community participants. It is not an appropriate model for all offenses. Because it is labor intensive, many do not think it is appropriate for first offenders and minor offenses. Circle sentencing requires an extensive presession process that is designed to prepare the offender and make certain that he or she is serious about personal change. The presession process can

include meeting with a respected community member and beginning some work on a reparation plan. Circles can be canceled if the offender does not complete the preliminary steps. There is little research addressing the effectiveness of circle sentencing; however, a 1996 Canadian study found that recidivism was lower for offenders who participated in circle sentencing than for offenders who went through the standard justice process.

Restorative justice raises unique concerns. On a systemic note, will restorative justice programs be used primarily as diversions from the formal juvenile court process, and, if so, will they contribute to widening the net? What criteria will be implemented to determine which incidences are handled through restorative practices and which are handled through the formal system? If restorative programs are located in the formal justice system, what role does due process play? What legal protections should or must be available to a youthful offender in the restorative justice model? Because communities play a major role in restorative practices, care must be taken to protect against the tyranny of the community, especially in communities dominated by certain individuals or groups. Significant power differentials in a community hierarchy can be very harmful for more vulnerable, less powerful members involved in a restorative justice setting, whether as an offender or a victim.

Interest in restorative justice principles and practices is growing; however, with the exception of victim-offender mediation, there is limited research concerning the effectiveness of restorative programs. Experts in the field agree that the criteria for evaluating the new programs should include not only measures of offender recidivism but also measures of community involvement and empowerment, victim restitution and satisfaction, and the success of reintegrative shaming. Additional and more appropriate standards are needed for evaluating restorative programs and for comparing them to traditional justice process systems.

Barbara A. Belbott

See also Mediation

Bibliography

Bazemore, G. 2000. Community justice and a vision of collective efficacy: The case for restorative conferencing. Pp. 225–297 in J. Horney (ed.), *Criminal Justice 2000,*

Vol. 3. Washington, DC: U.S. Department of Justice, Office of Justice Programs, National Institute of Justice.

Bazemore, G., and M. Umbreit. 1997. *Balanced and Restorative Justice for Juveniles: A Framework for Juvenile Justice in the 21st Century*. Washington, DC: U.S. Department of Justice, Office of Justice Programs, Office of Juvenile Justice and Delinquency Prevention.

Bazemore, G., and L. Walgrave (eds.). 1999. *Restorative Juvenile Justice: Repairing the Harm of Youth Crime*. New York: Criminal Justice Press.

Braithwaite, J. 1989. *Crime, Shame, and Reintegration*. New York: Cambridge University Press.

Van Ness, D., and K. H. Strong. 1997. *Restoring Justice*. Cincinnati, OH: Anderson.

 # RUNAWAYS

The act of running away from home by children is not new. For generations, the desire to leave the home behind and embrace the adventure that the wide world offers has been a great allure to the young. The runaway traditionally has been admired as embodying the American pioneering spirit, seeking freedom from constraints and the opportunity to make one's fortune or one's own way in the world. Indeed, for much of our country's history, vagabonds have been seen as ones who live life on their own terms, moving from place to place with a freedom that others can never have.

As much as the pull of adventure, the push of harsh home conditions also causes many to flee home at an early age. Runaways almost universally have conditions or situations in their homes or families that contribute to their running away. The conditions may be as severe as physical, emotional, or sexual abuse by a family member, or as relatively benign as a disagreement with parents. Regardless, the juvenile comes to view the streets as preferable to home. Mark Twain best captured the push-pull influences on the runaway. As the seemingly incorrigible and adventuresome youth Huckleberry Finn said, "it was rough living in the house all the time . . . and so when I couldn't stand it no longer, I lit out. I got into my old rags and my sugar-hogshead again, and was free and satisfied."

This romanticized tradition, however, is far removed from today's reality. The runaways of today are often endangered, suffering from instability in their families and homes and facing an uncertain future. In addition to putting themselves in physical and developmental jeopardy, today's runaways are looked down on as a societal problem that the juvenile justice system must address.

CONSEQUENCES OF RUNNING AWAY

Running away seems also to have been a response to societal conditions. The Great Depression, World War II, the Vietnam War, and the 1960s have been recognized as eras during which America faced unprecedented challenges and large numbers of runaways roamed the country (Lipschutz, 1977). For some youths, apparent instability in society seems to provide a cue to seek change for themselves and redefine their relationship with the world in which they live. Runaways see leaving home as a mechanism within their ability that allows them to accomplish the desired change.

Legally, running away is a juvenile offense. The concepts of mental incompetence and lack of accountability define the status of minors, and the juvenile is therefore required to remain under adult supervision during the period of minority. Many state laws proscribe incorrigibility and waywardness by juveniles, and the act of running away is considered to be contrary to their own "best interests." Runaways therefore are subject to court sanction for their defiant act of leaving home, with the ostensible goal of protecting the juvenile and providing for his or her rehabilitation.

Apart from the legal consequences of running away, however, are the human consequences. Young runaways are generally prohibited from participating in a variety of social rights and privileges, such as voting, driving, holding jobs, finding housing, and obtaining medical benefits. Their status as runaways therefore creates tremendous barriers to survival. The need for survival thus forces the majority of runaways into illicit behavior, nearly always at great risk to their psychological development and physical safety. The longer runaways are on the streets, the more clearly they come to understand that there is little romance in running away.

CLASSIFICATION AND INCIDENCE OF RUNAWAYS

The runaway is usually classified as a "missing" child. A missing child, quite simply, is understood to be one who is missing from home. However, children may be missing for many reasons, such as being abducted, lost, or injured. Due to the efforts of Congress in passing the Missing Children's Assistance Act (Title IV of the Juvenile Justice and Delinquency Prevention Act of 1974, as amended), as well as ongoing studies conducted by the federal Office of Juvenile Justice and Delinquency Prevention (OJJDP), much is now known about missing children, including runaways. The National Incidence Studies of Missing, Abducted, Runaway, and Thrownaway Children (NISMART 1) was first conducted in 1988 and published in 1990 (Finkelhor, Hotaling, and Sedlak, 1990). A second NISMART is now available. As the most comprehensive study on missing children, NISMART identifies the runaway as a specific type of missing child. NISMART defines runaways as those children who leave home voluntarily without the knowledge or permission of their parents or guardians and who stay away at least overnight. This category of missing child can be distinguished from thrownaways (sometimes called throwaways), who are children who do not leave home voluntarily but (1) are abandoned, (2) are forced from their homes by parents or guardians and are not allowed to return, or (3) sporadically come and go completely unsupervised. However, distinguishing between runaways and thrownaways is often difficult because the combination of factors that culminates in the child leaving home often makes the child's wish to flee as great as the parent's desire to banish the child.

In 1998, more than 70 million Americans (about 26 percent of the population) were considered juveniles — under the age of 18. From the 1988 NISMART, it was estimated that more than 450,000 juveniles were runaways at some time during that year. Most estimates today place the number of runaways from 500,000 to 1 million. Regardless of the precise figure, it is generally accepted that one half to one percent of juveniles may be considered runaways at any time. About half of these runaways are gone from home for only one or two days, and in half of the cases, a parent or guardian knew of the child's whereabouts at some point during the time they had run away. Many runaways are picked up by police and returned home; many return home on their own. The runaway "problem" can probably best be characterized as those juveniles who remain missing and become homeless or exploited.

THE REALITY OF RUNNING AWAY

A majority of runaways, at the time of running away, were from homes with divorced or single parents. Fewer than one third of runaways fled a home where both parents were present. Despite this statistic, it has been difficult to identify specific characteristics of the home or parents that may explain runaway behavior. In general, the mental health and emotional needs of most runaways have been identified as a source of their behavior, as well as the family problems or stresses of home life. Physical and sexual abuse by parents or family members have also been identified as reasons why runaways leave home.

Apart from the desire to escape what the child comes to see as intolerable conditions at home, the lure of the streets and desire for independence remain significant factors in a juvenile's decision to run away. The excitement of the unknown, however, commonly turns to disillusionment as the juvenile faces the harshness of street life. This includes the realties of finding food, a place to sleep, shelter from the elements, and the risks of being robbed, assaulted, or otherwise victimized. Runaways often discover that the problems from which they were running are replaced with new problems that become overwhelming.

Most runaways are girls in their teens. There is considerable evidence that female runaways, particularly those who are gone from home for extended periods, are at high risk for exploitation by pimps and others who seek targets for the prostitution trade (Chapman, 1976; Finkelhor et al., 1990). Runaway girls are vulnerable because of their need for emotional support, as well as their practical needs for food and shelter. These girls have also been found to be at significant risk for violence and assault, including sexual assault. While such victimization is not limited to girls, their status as a majority of runaways and their vulnerability increases their likelihood of becoming targets.

Throughout the United States, running away is a status offense that constitutes delinquent behavior. In 1999, approximately 150,000 juveniles were arrested for the act of running away. The status offense of running away tends not to be a focus of police efforts but usually results when a juvenile is arrested for another offense. Although not universal, police tend to exercise discretion in favor of finding a safe haven for the child outside the juvenile justice system. Further, juvenile court judges seem to favor interventions that may benefit the child by improving his or her living situation rather than employing a penal approach.

In addition to their delinquent status as runaways, however, juveniles who run away also tend to be involved in other criminal behavior (Armstrong, 1932). Prostitution, drug possession and distribution, and petty theft are all crimes in which runaways have regularly been found to be involved. Such criminal behavior is not surprising, given the need to survive on the streets and the lack of other means to do so. Criminal activity is also consistent with the runaway's adopted lifestyle; crime, whether prostitution, theft, or drug sales, is seen as easy work within the abilities of the unskilled runaway that produces immediate cash on the runaway's own terms.

Runaways seek out others like themselves, at least in part to satisfy their need for emotional support. Equally important is the interdependence and mutual support that develops when runaways connect with other runaways. Runaways frequently form street "families" to satisfy the needs that were missing in their own homes. Connecting with others also creates in runaways a sense of security, although the safety it offers is in large part imagined. To find others like themselves, most runaways gravitate toward cities and urban centers. In the runaway's perspective, more opportunity for adventure and living as part of a community exists in these locations. Unfortunately, just as the crime rates of such areas tends to be higher, the likelihood of juvenile involvement in crime increases as well.

Not all runaways turn to city streets, however. A large proportion of runaways stay with friends, acquaintances, or other relatives. Such runaways usually are fleeing instability in the home (such as violence or substance abuse by parents) or a precipitating circumstance (such as an argument with parents). These runaway episodes are usually of short duration, resulting from impulse. Runaways rarely plan their leaving, and they usually give little thought to financial needs or immediate destinations.

CONCLUSION

Many efforts to assist runaways have been and continue to be made. These efforts focus on providing runaways with safe shelter and food. Most interventions involve some attempt to return the juvenile to his or her parents, a family member, or another responsible adult. Most major cities have organizations formed to assist runaways, such as Covenant House founded in New York, which provides a range of services from finding shelter to coordinating with law enforcement and the courts to return of the children to their homes (see Ritter, 1988). Further, the OJJDP coordinates the Missing and Exploited Children's Program, which includes a variety of programs and services to assist missing children and runaways. Perhaps the most important of these is the National Center for Missing and Exploited Children (NCMEC). Among other services, NCMEC provides a toll-free telephone hotline for reporting the location of missing children as well as obtaining assistance for runaways and their parents or guardians.

Even after nearly 200 years, runaways remain a concern in this country. This concern is in sharper focus today than perhaps at any earlier time, and significant efforts are now being made to study the runaway problem. The combination of additional research on the causes of runaway behavior and further support for intervention in the lives of runaways is likely to have a significant impact on the juvenile and criminal justice systems and American society itself.

Jeffrey A. Jenkins

See also Children's Aid Society; Missing Children; Pregnancy, Teenage; Status Offenders

Bibliography

Armstrong, C. 1932. *660 Runaway Boys*. Boston: B. Humphries.

Chapman, C. 1976. *America's Runaways*. New York: William Morrow.

Finkelhor, D., G. T. Hotaling, and A. Sedlak. 1990. *Missing, Abducted, Runaway, and Thrownaway Children in America*. First Report: Numbers and Characteristics, National Incidence Studies. Washington, DC: Office of Juvenile Justice and Delinquency Prevention.

Lipschutz, M. R. 1977. Runaways in history. *Crime and Delinquency* 23:321–332.

Ritter, B. 1988. *Sometimes God Has a Kid's Face: The Story of America's Exploited Street Kids*. New York: Covenant House.

S

SCARED STRAIGHT

Scared Straight is the name of what is arguably the most well known juvenile crime prevention program in the United States. It exploded on the juvenile justice scene in 1976 and spread rapidly throughout departments of correction across the nation. Fueled by media attention and the public's fear of juvenile crime, Scared Straight was regarded as a cure-all for the problem of juvenile crime in this country.

PROGRAM BACKGROUND

To understand Scared Straight as an instrument of crime prevention, one must first understand the philosophy of the program. Central to the philosophy of the Scared Straight program is deterrence theory. Deterrence theorists assume that humans are rational beings. Before taking part in a behavior, humans rationally contemplate the potential costs and benefits of an action. Behaviors that are perceived to have more benefits than costs are accepted, and those perceived to have more costs than benefits are rejected. According to a rational choice perspective, crime occurs when the actor perceives more benefits than costs from breaking the law. Thus juveniles commit criminal and delinquent acts because they perceive such acts to be personally beneficial rather than costly.

Deterrence theorists assert that to prevent criminal behavior, punishment must be used to illustrate the costs of such behaviors. To achieve deterrence, punishment must be certain, swift, and severe. Certainty refers to the likelihood of being apprehended for a criminal or delinquent act. Swiftness is related to the amount of time between the act and the punishment for the act. Severity refers to the harshness of the punishment in relation to the act. It is believed that punishments administered in a certain, swift, and severe manner can achieve specific and general deterrence.

Specific deterrence occurs when juveniles who have been caught and punished for a crime do not take part in future criminal behavior for fear of being punished again. General deterrence occurs when others learn of the punishments offenders have received and do not take part in criminal behavior for fear of similar punishment. According to Finckenauer and Gavin (1999), a third type of deterrence, repressive deterrence, was also used in Scared Straight. Repressive deterrence was the product of the aversive experience of entering prison and being confronted with the harsh realities of prison life.

PROGRAM INGREDIENTS

The design and mission of the program commonly referred to as Scared Straight is most often associated with a group of inmates at Rahway State Prison in New Jersey. The group called themselves the Lifers' Group because all members were serving sentences of 25 years or longer. The group was committed to changing the stereotypical images of inmates portrayed by Hollywood and accepted by the American public (Finckenauer, 1982). To accomplish their goal, group members took part in charitable activities to prove that they were useful and worthwhile people despite their incarceration.

The Scared Straight premise developed within the Juvenile Intervention Committee, a subgroup of the

Lifers' Group. The committee was searching for a way to keep kids out of trouble. One day, while watching a group of college students tour the institution, then president of the Lifers' Group Richard Rowe conceived of the idea of bringing juveniles to the institution to see what prison was really like. With approval from the prison superintendent, the first group of juveniles to take part in the Juvenile Awareness Project (JAP) entered Rahway State Prison in September 1976.

"There was no overt attempt to intimidate or terrorize the youths at first, but this later became a more prominent and dramatic feature of the project" (Finckenauer and Gavin, 1999:21). Initially, the program followed a relatively calm progression. A correctional officer greeted each group of juveniles, briefed them about the program, and processed them through prison security. Once inside the prison, the inmates talked with the youths about prison life. The inmates discussed all the gruesome details and harsh realities of life behind bars, including the assaults, murders, rapes, and suicides that take place in prison. They told the youths about the poor living conditions, rigid schedule, and impersonal atmosphere of prison. The youths were allowed to ask the inmates questions and to take part in an open discussion about prison realities. After the discussion portion of the program, the group was given a tour of the facility, including the solitary confinement unit. The youths were told that even slight infractions within the institution could result in an inmate being placed in solitary confinement (Finckenauer, 1982).

The original design of the program was to use the prison experience as a form of counseling. The inmates approached the groups of young people with a "big brother" attitude. The show-and-tell experience was intended to give the youths a realistic look at prison and where they might end up if they took part in a life of crime. The ultimate goal was to deter the youths from taking part in criminal behavior for fear of being sent to prison. The inmates soon came to believe that their low-key big brother approach was not reaching many of the juveniles and thus adopted a more harsh and shocking style to get the attention of the youths (Finckenauer and Gavin, 1999). The better-known version of the JAP—in your face, intimidating, and marked by harsh language—soon emerged.

It was this version of the JAP that garnered national media attention and was presented to the public in numerous newspaper and magazine articles and an award-winning documentary titled *Scared Straight!*, which publicly proclaimed the effectiveness of the program. In November 1978, *Scared Straight!* was first broadcast in Los Angeles. Reviews of the film were so overwhelming that in March 1979, it was televised from coast to coast. That same year, the film won an Oscar award from the Academy of Motion Picture Arts and Sciences and an Emmy award. Despite the entertainment world's enthusiasm for the documentary and the public's fascination with prison life, the program was not without its critics. Beyond outrage about the harsh language and questionable content of the film, strong criticism of the program's effectiveness surfaced.

PROGRAM EFFECTIVENESS

Questions about the effectiveness of the program could only be answered through program evaluation. The goal of the Juvenile Awareness Project was to deter juveniles from taking part in crime. To evaluate the effectiveness of the program, researchers had to determine who was taking part in the program. Three types of juveniles were taking part in the JAP. First, the "good," were youths who did not have records of criminal involvement. Second, the "bad," were young people who had been found guilty of minor infractions. Third, the "ugly," were youths who had been involved in serious criminal behaviors. The program was intended to have the greatest impact on the "ugly" group, as they were the ones closest to being incarcerated (Vito, Tewksbury, and Wilson, 1998). Interestingly, Finckenauer (1982) determined that 41 percent of the juveniles who visited Rahway had no prior record and thus were members of the "good" category.

James Finckenauer evaluated the effectiveness of Scared Straight and published his findings in a 1982 book titled *Scared Straight! and the Panacea Phenomenon*. He evaluated the program's deterrent effect using a quasi-experimental research design. Through his research, he determined that the program was not serving as a deterrent. In fact, juveniles who took part in the program were more likely to recidivate (41.3 percent) than those who had not gone through the program (11.4 percent). In addition, juveniles with prior criminal records who completed the program had higher recidivism rates than those with prior criminal records who did not go through the program (48.2 percent versus 21.4 percent). New offenses committed by the participants also tended to be more serious compared with the new offenses committed by nonparticipants. Using questionnaires, Finckenauer was able to ask the juveniles questions about their perceptions of punishment severity. He concluded that going through the program did not alter juveniles' perceptions of the severity of punishment. It appeared that the program was somehow having a negative impact on juvenile crime rather than a positive impact on deterrence.

SIMILAR PROGRAMS

One of the first programs in the Scared Straight genre took place 15 years prior to the program at Rahway State Prison. The Michigan Reformatory Visitation Program operated from 1960 to 1967. Although little is known about the scare tactics used in the program, program evaluation results were strikingly similar to those found by Finckenauer in his evaluation of the JAP. The juvenile court records of youths randomly assigned to either experimental or control groups were evaluated six months after visiting the institution. The results of the evaluation concluded that 43 percent of the individuals who participated in the program had a court petition or probation violation within six months after taking part in the program. Only 17 percent of the control group, individuals who did not take part in the program, recidivated within six months (Michigan Department of Corrections, 1967).

A second attempt by the Michigan Department of Corrections to scare juveniles straight was entitled Juvenile Offenders Learn Truth (JOLT). One unique feature of this program was that youths were accompanied to the program by their parents or guardians. The adults and children were separated after touring the facility, and the juveniles took part in an intensive confrontation session. Though the program evaluation results of JOLT were no more encouraging than the Rahway results, recidivism rates for experimental and control groups were more similar in this program. Six months after taking part in the program, 30.8 percent of participants and 28.9 percent of nonparticipants had recidivated (Homant and Osowski, 1981). A similar program in Virginia, the Insiders Juvenile Crime Prevention Program, also yielded high recidivism rates and no difference between program participants and nonparticipants (Lundman, 1993).

Researchers have concluded that intensive confrontation programs that rely on scare tactics to deter juvenile crime are not effective at deterring juveniles from committing crime. As one group of researchers stated, "the programs are little more than a field trip of horrors" (Vito et al., 1998:155). Recent programs have attempted to distance themselves from the Scared Straight stigma by stressing the use of education and communication rather than scare tactics. The San Quentin Utilization of Inmates Resources, Experience and Studies (SQUIRES) Program was started in 1963 and once sought recognition as the basis for Rahway's program. Today the group is quick to distance itself from Scared Straight by touting itself as a counseling program, not a scare program. The inmates discuss a variety of topics such as drug use, AIDS education, and family relations rather than simply intimidating the youths (Finckenauer and Gavin, 1999). Additional Scared Straight spin-off programs that do not rely on scare tactics include the See Our Side Program, Stay Straight, SHAPE-UP, Project Aware, and the Massachusetts Prevention Program. However, the results of these new, less abrasive programs are the same as the hard-hitting Scared Straight confrontations of the past. Little evidence exists that supports the notion that these programs effectively achieve deterrence.

Researchers have found some secondary benefits of involvement in juvenile crime prevention programs. Inmates involved in such programs have been found to adopt new positive self-images after taking part in the programs. Keller (1993) concluded that the inmates' new role as counselors overshadowed their negative status as inmates. After evaluating the JOLT program, Homant and Osowski (1981) concluded the program had positive impacts on the inmate counselors and included this as one of the rationales for continuing the program, despite its lack of effectiveness as a deterrent.

Despite the lack of evidence that programs like Scared Straight achieve deterrence, they continue. Perhaps it is the idea of a panacea or cure-all for the juvenile crime problem that fuels such programs. Perhaps it is the fact that the basic premise of the program seems so logical that some find it hard to believe that an experience of this nature wouldn't keep kids out of trouble. Or maybe the secondary benefits of these programs are important enough to maintain their place in the crime prevention repertoire.

Amie R. Scheidegger

See also Boot Camps; Mentoring Programs; Wilderness Programs

Bibliography

Finckenauer, J. O. 1982. *Scared Straight! and the Panacea Phenomenon*. Englewood Cliffs, NJ: Prentice Hall.

Finckenauer, J. O., and P. W. Gavin. 1999. *Scared Straight!—The Panacea Phenomenon Revisited*. Prospect Heights, IL: Waveland.

Homant, R. J., and G. Osowski. 1981. Evaluation of the "Scared Straight" model: Some methodological and political considerations. *Corrective and Social Psychiatry and Journal of Behavior Technology Methods and Therapy* 27(3):130–134.

Keller, R. L. 1993. Some unanticipated positive effects of a juvenile awareness program on adult inmate counselors. *International Journal of Offender Therapy and Comparative Criminology* 37(1):75–83.

Lewis, R. V. 1983. Scared straight—California style: Evaluation of the San Quentin Squires program. *Criminal Justice and Behavior* 10(2):209–226.

Lundman, R. 1993. Scared straight. Pp. 168–181 in R. J. Berger (ed.), *The Sociology of Juvenile Delinquency*, 2nd ed. Chicago: Nelson-Hall.

Michigan Department of Corrections. 1967. A six month follow-up of juvenile delinquents visiting the Ionia Reformatory. Pp. 59–61 in J. O. Finckenauer (ed.), *Scared Straight and the Panacea Phenomenon*. Englewood Cliffs, NJ: Prentice Hall.

Vito, G. F., R. Tewksbury, and D. G. Wilson. 1998. *The Juvenile Justice System: Concepts and Issues*. Prospect Heights, IL: Waveland.

SCHOOL VIOLENCE

 I. Offenses and Incidence

Following on the heels of a frantic attempt to stem the tide of gangs and drugs in school, the high-profile and tragic school shootings since the early 1990s have sent shock waves through school administrations. The U.S. Department of Education, Department of Justice, and a host of education, criminal justice, and policy organizations have scrambled to provide information concerning school violence and possible ways of controlling that violence.

In this time of unprecedented cooperation, those in criminal justice and criminology have been called on to share information concerning juvenile crime that could be used in controlling school violence. This entry presents an overview of information concerning the incidence and characteristics of school violence and some of what is known about possible reasons for the violence.

SCHOOL VIOLENCE

It is difficult to determine exactly how much crime and violence occurs within American schools because schools are not required to report such incidents to any national reporting system (Arnette and Walsleben, 1998). This trend is changing as a result of the need for information on school violence following the school shootings since the early 1990s. For now, however, most of what is known about school violence is obtained from rather small samples of research in particular schools or from official reports to the police (only if an event rises to the level of needing police intervention). Because of the small samples and other methodological problems, most of what is known about school violence comes in the aftermath of a school shooting or other violent encounter.

Although the violent episodes of the previous few years have brought school violence and weapons use to the forefront of American concern, it should be noted that schools are, and always have been, relatively safe places for children. During the 1996-97 school year, 10 percent of schools reported one or more serious violent crimes (murder, sexual assault, suicide, aggravated assault, or robbery) to police. However, 43 percent of schools did not report any serious crimes of any type (Riley and McDaniel, 1999). Of all crimes reported to the police in 1997, according to the Department of Justice (1998), the most frequent type was a physical attack or fight without a weapon.

The drop in the number of violent incidents reported to the police coincided with a decline in the number of victimizations. Victimizations of juveniles aged 12 to 18 dropped slightly from 1992 to 1996, from about 164 incidents per 1,000 students to about 128; and the decline was similar for serious violent crimes during this same time (Department of Justice, 1998). Furthermore, more students aged 12 to 18 were victims of nonfatal, serious, violent crimes away from school than at school. However, 37 percent of all violent crimes experienced by juveniles aged 12 to 15 occurred on school grounds (Whitaker and Bastian, 1993). Snyder and Sickmund (1995) noted that this school-based concentration of juveniles has no counterpart among adults. This underscores the seriousness of even small amounts of serious violence at schools.

The most serious form of violence, homicide, shows similar patterns to nonfatal violence. Less than 1 percent of all homicides involving school-age children occur at school. Furthermore, 90 percent of all children under 12 who are victims of homicide are killed by adults, not other children, and 75 percent of children aged 12 to 17 are killed by adults. Most of these are the victims of family violence (Department of Justice, 1998).

Though the 1997-98 school year (the year of shootings in Pearl, Mississippi; Paducah, Kentucky; and Jonesboro, Arkansas) seemed to be a horrendous aberration of school violence and death, it was actually not completely out of the ordinary. Since 1992, the annual death toll from school shootings ranged from 21 (1994-95) to 54 (1992-93). There were 44 students killed in 1997-98. The devastating part, though, was that the number of multiple homicide events at schools rose from two in the 1992-93 school year to eight in 1997-98 (the 1994-95 school year had no multiple homicide incidents). That aberration has not repeated itself since the 1997-98 school year, even taking the Columbine shooting into account, and even though there continue to be multiple homicide events each school year.

The drop in violence and victimization (with the exception of the number of multiple homicide incidents) seemed to relate to an overall lower number of schoolchildren carrying weapons, especially guns, to school. Contrary to public opinion, there was a decline (from almost 12 percent to 8.5 percent) in the number of students in Grades 9 to 12 who reported carrying a weapon to school between 1992 and 1995 (Department of Justice, 1998). The rate at which high school seniors reported carrying guns remained fairly constant, however, at about 3 percent. Weapon possession at school is still a serious issue, however. During the 1996-97 school year, more than 6,000 students were expelled for bringing firearms to school.

Possibly related to the exposure by the media of high-profile shootings, a large number of students reported being fearful at school and while going to and returning from school. In 1995, approximately 9 percent of students aged 12 to 19 reported fearing being harmed at school. This was up from 6 percent in 1989 (Kaufman et al., 1998). In another study, 29 percent of elementary, 34 percent of middle, and 20 percent of high school students reported being worried

about violence or victimization at school (Nolin and Davies, 1995). This number certainly rose after the violence in 1997 and presents a potential for disaster, as fearful students may begin to carry weapons for self-protection.

It is also interesting to note that most of the juvenile crime reported under the FBI's National Incident Based Reporting System (NIBRS) occurs immediately following school (Office of Juvenile Justice and Delinquency Prevention, 1999). According to these data, almost 10 percent of all serious violent crime, and particularly aggravated assault, occurs at approximately 3:00 p.m. This peak in violence is particularly pronounced on school days, with serious violent crime on nonschool days being much more evenly spread and peaking at about 8:30 p.m. While these data show that most juvenile violence occurs after school hours, it does not diminish the seriousness for schools, because the violence occurs immediately after school and may be located at or near school.

SCHOOL HOMICIDES

Only a few years ago, any discussion such as this would have immediately begun to detail some of the high-profile shootings that occurred in schools. Although this entry does some of that, it is no longer possible to draw attention to each case in which multiple assailants, multiple weapons, and multiple victims are involved. The number of school-related deaths has risen to the point where each event cannot be chronicled and incidents must be stated in terms of numbers and statistics.

The recent focus on school violence and school shootings took a rather strange path to the public spotlight. It can be argued that the public and media attention on school shootings began when a 14-year-old boy in Paducah, Kentucky, shot and killed three students and wounded five others as they participated in a prayer circle at the high school. That was in December 1997. That same month in Stamps, Arkansas, a 14-year-old boy wounded two students in a school parking lot while he hid in the woods. The media then began exploring the phenomenon of school shootings and quickly focused on a story that had gained only minimal attention previously. A 16-year-old boy, a few hours after slitting his mother's throat, killed two students and wounded seven others in Pearl, Mississippi, in October 1997. He was reportedly a part of an outcast group who worshipped Satan.

According to a report from the National School Safety Center (NSSC; 2001), however, these shootings were neither the first nor the worst school shootings. The NSSC prepares a report, available on the Web, that tracks all known school-related deaths, beginning in September 1992 and continually updated as new school violence arises. According to this report, there were 52 violent incidents at school during the 1992-93 school year. As previously stated, 2 of those incidents involved multiple assailants and multiple victims (a total of 4 deaths for that school year). This report found a similar trend in school-related deaths the following school year, with 52 violent incidents again that year. There was one fewer incident with multiple assailants, but there was one incident where a lone assailant committed multiple homicides, for a total of 6 deaths. Interestingly, there were only 22 violent incidents reported by the NSSC in the 1994-95 school year and no multiple-assailant or multiple-victim incidents. The following year, there were 31 violent incidents, but the number of multiple-assailant incidents rose to 5 and the number of multiple-victim incidents rose to 6, resulting in 13 deaths. In the 1996-97 school year, there were actually fewer violent incidents than the year before (23) and only 2 multiple assailant incidents, resulting in 4 deaths. That would be the last year for a generally low level of violent deaths at school, however.

In 1997, the year that public attention began to focus on school violence because of the shootings in Paducah, Kentucky, the pattern of school-related homicides began to change. Although there were fewer incidents (33 violent incidents compared with 52 in the 1992-93 and 1993-94 school years), the multiple-assailant incidents (8) and multiple victims (22) climbed dramatically, as did the number of incidents where multiple weapons were used. The incident drawing the most public attention, and the one that seemed to set the stage for what was to come, occurred on March 24, 1998, when two students in Jonesboro, Arkansas, pulled a fire alarm at the Westside Middle School. As the students and teachers filed out of the school, the boys, aged 11 and 13, began shooting with the seven guns they brought for their task. Four students and a teacher were killed in that shooting, and 15 others were wounded.

A year later, the worst act of school violence to date occurred at Columbine High School in Littleton, Colorado. There, two boys, aged 17 and 18, put in motion a plot to kill "at least 500" students and blow up their high school. Although their plan would not be completely carried out, they did kill 12 students and a teacher and wounded 23 others before turning their guns on themselves. These boys were a part of the now infamous Trenchcoat Mafia and were reportedly often taunted by other students. In total in 1998-99, there were 14 incidents of school violence and 3 incidents involving multiple assailants and multiple victims (resulting in 19 deaths). This would have been good news for school violence had it not been for the Columbine shooting.

The shock of the Columbine shooting put students, school administrators, and the criminal justice system on high alert for school violence. Many schools that were not already using magnetometers and random searches for weapons began to do so. Some schools also began a zero-tolerance policy for violence, which often got students expelled from school or even jailed for making any threats of violence. These tactics seemed to work. In the 1999–2000 school year, only 15 incidents of school violence were reported by the NSSC; and only one of the incidents involved multiple victims (a total of three victims in which two died), and no incidents involved multiple assailants. There is no reason to believe that these tactics will completely control school violence, however. Although at the time of this writing there have been only 6 school-related death incidents in the 2000-01 school year, 2 serious incidents in suburban San Diego, California, serve as a grim reminder that school-aged children are still willing and capable of bringing multiple weapons to school and using them.

RESEARCH ON GUNS IN SCHOOL

Each school shooting described in this entry was different, but in many respects they were very similar. Although some of the persons perpetrating violence were outcasts, others were active members of school organizations and groups. While some of the shooters had previous disciplinary and legal problems, others were considered good students and had not demonstrated violent tendencies. What these students had in common, however, was that they saw violence and killing as a viable resolution to their interpersonal problems and likely their internal frustrations.

Research estimates that between 0.5 percent (Chandler, Chapman, Rand, and Taylor, 1998) and 9 percent (Sheley and Wright, 1993) of students may be carrying a weapon at any given time. This is not a small number of problem kids either. More frequently, juveniles who have never been convicted of a crime and who are generally thought of as good students are carrying guns and may be prone to violence. There are a variety of reasons for this. One of the significant reasons is that with so many juveniles carrying guns and using them to solve personal problems, a substantial number of juveniles are carrying guns for self-protection (see Arnette and Walsleben, 1998; Nolin and Davies, 1995).

Another possible reason for school violence may follow the lines of Travis Hirschi's (1969) theory involving social bonds. The importance of social bonds in school violence is shown in the research by May (1999). In this research on schoolchildren in Mississippi, May found that those who scored lower on a social bond scale were much more likely to carry weapons to school. When bonds are broken, juveniles are free to commit a variety of nonnormative acts. When students have not found a place or group at school where they feel they belong, the bond to conventional activities may break down, and the juveniles may fall into a fringe group where nonnormative behavior is more likely. This breakdown in bonds may also result in the person feeling that he or she is an outcast. The result can be an attack on the source of frustration, including school violence.

Arnette and Walsleben (1998:7) report that "carrying weapons to school has become an acceptable risk for many students, both those who are fearful and those who intend to exploit others." Irrespective of the reason, if juveniles are carrying weapons, and given their heightened sensitivity to interpersonal issues, it is likely that some will turn to violence as a means of solving interpersonal conflicts. This seems to be the case in several of the high-profile shootings of the previous few years.

Solutions offered for school violence often work to exacerbate this problem. For example, one of the "characteristics of a school that is safe and responsive to all children," as put forth by Dwyer, Osher, and Warger (1998:3) in their guide to safe schools, is to "focus on academic achievement." Even though it is certainly a priority of schools to focus on academics, an overemphasis can create frustration in those juveniles who have trouble in this area, and it can result in juveniles becoming a part of a nonnormative group. As Albert Cohen (1955) argued, using academic standards to evaluate all students may often lead to frustration that can ultimately result in subculture (gang) formation and criminal behavior.

CONCLUSION

Although school violence overall was down by the final years of the 1990s, several high-profile shootings and other dramatic incidents of school violence brought this form of behavior to the forefront of public and student attention. Although the serious rise of school violence in the United State that the public perceives has not occurred, the number of multiple-homicide incidents at schools causes serious concern for parents and institutions alike. It is now incumbent on all who have some knowledge or responsibility for schoolchildren to redouble their efforts at finding ways to reduce this kind of crime. This includes criminologists who seek the reasons why juveniles are turning to this kind of violence, school administrators tasked with the day-to-day control of the children, mental heath professionals who must deal with the range of emotional issues exhibited by these children, and members of the criminal justice system who must determine how to handle offenders who do not fit into the juvenile or adult systems of justice.

Jeffery T. Walker

See also At-Risk Youth; Theories of Delinquency

Bibliography

Arnette, J. L., and M. C. Walsleben. 1998. *Combating Fear and Restoring Safety in Schools.* Washington, DC: Office of Juvenile Justice and Delinquency Prevention.

Chandler, K. A., C. D. Chapman, M. R. Rand, and B. M. Taylor. 1998. *Students' Reports of School Crime: 1989 and 1995.* Washington, DC: Department of Education.

Cohen, A. K. 1955. *Delinquent Boys: The Culture of the Gang.* New York: Free Press.

Department of Justice. 1998. *Annual Report on School Safety.* Washington, DC: Departments of Education and Justice.

Dwyer, K., D. Osher, and C. Warger. 1998. *Early Warning, Timely Response: A Guide to Safe Schools.* Washington, DC: Department of Education.

Hirschi, T. 1969. *Causes of Delinquency.* Berkeley: University of California Press.

Kaufman, P., X. Chen, S. P. Choy, K. A. Chandler, C. D. Chapman, M. R. Rand, and C. Ringel. 1998. *Indicators of School Crime and Safety, 1998.* Washington, DC: Departments of Education and Justice.

May, D. C. 1999. Scared kids, unattached kids, or peer pressure: Why do students carry firearms to school? *Youth and Society* 31(1):100–127.

National School Safety Center (NSSC). 2001. *School Associated Violent Deaths*. Available at http://www.nssc1.org/savd/savd.pdf.

Nolin, M. J., and E. Davies. 1995. *Student Victimization at School*. Washington, DC: National Center for Educational Statistics.

Office of Juvenile Justice and Delinquency Prevention. 1999. *Violence After School*. Washington, DC: Office of Juvenile Justice and Delinquency Prevention.

Riley, P., and J. McDaniel. 1999. *Youth Out of the Education Mainstream: A North Carolina Profile*. Washington, DC: Office of Juvenile Justice and Delinquency Prevention.

Sheley, J. F., and J. D. Wright. 1993. *Gun Acquisition and Possession in Selected Juvenile Samples*. Washington, DC: National Institute of Justice.

Snyder, H. N., and M. Sickmund. 1995. *Juvenile Offenders and Victims: A Focus on Violence*. Washington, DC: Office of Juvenile Justice and Delinquency Prevention.

Whitaker, C. J., and L. D. Bastian. 1993. *Teenage Victims: A National Crime Survey Report*. Washington, DC: Government Printing Office.

SCHOOL VIOLENCE

 ## II. School Responses

Crime and violence in schools is a problem that has received considerable attention. Although students are generally safer at school than elsewhere in their neighborhoods, they are subjected to bullying and threats at school that create a fearful climate and disrupt the learning process. Student surveys indicate that most youth in junior and senior high schools are affected in some way by bullying, as participants, witnesses, or victims. Bullying has come to be viewed as a serious problem in schools because of the fear and disruption it causes, and because victims of bullying occasionally bring weapons to school for self-defense and may retaliate with deadly consequences. School shooting incidents have received extensive news media coverage, and concerned parents and citizens have demanded that police, school administrators, and juvenile justice officials implement policies to ensure that students are safe in school. This entry summarizes the responses taken by school and justice officials to reduce school crime.

SCHOOL CRIME PREVENTION

The first step officials must take in responding to school crime is a careful assessment of the frequency and seriousness of bullying, threats, assaults, and other crimes at school. Two primary sources provide this information: official reports and surveys. School records and police reports are helpful sources but are limited to incidents reported by students and teachers. Many students are reluctant to report victimization incidents, and teachers and principals often only report the more serious incidents in which disciplinary actions are taken. Self-administered surveys of students and teachers provide a more complete assessment of both reported and unreported incidents of bullying, assaults, and fights. These confidential surveys may be administered to a sample of students and teachers. As with any social scientific research, caution must be used in reporting survey findings. Accurate results depend on sample selection and size, response rate, and the extent to which the sample represents the school population. Victimization surveys are invaluable tools for assessing the nature and seriousness of crime problems and are essential sources of information for developing school crime prevention strategies. A thorough review of the school reports, police reports, and survey results should indicate the extent and seriousness of school crime, who the victims and offenders are, and the times and places where incidents occur in and around schools.

The second step in responding to school crime is a physical security assessment of school buildings and grounds, using information regarding assault, theft, and vandalism incidents. A physical security assessment should include the number and location of entrances and exits, lighting around the buildings and parking lots, and inventory control of all school supplies and equipment. School administrators must determine if law enforcement or security personnel should be hired to patrol school buildings and grounds and, if so, how they are to be selected. School staff and law enforcement or security officers should communicate regularly and work together closely to identify security needs. Administrators and school staff must work together to identify safety and discipline concerns and then implement policies and strategies to address those concerns. Resources and training opportunities should be made available for school staff to improve their skills in discipline, classroom management, and conflict mediation. Developing consistent expectations for student behaviors and establishing clear policies for misbehavior will help improve the school climate. School staff, students, and parents must see that policies are fair, equitable, and consistently applied and that administrators are serious about maintaining a safe and orderly school environment.

SCHOOLS AND JUVENILE JUSTICE

Juvenile justice professionals play a special role not only in preventing school crime but also in working with youthful offenders who are students. Police officers have worked closely with schools in the Drug Abuse Resistance Education (DARE) programs for years, and many schools now have school resource officers. Juvenile courts have long recognized the importance of regular school attendance and successful school performance in making satisfactory adjustment on probation supervision. Juvenile probation officers often work closely with school staff as they supervise and monitor their probation clients.

Police and Schools

Police have always been available to assist schools, both through regular patrol activities and through calls to respond to specific crime incidents. Police presence in many schools has been increased through DARE programs, although that is generally limited to fifth- and sixth-grade students and is primarily an educational role. Research on DARE programs shows mixed results in terms of long-term drug and delinquency prevention, but the programs are widely supported by educators and police departments. Many schools and police departments have worked together to expand the role of police by placing police-school liaison officers or school resource officers in schools. The responsibilities of these officers include an educational role but focus equally on security and law enforcement functions throughout school buildings and school grounds (Lawrence, 1998:174–175).

Juvenile Courts and Schools

These two institutions both work for the best interests of children. The courts enforce truancy laws and adjudicate youth charged with more serious offenses. School officials are often called on to testify in court offering information on school attendance and behavior of juveniles being sentenced. Judges recognize the importance of education in the rehabilitation process and consistently order juveniles on probation to attend school regularly and obey school rules. De-

spite what seems to be a close and cooperative working relationship, however, the courts and schools until recently, had been reluctant to disclose information in records that are considered confidential. Teachers and juvenile court officers faced a real dilemma. Out of concern for their safety, teachers wanted to know about the delinquency records of students. However, juvenile statutes generally forbade courts to disclose such information in the interest of maintaining privacy and confidentiality of juvenile offenders. In writing court reports and recommendations to the judge regarding youthful offenders, probation officers were expected to include youths' school attendance, behavior, and achievement. But school officials refused to share those confidential records without a court order and/or parents' permission. Both institutions believed they were working "in the best interests" of the child, but their privacy policies ultimately got in the way.

This dilemma was resolved by the federal Family Educational Rights and Privacy Act (FERPA). The original 1974 act was amended in 1994 under the Improving America's Schools Act to promote active information sharing by educators and juvenile justice personnel. The Act allows educators to share information with juvenile justice agencies with parents' consent. Educators may share information *without* parental consent under any or all of the following conditions:

1. A court orders it.

2. The school is taking legal action against a student.

3. The information is needed by a juvenile justice agency providing services to a student, prior to adjudication, under state law.

4. It is a law enforcement record created and maintained by a school resource officer.

5. The disclosure is in connection with an emergency and is necessary to protect the health or safety of the student or other persons.

6. It is part of the school district's "directory information" (Medaris, Campbell, and James, 1997).

Law enforcement officials are also authorized to notify educators when students are arrested for truancy and other crimes relating to school status. Probation officials are encouraged to inform school officials about the court status and disposition of students. FERPA has taken a positive step in promoting efforts to share information and resources for working with youthful offenders.

Probation Officers and Schools

As representatives of the juvenile court, probation officers have faced most of the same limitations to working closely with schools as previously discussed. With increased sharing of information and records and the recognition that it is mutually beneficial to work together, probation agencies and schools are now establishing formal working relationships and shared activities. Many county juvenile probation agencies and school districts have established formal working arrangements and agreements. Many schools provide an office for probation officers to share on a part-time basis, often with the school counselor or school resource officer. Pennsylvania developed a school-based probation program to work with youthful offenders in schools. The school-based probation officer (1) monitors probation clients' attendance and behavior; (2) assists school officials in imposing sanctions for school violations; (3) develops alternatives to suspension; (4) offers tutoring and organizes study and homework groups for clients; (5) encourages students' participation in after-school activities; (6) conducts conflict resolution and mediation skills classes for all students; (7) visits classes and provides information on juvenile law and the justice process; (8) attends reentry conferences with school officials and parents to review probationers' cases; (9) makes home visits and encourages parental support; and (10) monitors required community service for probationers suspended from school (DeAngelo, 1999; Metzger and Tobin-Fiore, 1997). The Pennsylvania program has been well received and supported by schools and probation agencies.

Corrections, Offender Reintegration, and Schools

Perhaps one of the greatest challenges for schools is working with youthful offenders who are returning to the community after spending time in a correctional facility. Because these youth may have a history of violence or frequent juvenile offenses, school personnel tend to express concerns for the safety of teachers and other students. Their concern is understandable,

but in reality, the number of juvenile offenders returning from correctional facilities to public schools is relatively small, and they are generally under more intense parole or aftercare supervision than students on probation supervision. Research has shown that one of the most important factors in preventing youthful offenders from recommitting crimes after their release is successful reintegration into the community through education, job training, and employment. The "balanced approach" to juvenile corrections emphasizes juvenile accountability, competency, and community protection (Bazemore and Day, 1996). Schools play a vital role in reintegration of youthful offenders and in development of competency through promoting education and skills needed for employment (Altschuler and Armstrong, 1996). When equal emphasis is placed on community protection and juvenile accountability, youthful offenders are required to comply with the conditions of release while being closely monitored and supervised. Juvenile offenders who are under correctional supervision with the threat of severe sanctions for violating conditions of their release generally pose less of a threat to school safety than do other students.

SCHOOL-BASED DELINQUENCY PREVENTION PROGRAMS

Schools are valuable resources for delinquency prevention. They provide access to virtually all students throughout their developmental years and can help to counter the adverse influences to which young people are exposed in the community. School staff are well equipped to help students develop prosocial values and positive thinking and communication skills. Research supports the importance of education and school involvement in helping youth avoid delinquent behavior. Numerous programs directed at reducing school crime have been implemented in schools. Programs that have shown positive results are those aimed at clarifying acceptable behavioral norms, establishing and consistently enforcing school rules, and initiating schoolwide campaigns to reduce bullying and drugs in schools. The most effective school programs are comprehensive instructional programs that focus on social competency skills (self-control, responsible decision making, problem solving, and communication) and that are delivered over a period of time to continually reinforce those skills (Gottfredson, 1997:5–55).

CONCLUSION

Maintaining safe and drug-free schools requires regular reassessment and evaluation of policies and strategies. Administrators, security, and law enforcement personnel should monitor and record all school crime incidents and share that information. A reluctance to share information has allowed some high-risk, angry youth to carry out school violence that might have been prevented. The highly publicized school shooting incidents have served as a wake-up call, resulting in greater sharing of information among school staff, students, law enforcement, and the community. Although the public's tendency to blame schools for violent incidents remains, most recognize that it is a community problem that cannot be solved without the collaborative efforts of students, parents, school staff, security, and law enforcement officials.

Richard Lawrence

See also DARE; Self-Report Studies

Bibliography

Altschuler, D. M., and T. L. Armstrong. 1996. Aftercare not afterthought: Testing the IAP model. *Juvenile Justice* 3(1):15–22.

Bazemore, G. and S. E. Day. 1996. Restoring the balance: Juvenile justice and community justice. *Juvenile Justice* 3(1):3–14.

DeAngelo, A. J. 1999. School-based probation: The successful partnership between education and juvenile probation. *APPA Perspectives* 24(Winter):24–27.

Gottfredson, D. C. 1997. School-based crime prevention. Pp. 5-1–5-74 in L. Sherman, D. Gottfredson, D. MacKenzie, J. Eck, P. Reuter, and S. Bushway (eds.), *Preventing Crime: What Works, What Doesn't, What's Promising.* Washington, DC: Department of Justice.

Lawrence, R. 1998. *School Crime and Juvenile Justice.* New York: Oxford University Press.

Medaris, M. L., E. Campbell, and B. James. 1997. *Sharing Information: A Guide to the Family Educational Rights and Privacy Act.* Washington, DC: Departments of Education and Justice.

Metzger, D. S., and D. Tobin-Fiore. 1997. *School-Based Probation in Pennsylvania—Final Report.* Philadelphia: University of Pennsylvania.

 ## SELF-REPORT STUDIES

Self-report surveys are data-gathering procedures that involve asking subjects to recall or admit to various types of behavior. As an attempt to overcome some of the shortcomings of reliance on official statistics, researchers have developed studies in which the respondents are asked to admit to various delinquent or criminal acts. Most studies have been conducted in the United States, primarily in delinquency studies of schoolchildren and high school and college students.

HISTORY AND FINDINGS

In 1947, a sample of adults was mailed a self-report survey, and 99 percent of the respondents admitted to having committed at least one offense. In another such study, admitted delinquency among Texas college students was found to be as high as officially processed delinquents. However, it was a 1957 study of Nashville students by James F. Short Jr. and F. Ivan Nye that set the tone for most of the self-report studies to come. These students committed more crimes than were reported to the police, and most students reported having committed crimes. Such results were taken as an indication of a higher rate of deviance and crime among a general population of "noncriminals." Further, the picture painted by official statistics (the *Uniform Crime Reports,* or UCR, primarily), which suggested that lower-class juveniles were far more delinquent than juveniles from other, higher classes, was shown to be false. While lower-class youth committed slightly more serious, and more frequent, delinquencies, middle- and upper-class youth also reported a substantial amount of delinquent acts. The only official-statistic picture that remained the same was the gender difference, with males reporting about nine offenses for every one committed by females.

Some methods that have been employed in self-report surveys have included totally anonymous questionnaires, confidential questionnaires in which the respondent is identifiable and can be later checked by interviews and police records, and signed questionnaires that can be validated against official records. Other variations include anonymous questionnaires with an identifying number that can be later validated by follow-up interviews and threat of polygraph (lie detector test), interviews, and interviews that can be checked against official records. In all of these approaches, "what people claim" is checked against independent criteria or "what people do."

MODERN SELF-REPORT SURVEYS

Self-report surveys have been used in a variety of settings and populations. Inmate reports of past conduct have been used to construct parole prediction (risk) scales. Such crime admissions by inmates have been found to complement official data. Surveys of youth drug use have commonly used self-report data. The best known of these is the National Youth Survey. This survey examines 11- to 17-year-olds and features a national probability sample and a multicohort design. The National Youth Survey was found to yield valid (accurate) and reliable (consistent) results and indicated delinquency/crime levels higher than the National Criminal Victimization Survey or the UCR.

A particularly innovative example of the use of self-report data was the Drug Use Forecasting Program, which is now called Arrestee Drug Abuse Monitoring (ADAM). In this annual program sponsored by the National Institute of Justice (NIJ), volunteer arrestees in various cities are asked details about their current and past drug usage at the time of their arrest. Such subjects are guaranteed anonymity and assured that none of the information that is provided will be used against them. Obviously, arrestees would not normally be viewed as the most honest in answering such questions. The program asked those surveyed to provide urine specimens to be tested for drugs. Begun in 1987 with 23 cities, plans are to expand the program to 75 cities. Also in 1998, the NIJ launched International ADAM, involving a partnership with criminal justice agencies in many countries and providing a framework for the global assessment of drug use and for strengthening drug control policies and their coordination. In 2000, the NIJ began plans for publishing an annual report based on ADAM that includes trends in drug use, gun markets, gang migration, the suburbanization of crime, and drug treatment availability.

CRITICISMS OF SELF-REPORT SURVEYS

Critics of quantitative research have pointed out that often there is little relationship between attitude or claimed behavior and actual behavior. A classic 1934 study in this regard was Richard La Pierre's "Restaurant Study." La Pierre traveled with a Chinese couple to a large number of restaurants on the West Coast and recorded the treatment they received. While only one of 251 establishments had refused service, a

subsequent self-report survey found 90 percent of the establishments indicated they would refuse service to a Chinese couple. This disparity between "words" (what people say they have done, or would do) and "deeds" (what people actually do) illustrates the hazards of attitudinal measurement of behavior.

Other studies have shown people to be inaccurate in recalling or reporting voting behavior, time of vaccination of children, money in savings accounts, level of loan debt, sexual activity, class attendance, school grades, and even crime victimization that they had already reported to the police. This raises the issue that, if individuals are incorrect in recalling less sensitive past behavior, higher accuracy in recalling past deviant and criminal behavior may be equally suspect.

Many criticisms of self-report surveys have been concerned with issues such as inaccurate reporting, the use of poorly designed or inconsistent instruments, poor research designs, and poor choice of subjects or settings. Europeans have been critical of U.S. self-report surveys of delinquency because they charge that such studies overestimate delinquency by including behavior that would not have been considered criminal had an adult committed it. Some additional problems that have been pointed out include the use of small or unrepresentative samples, lying, poor memory, and "telescoping." The latter refers to the tendency to move past incidents inappropriately into the period of study. Self-report studies have also been attacked for a lack of replication (repeating the studies) as well as featuring "one-shot case studies" and for not using similar questions.

STRENGTHS OF SELF-REPORT SURVEYS

Despite these criticisms, an impressive literature exists that argues for the strengths of self-report surveys. The validity (accuracy) of self-report studies can be strengthened by using other data as validity checks, using other observers for verification, using or threatening to use a polygraph, using a "known group" approach, using "lie scales" or "truth scales," using measures of internal consistency, and rechecking reports with follow-up interviews. Self-reports can be checked against other criteria such as police records, school records, or as in the case of ADAM, urinalysis. A murder suspect's plea of innocence can now be checked against DNA evidence. Results have been mixed regarding self-reports that have been checked against official records. Another way of verifying self-reports is to use other informants, peers, or people who can speak knowingly of the subject's behavior. The use or threat of the polygraph has been used, as well as a procedure called "known group validation." The latter involves studying groups whose behavior is already a matter of public record (reverse record checks) and comparing self-admissions with what is already known. Many transgressions may, of course, lack official records.

Another means of validating self-reports involves using "lie scales" or "truth scales." These are a series of interconnected questions that assess truthfulness by asking a respondent to admit to behavior that it is assumed no one person could have performed or crossing up the subject by eliciting inconsistencies in his or her responses. These types of questions are quite commonly used in personality inventories to check on those who appear to be lying. Interlocking items may also be used to denote internal consistency in response. Questions may be posed in pairs, such as first asking if the respondent agrees with "I always tell the truth" and later asking "I never tell a lie." Inconsistencies in the responses to such questions are taken as an indication of the lack of truthfulness in response. The use of reversal questions, stating some questions in a positive manner and some in a negative manner, is another means of ensuring the accuracy of response. Reinterviews of the same subjects operate as another validity check.

CONCLUSION

While some question the validity of self-report surveys, various checks have been discussed to address these objections. For the past 40 years, the methodology has provided the majority of information on delinquency. Theories of delinquency and governmental delinquency prevention programs have been built around self-report data.

Although self-report surveys are not without their shortcomings, they provide another important measure of delinquency that overcomes the reliance on official statistics and victim surveys. It has even been suggested that the National Institute of Justice should begin an annual self-report survey.

Frank E. Hagan

See also James Franklin Short Jr.; Theories of
Delinquency—Sociological

Bibliography

Nye, F. I., and J. F. Short Jr. 1957. Scaling delinquent behavior. *American Sociological Review* 22:326–331.

Nye, F. I., J. F. Short Jr., and V. Olson. 1958. Socioeconomic status and delinquent behavior. *American Journal of Sociology* 63:381–389.

SELLIN, JOHAN THORSTEN (1896–1994)

Johan Thorsten Sellin was born in Sweden in 1896 and moved with his family to Canada at the age of 17. He moved to the United States shortly after that and completed his undergraduate education in Rock Island, Illinois, at the Swedish-American Augustana College. In 1922, Sellin completed his doctoral work in sociology at the University of Pennsylvania. He then joined the faculty at Penn and continued to teach there for nearly five decades, becoming Professor Emeritus in 1967. From this academic home, Sellin produced more than 200 publications, the thrust of which were to assist in the development of criminology as a science. In the words of his student and later colleague, Marvin Wolfgang (1968:viii), "The meaning of criminology as an area of disciplined attention, training, and knowledge is a topic to which Sellin addressed himself in major ways throughout his writings."

THE CONTRIBUTIONS OF SELLIN

Among the many published works of Sellin are books, articles, reports, and essays that address theory and measurement, criminal statistics, penology and the death penalty, and crime on an international level. He was particularly interested in the history of prisons and argued that they arose as mercantilism changed the nature of labor relations in general and, more specifically, with the dislocation of workers (Sellin, 1944). Individuals who turned to "begging, wandering, idleness, and petty thievery," according to Sellin, soon found themselves placed in "workhouses" and forced to produce goods that were then sold in the rising capitalist market (Sellin, 1944:9–22).

Sellin was opposed to the death penalty. His opposition was probably based on a humanistic philosophy, but in his writings, he sought to show that capital punishment simply is not effective. In his work comparing annual homicide rates for capital punishment states with noncapital punishment states, Sellin (1980) concluded that executions have no discernible effect on homicide death rates.

The recognition that there is something to be gained by the sharing of knowledge among different countries did not escape Sellin. He spent a great deal of his career working to broaden international connections through contacts with scholars and criminal justice practitioners, seeking to understand better the issue of crime and/or delinquency. His contribution on the international market and his recognition as an expert in the field of criminology and criminal justice is underscored by the fact that many of his works have been translated into Spanish, French, Japanese, and German, to name a few languages. Further, many of his works are published in journals and government reports of other countries around the globe.

CULTURE CONFLICT AND CRIME

In the first decades of the 20th century, the field of criminology was a relatively new social science. The massive works that have been produced since that time owe a great debt to early scholars who sought to apply the scientific method to the study of crime and/or delinquency. Influenced by the scholars of the Chicago School, so named because these scholars were located at the University of Chicago, Sellin set out to contribute to the development of criminology as a scientific discipline from his home base in Pennsylvania. The context of *Culture Conflict and Crime* (1938) included a recognition that immigration and industrialization had produced a disproportionate amount of juvenile delinquents in major U.S. cities. The term *culture conflict* reflected the notion that "old world" traditions did not always align with those of the "new world," and when the two came in contact with each other, conflict was a natural result. In the 1930s, the Social Science Research Council sought to solicit a study on the etiology of delinquency as related to culture conflict, and it was Sellin who presented the council with just such a study in 1938.

In *Culture Conflict and Crime*, Sellin argued that different cultures have different conduct norms, rules that require individuals located within those cultures to act in specific ways in certain circumstances. He states that "man is born into a culture" (1938:25). Throughout the course of a lifetime, an individual learns to attach meanings to customs and beliefs and to interact with others according to those meanings.

Sellin (1938:30) defines a conduct norm as "a normal (right) or abnormal (wrong) way of reacting, the norm depending upon the social values of the group which formulated it."

In a simpler society, one that is primarily homogeneous, the laws represent a consensus in society. They are, in fact, a reflection of the conduct norms of the culture. In a society that is not homogeneous in nature, with increasing overlap and contradictions between the conduct norms among different groups or cultures, conflict is the more likely result. According to Sellin (1938:21), "In some states, these groups may comprise the majority, in others a minority, but the social values which receive the protection of the criminal law are ultimately those which are treasured by dominant interest groups."

Sellin distinguished between "primary cultural conflicts" and "secondary cultural conflicts." In the former, conflict occurs between two different cultures, as in migration, when members of one cultural group move into the territory of another. Secondary cultural conflicts occur when a single culture evolves into several different subcultures, each having its own conduct norms. In either case, law would not represent a consensus of the various members of the society but would reflect the conduct norms of the dominant culture.

Because of his strongly held belief that conflict is a result of the violation of some conduct norm, Sellin called for scientific studies that operationalized the dependent variable as such. To study crime using legal definitions only serves to "restrain, frustrate, or fix the social ends of scientific research" (Sellin, 1938:23). Sellin continues:

If a science of human conduct is to develop, the investigator in this field of research must rid himself of shackles which have been forged by the criminal law. . . . Confinement to the study of crime and criminals and the acceptance of the categories of specific forms of "crime" and "criminal" as laid down in law renders criminological research theoretically invalid from the point of view of science.

THE CRIMINALITY OF YOUTH

Applying culture conflict to the study of delinquency, Sellin, in *The Criminality of Youth* (1940), noted that his generation was not the first to see young people as a problem. He quoted from an unknown writer of ancient Egypt who said that the world is going to the dogs because children disobey their parents. Before accepting that youth are terribly criminal, though, Sellin suggested that social scientists must look at the data from which such an assumption is drawn. He urged caution in this area of inquiry and was one of the first theorists to call attention to the problems associated with the use of official data.

Using data from several cities and various age and crime classifications, Sellin set out to answer the following questions: (1) To what extent are youths found among those who get into conflict with the law; and (2) what is the incidence of criminality at various age levels? He was able to conclude that across all crime categories, young people did not show excessive participation. In crimes against property, however, he noted that the offense rates of youth were abnormally high and, since these offenses constitute the majority of serious crimes, the rates for juvenile crime were "very unfavorable to the youth group." He further noted that within the 16- to 20-year-old group, the rates involving serious crimes tended to rise with age. Eighteen- to 20-year-olds were more criminal than the 16- to 17-year-olds, and the 19-year-old group crime rate was particularly high.

Sellin then addressed the policy implications of his findings and articulated in the second part of *The Criminality of Youth* a means of dealing with young people in society. Looking at the various methods of handling the delinquent youth (execution, incarceration, or rehabilitation), Sellin argued for a treatment approach to the problem. That is, he was able to show that the likelihood of a person becoming a second offender is many times greater than that of becoming a first offender. He further noted that the probability of a person committing a subsequent crime increases with each conviction. Because of this finding, Sellin (1940:116) suggested, "If this conclusion is sound, adequate treatment measures for the youth group are needed, and if they can be made successful the offense rates of later age groups should in the course of time show considerable declines."

MEASURES OF DELINQUENCY

Over the course of his academic career, Sellin worked to improve the available data on delinquency. Along with Marvin Wolfgang and as discussed in *The Measurement of Delinquency* (1964), he developed what came to be called the Sellin-Wolfgang index.

The index has since been used by researchers, including Sellin himself in the often-cited work *Delinquency in a Birth Cohort*, published in 1972 with Wolfgang and Robert Figlio. In the words of Wolfgang (1968:ix), "Probably no topic has been of such abiding concern to Professor Sellin throughout his professional career as has that of criminal statistics."

RECOGNITION

Professor Sellin died in 1994, just short of his 98th birthday. His contribution to criminology and the study of delinquency will forever serve as a grounding force for both new students of criminology and the more seasoned modern-day scholars of the same. Sellin not only worked diligently at applying the scientific method to the study of crime and delinquency, he worked just as hard to argue for the rehabilitation of youthful offenders and against harsh sentencing practices such as those currently being used in the juvenile justice system. In 1960, Professor Sellin received the first of the distinguished Edwin H. Sutherland Awards given by the American Society of Criminology. In an even greater show of recognition, in 1973, the society conamed its international award after him (with Sheldon Glueck).

Barbara Sims

See also Philadelphia Birth Cohort; Theories of Delinquency; Marvin Wolfgang

Bibliography

Sellin, T. 1938. *Culture Conflict and Crime*. New York: Social Science Research Council.

Sellin, T. 1940. *The Criminality of Youth*. Philadelphia: The American Law Institute.

Sellin, T. 1944. *Pioneering in Penology: The Amsterdam Houses of Correction in the Sixteenth and Seventeenth Centuries*. Philadelphia: The American Law Institute.

Sellin, T. 1980. *The Penalty of Death*. Beverly Hills, CA: Sage.

Sellin, T., and M. E. Wolfgang. 1964. *The Measurement of Delinquency*. New York: Wiley.

Wolfgang, M. E. (ed.). 1968. *Crime and Culture: Essays in Honor of Thorsten Sellin*. New York: Wiley.

Wolfgang, M. E., R. M. Figlio, and T. Sellin. 1972. *Delinquency in a Birth Cohort*. Chicago: University of Chicago Press.

SERIOUS AND VIOLENT JUVENILE OFFENDERS

Serious, violent juvenile offenders are youth who have committed crimes that fall into the categories set forth in the juvenile violent crime index as classified by the Federal Bureau of Investigations' *Uniform Crime Reports*. These crimes include murder, forcible rape, robbery, and aggravated assault.

The heinous nature of the crimes committed by these juveniles, coupled with the extensive media attention focused on high-profile incidents such as school shootings and gang violence, has led society to conclude that the problem of serious and violent juvenile offenders is extensive and that grave measures should be taken to remedy the problem. One of the key measures has been the development of a "get tough" attitude. This attitude became prevalent among both citizens and lawmakers and resulted in changes that significantly affected the juvenile justice system.

AMOUNT OF SERIOUS, VIOLENT JUVENILE CRIME

The Office of Juvenile Justice and Delinquency Prevention (OJJDP) estimates that between the early 1980s and early 1990s, juvenile arrest rates for violent crime index offenses increased nearly 60 percent compared with a 47 percent increase for adults. This era represented the peak increase in serious and violent juvenile offending. Statistics show that the period between the mid- and late 1990s represented a period of decline for serious, violent juvenile offending, as evidenced by the 36 percent decrease in the juvenile arrest rates for violent crime index offenses. The 1999 statistics made available by the OJJDP revealed that, of all violent index crimes cleared by arrest, juveniles committed 6 percent of the murders, 12 percent of the forcible rapes, 15 percent of the robberies, and 12 percent of the aggravated assaults. These statistics are indicative of the fact that even though serious, violent juvenile offenses have declined, there is a grave problem that must be addressed.

CHARACTERISTICS OF SERIOUS, VIOLENT JUVENILE OFFENDERS

One of the most difficult questions for criminal justice professionals to answer is "Who among adolescents is most likely to become a serious violent juvenile offender?" While research has had some success in determining the characteristics of adolescents who are most likely to become delinquent, it has not yet determined who among adolescents is most likely to become a serious and violent offender. Part of the difficulty lies in the fact that, in many instances, the serious, violent juvenile offender has no prior record of offending. Attempts at profiling such offenders are complicated by the fact that these juveniles often do not fit the profile. As in the case with several of the juveniles involved in school shootings, the serious, violent juvenile offender is often a very good student and has a low profile within the student body. Another difficulty is that the particular offense committed is often the first offense of record by the juvenile. In such cases, there is no record of a progression of offenses or other indicators that the juvenile had the potential to become a serious, violent offender.

Criminal justice professionals are also cognizant of, and alarmed by, the fact that the age at onset of serious, violent juvenile offending is decreasing. A common response has been to transfer these offenders to adult courts. Although most states have a minimum age for adult certification, several states do not, thus allowing a juvenile to be tried as an adult regardless of his or her age. The transfer of juveniles from the juvenile justice system to the adult justice system has imposed problems and created new issues for the adult criminal justice system that have yet to be resolved.

In relation to gender, statistics show that males account for the majority of all serious, violent juvenile offenses committed. However, female involvement in serious, violent juvenile offending is increasing at alarming rates. In addition, statistics show that females are often the recipients of more leniencies offered by the justice system. Even during a period with a significant increase, females were less likely than males to have their cases petitioned. Of the petitioned cases, females were less likely than males to be adjudicated. Females were also less likely than males to be placed on formal probation or to be ordered to an out-of-home placement. This disparate treatment is indicative that even the justice system has not yet realized the gravity of female involvement in serious, violent juvenile offending.

CONTEMPORARY RESEARCH

The increase in serious, violent juvenile offending has generated a multidisciplinary approach to the study of the problem. Criminal justice professionals, educators, public health officials, religious organizations, and various other groups have initiated research into solutions. Traditionally, criminal justice professionals believed that young adults represented the most violence-prone age-group; however, the increase in violence among adolescents has called this belief into serious question and has reshaped the focus of research priorities. The outcomes of recent research have spawned various findings and have indicated that both prospective and retrospective approaches to the study of serious violent juvenile offending must be applied.

Generally, researchers have concluded that early identification of potential serious, violent juvenile offenders is crucial. Effective age-appropriate strategies for violence prevention, intervention, and control need to be developed and implemented at an early age. Researchers further suggest that among the strongest prevention and early intervention approaches is reducing identified risk factors by enhancing the strength and protection the child receives from the family, the school, peers, and the community.

Researchers have also admonished mental health professionals, school counselors, youth group workers, and the like to critically analyze the potential for serious, violent juvenile offending when psychologically assessing or otherwise working with adolescents. It is further suggested by researchers that a profile of the serious, violent juvenile offender be developed so adolescents at risk can be identified. This would allow interventions to be employed at a very early age in an attempt to prevent the behavior of serious, violent juvenile offending.

Peggy A. Engram

See also Arson; Cycle of Violence; Delinquency—Trends and Data; Gangs, Juvenile; Matricide and Patricide; School Violence

Bibliography

Hawkins, D. F., J. H. Laub, J. L. Lauritsen, and L. Cothern. 2000. *Race, Ethnicity, and Serious and Violent Juvenile Offending. Juvenile Justice Bulletin*, June. Washington, DC: Office of Juvenile Justice and Delinquency Prevention.

Loeber, R., and D. P. Farrington. 1997. *Never Too Early, Never Too Late: Risk Factors and Successful Interventions for Serious and Violent Juvenile Offenders.* Washington, DC: Office of Juvenile Justice and Delinquency Prevention.

Loeber, R., and D. P. Farrington (eds.). 1998. *Serious and Violent Juvenile Offenders: Risk Factors and Successful Interventions.* Thousand Oaks, CA: Sage.

 SEX OFFENDERS

Until the 1980s, juveniles who had committed sex offenses received little attention in the research literature. Their behavior was often explained as normal experimentation or developmental curiosity, while the focus of investigation of deviant sexual behavior was on adult sex offenders. However, crime reports and surveys have indicated that adolescents are responsible for about 20 percent of rapes and 30 percent to 50 percent of cases of child sexual abuse. Current estimates suggest that more than 70,000 boys and 110,000 girls are victims of adolescent perpetrators each year. Over the past decade, the phenomenon of adolescents and children being the perpetrators against younger children has become increasingly recognized.

These figures most likely underestimate the actual number of juvenile sex offenders because many of these incidents go unreported and only a small number result in an arrest. Furthermore, studies of adult sex offenders indicate that about half of adult offenders report that their first sex offense occurred as a juvenile, and often offenses escalated in frequency and severity over time. Because of these findings, juveniles who sexually abuse have been recognized as a distinct population for study, and efforts to identify and treat the group have increased.

THE NATURE AND EXTENT OF JUVENILE SEX OFFENDING

The research literature indicates that juvenile sex offenders are a heterogeneous population with diverse characteristics and treatment needs. For example, while some juveniles may begin their behaviors with the onset of puberty, some begin at very young ages. They vary in the ages of their victims and whether or not their offenses involve psychological coercion, violence, or both. Generally, three groups of juvenile sex offenders can be identified: (1) sexually assaultive juveniles, (2) pedophilic juveniles whose victims were three or more years younger, and (3) a mixed group that includes juveniles who perpetrate more than one class of sex offense.

Prior sexual victimization of sex offenders has been a consistent finding across the adult and juvenile literature, despite considerable differences in sample selection and data collection. In a national sample of adolescent sex offenders undergoing treatment (a database developed by the National Adolescent Perpetrator Network), nearly 40 percent of the adolescent sex offenders were known to have been sexually abused before further disclosures or discoveries during treatment. A study of very young perpetrators suggested that at least 49 percent had been sexually abused. Other studies have found even higher rates (50 percent to 80 percent) of sexual victimization. However, recent studies do not find a relationship between prior sexual victimization and later recidivism in sex offenders.

In examining the relationship between juvenile sex offending and prior victimization, several studies have examined the victimization behaviors and the characteristics of the victims of juvenile sex offenders. In a national sample, 35 percent had engaged in vaginal or anal penetration, 14.7 percent in oral genital contact, and 17.9 percent in both types of contact. Thus about two thirds involved one or both of these behaviors. With respect to the gender of victims, a study reported in a national sample that twice as many females as males were victims. Most other studies support these findings for juvenile sex offenders, with females constituting approximately 70 percent of the victims. However, it should be noted that when the victim was a child, the proportion of male victims increased, up to 63 percent.

The literature indicates that adolescent males who commit child molestation offenses tend to have young victims. The majority (more than 60 percent) of the victims were less than 12 years old, and two thirds of this percentage were less than 6 years old. In a national sample, 63 percent were younger than 9, and the modal age was 6. Adolescent male rapists, however, are more likely to select victims their own age or older.

Studies of relationships indicate that, generally, adolescent sex offenders know their victims. One study found that in their sample, the victims were blood relations in 38.8 percent of the cases, while in another sample of young perpetrators about 46 percent involved family members. A study comparing incest versus nonincest cases found that sibling offenders were more likely to have assaulted younger children than nonsibling offenders.

The relationship between early sexual victimization and later sex offending is undoubtedly complex. The reasons some victimized youths later perpetrate and others do not have yet to be fully explored. Emerging developmental literature is focusing on the cognitive and psychophysiological effects of trauma on youths. Mechanisms that are thought to contribute to this "cycle of abuse" or "vampire syndrome" include a reenactment of the abuse, an attempt to achieve mastery over resulting conflicts, and the subsequent conditioning of sexual arousal to assaultive fantasies. Prior traumatization might be one of a number of precursors to sexual perpetration, with other predisposing factors including social inadequacy, lack of intimacy, and impulsiveness. The high incidence of child victimization might be the result of a reactive, conditioned, or learned behavior pattern, and a progression of sexual acts might reflect the reinforcing pattern in the development and perpetration of sexually abusive behaviors.

CHARACTERISTICS OF JUVENILE SEX OFFENDERS

Several studies that have described the backgrounds of male juvenile sex offenders have found an overlap among adolescent sex offenders, juvenile delinquents, boys from abusive and neglectful families, and socially isolated boys. Although the samples are only partially comparable and studies differed in methods of data collection and analysis, the following characteristics of adolescent sex offenders have been repeatedly described:

1. A history of severe family problems, separation from parents, and placement away from home.
2. Experience of sexual abuse.
3. Neglect or physical abuse.
4. Social awkwardness or isolation.
5. Academic or behavioral problems at school.
6. Psychopathology.

Proportions of juvenile sex offenders who experienced physical abuse as children range from 25 percent to 50 percent. In addition, factors such as family instability, disorganization, and violence have been found to be prevalent among juveniles who engage in sexually abusive behavior. Studies have found that less than one third of juvenile sex offenders resided with both birth parents. Research on family communication styles have found that supportive communication and comments are limited in the families of both juvenile sex offenders and violent offenders, whereas negative communication, such as aggressive statements and interruptions, are frequent. Not surprisingly, adequate support and supervision appear to be lacking in the families of these juveniles.

Research repeatedly documents that juveniles with sexual behavior problems have significant deficits in social competence. Inadequate social skills, poor peer relationships, and social isolation are some of the difficulties identified in these juveniles. The juveniles who had committed child molestation offenses were more socially maladjusted than other sex offenders or other delinquents and evidenced more social anxiety and fear of heterosexual interactions.

Juveniles who sexually offend typically have experienced academic difficulties, including disruptive behavior, truancy, and/or learning disabilities. The incidence of attention deficit disorders in juveniles with sexual behavior problems has not been well established; studies indicate that 30 percent to 60 percent of juvenile sex offenders evidenced some symptoms of an attention deficit disorder. Juvenile sex offenders with lower IQ scores showed significantly more inappropriate sexual behaviors than did those with higher scores.

Juvenile sex offenders have been noted to have poor impulse control and poor judgment and problem-solving skills. Cognitive distortions, such as blaming the victim, have been associated with increased rates of sexual reoffending among juveniles who committed sex offenses. They have more difficulty recognizing appropriate emotions in others and have difficulty in taking the other person's perspective.

Some studies have investigated possible neurological deficits in juvenile sex offenders and comparison groups of nonsex offenders. Neurological impairments were found at higher rates in groups of juvenile sex offenders and juvenile violent nonsex offenders. It appears that deficits in verbal cognitive functioning, which can be seen indirectly in higher rates of impulsivity and poor judgment, might contribute to inappropriate sexual and other delinquent behaviors among juveniles.

Overall, juveniles who commit sex offenses and juveniles who commit other types of offenses share many characteristics. Follow-up studies of juvenile sex offenders have indicated that recidivism in terms of sex offenses is not particularly high and consists of both sex and nonsex offenses. This suggests that when a longitudinal perspective is used, sex offending among juveniles is often part of a pattern of general delinquency.

TYPOLOGIES OF JUVENILE SEX OFFENDERS

As stated previously, the general consensus among researchers is that juveniles who have committed sex offenses are a heterogeneous group. Consequently, for both theoretical and practical reasons, there is a need to develop reliable and valid typologies. Unfortunately, the typologies developed to date have largely been intuitively derived, and they have not been empirically validated. Some typologies have been offense driven (e.g., rapists, child molesters), while others have been personality driven (e.g., disturbed impulsive, pseudosocialized). Progress in the field will be significantly enhanced once reliable and empirically validated typologies emerge. Typologies based on combining type of offense with individual personality characteristics would appear to hold the most promise.

ASSESSMENT AND TREATMENT OF JUVENILE SEX OFFENDERS

Because of the heterogeneous nature of juveniles who have committed sex offenses, each offender should undergo a comprehensive clinical assessment before an individualized treatment plan is developed and implemented. Such a comprehensive clinical assessment should, at a minimum, identify strengths and weaknesses in the following six areas: (1) intellectual and neurological, (2) personality and psychopathological, (3) social and behavioral, (4) sexual, (5) history of victimization, and (6) substance use.

A thorough intellectual assessment is necessary for at least two reasons. First, cognitive-behavioral techniques need to be modified when used with juveniles with less than average intelligence. Second, studies have empirically demonstrated a relationship between lower intelligence, poor academic performance, truancy, and recidivism among juveniles who commit sex offenses. Since some studies maintain that as many as one third of juvenile sex offenders have some indication of a neurological deficit, it seems prudent to routinely include some form of neurological or neuropsychological screening as part of a comprehensive clinical assessment.

The comorbidity of sex offending and various forms of psychopathology also warrants the inclusion of assessment techniques designed to detect the presence of an accompanying psychopathological condition. Needless to say, if any such condition were to be identified, it would need to be treated as well. As a group, juveniles who commit sex offenses are quite likely to be deficient in a variety of social skills, so a thorough assessment of these deficits will aid in the development of an individualized treatment plan. Since the commission of a sex offense is what brought the juvenile to the attention of treatment personnel, a truly individualized treatment plan cannot be developed without an extensive investigation of the offender's sexual history.

As stated previously, studies indicate that significant proportions of juveniles who commit sex offenses have been the victims of emotional, physical, or sexual abuse. Before the traumatic consequences of such experiences can be resolved, their nature and extent must be thoroughly investigated. Finally, it is important to assess whether the juvenile has a substance abuse problem, because from a pharmacological standpoint, most psychoactive substances have a disinhibiting effect that might contribute to future reoffending.

Three other assessment issues have been raised in the research literature on juveniles who commit sex offenses. The first issue is whether lie detectors should be used in an attempt to enhance the veracity of an offender's statements regarding his or her sex offending behaviors. Due to the inherent questionable reliability of lie detectors at the present time, the general consensus in the research community is that they should not be used routinely. The second issue is whether phallometric assessment should be used to assess deviant sexual arousal. Because of the ethical problems associated with the use of phallometric assessment, the general consensus is that its use should not be routinely employed. The third issue is the need to obtain information from multiple sources, including self-reports, interviews, psychological tests, interviews with family members and victims, and official records.

Because of the nature of their offenses, the treatment of juvenile sex offenders must address both the needs of the individual and the needs of the community.

Although it has been argued that a continuum of treatment models using the concept of the least intrusive setting should be developed, most treatment programs for juveniles who have committed sex offenses are long term (12 to 24 months), specialized residential programs. Thus the need to protect the community from further offending has generally taken precedence over the needs of the individual.

To date, very little research has been conducted that conclusively demonstrates the effectiveness of particular treatment programs, or specific treatment interventions, for juveniles who have committed sex offenses. Most treatment programs have been modeled after treatment programs empirically proven to be effective with adult sex offenders, but it remains to be established whether such programs are in fact effective with juveniles. However, at this time, a reasonable approach would be to use interventions proven to be effective with adult sex offenders, after making the necessary modifications to ensure that they are appropriate for juveniles. Such treatment would still need to be empirically validated.

Consequently, most treatment programs for juveniles who have committed sex offenses use cognitive-behavioral techniques conducted in groups. Target areas for treatment typically include the following:

1. Decreasing cognitive distortions.

2. Increasing empathy.

3. Enhancing problem-solving skills.

4. Decreasing deviant sexual arousal.

5. Enhancing age-appropriate social skills, including dating skills.

6. Resolving traumatic consequences associated with being victimized.

7. Enhancing management of emotions, such as anger.

A particularly problematic issue in the treatment of juvenile sex offenders is the selection of an intervention designed to decrease deviant sexual arousal. Numerous researchers have raised ethical concerns related to the use of aversive conditioning techniques involving electric shock and noxious chemicals. The effectiveness of covert sensitization and masturbatory conditioning with juveniles has not been adequately empirically demonstrated. A promising intervention is vicarious sensitization, in which juveniles are exposed to a taped crime scenario designed to stimulate arousal, and then immediately afterward, they view an aversive video that presents the negative social, emotional, and legal consequences of sexually abusive behavior. However, the effectiveness of vicarious sensitization needs to be empirically established.

Most treatment programs also incorporate a relapse prevention component. Though theoretically sound, no empirical studies have been conducted to investigate the effectiveness of using this approach with juvenile sex offenders. Finally, noting the similarities between juveniles who commit general delinquent, nonsexual acts and juveniles who commit sex offenses, several researchers have argued that relevant empirically based treatment interventions for juvenile delinquents should be used with those who commit sex offenses, whenever the interventions appear to be indicated.

Carol Veneziano and Louis Veneziano

See also Serious and Violent Juvenile Offenders

Bibliography

National Adolescent Perpetrator Network. 1993. The revised report from the National Task Force on Juvenile Sexual Offending. *Juvenile and Family Court Journal* 44(4):1–120.

Righthand, S., and C. Welch. 2000. *Juveniles Who Have Sexually Offended.* Washington, DC: Office of Juvenile Justice and Delinquency Prevention.

Schwartz, B., and H. Cellini (eds.). 1995. *The Sex Offender, Vol. 1. Corrections, Treatment and Legal Practice.* Kingston, NJ: Civic Research Institute.

SHAW, CLIFFORD R. (1895–1957)

The resolute study of the field of juvenile delinquency from a sociological perspective began in the late 1920s with the work of Clifford R. Shaw and his colleague Henry D. McKay. Before then, that field was firmly in the hands of psychologists and psychiatrists, as was all of criminology. That domination encompassed empirical research, theorizing, and the practical applications of the deductions from those theories.

Shaw was born in 1895 in the tiny farm community of Luray, Indiana. After years of uncertainty as to whether his future was to be in farming or something more academic, he decided to study for the ministry at Adrian College in Michigan. On completing his junior year there, he enlisted in the U.S. Navy, where he remained until the conclusion of World War I. When he returned to Adrian to complete his bachelor's degree, his second set of experiences at Adrian created disillusionment with religion and a career in the ministry. He then enrolled, in 1919, as a graduate student in sociology at the University of Chicago where he received a master's degree. In Chicago, he lived in an immigrant neighborhood near the inner city, an experience that was important in awakening sensitivity to the problems and needs of the poor. Between 1921 and 1926, he was further exposed to the difficulties of life in Chicago, first in his position as a parole officer and then as a juvenile probation officer.

CONTRIBUTIONS TO CRIMINOLOGY AND DELINQUENCY

At the start of the 20th century, the earlier sociological work of people like Guerry, Quetelet, and Durkheim was swamped by the widespread appeal of biological determinism to explain criminal behavior. That direction was strengthened by the spread of the intelligence-testing movement in the United States and the uses of various tests concluding that delinquents had inferior intellects (some people assumed that the majority of delinquents were "feebleminded").

When the first juvenile court in the United States was established in 1899 in Chicago, with an orientation toward rehabilitation rather than punishment, it was natural to think of individually based treatment. That led to the establishment of the Chicago Juvenile Psychopathic Institute, which accepted referrals from the juvenile court. The Institute's first Director was William Healy, a psychiatrist, who published several books and articles on juvenile delinquency as sole author and later with his associate, Augusta Bronner, a psychologist. They later became Director and Assistant Director, respectively, of the Judge Baker Foundation for young offenders in Boston.

In the 1920s, the Juvenile Psychopathic Institute, now officially a state establishment, was renamed the Institute for Juvenile Research, and Clifford Shaw became its Director in 1926. At the Institute Shaw (and McKay) conducted research that would eventually make sociology the dominant academic discipline in the field of juvenile delinquency.

Although the Department of Sociology at the University of Chicago was founded in 1892, it did not achieve a position of national domination until about 1918, under the influence of Robert Park and Ernest Burgess. The Department became the center of a school of thought in terms of commitment to empirical research, much of it focused on the urban problems of Chicago, and the development of theory in an organized fashion by a community of scholars. Among the emphases in the Chicago School were the uses of personal documents and personal histories as basic data for the formulation of theory. Moreover, the School was associated with field research based on an ecological perspective of cities, with heavy emphasis on Chicago.

Both factors influenced Shaw during his studies as a graduate student. In addition, his personal exposure to the problems of life in Chicago, primarily its immigrant and inner-city neighborhoods, enhanced the resulting scholarly tendencies. Shaw used personal materials in the preparation of two life histories of persistent young offenders, works for which he may be best known: *The Jack-Roller: A Delinquent Boy's Own Story* (1930) and *The Natural History of a Delinquent Career* (1931). Showing the influence of the Chicago School further, he most effectively adopted the ecological perspective in his field research, relying heavily on the notion advanced by Burgess of concentric zones of decreasing social pathology emanating from the central city. That led to Shaw's classic works, written with McKay: *Social Factors in Juvenile Delinquency* (1931) and *Juvenile Delinquency and Urban Areas* (1942).

CONTRIBUTIONS TO PREVENTION AND TREATMENT

In addition to those accomplishments on behalf of sociology in the academic world, Shaw led the first major sociological challenge to the dominance of psychiatry and psychology in the practical realm of prevention and treatment. He tested his sociology-based ideas regarding delinquency and its control in three areas of Chicago with high concentrations of young offenders. The vehicle for that effort was the Chicago Area Project (CAP), which started in the early 1930s. The approach depended on the operation of local councils, formed by CAP, to organize the areas for civic improvement and the social control associated with well-functioning communities. Specific activities included recreational

programs, counseling gang members, and motivating general adult participation in the development and supervision of the activities of youths.

Arnold Binder

See also Augusta Fox Bronner; Chicago Area Project; William Healy; Solomon Kobrin; Henry D. McKay; Theories of Delinquency—Sociological

Bibliography

Blumer, M. 1984. *The Chicago School of Criminology.* Chicago: University of Chicago Press.

Schlossman, S., and M. Sedlak. 1983. The Chicago Area Project revisited. *Crime and Delinquency* 29:398–462.

Shaw, C. R. 1930. *The Jack-Roller: A Delinquent Boy's Own Story.* Chicago: University of Chicago Press.

Shaw, C. R. 1931. *The Natural History of a Delinquent Career.* Chicago: University of Chicago Press.

Shaw, C. R., and H. D. McKay. 1931. *Social Factors in Juvenile Delinquency. Report on the Causes of Crime to the Wickersham Commission*, Vol. 2. Washington, DC: Government Printing Office.

Shaw, C. R., and H. D. McKay. 1942. *Juvenile Delinquency and Urban Areas.* Chicago: University of Chicago Press.

Snodgrass, J. 1976. Clifford R. Shaw and Henry D. McKay: Chicago criminologists. *British Journal of Criminology* 16(1):1–19.

 SHORT, JAMES FRANKLIN, JR. (1924–)

By the late 1940s, the Department of Sociology at the University of Chicago had firmly established its reputation and was known simply as the Chicago School. In this academic environment and tradition, James F. Short Jr. received both his Master's (1949) and his Ph.D. (1951) in Sociology. For the next five decades, he pursued a career as a sociologist and criminologist.

Short was born in Illinois on June 22, 1924. His college career began at Shurtleff College in 1942 and, before completing his baccalaureate degree at Denison University in 1947, he served on active duty in the U.S. Marine Corps Reserve, attaining the rank of second lieutenant.

Before completing his doctorate, Short's career as an educator began in 1950 with his first position as an instructor at the Illinois Institute of Technology. Shortly afterward, he became an instructor at Indiana

University at South Bend that same year. Then in 1951, he took a faculty appointment to the Department of Sociology at Washington State University, where he is currently Professor Emeritus. In addition to his instructional positions during his tenure at Washington University, Short has served as dean of the graduate school and as director of the Social Research Center.

EARLY CAREER

During his career, Short has focused on the areas of violence, juvenile delinquency, gangs, risks, and research. He has authored, edited, and contributed to various books, chapters, and professional articles in these areas. He acknowledges many influences by such notables from the Chicago School as W. F. Ogburn, Ernest Burgess, Clifford Shaw, Henry McKay, Solomon Korbin, and Tony Sorrentino; many others associated with the Institute for Juvenile Research and the Chicago Area Project; and Harvard scholars Albert K. Cohen and Fred L. Strodtbeck.

One of his earliest published articles (1952) resulted from the influence of W. F. Ogburn and Ernest Burgess. Short studied the correlation between the amount of relief offered during the Depression of the 1930s and the amount of crime reported in the newly established *Uniform Crime Reports* (UCR) by the Federal Bureau of Investigation. This study suggested a negative correlation between the level of relief programs and the incidences of burglary and robbery. In addition, the review indicated relief programs could function as a social force in influencing the levels of burglary and robbery.

In 1954, Short and Andrew Henry coauthored a book in which they studied suicide and homicide within the context of the health of the social economy. They hypothesized that suicide rates related to the health of society's economy, increasing in frequency as the economy became depressed and decreasing as it recovered. However, Short and Henry found a direct relationship between homicide rates and the economy. Homicide rates appeared tied to the level of social frustration experienced due to the economy.

MEASUREMENT OF DELINQUENCY

The Chicago School was known for the use of official data and life histories in studying juvenile delinquency. Today there are three major ways of measuring delinquency: (1) official statistics, such as the UCR, developed during the 1920s; (2) self-reported data, developed in the 1950s; and (3) victimization data as reported in the National Crime Victimization Survey, developed in the 1970s. These three sources of data have become the primary sources for research in juvenile delinquency.

Clifford Shaw, recognizing the importance of a Kinsey-type report of self-reported data, suggested this approach to Short (1982:146). Short, with F. Ivan Nye, refined the methodology by applying their previous work in scale development. In 1957 and 1958, Short and Nye published articles (one with Olson) using the self-report methodology, which helped usher in one of the three major methods of knowing about delinquency. In his many research projects, Short always made the effort to ensure the reliability and validity of the self-report methodology, as well as the importance of experimental research in the criminal justice venue.

GANG STUDIES

Short's introduction into the study of gangs was through invitation by F. L. Strodtbeck, at the request of the Department of Sociology at the University of Chicago. He was invited to lead a research study of the "detached workers" program established by the Young Men's Christian Association (YMCA) in Chicago.

The results of this and various other gang studies by Short and colleagues challenged previously held theoretical explanations of gangs. The first Chicago gang study refuted the theory of crime-oriented gangs, though gangs did participate in delinquent behavior (Short and Strodtbeck, 1963). Short stressed that the accumulated information on gangs was primarily related to individual gang members and that less was known about gangs as a group. Other areas he presented as needing more inquiry included gang formation, transition, and gang interaction with other gangs and the gang's community (Short, 1997).

A second Chicago gangs study was an important test of Richard A. Cloward and Lloyd E. Ohlin's opportunity structure theory. This theory assumes that the lack of opportunities in communities leads to delinquency. Short's study suggested delinquency preceded the level of opportunities perceived by the individual (Short, Rivera, and Tennyson, 1965). Regarding status within gangs, another of Short's studies found that purposely damaged or destroyed property was more likely to be an act of higher-status males. Lower-status males were more likely to commit car theft, and higher-status girls were more likely to be runaways (Nye, Short, and Olson, 1958).

Gang leader behavior was another area that Short studied. A leader of a gang might use aggressive behavior to deal with a challenge to his status within the gang, but the leader would be selective in how he used it. A gang leader is more apt to focus aggressive behaviors outside the gang, such as toward other gangs. One of the interesting discoveries from this study about gang leaders was that "the overwhelming preponderance of their actions are co-ordinating and nurturant" (Short and Strodtbeck, 1963:578).

OTHER INTERESTS

Another of Short's interests was presented in his 1984 presidential address before the American Sociological Association. In his speech, he suggested focusing on developing a sociology of risks. He argued the field of sociology needed to explore an understanding of risks—the positives and negatives, gains and losses for the individual (Short, 1984). Another aspect of risk analysis he thought ought to be considered is rational choice (Short, 1997). Building on his address almost a decade later, Short and Lee Clarke (1993) further discussed and developed a rationale for analyzing interaction among technological and cultural risks.

RECOGNITION

"Intellectual attention" has been a motivating force for Short throughout a career that has spanned five decades and bridged a major tradition in criminal justice into a new century. During his career, Short has been the recipient of numerous visiting professorships, honors, and awards. His visiting professorships were at such institutions as the University of Chicago, Stanford University, Texas Christian University, and the University of Colorado. His scholarly awards include the Paul W. Tappan Award from the Western Society of Criminology, the Edwin H. Sutherland Award from the American Society of Criminology, and the Bruce Smith Award from the Academy of Criminal Justice Sciences. Also, he was honored by the establishment of the James F. Short Jr. Best Article

Award by the Crime, Law, and Deviance Section of the American Sociological Association.

As a member of many professional societies, Short has served in elected offices and appointed positions. He has been President of the Pacific Sociological Association, the Sociological Research Association, the American Sociological Association, the American Sociological Foundation, and the American Society of Criminology. In addition, he has served on the editorial staff of many of the most prestigious scholarly publications. James F. Short Jr. continues to live and work in Pullman, Washington.

Richard McWhorter

See also Chicago Area Project; Albert K. Cohen; Gangs, Juvenile; Henry D. McKay; Self-Report Studies

Bibliography

Clarke, L., and J. F. Short Jr. 1993. Social organization and risk: Some current controversies. *Annual Review of Sociology* 19:375–399.

Cohen, A. K., and J. F. Short Jr. 1958. Research in delinquent subcultures. *Journal of Social Issues* 14(3):20–37.

Henry, A. F., and J. F. Short Jr. 1954. *Suicide and Homicide: Some Economic, Sociological, and Psychological Aspects of Aggression*. Glencoe, IL: Free Press.

Nye, F. I., J. F. Short Jr., and V. Olson. 1958. Socioeconomic status and delinquent behavior. *American Journal of Sociology* 63:381–389.

Short, J. F., Jr. 1982. Life history, autobiography and the life cycle. Pp. 135–152 in Jon Snodgrass (ed.), *The Jack-Roller at 70*. Lexington, MA: D. C. Heath.

Short, J. F., Jr. 1984. The social fabric at risk: Toward a social transformation of risk analysis. *American Sociological Review* 49:711–725.

Short, J. F., Jr. 1997. The place of rational choice in criminology and risk analysis. *The American Sociologist* 28(2):61–72.

Short, J. F., Jr., and F. I. Nye. 1958. Extent of unrecorded juvenile delinquency: Tentative conclusions. *Journal of Criminal Law, Criminology, and Police Science* 49:296–302.

Short, J. F., Jr., R. Rivera, and R. A. Tennyson. 1965. Perceived opportunities, gang membership, and delinquency. *American Sociological Review* 30:56–67.

Short, J. F., Jr., and F. L. Strodtbeck. 1963. The response of gang leaders to status threats: An observation on group process and delinquent behavior. *American Journal of Sociology* 68:571–579.

SILVERLAKE EXPERIMENT

The Silverlake Experiment grew out of the Provo Experiment, both of which were under the leadership of LaMar T. Empey. The Silverlake Experiment was a juvenile delinquency residential program operated in Los Angeles, California, from 1964 to 1968, providing intensive supervision as a delinquency control strategy. The experiment was conducted for a period of three years, followed by an additional year in which follow-up data were collected.

Although this experiment operated on the same premise as the Provo Experiment, two basic changes were made in the program. First, the Silverlake Experiment took place in populous Los Angeles; thus the juveniles could not live at home and were required to attend daily group meetings, which were the major focus of the experiment. Second, as learned from the Provo Experiment, the boys could not be assured decent jobs unless they acquired educational skills. Therefore, the boys attended the local high school and were assisted by a tutor, which Silverlake provided. These changes made Silverlake a residential program, located in a middle-class, white residential neighborhood near downtown Los Angeles. The boys had to live at Silverlake during the week but could return home on the weekends.

DETAILS OF THE PROJECT

The Silverlake Experiment had three objectives:

1. Determine the capacity of a particular theory of delinquency to explain delinquent behavior and suggest effective measures for intervention.

2. Learn about the operational and organizational problems of a delinquency reduction effort based on that theory.

3. Study the problems with a *field experimental model* (FEM) as a knowledge-generating device.

Experimental and control subjects were selected randomly from a common population of offenders in Los Angeles County. Experimentals were assigned to the new community program (Silverlake), controls were assigned to the traditional program of the California Boys Republic. Only repeat offenders aged 15 to 17 were accepted into Silverlake. Offense histories varied, with the only exclusions being serious sex offenders, narcotics addicts, and seriously retarded or psychotic boys. No more than 20 boys were in the experiment at any given time with an average stay of six months, with the premise that too many would make it difficult to establish a unified and cohesive system. Unlike the boys in the Provo Experiment, the Silverlake boys were ethnically mixed, with 75 percent white, 10 percent African American, and 10 percent Hispanic.

The experiment focused on three main program components: (1) daily group meetings, (2) attendance at school, and (3) limited work and tutorial activities. Group meetings were held five times a week and were the major component of the experiment. Guided group meetings became the primary mechanism through which attempts at collaboration and problem solving were implemented. Guided group interaction attempted to make the group both the target and the medium of change. This method emphasized the development of the group as a means of producing change for its members. The role of the adult group leaders was extremely important. It was their job to become functional rather than act as an authoritarian member of the group. The fundamental objectives of the groups were to find and document the problems faced by group members, to search for and find sufficient alternatives, and to provide group support and personal rewards for seeking alternatives.

School attendance was the second major component of the experiment. Community linkage was vital to the experiment, and the boys' mandatory attendance at the local high school was seen as the primary way to achieve that link. A tutor was also assigned to assist the boys with any academic classes.

Work activities were the third component of the experiment and consisted mainly of housekeeping activities. The boys were responsible for the daily chores of the residential program, such as washing dishes, yard work, and cleaning their bedrooms. Assigning the boys these chores was an attempt to improve their work skills and to form a foundation for understanding personal and group problems.

PROJECT DIFFICULTIES

A major concern for the Silverlake Experiment was the ardent resistance of the local neighborhood school to accept the boys. From the onset, the boys were rejected, isolated, identified, and scrutinized. This was not the ideal situation, and recurrent problems continued for the duration of the experiment. The school had wanted the boys of Silverlake to attend an alternative program, but Silverlake staff were emphatic that the boys attend school in a "normal" setting with "normal" youth. The school enacted strict truancy rules for the residents of Silverlake that did not apply to the general population. As problems with the school continued to mount, the issue became the focus of group meetings.

With most discussions centered on resolving school conflicts, daily group meetings veered from their intended purpose of changing the boys' attitudes toward delinquency. Because of the punitive stance of the school regarding truancy, Silverlake had to enact strict and punitive measures for the boys; for example, any boy who ran away once would be removed from the program and recommended for incarceration. Silverlake was under intense pressure from the school, and that pressure resulted in a punitive group home model, far from the original ideal.

It is for these reasons that attention was drawn to the experiment regarding such issues as whether the research could be conducted objectively, whether conflicts between action and research were disruptive, how the research may have posed insoluble conflicts for delinquents, and how external pressures may have thwarted the objectives of the FEM. It was significant that the most effective relationships of the experiment were with the legal systems—specifically, the police, the courts, and probation. The least effective link during the experiment was with the schools. The failure of the experiment to address family problems was seen as a serious omission. The failure to effectively link offenders with external systems was perhaps its most significant failure.

EVALUATION OF THE PROJECT

The Silverlake Experiment consisted of 261 participants, 140 boys in the experimental group and 121 boys in the control group. Findings concluded that the effectiveness of the community-based treatment program was questionable. There were no important differences between the experimental and control group subjects in rates of recidivism. Thus the Silverlake Experiment was not more effective than institutionalization, but neither was it less effective. Runaway rates and in-program failures were high for both groups. In a two-and-a-half-year period, there was a 37 percent runaway rate for the experimental group

and a 40 percent runaway rate for the control group. The postprogram recidivism rates for experimentals were about the same as those for controls. Yet when before and after recidivism rates were considered, it appeared that both programs might have had a significant impact on delinquency.

CONCLUSION

The Silverlake Experiment resulted in three major observations: (1) Community-based programs have considerable inherent potential for reducing correctional costs, (2) such programs may not pose much increased danger to the community, and (3) it may be possible to help many offenders in much shorter periods without the effects of total long-term incarceration. In addition, overall findings indicated that any program using a field experimental model must take into consideration community linkage. School systems must be an integral part of the model for it to be successful, and the lack of school integration may have been the principal cause of Silverlake's inability to demonstrate greater success.

Terry A. Snow

See also LaMar Taylor Empey; Group Therapy; Provo Experiment

Bibliography

Binder, A., G. Geis, and D. D. Bruce. 1997. *Juvenile Delinquency: Historical, Cultural and Legal Perspectives*. Cincinnati, OH: Anderson.

Empey, L. T. 1978. *American Delinquency: Its Meaning and Construction*. Homewood, IL: Dorsey.

Empey, L. T., and S. G. Lubeck. 1971. *The Silverlake Experiment*. Chicago: Aldine.

Lundman, R. J. 1993. Community treatment. Pp. 187–193 in R. Lundman (ed.), *Prevention and Control of Juvenile Delinquency*. New York: Oxford University Press.

 ## STATUS OFFENDERS

Status offenses have been part of the juvenile justice system in the United States since its inception. These violations of juvenile codes at times have been considered criminal (that is, part of the definition of delinquency) and at times have been considered something other than, and less than, delinquency. To fully understand status offenses, it is necessary to provide a definition, a brief history of the role status offenses have played in the juvenile justice system, and a look at the potential legal standing of status offenses.

THE ORIGIN OF STATUS OFFENSES

When the first juvenile court was created in Cook County, Illinois, in 1899, the court's jurisdiction clearly was distinct from its adult criminal court counterpart. The proceedings were confidential, informal, and nonadversarial. In terms of subject matter jurisdiction, the juvenile court had responsibility for three kinds of cases: delinquency, dependency, and neglect. Dependency and neglect cases did not deal with what a child had done but with the situation in which the child was found. In reality, these types of cases were directed more at parents and guardians than at youngsters. Children were not offenders in these circumstances; they were more often viewed as victims.

This perspective did not exist for delinquency. In the broadest definition of the term, delinquency involved any offense that would be a crime (felony or misdemeanor) for an adult. However, the original juvenile court's definition of delinquency also included violations of the law that would not be offenses for adults. These are status offenses. Status offenses are defined primarily in terms of the child's age status (a person under the legal age of majority), and they are any violation of the law for a child—in the majority of states someone under the age of 18— that would not be a crime if committed by an adult. Specific examples, along with definitions, will give further clarification.

TYPES OF STATUS OFFENSES

Several status offenses have dominated the consideration of these legal transgressions. The most common status offenses have almost always been truancy, running away, curfew violations, alcohol-related offenses, tobacco use, underage gambling, and virtually any form of sexual intercourse. Once again, it is essential to remember that these activities are not law violations for adults under most circumstances.

Truancy

At about the time the first juvenile court was established, states, beginning with Colorado, adopted mandatory school attendance laws. These laws were designed to keep children in school and out of the workforce, typically until their 16th birthdays. Compulsory school attendance laws were intended not only to protect children but also to protect jobs for adults. Therefore, to enforce school attendance laws, states mandated that children who habitually failed to attend school were truant. Because most public school systems in the United States receive their funding based on average daily attendance figures, it clearly was in the best interests of the schools to have as many students present as possible every day. To enforce school attendance laws, school systems hired attendance enforcement officials, frequently known as truant officers. In some instances, the schools would go to the juvenile courts to file petitions for habitually truant children, and this often brought the police into the school attendance picture. Children who habitually were truant could be found to be delinquent, and they could be incarcerated by the juvenile court "in their best interests." The result was that children who failed to go to school—for whatever reasons—could be locked up in juvenile correctional facilities along with youngsters who had committed criminal offenses.

Running Away

Running away from home was another of the common status offenses from the very beginning of the juvenile justice system. It continues to be an issue with which justice and social services agencies deal today. Runaways have presented problems for many decades. First, like truant children, runaways who were apprehended were subject to incarceration. This typically did not occur the first time a child ran away from home, but repeatedly running away could result in court action. Second, the status offense of running away reflected the juvenile justice system's paternalistic attitudes. The view was that status offenders should be subject to legal intervention to prevent them from causing harm to themselves. One of the major concerns regarding status offenders has been that they would be subject to physical or sexual abuse during the time they are away, or that they might have to resort to criminal activity (selling drugs or prostitution) to support themselves while they are absent from home. Third, it has become apparent since the late 1960s that a great many runaways suffer from some type of abuse or neglect in the home, typically at the hands of a parent or guardian. This particular status offense continues to draw attention from the juvenile

Photo 10. Cauliflower field, State Industrial School for Boys, Kearney, Nebraska, circa 1908. Many youth were sent to state-run camps and schools to do farming and industrial work even though they had committed very minor offenses or status crimes.

SOURCE: Nebraska State Historical Society [RG2608]. Used with permission.

courts, but today runaways are no longer treated as criminal offenders.

Curfew Violation

In some instances, adults and juveniles may be subject to curfews. However, many communities have had curfew laws that relate to youngsters but not adults. Therefore, curfew violations fit within the definition of status offenses. Interestingly, after decades of nonexistence or nonenforcement, curfew laws were instituted or reinstituted in many communities nationwide during the 1980s and 1990s as one way to address the gang problem and offenses such as "tagging" (painting graffiti on walls and buildings). There have been legal challenges to these laws, but many

communities have relied on curfews as one way to keep youngsters off of the streets after certain hours.

Alcohol Use

Alcohol use presents a unique problem to the justice system. For adults, most uses of beverage alcohol are completely legal (there are exceptions, such as driving under the influence). In the case of minors, virtually anything dealing with alcohol is illegal. This includes sale, transportation, consumption, and even possession of alcoholic beverages. An interesting facet of the alcohol issue is that most states extend the prohibition beyond the age of majority (currently 18 in most states) up to age 21. Therefore, the use of alcohol provides a status offense category for individuals 18 to 20 years old. This particular offense demonstrates the difficulties that can result when trying to distinguish adult status from child status.

Tobacco Use

Tobacco use somewhat parallels that of alcohol. However, not all states prohibit tobacco purchase and use by children. Increasingly, as tobacco use has come under criticism from many segments of society because of health risks, states have moved to prohibit the sale of tobacco products to children. This qualifies violations of tobacco-related laws as status offenses.

Gambling

Gambling went through a period where it was illegal for adults and juveniles throughout much of the United States. Beginning in the 1970s, Atlantic City, New Jersey, followed by a number of other states and individual communities, legalized various forms of gaming, including casino gambling. As gambling has expanded throughout the country, there has been a concerted effort to prevent juveniles from engaging in illegal betting. Some studies have shown that the younger a person begins to gamble and the more that person gambles, the more likely the individual will turn into a problem or pathological gambler. Therefore, because all states except two now have some form of legalized gambling (the most pervasive being the state lotteries), laws have mandated that gambling is not allowed for persons under age 18 or, in some cases (casinos, for instance), under age 21.

Sexual Activity

Perhaps one of the most persistent status offenses, and the one that may be the most difficult to enforce, involves prohibitions against sexual intercourse by minors. States have tried to attack this issue in a number of ways. Among the common approaches to dealing with "sexual promiscuity" have been establishing ages of consent. However, even here the paternalism (and perhaps chauvinism) of the juvenile justice system shows through. States with age-of-consent laws typically specify different (and lower) ages of consent for males than for females. Many states also have statutes that prohibit intercourse between juveniles and adults, but because this activity usually takes place in private, most cases go undetected.

CHANGING PERCEPTIONS OF STATUS OFFENSES

Changes in juvenile court jurisdiction began to occur in the 1970s. One of the biggest changes dealt with status offenses. For decades, discontent had been building regarding the treatment of status offenders by juvenile courts. On the one hand, there were critics who felt that these youngsters had no business in the justice system. Most of these behaviors were seen as aggravating or obnoxious, but they were not truly "criminal" in nature. On the other hand, there were critics who worried that if status offenses were not addressed early and decisively, these relatively innocuous behaviors inevitably would escalate into full-blown delinquency. Research conducted from the late 1960s through the 1980s uncovered some interesting facets of the status offender issue.

First, there is little evidence that, if left untreated, status offenders would escalate into more serious delinquent offenders. Many youngsters are never apprehended and processed by the justice system, yet they engage in a variety of status offenses. In this country, relatively few children reach the age of majority without experimenting with alcohol or tobacco. Truancy and running away, while they may be serious behaviors, actually affect a small population of juveniles. Second, research also found that delinquent youngsters often commit a range of offenses and that offense specialization is uncommon.

These factors led to two conclusions. First, although many children commit status offenses, not many go on to commit serious delinquent offenses. Thus there was little evidence to indicate that offense escalation was a problem. Most juveniles stop short of committing serious offenses, and different delinquency theories give us different clues as to why this may be. Second, youngsters who had histories of persistent delinquency did commit both status offenses and criminal offenses. For these juveniles, there is both escalation and de-escalation. As a combined result of this research, appellate court decisions, and passage by Congress of the Juvenile Justice and Delinquency Prevention Act of 1974, states started to give some consideration to eliminating status offense jurisdiction from the juvenile courts and to the deinstitutionalization of status offenders (DSO).

In some jurisdictions, status offenses now are treated as social service problems. Other states have redefined status offenses, treating offenders as dependent children or children in need of services or supervision (CHINS) instead of as delinquents. Furthermore, since passage of the Juvenile Justice and Delinquency Prevention Act, in most jurisdictions in the United States, status offenders cannot be incarcerated in juvenile correctional facilities. Nevertheless, there are some exceptions to this rule. For example, if a status offender is considered a dependent child and fails to abide by court orders (such as staying in school and not running away), the judge may have the option of incarcerating the child, not for being a status offender but for failing to obey a court order.

CONCLUSION

Status offense jurisdiction still is part of many juvenile codes and juvenile court systems in the United States. The good news is that status offenders, by definition, have committed some of the least serious juvenile offenses. The bad news is that there seems to be virtually no way to eliminate status offenses because much of the behavior is endemic to the teenage years. Youngsters from a variety of backgrounds and socioeconomic statuses engage in these behaviors. Many stop without detection and with no legal intervention. However, in quite a few cases, status offenses are important, not in themselves but because they are symptoms of more serious personal and family problems.

Status offense jurisdiction is not likely to totally disappear from the nation's juvenile justice system anytime soon. While most people involved in the system express frustration and dissatisfaction over status offense treatment, many of them still want to retain the option of legal intervention with status offenses to provide children and their families with the services they need, but might not seek out.

G. Larry Mays

See also At-Risk Youth; Curfew; Deinstitutionalization Movement; Runaways; Truancy

Bibliography

Bernard, T. J. 1992. *The Cycle of Juvenile Justice.* New York: Oxford University Press.

Garry, E. M. 1996. *Truancy: First Step to a Lifetime of Problems.* Washington, DC: Office of Juvenile Justice and Delinquency Prevention.

Mays, G. L., and L. T. Winfree Jr. 2000. *Juvenile Justice.* New York: McGraw-Hill.

Schwartz, I. 1989. *(In)Justice for Juveniles.* Lexington, MA: Lexington Books.

 # SUTHERLAND, EDWIN H. (1883–1950)

Edwin H. Sutherland is universally acknowledged as the father of American criminology. He wrote the first true textbook on criminology in 1924 and at the time of his death in October 1950 was considered the foremost criminologist of the century. He contributed one of criminology's major theories, differential association theory, and originated the study of white-collar crime.

THE EARLY YEARS

Born in Gibbon, Nebraska, Edwin Sutherland grew up in Ottawa, Kansas, and Grand Island, Nebraska. His father, George Sutherland, was a stern and devout Baptist clergyman and, at one point, was a teacher at and president of Grand Island College, where Sutherland received his bachelor's degree in 1904. On moving to Sioux Falls, South Dakota, Sutherland taught humanities courses at the local college for two years. While there, he took a University of Chicago correspondence course in sociology as part of a plan to attend graduate school to study history. In the summer of 1906, Sutherland enrolled at the University of Chicago, intending to gain a graduate degree in history. He took several courses, among them one in sociology. Finding the subject matter interesting, Sutherland revised his career plans and, in the fall, enrolled in the graduate sociology program. The Sociology Department at the University of Chicago was the preeminent department in the discipline and Sutherland had an opportunity to study with scholars who helped to create sociology, among them Albion Small, Charles Henderson, and W. I. Thomas. At the same time, Sutherland also joined and became an officer in the Juvenile Protective Association, thus furthering his lifelong interest in the study of juvenile delinquency.

During his graduate work, Sutherland became somewhat disenchanted with sociology, at least the reformist version being espoused by Henderson. An interest in political economy began to occupy more of Sutherland's time, and he took courses taught by, among others, Robert Hoxie and Thorsten Veblen.

From 1908 to 1911, Sutherland returned to his teaching position at Grand Island College, where he taught economics, sociology, and psychology. On his return to the university, he studied primarily under W. I. Thomas, whose influence would appear later in the theory of differential association. By the time Sutherland received his Ph.D. in 1913, he had developed a major in both sociology and political economy and a minor in psychology (with at least one course each from Charles Herbert Mead and John Watson).

Sutherland's first teaching assignment after earning his doctorate was at William Jewel College in Liberty, Missouri. From all accounts, this position was one he took rather grudgingly and in which he was discontent from the start. One of his first courses was on crime and delinquency, which he taught in the usual manner of the day as "charities and corrections" and continued to teach each year. While he was able to teach the courses he wanted, as well as an occasional course at the University of Chicago or the University of Kansas, Sutherland found himself relatively isolated and published only one article during his six years at William Jewel. One noteworthy event, however, occurred in 1918—Sutherland married Myrtle Crews, from the local town.

THE MIDDLE YEARS

In 1919, Sutherland received and accepted an offer of a position in the Sociology Department at the University of Illinois. The chair of the department was E. C. Hayes, who also edited the Lippincott sociology series. The position not only moved Sutherland to a better school but gave him an opportunity to write a criminology textbook. In 1921, in his capacity of editor, Hayes asked Sutherland to write the book, which was published in 1924 as *Criminology*. In one sense, writing the book allowed Sutherland to define himself as a criminologist and began what would be a lifetime primary interest in crime and delinquency.

Criminology, as it was written, was quite a different book from most of those passed off as criminology books. The dominant way of explaining crime and delinquency had been based on the Lombrosian model of biological causality, with some acknowledgment of what was then called "multi-factor" theory. Sutherland's book offered a searing critique of these approaches and was the first criminology text to focus on the sociological perspective of crime and delinquency. Widely acknowledged and well received among sociologists, the book established Sutherland's reputation as a criminologist. It also contained what were to be considered characteristics of Sutherland's work throughout his career—careful scholarship, thoughtful analysis, and healthy skepticism.

During his tenure at Illinois, Sutherland began producing articles as well. His first two articles were noncriminological, but virtually all his published materials after 1926 were on the subject of crime and delinquency or the criminal justice system. Also while in Illinois, Sutherland was introduced to Henry D. McKay, who had arrived in 1924 as a graduate assistant and stayed until Sutherland left in 1926. The two became good friends.

Primarily because of the reputation gained by his book, Sutherland received a prestigious offer of a position at the University of Minnesota beginning in the fall of 1926. Not only did he receive a substantial increase in pay, but he was also hired as a full professor. Spending three years at Minnesota, Sutherland wrote articles focusing on the importance of sociology for criminology. He was also encouraged to produce scholarly work, primarily because the Sociology Department at the University of Minnesota was considered one of the premier departments. His colleagues at the time were such luminaries as F. Stuart Chapin and Pitirim Sorokin. Graduate students, who would later have recognizable names in criminology, were George Vold and Elio Monachesi. However, the department was not particularly collegial, and a good degree of strife was present. When Chapin, the chair of the department, took a one-year leave in 1928, Sutherland was asked to serve as the interim chair. The resulting unpleasant experience, as much as anything, pushed him to take a leave of absence and a one-year position to do research at the Bureau of Social Hygiene in New York in 1929. He never returned to Minnesota.

In 1930, Sutherland moved to the University of Chicago in a research position with the rank of full professor. The position apparently offered several incentives for him: an opportunity to focus on criminological research, good resources, a department that was ranked as number one in sociology, and a place where a number of his friends already worked. Even as a research professor, Sutherland taught every year he was there. He also completed the second edition of his textbook, now entitled *Principles of Criminology* (1934), which further enhanced his reputation in the field. From all reports, he was happy at Chicago, but in 1935, the Department Chair Ellsworth Farris recommended that his contract not be renewed. Sutherland promptly moved to Indiana University as Chair of the Sociology Department there. He remained at Indiana for the rest of his career. Although he had been productive during his years at Minnesota and Chicago, the time at Indiana was to be the period of his greatest scholarly productivity.

THE LATER YEARS AND THE THEORY OF DIFFERENTIAL ASSOCIATION

During the last years at Chicago, Professor Sutherland began work on two books. One was coauthored with a friend, Harvey Locke, and was about the homeless (*Twenty Thousand Homeless Men*, 1936), and the other was about a professional thief, Chic Conwell. The book, titled *The Professional Thief* (1937), was ostensibly an "as told to" work, incorporating elements of the Chicago School's life history methodology. The book also incorporated some elements of Sutherland's thinking about a new theory of delinquency, which had previously taken only rudimentary form in the second edition of his textbook. From this, Sutherland began a third revision of his *Principles of Criminology* and produced the first explicit version of his delinquency theory—differential association.

Three scholars—Alfred Lindesmith, Thorsten Sellin, and Frank Sweetser—were helpful in generating differential association theory. Lindesmith, a newly recruited faculty member at Indiana, served as a sounding board for Sutherland and introduced him to a method of theory and evidence called analytic induction. Sellin, with whom Sutherland worked on a Social Science Research Council project, wrote a project report (later to be published as *Culture Conflict and Crime*). The content of the report contained theoretical issues to which Sutherland mildly objected, and this reaction likely set the stage for differential association as an answer. Finally, Frank Sweetser, who was another new faculty member at Indiana, may have helped move Sutherland to a general theory of delinquency and crime through discussions with Sutherland and Lindesmith.

The theory of differential association was published in two versions, the first in 1939 and the second in 1947. The major difference between the two versions was that Sutherland, ever the cautious scholar, was reluctant to state the generality of the theory in the first version. Drawing on a combination of W. I. Thomas's interactionist approach, culture conflict, and social disorganization, the theory could be characterized as representing a culmination of the work of the Chicago School. In its final version, Sutherland viewed the learning of delinquent behavior as a general process created through interaction with intimate others. Those others provided values and rationalizations for behavior. When criminal values and rationalizations (referred to as definitions) outweighed conventional values, delinquent behavior would occur.

Sutherland's final contribution was the concept of white-collar crime. He proposed the idea of business-related crime in a 1945 article and argued that such behaviors were as criminal as those traditionally held to be crimes. In 1949, he published *White Collar Crime*, a book that became a classic in the field and ushered in the study of executive and corporate crime. He also used his newly revised theory of differential association to explain white-collar crime, in one sense testing the theory against a new form of behavior.

CONCLUSION

Edwin H. Sutherland was arguably the foremost criminologist of the 20th century. He helped anchor the discipline of criminology in sociology, contributed to its change into a scientific discipline, authored one of the most famous theories of delinquency and criminality, and created the concept of white-collar crime. His differential association theory remains, 60 years after it was first created, one of the most influential criminological theories with various offspring. In his home field of sociology, Sutherland was recognized through his election to president of the American Sociological Association in 1939 and of the Sociological Research Association in 1940. The American Society of Criminology named their most prestigious scholarly award in his honor.

Frank P. Williams III

See also Chicago Area Project; Henry D. McKay; Theories of Delinquency—Sociological

Bibliography

Gaylord, M., and J. Galliher. 1988. *The Criminology of Edwin Sutherland*. New Brunswick, NJ: Transaction Books.

Geis, G., and C. Goff. 1983. Introduction. Pp. ix–xxxiii in E. H. Sutherland, *White Collar Crime: The Uncut Version*. New Haven, CT: Yale University Press.

Schuessler, K. 1973. *Edwin H. Sutherland: On Analyzing Crime*. Chicago: University of Chicago Press.

Snodgrass, J. 1972. The criminologist and his criminal: The case of Edwin H. Sutherland and Broadway Jones. *Issues in Criminology* 8(Spring):1–17.

Sutherland, E. H. 1924. *Criminology*. Philadelphia: Lippincott.

Sutherland, E. H. 1934. *Principles of Criminology*, 2nd ed. Philadelphia: Lippincott.

Sutherland, E. H. 1937. *The Professional Thief*. Chicago: University of Chicago Press.

Sutherland, E. H. 1939. *Principles of Criminology*, 3rd ed. Philadelphia: Lippincott.

Sutherland, E. H. 1947. *Principles of Criminology*, 4th ed. Philadelphia: Lippincott.

Sutherland, E. H. 1949. *White Collar Crime*. New York: Dryden.

THEORIES OF DELINQUENCY

 ## I. Overview

A theory is an explanation of some event, no matter how simple or complex the explanation is. A scientific theory (that is, the usual form called a unit theory) differs from the public's usual use of the word *theory* in at least four ways. First, the theory must be based on empirical evidence—information derived from beliefs or intuition will not do. Second, the concepts used in the theory must be logically connected. Third, the theory must be empirically testable. Fourth, no matter how much evidence is available to support the theory, it remains a theory—in science, nothing is ever "proven" to be always true. The public usually has the greatest difficulty with the final requirement; in normal usage, the term *theory* suggests that something has no basis in fact. Scientific theories are designed to match empirical fact and if not supported are discarded.

Theories of delinquency are virtually synonymous with theories of criminality. For more than two centuries, criminologists have proposed explanations of delinquent and criminal behavior from various perspectives. For good or ill, the dominant perspective of the past century is a sociological one. The fact of sociological dominance, however, does not mean that other disciplines have not been contributing to our understanding of delinquent behavior. As the entries under this general topic suggest, a substantial amount of work has taken place in biogenetic and psychological disciplines.

On the whole, the emergence of criminal/delinquent theories has reflected the passage of time and the positions popular at various historical points. The first theories were oriented toward sin and "illness" and reflected on the dominant religious teachings of the period. Those who committed crimes had somehow failed to achieve proper religious values and morality. Following these approaches, a new form of explanation was ushered in with the European Renaissance: Humans were held to be rational, thinking beings who act to achieve pleasure and avoid pain. By the 1770s, a group of philosophers, referred to collectively as the Classical School, argued that this human self-interest required control through the passage of laws that would serve to deter criminal acts.

A new criminological school arose in response to the general popularity of science and its advances in the biological and physical sciences. From the 1830s to the 1920s, a "positivist" criminology was characterized by scientific studies of criminals. Scientists variously looked at the relationship between crime and the geographical environment, the biological and genetic features of the offenders, and the psychological characteristics of the offenders. While this work was mostly dominant until about 1920, geographical, psychological, and biological studies and theories remain today (as sections III and IV of this entry will discuss).

By the 1920s, a new scientific approach, the sociological one, emerged and quickly became dominant. The new theorists believed that delinquency could be best explained by social structures and interactions. For instance, some of these theorists explained delinquency as the product of following subcultural rules that were in opposition to the dominant culture (which defined delinquent acts). Others explained delinquency as the result of interaction with people who emphasized delinquent values. Still others theorized that inability to reach important social goals creates strain, which results in deviance. In whatever form, these sociological theories ruled explanations of delinquency until the present day.

Today's theories tend to be more complex approaches to human behavior than has been the case in the past. It is not uncommon to see theories that integrate, either in whole or in part, several other theories to create a new and more complex version. We are also beginning to see theories that bring together biology, psychology, and sociology in a single explanation of delinquency. However, these theories are still predominantly sociological, and we have yet to see an empirically supported and comprehensive explanation of delinquent behavior. We know that certain factors are related to delinquency and criminality, but these factors are not capable of explaining even a *majority* of delinquent acts. One critical problem is that delinquency is defined legally, not behaviorally, and over time, acts defined as delinquent change. Another critical problem is the reactive nature of delinquency—if not reacted to (by authorities), no official, legal delinquency has occurred. Thus we have juveniles who have committed delinquent acts but are not defined as delinquents because they have not been caught. Delinquency theories, then, describe behavioral (not legal) acts and do not necessarily assume that these acts have been reacted to. Producing evidence to evaluate them is difficult, at best.

Frank P. Williams III

Bibliography

Akers, R. L. 2000. *Criminological Theories: Introduction, Evaluation, and Application*, 3rd ed. Los Angeles: Roxbury.

Lilly, J. R., F. T. Cullen, and R. A. Ball. 2002. *Criminological Theory: Context and Consequences*, 3rd ed. Thousand Oaks, CA: Sage.

Vold, G., T. Barnard, and J. Snipes. 1998. *Theoretical Criminology*, 4th ed. Cambridge, MA: Oxford University Press.

Williams, F. P., III, and M. D. McShane. 2003. *Criminological Theory*, 4th ed. Englewood Cliffs, NJ: Prentice Hall.

THEORIES OF DELINQUENCY

 II. Sociological

Sociological theories of delinquency are characterized by an assumption that the most important factors in explaining behavior are social in nature. Thus such factors as social interaction, stress caused by an inability to reach one's goals, low socioeconomic status, a lack of proper socialization, poor education, and bad parenting are frequently implicated in these theories. As noted in the introduction, sociological theories have dominated explanations of delinquency since at least the 1920s and show no signs of yielding to other disciplines at present. This part of the Theories of Delinquency entry examines the most important of those explanations, largely in a chronological fashion, and describes the way in which they might be used in delinquency prevention programs. Interested readers will want to consult a book on criminology or delinquency theory for many more perspectives not mentioned in this summary.

EARLY SOCIOLOGICAL THEORIES

The French School

The earliest theories to describe criminality ("delinquency" had not yet been invented) in a social fashion were two French versions in the late 1800s. Gabriel Tarde, a French magistrate, said that criminal behavior spreads in a process of imitation. New forms of criminal acts (such as females committing murder by poison) occur first in the large, sophisticated cities and then are imitated by those in the towns and rural areas. A more well-accepted version was proposed by French sociologist Emile Durkheim, who said that crime occurs in every society and therefore is natural. However, when too much or too little crime is present in a society, an abnormal situation is present, and social control becomes an issue. Durkheim also assumed that crime (and deviance) is a product of a lack of regulation in society. As societies move from primitive to modern, the number of social relations increases and labor becomes more specialized. Thus people in modern societies cannot survive on their own and depend on a large number of others, with relationships always breaking down. When societal events—such as an economic depression—disrupt the social fabric, expected relationships between people become deregulated and crime increases. This deregulation is referred to as anomie, which will be described later in this entry.

The Chicago School and Its Relatives

The next popular sociological versions occurred with the rise of the Department of Sociology at the University of Chicago, primarily during the period of 1915 to 1940.

Symbolic Interactionism. The first approach to come out of the Chicago School was known as symbolic interactionism. Based on the work of George Herbert Mead, Charles Horton Cooley, and W. I. Thomas, symbolic interactionism was a preeminently social theory in a day when biological and psychological theories were dominant. The idea is that people act according to the communicated symbols they receive from others. These symbols can be verbal or nonverbal but must be interpreted by the person receiving them. In short, people interact with each other and provide symbolic communication. This communication requires interpretation and results in a person constructing his or her self-image according to the way he or she thinks others see them. The person then acts according to the self-image and the anticipated expectations of others. For delinquency, this means that communicated social values create behavior. When a juvenile is around enough communicated values that approve of delinquency, she or he will behave accordingly.

Ecological Theory. Robert Park and Ernest Burgess, using a view of cities derived from a then-popular biological perspective called ecology, proposed that a city has areas with dominant patterns and uses. These areas tend to follow an ecological pattern of succession and dominance in which other areas are "invaded" and taken over. For instance, industrialized areas tend to encroach on those bordering them and ultimately expand into new territory. Clifford Shaw and Henry McKay added to this picture by mapping delinquency against areas of Chicago and demonstrated that, as one moved away from the central area of the city, delinquency decreased. This perspective came to be known as concentric zone theory. The area (zone) in the most turmoil is the one between the business/industrial area and the residential area. This is the zone of transition, a place that is undesirable for living but where housing is cheap. In Chicago, when Park and Burgess developed this theory, people who had just moved to Chicago (mostly immigrants) could not afford to live elsewhere, and the location was near the factories where they found jobs. Delinquency was high in this area and is still high today.

Social Disorganization. Attempting to explain the phenomenon of concentric zones, Shaw and McKay developed a theory of social disorganization. In neighborhoods with rapid turnover and undergoing conversion from residential to industrial, there is little cohesion left among social institutions. Families have difficulty taking care of their children; churches, schools, recreational opportunities, and the like break down. In other words, these neighborhoods are deteriorating and so are the social values of the people in them. Thus the neighborhoods are socially disorganized. In addition, the values transmitted to children by their elders in disorganized areas tend to be deviant ones.

Culture Conflict. In communicating with Chicago School scholars, particularly Edwin Sutherland, Thorsten Sellin developed an alternative explanation for high delinquency rates seen in zones of transition. He suggested that immigrants arriving in Chicago bring their home cultures with them. These cultural values do not necessarily fit in with those already established in Chicago and, in some cases, cause conflict. The immigrants expect to engage in behavior according to their home culture, but in some situations, different behavior is mandated by the culture of Chicago (or America). Indeed, the difference between the two cultural values may result in criminal or delinquent behavior. Culture conflict is, then, an explanation of delinquent behavior. This form of delinquency is called primary conflict—someone from one culture runs afoul of another culture's laws. Another form is secondary conflict, in which a subculture within a larger culture has values opposed to those of the larger culture.

Differential Association. In 1939, and in a revised version in 1947, Edwin Sutherland developed a theory that was, in one sense, the culmination of the Chicago School. Combining symbolic interactionism, social disorganization, and culture conflict, Sutherland proposed that delinquent behavior is learned from others through a process of communication. This learning occurs mostly from those who are most important to a person: family, friends, and intimate others. The content of what is learned comprises both techniques of how to commit a crime and the values and rationalizations supportive of the behavior. The latter were rephrased as "definitions," which Sutherland said are favorable or unfavorable to criminal law. Greater weight given to definitions favorable to violation of law allows a youth to commit a delinquent act. Finally, these definitions provided by one's associates are affected by the importance of, and amount of time spent with, those associates. Sutherland's differential association theory became the most widely accepted explanation of delinquency for many years. He revised it in 1947, and it is that version that is described here.

Anomie. An altogether different theory was proposed by Robert Merton in 1930. While not directly a theory of delinquency or crime, Merton's theory is important because of delinquency theories that subsequently relied on it. Borrowing Durkheim's concept of anomie, Merton suggested that there are highly emphasized cultural values resulting in society-wide goals that individuals should attain (such as financial success). In addition, the goals are achieved by standard methods (which Merton called legitimate means). However, not everyone has equal access to these standard means of achieving society-wide goals. The lower classes in general have little access and therefore find ways of adapting to this problem.

Merton proposed five deviant modes of adaptation, which were based on the individual's level of acceptance of the standard means and goals: conformity, innovation, ritualism, retreatism, and rebellion. Conformity is the product of continuing to strive toward the goals and attempting to use standard means, even though, in this case, the means will never gain the goals. Merton believed this adaptation is the most common. Innovation involves acceptance of the goals but not the means; therefore, much of crime and delinquency is this form of adaptation. Ritualism represents focusing on the means but giving up on the goals as being out of reach (e.g., bureaucratic behavior and some religious fanaticism). Retreatism is giving up on both the goals and the means, as a hermit does or perhaps a skid-row bum. Finally, rebellion means substituting for both the goals and the means, seeking new goals and new means to attain them.

Merton's anomie theory was the only true competitor for differential association for about three decades, although Merton has recently said that the two do not conflict but are complementary. In addition, anomie theory was important to gang subculture theories of the 1950s, as discussed in the next section.

GANG SUBCULTURE THEORIES

Both differential association and anomie theory were critical to the development of the theories of the 1950s. The chief architects of these theories, Albert Cohen, Richard Cloward, and Lloyd Ohlin, shared not only an interest in the two major theories but had actually studied under either Sutherland or Merton (or both). In fact, the new theories were attempts to integrate differential association and anomie. For better or worse, the 1950s were a period of intense interest in gangs, and most criminologists were convinced that lower-class, urban, minority delinquency represented most of delinquent behavior.

The Delinquent Subculture

In 1955, Albert K. Cohen developed the first of the gang subculture theories. Having studied with both Sutherland and Merton, Cohen proposed that a lack of status (the goal) paired with a subcultural learning environment (differential association's definitions) created gang delinquency. The lack of status is the product of lower-class children's inadequate preparation for the tasks of school, a middle-class institution. Falling further and further behind, a high degree of frustration sets in until, in reaction, the juveniles opt for a method of gaining status that they can reach— the gang subculture. The critical point about the gang subculture is that it espouses anti-middle-class values, which almost automatically result in delinquency.

By the 1950s, the gang subculture had already existed for some time; thus it was merely a matter of lower-class juveniles choosing a handy alternative. Cohen explained its development as a process of historical collective solutions to the problem of how to gain status. In other words, at some past point, lower-class children struggled with the issue of lost status and slowly developed alternative solutions, which collectively became the gang subculture. After that point, the gang subculture will continue to exist as long as some children accept the existing subcultural alternative.

Differential Opportunity

Another approach to explaining subcultural gang delinquency was developed by Richard Cloward and Lloyd Ohlin. Cloward had studied with Merton and Ohlin with Sutherland. Together they proposed that, in addition to the legitimate opportunity structure (means) Merton had noted, an illegitimate opportunity structure exists and has unequal access (such as organized crime). This time, though, it is the lower class that has greater access. Cloward and Ohlin also noted that a key to delinquency is the degree of control exerted by adults in the neighborhood. The greatest amount of control over children (in urban areas) occurs in a lower-class neighborhood where both opportunity structures exist and are integrated—one can "cross over" between the two. Their argument was that even organized crime has an interest in controlling juvenile activity. Thus most of the delinquency in such a community will also be of a controlled variety, with gangs serving primarily as an "apprentice" structure for organized crime. When a community lacks integration, more conflict exists among juveniles, resulting in conflict-oriented gangs. Cloward and Ohlin also posited a final gang subculture: a retreatist gang. These juveniles are unsuccessful in both legitimate and illegitimate worlds and, literally, drop out to a world of drug use.

Focal Concerns

A third form of subculture theory developed during the 1950s, independent of the Sutherland-Merton heritage. Walter Miller, an anthropologist, proposed that urban lower classes simply had a different culture—one that is, in some instances, opposed to dominant middle-class values. For lower-class males, growing up in a female-dominated household creates a situation where male role models are valued. Gangs provide a place for such role models and exhibit behavior that focuses on male traits. Miller called these traits focal concerns and identified six of them with such attributes as trouble, toughness, excitement, smartness, fate, and autonomy. In other words, these values teach that a male should be in control of himself and all challenges should be met. Such values and traits automatically bring these lower-class urban juveniles into conflict with the law and legal authorities and result in higher rates of delinquency.

LABELING AND CONFLICT

Relying on officially collected crime reports, the theories just discussed strove to explain why certain groups of juveniles have higher rates of delinquency (always urban, lower-class, minority youth). At the end of the 1950s, a new method of locating evidence of delinquency was developed: the self-report study. The self-report methodology actually asked youths what delinquent behaviors they had engaged in. The results were somewhat different from those of official statistics: Lower-class and minority juveniles are about as likely to commit delinquent acts as are middle-class kids. Thus a new question was born: Why did official statistics report that lower-class minority juveniles were so delinquency prone?

Labeling theory developed as an answer to that question. Its answer was that, while many juveniles committed delinquent acts, it is the process of reaction to those acts that defines delinquency. In one sense, the acts that are reacted to are matched by those that aren't. On the whole, labeling says that those who are less powerful (i.e., the lower classes and minorities) are most likely to be reacted to and labeled by authorities as delinquent. Middle-class and white children are more likely to have their delinquent acts go unnoticed (or at least not officially reacted to). Further, labeling suggests that those who receive attention are more likely to be seen as "delinquents" and subsequently watched more carefully. This process ultimately results in a loss of life opportunities for those labeled. Thus the label itself is likely to precipitate more reactions and a "career" of delinquency and crime.

Carrying the picture drawn by labeling a bit further, conflict theories suggest that reaction by authorities is an intentional action to keep the powerless in their place. Higher classes are assumed to have created laws and legal process in such a manner as to further their interests at the expense of the lower classes. The various conflict theories range from assumptions that there are many groups competing for power at the expense of each other, to a version with only two classes, the elite and the working classes. Various subtleties in this process include such factors as the creation of conflict-oriented workplace relations in the family, frustration as a result of an inability to get ahead in life, and the use of the criminal/juvenile justice system as a way to control surplus labor. In all versions, however, the central idea is that delinquents are drawn from the losers in either group or class warfare.

SOCIAL LEARNING

Using Sutherland's theory of differential association, Ronald Akers authored the dominant version of social learning theory in the 1970s. The core of the theory is that reinforced behaviors are more likely to occur. Subcultural groups tend to reinforce more values supportive of delinquent acts, a process resulting in greater levels of delinquency. Akers's approach says that individuals do not need to be reinforced directly; learning can occur by observing others being rewarded for a behavior. Thus juveniles can model the behavior of those already delinquent. In addition, the values and statements that reinforce delinquency can come from conventional others, not just those who are delinquent and criminal.

SOCIAL CONTROL AND SELF-CONTROL

Another brand of delinquency theory is based on the assumption that everyone is self-interested and therefore needs to be controlled before proper behavior will occur. In short, delinquency is "normal" and conformity needs to be supported. Travis Hirschi, with a control theory popular in the 1970s, said that the necessary factor in decreasing delinquency is to have a strong bond to the moral order. This moral order is composed of four elements: attachment, involvement, commitment, and belief. The characteristics associated with the four elements include such factors as ties to parents and friends, time spent in conventional activities, investment in education, and approval of and cooperation with conventional pursuits. These elements, when present, serve to create conformity within an individual, and when absent, increase the likelihood of delinquency.

A more recent version, variously called the general theory of crime or low self-control theory, was developed by Michael Gottfredson and Travis Hirschi in 1990. They postulated that crime itself is merely part of self-interested behavior. The theory also acknowledges that delinquency and crime are only one form of impulsive and risky behaviors; with lack of self-control, any of a group of such behaviors can occur. A

person's degree of control over his or her self-interested behavior, characterized as impulsiveness, becomes a critical factor. Low self-control is generally a product of poor parenting, particularly a lack of proper discipline at an early age. Finally, Gottfredson and Hirschi state that low self-control does not come and go; once in place, it remains throughout life. Individuals with low self-control have higher rates of delinquency and crime (and analogous behavior) than do others.

CONTEMPORARY THEORIES

While there are many new versions of delinquency theory, most are based on some version of control theory. The question has become where to go from there. Two theories, coupled with Gottfredson and Hirschi's self-control theory, present a good picture of contemporary delinquency theory.

The major competitor to low self-control theory is the developmental or life-course approach, with one of the more popular versions proposed by Robert Sampson and John Laub. Instead of agreeing with low self-control theory that propensity for delinquency and crime is a trait that remains over the course of one's life, Sampson and Laub argued that different paths and trajectories over time create an ebb and flow for criminal behavior. Borrowing from general control theories, they posited that various factors serve to increase or decrease the social bonds affecting delinquency and criminality. Previous behavioral choices can also affect present and future social bonds, leading to continuity in delinquent and criminal behavior. Further, there are normal points in life where most people enter various criminality-reducing life paths, such as college, marriage, and a career. These various life paths are important to both conformity and deviance. For instance, marriage serves to reduce criminality; divorce serves to increase it. The important message in developmental theories is that the form of important social bonds varies throughout life, thus one's propensity for delinquency and crime also varies.

Robert Agnew proposed a new version of strain theory. Noting that Merton's anomie theory was broadly constructed and spoke to the way society was structured, Agnew brought the explanation of strain to the individual level. Juveniles may not partake of societal goals and means, yet they have similar strivings at school, just with more immediate and youthful goals such as popularity or doing well in school. For school-age juveniles, strain is likely to be a product of personal circumstances, such as lost popularity or a failed dating relationship, or when adverse situations occur, such as a family conflict. The degree of strain, and the ability to cope with it, is mitigated by several other conditions, such as supportive others, the juvenile's own ability to bear up under stress, the availability of acceptable alternatives, or even the usual social control variables. If the ability to cope is poor, frustration or humiliation may lead to anger, and delinquent acts become much more likely.

CONCLUSION

Sociological theories of delinquency tend toward identifying some type of socialization as the cause of delinquent acts. Over the last few decades, this socialization has primarily taken the form of parenting and school-based education. One can also observe that from the simple causes of delinquency proposed in the early theories of delinquency, theorists are now proposing versions that are much more complex. Some of the current theories, such as Charles Tittle's control balance theory, are so complex that testing them is very difficult. On the other hand, these complex theories probably are much more accurate in their reflection of real-life causes of delinquency. At the same time, even the currently complex versions tend to remain sociological in their focus; that is, they generally ignore both biogenetic and psychological factors. Perhaps it is time to put disciplinary emphases aside in favor of a truer but even more complex understanding of delinquency.

Frank P. Williams III

See also Richard A. Cloward; Albert K. Cohen; Travis Hirschi; Henry D. McKay; Walter B. Miller; Lloyd E. Ohlin; Johan Thorsten Sellin; Clifford R. Shaw; Self-Report Studies; Edwin H. Sutherland

Bibliography

Gibbons, D. C. 1979. *The Criminological Enterprise: Theories and Perspectives.* Englewood Cliffs, NJ: Prentice Hall.

Martin, R., R. Mutchnick, and T. Austin. 1990. *Criminological Thought: Pioneers Past and Present.* New York: Macmillan.

Williams, F. P., III, and M. D. McShane. 2003. *Criminological Theory*, 4th ed. Englewood Cliffs, NJ: Prentice Hall.

THEORIES OF DELINQUENCY

 ## III. Psychological

Theorists have attempted to explain delinquent behavior from a variety of perspectives, but the psychological approach is most introspective in nature. This approach uses the knowledge of psychological theorists to analyze the minds and thought processes of individuals who engage in delinquent acts. Theories range from psychoanalysis and behaviorism to social learning and intelligence. From the notion of rewards and punishments, learned expectations and assimilation, and accommodation, a psychological presence in delinquent behavior is quite evident. But to what extent can we truly attribute psychologjcal developments to crime, and exactly what do they mean?

PSYCHOANALYTIC THEORIES

The influence of psychoanalysis on criminal behavior is associated with the work of Sigmund Freud and the extension of his work by his pupils Alfred Adler and Carl Jung. Psychoanalysis rests on the notion that all actions people engage in are a direct result of what is going on in their unconscious mind (Allen, 1997). Freud believed that all individuals go through five psychosexual stages, beginning at birth and ending in adolescence. Individuals who do not properly progress through each stage can become fixated at one stage and spend the rest of their lives unconsciously acting out behaviors associated with that stage (Berk, 1996).

This psychosexual theory encompasses the notion that poorly developed sexual and aggressive drives can lead to unhealthy personality development. Thus the three driving forces of the id, ego, and superego—which represent impulsivity, rationality, and morality, respectively—may be unable to work out the inner struggle going on within an individual's mind (Allen, 1997). For example, a rapist may engage in criminal activity because he is stuck in the anal psychosexual stage of development, which deals with the issues of power and control. This fixation, coupled with a poorly developed personality, does not allow his rational ego to overrule his impulsive id, forcing him into an unconscious pattern of deviant behavior.

Similarly, Carl Jung, one of Freud's students and followers, also believed personality developed as a result of the unconscious. Jung rejected Freud's idea of sexualism and focused on how the total personality could only be developed through the unity of the conscious and collective unconscious. He equated it to a teeter-totter in that too much of the conscious would tilt it one way and too much of the unconscious would tilt it the other way. Therefore, an individual had to find a balance to help unify the development of "self." This balance usually was in reference to opposing forces within a person. In a poorly developed self, this balance was unequal, resulting in psychological ills. From Jung's perspective, individuals engage in delinquent behavior because they cannot find the balance between the conscious and unconscious mind. Thus the rapist in the previous example has a poorly developed personality, characterized by the inability to overcome the opposing forces within him and to find his total self, which leads him to engage in delinquent acts.

Psychoanalytic theorists support the concept that delinquent behavior is the result of past experiences that are repressed and expressed later in life through criminal behavior. Delinquency is the result of a slightly unbalanced conscious and unconscious mind and poorly developed id and superego. These theorists tend to support testing juveniles for past traumatic incidents that may have led to repression, or any childhood abnormalities that could have left them fixated at a certain stage of development or unable to properly develop their personality. The problem is that there are no tests able to measure id and ego development or relationships between early experiences and future behavior. Psychoanalytic theorists use psychotherapy to help offenders locate and understand the origin of their emotional disturbances.

BEHAVIORAL THEORIES

Behaviorism is tied to the works of Ivan Pavlov, John B. Watson, and B. F. Skinner. It is concerned with the idea of learning being accomplished through associations of stimuli with responses. B. F. Skinner argued that the environment shapes behavior, thus placing behavior on forces *outside* the individual. All individuals and their behaviors are governed by the pursuit of pleasure and the avoidance of pain. Accordingly, individuals act certain ways within their environment to elicit these pleasurable responses. This pattern of individual behavior, called operant conditioning, is based on a system of reinforcements and punishments. Skinner believed that an individual learns how to get what he or she wants

from an environment by trial and error. If a behavior produces a good consequence, it is increased; if it produces a bad consequence, it is decreased.

Behavioral theories of delinquency are based on the assumption that delinquency will occur as long as it produces pleasurable responses. For example, a juvenile may decide to rob a convenience store based on the assumption of the pleasurable response of obtaining money. If the juvenile robs the store and does not get caught, the pleasurable response is reinforced, and the behavior is likely to continue. If the juvenile gets caught, the robbery is likely to be associated with an unpleasurable response, thus decreasing the likelihood of the behavior. Theorists supporting this notion contend that the basis for deterring criminal behavior and delinquency lies in manipulating reinforcements. They believe if the reinforcer is controlled, the behavior can be controlled (Bolles, 1993).

SOCIAL LEARNING THEORIES

If a person were to observe a college student progress from freshman year to senior year, through graduate school and a Ph.D. program, and say, "I'd like to be successful like that someday," the observer would have just demonstrated social learning theory. This theory emphasizes that behavior is reinforced not only through rewards and punishments but also through expectations that are learned by watching what happens to other people. Gabriel Tarde was the first to recognize this tendency in 1890. He believed that people learn criminal behavior by imitating the behaviors of others, especially those who are defined as "superior." In 1969, Albert Bandura developed more elaborate explanations of this concept. Bandura's work illustrates the process of observational learning, showing how children learn by watching and imitating others. Children take what they see, model it and "turn it over" in their minds by relating it to information they already have. They then translate this model into a behavior that they continue or stop depending on reinforcements and incentives.

Ronald Akers's (1985) social learning theory of deviant behavior closely resembles the reinforcement theories of Albert Bandura and William Rotter. Often referred to as differential reinforcement theory, it is based on the premise that the strength of deviant behavior is directly related to the amount, frequency, and probability of its reinforcement. For example, a juvenile perceives various types of behaviors in the surrounding subculture. Behaviors exhibited by the people closest and most important to the juvenile become examples of desirable (i.e., reinforced) behavior. If the juvenile's associates engage in delinquent behaviors, they provide social reinforcements and sources of imitation for the juvenile. Based on these reinforcements (rewards and punishments), the youth decides whether to continue imitating the behaviors. If the reinforcements do not provide the type of consequences the juvenile is looking for, the behaviors will stop. If the reinforcements do produce favorable consequences, the criminal behavior will continue (Akers, 1985). According to Akers's theory, the juvenile has learned delinquent behaviors by watching the consequences those behaviors have on others. Thus social learning theory encompasses observational learning and emulation as the cause of crime and delinquency.

INTELLIGENCE THEORIES

Intelligence has also been widely used to explain the concept of delinquent and criminal behavior. From the explanations of Charles Goring (lack of intelligence results in uncontrolled actions) to Henry Goddard's misuse of intelligence testing, theorists have played on this concept for more than a century.

In the early 1900s, testing of the intelligence of prisoners indicated that prisoners had relatively higher IQs than World War I draftees. This led to the dismissal of Goddard's theory of IQ being used to classify individuals as "feebleminded," "morons," and "high-grade defectives" (Vold, Bernard, and Snipes, 1998). Unfortunately, by then, this theory had already resulted in over 20,000 forced sterilizations and trauma for countless immigrants who were prevented from entering the United States.

Recently, theorists Travis Hirschi and Michael Hindelang supported the IQ/delinquency theory with a different approach. They believed that individuals with low IQs will not be prepared for school or school achievements. This lack of preparation leads to few school-related attachments, few positive academic rewards, and consequently, school failure. This chain of events results in a lack of control over antisocial and delinquent behaviors, making them more likely.

Other theorists have posited a more direct relationship between IQ and delinquency. Robert Gordon, for instance, makes the assumption that IQ scores measure innate intelligence controversially arguing that

blacks commit more crime and delinquency than do whites because they have lower IQs. Similarly, James Q. Wilson and Richard Herrnstein agree that low IQ directly contributes to crime and delinquency because it is associated with poor moral reasoning.

In recent years, educational research has generally concluded that IQ is a better indicator of cultural background and learning environments. Aside from publications such as *The Bell Curve* by Herrnstein and Murray (which attempts to explain how American society is becoming less intelligent), the overall conclusion is that variations in IQ scores between delinquent and nondelinquent individuals are probably a reflection of environmental factors rather than genetic factors. Thus having a low IQ does not indicate one will become a delinquent.

CONCLUSION

Of all the psychological theories presented, each has its own unique explanation of why individuals engage in delinquent behavior. It may be due to the unconscious mind, the result of positive reinforcements, or the result of favorable consequences. Some sound a bit far-fetched, some are better supported than others, and some have had more research conducted on them than others. But all psychological theories share three common ideals: (1) Delinquency is a result of some type of thought process by the individual engaging in the act, (2) delinquency does not just happen but involves cognition, and (3) no individual is predisposed to delinquency. Specifically identifying which of the theories best explains delinquency is nearly impossible because delinquency seems to encompass some of each theory in its origin. At best, researchers can focus on the specifics of each theory in hopes of unifying and solidifying the entire psychological perspective of why delinquent behavior occurs.

Laura J. Bailey

See also Augusta Fox Bronner; Community Treatment Project; William Healy; Mental Health

Bibliography

Akers, R. 1985. Social control and delinquent behavior. *Criminology* 23:47–61.
Allen, B. P. 1997. *Personality Theories: Development, Growth, and Diversity*, 2nd ed. Boston: Allyn & Bacon.

Bartol, C. R. 1999. *Criminal Behavior: A Psychosocial Approach*, 5th ed. Upper Saddle River, NJ: Prentice Hall.

Berk, L. E. 1996. *Infants, Children, and Adolescents*, 2nd ed. Boston: Allyn & Bacon

Bolles, R. C. 1993. *The Story of Psychology: A Thematic History*. Pacific Grove, CA: Brooks/Cole.

Vold, G. B., T. J. Bernard, and J. B. Snipes. 1998. *Theoretical Criminology*, 4th ed. New York: Oxford University Press.

THEORIES OF DELINQUENCY

 ## IV. Biological

Biological theories were among the earliest of scientific explanations for deviant and delinquent behavior. A physiognomist of the 16th century, J. Baptiste della Porte, related characteristics of the body to criminality. However, the study of biological characteristics more properly can be traced to the mid-19th century science of phrenology and its relationship to crime. Franz Gall, the father of phrenology, believed that criminals could be identified by bumps on their skulls.

The most important criminological theorist of the 1800s in Europe and the United States, Cesare Lombroso (1835–1909), was heavily influenced by the work of Gall. While performing an autopsy on a violent criminal, Lombroso noticed that the skull was more suited to an animal than a human. He then developed the theory that criminals were not as far along the evolutionary ladder as normal people. Lombroso referred to these born criminals as atavists, or biological throwbacks to an earlier stage of development. Atavistic people share a number of characteristics, such as chimpanzee-like ears, shifty eyes, and large jaws. His students and colleagues, Enrico Ferri and Raffael Garofalo, continued his work and added factors other than physical ones to describe criminals.

As a result of Lombroso's work, many subsequent studies attempted to link biological traits to criminality. Some of these studies included eugenics (which concentrated on population control), genetics (which concentrated on the evolution of the human species), and body types.

In the late 19th and early 20th centuries, family studies were conducted to identify degenerate clans or families in hopes of preventing those with bad genes from breeding, thereby cleansing society of social problems. Earlier in the 1860s, the eugenics movement had started in England with Sir Francis Galton, a cousin of Charles Darwin. The eugenics movement provided the basis for many governmental policies and provisions, including how to deal with the poor, feebleminded, lazy, and other similar groups in society.

The ultimate goal of those who studied eugenics was to prove that poor, undereducated families produced an overabundance of criminals and otherwise were liabilities and menaces to society. Eugenicists believed they could identify these degenerates, who usually represented entire branches of family trees. Once identified, degenerate families would not be allowed to reproduce, and soon society would be cured of its ills. This kind of thinking helped support and justify an ideology of power based in biology.

After studying families of delinquents and criminals, Richard Dugdale and Charles Goring, for instance, both suggested that delinquency and criminality were passed down genetically from generation to generation. From such research, the term *feeblemindedness* was coined to describe a genetic disposition to low intelligence that delinquents were assumed to have. Goring concluded that criminals were born with a defective physique and a defective intelligence that differentiated criminals from noncriminals. Dugdale believed that, if left alone, defective lines of people would naturally become extinct.

Another genetic theorist of the time, Oscar M'Culloch (1888), urged social workers not to give aid to tribes such as the Ishmaels and soon they would die out. The Ishmaels were dark-skinned people whom M'Culloch believed were inferior because of their dark skin. Many eugenicists took the position that keeping the poor, criminal, and feebleminded locked up would save society from having additional dependents and higher liabilities. Family studies were supported and financed by wealthy people who thought that social problems were linked to biological problems. The poor, the criminal, and the feebleminded were looked upon as being social sores who, if not subjected to the eugenic cure, would infect society.

In 1939, Ernest Hooton claimed anew that there were important biological differences between criminals and noncriminals. Like Lombroso, Hooton suggested that biological features characterized delinquents and criminals. For instance, he concluded through his research that burglars have short heads, blond hair, and nonprotruding jaws; robbers have long wavy hair, short ears, and broad faces.

A decade later, William Sheldon identified varieties of delinquent youth with different body types. His "somatic typology" listed three major somatotypes (or body types). Endomorphs were characterized as obese, soft, and rounded people and were thought to be fun loving and sociable. Mesomorphs were considered muscular and athletic, assertive, vigorous, and bold. Ectomorphs were characterized as tall and thin with well-developed brains and were thought to be introverted, sensitive, and nervous. Sheldon theorized that mesomorphs were most likely to become delinquents.

Modern biologically oriented theorists tend to mix the environment with biological factors in more complex versions of delinquency theory. Biological factors also tend to be identified as neurochemical and enzyme-related, rather than the body-feature perspectives of the past. Criminologist C. Ray Jeffery, for instance, talks about a mixture of physical and social environments interacting with the body's neurochemistry. His position is that behavior is a product of the brain. When certain hormones or enzymes (or a lack thereof) affect the brain, misinterpretation of the environment may occur and result in deviance. Similarly, a toxic or harmful physical environment may produce certain neurochemicals, resulting in abnormal brain-produced behaviors.

In another example of modern biological research, Keith Burnett has linked boys aged 7 to 12 with low levels of the stress hormone cortisol to extremely aggressive behavior. If he is correct, in the future, a simple saliva test may serve to predict which boys will have some of the worst behavior problems. Other researchers have argued much the same point for other neurochemicals, toxins, and nutrients.

Such predictions exemplify the primary attraction of biological research: a simple "test" to determine who will become delinquent. Biological theories have always promised to identify predelinquents, but their biggest obstacle is that they tend to remain indifferent to the fact that delinquency is a socially defined, not biologically defined, phenomenon. Once these theories integrate social factors into their various positions, it should be clear that they have something to add to explanations of complex behaviors like delinquency.

Tracy Andrus

See also At-Risk Youth; Body-Type Theories; Learning Disabilities; Race and Processing of Juvenile Offenders

Bibliography

Horton, D. M. 2000. *Pioneering Perspectives in Criminology*. Incline Village, NV: Copperhouse.

Jeffery, C. Ray. 1997. *Criminology: An Interdisciplinary Approach*. Englewood Cliffs, NJ: Prentice Hall.

Mednick, S. A., T. E. Moffitt, and S. A. Stack. 1987. *The Causes of Crime: New Biological Approaches*. New York: Cambridge University Press.

Rafter, N. H. 1997. *Creating Born Criminals*. Urbana: University of Illinois Press.

THRASHER, FREDERIC M. (1892–1962)

Frederic Milton Thrasher's Ph.D. dissertation, *The Gang: A Study of 1,313 Gangs in Chicago*, was published by the University of Chicago Press in 1927 as one of the 18 volumes contained in the renowned Chicago Sociological Series. Within its first year, *The Gang* went through four printings. A second edition was released in 1936, and in 1963, James F. Short Jr. contributed a preface to the book and cut some dated material. That edition sold a hefty total of slightly more than 27,000 copies before it went out of print in 1969. In 2000, a small press reprinted the initial edition of *The Gang*, complete with the spot map that pinpointed the locations of gang activity in Chicago.

Today *The Gang* often is labeled as a "pioneering," "seminal," and "classic" study. One commentator has called it "unparalleled in the field" (Hardman, 1967:6), and 34 years after its publication, David Bordua (1961:130) regarded it as "still the best book on gangs and gang delinquency." The persisting significance of Thrasher's scholarship is testified to by a citation count. Seventy-one years after the book's appearance, 14 references to *The Gang* appeared in the *Social Science Citation Index*. Since 1981, when the index began, Thrasher's work has received slightly more than 200 references.

The Gang is perhaps best known for its focus on the ecology of gang development—that is, the relationship between ganging and the surrounding physical environment. Thrasher maintained that gangs tended to come into being primarily in interstitial areas—deteriorated sites near the central city where speculators refused to upgrade the housing and other amenities because they presumed that, in time, they would be able to sell their holdings at a considerable profit to meet the needs of the expanding central city.

Thrasher's monograph was the product of extensive fieldwork with gang members, law enforcement personnel, and social service providers. Perhaps its least successful element was its failure to pinpoint precisely what was meant by the term *gang*. Thrasher suggests that gangs are formed spontaneously and then integrated through conflict with outsiders, and that they are characterized by face-to-face meetings, milling, movement through space as a unit, and a degree of planning. Such collective behavior is said to lead to traditions, solidarity, and attachment to a local territory. Critics have pointed out that it would be but a slight exaggeration to suggest that according to Thrasher's definition, the Harvard and Notre Dame football teams as well as most other teams and Mardi Gras revelers could be regarded as gangs.

A MIDWEST UPBRINGING AND EDUCATION

Frederic M. Thrasher was an only child, born in Shelbyville, Indiana, on February 19, 1892, to Milton Brown Thrasher and Eva Lacy Thrasher in the 14th year of their marriage. He could trace his American ancestry back to the Revolutionary War. Thrasher's father, after leaving school at 16 because of the death of his mother, worked his way up from a succession of mercantile jobs to the ownership of the largest department store in Frankfort, Indiana, and to a position as "one of the city's best-loved citizens" (*Frankfort Morning Times*, 1937:5). Milton Thrasher's greatest moment of notoriety came in 1934 when he was featured in the 4,000 newspapers that printed Robert Ripley's "Believe It or Not" column. His feat was jumping off a 15-foot diving board at the municipal swimming pool on his birthday each year, even though he was then into his 80s. Thrasher's mother was a civic leader, a member of the Women's Christian Temperance Union, and active in literary clubs as a writer of poetry. Both parents were dedicated members of the Methodist Episcopalian church.

Frederic attended public and high school in Frankfort from 1899 to 1911. He later would take a certain pride in the fact that he engaged in no sports during these years—and apparently thereafter as well. During his senior high school year, he worked as a reporter for the local newspaper, an experience that may have played a role in capturing the attention of the eminent Chicago sociologist, Robert Park, who would be his dissertation supervisor. Park himself had been a reporter and editor on big-city newspapers for almost a dozen years before he joined the University of Chicago sociology department.

In the fall of 1911, Thrasher entered DePauw University in Greencastle, Indiana, and remained there until his graduation four years later. Tuition was $30 a semester and the university bulletin pointed out that a thoroughly neat and comfortable room could be had for a dollar and a quarter a week. By the time he graduated, Thrasher had become a tutor in English and held an assistantship in the sociology department.

In 1915, Thrasher began his work at the University of Chicago, without question the leading site for the study of sociology in the world, and he remained there for two years. His master's thesis was titled *The Boy Scout Movement as a Socializing Agency*. Thrasher did not see military service in World War I, though of susceptible age, perhaps because of his poor eyesight. He took a teaching position at Ohio State University in 1918 for one year and then accepted a job as director of the Cincinnati Home Service Institute, a division of the Red Cross, and head of the sociology department at the University of Cincinnati.

After the armistice in November 1919, Thrasher returned to Chicago for three more academic years. Then, in 1923, he took a position in the sociology department at Illinois Wesleyan University in Bloomington, Illinois, and remained there until 1926. After that, he became a founding member of the educational sociology department at New York University, retaining that position for a third of a century.

THE GANG

The Gang received fine reviews, though Nels Anderson, a fellow graduate student with Thrasher, felt compelled to point out that unlike his own dissertation (*The Hobo*, 1923), many persons had helped to provide material for Thrasher's work. He also noted that the Chicago newspapers had "made sport" of 1313—the precise number of gangs noted in *The Gang*'s subtitle. Solomon Kobrin, who worked for years with Chicago gangs, contended that it was Thrasher's research assistants who had specified the total as an in-joke, and that it was the house number of a nearby brothel.

In other reviews, Thorsten Sellin (1927:192) noted that *The Gang* was written in "an entertaining as well as an instructive manner," while John Gillin (1927:69) observed that "on the whole the book is one of the most worthwhile in recent sociological literature."

The writing in *The Gang* is unusually good for an academic study. Characteristic of some of the better prose style, for instance, is this description of a slum area:

There is nothing fresh or clean to greet the eye; everywhere are unpainted, ramshackle buildings, blackened and besmirched with the smoke of industry. In this sort of habitat the gang seems to flourish best. (Thrasher, 1927:9)

The book provides readers with a great deal of information—perhaps too much—about all sorts of matters that Thrasher rather haphazardly denotes as characteristics of gang behavior. Particularly notable is the pure pleasure that Thrasher so often attributes to gang membership. Given his religious training (though he backslid considerably as an adult), Thrasher might well have been morally outraged by "irresponsible" gang activities. Instead, he focuses on the freedom (a word he much favors) and the pursuit of fun by gang boys. It is a lifestyle, he observes, "far removed from the humdrum existence of the average citizen" (Thrasher, 1927:3).

NEW YORK UNIVERSITY

Thrasher continued gang research during the earlier part of his career at New York University, heading two major research projects. The first involved a three-year evaluation of the West Side Boys' Club of Manhattan. Thrasher produced a major article based on this work, though a promised monograph never made it into print. The research demonstrated that the provision of an elegant $750,000 facility to help boys in a heavily delinquent area failed to have a significant impact. "Crime prevention turns out to be not the function of a single preventive agency," Thrasher (1936a:78) concluded, "but a problem requiring the concerted attack of a coordinated community program" (see also Thrasher, 1932).

Subsequently, Thrasher became involved in the Lower East Side Project, a program that sought to implement his own blueprint for delinquency prevention by forming a coalition of relevant service providers to deal with youngsters seemingly headed for trouble. He supervised several dissertations by NYU students to map out conditions in the target area, and he sought to enlist agencies wont to go their own way into complementary efforts. "The hope," Thrasher (1936b:67) wrote, "is that agencies and community groups would eventually . . . adopt more definite measures to achieve a real concentration of responsibility for crime prevention with a consequent plan for cooperation and coordination of activities."

There is no published report on how this project worked out, though it is likely that it floundered. Perhaps disheartened, Thrasher thereafter turned his attention to other endeavors, most notably an involvement with motion pictures. He became technical director of the Motion Picture Council, organized a motion picture study institute at N.Y.U., and produced a coffee table picture book dealing with the advent of talking films.

Thrasher retired in 1959, but shortly after that he suffered serious brain injuries while a passenger on a New York bus that was hit by a truck (Knox, 1999). He remained hospitalized in Central Islip State Hospital, a mental institution on Long Island, until his death, reportedly of pneumonia, on March 24, 1962.

Mary Dodge and Gilbert Geis

See also Chicago Area Project; Gangs, Juvenile; Solomon Kobrin

Bibliography

Bordua, D. 1961. Delinquent subcultures: Sociological interpretations of gang delinquency. *Annals of the American Academy of Political and Social Science* 338:119–136.

Frankfort (IN) Morning Times. 1937. M. B. Thrasher, City's Oldest Merchant, Dead. March 4:1, 5.

Geis, G., and M. Dodge. 2001. Frederic M. Thrasher (1892–1962) and *The Gang* (1927). *Journal of Gang Research* 8(1):1–49.

Gillin, J. L. 1927. Human ecology. *Saturday Review of Literature* 4(August 27):69.

Hardman, D. G. 1967. Historical perspectives of gang research. *Journal of Research in Crime and Delinquency* 4:5–27.

Knox, G. 1999. Thrasher, Frederic Milton. Pp. 616–617 in *American National Biography*, Vol. 22. New York: Oxford University Press.

Sellin, T. 1927. Book review. *Annals of the American Academy of Political and Social Science* 130(May):192.

Thrasher, F. M. 1927. *The Gang: A Study of 1,313 Gangs in Chicago*. Chicago: University of Chicago Press. (Reissued in 2000, Peotone, IL: New Chicago School Press.)

Thrasher, F. M. 1932. The Boys' Club study. *Journal of Educational Sociology* 6:4–16.

Thrasher, F. M. 1936a. The Boys' Club and juvenile delinquency. *American Journal of Sociology* 41:66–80.

Thrasher, F. M. 1936b. The Lower East Side crime prevention program, New York City. Pp. 46–67 in S. Glueck and E. Glueck (eds.), *Preventing Crime: A Symposium.* New York: McGraw-Hill.

 # TRAINING SCHOOLS

Before the 1800s, society viewed children as little adults and treated them as little adults on many different levels, including meting out adult punishments. While society looked to the family to guide the child and oversee his or her moral development, due to the negligence or absence of some parents, a number of children did not have parental supervision. These children often lived as vagrants in the city and would at times engage in delinquent acts for survival purposes. Toward the late 1700s, society's view of children began to shift. This shift was due in part to urbanization and the many vices that were attributed to city life. The leaders of the child-saving movement, predominantly middle-class women, were concerned with what they deemed the evil temptations available in the city, such as alcohol, comic books, and brothels. They believed that children were growing up too fast and were exposed to many unwholesome and immoral things.

With the family structure no longer guaranteed and cities expanding and offering numerous vices, society began to experience an upheaval in social control. The response was to establish reformatories where these young delinquents could be housed and where they would receive the moral teachings and discipline their parents had not given them. The first reformatory, known as New York House of Refuge (Platt, 1969), was established specifically to teach delinquent juveniles how to live properly and morally and taught this lesson through strict discipline and structure. Youth were assigned daily responsibilities and followed a rigid daily schedule. Along with the uniformity of their dress, the building was designed in a way that reinforced conformity to the rules and regulations of the institution.

In the 1850s, those who were involved in the juvenile justice system became disillusioned with reformatories due to the difficulty in implementing moral teachings. This difficulty was exacerbated by a lack of appropriate funding, overcrowded facilities, staff shortages, poor or inadequate programming, and inadequate physical structures.

As a response to these concerns, the idea of training schools was developed. Training schools, also referred to as industrial schools, solved several problems. First, juveniles learned a skill or trade they could use once they returned to society, and they received an academic and a moral education. Second, the working juveniles provided a source of revenue for the institutions, purportedly to offset the cost of housing them. Third, they provided a way to meet the demand for labor that had been a challenge for many of the factories and industrial companies.

Training schools were typically styled in the manner reminiscent of a home or cottage. Instead of having the feel of an institution, training schools were designed to create the feel of a home. The chores included farming duties and household responsibilities. Training schools located within the city typically taught juveniles any of the local trades. Vocational training for vagrant and delinquent youth was particularly important to the women involved in the child-saving movement who felt it was their calling to give these alleged wayward youth parental, spiritual, and moral guidance as well as secure housing and job skills. It was their belief that a key ingredient was missing from the children's lives and that was a maternal influence.

To this end, the women began organizing their movement to ensure that these urban vagrants were housed in cottages when appropriate so that they could have the benefit of parental influence, country living, and moral and spiritual values. Using their finances and family influences, the child-savers established these benefits for wayward children. It was not uncommon for women in the movement to call on husbands or fathers with social status to further their cause.

It was a commonly held belief that women were largely responsible for the care and rearing of children; further, they were responsible for children's moral and spiritual development. The child savers worked diligently with judges as the structure of residential services was created for vagrant and delinquent children. They were able to devote their time largely due to the restricted professions available to women during those times. With time on their hands, they looked to their child advocacy efforts as a way to meet a personal need. While they worked to establish training schools, some of their greatest work was done

Photo 11. The Lyman School, Westborough, Massachusetts.
SOURCE: Photo by Marilyn D. McShane.

via political methods. The child savers advocated for greater government control of children and their activities. Specifically, they worked to ensure that there were laws that prohibited children from having access to activities that they deemed were unacceptable for children.

Every northern state had a refuge or reform school in operation by 1890 (Del Carmen et al., 1998:3). However, the quality of the institutional life for delinquents was less than acceptable; children continued to be jailed with adult criminals in contradiction to the Illinois Juvenile Court Act of 1899 that specified otherwise (Platt, 1969:146). City and county efforts coupled with the concerns of women's organizations worked to improve the conditions, but soon, unsupervised philanthropy no longer had a place in the child-saving

efforts due to establishment of the Juvenile Protection League (Platt, 1969:147–148).

The use of the term *school* to refer to juvenile institutions continued through the 1970s. Whether training school or reform school, the concept was that delinquents were being educated academically, morally, and vocationally. In reality, there was very little education taking place. On the whole, the concept of a cottage-style home with caring staff was a fiction that soon disappeared. Training schools were primarily institutions dedicated to controlling delinquents and instilling discipline.

Tonya Y. Willingham

See also Alternative Schools; Child-Saving Movement; Reformatories and Reform Schools

Bibliography

Del Carmen, R., M. Parker, and F. Reddington. 1998. *Briefs of Leading Cases in Juvenile Justice*. Cincinnati, OH: Anderson.

Platt, A. M. 1969. *The Child Savers: The Invention of Delinquency*. Chicago: University of Chicago Press.

 # TRUANCY

Truancy is considered a status offense—a behavior that is illegal only because of the child's age. Truancy is when a youth demonstrates a pattern of missing school, missing certain classes, or missing certain times of the school day. Today there is a growing concern as to the potential problems associated with chronic truancy among youth. This entry explores various aspects of truancy, including a brief history of truancy, the extent of truancy, problems associated with truant youth, and programs to address truancy.

HISTORICAL BACKGROUND

For more than 50 years, compulsory school attendance statutes have been in effect in the United States. Generally, these statutes require children to attend school until a certain age, usually 16 or 17 years old. In some instances, violations of these compulsory attendance statutes have resulted in litigation.

One well-known case challenging compulsory school attendance was *Pierce v. Society of Sisters* (268 U.S. 510, 1925). This case challenged the Oregon Compulsory Education Act (Oreg. Ls. § 5259), which required all children between the ages of 8 and 16 years to attend the public schools. An overriding argument supporting compulsory education of children in public school was the need to "Americanize" immigrant children by teaching them the English language and the character of American institutions and government. In addition, the voters of Oregon adopted this act on the belief that the increase in juvenile crime in the United States was associated with the increasing number of children who were not attending public school. The U.S. Supreme Court, however, ruled that the act was unconstitutional: The state could not require children to attend public schools rather than private schools.

The association between school and delinquency has been a central focus of the juvenile justice system as well as the study of delinquency. In his study on gangs, Frederic Thrasher (1927:259) noted that "although playing hookey seems innocuous to the casual observer, under city conditions of the gangland type, it contains the germs of later delinquencies." Many early criminologists emphasized the relation between school and delinquent behavior. Robert Merton viewed American society as being extremely productive but at the same time creating frustration and strain because all groups do not have equal access to the institutionalized means of legitimately achieving societal goals. These societal goals include wealth and success; one of the legitimate means for achieving these goals is education. Thus youth who do not achieve educational success have an increased likelihood to obtain societal goals through illegitimate, rather than legitimate, means.

Travis Hirschi developed a theory not to explain why some youth break the law but to explain why they obey the law. He focused on an individual's bonds to conventional society. The bond consists of attachment to parents, commitment to education or other legitimate goals, involvement in conventional activities, and belief in legitimate values. In the context of school, Hirschi maintained that this strong bond helps insulate youth from delinquent behavior. Consequently, delinquent youth are more likely to have weak bonds to conventional society.

Albert Cohen maintained that the problem of delinquency was mainly a working-class male phenomenon. He argued that working-class boys are not adequately equipped to deal with the competitive struggle that occurs in middle-class institutions, such as school. These youth have difficulty meeting the standards, or middle-class measuring rods, set by authority figures in these institutions. Due to this frustration, they react against those institutions they believe are representative of an environment that is too demanding, given the preparation they have received. Working-class males, therefore, may become involved in delinquent activity involving other working-class males. These peer groups legitimize and support behavior that renounces middle-class institutions. Involvement in such a group is essential to a youth because it reinforces negative attitudes toward middle-class institutions while also diverting feelings of inadequacy.

Truancy has been a central focus when attempting to address and understand delinquency. The following section illustrates the importance of this continuing focus by examining the extent of truancy among youth.

EXTENT OF TRUANCY

Nationwide, a number of children from elementary to high school are staying away from school for various reasons. Some have learning difficulties, some lack personal and educational goals due to an absence of an academic challenge, some fear violence, and some have parents who neglect to support their children's educational endeavors (Ingersoll and LeBoeuf, 1997:4). Although there are no national data on the extent of truancy, many cities report that unexcused absences among youth are a major problem:

1. In New York City, the country's largest school system, approximately 150,000 of the 1 million public school students are absent on a typical day. School officials are unsure as to how many of these absences are excused.

2. In the Los Angeles United School District, the country's second largest school system, approximately 10 percent of its enrollment is absent. About half of the absent students return with a written excuse.

3. In Detroit, 40 public school attendance officers investigated 66,440 chronic absenteeism complaints during the 1994–95 school year (Garry, 1996:1).

4. Pittsburgh reported that on an average day, approximately 3,500 students are absent; this is about 12 percent of the student population. Of these, about 70 percent are unexcused.

5. In Philadelphia, approximately 2,500 students are absent without an excuse (Departments of Education and Justice, 1996).

These statistics reveal that truancy is a major problem in this country. Further, truancy may be the beginning of a lifetime of problems for youth who are routinely absent from school (Garry, 1996:1).

PROBLEMS ASSOCIATED WITH TRUANT YOUTH

For youth who are regularly absent from school, truancy can be the "steppingstone" to a lifetime of problems. Due to their chronic absenteeism, these students soon fall behind in their schoolwork. Rather than trying to catch up, they drop out of school. Research has

revealed that youth who do not complete high school face several obstacles that can potentially influence their adult lives, including an increased chance of unemployment and receipt of public assistance. In addition, a disproportionate number of prison and death row inmates in this country are high school dropouts (Harlow, 1994). There are also social consequences to high dropout rates among youth. These social consequences include a decrease in national income, a decrease in tax revenues for the support of government services, increased demand for social services, a lower level of political participation, a reduced potential for intergenerational mobility, lower levels of health, and an increase in crime (Levin, 1972:41–48).

Various factors have been associated with dropping out of school (Lawrence, 1998:94–97). Support from parents and family is essential in determining whether youth remain in school. Additional parental- and familial-related factors that are associated with higher dropout rates include youth from single-parent families, low educational and occupational levels of parents, and absence of parental supervision and monitoring. In fact, parental neglect has been cited as the most common cause of truancy (Garry, 1996). Some children are kept at home to either work or baby-sit preschool siblings. Other children avoid attending school because of problems at home, at school, or in the neighborhood. Recognizing the importance of support from parents and family, many programs emphasize parental accountability. Some cities have passed ordinances that allow police to issue a citation to a truant child's parents. This can ultimately result in a $500 fine or 30 days in jail. In addition to these sanctions, courts can order parents to attend parenting classes. In some instances, the court can remove the child from the parents and make the child a ward of the court (Ingersoll and LeBoeuf, 1997:4–5).

Peers also have a strong influence on whether an individual stays in school. Youth who drop out of school are more likely to have peers that have also dropped out. These individuals often experience feelings of alienation from school life and therefore have a tendency to seek friends who have lower education aspirations and also feel alienated from school.

Truancy is considered a "gateway" to criminal and delinquent activity. As noted by the California District Attorney Kim Menninger, "I've never seen a gang member who wasn't a truant first." The U.S.

Department of Education emphasized that high rates of unexcused absences are associated with high daytime burglary rates and vandalism:

1. During a recent sample period, Miami reported that more than 71 percent of the 13- to 16-year-old youths prosecuted for criminal violations had been truant.

2. In Minneapolis, the daytime crime rate dropped 68 percent after police began citing truant students.

3. San Diego reported that 44 percent of violent juvenile crime occurs between 8:30 a.m. and 1:30 p.m.

4. In Van Nuys, California, a three-week truancy sweep effort coincided with a 60 percent reduction in shoplifting arrests.

Research has also revealed that students who are chronically truant are at a higher risk of being involved in substance and alcohol abuse. For instance, one study noted that 51 percent of female juvenile detainees not in school during their arrests tested positive for drug use (Wish, Gray, and Levine, 1996). Another study revealed that more than half of a group of male juvenile arrestees sent to juvenile hall in San Diego, California, tested positive for drug use. Those youth who did not attend school were more likely to test positive for drug use compared with youth who did attend school (67 percent and 49 percent, respectively; San Diego Association of Governments, 1996).

PROGRAMS TO ADDRESS TRUANCY

In its *Manual to Combat Truancy* (1996), the Department of Education, in cooperation with the Department of Justice, emphasized the importance of reducing truancy rates as one approach to preventing delinquency. The manual outlined five essential elements of a comprehensive community and educational strategy to address truancy. These elements included (1) involving parents in all truancy prevention activities, (2) ensuring that students face firm and decisive sanctions for truancy, (3) creating meaningful incentives for parental responsibility, (4) establishing ongoing truancy prevention programs in school, and (5) involving local law enforcement agencies in truancy reduction efforts.

The manual also briefly described some model truancy reduction initiatives that have been implemented in various cities across the country. A few of these model initiatives are described in the following paragraphs.

Rohnert Park, California

Program Elements. The Stop, Cite and Return Program is designed to reduce truancy and juvenile crime in the community as well as to increase the average daily attendance for the schools. Patrol officers issue citations to suspected truants contacted during school hours. The students, along with their parents, return to school to meet with the vice principal. Two citations are issued without penalty; the third citation results in a referral to the appropriate support services.

Results. Due in large part to this initiative, the daytime burglary rate is 75 percent below what it was in 1979. Haynes Hunter, who has been involved in reducing truancy in this community, noted that the program is effective because of its high visibility. Specifically, he stated that "being on the street, being in contact with the kids makes them aware of the fact that we care. We want them to get their education."

New Haven, Connecticut

Program Elements. The Stay in School Program targets middle school students who have started to demonstrate some problem behavior. Targeted students are sent to truancy court. Truancy court is made up of a panel of high school students who ask these younger students questions and try to provide solutions to some of their problems. After the court, youth and attorney mentors are assigned to each student to provide support. Both the student and the court sign a written agreement. After two months, the students return to the court to review their contract and report on their progress.

Results. Denise Keyes Page, who recruits and trains mentors for the Stay in School Program, stated that this program is successful because it embraces the positive aspects of peer pressure. These truant youth are judged and mentored by their peers rather than by adults who may appear to be distant and unconnected.

Milwaukee, Wisconsin

Program Elements. Parents, police, and the school system emphasize the causes of truancy in the Truancy Abatement and Burglary Suppression (TABS) program in Milwaukee. Attendance is taken every period in all high schools. Local law enforcement officers pick up truant students and bring them to a Boys and Girls Club for counseling. Parents are automatically called at home every night if their child did not attend school that day. If the parent is not supportive of regular school attendance, the district attorney is contacted.

Results. In a recent sample of students who went through the TABS program, 73 percent returned to school the next day, 66 percent remained in school on the 15th day, and 64 percent continued to remain in school on the 30th day. Furthermore, since the TABS program, daytime burglary in Milwaukee has decreased 33 percent, and daytime aggravated battery has decreased 29 percent. Aquine Jackson, director of the Parent and Student Services Division of the Milwaukee public schools, commented that the TABS program's success is due in part to the enhanced collaborative efforts between the Milwaukee public schools, the Milwaukee Boys and Girls Clubs, the Milwaukee Police Department, and the county sheriff.

Atlantic County, New Jersey

Program Elements. The Atlantic County Project Helping Hand receives referrals from six Atlantic City and four Pleasantville elementary schools for youth from kindergarten through eighth grade who have between 5 and 15 days of unexcused absences. A truancy worker meets with the youth and his or her family to provide short-term family counseling. Referrals to additional social services are made if needed. If the family fails to keep appointments, home visits are made to encourage cooperation. Once a truancy problem is successfully addressed, the case is closed and the youth is placed on aftercare or monitoring status for three months.

Results. During the previous school year, 84 percent of the students who participated in the program did not continue in their truant behavior. Colleen Denelsback of project Helping Hand maintained that

the major philosophy of the project was early intervention, both at the age level and the number of unexcused absences. She emphasized that early intervention will prevent truancy and potential delinquent behavior.

To continue efforts to address the problems associated with chronic absenteeism, eight communities established Truancy Reduction Demonstration Programs funded by the Office of Juvenile Justice and Delinquency Prevention. These eight sites have implemented truancy reduction strategies that include the following:

1. Prevention, including public awareness campaigns to educate youth and the greater community about the importance of combating truancy.

2. Intervention, including enhanced enforcement of compulsory attendance laws and providing education and support services to truant youth and their families.

3. Coordination, fostering collaborative efforts between schools, police departments, probation departments, juvenile courts, community organizations, parents, and teachers.

CONCLUSION

While truancy is designated as a status offense, it is considered a steppingstone to a lifetime of problems, including delinquent and criminal activity as well as diminished quality of life. Thus it is essential to identify truant youth before they become involved in more serious delinquent behavior. As this entry illustrates, many programs that address the problem of truancy recognize the importance of such preventive measures. Further, a common theme among these various programs is the importance of collaboration. To adequately and successfully prevent chronic truancy among youth, various agencies need to be involved, including parents, schools, police departments, juvenile courts, and policymakers.

Pamela Schram

See also At-Risk Youth; Curfew; Individuals With
   Disabilities Education Act; Learning Disabilities;
   Theories of Delinquency

Bibliography

Departments of Education and Justice. 1996. *Manual to Combat Truancy*. Available at http://www.ed.gov/pubs/Truancy.

Garry, E. M. 1996. *Truancy: First Step to a Lifetime of Problems*. Washington, DC: Department of Justice.

Harlow, C. W. 1994. *Comparing Federal and State Prison Inmates, 1991*. Washington, DC: Department of Justice.

Ingersoll, S., and D. LeBoeuf. 1997. *Reaching Out to Youth Out of the Education Mainstream*. Washington, DC: Department of Justice.

Lawrence, R. 1998. *School Crime and Juvenile Justice*. New York: Oxford University Press.

Levin, H. M. 1972. *The Effects of Dropping Out*. U.S. Senate Select Committee on Equal Educational Opportunity. Washington, DC: Government Printing Office.

San Diego Association of Governments. 1996. *Drug Use Among San Diego Arrestees*. San Diego, CA: San Diego Association of Governments.

Thrasher, F. M. 1927. *The Gang: A Study of 1,313 Gangs in Chicago*. Chicago: University of Chicago Press.

Wish, E. D., T. A. Gray, and E. B. Levine. 1996. *Recent Drug Use in Female Juvenile Detainees: Estimates From Interviews, Urinalysis, and Hair Analysis*. College Park, MD: Center for Substance Abuse Research, University of Maryland.

VICTIMIZATION

In recent times, and particularly within the past decade, the issue of juvenile victimization has become a dominant theme among the public. In addition to concern about drunk drivers, missing children, and child abuse, the prevalence of school gun violence and its aftermath have struck the media fancy. Except for this latter form of victimization, the public assumption is that adults are the ones responsible. However, adolescents are equally responsible for crimes against their fellow youth. The fact is that teenagers between the ages of 13 and 18 account for approximately 20 percent of all murder arrests in the United States, including juveniles as victims. When all offenses are examined, the common finding is that juveniles are usually the victims of other juveniles. Because recent juvenile gun violence in schools has raised the specter of danger in places that were previously considered safe, policymakers at all governmental levels have expressed concern for the victimization of children in the United States.

TRENDS IN JUVENILE VICTIMIZATION

The best evidence of juvenile victimization is the National Crime Victimization Survey (NCVS). Begun in 1972, the NCVS demonstrated that juveniles (ages 12 to 17) were the most likely victims of most types of crime. For a number of years (1972 to 1993) juvenile victimization rates were either flat or on the rise. Since 1993, those rates have dropped substantially to what are now referred to as "all-time lows," particularly

where violent victimizations are concerned (Klaus and Rennison, 2002). However, juveniles continue to have higher victimization rates than adults.

Violent Victimization

Homicide is an exception to the overall truism that juveniles are the most frequent victims of crime. Those aged 12 to 17 are about half as likely as adults to be homicide victims. Even so, juveniles are not rare victims. For the very young (under age 4), homicide is a major cause of death (Osofsky, 2001). For instance, the National Center for Health Statistics lists homicide as the third leading cause of death for these children. Most of these cases are at the hands of parents and caretakers. Indeed, death at the hands of strangers is relatively rare. Even where older juveniles are concerned, the statistics remain essentially the same.

Victims of nonfatal violence have also experienced a dramatic decrease in the likelihood of victimization. According to the NCVS, older juveniles (ages 12 to 17) have seen a 47 percent decrease in their rate of nonfatal violence since 1991. However, these juveniles still remain about twice as likely as adults to be victims. In addition, they are likely to know their offenders (either a friend, relative, or acquaintance), and this is more often the case for assaults (about 70 percent) than for robberies (about 45 percent). Single-offender victimizations are also much more common than those with multiple offenders.

A special case of violent victimization, reserved for juveniles, is that of missing children. The public assumes that a missing child is one taken by a stranger for violent and abusive purposes. This image is largely created by the media reporting on sensational cases. It is also false. Most missing children are either run-aways, throwaways, or parental abductions. The public image, that of a stranger abduction, is a rare event (see the Missing Children entry). Therefore, this is not truly a "violent victimization." Of the thousands of children reported missing each year, best estimates of the number of violent cases suggest there are no more than about 200. The true number may be even lower.

Property Crime Victimization

According to the NCVS, property crime victimization rates are even higher for juveniles than for other types of crimes. According to Finkelhor and Ormrod (2000), 1997 victimization figures show that one in six juveniles aged 12 to 17 was a victim of a property crime. This rate is substantially higher than the rate for adults. Overall, the trend since the 1970s is similar to victimization by crimes of violence—the rate began decreasing in the 1990s. Official statistics, such as the FBI's *Uniform Crime Reports*, have proven to be poor measures of property crimes against juveniles because the victimizations are rarely reported to the police.

Child Abuse and Neglect

Juveniles can be victims of a special category of offenses that cannot be committed against adults: child abuse and neglect. Reports of this type of victimization largely come from agencies specializing in the offense: child protective services agencies. In 1999, a little over one quarter of almost 3 million victimization reports were substantiated. These victims had primarily suffered neglect (mostly children under age 4) and minor physical abuse, but there were more serious forms of crime. Sexual abuse was predominantly suffered by girls, with those who were 12 to 15 years old most likely to be abused. As with other forms of violent victimization, the most likely offenders are parents, relatives, and friends. Males are more likely to be seriously physically abused, with 4- to 11-year-olds the most frequent victims.

Hate Crime Victimization

A final category of juvenile victimization is hate crime. This category is usually defined as victimization by crimes committed against persons because of their ethnic, cultural, religious, or socioeconomic background or sexual orientation. In schools, hate crime can mean some discriminatory practices by educators and students, such as malicious graffiti on walls, lockers, papers, books, and interpersonal confrontation (Kaufman et al., 1998). Children are particularly sensitive to hate crimes because of the importance they attach to peer esteem.

CONSEQUENCES OF VICTIMIZATION

Crime victims generally experience one of four types of effects: physical, emotional, behavioral, and economic (Menard, 2002). Victimization of juveniles tends to leave long-term psychological scars. Children who are subject to repeated victimization, especially those who witness violence and do not get immediate help, are at high risk of developing a tendency to use violence as a means of dealing with their own conflicts. Victims of violent school crime, for instance, are likely to suffer physical ailments, withdraw from peer relations, and display indifference to cooperative situations. They are also likely to engage in alcohol and drug abuse, which may contribute to a lack of learning and poor educational performance, cognitive growth, and development. Juvenile victims who are subject to repeated domestic violence, rape, incest, and sexual assault are likely to be overwhelmed by "emotional overload." They are also likely to suffer from rape-related posttraumatic stress disorder, unwanted pregnancy, withdrawal from social activities, distrust of peers and others, and physical injuries (National Crime Prevention Council, 1995). Further, suicidal ideation may be considered an option, and some may turn to alternative sexual lifestyles. Finally, there is substantial evidence that victimization, particularly repeated victimization, tends to lead to involvement with the juvenile justice system as an offender.

REDUCING JUVENILE VICTIMIZATION

Several victimization reduction programs have been implemented and supported nationally under the auspices of the Coordinating Council on Juvenile Justice and Delinquency Prevention. For a list and summary of such programs, see a federal publication by Osofsky (2001). Garbarino (1996) has identified and suggested five priority areas to protect juveniles from victimization: (1) controlling family violence, (2) establishing and maintaining high standards for the care of children and youths, (3) developing community activities that demonstrate interest in children and their families, (4) supporting social values and structures that strengthen families over time, and (5) improving research-based knowledge about the human ecology of child and adolescent maltreatment. To these we would add control of older juveniles' routine activity when they have roles that require frequent social activities outside the home, particularly at night. Similarly, the roles of parents, guardians, and significant others are vital in the effort to reduce juvenile crime and victimization. Close supervision and monitoring of youth after school hours are essential, both for preemptive prevention of crime and as a deterrent to crime victimization.

Eric E. Azubuike

See also Child Abuse; Child Sexual Abuse; Cycle of Violence; Guardians *Ad Litem;* Mediation; Missing Children; Runaways

Bibliography

Finkelhor, D., and R. Ormrod. 2000. *Juvenile Victims of Property Crimes*. Washington, DC: Office of Juvenile Justice and Delinquency Prevention.

Garbarino, J. 1996. *Adolescent Maltreatment Youth as Victim of Abuse and Neglect*. Eugene, OR: Oregon Health Division, Injury Prevention and Epidemiology.

Kaufman, P., X. Chen, S. P. Choy, K. A. Chandler, C. D. Chapman, M. R. Rand, and C. Ringel. 1998. *Indicators of School Crime and Safety, 1998*. Washington, DC: Departments of Education and Justice.

Klaus, P., and C. M. Rennison. 2002. *Age Patterns in Violent Victimization, 1976–2000*. Washington, DC: Bureau of Justice Statistics.

Menard, S. 2002. *Short- and Long-Term Consequences of Adolescent Victimization*. Youth Violence Research Series Bulletin. Washington, DC: Office of Juvenile Justice and Delinquency Prevention.

National Crime Prevention Council. 1995. *How Communities Can Bring Up Youth Free From Fear and Violence*. Washington, DC: National Crime Prevention Council.

Office of Juvenile Justice and Delinquency Prevention. 2000. *Children as Victims*. Washington, DC: Office of Juvenile Justice and Delinquency Prevention.

Osofsky, J. D. 2001. *Addressing Youth Victimization*. Action Plan Bulletin. Washington, DC: Departments of Education and Justice.

Snyder, H. N., and M. Sickmund. 1999. *Juvenile Offenders and Victims: 1999 National Report*. Washington, DC: Office of Juvenile Justice and Delinquency Prevention.

W

WAIVER TO ADULT COURT

In modern times, transferring juvenile offenders to adult criminal court has become a very popular approach for responding to youthful offending. A number of terms generally are used interchangeably to denote this process of jurisdictional change, including transfer, waiver, certification, and remand. Although state legal codes often exhibit wide variation in the age limitations placed on juvenile court jurisdiction, all states currently do have provisions that allow juveniles to be tried in adult court, and many states have amended their juvenile codes to facilitate waiver procedures. This legislative action has resulted in increasing numbers of juveniles being sent to adult court, particularly for violent offenses. In general, it is believed that these youthful offenders will receive harsher treatment in adult court, which in turn will have a beneficial impact on juvenile crime through both greater deterrence and longer incapacitation.

The increasing use of and optimistic belief in transferring juveniles to the adult system corresponds with contemporary criticisms of the juvenile court. During the past 30 years, there has been vigorous debate over the juvenile justice system's philosophy, structure, and procedures. Critical attacks have come from a variety of angles, focusing on such issues as insufficient enforcement of due process rights, inadequate treatment and rehabilitation services, abuse of the juvenile court's power, lenient treatment of offenders, and an overall lack of direction in dealing with juvenile crime. These criticisms, combined with increasing concern over youth violence, have led to an erosion of the traditional juvenile court's philosophy and authority. A "get tough" ideology, which originated in the adult criminal system in the 1970s, now extends to the juvenile system as well. A central issue is the transfer of juveniles to adult court, which is often described as a move toward "criminalizing" delinquent behavior.

HISTORICAL CONTEXT

Equating youthful offending with adult criminal behavior contrasts with the foundational principles of the juvenile justice system, which declared children and adolescents to be immature, limited in their reasoning and moral judgment capabilities, and undeserving of fully administered retributive punishments. To a certain extent, the idea that "children are different" dates back approximately 600 years. By the late 14th century, English common law began to recognize the defense of infancy or immaturity. Children under the age of 7 could not be found guilty of a crime. From ages 7 through 14, children were presumed to lack any criminal capacity, but this presumption could be rebutted. Anyone over the age of 14 could not raise infancy or immaturity as a defense and was treated as an adult. During the colonial period, American legal doctrine similarly recognized the age of law violators. However, the creation of a separate system of juvenile justice is most often associated with the establishment of houses of refuge in the 1820s, which sought to provide separate correctional quarters exclusively for young people in need of guidance and supervision.

Unfortunately, many youths were placed in houses of refuge without having committed any criminal offenses, and the courts that did so also generally failed to provide any due process rights. Thus constitutional challenges arose. By the late 19th century, a "progressive" reform effort led to the establishment of a separate court system that was to take into account that juveniles lacked the reasoning ability and moral development of adults. When the first juvenile court opened in Chicago in 1899, it was based on the doctrine of *parens patriae*. Theoretically, the juvenile court's proceedings were designed to identify the underlying causes of youthful misbehavior and provide the treatment necessary to prevent more serious criminal behavior from happening in the future. In spite of this orientation, it is important to note that juvenile court judges were also given the discretion to transfer serious young offenders to adult criminal court. Therefore, the idea of treating juvenile offenders as adults is not something new. However, until modern times, transfer procedures were used sparingly, as the *parens patriae* philosophy ensured that most young offenders would remain within the juvenile system.

MODERN SOCIAL FORCES

In the 1950s and 1960s, critics became increasingly vocal about the deficiencies of the juvenile system. The first round of criticisms focused on the lack of procedural safeguards granted to youthful offenders in juvenile court (Bernard, 1992). During the "due process revolution" of the late 1960s and early 1970s, several U.S. Supreme Court decisions established that juveniles could not be totally cut off from fundamental constitutional rights under the guise of "individualized justice." Although the Supreme Court stopped short of extending to juveniles all the procedural safeguards given to adults, these and other cases moved the juvenile court away from its original progressive orientation and toward a more procedurally formal system that emphasized substantive justice.

While initial criticisms of the juvenile court focused on constitutional rights and procedural fairness, a second round of criticisms and reforms that emerged in the 1970s and 1980s targeted the goals and structure of the juvenile system. Specifically, critics focused on the perceived ineffectiveness of rehabilitation programs and rapidly rising crime rates.

In the 1970s, several influential reviews of rehabilitation programs seemed to suggest that "nothing works." In addition to the apparent inability of the juvenile system to provide effective rehabilitative services, crimes committed by young people increased

rapidly from the mid-1960s through the mid-1970s. By the early 1980s, the popular view emerged that the juvenile court was too lenient, particularly with serious and violent offenders. The response was a rapid shift toward a more punitive system that emphasized accountability, deterrence, and incapacitation. It was hoped this would be an effective response to the increasing concern over juvenile crime.

Unfortunately, in the mid-1980s, two disturbing trends emerged that served to heighten fears about youthful offending. Beginning in 1985 and continuing through 1994, the juvenile violent crime arrest rate increased dramatically. Furthermore, demographic influences added even more to a perceived need to "do something" about violent juvenile crime. Beginning in the 1980s, the children of baby boomers (i.e., the "echo boom" generation) started to reach adolescence. Youths aged 18 and under currently rival baby boomers for the greatest percentage of the United States population, and this age group is expected to remain large over the next decade. Based on the projected size of the at-risk population of 14- to 17-year-olds, total juvenile arrests for violent offenses are also expected to remain high and even increase. The number of total arrests will depend greatly on youth violence rates over the same period.

Despite a recent downturn in the juvenile violent crime arrest rate (Snyder and Sickmund, 1999) and the possibility that forecasts of severe youthful offending could be incorrect, descriptions of future juvenile "superpredators" flooding the nation's streets have been very influential on public policy. Many states have moved to improve juvenile court records and make them more accessible, allow police to fingerprint and photograph specified juveniles, and open juvenile court hearings to the public. The use of mandatory sentencing and "blended sentencing," which combines juvenile and adult correctional alternatives, constitutes additional juvenile court reforms. Finally, probably the biggest area of change has occurred in jurisdictional authority, or altering the boundaries of juvenile and adult courts. To this end, from 1992 through 1997, laws were passed in 44 states and the District of Columbia that sought to ease the process of sending juvenile offenders to adult criminal court (Bishop, 2000).

METHODS OF TRANSFER

There are three primary ways to remove a youth from juvenile court jurisdiction: judicial waiver, prosecutorial waiver, and legislative waiver. Each represents a different way to identify which young offenders to process as adults, and these procedures are often used in various combinations. Judicial waiver historically has been the most commonly used method of transferring juveniles to adult criminal court, whereby a juvenile court judge makes the key decision in the transfer process. States vary in the amount of discretion granted to judges, but in general, judicial waiver is based on a consideration of such factors as the youth's amenability to treatment, age, offense seriousness, prior record, and the need for public safety. Currently, all but four states use some form of judicial waiver (Bishop, 2000; Snyder and Sickmund, 1999).

The Supreme Court addressed the practice of judicial waiver in *Kent v. U.S.* (1966) and *Breed v. Jones* (1975). Although these cases established a procedural framework for judges to use in making the transfer decision, critics contend that waiver laws containing vaguely stated criteria allow for inequities and disparities to occur. Research addressing this concern has revealed that an older age at the time of offense will often predict judicial certification to criminal court (Bishop, 2000; Myers, 2001). This practice is undoubtedly influenced by the length of time remaining within the juvenile court's jurisdiction. In addition, this same research generally suggests that inconsistent judicial interpretation and application of waiver laws often creates a situation of "justice by geography," whereby rural youths are more likely to be judicially waived than comparable urban offenders. Finally, a juvenile's gender and race may affect a judge's waiver decision, as youths transferred to adult court are disproportionately male and nonwhite. However, researchers who have employed multivariate statistical techniques to better control for critical legal variables (e.g., offense seriousness and prior record) have subsequently failed to find direct gender or racial bias toward males and minority offenders.

The second major method of transfer, prosecutorial waiver, is also sometimes referred to as concurrent jurisdiction or direct file. This strategy allows a prosecutor to file charges in either juvenile or adult court, with limits often imposed based on offense (e.g., violent crimes), age, and prior record. Furthermore, states allowing for this practice commonly permit a criminal court judge to send a case back to juvenile court if deemed appropriate, a process known as reverse waiver or decertification. Prosecutorial waiver is used in only

15 states, and it is probably the most controversial method of transfer (Bishop, 2000; Myers, 2001).

Research on prosecutorial waiver has been confined, for the most part, to the state of Florida, where prosecutors appear to enjoy the authority they are granted and feel it expedites the transfer process. However, opponents argue that prosecutors can be too easily influenced by a perceived public demand for punishment, especially if there is no opportunity for appellate review. Furthermore, the shift in discretion that takes place, from juvenile court judges to prosecutors, may actually introduce additional variability among jurisdictions in the use of transfer.

Over the past decade, literature has been building in opposition to both judicial and prosecutorial waiver, with calls for more objective criteria to be applied to the transfer process. Perhaps in response to these efforts, there has been increasing political support for the third method of transfer, legislative waiver. Also known as statutory exclusion, this popular approach places eligible youths into the adult system at the time of arrest, thereby removing the initial discretionary power of juvenile officials (Myers, 2001; Singer, 1996). Supporters of this policy contend that, compared with the highly discretionary practices of judicial and prosecutorial waiver, there is improved uniformity in determining the correct court of jurisdiction. However, others point out that the process can be rigid and overinclusive, as some excluded offenders may benefit from the treatment services offered in the juvenile system. Moreover, legislative waiver simply may switch discretionary decision making from juvenile court to adult criminal court. This argument is based on the fact that most states with legislative waiver provisions also allow cases to be certified back to juvenile court for adjudication, disposition, or both (Bishop, 2000; Myers, 2001).

Legislatures in 28 states have excluded certain offenses, offenders, or both from juvenile court jurisdiction, 13 states have set the minimum age for adult court jurisdiction below the age of 18, and 31 states have adopted a general policy of "once an adult, always an adult" (Bishop, 2000; Snyder and Sickmund, 1999). The most common statutorily excluded crimes are murder and other serious crimes against persons, while youth who are charged with a felony and have a prior adjudication of delinquency may also be identified. In recent years, states that made changes to the boundaries of their juvenile court jurisdictions most often did so through the use of legislative waiver. It is therefore ironic that the most rapidly expanding method of transfer is also the one that has received the least amount of research attention.

The increasing use of legislative waiver laws, which tend to focus on serious and violent offenders, corresponds with a shift in the offense characteristics of juveniles transferred to adult court (Bishop, 2000; Myers, 2001). Surprisingly, a great deal of past research revealed that waived youths were not usually charged with violent offenses or crimes against persons, but they instead appeared to be chronic property offenders. However, more recent studies show that this situation has changed, as juveniles charged with personal or violent crimes now make up the largest percentage of waived cases. This switch is associated with the growing concern over youth violence during the past 15 years. With the increasing adoption and expansion of legislative waiver laws, it is likely that violent offenses will continue to be targeted for transfer, as they are the charges most commonly excluded from juvenile court jurisdiction.

FREQUENCY AND RATES OF TRANSFER

Reliable national figures for the number of juvenile offenders who are waived to adult court are available only for youth who are transferred by judicial waiver. The total number of cases waived to adult court by a juvenile court judge rose from 7,000 to 12,300 between 1988 and 1994 (an increase of 75 percent), although the percentage of petitioned delinquency cases that resulted in transfer during this period remained fairly even at about 1.4 percent (Bishop, 2000).

In 1995 and 1996, the use of judicial waiver declined, undoubtedly due to the expanded use of other transfer methods. It is important to note that judicially waived cases represent less than 10 percent of all juveniles under the age of 18 who are handled in the adult criminal system (Bishop, 2000; Howell, 1997). The other 90 percent to 95 percent are tried in adult court under legislative and prosecutorial waiver provisions. With this in mind, a recent national estimate (based on a variety of data sources) indicated that 210,000 to 260,000 offenders under the age of 18 are prosecuted annually in adult criminal courts, which constitutes about 20 percent to 25 percent of the yearly total of offenders under the age of 18 (Bishop, 2000).

Although complete national statistics are not available on youths who are statutorily excluded from juvenile court jurisdiction, police dispositions of juvenile offenders that result in referral to adult court would appear to reflect the use of legislative waiver, as these youths are treated as adults at the time of arrest. Therefore, with the current expanded use of legislative waiver, one would expect that police would refer an increasing number of juvenile offenders to adult court and that an increasing percentage of police dispositions of juvenile offenders would result in an adult court referral. Nationwide figures support these expectations, as police referred nearly 91,300 juvenile offenders to adult court in 1997, representing more than 6.5 percent of the total police dispositions for juvenile offenders during that year (Federal Bureau of Investigation, 1998). In 1988, police referred less than 47,000 juveniles to adult court, representing about 4½ percent of all police dispositions of juvenile offenders for that year (Federal Bureau of Investigation, 1989).

Finally, current national statistics also are not available on young offenders who end up in adult court as a result of prosecutorial waiver, but in states that employ this method, juveniles waived by a prosecutor are likely to outnumber judicially waived youths by a large margin. For example, estimates in Florida indicated that prosecutorial transfers accounted for more than 80 percent of the youths under the age of 18 who were handled in adult court in that state in 1993 (Snyder and Sickmund, 1995). Furthermore, as another sign of the increasing use of transfer, waivers in Florida increased 216 percent between 1981 and 1993. Finally, it is noteworthy that an estimated 2,000 prosecutorial transfers occurred nationwide in 1982, while in 1993, Florida prosecutors alone filed charges in adult court for approximately 7,000 cases involving offenders under the age of 18.

THE EFFECTIVENESS OF TRANSFER

While transferring youthful offenders to adult court has emerged as a popular approach for responding to juvenile crime, there is much debate about the effectiveness of this practice. Essentially, there are two competing arguments surrounding the issue. First, juvenile transfer may have a beneficial impact on juvenile offending through the imposition of punishment that provides greater accountability, lengthier incapacitation, stronger deterrence, and enhanced public safety. On the other hand, treating young offenders as adults may make little difference or might actually make things worse by producing criminals who are more hardened and motivated. Over the past 20 years, a growing body of research has examined these contrasting positions through the use of a variety of research designs within a number of jurisdictions.

A number of studies have focused on conviction rates to assess the certainty of punishment for juveniles transferred to adult court. Most studies find high conviction rates among transferred youths, generally in the range of 65 percent to 95 percent (Bishop, 2000; Howell, 1997; Myers, 2001). However, most studies on this topic have been descriptive and did not include any comparison group of youthful offenders retained in juvenile court. Based on much more limited comparative research, the evidence does not suggest that the certainty of punishment for similar offenders is much greater in adult criminal court than in juvenile court.

For example, Fagan (1995) examined 15- and 16-year-old robbery and burglary defendants from New York and New Jersey who were arrested during 1981 and 1982. Four hundred youths from two counties in New York whose cases originated in criminal court were compared with 400 youths from two matched counties in New Jersey whose cases were handled in juvenile court. The findings indicated that the burglary conviction rate in New Jersey's juvenile courts (66 percent) was insignificantly greater than the burglary conviction rate in New York's criminal courts (63 percent), while robbery cases in New Jersey's juvenile courts were significantly less likely (46 percent conviction rate) to result in conviction than were robbery cases in New York's criminal courts (56 percent conviction rate). These mixed results led Fagan to conclude that accountability for adolescents in criminal court was no greater than for similar youths in juvenile court.

Another expectation in the move toward transferring more juvenile offenders to adult court is that these youths will receive harsher punishment than they would have in the juvenile system. Contrary to what one might expect, the evidence indicates that harsher sanctioning in adult criminal court is not guaranteed (Bishop, 2000; Howell, 1997; Myers, 2001). Some earlier studies found evidence of a "leniency gap" for juveniles waived to criminal court, as these youths appeared to receive less severe sentencing based on their younger age and relative inexperience. However, more recent comparative research has begun to clarify this situation. Concerning the type of sentence imposed, studies show that

youthful property offenders tend to be treated more leniently in criminal court, while juveniles convicted of violent offenses appear to be treated more harshly. For instance, Barnes and Franz (1989) examined data on all 206 youth considered for transfer between 1978 and 1983 in a northern California metropolitan area. Almost half (47 percent) of the juveniles were transferred, and the rest remained in juvenile court. Violent offenders were found more likely to be incarcerated in adult court than in juvenile court, while property offenders were less likely to be incarcerated in adult court than in juvenile court. Somewhat similar findings were uncovered in Fagan's (1995) previously mentioned research.

Research on a second dimension of sanction severity, length of incarceration, has produced comparable results (Bishop, 2000; Howell, 1997; Myers, 2001). Various studies have shown that lengthy sentences are common for transferred youths who are incarcerated, often in the range of one to four years, with the longest sentences imposed on violent offenders. However, the next question would be whether periods of incarceration issued in criminal court are longer than those prescribed for similar offenders in juvenile court. Studies do tend to support that lengthier sentences are imposed in adult criminal court, at least for violent offenders. To illustrate, Podkopacz and Feld's (1996) study of juvenile violent and property offenders considered for waiver in Minnesota found that youths convicted as adults on violent offenses experienced longer sentences of incarceration than those imposed on offenders retained and adjudicated in juvenile court. On the other hand, youths convicted in adult court on property offenses received shorter sentences of incarceration than did similar offenders retained in the juvenile system.

Compared with the certainty and severity of punishment for juveniles transferred to adult court, the swiftness of their punishment has been much less studied. Research suggests that the most serious cases in juvenile court take the longest time to process, often requiring three to four months or more to reach disposition (Myers, 2001). Although case-processing time for these offenders might seem lengthy at first glance, juveniles waived to adult court may be subjected to even longer waiting periods. Among its other findings, Fagan's (1995) study uncovered much swifter action in juvenile court, as cases took 100 days on average to be disposed in New Jersey juvenile courts and 145 days to reach sentencing in New York's criminal courts. This evidence is consistent with that obtained through other research that has considered the case processing times of comparable cases in juvenile and adult court (Myers, 2001).

Finally, along with accountability and incapacitation, the principle of deterrence has been used as a primary justification for transferring increased numbers of youthful offenders to adult court. It commonly is assumed by policymakers and the general public that treating adolescents as adults will reduce overall juvenile crime (i.e., have a general deterrent effect) and also reduce or eliminate the future offending of those transferred to criminal court (i.e., have a specific deterrent effect). This expectation of greater deterrence seems based on the perception that juvenile courts are too lenient and that criminal courts can provide increased accountability and stronger punishment, which will reduce youthful offending.

In terms of general deterrence, very limited evidence suggests that expanded juvenile transfer laws have little or no impact on aggregate adolescent crime rates (Bishop, 2000; Howell, 1997; Myers, 2001), contrary to the expectations of supporters of this policy. Furthermore, by comparing similar youths processed and released by the juvenile and adult court systems, recent research consistently has uncovered greater, more serious, and faster recidivism on the part of waived youths (Bishop, 2000; Howell, 1997; Myers, 2001). These findings appear to refute the suggestion that treating juvenile offenders as adults will enhance specific deterrence. Moreover, it appears likely that juvenile court treatment services may be more effective and that less stigmatization occurs in the juvenile system, while the adult criminal system might actually train (through criminal associations and personal victimization) young offenders for lengthier and more serious criminal careers.

THE FUTURE OF TRANSFER

Modern efforts to "criminalize" delinquent behavior have been combined with calls for the abolishment or wholesale reconceptualization of the juvenile court. However, vocal supporters of the juvenile system strongly oppose these efforts, and research findings tend to support their position. Furthermore, there is much that is not yet clear about the consequences of transferring large numbers and broad categories of young offenders to the adult system. It seems likely that the already strained resources of adult courts and correctional agencies will be further taxed by the influx of juvenile offenders (Bishop, 2000). These adolescents commonly exhibit greater individual needs than adults, and the criminal system appears ill equipped to deal with this population.

A less obvious issue pertains to the movement of cases between juvenile and adult courts. Recent legislative efforts have focused on reducing or eliminating judicial discretion at the juvenile court level, but this often has resulted in adult court judges being forced to determine whether cases should remain in criminal court. Questions have arisen regarding the ability of criminal court judges to decide on this matter. It is also possible that these judges may reverse waive many of the cases that would have previously remained in juvenile court. Finally, the issue of bail for transferred offenders has been greatly ignored, but some evidence indicates that waived youths are more likely to be returned to the street with the opportunity to reoffend soon after their transfers, compared with similar offenders retained in juvenile court (Myers, 2001).

All things considered, as a juvenile crime control policy, transfer to adult court generally appears counterproductive and misguided (Bishop, 2000). Therefore, rather than continuing or increasing efforts to transfer as many youths as possible to adult court (or ending juvenile court jurisdiction altogether), it seems more likely that most youthful offenders will be treated as juveniles in the future. In the face of research findings showing the limited effectiveness (or ineffectiveness) of transfer, more states may raise the maximum age at which their juvenile courts can retain jurisdiction of cases (e.g., to age 24), thereby allowing for lengthier confinement, treatment, and supervision but avoiding the adverse consequences associated with sending youths to adult court. A somewhat similar alternative is to create a "blended jurisdiction" between juvenile and adult courts, or an intermediate system for handling serious and violent young offenders, which is currently being employed in a number of states (Snyder and Sickmund, 1999). While the right to move certain cases to the adult system is preserved, the overriding purpose behind these schemes is to maintain access to juvenile correctional services and provide longer periods of supervision and control under the jurisdiction of the juvenile court.

Of course, as long as there is some separate system for dealing with juvenile offenders, there will always be a need and desire to treat some of them as adults. Few would argue that there are not certain chronically, violent youths who, for the sake of public safety, should be removed from society for long periods. However, all indications are that extending the transfer of youthful offenders beyond those who are the most serious and violent is not good public policy. Youths of a specified age, such as 14 and older, who are charged with murder will undoubtedly continue to be targeted for transfer. However, for most other offenders, an older minimum age (e.g., 16) for waiver appears more appropriate. This would ensure that younger adolescents could receive juvenile correctional services and also avoid the potential negative consequences of contact with adult criminals and public labeling in the adult system.

Next, instead of including all types of violent (and nonviolent) offenses under broad waiver laws, a focus on firearms seems more justified. From a public safety standpoint, transferring violent firearm users would seem to provide the best chance of producing both immediate and longer-term protection. However, identifying some other factor or factors to consider in combination with firearm use may be appropriate in determining which offenders require longer-term periods of incapacitation in the adult system, and a youth's prior offending history may supply the needed information. Much research suggests that adolescents with an earlier onset and substantial history of offending are likely to continue their chronic behavior into young adulthood, even in the face of harsher punishment (Myers, 2001).

Finally, the use of transfer for the "most deserving" young offenders is not a complete approach. In combination with this tactic, a future emphasis on combining earlier intervention for troubled youths with scientifically supported prevention strategies is likely. There has been growing support for a "comprehensive strategy" for dealing with serious and violent juvenile offenders (Howell, 1997), which is based on sound research regarding effective correctional programs and the causes and correlates of delinquency. Rather than responding to youth violence after it has escalated to a high level (as is done with transfer to adult court), the evidence suggests that reducing risk factors that predict serious and violent youthful offending and increasing protective factors that shield adolescents from problem behavior can be a much more effective strategy. In addition, in conjunction with early and immediate intervention, an emphasis on individualized treatment and expanding the scope of dispositional alternatives available to juvenile courts appears appropriate (Howell, 1997).

Future research should continue to explore differences in the treatment and experiences of youths in both the juvenile and adult systems. Special facilities are being built (some have opened) for transferred youths, and new programs are constantly being developed. These efforts will provide researchers with natural laboratories to test hypotheses pertaining to the practice of treating juveniles as adults. Studies also should consider adolescents' perceptions and attitudes toward the treatment they are receiving in the juvenile and adult systems and then further assess how these views might affect the behavior of youths both during their correctional stay and in the community following their release. This research will allow for the further specification of the effectiveness of the juvenile transfer approach.

David L. Myers

See also Courts, Juvenile—Current Status; Death Penalty; Delinquency—Trends and Data; Law, Juvenile; Serious and Violent Juvenile Offenders

Bibliography

Barnes, C. W., and R. S. Franz. 1989. Questionably adult: determinants and effects of the juvenile waiver decision. *Justice Quarterly* 6:117–135.

Bernard, T. J. 1992. *The Cycle of Juvenile Justice.* New York: Oxford University Press.

Bishop, D. M. 2000. Juvenile offenders in the adult criminal justice system. Pp. 81–167 in M. Tonry (ed.), *Crime and Justice: A Review of Research*, Vol. 27. Chicago: University of Chicago Press.

Fagan, J. 1995. Separating the men from the boys: The comparative advantage of juvenile versus criminal court sanctions on recidivism among adolescent felony offenders. Pp. 238–260 in J. C. Howell, B. Krisberg, J. D. Hawkins, and J. J. Wilson (eds.), *A Sourcebook: Serious, Violent, & Chronic Juvenile Offenders.* Thousand Oaks, CA: Sage.

Federal Bureau of Investigation. 1989–1998. *Uniform Crime Reports for the United States.* Washington, DC: Government Printing Office.

Howell, J. C. 1997. *Juvenile Justice and Youth Violence.* Thousand Oaks, CA: Sage.

Myers, D. L. 2001. *Excluding Violent Youths from Juvenile Court: The Effectiveness of Legislative Waiver.* New York: LFB Scholarly Publishing.

Podkopacz, M. R., and B. C. Feld. 1996. The end of the line: An empirical study of judicial waiver. *The Journal of Criminal Law and Criminology* 86:449–492.

Singer, S. I. 1996. Recriminalizing *Delinquency: Violent Juvenile Crime and Juvenile Justice Reform.* New York: Cambridge University Press.

Snyder, H. N., and M. Sickmund. 1999. *Juvenile Offenders and Victims: 1999 National Report*. Washington, DC: Office of Juvenile Justice and Delinquency Prevention.

Thomas, C. W., and S. Bilchik. 1985. Prosecuting juveniles in criminal courts: A legal and empirical analysis. *The Journal of Criminal Law and Criminology* 76:439–479.

WILDERNESS PROGRAMS

Wilderness therapy programs are structured around a series of tasks that may appear insurmountable and dangerous to the youth, but the challenges are designed to be safe and eventually solved. Solutions, however, require students to use their own physical, emotional, and cognitive resources as well as to work with others collaboratively. Wilderness therapy is not an individual process but the result of the supportive participation of a group of 6 to 14 youths. Some experts argue that the tasks of the adventure should be incremental, increasing in complexity and skill as the youth masters each graduated level of difficulty. The result of these challenges and group processes is a feeling of personal empowerment and a sense that others can be trusted.

HISTORICAL BACKGROUND

Wilderness programs as a treatment strategy for delinquent youth have roots in several early interventions. First, California developed forestry camps in the 1930s to provide work and housing for delinquent boys. The crews performed conservation work, park development, and road construction. Counseling, education, and religious activities were also included in the schedules. The second source was Kurt Hahn, a German educator and pioneer in experimental education, who founded the Salem School in Germany during the 1920s. The school was based on learning by doing. Hahn believed that modern youth suffered from the "misery of unimportance." He saw the Western world as information rich and experience poor. Adolescents in Hahn's view were not initiated into adulthood through increasing levels of responsibility. Rather, they were given no significant duties and received a level of recognition only barely greater than that of young children.

Programs developed from Hahn's premises attempted to elicit prosocial values through a series of challenging experiences. On the basis of this philosophy, an Outward Bound model was first used by the Welsh to train their merchant seamen to survive in lifeboats on the open sea. Their curriculum focused on group pride, teamwork, trust, and self-discipline.

The wilderness concept was brought to the United States in the 1960s as programs for youth. It was applied to various adolescent groups and, naturally, found its way to programs for adjudicated youth. However, this model has also been adopted by American businesses. Trips into the mountains and deep woods are often used to expose executives and managers to the benefits of building teams and solving unusual problems. Although the problems may seem totally unrelated to the office, in reality, these highly structured retreats often have implications for creative thinking, innovative management, and enhanced personnel relations.

WILDERNESS PROGRAMMING FOR JUVENILES TODAY

Wilderness or challenge programs for juveniles are usually designed in two phases. The first phase is to complete successfully a series of strenuous physical and mental challenges that the youths are unlikely to have experienced. The expectation is that achievement in these tasks, in both group and individual exercises, will build self-esteem and confidence. This is then applied to tasks in the second phase, where the goal is to have the young people master tasks in their own lives, families, schools, and neighborhoods using the same decision-making and problem-solving skills they learned in the programs.

The programs are carefully structured to provide juveniles with opportunities to experiment with their own creative solutions. The juveniles are encouraged to explore new behavioral responses and to capitalize on their personal strengths. Confidence building is important because many theorists have assumed that juveniles have low levels of self-esteem and self-confidence. According to these theorists, gang activity often results from adolescent insecurity. A completely different and unknown environment, away from peers, is believed to be helpful in changing such youths. It may also be that the survivalist nature of the wilderness experience forces them to change. Otherwise, under normal daily circumstances, there would be no motivation to change.

The Spectrum Wilderness Program is operated out of Southern Illinois University. Activities include backpacking, canoeing, caving, rock climbing, and ropes courses. The youth progress through phases that include a training expedition and a solo expedition. They also participate in counseling, most often using the circle method for discussing and solving daily problems. Academics are another important component, and the youth are encouraged to write in journals. Seven to 11 youngsters participate in each group, with an average of three to four staff members supervising. Results at the end of a seven-month follow-up indicated that, compared with a control group, the Spectrum graduates had fewer and less serious subsequent petitions in the court and measured fewer asocial behaviors.

Another program, the Associated Marine Institutes, served juveniles who were on the verge of being incarcerated. The program combined marine skills, such as sailing and chart and map reading, with such related courses as Red Cross lifesaving, CPR, and boat restoration. Although most participants had never sailed before, they were given increasing responsibilities as classes progressed. The youngsters lived at home and attended the program during the day. Those who dropped out or failed risked being sent to traditional secure facilities. School subjects were also taught, and the student-staff ratio was 6 to 1. Criteria for success in the program included completing 54 courses, two weeks of perfect attendance before graduation, moving up two successive GED levels, and obtaining full-time employment. This program was offered in Florida, South Carolina, Delaware, Louisiana, and Texas and claimed that their 20 percent to 30 percent recidivism rates were much lower than other programs targeting this population.

Eckerd Family Youth Alternatives in Maryland and Florida also offered challenge programs that included hiking, canoe trips, and ropes courses to build self-esteem and skill confidence. This particular residential program also included community service projects, such as painting shelters for the homeless, collecting food for the needy, and washing police cars. The second phase of this program had the youth living at home and continuing to take part in outdoor activities and community service projects.

MEASURING THE SUCCESS OF WILDERNESS PROGRAMS

As with other program evaluations, studies on the outcome of wilderness activities suffer from many weaknesses. One problem is that there are limited measures of program success. For example, only subsequent arrests or incarcerations are used to determine whether participation was positive or worthwhile. Second, the numbers of participating youth are usually very small, making it hard to generalize about the effects of the program. Third, the program may not run long enough to accumulate a sufficiently sized group of past participants for tracking purposes. A fourth potential problem is that results may be measured soon after the program has ended, which does not allow evaluators to determine if the results, usually positive, will hold up over time. A fifth problem is that many youths drop out of these programs. Often researchers do not factor these cases of attrition into the evaluation so that success rates are biased by the fact that only those who complete (which is already an indicator of success) are tracked over time. Finally, a sixth problem is that, when the program graduates are compared with youngsters who did not go through the program, it is not always evident that the two groups being compared were equal to start with. The wilderness groups may have been more or less seriously involved in crime, or they may be older or from different backgrounds. If so, then their later behavior could result from original differences rather than any effect of the program itself.

Some research studies of wilderness programs show that not all programs result in similar rates of recidivism. Programs with higher levels of danger and excitement may be more successful than those focusing more on skill mastery and interpersonal relationships. In addition, juveniles who made their first court appearances at an older age and those who came from two-parent families seemed to be more successful in the wilderness programs. One study also determined that chronic runaways were more likely to recidivate following these programs than those who had been processed for other offenses.

Another study found that although the effects of the wilderness program seemed dramatic at first, the effects eroded over time. The youths in the study appeared to be seriously delinquent. Furthermore, they were entering the wilderness program at what could be called the peak of their delinquent activity. Those who successfully completed the program experienced immediate reductions in arrest that lasted about one year. Seventy-five percent were rearrested within two years. However, positive results also could be interpreted by the fact that program graduates who were arrested seemed to be involved in less serious crimes than before their wilderness experiences.

WILDERNESS PROGRAMS FACE DIFFICULT TIMES

Wilderness programs are relatively expensive programs to operate and have lower client-staff ratios than most other interventions. The Therapeutic Wilderness Program for Boys operated out of the Davy Crockett National Forest in Texas recently lost its state funding after operating for almost 30 years. The program served 12- to 16-year-old youth who were either referred by county juvenile probation departments, social and protective services, or directly from parents of troubled and high-risk kids. Officials estimated that it cost approximately $3,200 per month to house, feed, and counsel a camper.

Other camp programs have been closed by problems arising from lawsuits when teens die or are injured during the exercises. While some programs have been exposed for brutal treatment, failure to provide essential emergency medical care, and engaging in unnecessarily harmful activities, others have been guilty of less concrete violations such as failing to properly train staff and avoiding unnecessary risks. In some cases, youth have died from overexposure, malnutrition, heatstroke, pneumonia, and injuries suffered in falls or fires. Wilderness program advocates would argue that these unfortunate incidents run contrary to the philosophy of the experience where the goal is to build youth up, not break them down as many boot camp programs may do.

RELATED PROGRAM APPROACHES

Today the California Youth Authority still conducts wildfire-fighting training for select youth incarcerated by the state. This elite corps of skilled young men is on call to assist the forestry service in fighting fires in many states across the western United States. Although accessing the wilderness is not always practical or affordable, ropes courses, obstacle courses, rapelling, and bungee jumping can often be conducted in closer urban settings or on institutional grounds. These exercises in high-risk challenges seem to appeal to youth, and some may eventually lead to jobs, such as oil well fire fighting and off-shore drilling repair, as well as lifetime hobbies, such as skydiving and sailing.

Marilyn D. McShane

Bibliography

Krisberg, B., E. Currie, D. Onek, and R. G. Wiebush. 1995. Graduated sanctions for serious, violent, and chronic juvenile offenders. Pp. 142–170 in J. C. Howell, B. Krisberg, J. D. Hawkins, and J. J. Wilson (eds.), *Serious, Violent, and Chronic Juvenile Offenders: A Sourcebook*. Thousand Oaks, CA: Sage.

Stepanik, R. 1991. The Eckerd Youth Program: Challenging juveniles to change. *Corrections Today* 53(1):48.

Stewart, R. 2001. Lights out for troubled youth camps. *Houston Chronicle*, 13 August:1A, 4A.

WOLFGANG, MARVIN EUGENE (1924–1998)

Marvin Eugene Wolfgang is a giant in the history of criminology. He is recognized around the world for his groundbreaking contributions to our understanding of criminal violence and juvenile delinquency and to the development of criminology as a scientific discipline. Contrary to the frequent stereotyping of "mainstream" criminologists as amoral careerists merely serving the ruling class, Marvin Wolfgang was deeply concerned with the moral issues embedded in the assessment and reaction to criminality. A lifelong opponent of capital punishment, his research on the racially biased application of the death sentence over 20 years across the South helped convince the U.S. Supreme Court in 1972 (*Furman v. Georgia*) that state laws then in place were unconstitutional.

Wolfgang was born November 14, 1924, in Millersburg, Pennsylvania. After serving in the United States Army in Italy during World War II, he received his undergraduate degree in 1948 from Dickinson College and began teaching at Lebanon Valley College in Annville, Pennsylvania. He went on to graduate studies at the University of Pennsylvania, completing his doctorate in 1955 under the supervision of the internationally distinguished criminologist Thorsten Sellin. Over the half century of his tenure at Penn, Wolfgang became the founding director of the Sellin Center for Studies in Criminology and Criminal Law, for years arguably the premier facility for criminological research.

CONTRIBUTIONS

Wolfgang was enormously influential in both producing major studies of violence and eliciting governmental and private support for violence research. One of his first contributions was a scholarly analysis of the ferocious conflict between the Guelph and Ghibelline political parties of Florence in the late 13th and early 14th centuries (1954). His doctoral research on 558 Philadelphia murders culminated in a book (1958) that revitalized the field of victimology, introducing the term *victim-precipitated homicide* in reporting that one in four of the homicides resulted from violent conflicts initiated by the eventual victims.

Subculture of Violence

A decade later, his collaboration with the noted Italian criminologist Franco Ferracuti produced an analysis (1967) of correlates and sources of violent behavior. The analysis explained much violence as the consequence of socialization into an environment (a "subculture of violence") that encouraged the use of violence to resolve interpersonal and intergroup conflicts. Wolfgang served on numerous international and national bodies concerned with the reduction of criminal violence. In his role as Research Director (with James F. Short Jr.) for the 1960s Presidential Commission on the Causes and Prevention of Violence, he was markedly successful in enlisting an impressive list of scholars to compile authoritative summary analyses of the research literature. Further, he was one of the first to promote the vision of systematic large-scale and long-range research programs to better understand violence and to develop more effective—and humane—control policies.

MEASUREMENT OF CRIME SERIOUSNESS

Building on Sellin's insights of some 30 years earlier, Wolfgang and Sellin grounded those insights in an empirical study (1964) that challenged the common assumption that the prevalence and incidence of criminality could be directly inferred from police and court statistics. Emphasizing the problematic and interpretative nature of criminal statistics, they argued instead that criminologists should generate their own analyses independent of the legal and extralegal factors influencing official compilations. To this end, they went directly to the investigative files of the Juvenile Aid Division of the Philadelphia Police Department and used the information to produce a multivariate index of the relative seriousness of offenses as defined primarily by the presence/absence of physical injury,

property theft, and property damage. The Sellin-Wolfgang seriousness scale subsequently became the model for many replications and adaptations by researchers throughout the world.

The Philadelphia Birth Cohort Study

Probably Wolfgang's crowning achievement was his (1972) pioneering longitudinal study with his Penn research staff of the criminal careers of 10,000 boys born in Philadelphia in 1945. While one third had police records by age 18, the most startling and controversial finding was that only 6 percent accounted for 52 percent of the total number of offenses. Against the politically popular rush to detect and incapacitate the 6 percent in their childhood, Wolfgang argued that identification of which specific individuals would become "career criminals" was not only methodologically dubious but also legally and ethically questionable. In addition to a second birth cohort study undertaken in Philadelphia, cohort studies have been conducted or initiated in several other sites—including the study in the People's Republic of China on which Wolfgang was working at the time of his death.

Evaluating Criminology

Reflecting his lifetime commitment to the scientific advancement of criminology, Wolfgang and his colleagues published the two-volume *Criminology Index* (1975). The mammoth resource is a comprehensive listing and cross-referencing of 3,132 articles and 556 books in the field published between 1945 and 1972 in the United States. It provides an invaluable reference tool for locating works relevant to a particular topic and tracking their citation histories—that is, the extent to which they were recognized by subsequent investigators in the topical area. The *Index* was precursor to the monumental effort by Wolfgang and his staff to "evaluate the scientific quality of criminology" (1978:1). After an exhaustive search of the literature, 3,690 publications were selected as the American literature in scientific criminology published from 1945 to 1972. Combining citation index analysis, peer evaluation by a sample of 500 criminologists, and content analysis resulted in the identification of the "best works" in several categories.

Wolfgang observed both the high degree of consensus on what constituted the best and the limited impact of criminological research on criminal justice policy. In conclusion, he argued that although criminologists should be cautiously responsive to the interests of funding and decision-making agencies, they "should avoid being seduced by the imminent needs of such agencies" (1978:268). Wolfgang was adamant that the integrity of the scientific enterprise must not be compromised, even as he advocated methodological flexibility in researching inadequately explored areas of inquiry such as corporate and white-collar crime, criminal violence, and race and crime.

RECOGNITION

Marvin Wolfgang saw no conflict between the scientific enterprise and the struggle for justice. Indeed, he worked on myriad fronts to improve the scientific rigor of criminology. In doing so, his goal was not merely the intellectual challenge. More important, Wolfgang had the conviction that good research can and should be a major resource for encouraging and assisting efforts to end the racist and other oppressive features of criminal justice institutions. An erudite intellectual, he was at the same time an eminently down-to-earth researcher who always intended the fruits of his labors to be used to support progressive reforms, not merely to add to the accumulation of works on library shelves.

Professor Wolfgang's many accomplishments were recognized twice by his colleagues in the American Society of Criminology. In 1960, he received the August Vollmer Award and, in 1989, the Society named him the recipient of its prestigious Edwin H. Sutherland Award.

Austin T. Turk and Ruth-Ellen M. Grimes

See also Philadelphia Birth Cohort; Johan Thorsten Sellin

Bibliography

Wolfgang, M. 1954. Political crimes and punishments in Renaissance Florence. *Journal of Criminal Law, Criminology, and Police Science* 44:555–581.

Wolfgang, M. 1958. *Patterns in Criminal Homicide*. Philadelphia: University of Pennsylvania Press.

Wolfgang, M., and F. Ferracuti. 1967. *The Subculture of Violence*. London: Tavistock.

Wolfgang, M., R. M. Figlio, and T. Sellin. 1972. *Delinquency in a Birth Cohort*. Chicago: University of Chicago Press, 1972.

Wolfgang, M., R. M. Figlio, and T. P. Thornberry. 1975. *Criminology Index*, Vols. 1 and 2. New York: Elsevier.

Wolfgang, M., R. M. Figlio, and T. P. Thornberry. 1978. *Evaluating Criminology*. New York: Elsevier.

Wolfgang, M., and T. Sellin. 1964. *The Measurement of Delinquency*. New York: Wiley.

Appendix 1
Print and Online
Resources for Juvenile Justice

The field of juvenile justice is complex in its subsystems, but in general, the field comprises the following three categories: juvenile delinquency and education, youth crime and victimization, and the juvenile justice system. Further distinctions can be made within these categories. For instance, programmatic research in the correctional area of the juvenile justice system may be designated as community-based programs, residency programs, and boot camps. Specific research topics are as varied as media portrayals of violence to body mutilation and may cut across the categories and subcategories.

Given the complexity of the juvenile justice system, coupled with the complexity of today's libraries, it is no wonder students sometimes feel lost. The intent of this entry is to guide the student to find resources more easily.

Resources that are valuable for researching juvenile justice topics are as varied as the topics themselves. While the Internet is one easily accessed source of information, the library offers many other sources: books, including reference sources such as dictionaries, encyclopedias, statistical materials, and standards; journals; databases; and newspapers and news broadcasts.

BOOKS

The most basic tool of a library is the catalog. Basically, a library catalog lists the materials the library owns, both book and journal titles. In the past, library catalogs were paper card catalogs. Electronic catalogs have taken the place of printed cards in most libraries today. These electronic catalogs are searchable by title, author, subject headings, and keyword. Because subject headings prescribed by the Library of Congress are long and complicated, a better alternative

is to use the keyword search option if available. However, there is a disparity of indexing terms among catalogs, indexes, abstracts, and databases. Most electronic catalogs can be searched from any Internet connection.

Juvenile justice resources are found in the Library of Congress call numbers H through K. The call number designation H includes the social sciences (sociology, economics, and business); J is the political sciences; and K is law. Depending on the focus of your topic, it is sometimes useful to browse these areas. Examples of books useful for juvenile justice research include the following:

1. American Correctional Association. 2000. *Juvenile and Adult Correctional Departments, Institutions, Agencies and Paroling Authorities.* Lanham, MD: American Correctional Association.

2. Benemati, D., A. Bouloukos, G. Newman, and P. Schultze. 1997. *Criminal Justice Information: How to Find It, How to Use It.* Westport, CT: Greenwood.

3. Nelson, B. 1997. *Criminal Justice Research in Libraries and on the Internet.* Westport, CT: Greenwood.

4. O'Block, R., L. Parker, and Q. Thurman. 2000. *Criminal Justice Research Sources,* 4th ed. Cincinnati, OH: Anderson.

Reference Sources

Dictionaries, handbooks, and encyclopedias offer quick and easy access to basic information about research topics. Some excellent examples of these resources include the following:

1. Champion, D. (ed.). 2001. *American Dictionary of Criminal Justice, Key Terms and Major Court Cases*, 2nd ed. Los Angeles: Roxbury.

2. Gale Group (ed.). 2001. *Encyclopedia of Crime and Justice*, 2nd ed. Farmington Hills: Gale Group.

3. Johnson, E. (ed.). 1987. *Handbook of Crime and Delinquency Prevention*. Westport, CT: Greenwood.

4. Knox, G. (ed.). 1995. *National Gangs Resource Handbook, An Encyclopedic Reference*. Bristol, VA: Wyndham Hall.

5. Meagher, R. 1996. *Crime and Justice in America*. Fort Worth, TX: Harcourt.

6. Office of Juvenile Justice and Delinquency Prevention. 1991. *Handbook for Juvenile Justice Advisory Boards*. Lanham, MD: American Correctional Association.

7. Rush, G. F., and S. Torres. 1998. *The Encyclopedic Dictionary of Criminology*. Incline Village, NV: Copperhouse.

8. Shoemaker, D. (ed.). 1996. *International Handbook on Juvenile Justice*. Westport, CT: Greenwood.

Visit your library's reference room or check the electronic catalog to find these titles.

Standards

Standards are written to provide guidelines for professionals in the provision of services to juveniles. Standards assure quality of service and provide checks and balances for governing bodies. The following are two examples of standards publications published by the American Correctional Association:

1. Commission on Accreditation for Corrections Staff. 1991. *Standards for Juvenile Detention Facilities*, 3rd ed. Lanham, MD: American Correctional Association.

2. Commission on Accreditation for Corrections Staff. 1991. *Standards for Juvenile Training Schools*, 3rd ed. Lanham, MD: American Correctional Association.

The American Correctional Association publishes many other standards publications dealing with various aspects of juvenile justice and corrections. See also the National Council of Juvenile and Family Court Judges for various court-related standards.

Statistics

The federal government is a prolific producer of statistics in juvenile justice. The Bureau of Justice Statistics (BJS) is an organization that operates under a mandate from Congress and collects and disseminates statistics on various facets of crime in the United States. The BJS produces many publications, most notably in the form of newsletters. Typically, BJS publications are found in the government documents sections of libraries, but some libraries maintain special collections of government publications pertinent to the libraries' clientele. The *Sourcebook of Criminal Justice Statistics* (2001), 27th edition, is an excellent, comprehensive resource published by BJS. Aside from providing print resources, the BJS has a comprehensive Web site at http://www.ojp.usdoj.gov/bjs.

Another resource for juvenile justice statistics is the *Uniform Crime Reports* (also known as *Crime in the United States*), published annually by the Federal Bureau of Investigation. In addition, most states collect and compile their own criminal justice statistics and make them available either in print or electronic format.

Journals

Professionals in the field of juvenile justice often publish their research findings in journals. The currency of journal articles makes them one of the most important sources of information for the juvenile justice researcher.

Databases, indexes, and abstracts, either print or electronic, allow a researcher to locate articles within journals by keyword or subject. These resources give citation information that will allow you to access articles. Some electronic databases give the full text of the article. If full text databases are not available, check the library catalog to see if the journal is in the library's collection. Keep in mind that library catalogs index journal titles, not the titles of the articles within the journals.

The following are some outstanding journals in the field of juvenile justice:

1. *Adolescence,* published by Libra Publishers, beginning in 1966.

2. *Child Welfare,* published by Transaction Publishers, beginning in 1920.

3. *Journal of Adolescent Chemical Dependency,* published by Haworth Press, beginning in 1990.

4. *Journal of Research in Crime and Delinquency,* published by Sage Periodicals Press, beginning in 1964.

5. *Juvenile and Family Court Journal,* published by the National Council of Juvenile and Family Court Judges, beginning in 1978.

6. *Juvenile and Family Law Digest,* published by the National Council of Juvenile and Family Court Judges, beginning in 1981.

7. *Juvenile Justice Digest,* published by Washington Crime News Services, beginning in 1972.

8. *Social Problems,* published by the University of California Press, beginning in 1953.

Due to the interdisciplinary nature of juvenile justice, other disciplines, including criminal justice and sociology, cover juvenile justice issues as well.

DATABASES

Databases are electronic collections of information. Searchable by keywords, databases are usually produced for specific audiences such as juvenile justice researchers. Databases are either in CD-ROM format or are delivered over the Internet.

Juvenile justice researchers are fortunate to have several outstanding databases available for their use. *Criminal Justice Abstracts,* published by Sage Publications and produced electronically by Silver Platter, covers journals, books, reports, and dissertations. However, *CJ Abstracts* does not contain full text of these materials, only the abstracts. *Crime Justice Periodical Index (CJPI),* published by UMI and produced by ProQuest, focuses its content on crime prevention, juvenile delinquency, and courtroom

procedures. *CJPI* does contain a significant amount of full-text articles. The National Criminal Justice Reference Service (NCJRS) provides free Internet access to their database of abstracts available at http://www.ncjrs.org. The NCJRS database contains many hard-to-find public agency publications and is of interest to juvenile and criminal justice research scholars, policymakers, and practitioners.

The content of a database varies depending on the subscription limitation. Many databases are available in print as well as electronic format.

NEWSPAPERS AND NEWS BROADCASTS

Currency is always an issue for researchers. Newspapers and news broadcasts are excellent venues to learn about current, popular trends and issues concerning juveniles. Current events are transmitted to a large audience via these resources quickly, nearly as soon as the information is available, and sometimes as the situation is unfolding. To stay abreast of the latest trends and issues, the popular media is an adequate source of information. Both newspapers and television stations have very thorough Web sites that offer searchable archives. Do not overlook these valuable resources.

INTERNET

While the Internet is an incredible resource for researchers, it is advisable to use discretion when collecting information from it. Ask yourself the following questions to judge the quality of information found on a Web site:

1. Accuracy: How do you know the information is accurate?

2. Authority: Can you trust the information presented?

3. Authorship: Who is the author and is she or he an expert on the topic?

4. Currency: Is the page updated regularly for changes in content? If a page is not updated regularly, the information may be questionable.

5. Objectivity or point of view: Does the site consider all perspectives or focus solely on one perspective of an issue?

6. Scope and purpose of the site: Does the site have a motive for existing other than simply communicating information? Does the site advance an agenda?

Many Web sites offer e-mail updates, online news updates, and listservs to help keep researchers on top of the latest developments and to keep them engaged in a continuing dialogue with their colleagues. When used in conjunction with library resources, the Internet is a rich resource. However, the Internet should not be relied on as a sole source of information due to its increasingly commercial nature.

INTERLIBRARY LOAN

Researchers should also note the availability of inter-library loan services at their public or academic libraries. Nearly all libraries today participate in agreements that partner them with other libraries for sharing resources. If a researcher is unable to get a particular book, article, or other information source at his or her library, he or she may be able to request the resources from another library. Sharing resources in such a way makes researching limitless in terms of quantity of information.

CONCLUSION

Even though the modern library, with its rows of computers, may seem confusing and daunting at first, it is actually easier now to find and use information than ever before. A single networked computer can substitute for many library tools of the past, such as card catalog, indexes, abstracts, encyclopedia, almanacs, and the like. Although the computer makes searching for and using information fast and easy, become acquainted with the librarian and ask for her or his assistance. Librarians are the single best source of information in the library.

Verna Casey and Betina Gardner

Appendix 2
Internet Resources
for Juvenile Justice

ADOPTION AND FOSTER CARE

Administration on Children, Youth and Families
(ACYF)
http://www.acf.dhhs.gov/programs/acyf

Children's Bureau
http://www.acf.dhhs.gov/programs/cb

Interstate Compact on Adoption and Medical
Assistance (ICAMA)
http://aaicama.aphsa.org

National Adoption Information Clearinghouse
(NAIC)
http://www.calib.com/naic

National Resource Center for Foster Care and
Permanency Planning
http://www.hunter.cuny.edu/socwork/nrcfcpp

National Resource Center for Special Needs
Adoption
http://www.spaulding.org/adoption/NRC-
adoption.html

ALCOHOL ABUSE

National Institution on Alcohol Abuse and
Alcoholism (NIAAA)
http://www.niaaa.nih.gov

CHILD ABUSE AND NEGLECT

American Professional Society on the Abuse of
Children (APSAC)
http://www.apsac.org

Childhelp USA
http://www.childhelpusa.org

National Abandoned Infants Assistance Resource
Center (NAIARC)
http://socrates.berkeley.edu/~aiarc

National Center for the Prosecution of Child
Abuse
http://www.ndaa apri.org/apri/programs/
ncpca/index.html

National Children's Alliance
http://www.nca-online.org

National Clearinghouse on Child Abuse and
Neglect Information
http://www.calib.com/nccanch

National Court Appointed Special Advocate
Association (CASA)
http://www.nationalcasa.org
http://www.casanet.org (for professionals)

National Data Archive on Child Abuse and
Neglect
http://www.ndacan.cornell.edu

National Exchange Club Foundation for the
Prevention of Child Abuse
http://www.preventchildabuse.com

National Resource Center on Child
Maltreatment
http://www.gocwi.org/nrccm

Prevent Child Abuse America
http://www.preventchildabuse.org

DATA AND STATISTICS ON JUVENILE CRIME

Bureau of Justice Statistics (BJS)
http://www.ojp.usdoj.gov/bjs

Government Printing Office
http://www.gpo.gov

Justice Research and Statistics Association
http://www.jrsainfo.org

National Archives and Records Administration (NARA)
http://www.archives.gov/index.html

National Criminal Justice Reference Service
http://www.ncjrs.org

Sourcebook of Criminal Justice Statistics
http://www.albany.edu/sourcebook

Statistical Abstract of the United States
http://www.census.gov/statab/www

DELINQUENCY AND CRIME THEORY

Criminological Theory
http://www.crimetheory.com

DRUGS

Center for Substance Abuse Treatment (CSAT)
http://www.samhsa.gov/centers/csat2002/csat_frame.html

National Clearinghouse for Alcohol and Drug Information (NCADI)
http://www.health.org

National Drug Intelligence Center (NDIC)
http://www.usdoj.gov/ndic

National Institute on Drug Abuse (NIDA)
http://www.nida.nih.gov

Substance Abuse and Mental Health Services Administration (SAMHSA)
http://www.samhsa.gov

EDUCATION AND CHILD WELFARE

Administration on Developmental Disabilities (ADD)
http://www.acf.dhhs.gov/programs/add

Black Administrators in Child Welfare (BACW)
http://www.cwla.org/programs/bacw

Children's Bureau
http://www.acf.dhhs.gov/programs/cb

Child Welfare League of America (CWLA)
http://www.cwla.org

Department of Education
http://www.ed.gov

Interstate Compact on the Placement of Children (ICPC)
http://icpc.aphsa.org

National Child Welfare Resource Center on Legal and Judicial Issues
http://www.abanet.org/child/rclji/home.html

National Child Welfare Resource Center for Organizational Improvement
http://muskie5.musk.usm.maine.edu/helpkids

National Indian Child Welfare Association
http://nicwa.org

National Information Center for Children and Youth With Disabilities (NICHCY)
http://www.nichcy.org

National Resource Center for Information Technology in Child Welfare
http://www.nrcitcw.org

National Resource Center for Youth Development
http://www.nrcys.ou.edu/nrcyd.htm

Office of Educational Research and Improvement (OERI)
http://www.ed.gov/offices/OERI

Office of Elementary and Secondary Education (OESE)
http://www.ed.gov/offices/OESE

Office of Special Education and Rehabilitative Services (OSERS)
http://www.ed.gov/offices/OSERS

FAMILY ISSUES

Administration for Children and Families (ACF)
http://www.acf.dhhs.gov/index.html

Administration on Children, Youth and Families (ACYF)
http://www.acf.dhhs.gov/programs/acyf

AVANCE Family Support and Education Program
http://www.avance.org

Military Family Resource Center (MFRC)
http://mfrc.calib.com

National Child Care Information Center
http://nccic.org

National Child Welfare Resource Center for Family-Centered Practice
http://www.cwresource.org

National Clearinghouse on Families and Youth (NCFY)
http://www.ncfy.com

National Resource Center for Community-Based Family Resource and Support Programs (FRIENDS)
http://www.chtop.com/FRIENDS

Office of Family Assistance
http://www.acf.dhhs.gov/programs/ofa

FAMILY AND SOCIAL SERVICES

Administration for Children and Families (ACF)
http://www.acf.dhhs.gov/index.html

American Public Human Services Association (APHSA)
http://www.aphsa.org

ARCH National Resource Center for Respite and Crisis Care Services
http://www.chtop.com/ARCH/ARCHserv.htm

Child Care Bureau (CCB)
http://www.acf.dhhs.gov/programs/ccb

Department of Housing and Urban Development (HUD)
http://www.hud.gov

Department of Labor (Women's Bureau)
http://www.dol.gov/wb

Family and Youth Services Bureau (FYSB)
http://www.acf.dhhs.gov/programs/fysb

Office of Community Services
http://www.acf.dhhs.gov/programs/ocs

Office of Human Services Policy (HSP)
http://aspe.hhs.gov/hsp/index.htm

GANGS

Gang Crime Prevention Center
http://www.gcpc.state.il.us

Gangs in Los Angeles County
http://www.streetgangs.com

National Gang Crime Research Center
http://www.ngcrc.com

National Youth Gang Center (NYGC)
http://www.iir.com/nygc

Texas Gang Investigators Association
http://www.tgia.net/index.html

JUVENILE JUSTICE PROGRAMS AND SERVICES

Bureau of Justice Assistance
http://www.ojp.usdoj.gov/BJA

Department of Justice
http://www.usdoj.gov

Juvenile Justice Evaluation Center
http://www.jrsa.org/jjec/index.html

National Council of Juvenile and Family Court Judges
http://www.ncjfcj.unr.edu/index.html

Office of Juvenile Justice and Delinquency Prevention (OJJDP)
http://ojjdp.ncjrs.org

Office of Justice Programs (OJP)
http://www.ojp.usdoj.gov

Texas Youth Commission Home
http://www.tyc.state.tx.us

LAW ENFORCEMENT AND JUDICIAL AGENCIES

Department of Justice
http://www.usdoj.gov

Federal Bureau of Investigation (FBI)
http://www.fbi.gov/homepage.htm

Institution for Law and Justice
http://www.ilj.org

National Institution of Justice (NIJ)
http://www.ojp.usdoj.gov/nij

Texas Attorney General
http://www.oag.state.tx.us

LEGAL RESEARCH

Georgia State University College of Law—Meta-Index for U.S. Legal Research
http://gsulaw.gsu.edu/metaindex

MegaLaw Legal Research
http://www.megalaw.com

National Archives and Records Administration (NARA)
http://www.archives.gov/index.html

MEDICAL AND HEALTH ISSUES

Center for Mental Health Services (CMHS)
http://www.mentalhealth.org/cmhs

Centers for Disease Control and Prevention (CDC)
http://www.cdc.gov

Department of Health and Human Services
http://www.dhhs.gov

Health Resources and Services Administration (HRSA)
http://www.hrsa.gov

Maternal and Child Health Bureau (MCHB)
http://www.mchb.hrsa.gov

National Center for Education in Maternal and Child Health (NCEMCH)
http://www.ncemch.org

National Institute of Child Health and Human Development (NICHD)
http://www.nichd.nih.gov

National Institute of Mental Health (NIMH)
http://www.nimh.nih.gov

National Institutes of Health (NIH)
http://www.nih.gov

National Maternal and Child Health Clearinghouse
http://www.nmchc.org

National Mental Health Information Center
http://www.mentalhealth.org

National Sudden Infant Death Syndrome Resource Center (NSRC)
http://www.sidscenter.org

Office of Minority Health Resource Center
http://www.omhrc.gov/omhhome.htm

Office of Public Health and Science (OPHS)
http://www.surgeongeneral.gov/ophs

World Health Organization (WHO)
http://www.who.int

PREVENTION PROGRAMS

Head Start Bureau
http://www.acf.dhhs.gov/programs/hsb

National Crime Prevention Council
http://www.ncpc.org/ncpc1.htm

Office of Juvenile Justice and Delinquency Prevention (OJJDP)
http://ojjdp.ncjrs.org

Partnerships Against Violence Network (PAVNET)
http://www.pavnet.org

RESEARCH ON JUVENILES AND JUVENILE CRIME

ABA Center on Children and the Law
http://www.abanet.org/child

Children's Defense Fund
http://www.childrensdefense.org

The 'Letric Law Library's Constitutional Law and Rights Topic Area
http://www.lectlaw.com/tcon.htm

National Criminal Justice Reference Service (NCJRS)
http://www.ncjrs.org

SPECIAL TOPICS

Academy of Criminal Justice Sciences
http://www.acjs.org

Administration for Native Americans
http://www.acf.dhhs.gov/programs/ana

American Humane Association
http://www.americanhumane.org

American Society of Criminology
http://www.asc41.com

Cooperative State Research, Education, and Extension Service
http://www.reeusda.gov

Court TV
http://www.courttv.com/index.html

Criminal Justice Policy Council
http://cjpc.state.tx.us

Cybrary Criminal Justice Directory
http://talkjustice.com/cybrary.asp

Famous Trials, Compiled by Douglas Linder, professor of law at the University of Missouri–Kansas City Law School
http://www.law.umkc.edu/faculty/projects/ftrials/ftrials.htm

FindLaw
http://www.findlaw.com

Juvenile Delinquency: Causes and Control
http://www.roxbury.net/jdcchout.html

MegaLinks in Criminal Justice
http://faculty.ncwc.edu/toconnor

National Self-Help Clearinghouse
http://www.selfhelpweb.org

Office of Assistant Secretary for Planning and Evaluation (ASPE)
http://aspe.os.dhhs.gov

Office of Planning, Research and Evaluation (OPRE)
http://www.acf.dhhs.gov/programs/opre

The Origin of Prisons
http://www.notfrisco.com/prisonhistory/origins/index.html

Punishment and the Death Penalty
http://ethics.acusd.edu/death_penalty.html

Thomas: Legislative Information on the Internet
http://thomas.loc.gov

University of Missouri–St. Louis Department of Sociology
http://www.umsl.edu/~sociolog

Women's Bureau Clearinghouse
http://www.dol.gov/wb

VIOLENCE AND VICTIMS

National Center for Missing and Exploited Children
http://www.missingkids.org

Office for Victims of Crime (OVC)
http://www.ojp.usdoj.gov/ovc

Office for Victims of Crime Resource Center
http://www.ojp.usdoj.gov/ovc/ovcres/welcome.html

Violence Against Women Office (VAWO)
http://www.ojp.usdoj.gov/vawo

Dalila Mebane

Index

DATE DUE

11/28/11	ENR		

DEMCO 38-296